JOHN MILTON'S *AN APOLOGY*

ILLINOIS STUDIES IN LANGUAGE AND LITERATURE, VOL. XXXV, NOS. 1-2
PUBLISHED FOR THE GRADUATE COLLEGE, UNIVERSITY OF ILLINOIS

John Milton's

AN APOLOGY

Against a Pamphlet

CALLED

A Modest Confutation

of the Animadversions upon

the Remonstrant against

Smectymnuus

Critical Edition by MILFORD C. JOCHUMS

University of Illinois Press, Urbana, 1950

Foreword

THE PURPOSE of this study is to present a critical edition of John Milton's *Apology*. The study provides a brief introduction to the pamphlet, a critical facsimile text of the pamphlet based upon an examination of the original copies available in the libraries of this country, and critical notes and commentary on the contents of the pamphlet.

Concerning the study, a number of general comments are in order. All references to Milton's *Apology* in this study are made by page and line to the facsimile text presented in this edition. Since the lines in the original edition were unnumbered, the line numbers are mine. For the convenience of the user of this edition, a conversion chart to the *Apology* in the Columbia edition of Milton's complete works has been provided on page 220. All references to the rest of Milton's works are, unless otherwise indicated, to the Columbia edition. Because of the strategic importance to this study of the original edition of Milton's *Animadversions* (1641), references to the *Animadversions* frequently include the page number or page numbers in the original edition. The presence of brackets around a signature designation in a reference indicates that the signature is not printed. Those *recto*

signatures, therefore, that are unprinted and all *verso* signatures are placed within brackets. No attempt has been made in citing from early source materials, in the critical notes and commentary, to preserve the ligatures and long *s* forms.

This study, in its original form, was a doctoral dissertation submitted in August, 1948, at the University of Illinois.

The debts one owes to others in a work of this kind are both considerable and inevitable. To the librarians of the University of Illinois, particularly to Miss Isabelle Grant and Miss Georgia Coffin of the Rare Book Room, I express my appreciation for their patience and encouragement. I am grateful for the aid given me by Drs. Marvin T. Herrick, Edwin Robbins, and Marian Harman in connection with the Latin and Greek passages in this study. I acknowledge with thanks the assistance which Dr. Marguerite Little gave me upon many occasions, and the many helpful suggestions which Dr. Gwynn B. Evans generously offered. It has been my privilege to prepare this edition under the direction of Professor Harris F. Fletcher, whose criticisms, advice, and inspiration have been "my strength and my fortress."

MILFORD C. JOCHUMS

Contents

List of Abbreviations

REF	[John Milton]. *Of Reformation Touching Chvrch-Discipline In England: And the Cavses that hitherto have hindred it.* (1641)
PRE	[John Milton]. *Of Prelatical Episcopacy, And VVhether it may be deduc'd from the Apostolical times . . . .* (1641)
ANIM	[John Milton]. *Animadversions Upon The Remonstrants Defence, Against Smectymnvvs.* (1641)
RCG	John Milton. *The Reason Of Church-governement Urg'd against Prelaty By Mr. John Milton.* (1641)
Apology	[John Milton]. *An Apology Against a Pamphlet Call'd A Modest Confutation of the Animadversions upon the Remonstrant against Smectymnuus.* (1642)
Hall, *Humble Remonstrance*	[Joseph Hall]. *An Humble Remonstrance To The High Covrt Of Parliament, By A dutifull Sonne of the Church.* (1640)
Hall, *Defence*	[Joseph Hall]. *A Defence Of The Humble Remonstrance, Against the frivolous and false exceptions of Smectymnvvs.* (1641)
Hall, *Short Answer*	[Joseph Hall]. *A Short Answer To The Tedious Vindication Of Smectymnvvs.* (1641)
Modest Confutation	[Joseph Hall?]. *A Modest Confutation Of A Slanderous and Scurrilous Libell, Entitvled, Animadversions Vpon The Remonstrants Defense Against Smectymnuus.* (1642) (A facsimile reproduction of the *Modest Confutation* is available in William R. Parker's *Milton's Contemporary Reputation*, published in 1940.)
Smectymnuus, *Answer*	Smectymnuus. *An Answer To A Book Entitvled, An Humble Remonstrance.* (1641)
Smectymnuus, *Vindication*	Smectymnuus. *A Vindication Of The Ansvver To The Hvmble Remonstrance . . . .* (1641)
Gardiner, *History*	Samuel R. Gardiner. *History of England From the Accession of James I. To The Outbreak of the Civil War 1603-1642.* (1894-1900, 10 vols.)

Hanford, *Handbook*	James Holly Hanford. *A Milton Handbook*. 4th edition. (1946)
Masson, *Life*	David Masson. *The Life of John Milton: narrated in connexion with the political, ecclesiastical, and literary History of his time*. (1859-96, 6 vols. and index. All references made to Volume I are to the 1881 revision.)
Col.	*The Works of John Milton* (Frank Allen Patterson, General Editor). (1931-38, 18 vols.)
DNB	*The Dictionary of National Biography*. (1937-38 reprint, 25 vols. and index.)
MLN	*Modern Language Notes*.
MLR	*Modern Language Review*.
MP	*Modern Philology*.
OED	*The Oxford English Dictionary*.
PMLA	*Publications of the Modern Language Association of America*.
PQ	*Philological Quarterly*.
SP	*Studies in Philology*.

Introduction to Milton's *An Apology*

JOHN MILTON'S fifth and last antiprelatical tract entitled *AN APOLOGY Against a Pamphlet CALL'D A Modest Confutation of the Animadversions upon the Remonstrant against SMECTYMNUUS,* has never before been edited and annotated as a separate work. Attention to it has usually been lightly textual for inclusion in collections of Milton's prose, restricted or complete.

The *Apology,* originally issued anonymously, was undoubtedly written by John Milton. The tract, published twice during Milton's lifetime, probably first appeared in April or May of 1642. It is probable that John Rothwell, the younger, who published and sold the tracts of the presbyterian ministers who signed themselves "Smectymnuus," also published and sold Milton's fourth antiprelatical pamphlet, *The Reason Of Church-governement,* and his *Apology.* Edward Griffin printed both of the Milton pamphlets. It was probably Edward Griffin's device, a flaming sun, which appeared on the title page of the *Apology.* It seems quite probable that neither *The Reason Of Church-governement* nor *An Apology* sold so well as had been anticipated, for when Milton's fame had become enhanced by his *Defence of the People of England* and *Second Defence of the People of England,* Rothwell decided to make use of copies of *The Reason Of Church-governement* and the *Apology* that remained on his shelves by reissuing both pamphlets under a single new title page, which read: *AN APOLOGY FOR SMECTYMNUUS. WITH THE REASON OF CHURCH - GOVERNMENT. BY JOHN MILTON, Gent. LONDON,* Printed for *John Rothwell,* at the Fountain and Beare in *Cheapside.* Although the reissue title was undated, evidence seems to point to the year 1654 as the reissue date.

Milton's five anti-episcopal pamphlets — *Of Reformation Touching Chvrch-Discipline In England; Of Prelatical Episcopacy, And VVhether it may be deduc'd from the Apostolical times; Animadversions Upon The Remonstrants Defence, Against Smectymnvvs; The Reason Of Church-governement Urg'd against Prelaty;* and *An Apology Against a Pamphlet Call'd A Modest Confutation* — indicate his position, theologically and politically, in the struggle between those who upheld the established form of church government and those who wished to reform it. Although Milton declared in 1641 that the only true, scriptural method of church government was by presbyters, he set up reservations to the strict presbyterian position which show his general agreement with the English presbyterians in their emphasis on congregationalism and which exhibit his tendencies toward Independency in politics and religion. As a result of Milton's awareness of the importance of the struggle, he became involved in the Smectymnuan controversy, contributing thereto his *Animadversions* and his *Apology.*

The Smectymnuan controversy had begun immediately after the appearance of Bishop Joseph Hall's anonymous *An Humble Remonstrance To The High Covrt Of Parliament, By A dutifull Sonne of the Church* (registered January 13, 1640/1), which had inspired Stephen Marshall, Edmund Calamy, Thomas Young, Matthew Newcomen, and William Spurstowe, the five presbyterian ministers writing under the pseudonym "Smectymnuus," thus giving inadvertently their name to the series of pamphlets, to take up the defense of the antiprelatical position with *An Answer To A Book Entitvled, An Humble Remonstrance.... Written by Smectymnvvs* (registered March 20, 1640/1). Hall was goaded by the Smectymnuan retort to write his anonymous *A Defence Of The Humble Remonstrance....By the Author of the said Humble Remonstrance* (registered April 12, 1641), which was answered both by the Smectymnuan *A Vindication Of The Ansvver To The Hvmble Remonstrance... By The Same Smectymnvvs* (registered June 26, 1641) and by John Milton's anonymous *Animadversions Upon The Remonstrants Defence, Against Smectymnvvs* (July 1641). Hall answered the Smectymnuan *Vindication* with the anonymous *A Short Answer To The Tedious Vindication Of Smectymnvvs. By The Avthor of the Humble Remonstrance* (registered July 28, 1641) in which he declared that he was quitting the controversy. Approximately a half year later the pamphlet *A Modest Confutation Of A Slanderous and Scur-*

rilous Libell, Entitvled, Animadversions Vpon The Remonstrants Defense Against Smectymnuus appeared anonymously in answer to Milton's *Animadversions*. The *Modest Confutation* became the occasion for Milton's writing of *An Apology*.

Since none of Milton's anti-episcopal tracts nor the *Modest Confutation* was registered, it is apparent that little more can be done in exact dating, by day and month, of the *Apology* than has been done without entering the realm of speculation. Masson noted the references in the *Apology* to the numerous anti-episcopal petitions to Parliament, including the Petition of Women of February 4, 1641/2. He further noted that the allusions to the exclusion of the bishops from the House of Lords, which became effective on the same date, had an immediacy that indicated that the act had just been completed or was in the process of being completed. He dated the piece "March or April 1642," conjecturing that "it *may* have been in print *before* the formal commencement of that year, *i.e.* before March 25."[1]

Although the *Modest Confutation* bears the imprint "Printed in the yeer M.DC.XLII.," a number of allusions in it led to Masson's conjecture that it was "written before February 1641-2," and to the assigning of the date "[Jan.] 1642" in the *Catalogue of the Pamphlets ... collected by George Thomason*. It seems probable that the author of the *Modest Confutation* was writing the pamphlet at approximately the same time that Milton was writing *The Reason Of Church-governement*, in fact, that the appearance of the *Modest Confutation* with its charges against Milton, perhaps while *The Reason Of Church-governement* was being printed, permitted Milton to add, as Frederick L. Taft suggests,[2] the preface to "The second Book" and the concluding pages of *The Reason Of Church-governement*. The allusions to the Bishops' Ejection Bill in both pamphlets seem to indicate that that Bill had not yet passed, and to set the limit February 4, 1641/2, the date of King Charles' assent to that Bill. Milton's attempts in *The Reason Of Church-governement* to redeem himself from the detraction of the *Modest Confutation* were far from satisfactory, for the connection between the two pamphlets was so illusive that his friends, as well as the scholars of succeeding centuries, failed to see it. Consequently, Milton felt impelled, in order to maintain his po-

sition as a leader of his group, to answer the *Modest Confutation* in such a fashion that there would be no mistaking his intent, his integrity, and his ability. In the *Apology*, therefore, he defended himself by eliminating the author of the *Modest Confutation* as a serious opponent, by continuing the self-aggrandizement, particularly in the autobiographical section of the *Apology*, that he had begun in the preface to "The second Book" of *The Reason Of Church-governement*, and by dwelling on several aspects of the church problem with considerable astuteness. He probably worked very carefully on the *Apology*, for his purpose was not only to destroy the author of the *Modest Confutation* but also to discountenance the great defender of Anglicanism, Bishop Joseph Hall, whom Milton had already buffeted in the *Animadversions*, and thereby to increase his own stature by several cubits. Time passed. All England suddenly became aware of the "miraculous and losselesse victories" in Ireland when, as Taft points out,[3] the King, on April 6, 1642, stated his intention of going to Ireland in order "to settle the Peace of that Kingdome, and the Security of this"[4] only to be advised by the Parliament that the Irish, weak, disheartened, and starved, would soon capitulate, and that, should the King, against the advice of Parliament, proceed to Ireland, the Parliament would not submit to any commissioner whom the King might choose to direct affairs in his absence.[5] The King decided to forego his resolution and to await the outcome of "some late and great Successes in that Kingdome" that he knew not of.[6] The considerable interest in the Irish situation that arose as a result of the pitting of King against Parliament may be reflected in Milton's "miraculous and losselesse victories" in the *Apology*, which seems, therefore, to have appeared in April or, as suggested in the *Catalogue of the*

---

[1] Masson, *Life*, II, 398 and note.
[2] Frederick Lovett Taft, *Milton and the Smectymnuus Controversy, 1641-42* (Unpublished Ph.D. dissertation in English, Western Reserve University, 1942), pp. 336 ff.
[3] *Ibid.*
[4] *An Exact Collection of all Remonstrances, Declarations, Votes, Orders, Ordinances, Proclamations, Petitions, Messages, Answers, and other Remarkable Passages betweene the Kings most Excellent Majesty, and his High Court of Parliament beginning at his Majesties return from Scotland, being in December 1641, and continued untill March the 21, 1643* (London, 1642 [*i.e.*, 1643]), p. 133.
[5] *Ibid.*, p. 143.   [6] *Ibid.*, p. 146.

Pamphlets . . . collected by George Thomason, in "[May], 1642."

Although the *Apology* is an antiprelatical tract, the church interest is secondary to Milton's vindication of himself from the charges of the author of *A Modest Confutation* who, drawing inferences from Milton's words and tone in the *Animadversions,* insisted, among other things, that Milton spent his youth *"in loytering, bezelling, and harlotting,"* that he was *"vomited out"* the University, that he frequented the "Play-Houses, *or the* Bordelli,"* and that he blasphemed *"God and the King, as ordinarily as erewhile he drank Sack or swore."* Such charges, Milton felt, could not be allowed to go unchallenged for they were hurtful not only to him as a person but also to the truth of anti-episcopacy with which he had "incorporated" himself. Therefore, Milton welcomed the opportunity to reveal how wrong the author of the *Modest Confutation* was in every charge that he had made.

The pamphlet to which the *Apology* is the reply has, on the basis of Milton's statements in the *Apology,* long been attributed to Bishop Joseph Hall and his oldest son, the Rev. Robert Hall. A careful consideration of the evidence in the *Apology* seems to indicate that Milton thought he saw Joseph Hall's hand in parts of the work, but that he attributed other parts as definitely to Hall's son, for Milton is usually very careful to distinguish Hall, the Remonstrant, from his son, the Confuter. From a study of the various allusions to the Confuter the feeling grows that Milton thought of the Confuter as a young scholar, recently graduated B. A., and still at the University, a scholar who had taken orders and had a living, who was teaching freshmen, and who was a true product of scholasticism. In the *Modest Confutation,* in response to Milton's demands that the *"Bishopricks and Deanaries to encourage [young Scholars] in their Studies"* be taken away, the Confuter answered that he was "one of those young Scholars." If the Confuter meant, as he seems to mean, that he has had the encouragement of a bishopric or deanery, that Confuter can be neither Bishop Joseph Hall nor his son Robert, for both had been *pensioners* at Emmanuel College, Cambridge. The Bishop's second son, Joseph, appears to have been a layman and to be disqualified. The third son, George, is ineligible for he was a *commoner* at Exeter College, Oxford. Of Hall's three younger sons, Samuel, who had taken his B. A. at Exeter College in 1634 and who had been made sub-Dean of Exeter in September, 1641, seems not quite to fit the situation. John's bent toward law seems to eliminate him. Edward, who probably took his B. A. in 1640 at Oxford, who had a fellowship until his death on December 24, 1642, and who apparently held the position of "Artium Professor" at Oxford, appears most nearly to fit Milton's description. Milton spends much of his time and vents much of his anger in repaying the Confuter for his bold charges against Milton. Milton's anger at having been accused of frequenting the bordelloes and of seeking a "rich Widow" seems to demand the annihilation of the Confuter. Milton taunts him with such terms as "rude Scavinger," "cursing *Shimei*," "Sophister," "obscure thorn-eater of malice and detraction," "lozel Bachelour of Art," "*matriculated confutant*," "cloister'd Lubber," and "inrag'd . . . hypocrite." Milton points out that the Confuter uses "foolish language," is a "tormenter of semicolons," borrows "word for word," and "demeanes himselfe in . . . dull expression." Milton, in his studied intent to belittle the Confuter, seems to follow him even into the digression eulogizing Parliament where the Confuter is by inference denied all the excellences attributed to the members of Parliament. Much of the bitterness of the *Apology* is pointed directly at the one who had attacked Milton's virtue. It is quite probable that few outside the Hall family realized the full force of Milton's viciousness. Milton's indignant charge that the Confuter had a "worse plague, in his middle entraile" than that which the Confuter claimed raged in Milton's *"Suburb sinke"* may indicate that Milton was aware that the Confuter was not well. If Edward was the Confuter, his death left much of the *Apology* rather pointless and rather egotistical.

Milton, as a consequence, in looking back upon the antiprelatical conflict in the *Second Defence of the English People,* preferred to emphasize that the *Apology* had been an attack upon a "bishop of reputation" and to minimize that it had been his vindication of his own reputation against the charges of a rather insignificant Confuter. Milton's emphasis does not alter the fact that the *Apology* is much less concerned with the church question than with the personal aspects of the controversy.

Milton's tone and sureness of touch in the *Apology* point toward his recognition of the entirely successful nature of his preceding pamphlets and toward his satisfaction with the reception and attention given them. The adulation which the presbyterian group with whom Milton had allied himself heaped upon him, and the success with which his antiprelatical efforts had been crowned, caused him to throw himself into the fray with the blind zeal that he exhibits in the *Apology*. As the defender of the truth, he felt the necessity of vindicating his name from the extravagant charges of the Confuter, lest the cause suffer. Consequently, he devoted much time to an account of his youth, his study habits, and his mental and spiritual growth, thereby contributing autobiographical data second to none as a record of the successive phases of his life, covering a period of about seventeen years, from his entry into Christ College in the spring of 1625 to the writing of the *Apology* in the spring of 1642. Milton is elated with the opportunity of attacking such men of learning as Archbishop Ussher and Bishop Hall, so elated that he constantly reminds his reader not only of the "blunted fame of his elder adversary" but also of his own youth and "small repute."

Milton, who has established himself in his own esteem and in that of his friends as a controversialist, has found himself maligned by an unimportant Confuter whose charges, because of their very grossness, jeopardize his leadership in his cause. Milton writes, therefore, with a fervor and frenzy bent toward the justification of himself and the complete discrediting of his opponents, particularly Hall and his son. He regularly and conventionally resorts not only to derision and vilification in his attempt to vindicate himself, but also to the well-known medium of self-exaltation. He welcomes the opportunity of proving that by nature he had a "reserv'dnesse of naturall disposition, and morall discipline" that, exclusive of his Christian training, guided him unerringly toward the highest goals. Because Milton's focal point is the establishment of his virtue with such finality that any charges against him will be incredible and that those who make the charges will seem the more insignificant for having made them, he turns to a revelation of his inmost thoughts to show the sort of irresistible grace that has impelled him constantly toward the highest values, and at the same time away from "those low descents of minde" to which one must succumb before he "can agree to salable and unlawfull prostitutions." Having once established his character upon bases that seem to him unassailable, he proceeds to discuss with some authority a number of the church problems the Confuter had raised.

The very vehemence of Milton's objections to the Confuter's charges that Milton had frequented the bordelloes and that he was searching for a "rich Widow" may indicate that those charges touched nearer home than we know. His own declarations have pretty much made his readers forget that the "rich Widow" may have been a real widow, and that, according to Edward Phillips, Milton would occasionally "so far make bold with his Body, as now and then to keep a Gawdy-day."

The recourse to extant allusions to Milton in order to prove that his reputation was small is illusive. One must not forget that he was appointed Latin Secretary, according to his own chronology, before February 9, 1648/9. It is very probable that Milton was, in 1642, already a person of some repute in the rather small world that was the London of his day. By virtue of his anti-episcopal tracts he was already a man of importance in the estimation of a considerable, though perhaps a rather inarticulate, group. That Milton is particularly proud of his *Animadversions* is evidenced by his frequent reference to it in the *Apology*. That Milton writes *An Apology* in order to maintain his pamphleteering leadership seems to be obvious. One must, therefore, remember that the *Apology* is written for a particular audience against those who would detract from Milton's leadership. Like other controversialists of the time, Milton brings to bear every resource at his disposal from the ennoblement of himself to the consummate degradation of his opponent in order to maintain his position. The biographical passages in *An Apology* are, no doubt, very valuable to the student of Milton, but they must be accepted with some reservations for they are propaganda. That the propaganda is based on actual experience is quite possible; that it is a precise and accurate record of Milton's experience is improbable. The very orderliness of the development of Milton's inner thought as portrayed in the *Apology* suggests retrospective rationalization.

The Text and Textual Notes

THE *Apology* was printed originally on sheets measuring at least 11 inches by 15 inches, falling into the general classification of cap paper or crown paper. The watermarks indicate that random lots of paper were used, for no copy examined shows any consistency in style of watermarks. A watermark that appears quite frequently in the copies examined consists of a double-handled pot, with initials that appear to be IGA, surmounted by three pedestals each supporting a crescent.[1] Another less frequently recurring watermark is a single-handled pot with the initial B, surmounted by a semicircle from which arise five pedestals, the two outside supporting clusters of three grapes(?) and the other three, single grapes. The center grape supports a flower which supports a crescent.[2] Other styles include an ornate two-handled pot on which rests a pyramid of grapes, which supports a flower which in turn supports a small crescent; a single-handled pitcher-type pot bearing the letters BTA(?) surmounted by a semicircle and proceeding by a series of circles to a crescent; and a pot on which rests a crown that supports a crescent.

The 11-inch by 15-inch sheets of paper were printed four pages to each side of the sheet, the four pages being made at one pull at the press, or worked and turned. These sheets were folded twice after printing on both sides, first in the middle of the 15-inch length, and then in the middle of the 11-inch width, forming a gathering or signature of four leaves. The foldings were cut at the top and trimmed. The side and bottom were trimmed. Occasional leaves were too short on the bottom to be trimmed and a very few too narrow to be trimmed on the side. The top edges in all copies examined were probably burnished when they were first stitched.

The first and second leaves only of the quarto sheet bore signature letters.[3] The normal page consisted of the running head separated from the text by approximately a line and a half, forty lines of print, and the catchword on the forty-first line. The page number appeared on the same line as the running title, and the signature, when it appeared, on the same line as the catchword.

The facsimile text of the *Apology* presented in this edition is actual size. All reproductions are photographs with the exception of State 1 of page 8, which is a photostatic reproduction. The word "state" as used here refers always to a particular resetting of any part of the type; that is, there must be evidence that the type has been intentionally reset before a second state is declared. Changes of type in the actual text only have been considered important enough to warrant duplicate reproductions of pages. Variations in pagination and in signatures are noted in the short discussion of variations within signatures immediately following and in the textual notes.

The text of the *Apology* is made up of eight gatherings or signatures, designated A, B, C, D, E, F, G, and H. The A to G signatures which were full quarto sheets are gatherings of four leaves; the H signature, which was a half sheet, consists of two leaves.

Signature A of the *Apology* seems to appear in three states. In State 1, page 5 is unnumbered; and on page 8, line 5, the word "prosopopaea" appears with an "ae" ligature. It is interesting to note that in every copy examined which has the "ae" ligature, the words "in derision," page 4, line 21, are not separated by a space. In State 2, page 5 is unnumbered; the word "prosopopoea" is spelled with an "oe" ligature; the words "in derision" are properly spaced. State 3 incorporates the corrections of State 2, and, in addition, page 5 is numbered. Only one copy of State 3 has been seen.

Signature B appears in two states. State 1 shows the following characteristics: On page 9, line 14, "*Symectymnuans*" is misspelled "*Smectymunans*"; on page 13, line 30, the words "false beards, nigh-walkers" appear; and page 16 is misnumbered 4. In State 2 the word "*Smectymnuans*" is correctly

---

[1] Somewhat similar in general outline to Illustration 89 of Edward Heawood, "Papers Used in England after 1600," *The Library*, Fourth Series, II (1931), 299.

[2] In general outline somewhat similar to Illustration 471 of W. A. Churchill, *Watermarks in Paper in Holland, England, France, etc., in the XVII and XVIII Centuries and their interconnection* (Amsterdam, 1935).

[3] Because the H Signature was a half sheet, the second leaf did not bear a signature.

spelled; the words "false beards, nigh-walkers" have been corrected to "falsbeards, night-walkers"; and page 16 is numbered correctly.

Signature C seems to appear in only one state.

Signature D appears in two states. In State 1, Signature "C2" is printed in error for "D2" on page 27. In State 2, the correction has been made.

Signatures E, F, and G seem to appear in only one state.

Signature H appears in at least two states. In State 1, page 59 is unnumbered; a heavy rule separates the last line of the text from the words "The End."; a light rule separates the words "The End." from the single erratum; the distance between the rules is less than that in State 2; and the spacing in the erratum is somewhat crowded. In State 2, page 59 is numbered; a light rule separates the last line of the text from the words "The End."; a heavy rule separates the words "The End." from the single erratum. The distance between the rules is greater than that in State 1. In the erratum the spacing between the words "speak *correct*" as well as between "*it* read" is greater than that in State 1.

The textual observations and notes in this edition are based on the direct collation of six original copies, one photostatic facsimile copy, and eleven film copies. Some of the variations and irregularities pointed to show only that the student of printing is beset by many problems: the type from various fonts, some of it worn, some of it battered, was by accident or design mixed together; the inking was frequently too heavy or not heavy enough; the pressure placed upon the paper was often too great, or not great enough; the aligning of the right hand margin was gained by the abbreviation of words, by the crowding of words, and by the doubling of final letters and/or the adding of *e* to words, as well as by inserting spaces between words and occasionally between letters of a word. The furniture in the chase sometimes became loose, permitting letters to separate and to become squabbled. No attempt has been made to indicate every faint, smashed, or squabbled letter, nor to show degrees of squabbling in various copies. There is no reason to assume that every variant has been found, although it is true that every variant indicated has been seen. Film copies have been compared carefully with actual copies before the evidence has been recorded, because there is sometimes difficulty in ascertaining

whether variations seen on film are real or whether they are the result of spots or marks on the paper, or of show-through from the opposite side of the sheet.

Of the six actual copies which have been used for the purposes of this study, five have title pages bearing the date "1642," the other, which is in no significant way different from the others in the text, is bound with the reissue title page, which is undated. The listing of the actual copies, all at the University of Illinois Library, together with the abbreviations used in the textual notes follows:

An Apology Against a Pamphlet.... 1642 —
        Copy 1........IU-1
        Copy 2........IU-2
        Copy 3........IU-3
        Copy 4........IU-4
        Copy 5........IU-5

An Apology For Smectymnuus With The Reason Of Church-Government....1654
        IU-1654

The copy used in photostatic facsimile is from the University of Texas Library. It follows together with the abbreviation used for it:

An Apology For Smectymnuus With The Reason Of Church-Government....1654
        TxU-1654

The film copies used, all of which have the 1642 title page, are from the following libraries and are abbreviated in the textual notes as follows:

An Apology Against a Pamphlet....1642

Ohio State	OU
Harvard	MH
New York Public	NN
University of Chicago	ICU
Union Theological Seminary	NU
University of California (Andrew Clark Memorial)	CLUC
Newberry	ICN
Yale — M642 — C641	CtY-1
Yale — M642 — M642g	CtY-2
Princeton — Ex 3859 — .3115	NjP-1
Princeton — Ex 3859 —.3115 — cop. 2	NjP-2

The facsimile text which appears in this edition was photographed from originals in the University of Illinois Library, except for the photostatic reproduction of page 8, State 1, which was reproduced from the University of Illinois negative photostatic facsimile of the University of Texas *Apology* bearing the reissue title page (1654?). The following tabulation indicates the originals from which this text was taken.

Page of this text	Reproduced from	Page of this text	Reproduced from
1642 title page	IU-4	11	IU-2
1	IU-1	12	IU-2
2	IU-1	13 (State 1)	IU-2
3	IU-1	13 (State 2)	IU-1
4	IU-1	14	IU-2
5	IU-1	15	IU-2
6	IU-1	16	IU-1
7	IU-2	17	IU-2
8 (State 1)	TxU-1654	18	IU-2
8 (State 2)	IU-2	19	IU-1
9 (State 1)	IU-2	20	IU-2
9 (State 2)	IU-1	21	IU-2
10	IU-2	22	IU-1
		23	IU-1
		24	IU-2

Page of this text	Reproduced from	Page of this text	Reproduced from
25	IU-2	44	IU-1
26	IU-2	45	IU-1
27	IU-2	46	IU-1
28	IU-1	47	IU-1
29	IU-1	48	IU-1
30	IU-1	49	IU-2
31	IU-2	50	IU-2
32	IU-2	51	IU-2
33	IU-2	52	IU-1
34	IU-1	53	IU-1
35	IU-1	54	IU-5
36	IU-2	55	IU-5
37	IU-2	56	IU-3
38	IU-2	57	IU-1654
39	IU-1	58	IU-3
40	IU-2	59 (State 1)	IU-5
41	IU-1	59 (State 2)	IU-3
42	IU-1	1654 title page	IU-1654
43	IU-1		

AN
APOLOGY
Againſt a Pamphlet
CALL'D
A Modeſt Confutation
of the Animadverſions upon
the Remonſtrant againſt
SMECTYMNUUS.

LONDON,
Printed by *E. G.* for *Iohn Rothwell,* and are
to be ſold at the ſigne of the Sunne
in *Pauls* Church-yard. 1642.

The title page dated 1642 appears in one form only. There is no significant difference in any of
the copies examined. Note that the rule marks are not parallel.

The *verso* of the 1642 title page is blank.

1

An Apology, &c.

IF, Readers, to that same great difficulty of well doing what we certainly know, were not added in moſt men as great a careleſſenes of knowing what they, and others ought to do, we had bin long ere this, no doubt but all of us much farther on our way to ſome degree of peace and happineſſe in this kingdome. But ſince our ſinfull neglect of practiſing that which we know to be undoubtedly true and good, hath brought forth among us, through Gods juſt anger ſo great a difficulty now to know that which otherwiſe might be ſoone learnt, and hath divided us by a controverſie of great importance indeed, but of no hard ſolution, which is the more our puniſhment, I reſolv'd (of what ſmall moment ſoever I might be thought) to ſtand on that ſide where I ſaw both the plain autority of Scripture leading, and the reaſon of juſtice and equity perſwading ; with this opinion which eſteemes it more unlike a Chriſtian to be a cold neuter in the cauſe of the Church, then the law of *Solon* made it puniſhable after a ſedition in the State. And becauſe I obſerve that feare and dull diſpoſition, lukewarmeneſſe & ſloth are not ſeldomer wont to cloak themſelves under the affected name of moderation ; then true and lively zeale is cuſtomably diſpareg'd with the terme of indiſcretion, bitterneſſe, and choler, I could not to my thinking honor a good cauſe more from the heart, then by defending it earneſtly, as oft as I could judge it to behoove me, notwithſtanding any falſe name that could be invented to wrong, or undervalue an honeſt meaning. Wherein although I have not doubted to ſingle forth more then once, ſuch of them as were thought the chiefe and moſt nominated oppo-

A   ſers

5

10

15

20

25

The ornament at the top of the page becomes progressively lighter from left to right.   1 **difficulty**] The first i is faint.   5 **this,**] Note the spacing between the t and h   7 **this**] The t is smeared in many copies.   8 **ctiſing**] The first i is missing in all copies examined except IU-4 where its presence is very doubtful.   9 **juſt**] Note the light u between the heavy j and the ſt ligature. 11 **hath**] Note that the t is dropped down and that the final h is raised above the line of type. 15 **leading,**] The d and n sit too high; the i is low; the n is faint between two heavy letters. **juſtice**] Note the heavy e   16 **ſwading;**] The i is faint.   20 **ſloth**] The o is faint between heavy letters.   21 **cted**] The c of the ligature ct is battered in such a manner that it resembles an **e** in all copies examined.   24 **I**] The serifs are worn off or broken off.   27 **once,ſuch**] There is no space after the comma in a crowded line.

12   *An Apology, &c.*

fers on the other fide, whom no man elſe undertooke: if I have
done well either to be confident of the truth, whoſe force is beſt
ſeene againſt the ableſt reſiſtance, or to be jealous and tender of
the hurt that might be done among the weaker by the intrapping

5   autority of great names titl'd to falſe opinions, or that it be lawfull to attribute ſomewhat to guifts of Gods imparting, which I
boaſt not, but thankfully acknowledge, and feare alſo leſt at my
certaine account they be reckon'd to me many rather then few, or
if laſtly it be but juſtice not to defraud of due eſteeme the weari-

10 ſome labours and ſtudious watchings, wherein I have ſpent and
tir'd out almoſt a whole youth, I ſhall not diſtruſt to be acquitted
of preſumption. Knowing that if heretofore all ages have receav'd
with favour and good acceptance the earlieſt induſtry of him that
hath beene hopefull, it were but hard meaſure now, if the free-

15 dome of any timely ſpirit ſhould be oppreſt meerely by the big
and blunted fame of his elder adverſary; and that his ſufficiency
muſt be now ſentenc't, not by pondering the reaſon he ſhewes,
but by calculating the yeares he brings. However, as my purpoſe is not, nor hath beene formerly, to looke on my adverſary

20 abroad, through the deceaving glaſſe of other mens great opinion of him, but at home, where I may finde him in the proper
light of his owne worth, ſo now againſt the rancor of an evill
tongue, from which I never thought ſo abſurdly, as that I of all
men ſhould be exempt, I muſt be forc't to proceed from the un-

25 fained and diligent inquiry of mine owne conſcience at home
(for better way I know not, Readers) to give a more true account
of my ſelfe abroad then this modeſt Confuter, as he calls himſelfe, hath given of me. Albeit that in doing this I ſhall be ſen-
ſible of two things which to me will be nothing pleaſant; the

30 one is, that not unlikely I ſhall be thought too much a party in
mine owne cauſe, and therein to ſee leaſt; the other, that I ſhall
be put unwillingly to moleſt the publick view with the vindication of a private name; as if it were worth the while that the people ſhould care whether ſuch a one were thus, or thus. Yet thoſe

35 I intreat who have found the leaſure to reade that name, however of ſmall repute, unworthily defam'd, would be ſo good and
ſo patient as to heare the ſame perſon not unneedfully defended. I
will not deny but that the beſt apology againſt falſe accuſers is
ſilence and ſufferance, and honeſt deeds ſet againſt diſhoneſt

40 words. And that I could at this time moſt eaſily, and ſecurely,
with

To the left of the page number the space work-up shows.   1 **undertooke:**] The colon is italic.
2 truth,] Note the battered u   **6 to**] The t of the first to is raised in all copies examined; in
some copies the t is normal in impression, in others heavy but clear, in still others heavy but not
clear. **attribute**] The a is smeared in this copy; it is very weak in some copies. **7 left**] In
some copies the ſ might be mistaken for an 'f' **11 I**] The I is wrong font. **24 exempt,**] The
first e is battered and raised. **25 inquiry**] The r is very faint. **26 (for**] The ink spot inside
the o occurs in all copies examined. **31 I**] The I is wrong font. **32 with**] Note the squabbled **w** **33 private**] Note the battered **a** and **e** **name;**] The a is illegible. **34 thus, or**] Note
the crowding. **36 ſmall**] The a is illegible in some copies and faint in others. **37 ſo**] Note
the battered ſ and broken o **defended. I**] Note the crowding. The last five lines of this page
become progressively poorer in every copy examined, partially because of show-through from
the opposite side of the leaf.

An Apology, &c. 3

with the least losse of reputation use no other defence, I need not
despaire to win beliefe. Whether I consider both the foolish contriving, and ridiculous aiming of these his slanderous bolts,
shot so wide of any suspicion to be fastn'd on me, that I have oft
with inward contentment perceav'd my friends congratulating   5
themselves in my innocence, and my enemies asham'd of their
partners folly. Or whether I look at these present times wherein
most men now scarce permitted the liberty to think over their
owne concernments have remov'd the seat of their thoughts
more outward to the expectation of publick events. Or whether   10
the examples of men, either noble or religious, who have sat
downe lately with a meeke silence and sufferance un er many li-
bellous endorsements, may be a rule to others, I might well appease my self to put up any reproaches in such an honourable society of fellow-sufferers using no other defence. And were it that 15
slander would be content to make an end where it first fixes, and
not seek to cast out the like infamy upon each thing that hath but
any relation to the person traduc't, I should have pleaded against
this Confuter by no other advocates, then those which I first
commended, Silence, and Sufferance, and speaking deeds against   20
faltering words. But when I discern'd his intent was not so
much to smite at me, as through me to render odious the truth
which I had written, and to staine with ignominy that Evangelick doctrine which opposes the tradition of Prelaty, I conceav'd my selfe to be now not as mine own person, but as a mem-   25
ber incorporate into that truth whereof I was perswaded, and
whereof I had declar'd openly to be a partaker. Whereupon I
thought it my duty, if not to my selfe, yet to the religious cause
I had in hand, not to leave on my garment the least spot, or blemish in good name so long as God should give me to say that   30
which might wipe it off. Lest those disgraces which I ought to
suffer, if it so befall me, for my religion, through my default religion be made liable to suffer for me. And, whether it might
not something reflect upon those reverent men whose friend I
may be thought in writing the Animadversions, was not my last   35
care to consider, if I should rest under these reproaches having
the same common adversary with them, it might be counted
small credit for their cause to have found such an assistant, as this
babler hath devis'd me. What other thing in his book there is
of dispute, or question, in answering thereto I doubt not to be   40
A 2   justifi'd

7 I] The serifs have been worn off or broken off.   10 Or] The O is upside-down in every copy
examined.   11 who] The w is squabbled and battered.   12 under] The d is unprinted in all
copies examined except IU-3, IU-5, OU, and ICU: in IU-3 and ICU it appears as a very faint
trace; in IU-5 and OU it is legible.   19 advocates,] The second a is illegible.   25 person,] The
p is faint and broken; the r is faint.   29 leave] The a sits high.   30 good] The first o is raised
and faint.   31 I] The I is from the wrong font.   35 last] Note the space between the a and s
38 for their] Note the meager spacing between the words.

4   *An Apology, &c.*

juſtifi'd ; except there be who will condemne me to have waſted
time in throwing downe that which could not keepe it ſelfe up.
As for others who notwithſtanding what I can allege have yet
decreed to miſ-interpret the intents of my reply , I ſuppoſe they
5   would have found as many cauſes to have miſconceav'd the reaſons of my ſilence.

TO beginne therefore an Apology for thoſe animadverſions
which I writ againſt the Remonſtrant in defence of *Smectym-*
nus, ſince the Preface, which was purpoſely ſet before them, is
10   not thought apologeticall anough ; it will be beſt to acquaint ye,
Readers, before other things, what the meaning was to write
them in that manner which I did. For I do not look to be askt
wherefore I writ the book , it being no difficulty to anſwer that
I did it to thoſe ends which the beſt men propoſe to themſelves
15   when they write. But wherfore in that manner neglecting the
maine bulk of all that ſpecious antiquity, which might ſtunne
children , but not men, I choſe rather to obſerve ſome kinde of
military advantages to await him at his forragings , at his wa-
trings , and when ever he felt himſelfe ſecure to ſolace his veine
20   in deriſion of his more ſerious opponents. And here let me have
pardon , Readers , if the remembrance of that which he hath licenc't himſelfe to utter contemptuouſly of thoſe reverend men
provoke me to doe that over againe which ſome expect I ſhould
excuſe as too freely done ; ſince I have two provocations, his la-
25   teſt inſulting in his ſhort anſwer, and their finall patieuce. I had
no fear but that the authors of *Smectymnus* to all the ſhew of ſo-
lidity which the Remonſtrant could bring, were prepar'd both
with ſkill and purpoſe to returne a ſuffizing anſwer, and were
able anough to lay the duſt and pudder in antiquity , which he
30   and his, out of ſtratagem, are wont to raiſe ; but when I ſaw his
weake arguments headed with ſharpe taunts, and that his deſigne
was, if he could not refute them, yet at leaſt with quips and ſnap-
ping adagies to vapour them out , which they bent only upon
the buſineſſe were minded to let paſſe, by how much I ſaw them
35   taking little thought for their own injuries, I muſt confeſſe I took
it as my part the leſſe to endure that my reſpected friends through
their own unneceſſary patience ſhould thus lye at the mercy of
a coy flurting ſtile ; to be girded with frumps and curtall gibes,
by one who makes ſentences by the Statute, as if all above three
inches

---

2 **not**] The broken and smeared **n** in this copy is sharp and whole in many copies.   4 **intents**]
The first **n** is faint in all copies examined.   5 **miſconceav'd**] The **e** is battered; part of the **a**
is faint.   7 **Apology**] The **A** is battered in most copies.   8-9 *Smectymnus,*] Note spelling.
10 **acquaint**] Note space between **c** and **q**   12 **manner**] The **m** is raised and battered.
20 **in deriſion**] There is no space between **in** and **deriſion** in CLUC, ICN, CtY-2, and TxU-1654.
23 **I**] The **I** is very badly battered.   25 **patieuce.**] The upside-down 'n' appears in all copies
examined.   26 *Smectymnus*] Note spelling.   33 **adagies**] The second **a** is battered.   36 **it as**]
The two words are illegible in IU-2 and faint in most of the other copies examined; this is the
best copy seen.   37 **unneceſſary**] The two **e**'s range from legibility to illegibility in the copies
examined. **patience**] The **c** is battered.   39 **ſentences**] The top of the **ſ** is broken.

An Apology, &c.

inches long were confiscat. To me it feem'd an indignity, that
whom his whole wifdome could not move from their place,
them his impetuous folly fhould prefume to ride over. And if I
were more warme then was meet in any paffage of that booke,
which yet I do not yeild, I might ufe therein the patronage of   5
no worfe an author then *Gregory Nyffen,* who mentioning his
fharpneffe againft *Eunomius* in the defence of his brother *Bafil,*
holds himfelfe irreprovable in that it *was not for himfelfe, but in
the caufe of his brother ; and in fuch cafes,* faith he, *perhaps it is wor-
thier pardon to be angry, then to be cooler.* And whereas this Con-   10
futer taxes the whole difcourfe of levity, I fhall fhew ye, Readers,
wherefoever it fhall be objected in particular that I have anfwer'd
with as little lightneffe as the Remouftrant hath given example.
I have not beene fo light as the palme of a Bifhop which is the
lighteft thing in the world when he brings out his book of Ordi-   15
nation: For then contrary to that which is wont in releafing out
of prifon, any one that will pay his fees is layd hands on. Another reafon, it would not be amiffe though the Remonftrant
were told, wherefore he was in that unufuall manner beleaguer'd ;
and this was it, to pluck out of the heads of his admirers the con-   20
ceit that all who are not Prelaticall, are groffe-headed, thick
witted, illiterat, fhallow. Can nothing then but Epifcopacy
teach men to fpeak good Englifh, to pick & order a fet of words
judicioufly? Muft we learne from Canons and quaint Sermo-
nings interlin'd with barbarous Latin to illumin a period, to   25
wreath an Enthymema wth maiftrous dexterity? Irather encline,
as I have heard it obferv'd, that a Jefuits Italian when he writes,
is ever naught, though he be borne and bred a *Florentine,* fo to
thinke that from like caufes we may go neere to obferve the fame
in the ftile of a Prelat. For doubtleffe that indeed according to   30
art is moft eloquent, which returnes and approaches neereft to
nature from whence it came; and they expreffe nature beft, who
in their lives leaft wander from her fafe leading, which may be
call'd regenerate reafon. So that how he fhould be truly eloquent
who is not withall a good man, I fee not. Never the leffe as oft   35
as is to be dealt with men who pride themfelves in their fuppo-
fed art, to leave the unexcufable wherin they will not be better'd
there be of thofe that efteeme Prelaty a figment, who yet can
pipe, if they can dance, nor will be unfurnifht to fhew that what
the Prelats admire and have not, others have and admire not.   40
                                            The

Page 5 is unnumbered in every copy examined except NjP-2.   Running Head. **&c.**] The period
is battered in IU-1, IU-5, OU, MH, NU, ICN, CtY-2, NjP-1, NjP-2.   11 **I**] The I is wrong
font.   13 **Remouftrant**] A u is printed for an 'n'   17 **Ano-**] Note the space between the A
and n   26 **wth**] An abbreviated form is used in the crowded line.   **Irather**] There is no space
between the two words.   27 **I**] The I is wrong font.   **Jefuits**] The J is a swash letter.   **Italian**]
The capital I is wrong font; the small i is undotted.   33 **fafe**] The top of the f has been broken
off.   37 **thē**] Note the abbreviated form. The many obvious cases of misalignment on the page
have not been indicated because every line on the page gives evidence of poor alignment.

6   *An Apology, &c.*

The knowledge whereof, and not of that only, but of what the
Scripture teacheth us how we ought to withstand the perverters
of the Gospell were those other motives which gave the animadversions no leave to remit a continuall vehemence throughout the
5   book. For as in teaching, doubtlesse the Spirit of meeknesse is
most powerfull, so are the meeke only fit persons to be taught :
as for the proud, the obstinate, and false Doctors of mens devices, be taught they will not; but discover'd and laid open they
must be. For how can they admit of teaching who have the con-
10   demnation of God already upon them for refusing divine instruction; that is, to be *fill'd with their own devices,* as in the Proverbs we may reade; therefore we may safely imitate the method that God uses; *with the froward to be froward, and to
throw scorne upon the scorner,* whom if any thing, nothing else
15   will heale. And if *the righteous shall laugh at the destruction of the
ungodly,* they may also laugh at their pertinacious and incurable
obstinacy, and at the same time be mov'd with detestation of
their seducing malice, who imploy all their wits to defend a Prelaty usurpt, and to deprave that just government, which pride
20   and ambition partly by fine fetches and pretences, partly by
force, hath shoulder'd out of the Church. And against such kind
of deceavers openly and earnestly to protest, lest any one should
be inquisitive wherefore this or that man is forwarder then o-
thers, let him know that this office goes not by age, or youth,
25   but to whomsoever God shall give apparently the will, the Spirit, and the utterance. Ye have heard the reasons for which I
thought not my selfe exempted from associating with good men
in their labours toward the Churches wellfare: to which if any
one brought opposition, I brought my best resistance. If in re-
30   quitall of this and for that I have not been negligent toward the
reputation of my friends, I have gain'd a name bestuck, or as I
may say, bedeckt with the reproaches and reviles of this modest
Confuter, it shall be to me neither strange, nor unwelcome; as
that which could not come in a better time.
35   Having render'd an account, what induc't me to write those animadversions in that manner as I writ them, I come now to see
what the confutatiõ hath to say against thē; but so as the confuter
shall hear first what I have to say against his confutation. And because he pretends to be a great conjector at other men by their
40   writings, I will not faile to give ye, Readers, a present taste of
                                       him

---

1 **of**] The f of the first **of** is above the line of type in all copies examined. **that**] The first t is
badly worn.   4 **leave**] The final **e** is raised.   5 **teaching,**] Only a vestige remains of the dot
of the i   6 **powerfull,**] Note the faint comma which in NU and CtY-1 has not printed.   **taught :**]
The space before the colon, which is italic, justifies the line.   7 **Doctors**] The s is raised and
smeared.   8 **discover'd**] The **r** is broken.   10 **refusing**] The **f** is battered, and its crossbar
is missing.   11 *fill'd*] The top of the second *l* is broken off; the apostrophe is smashed.   13 *to*]
The space work-up shows after the first *to*   **froward,**] The *d* of the second *froward* is battered.
21 **the**] The **t** is wrong font.   24 **age,**] The descender of the g is broken in all copies examined.
35 **Having**] The **n** is battered and smeared.   36 **I**] The second **I** is wrong font.   37 **confutatiõ**]
Note the abbreviated form in a crowded line.   **thē;but**] Note the abbreviated form and the
crowding.   38 **confutation.**] The first t is raised and broken.   **And**] The A is raised and broken.
39 **cause**] The **a** is barely legible in a few copies; the battered u looks like an 'n' in a few copies.

An Apology, &c. 7

him from his own title ; hung out like a toling figne-poft to call
paffengers, not fimply *a confutation* but *a modeft confutation* with
a laudatory of it felfe obtruded in the very firft word. Whereas
a modeft title fhould only informe the buyer what the book con-
taines without furder infinuation, this officious epithet fo haftily
affuming the modefty wch others are to judge of by reading, not
the author to anticipate to himfelf by foreftalling, is a ftrong pre-
fumption that his modefty fet there to fale in the frontifpice, is
not much addicted to blufh. A furer figne of his loft fhame he
could not have given, then feeking thus unfeafonably to prepof-
feffe men of his modefty. And feeing he hath neither kept his
word in the fequel, nor omitted any kinde of boldneffe in flan-
dering, tis manifeft his purpofe was only to rub the forehead of
his title with this word *modeft*, that he might not want colour to
be the more impudent throughout his whole confutation. Next
what can equally favour of injuftice, and plaine arrogance, as to
prejudice and forecondemne his adverfary in the title for *flande-*
rous and fcurrilous, and as the Remonftrants fafhion is, for *frivo-*
lous, tedious, and falfe, not ftaying till the Reader can hear him
prov'd fo in the following difcourfe ; which is one caufe of a fu-
fpicion that in fetting forth this pamplet the Remonftrant was
not unconfulted with ; thus his firft addreffe was *an humble Re-*
monftrance by a dutifull fon of the Church, almoft as if he had faid
her white-boy. His next was *a defence* (a wonder how it fcapt
fome praifing adjunct) *againft the frivolous and falfe exceptions of*
Smectymnus, fitting in the chaire of his Title page upon his poore
caft adverfaries both as a Judge and Party, and that before the
jury of Readers can be impannell'd. His laft was *A fhort anfwer*
to a tedious vindication ; fo little can he fuffer a man to meafure either with his eye or judgement, what is fhort or what tedious
without his preoccupying direction : and from hence is begotten this *modeft confutation againft a flanderous and fcurrilous libell*.
I conceave, Readers, much may be gueft at the man and his book,
what depth there is, by the framing of his title, which being in
this Remonftrant fo rafh, and unadvifed as ye fee, I conceit him
to be neere a kin to him who fet forth a Paffion Sermon with a
formall Dedicatory in great letters to our Saviour. Although I
know that all we do ought to begin and end to his praife and glory, yet to infcribe him in a void place with flourifhes, as a man
in complement ufes to trick up the name of fome Efquire, Gentle-
man,

5

10

15

20

25

30

35

40

---

2 **not**] The o is raised.   6 **wch**] The abbreviated form is used in the crowded line.   16 **equally**]
The **a** is battered and broken. **favour**] The **v** is battered.   21 **pamplet**] Note the spelling.
26 *Smectymnus,* **fitting**] Note the spelling and the crowding.   27 **Judge**] The J is a swash
letter.   30 **eye**] The y is raised.   34 **what**] The t, probably from the wrong font, is raised.
35 **rafh,**] The **a** is battered.

8   *An Apology, &c.*

man, or Lord Paramont at Common Law, to be his book-patron with the appendant form of a ceremonicus prefentment, wil
ever appeare among the judicious to be but an an infuls and frigid affectation. As no leffe was that before his book againft the
5 Brownifts to write a Letter to a profopo xa a certain rhetoriz'd
woman whom he calls mother, and complains of fome that laid
whoredome to her charge; and certainly had he folded his Epiftle with a fuperfcription to be deliver'd to that female figure by
any Poft or Carrier who were not a Ubiquitary, it had beene a
10 moft miraculous greeting. We finde the Primitive Doctors as oft
as they writ to Churches, fpeaking to them as to a number
of faithfull brethren and fons, and not to make a cloudy tranf-
migration of fexes in fuch a familiar way of writing as an Epiftle
ought to be, leaving the track of common adreffe, to runne up,
15 and tread the aire in metaphoricall compellations, and many
fond utterances better let alone. But I ftep againe to this emblazoner of his Title page (whether it be the fame man or no I leave
it in the midft) and here I finde him pronouncing without re-
prieve thofe animadverfions to be *a flanderous and fcurrilous libell.*
20 To which I, Readers, that they are neither flanderous, nor fcurrilous, will anfwer in what place of his book he fhall be found
with reafon, and not inke only in his mouth. Nor can it be a libell more then his owne, which is both namelefle, and full of
flander, and if in this that it freely fpeaks of things amiffe in re-
25 ligion, but eftablifht by act of State, I fee not how *Wickleffe* and
Luther, with all the firft Martyrs, and reformers, could avoid
the imputation of libelling. I never thought the humane frailty
of erring in cafes of religion infamy to a State, no more then to a
Councell; it had therefore beene neither civill, nor Chriftianly,
30 to derogate the honour of the State for that caufe, efpecially
when I faw the Parlament it felfe pioufly and magnanimoufly
bent to fupply and reforme the defects and overfights of their
forefathers, which to the godly and repentant ages of the Jewes
were often matter of humble confeffing and bewailing, not of
35 confident afferting and maintaining. Of the State therefore I
found good reafon to fpeak all honourable things, and to joyne
in petition with good men that petition'd: but againft the Prelats who were the only feducers and mif-leaders of the State to
conftitute the government of the Church not rightly, me thought
40 I had not vehemence anough. And thus, Readers, by the example

STATE I

1 **book-pa-**] The first hyphen appears to be a raised period in IU-3, MH, CLUC, and CtY-1.
2 **ceremonious**] The second o is broken.   3 **an an**] Note the repetition.   5 **profopopæa**] The
third p is faint in all copies examined in which the æ ligature appears; the æ ligature appears
in CLUC, ICN, CtY-2, and TxU-1654.   12 **faithfull**] The second f sits too high.   15 **and**]
In the first **and** the n is broken and the d sits above the line of type.   **compellations**] The s is
battered.   19 **animadverfions**] The first i is smashed and sits too high.   20 **flanderous**] The
a is battered.   24 **flanders**] The s is very faint and broken in all copies examined.
31 **magnanimoufly**] The u is smashed.   35 **Of**] The f is broken and sits above the line of type.
36 **all**] The first l sits too low.   **joyne**] The y sits too high.   39 **conftitute**] The n is broken
and the i is faint in all copies examined.

This page is left blank so that the next facsimile page will appear correctly as a *verso*.

8   *An Apology, &c.*

man, or Lord Paramont at Common Law, to be his book-patron with the appendant form of a ceremonicus prefentment, wil
ever appeare among the judicious to be but an an infuls and frigid affectation. As no leffe was that before his book againft the
5   Brownifts to write a Letter to a profopopœa a certain rhetoriz'd
woman whom he calls mother, and complains of fome that laid
whoredome to her charge ; and certainly had he folded his Epiftle with a fuperfcription to be deliver'd to that female figure by
any Poft or Carrier who were not a Ubiquitary, it had beene a
10   moft miraculous greeting. We finde the Primitive Doctors as oft
as they writ to Churches, fpeaking to them as to a number
of faithfull brethren and fons, and not to make a cloudy tranf-
migration of fexes in fuch a familiar way of writing as an Epiftle
ought to be, leaving the track of common adreffe, to runne up,
15   and tread the aire in metaphoricall compellations, and many
fond utterances better let alone. But I ftep againe to this emblazoner of his Title page (whether it be the fame man or no I leave
it in the midft) and here I finde him pronouncing without re-
prieve thofe animadverfions to be *a flanderous and fcurrilous libell*.
20   To which I, Readers, that they are neither flanderous, nor fcurrilous, will anfwer in what place of his book he fhall be found
with reafon, and not inke only in his mouth. Nor can it be a libell more then his owne, which is both namelefte, and full of
flanders, and if in this that it freely fpeaks of things amiffe in re-
25   ligion, but eftablifht by act of State, I fee not how *Wickleffe* and
Luther, with all the firft Martyrs, and reformers, could avoid
the imputation of libelling. I never thought the humane frailty
of erring in cafes of religion infamy to a State, no more then to a
Councell; it had therefore beene neither civill, nor Chriftianly,
30   to derogate the honour of the State for that caufe, efpecially
when I faw the Parlament it felfe pioufly and magnanimoufly
bent to fupply and reforme the defects and overfights of their
forefathers, which to the godly and repentant ages of the Jewes
were often matter of humble confefling and bewailing, not of
35   confident afferting and maintaining. Of the State therefore I
found good reafon to fpeak all honourable things, and to joyne
in petition with good men that petition'd : but againft the Prelats who were the only feducers and mif-leaders of the State to
conftitute the government of the Church not rightly, me thought
40   I had not vehemence anough. And thus, Readers, by the example

STATE 2

5 profopopœa] The œ ligature appears in IU-1, IU-2, IU-3, IU-4, IU-5, OU, MH, NN, ICU,
NU, CtY-1, NjP-1, NjP-2, and IU-1654. In all copies in which the œ ligature appears the spacing
of page 4, line 21 in derifion is normal; when the æ ligature appears, as in State 1, there is no
space between the words in derifion of page 4, line 21.

An Apology, &c. 9

ple which hee hath set mee I have given yee two or three notes of
him out of his Title page; by which his firstlings feare not to
guesse boldly at his whole lumpe, for that guesse will not faile
ye; and although I tell him keen truth, yet he may beare with
me, since I am like to chafe him into some good knowledge, and 5
others, I trust, shall not mis-spend their leasure. For this my
aime is, if I am forc't to be unpleasing to him whose fault it is, I
shall not forget at the same time to be usefull in some thing to the
stander by.

As therefore he began in the Title, so in the next leafe he makes 10
it his first businesse to tamper with his Reader by sycophanting
and misnaming the worke of his adversary. He calls it *a mime*
thrust forth upon the stage to make up the breaches of those solemne
Scenes betweene the Prelats and the Smectymnuans. Wherein while
he is so overgreedy to fix a name of ill sound upon another, note 15
how stupid he is to expose himselfe, or his own friends to the
same ignominy; likening those grave controversies to a piece of
Stagery, or Scene-worke where his owne Remonstrant whether
in Buskin or Sock must of all right be counted the chiefe Player,
be it boasting *Thraso*, or *Davus that troubles all things*, or one 20
who can shift into any shape, I meddle not; let him explicate
who hath resembl'd the whole argument to a Comedy, for *Tra-*
gicall, he sayes, *were too ominous.* Nor yet doth he tell us what a
Mime is, whereof we have no pattern from ancient writers except some fragments, which containe many acute and wise sen- 25
tences. And this we know in *Laertius*, that the Mimes of *Sophron*
were of such reckning with *Plato*, as to take them nightly to
read on and after make them his pillow. *Scaliger* describes a
Mime to be a Poem imitating any action to stirre up laughter. But
this being neither Poem, nor yet ridiculous, how is it but abu- 30
sively taxt to be a Mime. For if every book which may by chance
excite to laugh here and there, must be term'd thus, then may the
Dialogues of *Plato*, who for those his writings hath obtain'd
the surname of Divine, be esteem'd as they are by that detractor
in *Athenæus*, no better then *Mimes.* Because there is scarce one 35
of them, especially wherein some notable Sophister lies sweating
and turmoyling under the inevitable, and mercilesse dilemma's
of *Socrates*, but that hee who reads, were it *Saturne* himselfe,
would be often rob'd of more then a smile. And whereas he tels
us that *Scurrilous Mime was a personated grim lowring foole*, his 40
                               B   foolish

STATE 1

1 I] The I is wrong font.   4 I] The I is wrong font.   5 chafe] The Columbia editors rendered the word *chase*. IU-1, IU-2, IU-3, IU-5, ICU, NU, CtY-1, NjP-1, and NjP-2 show clearly
the f In IU-4, OU, MH, NN, CLUC, ICN, CtY-2, TxU-1654, and IU-1654, the f is not clear
enough to be distinguished with certainty from an 'f'   14 *Smectymnuans*.] This spelling is
found in IU-2 and ICU. The Signature B in which the *Smectymnuans* spelling occurs also shows
page 16 misnumbered 4   15 overgreedy] Both r's and the d are battered.   18 Stagery,] The
space between the t and a is found in IU-2 and ICU. In IU-3 and IU-1654 the space appears between the a and g Other copies show the a more or less evenly spaced between the t and g In
IU-1 and CLUC the a is faint; in NN, CtY-1, and TxU-1654 the a is missing. In CtY-2 the **ta**
is missing. In IU-5 and ICN, the t is missing, and the a shows only as an uninked impression.
21 shift] The sh as seen here is peculiar to IU-2.

This page is left blank so that the next facsimile page will appear correctly as a *recto*.

An Apology, &c.   9

ple which hee hath set mee I have given yee two or three notes of
him out of his Title page; by which his firstlings feare not to
guesse boldly at his whole lumpe, for that guesse will not faile
ye; and although I tell him keen truth, yet he may beare with
me, since I am like to chafe him into some good knowledge, and   5
others, I trust, shall not mis-spend their leasure. For this my
aime is, if I am forc't to be unpleasing to him whose fault it is, I
shall not forget at the same time to be usefull in some thing to the
stander by.

    As therefore he began in the Title, so in the next leafe he makes   10
it his first businesse to tamper with his Reader by sycophanting
and misnaming the worke of his adversary. He calls it *a mime*
thrust forth upon the stage to make up the breaches of those solemne
Scenes betweene the Prelats and the Smectymnuans. Wherein while
he is so overgreedy to fix a name of ill sound upon another, note   15
how stupid he is to expose himselfe, or his own friends to the
same ignominy; likening those grave controversies to a piece of
Stagery, or Scene-worke where his owne Remonstrant whether
in Buskin or Sock must of all right be counted the chiefe Player,
be it boasting *Thraso*, or *Davus that troubles all things*, or one   20
who can shift into any shape, I meddle not; let him explicate
who hath resembl'd the whole argument to a Comedy, for *Tra-*
gicall, he sayes, *were too ominous.* Nor yet doth he tell us what a
Mime is, whereof we have no pattern from ancient writers except some fragments, which containe many acute and wise sen-   25
tences. And this we know in *Laertius*, that the Mimes of *Sophron*
were of such reckning with *Plato*, as to take them nightly to
read on and after make them his pillow. *Scaliger* describes a
Mime to be a Poem imitating any action to stirre up laughter. But
this being neither Poem, nor yet ridiculous, how is it but abu-   30
sively taxt to be a Mime. For if every book which may by-chance
excite to laugh here and there, must be term'd thus, then may the
Dialogues of *Plato*, who for those his writings hath obtain'd
the surname of Divine, be esteem'd as they are by that detractor
in *Athenaeus*, no better then *Mimes*. Because there is scarce one   35
of them, especially wherein some notable Sophister lies sweating
and turmoyling under the inevitable, and mercilesse dilemma's
of *Socrates*, but that hee who reads, were it *Saturne* himselfe,
would be often rob'd of more then a smile. And whereas he tels
us that *Scurrilous Mime was a personated grim lowring foole*, his   40
                         B   foolish

STATE 2

10 **Title,so**] Note the crowding.   14 *Smectymnuans.*] The revised spelling appears in all copies
examined except those cited under page 9, State 1.   27 *Plato,*] The *P* is a swash letter.

10   *An Apology, &c.*

foolish language unwittingly writes foole upon his owne friend, for he who was there *perſonated*, was only the *Remonſtrant* ; the author is ever diſtinguiſht from the perſon he introduces. But in an ill houre hath his unfortunate raſhneſſe ſtumbl'd upon the

5 mention of miming. That hee might at length ceaſe, which he hath not yet ſince he ſtept in, to gall and hurt him whom hee would aide. Could he not beware, could he not bethink him, was he ſo uncircumſpeᄻ, as not to foreſee, that no ſooner would that word *Mime* be ſet eye on in the paper, but it would bring

10 to minde that wretched pilgrimage over *Minſhews* Diᄻionary call'd *Mundus alter & idem*, the idleſt and the paltrieſt Mime that ever mounted upon banke. Let him ask *the Author of thoſe toothleſſe Satyrs* who was the maker, or rather the anticreator of that univerſall foolery, who he was, who like that other princi-

15 ple of the *Maniches* the *Arch evill one*, when he had look't upon all that he had made and mapt out, could ſay no other but contrary to the Divine Mouth, that it was all very fooliſh. That grave and noble invention which the greateſt and ſublimeſt wits in ſundry ages, *Plato in Critias*, and our two famous countrey-

20 men, the one in his *Vtopia*,the other in his *new Atlantis* choſe, I may not ſay as a feild, but as a mighty Continent wherein to diſplay the largeneſſe of their ſpirits by teaching this our world better and exaᄻer things,then were yet known, or us'd, this petty prevaricator of *America*,the zanie of *Columbus*,(for ſo he muſt

25 be till his worlds end) having rambl'd over the huge topography of his own vain thoughts,no marvell, if he brought us home nothing but a meer tankard drollery, a venereous parjetory for a ſtewes. Certainly he that could indure with a ſober pen to ſit and deviſe laws for drunkards to carouſe by, I doubt me whether the

30 very ſoberneſſe of ſuch a one, like an unlicour'd *Silenus*,were not ſtark drunk. Let him go now and brand another man injuriouſly with the name of *Mime*, being himſelfe the looſeſt and moſt extravagant *Mime*, that hath been heard of; whom no leſſe then almoſt halfe the world could ſerve for ſtage roome to play the

35 *Mime* in.And let him adviſe againe with ·ir *Fr·ncis Bacon* whom he cites to confute others, what it is to *turn the ſinnes of Chriſtendome into a mimicall mockery, to rip up the ſaddeſt vices with a laughing countenance*, eſpecially where neither reproofe nor better teaching is adjoynd. Nor is my meaning, Readers, to ſhift off a

40 blame from my ſelfe, by charging the like upon my accuſer, but
                                       ſhall

---

1 foole] The f and second o sit above the line of type. friend,] The d is raised. 2 *Remonſtrant* ;] Note the space before the semicolon. 8 foreſee,] The r which in a number of copies is very faint, is worn. 9 Mime] The capital *M* is a swash letter. 14 univerſall] The n is battered and broken. 20 *Vtopia*,the] There is no space after the comma. *Atlantis*] Note the space between the *t* and the *is* ligature. 23 things,then] There is no space after the comma in a crowded line. 24 America,the] Note the crowding. *Columbus*,] The *C* is a swash letter. hemuſt] The words are crowded together. 26 thoughts,no] There is no space after the comma. 29 I] The I is wrong font. 30 very] The v and r are battered and worn. *Silenus*,were] Note the crowding. 35 in.And] There is no space between the period and the And Sir] The S is rudimentary or faint in every copy examined. 38 eſpecially] The second e is battered. 40 my . . . my] Note the variation between the y's of the two my's.

An Apology, &c. 11

fhall only defire, that fentence may be refpited, till I can come
to fome inftance, wheieto I may give anfwer.

Thus having fpent his firft onfet not in confuting, but in a
reafonleffe defaming of the book, the method of his malice hur-
ries him to attempt the like againft the Author: not by proofes
and teftimonies, but *having no certaine notice of me*, as he profeffes, *furder then what he gathers from the animadverfions*, blunders
at me for the reft, and flings out ftray crimes at a venture, which
he could never, though he be a Serpent, fuck from any thing that
I have written ; but from his own ftufft magazin, and hoard of
flanderous inventions, over and above that which he converted
to venome in the drawing. To me Readers, it happens as a fingular contentment, and let it be to good men no flight fatisfacti-
on, that the flanderer here confeffes, he has *no furder notice of mee
then his owne conjecture.* Although it had been honeft to have in-
quir'd, before he utter'd fuch infamous words, and I am credibly
inform'd he did inquire, but finding fmall comfort from the intelligence which he receav'd, whereon to ground the falfities
which he had provided, thought it his likelieft courfe under a
pretended ignorance to let drive at randome, left he fhould lofe
his odde ends which from fome penurious Book of Characters he
had been culling out and would faine apply. Not caring to burden me with thofe vices, whereof, among whom my converfati-
on hath been, I have been ever leaft fufpected ; perhaps not without fome futtlety to caft me into envie, by bringing on me a ne-
ceffity to enter into mine own praifes.In which argument I know
every wife man is more unwillingly drawne to fpeak, then the
moft repining eare can be averfe to heare. Neverthelefle fince I
dare not wifh to paffe this life unperfecuted of flanderous
tongues, for God hath told us rhat to be generally prais'd is wofull, I fhall relye on his promife to free the innocent from caufe-
leffe afperfions : whereof nothing fooner can affure me, then if
I fhall feele him now affifting me in the juft vindication of my
felfe, which yet I could deferre, it being more meet that to thofe
other matters of publick debatement in this book I fhould give
attendance firft, but that I feare it would but harme the truth, for
me to reafon in her behalfe, fo long as I fhould fuffer my honeft
eftimation to lye unpurg'd from thefe infolent fufpicions. And
if I fhall be large, or unwonted in juftifying my felfe to thofe
who know me not, for elfe it would be needleffe, let them confider

B 2

5

10

15

20

25

30

35

40

---

1 **fhall**] The a is barely legible. 2 **whereto**] The r is badly battered. 10 **ftufft**] The fft is raised and the final t is battered. 11 **flanderous**] The a is battered. 13 **flight**] The i is worn. 14 **flanderer**] The a is illegible; in a few copies it is missing. *furder*] The first r is battered. 17 **but**] The t is battered. 18 **falfities**] The fi is faint between heavily printed syllables. 20 **lofe**] The o is battered. 24 **I**] The I is wrong font and sits above the line of type. 26 **praifes.In**] Note the crowding. 30 **hath**] The t sits above the line of type. **that**] The first t may be a battered 'r' 31 **I**] The wrong font I sits below the line of type. 32 **nothing**] The **o** sits above the line of type. 38 **infolent**] The l may be a battered 'i' **And**] The A is broken.

1 2   *An Apology, &c.*

der, that a fhort flander will oft times reach farder then a long
apology : and that he who will do juftly to all men, muft begin
from knowing how, if it fo happen, to be not unjuft to himfelfe. I muft be thought, if this libeller (for now he fhewes himfelfe to be fo) can finde beliefe, after an inordinat and riotous
youth fpent at *the Vniverfity*, to have bin at length *vomited out*
thence. For which commodious lye, that he may be incourag'd
in the trade another time, I thank him; for it hath given me an
apt occafion to acknowledge publickly with all gratefull minde,
that more then ordinary favour and refpect which I found above
any of my equals at the hands of thofe curteous and learned men,
the Fellowes of that Colledge wherein I fpent fome yeares: who
at my parting, after I had taken two degrees, as the manner is, fig-
nifi'd many wayes, how much better it would content them
that I would ftay; as by many Letters full of kindneffe and lo-
ving refpect both before that time, and long after I was affur'd
of their fingular good affection towards me. Which being like-
wife propenfe to all fuch as were for their ftudious and civill life
worthy of efteeme, I could not wrong their judgements, and
upright intentions, fo much as to think I had that regard from
them for other caufe then that I might be ftill encourag'd to proceed in the honeft and laudable courfes, of which they appre-
hended I had given good proofe. And to thofe ingenuous and
friendly men who were ever the countnancers of vertuous and
hopefull wits, I wifh the beft, and happieft things, that friends
in abfence wifh one to another. As for the common approbation
or diflike of that place, as now it is, that I fhould efteeme or
difefteeme my felfe or any other the more for that, too fimple
and too credulous is the Confuter, if he thinke to obtaine with
me, or any right difcerner. Of fmall practize were that Phyfitian
who could not judge by what both fhe or her fifter, hath of long
time vomited, that the worfer ftuffe fhe ftrongly keeps in her fto-
mack, but the better fhe is ever kecking at, and is queafie. She
vomits now out of ficknesse, but ere it be well with her, fhe muft
vomit by ftrong phyfick. In the meane while that *Suburb finke*, as
this rude Scavinger calls it, and more then fcurriloufly taunts it
with the *plague*, having a worfe plague, in his middle entraile,
that fuburb wherein I dwell, fhall be in my account a more honourable place then his Univerfity. Which as in the time of her
better health, and mine owne younger judgement I never great-

                                                                    ly

2 apology:] The colon is italic.   7 *thence.*] The period is battered.   **commodious**] Note the
space between the two m's; note also the battered **u**   9 **publickly**] The letter k is battered.
with] The w is smashed.   10 **I**] The I is wrong font.   12 **yeares:who**] Note the crowding.
20 **upright**] The top part of the i proper has been broken off in many copies.   30 **practize**]
Note the heavy **ct** ligature.   34 **fickneffe,**] The comma is battered.   35 **phyfick.In**] There is
no space between the period and the **In**   37 **entraile,**] The battered final **e** makes the following comma appear to be a semicolon in some copies.

An Apology, &c. 1**3**

ly admir'd, fo now much leffe. But he followes me to the City,
ftill ufurping and forging beyond his book notice, which only
he affirmes to have had ; *and where my morning haunts are he wiffes*
not. Tis wonder, that being fo rare an Alchymift of flander, he
could not extrac̄t that, as well as the Univerfity vomit, and the   5
Suburb finke which his art could diftill fo cunningly, but becaufe his Limbeck failes him, to give him and enviethe more
vexation, Ile tell him. Thofe morning haunts are where they
fhould be, at home; not fleeping, or concoc̄ting the furfets of an
irregular feaft, but up, and ftirring, in winter often ere the found   10
of any bell awake men to labour, or to devotion ; in Summer as
oft with the Bird that firft roufes, or not much tardier, to reade
good Authors, or caufe them to be read, till the attention bee
weary, or memory have his full fraught. Then with ufefull and
generous labours preferving the bodies health, and hardineffe ;   15
to render lightfome, cleare, and not lumpifh obedience to the
minde, to the caufe of religion, and our Countries liberty, when
it fhall require firme hearts in found bodies to ftand and cover
their ftations, rather then to fee the ruine of our Proteftation,
and the inforcement of a flavifh life. Thefe are the morning pra-   20
c̄tifes ; proceed now to the afternoone ; *in Playhoufes*, he fayes,
and the Bordelloes. Your intelligence, unfaithfull Spie of Canaan?
he gives in his evidence, that *there he hath trac't me.* Take him at
his word Readers, but let him bring good fureties, ere ye dif-
miffe him, that while he pretended to dogge others, he did not   25
turne in for his owne pleafure ; for fo much in effec̄t he concludes againft himfelfe, not contented to be caught in every o-
ther gin, but he muft be fuch a novice, as to be ftill hamper'd
in his owne hempe. In the Animadverfions, faith he, I finde the
mention of old clokes, falfe beards, nigh-walkers, and falt lotion;   30
therefore the Animadverter haunts Playhoufes and Bordel-
loes ; for if hee did not, how could hee fpeake of fuch gear?
Now that he may know what it is to be a childe, and yet to meddle with edg'd tooles, I turne his *Antiftrephon* upon his owne
head ; the Confuter knowes that thefe things are the furniture of   35
Playhoufes and Bordelloes, therefore by the fame reafon the
Confuter himfelfe hath beene trac't in thofe places. Was it fuch a
diffolute fpeech telling of fome Politicians who were wont to
eavefdroppe in difguifes, to fay they were often lyable to a night-
walking cudgeller, or the emptying of a Urinall ? What if I   40
had

State 1

This page is left blank so that the next facsimile page will appear correctly as a *recto*.

An Apology, &c.   **13**

ly admir'd, fo now much leffe. But he followes me to the City,
ftill ufurping and forging beyond his book notice, which only
he affirmes to have had; *and where my morning haunts are he wiffes
not.* Tis wonder, that being fo rare an Alchymift of flander, he
could not extract that, as well as the Univerfity vomit, and the   5
Suburb finke which his art could diftill fo cunningly, but becaufe his Limbeck failes him, to give him and envie the more
vexation, Ile tell him. Thofe morning haunts are where they
fhould be, at home, not fleeping, or concocting the furfets of an
irregular feaft, but up, and ftirring, in winter often eré the found   10
of any bell awake men to labour, or to devotion; in Summer as
oft with the Bird that firft roufes, or not much tardier, to reade
good Authors, or caufe them to be read, till the attention bee
weary, or memory have his full fraught. Then with ufefull and
generous labours preferving the bodies health, and hardineffe;   15
to render lightfome, cleare, and not lumpifh obedience to the
minde, to the caufe of religion, and our Countries liberty, when
it fhall require firme hearts in found bodies to ftand and cover
their ftations, rather then to fee the ruine of our Proteftation,
and the inforcement of a flavifh life. Thefe are the morning pra-   20
ctifes; proceed now to the afternoone; *in Playhoufes,* he fayes,
and the Bordelloes. Your intelligence, unfaithfull Spie of Canaan?
he gives in his evidence, that *there he hath trac't me.* Take him at
his word Readers, but let him bring good fureties, ere ye dif-
miffe him, that while he pretended to dogge others, he did not   25
turne in for his owne pleafure; for fo much in effect he con-
c'udes againft himfelfe, not contented to be caught in every o-
ther gin, but he muft be fuch a novice, as to be ftill hamper'd
in his owne hempe. In the Animadverfions, faith he, I finde the
mention of old clokes, falfbeards, night-walkers, and falt lotion;   30
therefore the Animadverter haunts Playhoufes and Bordelloes; for if hee did not, how could hee fpeake of fuch gear?
Now that he may know what it is to be a childe, and yet to meddle with edg'd tooles, I turne his *Antiftrephon* upon his owne
head; the Confuter knowes that thefe things are the furniture of   35
Playhoufes and Bordelloes, therefore by the fame reafon the
Confuter himfelfe hath beene trac't in thofe places. Was it fuch a
diffolute fpeech telling of fome Politicians who were wont to
eavefdroppe in difguifes, to fay they were often lyable to a night-
walking cudgeller, or the emptying of a Urinall? What if I   40
had

STATE 2

24 **fureties**,] The small dot above the comma is peculiar to this copy.   25 **miffe**] The i is
smashed in many copies.   26 **turne**] The heavy t probably caused the left stem of the u to
fail to print.   27 **c'udes**] The heavy c probably caused the partially printed l the top of which
is very faint and the rest unprinted in many copies.   30 **falf beards, night-walkers,**] The long
f of **falf** has been retained. Note the correction to **night-walkers** which appears in all copies
examined except those listed under State 1.   39 **eavefdroppe**] Note the battered **a**

14   *An Apology, &c.*

had writ as your friend the author of the aforesaid *Mime, Mundus alter & idem*, to have bin ravisht like some young *Cephalus*
or *Hylas*, by a troope of camping Huswives in *Viraginia*, and
that he was there forc't to sweare himselfe an uxorious varlet,

5   then after a long servitude to have come into *Aphrodisia* that pleasant Countrey that gave such a sweet smell to his nostrils among
the shamelesse Courtezans of *Desvergonia*? surely he would have
then concluded me as constant at the Bordello, as the gally-slave
at his Oare. But since there is such necessity to the hear-say of a

10 Tire, a Periwig, or a Vizard, that Playes must have bin seene,
what difficulty was there in that? when in the Colleges so many
of the young Divines, and those in next aptitude to Divinity
have bin seene so oft upon the Stage writhing and unboning their
Clergie limmes to all the antick and dishonest gestures of Trin-

15 culo's, Buffons, and Bawds; prostituting the shame of that ministery which either they had, or were nigh having, to the eyes
of Courtiers and Court-Ladies, with their Groomes and *Mada-
moisellaes.* There while they acted, and overacted, among o-
ther young scholars, I was a spectator; they thought themselves

20 gallant men, and I thought them fools, they made sport, and
I laught, they mispronounc't and I mislik't, and to make up the
atticisme, they were out, and I hist. Judge now whether so many
good text men were not sufficient to instruct me of false beards
and vizards without more expositors; and how can this Con-

25 futer take the face to object to me the seeing of that which his reverent Prelats allow, and incite their young disciples to act. For
if it be unlawfull to sit and behold a mercenary Comedian perso-
nating that which is least unseemely for a hireling to doe, how
much more blamefull is it to indure the sight of as vile things a-

30 cted by persons either enter'd, or presently to enter into the ministery, and how much more fouleand ignominious for them to
be the actors.

    But because as well by this upraiding to me the Bordello's, as
by other suspicious glancings in his book he would seem privily

35 to point me out to his Readers, as one whose custome of life were
not honest, but licentious; I shall intreat to be born with though
I digresse; & in a way not often trod acquaint ye with the summe
of my thoughts in this matter through the course of my yeares
and studies. Although I am not ignorant how hazardous it will

40 be to do this under the nose of the envious, as it were in skirmish
                                                                        to

---

2 **ravisht**] The f is faint in all copies examined; the t is battered.   6 **Countrey**] The r is battered
and weak in many copies.   8 **concluded**] The first d is smashed.   9 **Oare.**] The quality of
the a varies from fairly legible to vestigial.   **hear-say**] The h is broken and smeared.   10 **Tire,**]
The T is very heavy.   14 **Clergie**] The C and final e sit above the line of type.   15 **Buffons,**]
The B and the two f's are smeared.   19 **I**] The I is wrong font.   22 **out,**] The t is badly battered.   23 **false**] The top of the f is missing.   26 **young**] Note the space between the y and o
31 **foule and**] The words are crowded.   35 **of life**] The apparent crowding is made more obvious by the long kern of the f in **of**   37 **in**] The n is battered and smeared.   **trod**] Note
the weak o

An Apology, &c. 1 5

to change the compact order, and instead of outward actions to
bring inmost thoughts into front. And I must tell ye Readers,
that by this sort of men I have bin already bitten at; yet shall
they not for me know how slightly they are esteem'd, unlesse they
have so much learning as to reade what in Greek Ἀπειροκαλία is, 5
which together with envie is the common disease of those who
censure books that are not for their reading. With me it fares
now, as with him whose outward garment hath bin injur'd and
ill bedighted; for having no other shift, what helpe but to turn
the inside outwards, especially if the lining be of the same, or, 10
as it is sometimes, much better. So if my name and outward demeanour be not evident anough to defend me, I must make tryall,
if the discovery of my inmost thoughts can. Wherein of two purposes both honest, and both sincere, the one perhaps I shall not
misse; although I faile to gaine beliefe with others of being such 15
as my perpetuall thoughts shall heere disclose me, I may yet not
faile of successe in perswading some, to be such really themselves,
as they cannot believe me to be more then what I fain. I had my
time Readers, as others have, who have good learning bestow'd upon them, to be sent to those places, where the opinion 20
was it might be soonest attain'd : and as the manner is, was not
unstudied in those authors which are most commended; whereof
some were grave Orators & Historians; whose matter me thought
I lov'd indeed, but as my age then was, so I understood them; o-
thers were the smooth Elegiack Poets, whereof the Schooles are 25
not scarce. Whom both for the pleasing sound of their numerous
writing, which in imitation I found most easie; and most agreeable to natures part in me, and for their matter which what it is,
there be few who know not, I was so allur'd to read, that no recreation came to me better welcome. For that it was then those years 30
with me which are excus'd though they be least severe, I may be
sav'd the labour to remember ye. Whence having observ'd them
to account it the chiefe glory of their wit, in that they were ablest
to judge, to praise, and by that could esteeme themselves worthiest to love those high perfections which under one or other 35
name they took to celebrate, I thought with my selfe by every
instinct and presage of nature which is not wont to be false, that
what imbolded them to this task might with such diligence as
they us'd imbolden me, and that what judgement, wit, or
elegance was my share, would herein best appeare, and best va- 40
lue

3 I] The I is unusually heavy.   29 there] The word there is followed by a space work-up.
not,I] There is no space after the comma.   read,that] Note the crowding.   30 welcome.For]
There is no space after the period.   those] The t is badly worn.   35 under] Note the partially
imprinted e followed by a heavily imprinted r   36 I] The I is wrong font.   39 wit ,] The
space between wit and the comma is unusually large.

16   *An Apology. &c.*

lue it felfe, by how much more wifely, and with more love of.
vertue I fhould choofe (let rude eares be abfe t) the objeƈt of
not unlike praifes. For albeit thefe thoughts to fome will feeme
vertuous and commendable, to others only pardonable, to a
5 third fort perhaps idle, yet the mentioning of them now will
end in ferious. Nor blame it Readers, in thofe yeares to pro-
pofe to themfelves fuch a reward, as the nobleft difpofitions a-
bove other things in this life have fometimes preferr'd. Whereof
not to be fenfible, when good and faire in one perfon meet, ar-
10 gues both a groffe and fhallow judgement, and withall an ungen-
tle, and fwainifh breft. For by the firme fetling of thefe perfwa-
fions I became, to my beft memory, fo much a proficient, that
if I found thofe authors any where fpeaking unworthy things of
themfelves; or unchafte of thofe names which before they had
15 extoll'd, this effeƈt it wrought with me, from that time forward their art I ftill applauded, but the men I deplor'd; and a-
bove them all preferr'd the two famous renowners of *Beatrice* and
Laura who never write but honour of them to whom they devote
their verfe, difplaying fublime and pure thoughts, without
20 tranfgreffion. And long it was not after, when I was confirm'd
in this opinion, that he who would not be fruftrate of his hope
to write well hereafter in laudable things, ought him felfe to bee
a true Poem, that is, a compofition, and patterne of the beft
and honourableft things; not prefuming to fing high praifes of
25 heroick men, or famous Cities, nnleffe he have in himfelfe the
experience and the praƈtice of all that which is praife-worthy.
Thefe reafonings, together with a certaine niceneffe of nature, an
honeft haughtineffe, and felf-efteem either of what I was, or what
I might be, (which let envie call pride) and laftly that modefty,
30 whereof though not in the Title page yet here I may be excus'd
to make fome befeeming profeffion, all thefe uniting the fupply
of their naturall aide together, kept me ftill above thofe low de-
fcents of minde, beneath which he muft dejeƈt and plunge himfelf, that can agree to falable and unlawfull proftitutions. Next,
35 (for heare me out now Readers) that I may tell ye whether my
younger feet wander'd; I betook me among thofe lofty Fables
and Romances, which recount in folemne canto's the deeds of
Knighthood founded by our viƈtorious Kings; & from hence
had in renowne over all Chriftendome. There I read it in the
40 oath of every Knight, that he fhould defend to the expence of his
                                   beft

All copies examined are numbered **16** except IU-2 and ICU which are numbered 4 2 abfent)] The
n is illegible in this copy.   6 **Readers,**] The top and bottom of the s failed to print.   8 **this life**]
Note the faint h and f   23 **Poem,**] Note the battered e   25 **nnleffe**] The first n should be
a 'u'   27 **nature,an**] There is no space after the comma.   28 **haughtineffe,and . . . was,or**]
Note the crowding.   34 **felf,that**] There is no space after the comma.   **agree**] Note the space
between the a and g   37 **Romances,**] The s is badly battered.   39 **over**] The right side of
the e probably failed to print because of the following heavy r   40 **oath**] The **a** is battered and
broken; in some copies it is missing.

An Apology, &c. **17**

beft blood, or of his life, if it fo befell him, the honour and chaftity of Virgin or Matron. From whence even then I learnt what
a noble veitue chaftity fure muft be, to the defence of which fo
many worthies by fuch a deare adventure of themfelves had
fworne. And if I found in the ftory afterward any of them by
word or deed breaking that oath, I judg'd it the fame fault of
the Poet, as that which is attributed to *Homer*; to have written
undecent things of the gods. Only this my minde gave me that
every free and gentle fpirit without that oath ought to be borne a
Knight, nor needed to expect the guilt fpurre, or the laying of
a fword upon his fhoulder to ftirre him up both by his counfell,
and his arme to fecure and protect the weakneffe of any attempted
chaftity. So that even thofe books which to many others have
bin the fuell of wantonneffe and loofe livi g, I cannot thinke
how unleffe by divine indulgence prov'd to me fo many incitements as you have heard, to the love and ftedfaft obfervation
of that vertue which abhorres the fociety of Bordello's.
Thus from the Laureat fraternity of Poets, riper yeares, and the
ceafeleffe round of ftudy and teading led me to the fhady fpaces
of philofophy, but chiefly to the divine volumes of *Plato*, and his
equall *Xenophon*. Where if I fhould tell ye what I learnt, of chaftity and love, I meane that which is truly fo, whofe charming
cup is only vertue which fhe bears in her hand to thofe who
are worthy. The reft are cheated with a thick intoxicating poti-
on which a certaine Sorcereffe the abufer of loves name carries
about; and how the firft and chiefeft office of love, begins and
ends in the foule, producing thofe happy twins of her divine generation knowledge and vertue, with fueh abftracted fublimities
as thefe, it might be worth your liftning, Readers, as I may one
day hope to have ye in a ftill time, when there fhall be no chi-
ding; not in thefe noifes, the adverfary as ye know, barking
at the doore; or fearching for me at the Burdello's where it may
be he has loft himfelfe, and raps up without pitty the fage and
rheumatick old *Prelateffe* with all her young *Corinthian Laity* to
inquire for fuch a one. Laft of all not in time, but as perfection
is laft, that care was ever had of me, with my earlieft capacity
not to be negligently train'd in the precepts of Chriftian Religion: This that I have hitherto related, hath bin to fhew, that
though Chriftianity had bin but flightly taught me, yet a certain
referv'dneffe of naturall difpofition, and morall difcipline learnt

C   out

5

10

15

20

25

30

35

40

---

2 I] The I is wrong font.   6 it] The dot of the i is missing in most copies.   8 this] The t is badly battered.   9 and] Note the illegible a   without] The final t is raised and battered.   11 him] The top of the i proper has been broken off.   12 fecure] The r is battered.   14 living,] The n of which vestiges are seen here, is missing in a few copies and is broken and battered in most.   18 Thus] Note the worn and crowded us   20 volumes] The o is battered and raised.   28 fueh] The third letter is plainly e in all copies examined except OU, MH, NN, and ICU, in which it is indeterminate. No doubt the word was intended to be *such*; Milton editors have rendered it so.   31 noifes,] The battered f has lost its crossbar.   34 young] The y is smeared in this copy.   38 on :] Note the space before the colon.   40 learnt] The t is blurred. Catchword out] The t is blurred.

18   *An Apology, &c.*

out of the nobleſt Philoſophy was anough to keep me in diſdain
of farre leſſe incontinences then this of the Burdello. But having
had the doctrine of holy Scripture unfolding thoſe chaſte and
high myſteries with timelieſt care infus'd, that *the body is for the*
5   *Lord and the Lord for the body,* thus alſo I argu'd to my ſelfe ; that
if unchaſtity in a woman whom Saint *Paul* termes the glory of
man, be ſuch a ſcandall and diſhonour, then certainly in a man
who is both the image and glory of God, it muſt, though commonly not ſo thought, be much more deflouring and diſhonou-
10   rable. In that he ſins both againſt his owne body which is the
perfeter ſex, and his own glory which is in the woman, and that
which is worſt, againſt the image and glory of God which is in
himſelfe. Nor did I ſlumber over that place expreſſing ſuch high
rewards of ever accompanying the Lambe, with thoſe celeſtiall
15   ſongs to others inapprehenſible, but not to thoſe who were not
defil'd with women, which doubtleſſe meanes fornication: For
mariage muſt not be call'd a defilement. Thus large I have purpoſely bin, that if I have bin juſtly taxt with this crime, it may
come upon me after all this my confeſſion, with a tenne-fold
20   ſhame. But if I have hitherto deſerv'd no ſuch opprobrious word,
or ſuſpicion, I may hereby ingage my ſelfe now openly to the
faithfull obſervation of what I have profeſt. I go on to ſhew you
the unbridl'd impudence of this looſe rayler, who having once
begun his race regards not how farre he flyes out beyond all truth
25   & ſhame; who from the ſingle notice of the animadverſions, as he
proteſts, will undertake to tell ye the very cloaths I weare, though
he be much miſtaken in my wardrobe. And like a ſon of Belial
without the hire of *Ieſabel* charges me *of blaſpheming God and the*
King, as ordnarily as he imagines *me to drink Sack and ſweare,*
30   meerely becauſe this was a ſhred in his common place-book, and
ſeem'd to come off roundly, as if he were ſome Empirick of falſe
accuſations to try his poyſons upon me whether they would
work or no. Whom what ſhould I endeavour to refute more,
whenas that book which is his only teſtimony returnes the lye
35   upon him ; not giving him the leaſt hint of the author to be either a ſwearer, or a Sack drinker. And for the readers if they
can believe me, principally for thoſe reaſons which I have alleg'd, to be of life & purpoſe neither diſhoneſt, nor unchaſte, they
will be eaſily induc't to thinke me ſober both of wine, and of
40   word ; but if I have bin already ſucceſſeleſſe in perſwading them,
                                                  all

10 **In**] The I is raised and wrong font.   11 **woman,and**] There is no space after the comma.
13 **himſelfe.**] Note the period.   20 **opprobrious**] The first r is heavy and sits high; the second
is battered.   26 **weare,though**] Note the crowding.   33 **refute**] The crossbar of the f is missing;
the t is broken.   38 **leg'd,to**] Note the crowding.   **unchaſte,they**] There is no space after
the comma.

An Apology, &c.   19

all that I can furder fay will be but vaine ; and it will be better
thrift to fave two tedious labours, mine of excufing, and theirs
of needleffe hearing.

Proceeding furder I am met with a whole ging of words and
phrafes not mine, for he hath maim'd them, and like a flye de-   5
praver mangl'd them in this his wicked Limbo, worfe then the
ghoft of *Deiphobus* appear'd to his friend *Æneas.* Here I fcarce
know them, and he that would, let him repaire to the place in
that booke where I fet them. For certainly this tormenter of
femicolons is as good at difmembring and flitting fentences, as   10
his grave Fathers the Prelates have bin at ftigmatizing & flitting
nofes. By fuch handy craft as this what might he not traduce?
Only that odour which being his own muft needs offend his fenfe
of fmelling, fince he will needs beftow his foot among us, and
not allow us to think he weares a Sock, I fhall endeavour it may   15
be offenceleffe to other mens eares. The Remonftrant having to
do with grave and reverend men his adverfaries, thought it became him to tell them in fcorne, that *the Biſhops foot had beene
in their book and confuted it*, which when I faw him arrogate, to
have done that with his heeles that furpaft the beft confideration   20
of his head, to fpurn a confutation among refpected men, I queftion'd not the lawfulneffe of moving his jollity to bethink him,
what odor a Sock would have in fuch a painfull bufineffe. And
this may have chanc't to touch him more neerly then I was aware;
for indeed a Biſhops foot that hath all his toes maugre the gout,   25
and a linnen Sock over it, is the apteft embleme of the Prelate
himfelfe. Who being a pluralift, may under one Surplice which
is alfo linnen, hide foure benefices befides the metropolitan toe, and fends a fouler ftench to heaven, then that which
this young queafineffe reches at. And this is the immediate   30
reafon here why our inrag'd Confuter, that he may be as perfet
an hypocrite as *Caiaphas*, ere he be a High Prieft, cries out, *horrid blaſphemy !* and like a recreant Jew calls for *ſtones.*I befeech ye
friends, ere the brick-bats flye, refolve me and your felves, is it
blafphemy, or any whit difagreeing from Chriftian meekneffe,   35
when as Chrift himfelfe fpeaking of unfavory traditions, fcruples
not to name the Dunghill and the Jakes, for me to anfwer a flo-
ven!y wincer of a confutation, that, if he would needs put his
foot to fuch a fweaty fervice, the odour of his Sock was like to
be neither musk, nor benjamin ? Thus did that foolifh Monk   40
C 2   in

---

5 flye] The f is smeared.   7 *Deiphobus*] The *D* is a swash letter.   *Ænæas.*] The *Æ* is a swash
ligature; the period is smashed.   8 know] Note the space between the kno and the battered **w**
32 *Caiaphas,*] The *C* is a swash letter.   33 Jew] The J is a swash letter.   *ſtones.*I] Note the
crowding.   36 as] The **s** is badly battered.   unfavory] Note the battered **u**

20   *An Apology, &c.*

in a barbarous Declamation accuse *Petrarch* of blasphemy for
dispraising the French wines. But this which followes is plaine
bedlam stuffe, this is the *Demoniack legion* indeed, which the
Remonstrant feard had been against him, and now he may see is

5   for him. *You that love Christ*, saith he, *and know this miscreant
wretch, stone him to death, lest you smart for his impunity.* What
thinks the Remonstrant? does he like that such words as these
should come out of his shop, out of his Trojan horse? to give
the watch word like a *Guisian of* Paris to a mutiny or massacre;

10   to proclame a *Crusada* against his fellow Christian now in this
troublous and divided time of the Kingdome? if he do, I shall
say that to be the Remonstrant is no better then to be a Jesuit.
And that if he and his accomplices could do as the rebels have
done in *Ireland* to the Protestants, they would do in *England*

15   the same to them that would no Prelats. For a more seditious
and Butcherly Speech no Cell of *Loyola* could have belch't a-
gainst one who in all his writing spake not, that any mans skin
should be rais'd. And yet this cursing *Shimei* a hurler of stones, as
well as a rayler, wants not the face instantly to make as though

20   he *despair'd of victory unlesse a modest defence would get it him.* Did
I erre at all, Readers, to foretell ye, when first I met with his
title, that the epithet of modest there, was a certaine red portending signe, that he meant ere long to be most tempestuously
bold, , and shamelesse? Neverthelesse *he dares not say but there*

25   *may be hid in his nature as much venemous Atheisme and profanati-*
on, as he thinks, *hath broke out at his adversaries lips, but he hath*
not the soare running upon him, as he would intimate *I have.* Now
trust me not, Readers, if I be not already weary of pluming
and footing this Seagull, so open he lies to strokes; and never

30   offers at another, but brings home the dorre upon himselfe. For
if the sore be running upon me, in all judgement I have scapt
the disease, but he who hath as much infection hid in him, as
he hath voluntarily confest, and cannot expell it, because hee
is dull, for venomous Atheisme were no treasure to be kept with-

35   in him else, let him take the part hee hath chosen, which
must needs follow, to swell and burst with his owne inward
venome.
    Sect. 1. But marke, Readers, there is a kind of justice observ'd
among them that do evill, but this man loves injustice in the ve-

40   ry order of his malice. For having all this while abus'd the good
                                              name

---

1 in] Note the raised i   barbarous] The first r is badly worn.   **Petrarch**] The P is not italic.
3 bedlam] The e is smeared.   5 *Christ*,] The C is a swash letter.   8 horse?] The question
mark is italic.   9 *Guisian*] Note the space between the G and u   Paris] The P is not italic.
12 Jesuit.] The J is a swash letter.   14 *Ireland*] The *I* is a swash letter.   18 stones,as] Note
the crowding.   24 bold, ,] Note the two commas.   25 *Atheisme*] The A is not italic.
26 *adversaries*] The d is battered.   34 dull,] The final l and the comma are fused as a result
of smearing.

An Apology, &c. 21

name of his adverſary with all manner of licence in revenge
of his Remonſtrant, if they be not both one perſon, or as I am
told, Father and Son, yet after all this he calls for ſatisfaction,
when as he himſelfe hath already taken the utmoſt farding. *Vio-*
lence hath been done, ſayes he, *to the perſon of a holy, and religious* 5
Prelat· To which, ſomething in effect to what S. *Paul* anſwer'd
of *Ananias*, I anſwer, *I wiſt not brethren that he was a holy and re-*
ligious Prelat; for evill is written of thoſe who would be Prelats.
And finding him thus in diſguiſe without his ſuperſcription or
Phylactery either of *holy* or *Prelat*, it were no ſinne to ſerve him 10
as *Longchamp* Biſhop of *Elie* was ſerv'd in his diſguiſe at *Dover*:
He hath begun the meaſure nameleſſe, and when he pleaſes we
may all appeare as we are. And let him be then what he will, he
ſhall be to me ſo as I finde him principl'd. For neither muſt Prelat or Arch-Prelat hope to exempt himſelfe from being reckon'd 15
as one of the vulgar; which is for him only to hope whom true
wiſdome and the contempt of vulgar opinions exempts, it being
taught us in the Pſalmes that he who is in honour and underſtan-
deth not is as the beaſts that periſh. And now firſt *the manner of*
handling that cauſe which I undertook, he thinks *is ſuſpicious*, as 20
if the wiſeſt, and the beſt words were not ever to ſome or other
ſuſpicious. But where is the offence, the diſagreement from Chriſtian meekneſſe, or the precept of *Solomon* in anſwering folly?
when the Remonſtrant talks of *froth and ſcum*, I tell him there is
none, and bid him *ſpare his Ladle*: when he brings in the meſſe 25
with *Keale, Beef, and Breweſſe*, what ſtomack in *England* could
forbeare to call for flanks and briskets? Capon and whitebroth
having beene likely ſometimes in the ſame roome with Chriſt
and his Apoſtles, why does it trouble him that it ſhould be now
in the ſame leafe, eſpecially, where the diſcourſe is not continu'd 30
but interrupt? And let him tell me, is he wont to ſay grace,
doth he not then name holieſt names over the ſteame of coſtlieſt
ſuperfluities? Does he judge it fooliſh or diſhoneſt to write that
among religious things, which when he talks of religious things
he can devoutly chew? is he afraid to name Chriſt where thoſe 35
things are written in the ſame leafe whom he fears not to name
while the ſame things are in his mouth? Doth not Chriſt himſelfe teach the higheſt things by the ſimilitude *of old bottles and*
patcht cloaths? Doth he not illuſtrate beſt things by things moſt
evill? his own *comming* to be *as a thiefe in the night*, and the righ- 40
teous

---

5 *perſon*] The descender of the *p* is battered.   *aud*] A *u* is printed for an '*n*'   6 *Prelat*·]
The *P* is a swash letter; the period is raised.   10 *Prelat*,] The *P* is a swash letter.   11 *Dover.*]
The dot above the period is a very faint point in some copies; it resembles a squabbled comma
in others.   14 **as**] The s is raised and badly battered.   19 **that**] The heavy h caused the
preceding t and the following a to be weak.   20 *handling*] The g is smeared.   21 **if**] The **f**
sits above the line of type.   26 *Beef . . . Breweſſe*] The B's are swash letters.   27 **briskets?**]
The final s is battered and raised.   29 **ſhould**] The ascender of the d is broken off.   40 *thiefe*]
The first *e* is poorly printed in most copies; in this copy the first *e* is illegible and the second
barely legible.

22   *An Apology, &c.*

teous mans *wisdome to that of an unjust Steward?* He might therefore have done better to have kept in *his canting beggars and heathen Altar* to sacrifice his thredbare criticisme of *Bomolochus* to
an unseasonable Goddesse fit for him call'd Importunity, and
5 have reserv'd his Greek derivation till he lecture to his fresh men,
for here his itching pedantry is but flouted.

But to the end that nothing may be omitted which may furder
satisfie any conscionable man, who notwithstanding what I
could explaine before the animadversions, remains yet unsatisfi'd
10 concerning that way of writing which I there defended, but
this confuter whom it pinches, utterly disapproves, I shall assay
once againe, and perhaps with more successe. If therefore the
question were in oratory, whether a vehement vein throwing out
indignation, or scorn upon an object that merits it, were among
15 the aptest *Id:as* of speech to be allow'd, it were my work, and
that an easie one to make it cleare both by the rules of best rhetoricians, and the famousest examples of the Greek and Roman
Orations. But since the Religion of it is disputed, and not the
art, I shall make use only of such reasons and autorities, as re-
20 ligion cannot except against. It will be harder to gainsay, then
for me to evince that in the teaching of men diversly temper'd
different wayes are to be try'd. The Baptist we know was a strict
man remarkable for austerity and set order of life. Our Saviour
who had all gifts in him was Lord to expresse his indoctrinating
25 power in what sort him best seem'd; sometimes by a milde and
familiar converse, sometimes with plaine and impartiall home-
speaking regardlesse of those whom the auditors might think he
should have had in more respect ; otherwhiles with bitter and
irefull rebukes if not teaching yet leaving excuselesse those his
30 wilfull impugners. What was all in him, was divided among
many others the teachers of his Church; some to be severe and
ever of a sad gravity that they may win such, & check sometimes
those who be of nature over-confident and jocond; others were
sent more cheeresull, free, and still as it were at large, in the
35 midst of an untrespassing honesty ; that they who are so temper'd
may have by whom they might be drawne to salvation, and they
who are too scrupulous, and dejected of spirit might be often
strengthn'd with wise consolations and revivings : no man being
forc't wholly to dissolve that groundwork of nature which God
40 created in him, the sanguine to empty out all his sociable live-
linesse,

---

14 **merits**] The r is badly battered.   19 **I**] The I is worn.   21 **diversly**] The r is badly worn.
28 **respect ;**] Note the large space before the semicolon.   29 **teaching**] The a is faint between
two heavy letters.   35 **are so**] The words are crowded together.   39 **of**] The o sits too low.

An Apology, &c. 23

linesse, the cholerick to expell quite the unsinning predominance
of his anger; but that each radicall humour and passion wrought
upon and corrected as it ought, might be made the proper mould
and foundation of every mans peculiar guifts, and vertues. Some
also were indu'd with a staid moderation, and soundnesse of ar- 5
gument to teach and convince the rationall and sober-minded;
yet not therefore that to be thought the only expedient course
of teaching, for in times of opposition when either against new
heresies arising, or old corruptions to be reform'd this coole un-
passionate mildnesse of positive wisdome is not anough to damp 10
and astonish the proud resistance of carnall, and false Doctors,
then (that I may have leave to soare a while as the Poets use:)
then Zeale whose substance is ethereal, arming in compleat diamond ascends his fiery Chariot drawn with two blazing Mete-
ors figur'd like beasts, but of a higher breed then any the Zodiack 15
yeilds, resembling two of those four which *Ezechiel* and S. *John*
saw, the one visag'd like a Lion to expresse power, high autority and indignation, the other of count'nance like a man to cast
derision and scorne upon perverse and fraudulent seducers; with
these the invincible warriour Zeale shaking loosely the slack reins 20
drives over the heads of Scarlet Prelats, and such as are insolent
to maintaine traditions, brusing their stiffe necks under his flaming wheels. Thus did the true Prophets of old combat with
the false; thus Christ himselfe the fountaine of meeknesse found
acrimony anough to be still galling and vexing the Prelaticall 25
Pharisees. But ye will say these had immediat warrant from God
to be thus bitter, and I say, so much the plainlier is it prov'd,
that there may be a sanctifi'd bitternesse against the enemies of
truth. Yet that ye may not think inspiration only the warrant
thereof, but that it is as any other vertue, of morall and generall 30
observation, the example of *Luther* may stand for all: whom
God made choice of before others to be of highest eminence and
power in reforming the Church; who not of revelation, but of
judgement writ so vehemently against the chiefe defenders of old
untruths in the Romish Church, that his own friends and fa- 35
vourers were many times offended with the fiercenesse of his spirit; yet he being cited before *Charles* the fifth to answer for his
books, and having divided them into three sorts, whereof one
was of those which he had sharply written, refus'd though
upon deliberation giv'n him to retract or unsay any word there- 40
in

2 each] The a is battered.   3 ought,might] There is no space after the comma.   6 sober-minded;]
The space before the semicolon justifies the line.   12 use)] The heavy s makes the impression
of the right stem of the u and of the left side of the e faint.   16 yeilds,] The i is broken.
John] The I is a swash letter.   30 morall] The r is broken.   31 all:] The colon is italic.
34 defenders] The n appears to be an 'h' with the ascender broken off.

24   *An Apology, &c*

in ; as we may reade in *Sleidn*. Yea he defends his eagernesse, as
being *of an ardent spirit, and one who could not write a dull stile:* and
affirm'd *hee thought it Gods will to have the inventions of men
thus laid open, seeing that matters quietly handled, were quickly
forgot.* And herewithall how usefull and available God had
made this tart rhetorick in the Churches cause, he often found by
his owne experience. For when he betook himselfe to lenity
and moderation, as they call it, he reapt nothing but contempt
both from *Cajetan* and *Erasmus*, from *Cocleus*, from *Ecchius* and
others, infomuch that blaming his friends who had so counsel'd
him, he refolv'd never to runne into the like error ; if at other
times he feeme to excufe his vehemence , as more then what was
meet, I have not examin'd through his works to know how farre
he gave way to his owne fervent minde ; it shall suffice me to
looke to mine own. And this I shall easily averre though it may
feeme a hard faying, that the Spirit of God who is purity it selfe,
when he would reprove any fault severely, or but relate things
done or said with indignation by others, abstains not from fome
words not civill at other times to be spok'n. Omitting that place
in Numbers at the killing of *Zimri and Cosbi* done by *Phineas* in
the heigth of zeal, related as the Rabbines expound, not without
an obfcene word, we may finde in Deuteronomy and three of
the Prophets, where God denouncing bitterly the punishments
of Idolaters, tels them in a terme immodest to be utter'd in coole
blood, that their wives shall be defil'd openly. But these, they
will fay were honest words in that age when they were spok'n.
Which is more then any Rabbin can prove, and certainly had
God been so minded, he could have pickt such words, as should
never have come into abufe. What will they fay to this. *David*
going againft *Nabal*, in the very fame breath when he had but
just before nam'd the *name of God*, he vowes not *to leave any alive
of Nabals house that pisseth against the wall.* But this was unadvi-
fedly spoke, you will anfwer, and fet downe to aggravate his infirmity. Turne then to the first of Kings where God himfelfe
ufes the phrafe ; *I will cut off from Ieroboam him that pisseth against
the wall.* Which had it beene an unfeemely speech in the heat of
an earneft expreffion, then we must conclude that *Ionathan*, or
Onkelos the Targumifts were of cleaner language then he that
made the tongue ; for they render it as briefly, *I will cut off all
who are at yeares of diferetion,* that is to fay fo much diferetion as
                                                        to

---

1 *Sleiden.*] The second *e* is very faint in all copies examined. The Columbia editors have spelled
the word *Sleidan*. 2 *stile:and*] Note the crowding. 6 **caufe,he**] Note the crowding. 11 **error ;**]
There is an unusually large space before the semicolon. 18 **others,**] The comma is battered.
35 **ufes**] The u is broken; the lower part of the f is broken off in all copies examined.

An Apology, &c.   25

to hide nakedneſſe. Whereas God who is the author both of purity and eloquence, choſe this phraſe as fitteſt in that vehement
character wherein he ſpake. Otherwiſe that plaine word might
have eaſily bin forborne. Which the *Maſoreths* and Rabbini-
call *Scholiaſts* not well attending, have often us'd to blurre the   5
margent with *Keri*, inſtead of *Ketiv*, and gave us this inſulſ
rule out of their *Talmud*, *That all words which in the Law are writ*
obſcenely, muſt be chang'd to more civill words. Fools who would
teach men to ſpeak more decently then God thought good to
write. And thus I take it to be manifeſt, that indignation againſt   10
men and their actions notoriouſly bad, hath leave and autority
oft times to utter ſuch words and phraſes as in common talke
were not ſo mannerly to uſe. That ye may know, not only as
the Hiſtorian ſpeaks, *that all thoſe things for which men plough,*
build, or ſaile, obey vertue, but that all words and whatſoever may   15
be ſpoken ſhall at ſome time in an unwonted manner wait upon
her purpoſes.

Now that the confutant may alſo know as he deſires, what
force of teaching there is ſometimes in laughter, I ſhall returne
him in ſhort, that laughter being one way of anſwering *A Foole*   20
according to his folly, teaches two ſorts of perſons, firſt the Foole
himſelfe *not to be wiſe in his own conceit*; as *Salomon* affirms, which
is certainely a great document, to make an unwiſe man know
himſelfe. Next, it teaches the hearers, in as much as ſcorne is one
of thoſe puniſhments which belong to men carnally wiſe, which   25
is oft in Scripture declar'd; for when ſuch are puniſht *the ſimple*
are thereby made wiſe, if *Salomons* rule be true. And I would ask,
to what end *Eliah* mockt the falſe Prophets? was it to ſhew his
wit, or to fulfill his humour? doubtleſſe we cannot imagine that
great ſervant of God had any other end in all which he there   30
did, but to teach and inſtruct the poore miſledde people. And we
may frequently reade, that many of the Martyrs in the midſt of
their troubles, were not ſparing to deride and ſcoffe their ſu-
perſtitious perſecutors. Now may the confutant adviſe againe
with Sir *Francis Bacon* whether *Eliah* and the Mattyrs did well   35
to turne religion into a Comedy, or Satir; *to rip up the wounds*
of Idolatry and Superſtition *with a laughing countenance.* So that
for pious gravity his author here is matcht and overmatcht, and
for wit and morality in one that followes.

              D   *--laughing*

---

1 **nakedneſſe.**] The two n's are badly battered. **God**] The G is battered in all copies examined;
the **d** is weak and broken in many. 4 ***Maſoreths***] The faint *o* is illegible in some copies and is
unprinted in others. 9 **ſpeak**] The erratum substitutes *read*. 10 **indignation**] The second **n**
is smeared in most copies and is hardly distinguishable from a 'u' in many. 20 ***A***] The ***A*** is
a swash letter. 22 ***conceit***;] Note the space before the semicolon. **affirms,which**] Note the
crowding. 31 **did,but**] There is no space after the comma. 34 **againe**] The **n** is battered
and faint.

26   *An Apology, &c.*

---laughing to teach the truth
What hinders? as some teachers give to Boyes
Iunkets and knacks, that they may learne apase,
Thus *Flaccus* in his first Satir, and in his tenth
5   *---Iesting decides great things*
Stronglier, and better oft then earnest can.

I could urge the same out of *Cicero,* and *Seneca,* but he may
content him with this. And hence forward, if he can learn, may
know as well what are the bounds, and objects of laughter and
10 vehement reproofe, as he hath knowne hitherto how to deserve
them both. But lest some may haply think, or thus expostulat with
me after all this debatement, who made you the busie Almoner
to deale about this dole of laughter and reprehension which no
man thanks your bounty for? To the urbanity of that man I shold
15 answer much after this sort? That I, friend objecter, having
read of heathen Philosophers, some to have taught, that whoso-
ever would but use his eare to listen, might heare the voice of his
guiding *Genius* ever before him, calling and as it were pointing
to that way which is his part to follow; others, as the Sto-
20 icks, to account reason, which they call the *Hegemonicon,* to
be the common *Mercury* conducting without error those that
give themselves obediently to be led accordingly, having read
this, I could not esteeme so poorly of the faith which I professe,
that God had left nothing to those who had forsaken all other
25 doctrines for his, to be an inward witnesse, and warrant of what
they have to do, as that they should need to measure themselves
by other mens measures how to give scope, or limit to their proper actions; for that were to make us the most at a stand, the
most uncertaine and accidentall wanderers in our doings, of all
30 religions in the world. So that the question ere while mov'd
who he is that spends thus the benevolence of laughter and reproofe so liberally upon such men as the Prelats, may returne
with a more just demand, who he is not of place and knowledge
never so mean, under whose contempt and jerk these men are not
35 deservedly falne ? neither can religion receive any wound by
disgrace thrown upon the Prelats, since religion and they surely were never in such amity. They rather are the men who have
wounded religion, and their stripes must heale her. I might also tell them, what *Electra* in *Sophocles,* a wise Virgin answer'd
40 her wicked Mother who thought her selfe too violently reprov'd
by her the daughter.
                                       Tis

---

2 *hinders?*] The question mark is not italic.   4 *Flaccus*] The *a* is battered.   5 *Iesting*] The *I* is a swash letter.   11 **both.Butlest**] Note the crowding. **think,or**] There is no space after the comma.   14 **for?To**] There is no space after the question mark. **shold**] Note the spelling. 15 **sort?**] The question mark may be a printer's error, for a period seems to be the logical punctuation here. **I**] The I is wrong font.   19 **his**] The h is broken; the s sits above the line of type.   22 **themselves**] The f is battered and broken. **read**] The a is faint before a heavy d 25 **warrant**] Note the weak letters.   26 **measure**] The first e is badly battered.   30 **So**] The S is battered and broken.   35 **falne ?**] Note the spelling as well as the space before the question mark.   36 **Prelats,**] The s is battered.   37 **They**] The T is weak; the e is battered. 39 *Electra*] The small e is vestigial.   41 **by her the daughter.**] These words are on the same line as the catchword *Tis*

An Apology, &c. **27**

T is you that say it, not I, you do the deeds,
And your ungodly deeds finde me the words.

If therefore the Remonstrant complaine of libels, it is because
he feels them to be right aim'd. For I ask againe as before in the
animadversions, how long is it since he hath dif-relifht libe's? 5
we never heard the least mutter of his voice against them while
they flew abroad without controul or check defaming the Scots
and Puritans. And yet he can remember of none but *Lysimachus*
Nicanor, and *that he mislikt and censur'd.* No more but of one can
the Remonstrant remember? What if I put him in minde of one 10
more? What if of one more whereof the Remonstrant in many
likelyhoods may be thought the author? Did he never see a Pamphlet intitl'd after his own fashion, *A survey of that foolish, sedi-*
tious, scandalous, profane libell the Protestation protested? The child
doth not more expresly refigure the visage of his Father, then 15
that book resembles the stile of the Remonstrant, in those idioms of speech, wherein he seemes most to delight: and in the
seventeenth Page three lines together taken out of the Remonstrance word for word, not as a citation, but as an author bor-
rowes from himselfe. Who ever it be, he may as justly be said to 20
have libell'd, as he against whom he writes: there ye shall finde
another man then here is made shew of, there he bites as fast
as this whines. *Vinegar in the inke* is there *the antidote of Vi-*
pers. Laughing in a religious controversie is there *a thrifty physick*
to expell his melancholy. In the meane time the testimony of Sir 25
Francis Bacon was not misalledg'd, complaining that libels on
the Bishops part were utter'd openly; and if he hop't the Prelats
had no intelligence with the libellours, he delivers it but as his favourable opinion. But had he contradicted himselfe, how could
I assoil him here, more then a little before, where I know not 30
how by entangling himselfe, he leaves an aspersiou upon *Iob,*
which by any else I never heard laid to his charge. For having
affirm'd that *there is no greater confusion then the confounding of jest*
and earnest, presently he brings the example of *Iob glancing at*
conceits of mirth, when he sate among the people with the gravity of 35
a Iudge upon him. If jest and earnest be such a confusion, then
were the people much wiser then *Iob,* for *he smil'd, and they be-*
liev'd him not. To defend Libels, which is that whereof I am
next accus'd, was farre from my purpose. I had not so little
share in good name, as to give another that advantage against 40

D 2 my

---

1 *I*] The *I* is a swash letter. 2 *words.*] The *r* is heavy. 5 dif-relifht] The second i is badly battered and undotted. libels?] The second l is vestigial. 7 **defaming**] The a is battered and smeared; the descender of the g is broken off. 9 *mislikt*] The second *i* is broken and undotted; the *k* is battered and broken; the *t* is broken. 10 I] The I is wrong font. put] The p is very faint and illegible here; in some copies it is squabbled. 12 **Pam-**] The P is smeared in all copies examined. 13 *foolish*,] Note the space before the battered comma. 14 *Protestation*] The *i* is undotted. 16 **Remonstrant,**] The line extending downward from the on is a flaw in the paper. 17 speech,] The c is battered. 23 *Vinegar*] The *e* is broken. *inke*] The k is battered. 31 aspersiou] The u is printed for an 'n' in all copies examined. 35 *conceits*] The *e* appears battered; the right side of it is unprinted because of the heavily imprinted *i* which follows. *the*] The t of the first *the* is battered. 39 little] The second t is illegible here. Catchword **my**] The y may have been changed in some copies, for two styles of y seem to appear: compare IU-1 and IU-1654 with IU-4 and IU-5. Signature **D2**] Signature **C2** appears for **D2** in IU-5, OU, NN, CtY-1, NjP-1.

28   *An Apology, &c.*

my felfe. The fumme of what I faid, was that a more free per-
miffion of writing at fome times might be profitable, in fuch a
queftion efpecially wherein the Magiftrates are not fully refolv'd;
and both fides have equall liberty to write, as now they have.
5   Not as when the Prelats bore fway, in whofe time the bookes of
fome men were confuted, when they who fhould have anfwer'd
were in clofe prifon, deny'd the ufe of pen or paper. And the
Divine right of Epifcopacy was then valiantly afferted, when he
who would have bin refpondent, muft have bethought himfelfe
10   withall how he could refute the *Clink*, or the *Gate-houfe*. If now
therefore they be perfu'd with bad words, who perfecuted o-
thers with bad deeds, it is a way to leffen tumult rather then to
encreafe it; when as anger thus freely vented fpends it felfe, ere
it break out into action, though *Machiavell* whom he cites, or
15   any *Machiavillian* Prieft think the contrary.
     Sect. 3   Now Readers I bring ye to his third Section; where-
in very cautioufly, and no more then needs, left I fhould take
him for fome Chaplaine at hand, fome Squire of the body to
his Prelat, one that ferves not at the Altar only, but at the Court
20   cup board, he will beftow on us a pretty modell of himfelfe;
and fobs me out halfe a dozen tizicall mottoes where ever he had
them, hopping fhort in the meafure of convulfion fits; in which
labour the agony of his wit, having fcapt narrowly, inftead of
well fiz'd periods, he greets us with a quantity of thum-ring po-
25   fies. *He has a fortune therefore good, becaufe he is content with it.*
This is a piece of fapience not worth the brain of a fruit-trencher;
as if content were the meafure of what is good or bad in the guift
of fortune. For by this rule a bad man may have a good fortune,
becaufe he may be oft times content with it for many reafons
30   which have no affinity with vertue, as love of eafe, want of fpirit
to ufe more, and the like. *And therefore content,* he fayes, *becaufe
it neither goes before, nor comes behinde his merit.* Belike then if his
fortune fhould go before his merit, he would not be content, but
refigne, if we believe him, which I do the leffe, becaufe he implyes
35   that if it came behinde his merit, he would be content as little.
Wheras if a wife mans content fhould depend upon fuch a *Therefore,* becaufe his fortune came not behinde his merit, how many
wife men could have content in this world? In his next pithy
fymbol I dare not board him, for he paffes all *the feven wife
40   Mafters of Greece,* attributing to himfelfe that which on my life
                                                    Salomon

---

1 felfe.] The final e is battered.   faid,] The comma, which is battered in this copy, appears
in some copies to be a period.   3 efpecially] The second e is broken.   wherein] The second e
appears smashed.   5 the] The t of the first the is badly battered.   6 men] The n is battered.
10 *Clink*,] The *C* is a swash letter.   11 perfu'd] The u is smashed and broken.   13 encreafe]
The long kern of the f faintly imprinted here, is in some copies rudimentary and in others unprinted.   14 *Machiavell*] The *M* is a swash letter.   15 the] The t is battered and squabbled.
16 I] The I is wrong font.   where-] The battered hyphen, which sits low, appears in some copies
to be a period.   19 Court] The o is poorly imprinted in many copies; in a few it is missing.
28 this] The h is battered and sits too high.   30 affinity] The n is battered.   31 the] The t
is badly battered and broken.   And] The left stem of the n is unprinted following a heavily
imprinted *A*   33 merit,] The r is battered; the i faint in many copies, is illegible here.
34 which] The c is broken.   35 little.] The first t missing in a few copies, is battered here.
36 Wheras] The battered s sits too high.

An Apology, &c.   29

Salomon durſt not ; *to have affections ſo equally temper'd, that they neither too haſtily adhere to the truth, before it be fully examin'd, nor too lazily afterward.* Which unleſſe he only were exempted out of the corrupt maſſe of *Adam*, borne without ſinne originall, and living without actuall, is impoſſible. Had *Salomon* (for it behoves me to inſtance in the wiſeſt, dealing with ſuch a tranſcendent Sage as this) had *Salomon* affections ſo equally temper'd, as *not adhering too lazily to the truth*, when God warn'd him of his halting in idolatry ? do we reade that he repented haſtily ? did not his affections lead him haſtily from an examin'd truth, how much more would they lead him ſlowly to it ? Yet this man beyond a *Stoick apathy* ſees truth as in a rapture, and cleaves to it. Not as through the dim glaſſe of his affections which in this frail manſion of fleſh are ever unequally temper'd, puſhing forward to error, and keeping back from truth oft times the beſt of men. But how farre this boaſter is from knowing himſelfe, let his *Preface* ſpeake. Something I thought it was that made him ſo quiekſighted to gather ſuch ſtrange things out of the Animadverſions, whereof the leaſt conception could not be drawne from thence, of *Suburb ſinks*, ſometimes *out of wit and cloaths*, ſometimes *in new Serge, drinking Sack, and ſwearing*, now I know it was this equall temper of his affections that gave him to ſee clearer then any fenell rub'd Serpent. Laſtly, he has reſolv'd *that neither perſon, nor cauſe ſhall improper him*. I may miſtake his meaning, for the word ye heare is *improper*. But whether if not a perſon, yet a good Perſonage, or Impropriation bought out for him would not *improper* him, becauſe there may be a quirk in the word, I leave it for a Canoniſt to reſolve.

Sect. 4. And thus ends this Section, or rather diſſection of himſelfe, ſhort ye will ſay both in breath, and extent, as in our own praiſes it ought to be, unleſſe wherein a good name hath bin wrongfully attainted. Right, but if ye looke at what he aſcribes to himſelfe, *that temper of his affections* which cannot any where be but in Paradiſe, all the judicious *Panegyricks* in any language extant are not halfe ſo prolixe. And that well appears in his next removall. For what with putting his fancy to the tiptoe in this deſcription of himſelfe, and what with adventuring preſently to ſtand upon his own legs without the crutches of his margent, which is the ſluce moſt commonly, that feeds the drouth of his text, he comes ſo lazily on in a Similie, with his

5

10

15

20

25

30

35

40

---

1 *they*] The *y* is raiſed.   4 *Adam*,] The *A* is a swash letter.   5 *Salomou*] The letter *u* is printed for an 'n'   6 inſtance] The left stem of the first n has not printed.   14 ever] The word is transcribed *every* by the Columbia editors.   21 *Serge*, ... *Sack*, ... *ſwearing*,] Note the varying quality of the commas.   32 if] The i is undotted.   33 *temper*] The *p* is battered.

30   *An Apology, &c.*

his *arme full of weeds*, and demeanes himſelfe in the dull expreſ-
ſion ſo like a dough kneaded thing, that he has not ſpirit anough
left him ſo farre to look to his *Syntaxis*, as to avoide nonſenſe.
For it muſt be underſtood there that *the ſtranger*, and not *he who*
5 *brings the bundle* would be *deceav'd in cenſuring the field*, which
this hip-ſhot *Grammarian* cannot ſet into right frame of conſtruction, neither here in the ſimilitude, nor in the following *reddi-*
tion thereof, which being to this purpoſe, that *the faults of the*
beſt pickt out, and preſented in groſſe, ſeeme monſtrous, this ſaith he,
10 *you have done, in pinning on his ſleeve the faults of others*; as if to
pick out his owne faults, and to pin the faults of others upon
him, were to do the ſame thing. To anſwer therefore how I
have cull'd out the evill actions of the Remonſtrant from his vertues, I am acquitted by the dexterity and conveiance of his non-
15 ſenſe, looſing that for which he brought his parable. But
what of other mens faults I have pinn'd upon his ſleeve, let
him ſhew. For whether he were the man who term'd the Martyrs *Foxian* confeſſors, it matters not; he that ſhall ſtep up before others to defend a Church-government, which wants al-
20 moſt no circumſtance, but only a name to be a plaine Popedome,
a government which changes the fatherly and everteaching diſ-
cipline of Chriſt into that Lordly and uninſtructing juriſdiction
which properly makes the Pope Antichriſt, makes himſelfe an
acceſſory to all the evill committed by thoſe, who are arm'd to
25 do miſchiefe by that undue government; which they by their
wicked deeds, do with a kinde of paſſive and unwitting obedience to God, deſtroy. But he by plauſible words and traditions
againſt the Scripture obſtinately ſeeks to maintaine. They by
their owne wickedneſſe ruining their owne unjuſt autority make
30 roome for good to ſucceed. But he by a ſhew of good upholding
the evill which in them undoes it ſelfe, hinders the good which
they by accident let in. Their manifeſt crimes ſerve to bring forth
an enſuing good and haſten a remedy againſt themſelves, and his
ſeeming good tends to reinforce their ſelfe-puniſhing crimes and
35 his owne, by doing his beſt to delay all redreſſe. Shall not all
the miſchiefe which other men do, be layd to his charge, if they
doe it by that unchurchlike power which he defends? Chriſt
ſaith, *be that is not with me is againſt me, and he that gathers not*
with me ſcatters. In what degree of enmity to Chriſt ſhall wee
40 place that man then, who ſo is with him, as that it makes more
againſt

---

2 kneaded] The k is battered; the ascender of the final d is broken off.   4 For] The F is smeared;
the o sits above the line of type.   5 field,] The *e* is illegible.   6 *Grammarian*] The *G* is a swash
letter.   18 tyrs] The letters ty are smeared; the s is battered.   *Foxian*] The *F* is smeared;
there is a space between the *F* and *o*   20 but] The u is broken in all copies examined.
33 themſelves, and] Note the crowding.

An Apology, &c. 3ɪ

against him, and so gathers with him, that it scatters more from
him ? shall it availe that man to say he honours the Martyrs memory and treads in their steps ? No, the Pharisees confest as much
of the holy Prophets. Let him and such as he when they are in
their best actions even at their prayers looke to heare that which 5
the Pharisees heard from *Iohn* the *Baptist* when they least expected, when they rather lookt for praise from him. *Generation of*
Vipers who hath warn'd ye to flee from the wrath to come ? Now
that ye have started back from the purity of Scripture which is
the only rule of reformation, to the old vomit of your traditi- 10
ons, now that ye have either troubl'd or leven'd the people of
God , and the doctrine of the Gospell with scandalous ceremonies and masse-borrow'd Liturgies, doe ye turne the use of that
truth which ye professe, to countenance that falshood which ye
gaine by ? We also reverence the Martyrs but relye only upon 15
the Scriptures. And why we ought not to relye upon the Martyrs I shall be content with such reasons as my confuter himselfe
affords me ; who is I must needs say for him in that point as officious an adversary as I would wish to any man. For *first,* saith
he, *there may be a Martyr in a wrong cause, and as couragious in* 20
suffering as the best : sometimes in a good cause with a forward am-
bition displeasing to God. Otherwhiles they that story of them out of
blind zeale, or malice may write many things of them untruly. If
this be so, as ye heare his own confession, with what safety can
the Remonstant rely upon the Martyrs as *Patrons of his cause,* 25
when as any of those who are alleg'd for the approvers of our
Liturgy or Prelaty might have bin though not in a wrong cause
Martyrs, yet whether not vainly ambitious of that honour, or
whether not misreported, or misunderstood, in those their opi-
ons God only knowes. The testimony of what we believe in re- 30
ligion must be such as the conscience may rest on to be infallible,
and incorruptible, which is only the word of God.

    Sect. 5. His fifth Section finds it selfe agriev'd that the Re-
monstrant should be taxt with the illegall proceedings of the
high Commission, and oath *Ex officio;* And first *whether they were* 35
illegall or no , tis more then he knowes. See this malevolent Fox ?
that tyranny which the whole Kingdome cry'd out against as
stung with Adders, and Scorpions, that tyranny which the Parlament in compassion of the Church and Commonwealth hath
dissolv'd, aud fetch't up by the roots, for which it hath receav'd 40
                             the

Running Head **&c.**] The period is battered.   **3 No;the**] Note the crowding.   **7 of**] The *f*
has a blot in many copies.   **11 either**] The i is very badly worn; the t is battered.   **20 Martyr**]
The *M* is a swash letter.   **21 best:**] Note the italic colon.   **25 Remonstant**] Note the spelling.
The Columbia editors spelled the word *Remonstrant.*   **Patrons**] The *P* is a swash letter.
29-30 opi-ons] The word is written *opinions* in the Columbia edition.   **34 should**] Note the
very faint o   **35 And**] The capital A which is heavy and squabbled, follows a semicolon.   **first**]
The **r** is smashed beyond recognition.   **40 aud**] The **u** appears to be an upside-down 'n'

32   *An Apology, &c.*

the publick thanks and bleſſings of thouſands, this obſcure thorn-
eater of malice and detraction, as well as of *Quodlibets* and *So-*
phiſms knowes not whether it were illegall or not. Evill, evill,
would be your reward ye worthies of the Parlament, if this So-
5   phiſter and his accomplices had the cenſuring, or the ſounding
forth of your labours. And that the Remonſtrant cannot waſh
his hands of all the cruelties exercis'd by the Prelats, is paſt
doubting. They ſcourg'd the confeſſors of the Goſpell, and he
held the ſcourgers garments. They executed their rage, and he,
10   if he did nothing elſe, defended the government with the oath
that did it, and the ceremonies which were the cauſe of it : does
he think to be counted guiltleſſe ?

   Sect. 6. In the following Section I muſt foretell ye, Readers,
the doings will be rough and dangerous, the bating of a *Satir.*
15   And if the work ſeeme more triviall or boiſtrous then for this
diſcourſe, let the Remonſtrant thank the folly of this confuter,
who could not let a private word paſſe, but he muſt make all this
blaze of it. I had ſaid that becauſe the Remonſtrant was ſo much
offended with thoſe who were tart againſt the Prelats, ſure he
20   lov'd toothleſſe Satirs, which I took were as improper as a toothed Sleekſtone. This Champion from behind the Arras cries out
that thoſe toothleſſe Satyrs were of the Remonſtrants making ;
and armes himſelfe heretooth and naile and *horne* to boot, to ſup-
ply the want of teeth, or rather of gumms in the Satirs. And for
25   an onſet tels me that the ſimily of a Sleekſtone *ſhewes J can be*
as bold with a Prelat as familiar with a Laundreſſe. But does it not
argue rather the laſcivious promptneſſe of his own fancy, who
from the harmeleſſe mention of a Sleekſtone could neigh out the
remembrance of his old converſation among the *Viraginian* trol-
30   lops ? For me, if he move me, I ſhall claime his owne oath, the
oath *Ex officio* againſt any Prieſt or Prelat in the kingdome to
have ever as much hated ſuch pranks as the beſt and chaſteſt of
them all. That exception which I made againſt toothleſſe Satirs
the Confuter hopes I had from the *Satiriſt,* but is farre deceav'd :
35   neither had I ever read the hobbling *diſtick* which he means. For
this good hap I had from a carefull education to be inur'd and
ſeaſon'd betimes with the beſt and eleganteſt authors of the learned tongues, and thereto brought an eare that could meaſure a
juſt cadence, and ſcan without articulating ; rather nice and hu-
40   morous in what was tolerable, then patient to read every drawl-
                                                            ling

1 **thouſands,this**] Note the crowding.   2 ***Quodlibets***] The *Q* is a swash letter.   7 **cruelties**]
The **r** is battered.   11 **it:**] The colon is italic.   19 **againſt**] The ſt ligature appears to be
smeared.   20 **Satirs,which**] There is no space after the comma.   I] The **I** is wrong font.
23 **heretooth**] The words are crowded together.   **boot,to**] Note the crowding.   25 ***I***] The *I*
is a swash letter.   34 **hopes**] The **o** is smeared; the **s** is battered.   *Satiriſt,*] The *ſ* is smeared.
35 **the**] The **h** is smeared.   *diſtick*] The *k* is battered.   39 **and**] The **n** is battered and smeared.

An Apology, &c.   33

ling versifier. Whence lighting upon this title of *toothleſſe Satirs*,
I will not conceale ye what I thought, Readers, that sure this
muſt be ſome ſucking Satir, who might have done better to have
us'd his corall, and made an end of breeding, ere he took upon him
to weild a Satirs whip. But when I heard him talk of *ſcouring the*
ruſted ſwords of elviſh Knights, doe not blame me, if I chang'd
my thought, and concluded him ſome deſperate Cutler. But
why *his ſcornefull muſe could never abide with tragick ſhoos her an-*
kles for to hide, the pace of the verſe told me that her maukin
knuckles were never ſhapen to that royall buskin. And turning   10
by chance to the ſixth Satyr of his Second book I was confirm'd;
where having begun loftily *in heavens univerſall Alphabet* he
fals downe to that wretched poorneſſe and frigidity as to talke
of *Bridge ſtreet in heav'n, and the Oſtler of heav'n*, and there wanting other matter to catch him a heat, (for certaine he was in the   15
frozen *Zone* miſerably benumm'd) with thoughts lower then any
Beadle betakes him to whip the ſigne poſts of *Cambridge* Alehou-
ſes, the ordinary ſubject of freſhmens tales, and in a ſtraine as pittifull. Which for him who would be counted *the firſt Engliſh*
Satyr, to abaſe himſelfe to, who might have learnt better among   20
the Latin, and Italian Satyriſts, and in our own tongue from the
viſion and Creed of Pierce plowman, beſides others before him, ma-
nifeſted a preſumptuous undertaking with weak, and unexamin'd
ſhoulders. For a Satyr as it was borne out of a *Tragedy*, ſo ought
to reſemble his parentage, to ſtrike high, and adventure dange-   25
rouſly at the moſt eminent vices among the greateſt perſons, and
not to creepe into every blinde Taphouſe that fears a Conſtable
more then a Satyr. But that ſuch a Poem ſhould be toothleſſe I
ſtill affirme it to be a bull, taking away the eſſence of that which
it calls it ſelfe. For if it bite neither the perſons nor the vices,   30
how is it a Satyr, and if it bite either, how is it toothleſſe, ſo that
toothleſſe Satyrs are as much as if he had ſaid toothleſſe teeth.
What we ſhould do therefore with this learned Comment upon
teeth and *horns* which hath brought this confutant into his *Pe-*
dantick kingdome of *Cornucopia*, to reward him for gloſſing upon   35
hornes even to the *Hebrew root*, I know not unleſſe we ſhould
commend him to be Lecturer in Eaſt-cheap upon S. *Lukes* day,
when they ſend their tribute to that famous hav'n by Detford.
But we are not like to ſcape him ſo. For now the worme of *Cri-*
ticiſme works in him, he will tell us the derivation of *German*   40
E   *rutters.*

---

4 **corall,and**] There is no space after the comma.   **breeding,ere**] The comma is faint and battered. Note the crowding.   6 *elviſh*] The ſ is smeared.   12 *Alphabet*] The *A* is a swash letter.
18 **ſes,**] The s sits high.   27 **Taphouſe**] The T is battered and squabbled.   **Conſtable**] The
C is battered.   31 **Satyr,and**] Note the crowding.   **either,how**] There is no space after the
comma.   34 *Pe-*] The *P* is a swash letter.   35 *Cornucopia,to*] The *C* is a swash letter; there is
no space after the comma.   38 **ſend**] The e is illegible here; in many copies it is faint but legible.

34   *An Apology, &c.*

ratters, of meat, and of ink, which doubtleſſe rightly apply'd
with ſome gall in it may prove good to heale this tetter of *Peda-*
goguiſme that beſpreads him, with ſuch a *tenaſmus* of originating, that if he be an Arminian and deny originall ſinne, all the
5   *etymologies* of his book ſhall witneſſe that his brain is not meanly
tainted with that infection.

    Sect. 7. His ſeventh ſection labours to cavill out the flawes
which were found in the Remonſtrants logick; who having layd
downe for a generall propoſition, that *civill polity is variable and*
10   *arbitrary*, from whence was inferr'd logically upon him that he
had concluded the polity of England to be arbitrary, for generall includes particular, here his defendant is not aſham'd to
confeſſe that the Remonſtrants propoſition was ſophiſticall *by a*
fallacy call'd ad plures iuterrogationes which ſounds to me ſome-
15   what ſtrange that a Remonſtrant of that pretended ſincerity
ſhould bring deceitfull and double dealing propoſitions to the
Parlament. The truth is he had let ſlip a ſhrewd paſſage ere he
was aware, not thinking the concluſion would turne upon him
with ſuch a terrible edge, and not knowing how to winde out
20   of the briars, he or his ſubſtitute ſeems more willing to lay the integrity of his Logick to pawn, and grant a fallacy in his owne
Major where none is, then be forc't to uphold the inference. For
that diſtinction *of poſſible and lawfull* is ridiculous to be ſought for
in that propoſition; no man doubting that it is poſſible to change
25   the forme of civill polity; and that it is held lawfull by that
Major, the word *arbitrary* implyes. Nor will this helpe him, to
deny that it is arbitrary *at any time or by any undertakers* (which
are two limitations invented by him ſince) for when it ſtands as
he will have it now by his ſecond edition *civill polity is variable*
30   *but not at any time or by any undertakers*, it will reſult upon him,
belike then at ſome time, and by ſome undertakers it may. And
ſo he goes on mincing the matter, till he meets with ſomething
in Sir *Francis Bacon*, then he takes heart againe and holds his
Major at large. But by and by as ſoon as the ſhadow of Sir *Fran-*
35   *cis* hath left him, he fals off again warping and warping till he
come to contradict himſelfe in diameter : and denies flatly that
it is *either variable or arbitrary, being once ſettl'd*. Which third
ſhift is no leſſe a piece of laughter. For before the polity was
ſettl'd how could it be variable when as it was no polity at all,
40   but either an *Anarchy* or a *Tyranny*. That limitation therefore of
                                                after

14 *iuterrogationes*] The *u* appears to be an upside-down '*n*'   24 proposition;no] There is no
space after the semicolon.   25 polity ;] Note the space before the semicolon.   32 matter,] The
mark under the ma is a paper flaw.   36 diameter :] Note the space before the colon. The colon
is italic.

An Apology, &c.   35

after setling is a meere *tautology.* So that in fine his former affertion is now recanted *and civill polity is neither variable nor arbitrary.*

Sect. 8. What ever elfe may perfwade me that this confutation was not made without fome affistance or advice of the Remonftrant, yet in this eighth Section that his hand was not greatly intermixt, I can eafily believe. For it begins with this furmife, that *not having to accufe the Remonftrant to the King, J do it to the Parlament,* which conceit of the man cleanly fhoves the King out of the Parlament, and makes two bodies of one. Whereas the Remonftrant in the Epiftle to his laft *fhort anfwer, gives his fuppofall that they cannot be fever'd in the rights of their feverall concernments.* Mark, Readers, if they cannot be fever'd in what is feverall (which cafts a Buls eye to go yoke with the toothleffe Satyrs) how fhould they be fever'd in their common concernments, the wellfare of the land, by due accufation of fuch as are the common grievances, among which I took the Remonftrant to be one. And therefore if I accus'd him to the Parlament, it was the fame as to accufe him to the King. Next he cafts it into the difh of I know not whom that *they flatter fome of the Houfe and libell others whofe confciences made them vote contrary to fome proceedings.* Thofe fome proceedings can be underftood of nothing elfe but the *Deputies* execution. And can this private concocter of malecontent, at the very inftant when he pretends to extoll the Parlament, afford thus to blurre over, rather then to mention that publick triumph of their juftice and conftancy fo high, fo glorious, fo reviving to the fainted Common-wealth with fuch a fufpicious and murmuring expreffion as to call it *fome proceedings?* and yet immediately hee falls to glozing, as if hee were the only man that rejoyc't at thefe times. But I fhall difcover to ye Readers, that this his praifing of them is as full of nonfenfe and Scolaftick foppery, as his meaning he himfelfe difcovers to be full of clofe malignity. His firft *Encomium* is that the *Sun looks not upon a braver nobler convocation then is that of King, Peers, and Commons.* One thing I beg of ye Readers, as ye beare any zeale to learning, to elegance, and that which is call'd *Decorum* in the writing of praife, efpecially on fuch a noble argument, ye would not be offended, though I rate this cloifter'd Lubber according to his deferts. Where didft thou learne to be fo agueifh, fo pufillanimous, thou lozel Bachelour of Art, as

E 2   againft

1 *tautology.*] The *a* is battered and broken.   6 monftrant,yet] There is no space after the comma.   8 *I*] The *I* is a swash letter.   11 *anfwer,*] The ʃ is battered.   17 I] The I is badly worn.   Remonftrant] The R appears to be smashed and squabbled.   19 King.] The K appears to be smashed and squabbled.   23 *Deputies*] The *D* is broken; the *t* appears to be smeared.   29 *proceedings?*] The question mark is italic.   35 ye] The y of the first ye is squabbled.   36 *De-*] The *D* is a swash letter. Some of the apparently squabbled letters on the left third of the page are the result of the rising of the slightly humpbacked lines.

36   *An Apology, &c.*

againſt all cuſtome and uſe of ſpeech to terme the high and ſovran
Court of Parlament, a Convocation ? was this the flower of all
thy *Synonyma's* and voluminous *Papers* whoſe beſt *folios* are
predeſtin'd to no better end then to make winding ſheetes
5   in Lent for Pilchers ? Could'ſt thou preſume thus with one
words ſpeaking to clap as it were under hatches the King with
all his Peeres and Gentry into ſquare Caps, and Monkiſh hoods?
How well doſt thou now appeare to be a Chip of the old block
that could finde *Bridge ſtreet and Al-houſes in heav'n* ; why didſt
10 thou not to be his perfect imitator , liken the King to the Vice-
chancellour & the Lords to the Doctors. Neither is this an indignity only but a reproach   to call that inviolable reſidence of juſtice and liberty, by ſuch an odious name as now a *Convocation*
is become; which would be nothing injur'd, though it were
15 ſtil'd the houſe of bondage, whereout ſo many cruell taſks , ſo
many unjuſt burdens, have been laden upon the bruſed conſcien-
ces of ſo many Chriſtians throughout the land. But which of
thoſe worthy deeds, whereof we and our poſterity muſt confeſſe
this Parlament to have done ſo many and ſo noble, which of
20 thoſe memorable acts comes firſt into his praiſes ? none of all, not
one. What will he then praiſe them for ? not for any thing doing, but for deferring to do , for deferring to chaſtiſe his leud
and inſolent *comprieſts*. Not that they have deferr'd all, but that
he hopes they will remit what is yet behind. For the reſt of his
25 oratory that followes, ſo juſt is it in the language of ſtall epiſtle
non ſenſe, that if he who made it can underſtand it, I deny not
but that he may deſerve for his pains a caſt Doublet. When a man
would looke he ſhould vent ſomething of his owne, as ever in a
ſet ſpeech the manner is with him that knowes any thing, he,
30 leſt we ſhould not take notice anough of his barren ſtupidity, declares it by Alphabet, and referres us to odde remnants in his
topicks. Nor yet content with the wonted room of his margent,
but he muſt cut out large docks and creeks into his text to unlade the fooliſh frigate of his unſeaſonable antorities, not where-
35 with to praiſe the Parlament , but to tell them what he would
have them do. What elſe there is, he jumbles together in ſuch a
loſt conſtruction, as no man either letter'd, or unletter'd will be
able to piece up. I ſhall ſpare to tranſcribe him , but if I do him
wrong, let me be ſo dealt with.
40   Now although it be a digreſſion from the enſuing matter, yet
because

An Apology, &c. 37

because it fhall not be faid I am apter to blame others then to
make triall my felfe, and that I may after this harfh difcord
touch upon a fmoother ftring, awhile to entertaine my felfe and
him that lift, with fome more pleafing fit, and not the left to
teftifie the gratitude which I owe to thofe publick benefactors 5
of their country, for the fhare I enjoy in the common peace and
good by their inceffant labours, I fhall be fo troublefome to this
declamer for once, as to fhew him what he might have better faid
in their praife. Wherein I muft mention only fome few things
of many, for more then that to a digreffion may not be granted. 10
Although certainly their actions are worthy not thus to be fpoken of by the way, yet if hereafter it befall me to attempt fomething more anfwerable to their great merits, I perceave how
hopeleffe it will be to reach the heigth of their prayfes at the ac-
complifhment of that expectation that weights upon their noble 15
deeds, the unfinifhing whereof already furpaffes what others
before them have left enacted with their utmoft performance
through many ages. And to the end we may be confident that
what they do, proceeds neither from uncertaine opinion, nor fud-
den counfels, but from mature wifdome, deliberat vertue, and 20
deere affection to the publick good, I fhall begin at that which
made them likelieft in the eyes of good men to effect thofe
things for the recovery of decay'd religion and the Commonwealth, which they who were beft minded had long wifht for,
but few, as the times then were defperat, had the courage to hope 25
for. Firft therefore the moft of them being either of ancient and
high Nobility, or at leaft of knowne and well reputed anceftry,
which is a great advantage towards vertue one way, but in refpect of welth, eafe, and flattery, which accompanies a nice and
tender education, is as much a hindrance another way, the good 30
which lay before them they took, in imitating the worthieft of
their progenitors, and the evill which affaulted their younger
yeares by the temptation of riches, high birth, and that ufuall
bringing up, perhaps too favourable and too remiffe, through
the ftrength of an inbred goodneffe, and with the helpe of divine 35
grace,that had markt them out for no meane purpofes,they nobly
overcame. Yet had they a greater danger to cope with; for being train'd up in the knowledge of learning, and fent to thofe
places, which were intended to be the feed plots of piety and the
Liberall Arts, but were become the nurferies of fuperftition, and 40
empty

1 **fhall**] The fh ligature is battered. 2 **I**] The I is badly worn. 6 **country,**] The o is weak after a heavy c; the u appears to be wrong font. **fhare**] Only the right side of the a is printed. **common**] The first o is broken. 7 **I**] The I is badly worn. 8 **once,as**] There is no space after the comma. 14 **reach**] The h is battered. 15 **expectation**] The p faint in this copy, is normal in many; the a is weak following a heavily imprinted ct ligature. 18 **confident**] The t is battered and weak. 20 **deliberat**] The d sits above the line of type; the i is undotted. 29 **welth,**] Note the spelling. 36 **grace,that**] There is no space after the comma. **purpofes,they**] No space follows the comma. 37 **danger**] The e is badly battered. 40 **offuperftition,**] The words are crowded together.

38 *An Apology, &c.*

empty speculation, as they were prosperous against those vices
which grow upon youth out of idlenesse and superfluity, so were
they happy in working off the harmes of their abused studies and
labours; correcting by the clearnesse of their owne judgement
5   the errors of their mis-instruction, and were as *David* was, wiser
then their teachers. And although their lot fell into such times,
and to be bred in such places, where if they chanc't to be taught
any thing good, or of their own accord had learn't it, they might
see that presently untaught them by the custome and ill example
10 of their elders, so farre in all probability was their youth from
being misled by the single power of example, as their riper years
were knowne to be unmov'd with the baits of preferment, and
undaunted for any discouragement and terror which appear'd
often to those that lov'd religion, and their native liberty.
15 Which two things God hath inseparably knit together, and
hath disclos'd to us that they who seek to corrupt our religion
are the same that would inthrall our civill liberty. Thus in the
midst of all disadvantages and disrespects (some also at last not
without imprisonment and open disgraces in the cause of their
20 countrey) having given proofe of themselves to be better made
and fram'd by nature to the love and practise of vertue, then o-
thers under the holiest precepts and best examples have been
headstrong and prone to vice, and having in all the trialls of a
firme ingrafted honesty not oftner buckl'd in the conflict, then
25 giv'n every opposition the foile, this moreover was added by favour from heav'n, as an ornament and happinesse to their vertue,
that it should be neither obscure in the opinion of men, nor e-
clipst for want of matter equall to illustrat it selfe; God and man
consenting in joynt approbation to choose them out as wor-
30 thiest above others to be both the great reformers of the Church,
and the restorers of the Common-wealth. Nor did they deceave
that expectation which with the eyes and desires of their countrey was fixt upon them; for no sooner did the force of so much
united excellence meet in one globe of brightnesse and efficacy,
35 but encountring the dazl'd resistance of tyranny, they gave
not over, though their enemies were strong and suttle, till they
had laid her groveling upon the fatall block. With one stroke
winning againe our lost liberties and Charters, which our forefathers after so many battels could scarce maintaine. And meet-
40 ing next, as I may so resemble, with the second life of tyranny
(for

---

1 prosperous] The us is battered.   5 *David*] The *D* is a swash letter; the *i* sits high.   7 such]
The top of the f is broken off.   8 learn't] The battered apostrophe sits too high.   it,they]
There is no space after the comma.   18 disadvantages] The dis is smeared.   disrespects] The
second e sits too high.   21 to] The t is battered.   23 of] The of is smeared.   24 then] The
e and n are battered and smeared.   31 restorers] The first r is battered; the second r is heavy.
36 suttle,] The first t is badly worn and sits high.   37 the] The t is smashed.   38 our] The
letters ur are smeared.

An Apology, &c.   39

(for ſhe was growne an ambiguous monſter, and to be ſlaine in
two ſhapes) guarded with ſuperſtition which hath no ſmall power to captivate the minds of men otherwiſe moſt wiſe, they neither were taken with her miter'd hypocriſie, nor terrifi'd with
the puſh of her beſtiall hornes, but breaking them immediately   5
forc't her to unbend the pontificall brow, and recoile. Which
repulſe only, given to the Prelats (that we may imagine how happy their removall would bē) was the producement of ſuch glorious effects and conſequences in the Church, that if I ſhould compare them with thoſe exploits of higheſt fame in Poems and *Pa-*   10
negyricks of old, I am certaine it would but diminiſh and impaire
their worth, who are now my argument. For thoſe ancient worthies deliver'd men from ſuch tyrants as were content to inforce
only an outward obedience, letting the minde be as free as it
could. But theſe have freed us from a doctrine of tyranny that   15
offer'd violence and corruption even to the inward perſuaſion.
They ſet at liberty Nations and Cities of men good and bad
mixt together: but theſe opening the priſons and dungeons cal'd
out of darkneſſe and bonds, the elect Martyrs and witneſſes of
their Redeemer. They reſtor'd the body to eaſe and wealth ;   20
but theſe the oppreſt conſcience to that freedome which is the
chiefe prerogative of the Goſpell; taking off thoſe cruell burdens impos'd not by neceſſity, as other tyrants are wont for the
ſafeguard of their lives, but laid upon our necks by the ſtrange
wilfulneſſe and wantonneſſe of a needleſſe and jolly perſecuter   25
call'd Indifference. Laſtly, ſome of thoſe ancient deliverers have
had immortall praiſes for preſerving their citizens from a famine
of corne. But theſe by this only repulſe of an unholy *hierarchy*
almoſt in a moment repleniſht with ſaving knowledge their
countrey nigh famiſht for want of that which ſhould feed their   30
ſouls. All this being done while two armies in the field ſtood ga-
zing on, the one in reverence of ſuch nobleneſſe quietly gave
back, and diſlodg'd; the other ſpight of the unrulineſſe, and
doubted fidelity in ſome regiments, was either perſwaded or
compell'd to disband and retire home. With ſuch a majeſty had   35
their wiſdome begirt it ſelfe, that whereas others had levied warre
to ſubdue a nation that ſought for peace, they ſitting here in
peace could ſo many miles extend the force of their ſingle words
as to overawe the diſſolute ſtoutneſſe of an armed power ſecretly
ſtirr'd up and almoſt hir'd againſt them. And having by a ſo-   40
lemne

---

1 **ſlaine**] The **a** is battered and broken.   6 **recoile.Which**] Note the crowding. The **c** of **Which**
is battered.   8 **glori-**] The hyphen is smashed.   9 **conſequences**] The first n is broken; the
ſe sits too high.   14 **outward**] The **o** is broken.   16 **offer'd**] The **r** is battered and broken.
18 **together:**] The colon is italic.   **priſons**] The letters **ns** are smeared.   **cal'd**] The apostrophe
sits too low.   27 **famine**] The **n** is battered and smeared.   28 **repulſe**] Note the smashed **u**
29 **with**] The **i** is broken and undotted.   31 **All**] The **A** is broken.   32 **ſuch**] The **u** is broken
and smeared and sits low.   36 **ſelfe,that**] There is no space after the comma.

40   *An Apology, &c.*

lemne proteftation vow'd themſelves and the kingdome anew to
God and his ſervice, and by a prudent foreſight above what
their Fathers thought on, prevented the diſſolution and fruſtra-
ting of their deſignes by an untimely breaking up, notwith-
5 ſtanding all the treaſonous plots againſt them, all the rumours
either of rebellion, or invaſion, they have not bin yet brought to
change their conſtant reſolution, ever to think fearleſly of their
owne ſafeties, and hopefully of the Common-wealth. Which
hath gain'd them ſuch an admiration from all good men, that
10 now they heare it as their ord'nary ſurname, to be ſaluted the
Fathers of their countrey; and ſit as gods among daily Petitions
and publick thanks flowing in upon them. Which doth ſo little
yet exalt them in their own thoughts, that with all gentle affability and curteous acceptance they both receave and returne that
15 tribute of thanks which is tender'd them; teſtifying their zeale
and deſire to ſpend themſelves as it were peice-meale upon the
grievances and wrongs of their diſtreſſed Nation. Inſomuch
that the meaneſt artizans and labourers, at other times alſo women, and often the younger ſort of ſervants aſſembling with
20 their complaints, and that ſometimes in a leſſe humble guiſe
then for petitioners, have gone with confidence, that neither
their meanneſſe would be rejected, nor their ſimplicity contemn'd, nor yet their urgency diſtaſted either by the dignity,
wiſdome, or moderation of that ſupreme Senate; nor did they
25 depart unſatisfi'd. And indeed, if we conſider the generall con-
courſe of ſuppliants, the free and ready admittance, the willing
and ſpeedy redreſſe in what is poſſible, it will not ſeeme much o-
therwiſe, then as if ſome divine commiſſion from heav'n were de-
ſcended to take into hearing and commiſeration the long reme-
30 dileſſe afflictions of this kingdome; were it not that none more
then themſelves labour to remove and divert ſuch thoughts, leſt
men ſhould place too much confidence in their perſons, ſtill referring us and our prayers to him that can grant all and appointing the monthly return of publick faſts and ſupplications. There-
35 fore the more they ſeeke to humble themſelves, the more does
God by manifeſt ſignes and teſtimonies viſibly honour their proceedings; and ſets them as the mediators of this his cov'nant
which he offers us to renew. Wicked men daily conſpire their
hurt, and it comes to nothing, rebellion rages in our Iriſh Pro-
40 vince, but with miraculous and loſſeleſſe victories of few againſt
                                                        many

---

2 **above**] The **b** and **v** are very weak.   3 **on,**] The comma is battered and faint in most copies
examined.   **diſſolution**] The **t** is particularly weak in this poorly imprinted word.   **fruſtra-**]
The **f** and **ſ** are only partially printed.   4 **breaking**] The **k** appears to be smashed.   6 **rebellion,**]
Note the battered comma.   **invaſion,**] The battered **a** is illegible in a few copies.   7 **of**] Part
of the **o** impression is uninked.   12 **doth**] The **o** is battered and sits high.   14 **curteous**] Note
the battered **r**   **they**] The descender of the **y** is broken off.   15 **tender'd**] The **r** is battered.
24 **ſupreme**] The **u** is raised and slightly squabbled.   40 **few**] The **w** is wrong font.

An Apology, &c.   **41**

many is daily difcomfited and broken; if we neglect not this
early pledge of Gods inclining towards us, by the flickneffe of
our needfull aids. And whereas at other times we count it ample
honour when God voutfafes to make man the inftrument and fub-
ordinate worker of his gracious will, fuch acceptation have their   5
prayers found with him, that to them he hath bin pleas'd to
make himfelfe the agent, and immediat performer of their de-
fires; diffolving their difficulties when they are thought inex-
plicable, cutting out wayes for them where no paffage could
be feene; as who is there fo regardleffe of Divine providence,   10
that from late occurrences will not confeffe. If therefore it be
fo high a grace when men are preferr'd to be but the inferior officers of good things from God, what is it when God himfelfe
condefcends, and workes with his owne hands to fulfill the re-
quefts of men; which I leave with them as the greateft praife that   15
can belong to humane nature. Not that we fhould think they are
at the end of their glorious progreffe, but that they will go on
to follow his Almighty leading, who feems to have thus cov'nan-
ted with them, that if the will and the endeavour fhall be theirs,
the performance and the perfeting fhall be his. Whence only it   20
is that I have not fear'd, though many wife men have mifcarried
in praifing great defignes before the utmoft event, becaufe I fee
who is their affiftant, who their confederat, who hath ingag'd
his omnipotent arme, to fupport and crowne with fucceffe their
faith, their forritade, their juft and magnanimous actions, till   25
he have brought to paffe all that expected good which his fer-
vants truft is in his thoughts to bring upon this land in the full
and perfet reformation of his Church.

Thus farre I have digreft, Readers, from my former fubject;
but into fuch a path, as I doubt not ye will agree with me, to be   30
much fairer and more delightfull then the rode way I was in. And
how to break off fuddenly into thofe jarring notes, which this
Confuter hath fet me, I muft be wary, unleffe I can provide a-
gainft offending the eare, as fome Muficians are wont skilfully
to fall out of one key into another without breach of harmony.   35
By good luck therefore his ninth Section is fpent in mournfull
elegy, certaine paffionat foliloquies, and two whole pages of
intergatories that praife the Remonftrant even to the fonetting
of *his frefh cheeks, quick eyes, round tongue, agil hand, and nim-*
ble invention.   40

F   In

---

1 **many**] The m is broken. **daily**] The l is worn.   5 **acceptation**] The p and second **a** because
of their positions between heavily imprinted letters, are weak.   7 **their**] Every letter in the word
is battered and worn.   13 **himfelfe**] The smeared **h** and **m** and the solid bowls of the two **e**'s
probably indicate dirty type.   14 **re-**] The **r** is battered.   15 **men;which**] There is no space after
the semicolon. **praife**] The **f** is battered. **that**] The first **t** is battered.   18 **leading,who**] There
is no space after the comma.   19 **theirs,**] The **e** is battered.   23 **confederat,**] The **c** appears
to be battered and smeared.   25 **forritude,**] The second **r** should be a **t** and is so written in the
Columbia edition.   27 **in**] The **i** of the second **in** appears to be undotted in most copies examined.
28 **reformation**] The left part of the crossbar of the **f** has been broken off.   29 **digreft,**] The
e is battered. **fubject;**] The **e** is faint in many copies.   30 **fuch**] The **f** is battered.   31 **I**]
The **I** is wrong font. **in.And**] Note the crowding and the smashed **A**   36 **Section**] The **ct**
ligature is smeared.   37 **whole**] The **l** appears to be battered and smeared.

42   *An Apology, &c.*

In his tenth Section he will needs erect figures, and tell fortunes. *I am no Bishop*, he fayes, *I was never borne to it*; let me tell therefore this wizzard fince he calculats fo right, that he may know there be in the world, and I among thofe who nothing admire his Idol a Bishoprick, and hold that it wants fo much to be a blessing, as that I rather deeme it the meereft, the falfeft, the most unfortunate guift of fortune. And were the punishment and misery of being a Prelat Bishop terminated only in the perfon, and did not extend to the affliction of the whole Diocesse, if I would wish any thing in bitternesse of foule to mine enemy, I would wish him the biggest and the fatteft Bishoprick. But hee proceeds; and the familiar belike informs him, that *a rich Widow, or a Lecture, or both, would content me*; whereby I perceave him to be more ignorant in his art of divining then any Gipfy. For this I cannot omit without ingratitude to that providence above, who hath ever bred me up in plenty, although my life hath not bin unexpenfive in learning, and voyaging about, fo long as it shall please him to lend mee what he hath hitherto thought good, which is anough to ferve me in all honeft and liberall occafions, and fomething over befides, I were unthankfull to that higheft bounty, if I should make my felfe fo poore, as to follicite needily any fuch kinde of *rich hopes* as this Fortuneteller dreams of. And that he may furder learne how his Astrology is wide all the houfes of heav'n in fpelling mariages, I care not if I tell him thus much profeftly, though it be to the lofing of my *rich hopes*, as he calls them, that I think with them who both in prudence and elegance of fpirit would choofe a virgin of mean fortunes honeftly bred, before the wealthieft widow. The feind therefore that told our *Chaldean* the contrary was a lying feind. His next venome he utters againft a prayer which he found in the animadverfions, angry it feemss to finde any prayers but in the Service Book. He diflikes it, and I therefore like it the better. *It was theatricall*, he fayes. And yet it confifted moft of Scripture language: it had no *Rubrick* to be fung in an antick Coape upon the Stage of a High Altar. *It was big-mouth'd* he fayes; no marvell; if it were fram'd as the voice of three Kingdomes: neither was it a prayer fo much as a hymne in profe frequent both in the Prophets, and in humane authors; therefore the ftile was greater then for an ordinary prayer: *It was an aftounding prayer.* I thank him for that confeffion, fo it was intended to aftound

---

2 *Bishop*,] The *B* is a swash letter.   *I*] The *I* is a swash letter.   7 punifhment] The fh ligature is battered and smeared.   11 fatteft] The ft ligature is smeared.   hee] The h is battered. 16 life] The f is battered.   24 I] The I is wrong font.   30 found] The u appears to be wrong font.   31 feemss] Note the irregular spelling.   32 I] The I is wrong font.   33 And] No copy examined has a small 'a' as the Columbia editor indicates in the notes to the *Apology, Col.* III, 521.   36 Kingdomes:] The colon is italic.   40 *prayer.*] The *e* and final *r* are battered. I] The wrong font I sits below the line of type.

An Apology, &c.   43

aftound and to aftonish the guilty Prelats ; and this Confuter
confeffes that with him it wrought that effect. But in that which
followes , he does not play the Soothfayer but the diabolick
flanderer of prayers. *It was made,* he fayes, *not so much to pleafe*
God, or to benefit the weale publick (how dares the Viper judge   5
that) *but to intimate,* faith he, *your good abilities, to her that*
is your rich hopes, your Maronilla. How hard it is when a man
meets with a Foole to keepe his tongue from folly. That were
miferable indeed to be a Courter of *Maronilla,* and withall of
fuch a haplefle invention, as that no way should be left me to pre-   10
fent my meaning but to make my felfe a canting Probationer of
orifons, The Remonftrant when he was as young as I could

   Toothleffe   *Teach each hollow Grove to found his love*
   Satyrs,   *Wearying eccho with one changeleffe word.*

And fo he well might, and all his auditory befides with his   15
teach each.

   Toothleffe   *Whether fo me lift my lovely thoughts to fing,*
   Satyrs,   *Come dance ye nimble dryads by my fide,*
             Whiles I report my fortunes or my loves.

Delicious ! he had that whole bevie at command, whether in   20
morrice or at May pole. Whileft I, by this figure-cafter muft be
imagin'd in fuch diftreffe as to fue to *Maronilla,* and yet left fo
impoverisht of what to fay, as to turne my Liturgy into my Ladies Pfalter. Believe it graduat , I am not altogether fo ruftick,
and nothing fo irreligious, but as farre diftant from a Lecturer,   25
as the meereft Laick, for any confecrating hand of a Prelat that
shall ever touch me. Yet I shall not decline the more for that, to
fpeak my opinion in the controverfie next mov'd. *Whether the*
people may be allow'd, for competent judges of a minifters ability. For
how elfe can be fulfill'd that which God hath promis'd,to power   30
out fuch abundance of knowledge upon all forts of men in the
times of the Gofpell? how should the people examine the doctrine which is taught them, as Chrift and his Apoftles continually bid them do? how should they *difcerne and beware of falfe*
Prophets, and try every fpirit, if they muft be thought unfit to   35
judge of the minifters abilities : the Apoftles ever labour'd to perfwade the Chriftian flock that they *were cah'd in Chrift to all per-*
fectneffe of fpirituall knowledge , and full affurance of underftanding
in the myftery of God. But the non-refident and plurality-gaping
Prelats the gulphs and whirle pools of benefices, but the dry   40

              F 2   pits

---

1 **aftound**] The u and n are battered. **aftonish**] The ft ligature is battered and broken and
smeared. 4 *It*] The *I* is battered. 7 *Maronilla.*] The *M* appears to be smeared; the *r* is heavy.
9 *Maronilla,*] The *M* is a swash letter. 12 orifons, **The**] Note the punctuation. The **T** is
battered and squabbled. **Remonftrant**] The **R** is squabbled. **young**] The **y** sits too high.
24 **ruftick,**] The **u** is smeared; the ft ligature is battered; the **k** is battered and smeared. 28 **next**]
The **e x** and **t** are battered. 29 *ability.*For] There is no space after the period. 30 **promis'd,to**]
There is no space after the comma. **power**] Note the spelling for 'pour.'

44   *An Apology, &c.*

pits of all sound doctrine, that they may the better preach
what they lift to their sheep, are still possessing them that they
are sheepe indeed, without judgement, without understanding,
the very beasts of Mount Sinai, as this Confuter calls them; which
5   words of theirs may serve to condemne them out of their owne
mouths; and to shew the grosse contrarieties that are in their
opinions. For while none thinke the people so void of knowledge as the Prelats think them, none are so backward and ma-
lignant as they to bestow knowledge upon them; both by sup-
10 pressing the frequency of Sermons, and the printed explanations
of the English Bible. No marvell if the people turne beasts, when
their Teachers themselves as *Isaiah* calls them, *Are dumbe and
greedy dogs that can never have anough, ignorant, blind, and cannot understand, who while they all look their own way every one for his
15 gaine from his quarter*, how many parts of the land are fed with
windy ceremonies instead of sincere milke; and while one Prelat enjoyes the nourishment and right of twenty Ministers, how
many waste places are left as darke as *Galile of the Gentiles,
sitting in the region and shadow of death*; without preaching Mi-
20 nister, without light. So little care they of beasts to make them
men, that by their sorcerous doctrine of formalities they take
the way to transforme them out of Christian men into *Iudaizing*
beasts. Had they but taught the land, or suffer'd it to be taught,
as Christ would it should have bin, in all plenteous dispensation
25 of the word, then the poore mechanick might have so accustom'd
his eare to good teaching, as to have discern'd betweene faithfull teachers and false. But now with a most inhumane cruelty
they who have put out the peoples eyes reproach them of their
blindnesse. Just as the Pharisees their true Fathers were wont;
30 who could not indure that the people should be thought competent judges of Christs doctrine, although we know they judg'd
farre better then those great Rabbies. Yet *this people*, said they,
that knowes not the law is accurst. We need not the autority of
Pliny brought to tell us, the people cannot judge of a minister.
35 Yet that hurts not. For as none can judge of a Painter, or Statuary but he who is an Artist, that is, either in the *Practick* or the
Theory, which is often separated from the practick, and judges
learnedly without it, so none can judge of a Christian teacher,
but he who hath, either the practize, or the knowledge of Chri-
40 stian religion, though not so artfully digested in him. And who
almost

Running Head *&c.*] The *c* is broken.   4 *Sinai,*as] There is no space after the comma.   7 while]
The w and h are separated; the i is undotted in most copies examined.   11 English] Note the
faint n   beasts,when] There is no space after the comma.   18 *Galile*] Note the spelling.
Gentiles,] The *G* is a swash letter; the *s* is battered.   25 word,then] There is no space after
the comma.   29 blindnesse.] Note the battered and broken first e   Just] The J is a swash
letter.   Pharisees] Note the badly worn P   their] Note the battered h   Fathers] The t
which is badly battered in this copy, is missing in IU-2, NN, CLUC, and CtY-2.   30 that]
The a is wrong font.   compe-] The hyphen is battered and sits low.   31 doctrine,] The o
missing in this copy, is faint or vestigial in many copies.   34 *Pliny*] The *P* is a swash letter.
judge] The heavily impressed, smashed j is followed by a faint, broken u   37 practick,] The
ract sits above the line of type; the i is squabbled.   39 practize,] Note the raised, battered i
40 him.] The smashed period appears to be a comma in some copies.

An Apology, &c. 45

almoſt of the meaneſt Chriſtians hath not heard the Scriptures
often read from his childhood, beſides ſo many Sermons and
Lectures more in number then any ſtudent hath heard in Philo-
ſohy, whereby he may eaſily attaine to know when he is wiſely
taught and when weakly. Whereof three wayes I remember are   5
ſet downe in Scripture. The one is to reade often that beſt of
books written to this purpoſe, that not the wiſe only but the ſimple and ignorant may learne by them; the other way to know
of a miniſter, is by the life he leads, whereof the meaneſt underſtanding may be apprehenſive. The laſt way to judge aright in   10
this point is when he who judges, lives a Chriſtian life himſelfe.
Which of theſe three will the Confuter affirme to exceed the capacity of a plaine artizan? And what reaſon then is there left
wherefore he ſhould be deny'd his voice in the election of his
miniſter, as not thought a competent diſcerner? It is but arro-   15
gance therefore, and the pride of a *metaphyſicall* fume, to thinke
that *the mutinous rabble* (for ſo he calls the Chriſtian congregation) *would be ſo miſtaken in a Clerk of the Vniverſity* that were to
be their miniſter. I doubt me thoſe Clerks that think ſo, are
more miſtaken in themſelves, and what with truanting and de-   20
bauſhery, what with falſe grounds and the weakneſſe of naturall faculties in many of them (it being a maxim in ſome men
to ſend the ſimpleſt of their ſonnes thither) perhaps there would
be found among them as many unſolid and corrupted judgements both in doctrine and life, as in any other two Corporati- 25
ons of like bigneſſe. This is undoubted that if any Carpenter
Smith, or Weaver, were ſuch a bungler in his trade, as the greater number of them are in their profeſſion, he would ſtarve for
any cuſtome. And ſhould he exerciſe his manufacture, as little
as they do their talents, he would forget his art: and ſhould he 30
miſtake his tools as they do theirs, he would marre all the worke
he took in hand. How few among them that know to write, or
ſpeak in a pure ſtile, much leſſe to diſtinguiſh the *idea's*, and various kinds of ſtile: in Latine barbarous, and oft not without *ſo-
leciſms*, declaming in rugged and miſcellaneous geare blown to- 35
gether by the foure winds, and in their choice preferring the
gay rankneſſe of *Apuleius*, *Arnobius*, or any moderne ſuſtianiſt,
before the native *Latiniſms* of *Cicero*. In the Greek tongue moſt
of them unletter'd, or unenter'd to any ſound proficiency in thoſe
Attick maiſters of morall wiſdome and eloquence. In the He-   40
brew

---

46   *An Apology, &c.*

brew text, which is fo neceffary to be underftood except it be
fome few of them, their lips are utterly uncircumcis'd. No leffe
are they out of the way in philofophy ; peftring their heads with
the fapleffe dotages of old *Paris and Salamanca.* And that which
5 is the main point, in their Sermons affecting the comments and
poftils of Friers and Jefuits, but fcorning and flighting the reformed writers. In fo much that the better fort among them
will confeffe it a rare matter to heare a true edifying Sermon in
either of their great Churches;and that fuch as are moft humm'd
10 and applauded there, would fcarce be fuffer'd the fecond hearing in a grave congregation of pious Chriftians. Is there caufe
why thefe men fhould overween, and be fo queafie of the rude
multitude, left their deepe worth fhould be undervalu'd for want
of fit umpires ? No my *matriculated confutant* there will not want
15 in any congregation of this Ifland, that hath not beene altogether famifht, or wholly perverted with Prelatifh leven,there will
not want divers plaine and folid men, that have learnt by the experience of a good confcience, what it is to be well taught, who
will foone look through and through both the lofty nakedneffe
20 of your *Latinizing* Barbarian, and the finicall goofery of your
neat Sermon-actor. And fo I leave you and your fellow *ftarres,*
as you terme them, *of either horizon,* meaning I fuppofe either *he-*
mifphere, unleffe you will be ridiculous in your aftronomy . For
the rationall horizon in heav'n is but one, and the fenfible hori-
25 zons in earth are innumerable ; fo that your allufion was as erroneous as your ftarres. But that you did well to prognofticat them
all at loweft in the horizon, that is either feeming bigger then
they are through the mift and vapour which they raife, or elfe
finking, and wafted to the fnuffe in their wefterne focket.
30 *Sect.* 11. His eleventh Section intends I know not what unleffe
to clog us with the refidue of his phlegmatick floth, difcuf-
fing with a heavie pulfe the *expedience of fet formes :* which no
queftion but to fome. and for fome time may be permitted, and
perhaps there may be ufefully fet forth by the Church a common
35 *directory* of publick prayer,efpecially in the adminiftration of the
Sacraments. But that it fhould therefore be inforc't where both
minifter and people profeffe to have no need, but to be fcanda-
liz'd by it, that, I hope, every fenfible Chriftian will deny. And
the reafons of fuch deniall the confuter himfelfe, as his bounty
40 ftill is to his adverfary, will give us out of his affirmation. Firft
        faith

Page number 46] The 46 like many other characters on the page, is smeared as a result of heavy
inking.   6 **Jefuits,**] The J is a swash letter.   7 **better**] The r is battered.   9 **Churches;and**]
There is no space after the semicolon.   11 **Is**] The I is wrong font.   13 **worth**] The r is battered and sits above the line of type.   16 **leven,there**] There is no space after the comma.
32 *expedience*] Note the battered *pe*   *formes:*] Note the italic colon.   35 **prayer,efpecially**]
There is no space after the comma.

An Apology, &c.   47

faith he, *God in his providence hath chosen some to teach others and pray for others, as ministers and Pastors.* Whence I gather, that however the faculty of others may be, yet that they whom God hath set apart to his ministery, are by him endu'd with an ability of prayer; because their office is to pray for others. And not to 5
be the lip-working deacons of other mens appointed words. Nor is it easily credible that he who can preach well should be unable to pray well; when as it is indeed the same ability to speak affirmatively, or doctrinally, and only by changing the mood to speak prayingly. In vaine therefore do they pretend to want ut- 10
terance in prayer, who can finde utterance to preach. And if prayer be the guift of the Spirit, why do they admit those to the Ministery, who want a maine guift of their function, and pre-scribe guifted men to use that which is the remedy of another mans want; setting them their tasks to read, whom the Spirit 15
of God stands ready to assist in his ordinance with the guift of free conceptions. What if it be granted to the infirmity of some Ministers (though such seeme rather to be halfe ministers) to help themselves with a set forme, shall it therefore be urg'd upon the plenteous graces of others ? and let it be granted to some peo- 20
ple while they are babes in Christian guifts, were it not better to take it away soone after, as we do loitering books, and *interline-ary* translations from children ; to stirre up and exercise that por-tion of the spirit which is in them, & not impose it upon congre-gations who not only deny to need it, but as a thing trouble- 25
some and offensive refuse it. Another reason which he brings for liturgie, is *the preserving of order, unity, and piety,* and the same shall be my reason against Liturgy. For I Readers, shall alwayes be of this opinion, that obedience to the Spirit of God, rather then to the faire seeming pretences of men, is the best and most 30
dutifull order that a Christian can observe. If the Spirit of God manifest the guift of prayer in his Minister, what more seemely order in the congregation, then to go along with that man in our devoutest affections ? for him to abridge himselfe by reading, and to forestall himselfe in those petitions, which he must either 35
omit, or vainly repeat, when he comes into the Pulpit under a shew of order, is the greatest disorder. Nor is unity lesse broken, especially by our Liturgy, though this author would almost bring the Communion of Saints to a Communion of Liturgicall words. For what other reformed Church holds communion 40
with

Page number 47] The 4 is smeared; the 7 is battered and smeared.   9 **affirmatively,or**] Note the crowding.   10 **In**] The **I** is wrong font; the **n** is battered and broken.   17 **to**] Note the battered **t**   21 **Christian**] The first **i** is undotted.   23 **por-**] The hyphen is battered and sits high.   24 **spirit**] The **s** is smeared.   **them,&**] Note the crowding.   34 **affections?**] The **a** is blotted in some copies; in others it is perfectly clear.   35 **petitions,**] A smear joins the first **ti** in a number of copies.   38 **this**] The **h** is squabbled; the **s** sits above the line of type.

48　　　*An Apology, &c.*

with us by our liturgy, and does not rather diſlike it? and a-
mong our ſelves who knowes it not to have bin a perpetuall cauſe
of diſunion. Laſtly, it hinders piety rather then ſets it forward,
being more apt to weaken the ſpirituall faculties, if the people
5　be not wean'd from it in due time; as the daily powring in of
hot waters qenches the naturall heat. For not only the body,
& the mind, but alſo the improvement of Gods Spiꝛit is quickn'd
by uſing. Wheras they who will ever adhere to liturgy, bring thē-
ſelves in the end to ſuch a paſſe by overmuch leaning as to looſe
10　even the legs of their devotion. Theſe inconveniencies and dangers follow the compelling of ſet formes: but that the toleration of the Engliſh Liturgy now in uſe, is more dangerous then
the compelling of any other which the reformed Churches uſe,
theſe reaſons following may evince. To contend that it is fanta-
15　ſticall, if not ſenſeleſſe in ſome places, were a copious argument,
eſpecially in the *Reſponſories*. For ſuch alternations as are there
us'd muſt be by ſeverall perſons; but the Miniſter and the people
cannot ſo ſever their intereſts, as to ſuſtaine ſeverall perſons; he
being the only mouth of the whole body which he preſents. And
20　if the people pray he being ſilent, or they ask one thing & he another, it either changes the property, making the Prieſt the people, and the people the Prieſt by turnes, or elſe makes two perſons and two bodies repreſentative where there ſhould be but one.
Which if it be nought elſe, muſt needs be a ſtrange quaintneſſe
25　in ordinary prayer. The like, or worſe may be ſaid of the *Litany*,
wherein neither Prieſt nor people ſpeak any intire ſenſe of themſelves throughout the whole I know not what to name it; only by the timely contribution of their parted ſtakes, cloſing up
as it were the *ſchiſme* of a ſlic't prayer, they pray not in vaine,
30　for by this means they keep life betweene them in a piece of gaſ-
ping ſenſe, and keep downe the ſawcineſſe of a continuall reboun-
ding nonſenſe. And hence it is that as it hath been farre from
the imitation of any warranted prayer, ſo we all know it hath
bin obvious to be the pattern of many a Jig. And he who hath but
35　read in good books of devotion and no more, cannot be ſo either
of eare or judgement unpractiz'd to diſtinguiſh what is grave, *patheticall*, devout, and what not, but will preſently perceave this
Liturgy all over in conception leane and dry, of affections empty
and unmoving, of paſſion, or any heigth whereto the ſoule might
40　ſoar upon the wings of zeale, deſtitute and barren: beſides errors,

7 **mind,but**] Note the crowding. **Spirit**] The r is battered. **quickn'd**] The k is battered and
sits above the line of type; the n sits below the line of type. 8 **uſing.Whereas**] Note the
crowding. **liturgy,bring**] There is no space after the comma. **thē-**] Note the abbreviated
form. The ē sits above the line of type. 10 **Theſe**] The T is heavy and battered and squabbled.
inconveniencies] The second c is battered. 11 **formes:**] The colon is italic. 15 **places,were**]
There is no space after the comma. 16 *Reſponſories*.] The i is heavy and raised. 20 **ſilent,or**]
There is no space after the comma. 24 **nought**] Note the battered u 31 **ping**] The space
work-up shows after the g **ſenſe,and**] There is no space after the comma. 34 **Jig.And**] The
J is a swash letter. There is no space after the period. 40 **barren:**] The colon is italic.

An Apology, &c. 49

rors, *tautalogies*, impertinences, as those thanks in the womans
Churching for her delivery from Sunburning and Moonblasting, as if she had bin travailing not in her bed, but in the deserts
of *Arabia.* So that while some men cease not to admire the incomparable frame of our Liturgy, I cannot but admire as fast 5
what they think is become of judgement, and tast in other men,
that they can hope to be heard without laughter. And if this
were all, perhaps it were a complyable matter. But when we remember this our liturgy where we found it, whence we had it,
and yet where we left it, still serving to all the abominations of the 10
Antichristian temple, it may be wonder'd how we can demurre
whether it should be done away or no, and not rather feare we
have highly offended in using it so long. It hath indeed bin pretended to be more ancient then the Masse, but so little prov'd,
that whereas other corrupt Liturgies have had withall such a see- 15
ming antiquity, as that their publishers have ventur'd to ascribe
them with their worst corruptions either to S. *Peter*, S. *James*,
S. *Mark*, or at least to *Chrysostome*, or *Basil*, ours hath bin never
able to find either age, or author allowable, on whom to father
those things therein which are least offensive, except the two 20
Creeds, for *Te Deum* has a smach in it of *Limbus Patrum.* As if
Christ had not *open'd the kingdome of heaven* before he had *overcome the sharpnesse of death.* So that having receav'd it from the
Papall Church as an originall creature, for ought can be shewn
to the contrary, form'd and fashion'd by work maisters ill to be 25
trusted, we may be assur'd that if God loathe the best of an Idolaters prayer, much more the conceited fangle of his prayer. This
Confuter himselfe confesses that a community of the same set
forme in prayers, is that which *makes Church and Church truly
one*; we then using a Liturgy farre more like to the Masse-book 30
then to any Protestant set forme, by his owne words must have
more communion with the *Romish Church*, then with any of the
reformed. How can we then not partake with them the curse
and vengeance of their superstition, to whom we come so neere
in the same set forme and dresse of our devotion? do we thinke 35
to sift the matter finer then we are sure God in his jealousie will?
who detested both the gold and the spoile of Idolatrous Cities,
and forbid the eating of things offer'd to Idols. Are we stronger
then he, to brook that which his heart cannot brook? It is not
surely because we think that praiers are no where to be had but at 40
G   Rome

The show-through is considerable on this page.   4 *Arabia.*] The *A* is a swash letter.   10 were]
The word is probably a printer's error for 'where.'   12 we] The w is wrong font.   15 withall]
The t is badly worn.   17 *Iames,*] The *I* is a swash letter.   18 *Basil,*] The *ſ* is battered.
21 *Deum*] The *D* is a swash letter.   27 conceited] The i is undotted. prayer.This] Note
the crowding.   30 Masse-book] The hyphen is smashed.

50 *An Apology, &c.*

Rome; that were a foule fcorne and indignity caft upon all the reformed Churches, and our own; if we imagine that all the godly Minifters of England are not able to new mould a better and more pious Liturgy then this which was conceav'd and infanted

5 by an idolatrous Mother : how bafely were that to efteeme of Gods Spirit, and all the holy bleffings and priviledges of a true Church above a falfe? Heark ye Prelats, is this your glorious Mother of England, who when as Chrift hath taught her to pray, thinks it not anough unleffe fhe adde thereto the teaching of An-

10 tichrift? How can we believe ye would refufe to take the ftipend of Rome, when ye fhame not to live upon the almes-basket of her prayers? will ye perfwade us that ye can curfe Rome from your hearts when none but Rome muft teach ye to pray? *Abraham* difdain'd to take fo much as a thred or a fhoo latchet from

15 the King of *Sodome*, though no foe of his, but a wicked King, and fhall we receave our prayers at the bounty of our more wicked enemies? whofe guifts are no guifts, but the inftruments of our bane? Alas that the Spirit of God fhould blow as an uncertaine wind, fhould fo miftake his infpiring, fo misbeftow his guifts pro-

20 mis'd only to the eleĉt, that the idolatrous fhou'd finde words acceptable to prefent God with and abound to their neighbours, while the true profeffors of the Gofpell can find nothing of their own worth the conftituting, wherewith to worfhip God in publick. Confider if this be to magnifie the Church of England, and

25 not rather to difplay her nakedneffe to all the world. Like therefore as the retaining of this Romifh Liturgy is a provocation to God, and a difhonour to our Church, fo is it by thofe ceremonies, thofe purifyings and offrings at the Altar, a pollution and difturbance to the Gofpell it felfe; and a kinde of driving

30 us with the foolifh *Galatians* to another gofpell. For that which the Apoftles taught hath freed us in religion from the *ordinances of men*, and commands that *burdens be not laid* upon the redeemed of Chrift, though the formalift will fay, what no decency in Gods worfhip? Certainly Readers, the worfhip of God fing-

35 ly in it felfe, the very aĉt of prayer and thankfgiving wirh thofe free and unimpos'd expreffions which from a fincere heart unbidden come into the outward gefture, is the greateft decency that can be imagin'd. Which to dreffe up and garnifh with a devis'd bravery abolifht is the law, and difclam'd by the Gofpell addes

40 nothing but a deformed uglineffe. And hath ever afforded a colourable

---

2 **Churches,and**] There is no space after the comma.   5 **Mother:**] The colon is italic. 8 **England,who**] Note the crowding.   13 **hearts,**] The comma which follows **hearts** in most copies is missing here. It is plainly visible in IU-1, IU-3, IU-4, and IU-1654. The comma has been omitted by the Columbia editors. **pray?**] The question mark is italic.   14 **difdain'd**] Note especially the broken f   19 **his**] The s of the first **his** is badly battered. **fo**] The f of the second **fo** is badly battered in this copy. There is no doubt that it is an f In IU-4 it shows clearly. The Columbia editors have mistaken the letter for a 't' Earlier editors have read the word correctly.   21 **prefentGod**] Note the crowding.   22 **profeffors**] The second o is broken and very faint in many copies; it is an uninked impression in IU-3.   24 **England,and**] There is no space after the comma.   31 **taught**] The first t is badly battered.   35 **with**] The t is battered beyond recognition.   39 **in**] The n which is smeared beyond recognition in this copy, is blurred in many copies.   40 **but**] Note the space between the **b** and **u**

An Apology, &c.   5**1**

lourable pretenſe to bring in all thoſe traditions and carnalities
that are ſo killing to the power and vertue of the Goſpell. What
was that which made the Jewes figur'd under the names of *Aho-*
lah and *Aholibah* go a whooring after all the heathens inventions, but that they ſaw a religion gorgeouſly attir'd and deſira-   5
ble to the eye? What was all, that the falſe Doctors of the Primitive Church, and ever ſince have done, but *to make a faire ſhew*
in the fleſh, as S. *Pauls* words are? If we have indeed given a bill
of divorce to Popery and ſuperſtition, why do we not ſay as to
a divors't wife; thoſe things which are yours take them all with   10
you, and they ſhall ſweepe after you? Why were not we thus
wiſe at our parting from Rome? Ah; like a crafty adultreſſe ſhe
forgot not all her ſmooth looks and inticing words at her parting; yet keep theſe letters, theſe tokens, and theſe few ornaments; I am not all ſo greedy of what is mine, let them preſerve   15
with you the memory of what I am? No, but of what I was,
once faire and lovely in your eyes. Thus did thoſe tender hear-
ted reformers dotingly ſuffer themſelves to be overcome with
harlots language. And ſhe like a witch, but with a contrary policy did not take ſomething of theirs that ſhe might ſtill have   20
power to bewitch them, but for the ſame intent left ſomething
of her own behind her. And that her whooriſh cunning ſhould
prevaile to work upon us her deceitfull ends, though it be ſad
to ſpeak, yet ſuch is our blindneſſe, that we deſerve. For we are
deepe in dotage. We cry out *Sacriledge and miſdevotion* againſt   25
thoſe who in zeale have demoliſh't the dens and cages of her uncleane wallowings. We ſtand for a Popiſh Liturgy as for the ark
of our Cov'nant. And ſo little does it appeare our prayers are
from the heart, that multitudes of us declare, they know not
how to pray but by rote. Yet they can learnedly invent a prayer   30
of their own to the Parlament, that they may ſtill ignorantly
read the prayers of other men to God. They object that if wee
muſt forſake all that is Rome's, we muſt bid adieu to our Creed;
and I had thought our Creed had bin of the Apoſtles; for ſo it
beares title. But if it be hers let her take it. We can want no   35
Creed, ſo long as we want not the Scriptures. We magnifie thoſe
who in reforming our Church have inconſideratly and blame-
fully permitted the old leven to remaine and ſoure our whole
lumpe. But *they were Martyrs*; True and he that looks well into the book of Gods providence, if he read there that God for   40

G 2   this

---

10 **all**] The **a** is battered.   31 **Parlament**,] Note the space between the **P** and the **a**   32 **prayers**]
Note the battered first **r**   **object**] The **j** is battered.   33 **Rome's**,] The **R** is battered and
ſquabbled; the **o** is broken.   38 **permitted**] The first **e** is ſmeared.   39 **True**] The **T** is capital
following a ſemicolon.

52   *An Apology, &c.*

this their negligence and halting, brought all that following
perfecution upon this Church, and on themfelves, perhaps will
be found at the laft day not to have read amiffe.

    Sect. 12. But now, Readers, we have the Port within fight;
5 his laft Section which is no deepe one, remains only to be foar-
ded, and then the wifht fhoare. And here firft it pleafes him much,
that he hath difcri'd me, as he conceaves, to be unread in the Counfels. Concerning which matter it will not be unneceffary to fhape
him this anfwer; That fome years I had fpent in the ftories of
10 thofe Greek and Roman exploits, wherein I found many things
both nobly done, add worthily fpoken: when comming in the
method of time to that age wherein the Church had obtain'd
a Chriftian Emperor, I fo prepar'd my felfe, as being now to
read examples of wifdome and goodneffe among thofe who were
15 formoft in the Church, not elfe where to be parallell'd: But to
the amazement of what I expected, Readers, I found it all
quite contrary; excepting in fome very few, nothing but ambition, corruption, contention, combuftion: in fo much that I
could not but love the Hiftorian *Socrates,* who in the proem to
20 his fifth book profeffes, *He was faine to intermixe affaires of State,*
for that it would be elfe an extreame annoyance to heare in a continu'd
difcourfe the endleff brabbles & counterplottings of the Bifhops. Finding therefore the moft of their actions in fingle to be weak, and
yet turbulent, full of ftrife and yet flat of fpirit, and the fumme
25 of their beft councels there collected, to be moft commonly in
queftions either triviall and vaine, or elfe of fhort, and eafie de-
cifion without that great buftle which they made, I concluded
that if their fingle ambition and ignorance was fuch, then certainly united in a Councell it would be much more; and if the
30 compendious recitall of what they there did was fo tedious and
unprofitable, then furely to fit out the whole extent of their tat-
tle in a dozen volumes, would be a loffe of time irrecoverable.
Befides that which I had read of S. *Martin,* who for his laft fix-
teene yeares could never be perfwaded to be at any Councell of
35 the Bifhops. And *Gregory Nazianzen* betook him to the fame re-
folution affirming to *Procopius,* that of any Councell, or meeting
of Bifhops he never faw good end; nor any remedy thereby of evill in
the Church, but rather an increafe. For, faith he, *their contentions*
and defire of Lording no tongue is able to expreffe. I have not there-
40 fore I confeffe read more of the Councels fave here and there, I
                                                                   fhould

---

Running Head *Apology, &c.*] The comma is smeared; the *c* is battered.   1 **halting,**] The **n** is
battered and faint; the descender of the **g** is broken.   4 **fight ;**] The space before the semicolon
justifies the line.   5 **is**] The battered **s** is probably upside-down.   7 **me,as**] There is no space
after the comma. **conceaves,to**] Note the crowding.   8 **fels.Concerning**] There is no space
after the period.   9 **That**] The **T** is capital following a semicolon.   11 **add**] The word is probably a printer's error for 'and.'   15 **parallell'd:**] The colon is italic; the smear preceding the
colon is show-through.   16 **expected,**] The **p** is faint.   18 **I**] The **I** is battered and smeared;
some of the blur is show-through.   21 *extreame*] The *m* is battered.   22 *endleff*] The final
e has apparently failed to print in all copies examined. *Bifhops.*Fin-] Note the crowding. The
battered **i** in **Fin-** is undotted.   23 **therefore**] Note the broken **o** 26 **triviall**] Note the weak
r v and **a** and the two strong **i**'s.   33 *Martin,*] The *M* is a swash letter. **fix-**] The hyphen
is smeared in this copy.   36 *Procopius,*] The *P* is a swash letter.   38 *Church,*] The *C* is a
swash letter.

An Apology, &c. **53**

should be forry to have bin fuch a prodigall of my time : but that which is better, I can affure this Confuter ; I have read into them all. And if I want any thing yet, I shall reply fomething toward that which in the defence of *Murena* was anfwer'd by *Cicero to Sulpitius* the Lawyer. If ye provoke me (for at no hand elfe will I undertake fuch a frivolous labour) I will in three months be an expert councelift. For be not deceav'd, Readers, by men that would overawe your eares with big names and huge Tomes that contradict and repeal one another, becaufe they can cramme a margent with citations. Do but winnow their chaffe from their wheat, ye fhall fee their great heape fhrink and wax thin paft beliefe. From hence he paffes to enquire wherefore I fhould blame the vices of the Prelats only, feeing the inferiour Clergy is known to be as faulty. To which let him heare in briefe ; that thofe Priefts whofe vices have been notorious, are all Prelaticall, which argues both the impiety of that opinion, and the wicked remiffneffe of that government. We hear not of any which are call'd *Nonconformifts* that have been accus'd for fcandalous living ; but are known to be pious, or at leaft fober men. Which is a great good argument, that they are in the truth and Prelats in the error. He would be refolv'd next *What the corruptions of the Univerfities concerne the Prelats ?* and to that let him take this, That the Remonftrant having fpok'n as if learning would decay with the removall of Prelats, I fhew'd him that while books were extant, and in print, learning could not readily be at a worfe paffe in the Univerfities then it was now under their government. Then he feeks to juftifie the pernicious Sermons of the Clergy, as if they upheld foveranty, when as all Chriftian foveranty is by law, and to no other end but to the maintenance of the common good. But their doctrine was plainly the diffolution of law which only fets up fov'ranty, and the erecting of an arbitrary fway according to privat will, to which they would enjoyne a flavifh obedience without law ; which is the known definition of a tyrant, and a tyranniz'd people. A little beneath he denies that great riches in the Church are the baits of pride & ambition : of which error to undeceave him, I fhall allege a reputed divine autority, as ancient as *Conftantine*, which his love to antiquity muft not except againft ; and to adde the more waight, he fhall learne it rather in the words of our old Poet *Gower* then

in

3 thing] The n is battered.   9 contradict] Note especially the badly worn first t   11 wheat,] The a is battered. fhrink] The ri is smeared.   13 the vices] Note the spacing. The s sits above the line of type.   14 which] The i is battered and faint.   15 Priefts] The r and e are badly battered. notorious,are] Note the crowding.   18 fcandalous] The two a's are battered; the da is smeared.   22 *Prelats?*] The question mark is italic.   23 fpok'n] The k and n are battered and broken.   26 Univerfities] The right stem of the v is not printed.   28 foveranty,] The f of the first foveranty is very badly worn; the f of the second foveranty is battered and broken. is] Note the battered i   33 flavifh] The left side of the a is unprinted.   36 bition:] The colon is italic.   38 adde] The second d is battered and broken.

54   *An Apology, &c.*

in mine, that he may fee it is no new opinion, but a truth deliver'd of old by a voice from heav'n, and ratify'd by long experience,

> This Conſtantine which heal hath found
> 5   within Rome anon let found
> Two Churches which he did make
> For Peter and for Pauls ſake :
> Of whom he had a viſion,
> And yafe therto poſſeſſion
> 10   Of Lordſhip and of worlds good ;
> But how ſo that his will was good
> Toward the Pope and his Franchiſe
> Yet hath it proved otherwiſe
> To ſee the working of the deed,
> 15   For in Cronick thus I read
> Anon as he hath made the yeft
> A voice was heard on high the left
> Of which all Rome was adrad
> And ſaid this day venim is ſhad
> 20   In holy Church, of temporall
> That medleth with the ſpirituall
> And how it ſtant in that degree
> Yet may a man the ſooth ſee.
> God amend it whan he will
> 25   I can thereto none other skill.

But there were beaſts of prey, ſaith he, before wealth was be-
ſtow'd on the Church. What though ? becauſe the Vulturs had
then but ſmall pickings ; ſhall we therefore go and fling them a
full gorge ? if they for lucre uſe to creepe into the Church un-
30   diſcernably, the more wiſdome will it be ſo to provide that no
revennu there may exceed the golden mean. For ſo, good Paſtors
will be content, as having need of no more, and knowing withall the precept and example of Chriſt and his Apoſtles, and alſo
will be leſſe tempted to ambition. The bad will have but ſmall
35   matter whereon to ſet their miſchiefe a work. And the worſt
and ſutleſt heads will not come at all, when they ſhall ſee the
crop

Most of the first line and part of the second are blurred.   1 ſee] The ſ is broken. Note the show-
through between the ſ and e   opinion,] The first o is broken and faint; the first i is vestigial.
2 heav'n,] The v is broken; the n is battered and broken.   31 For] The F is smashed and
squabbled.   Paſtors] The P is squabbled.   32 need] The second e sits above the line of type.

An Apology, &c. 55

crop nothing anſwerable to their capacious greedineſſe. For
ſmall temptations allure but dribling offendors ; but a great pur-
chaſe will call ſuch as both are moſt able of themſelves, and will
be moſt inabl'd hereby to compaſſe dangerous projects. But
ſaith he, *A widow's houſe will tempt as well as a Biſhops Palace.* 5
Acutely ſpok'n. Becauſe neither we, nor the Prelats can abo-
liſh widows houſes which are but an occaſion taken of evill
without the Church, therefore we ſhall ſet up within the
Church a Lottery of ſuch prizes as are the direct inviting cauſes of avarice and ambition, both unneceſſary and 10
harmefull to be propos'd, and moſt eaſie, moſt convenient,
and needfull to be remov'd. *Yea but they are in a wiſe diſpen-
cers hand.* Let them be in whoſe hand they will, they are moſt
apt to blind, to puffe up and pervert the moſt ſeeming good. And
how they have bin kept from Vultures, what ever the diſpen- 15
cers care hath bin, we have learnt by our miſeries. But this which
comes next in view, I know not what good vein, or humor
took him, when he let drop into his paper. I that was ere while
the ignorant, the loyterer, on the ſudden by his permiſſion am
now granted *to know ſomething.* And that *ſuch a volley of expreſ-* 20
ſion he hath met withall, *as he would never deſire to have them*
better cloth'd. For me, Readers, although I cannot ſay that I am
utterly untrain'd in thoſe rules which beſt Rhetoricians have
giv'n, or unacquainted with thoſe examples which the prime authors of eloquence have written in any learned tongu, yet true elo- 25
quence I find to be none, but the ſerious and hearty love of truth:
And that whoſe mind ſo ever is fully poſſeſt with a fervent deſire
to know good things, and with the deareſt charity to infuſe the
knowledge of them into others, when ſuch a man would ſpeak,
his words (by what I can expreſſe) like ſo many nimble and 30
airy ſervitors trip about him at command, and in well order'd
files, as he would wiſh, fall aptly into their own places. But
now to the remainder of our diſcours. Chriſt refus'd great riches,
and large honours at the Devils hand. But why, ſaith he, *as they*
were tendr'd by him from whom it was a ſin to receave them. Time- 35
ly remember'd : why is it not therefore as much a ſin to receave
a Liturgy of the maſſes giving, were it for nothing elſe but for the
giver ? *But he could make no uſe of ſuch a high eſtate,* quoth the
Confuter ; opportunely. For why then ſhould the ſervant take
upon him to uſe thoſe things which his maſter had unfitted him- 40
ſelfe

56   *An Apology, &c.*

ſelfe to uſe, that hee might teach his miniſters to follow his
ſteps in the ſame miniſtery. But *they were offer'd him to a bad
end.* So they prove to the Prelats; who after their preferment moſt uſually change the teaching labour of the
5   word, into the unteaching eaſe of Lordſhip over conſcien-
ces, and purſes. But hee proceeds, *God entic't the Iſra-lites
with the promiſe of Canaan.* Did not the Prelats bring as ſla-
viſh mindes with them, as the Jewes brought out of Egypt,
they had left out that inſtance. Beſides that it was then the
10   time, when as the beſt of them, as Saint *Paul* ſaith, *was
ſhut up unto the faith under the Law* their School-maiſter,
who was forc't to intice them as children with childiſh enticements. But the Goſpell is our manhood, and the miniſtery ſhould bee the manhood of the Goſpell, not to looke
15   after, much leſſe ſo baſely to plead for earthly rewards. *But
God incited* the wiſeſt man *Salomon with theſe means.* Ah Confuter of thy ſelfe, this example hath undone thee, *Salomon*
askt an underſtanding heart, which the Prelats have little
care to ask. He askt no riches which is their chiefe care :
20   therefore was the prayer of *Salomon* pleaſing to God : hee
gave him wiſdome at his requeſt, and riches without asking :
as now hee gives the Prelats riches at their ſeeking, and no
wiſdome becauſe of their perverſe asking. But hee gives not
over yet, *Moſes had an eye to the reward.* To what reward,
25   thou man that looks't with *Balaams* eyes, to what reward
had the faith of *Moſes* an eye to ? He that had forſaken all
the greatneſſe of *Egypt*, and choſe a troubleſome journey in
his old age through the Wilderneſſe, and yet arriv'd not at
his journies end : His faithfull eyes were fixt upon that in-
30   corruptible reward, promis'd to *Abraham* and his ſeed in
the *Meſſiah*, hee ſought a heav'nly reward which could
make him happy, and never hurt him, and to ſuch a reward every good man may have a reſpect. But the Prelats
are eager of ſuch rewards as cannot make them happy, but
35   can only make them worſe. *Iacob* a Prince borne, vow'd,
that if God would *but give him bread to eat and raiment to
put on, then the Lord ſhould be his God.* But the Prelats of meane
birth, and oft times of loweſt, making ſhew as if they were
call'd to the ſpirituall and humble miniſtery of the Goſpell,
                                           yet

---

2 **miniſtery.**] The second i is smeared.   6 *entic't*] The dot of the *i* is battered.   *Iſraelites*]
The first *e* is vestigial.   7 *promiſe*] The ſ is battered.   9 that] The first t of the first **that** is
badly battered.   12 forc't] The c is battered.   15 *But*] The *B* is a swash letter.   18 little]
The top of the i proper is broken off.   19 care :] Note the space before the colon.   20 God :]
Note the space before the colon.   22 Prelats] The r is badly battered.   ſeeking,] The mark
above the comma is show-through.   25 *Balaams*] The *B* is a swash letter.   26 *Moſes*] The *M*
is a swash letter.   29 end:] The colon is italic.   31 *Meſſiah*,] The *M* is a swash letter.

An Apology, &c. 57

yet murmur, and thinke it a hard service, unlesse contrary
to the tenour of their profession, they may eat the bread and
weare the honours of Princes. So much more covetous and
base they are then *Simon Magus*, for he proffer'd a reward
to be admitted to that work, which they will not be meanly hir'd to. But saith he, *Are not the Clergy members of Chrift,*
why fhould not each member thrive alike? Carnall textman!
As if worldly thriving were one of the priviledges wee
have by being in Chrift, and were not a providence
oft times extended more liberally to the Infidell then to
the Chriftian. Therefore muft the Minifters of Chrift not
be over rich or great in the world, becaufe their calling is fpirituall, not fecular; becaufe they have a fpeci-
all warfare, which is not to be intangl'd with many im-
pediments: becaufe their Maifter Chrift gave them this
precept, and fet them this example, told them this was
the myftery of his comming, by meane things and per-
fons to fubdue mighty ones: and laftly becaufe a middle
eftate is moft proper to the office of teaching. Whereas
higher dignity teaches farre leffe, and blindes the teacher.
Nay, faith the Confuter, fetching his laft indeavour, *The*
Prelats will be very loath to let go their Baronies, and votes
in Parlament, and calls it *Gods caufe,* with an unfuffera-
ble impudence. *Not that they love the honours and the means,*
good men and generous, *but that they would not have their*
countrey made guilty of fuch a facrilege and injuftice. A worthy Patriot for his owne corrupt ends! That which hee
imputes as facrilege to his countrey, is the only way left
them to purge that abominable facrilege out of the land,
which none but the Prelats are guilty of. Who for the
difcharge of one fingle duty receave and keepe that which
might bee anough to fatisfie the labours of many painefull Minifters better deferving then themfelves. Who pof-
feffe huge Benefices for lazie performances, great promotions, only for the execution of a cruell difgofpelling ju-
rifdiction. Who ingroffe many pluralities under a *non-*
refident and flubbring difpatch of foules. Who let hundreds of parifhes famifh in one *Dioceffe*, while they the

H   Prelats

---

4 **proffer'd**] The r is battered.   6 *Chrift,*] Note the heavy, battered comma.   8 **wee**] The
first **e** is battered and smeared.   10 **liberally**] The i is broken and undotted.   15 **pediments:**]
Note the italic colon.   22 *Baronies,*] The *B* is a swash letter; the comma is battered.
25 **generous,**] The second e is battered.   27 **ends!**] The exclamation point is apparently italic.
35 **cruell**] The r is battered.   **ju-**] The u is battered and broken.   36 **rifdiction.**] The first
i is smeared.   *non-*] The hyphen sits too high and is squabbled.   38 *Dioceffe,*] The *D* is a
swash letter; the two ſ's are battered.

58   *An Apology, &c.*

Prelats are mute, and yet injoy that wealth that would
furnish all those darke places with able supply, and yet
they eat, and yet they live at the rate of Earles, and yet
hoard up.   They who chafe away all the faithfull Shep-
heards of the flocke, and bring in a dearth of spirituall
food, robbing thereby the Church of her dearest treasure,
and sending heards of souls starvling to Hell, while they
feast and riot upon the labours of hireling Curats, con-
suming and purloyning even that which by their foundation is allow'd, and left to the poore, and to repa-
rations of the Church.   These are they who have bound
the land with the sinne of Sacrilege, from which mor-
tall ingagement wee shall never be free, till wee have totally remov'd with one labour as one individuall thing
Prelaty and Sacrilege. And herein will the King be a true
defender of the Faith, not by paring or leshning, but by
distributing in due proportion the maintenance of the
Church, that all parts of the Land may equally partake
the plentifull and diligent preaching of the faith, the scandall of Ceremonies thrown out, that delude and circum-
vent the faith. And the usurpation of Prelats laid lovell,
who are in words the Fathers, but in their deeds the oppugners of the faith. This is that which will best con-
firme him in that glorious title. Thus yee have heard,
Readers, how many shifts and wiles the Prelats have invented to save their ill got booty. And if it be true, as in
Scripture it is foretold, that pride and covetousnesse are the
sure markes of those false Prophets whicst are to come, then
boldly conclude these to bee as great seducers, as any of
the latter times. For betweene this and the judgement
day, doe not looke for any arch deceavers who in spight
of reformation will use more craft, or lesse shame to defend their love of the world, and their ambition, then these
Prelats have done. And if yee thinke that soundnesse of
reason, or what force of argument soever, will bring them
to an ingenuous silence, yee think that which will never
be. But if ye take that course which *Erasmus* was wont
to say *Luther* tooke against the Pope and Monks, if yee
denounce

3 they] The first **they** is fairly normal in this copy. In some copies the **the** is separated from
the **y** by a space, and the **y** is squabbled.   yet] The **y** of the first **yet** is broken in every copy
examined.   4 hoard] The word appears variously: in some copies the spacing is not normal;
in others one or more of the letters sit above the line of type; in others one or more of the letters,
most frequently the **a** are squabbled.   5 heards] In a few copies the **ard** slants sharply down
to the right; in others the **r** sits above the line of type; in others the **a** sits above the line of type.
13 to-] The **t** is battered and sits high.   15 Sacrilege.] The **S** is broken.   16 defender] The
first **e** is battered.   19 faith] The **i** is undotted.   24 title.] Note the battered period.
28 whicst] Note the spelling.   31 who] The **w** is battered and sits above the line of type.
35 reason,] The comma is battered and broken.   will] Note the battered, undotted **i**
37 *Erasmus*] The ſ is battered and broken.

An Apology, &c.

denounce warre againſt their Miters and their bellies, ye
ſhall ſoon diſcerne that *Turbant* of pride which they weare
upon their heads to be no *helmet of ſalvation*, but the meere
mettle and horn-work of Papall juriſdiction; and that
they have alſo this guiſt, like a certaine kinde of ſome   5
that are poſſeſt, to have their voice in their bellies, which
being well drain'd and taken downe, their great Oracle,
which is only there, will ſoone be dumbe, and the *Di-*
vine right of Epiſcopacy forthwith expiring, will put us
no more to trouble with tedious antiquities and diſputes.   10

The End.

Pag. 25. lin. 9. for ſpeak *correct* is read

STATE 1

There is no page number.   8 *Di*-] The *D* is a swash letter.   A heavy rule separates the text
from **The End.** A light rule separates **The End.** from the erratum. Note that the distance between
the rules is less in State 1 than in State 2. Compare the spacing of the words in the erratum of
State 1 with that of the words in the erratum of State 2.

This page is left blank so that the next facsimile page will appear correctly as a *recto*.

An Apology, &c. 59

denounce warre against their Miters and their bellies, ye
shall soon discerne that *Turbant* of pride which they weare
upon their heads to be no *helmet of salvation*, but the meere
mettle and horn-work of Papall jurisdiction; and that
they have also this guift, like a certaine kinde of some 5
that are possest, to have their voice in their bellies, which
being well drain'd and taken downe, their great Oracle,
which is only there, will soone be dumbe, and the *Divine right of Episcopacy* forthwith expiring, will put us
no more to trouble with tedious antiquities and disputes. 10

The End.

Pag. 25. lin. 9. *for* speak *correct it* read

STATE 2

The page is numbered. 2 **discerne**] The **i** is not legible. A light rule separates the text from
The End. A heavy rule separates **The End.** from the erratum. Note that the distance between
the rules is greater in State 2 than in State 1. Erratum: speak *correct it* read] There is greater
space between speak and *correct* and between *it* and **read** in State 2 than in State 1.

Page [60] is blank in all copies examined.

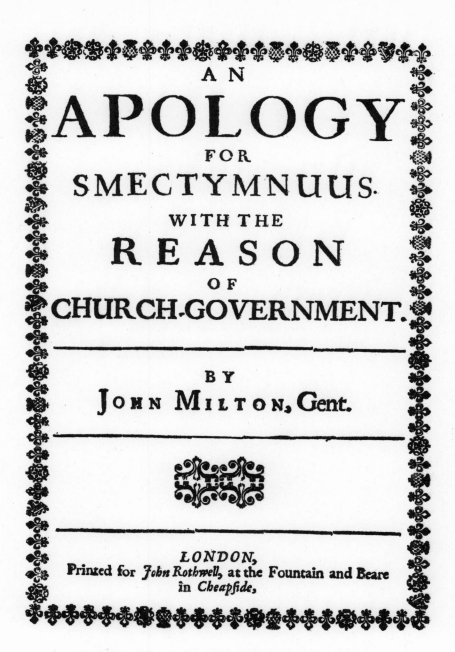

AN
APOLOGY
FOR
SMECTYMNUUS.
WITH THE
REASON
OF
CHURCH-GOVERNMENT.

BY
JOHN MILTON, Gent.

LONDON,
Printed for *John Rothwell,* at the Fountain and Beare
in *Cheapside,*

The reissue title page appears in only one form. It is undated.

The *verso* of the reissue title page is blank.

Critical Notes and Commentary

THE CHIEF PURPOSE of the critical notes and commentary which follow is to provide information and explanations which will be helpful to the student of John Milton's *Apology*. Comment has been made upon every word, phrase, sentence, or idea which offered a hindrance to the understanding or appreciation of the piece. Some students will judge that time has been wasted explaining the obvious; some will find that points of importance have not been mentioned or clarified. The selection of the items upon which critical comment is made is of necessity subjective.

References to the *Apology* in these Notes are made by page and line numbers to the facsimile text presented in this edition. The reference "3:45-48," for example, means page 3, lines 45-48. The title *"Apology"* may precede such a reference if there is likelihood of ambiguity. Page and line numbers prefixed by the word "Note" refer to the particular Note to which the numbers are pertinent. Should more than one Note bear identical page and line numbers, the identifying text is included. That identifying text is in these Notes printed in capital letters and consists of the word, phrase, or sentence upon which comment is being made. When the citation is lengthy, enough of the quotation is given to show the reader where the passage under consideration begins and ends. Medial words of particular significance are frequently included in the abbreviated citation.

The Notes have been divided into sections. The first section, which has been entitled "Milton's Preface to the Reader of *An Apology*," covers roughly the first twenty pages of the piece. The remaining sections are simply numbered from Section 1 through Section 12 in accordance with Milton's division of the rest of the *Apology* into twelve sections for the purpose of answering the similarly numbered sections in the *Modest Confutation*.

[MILTON'S PREFACE TO THE READER OF *AN APOLOGY*]

1:3-4 A CARELESSENES OF KNOWING WHAT ... TO DO — Milton shows impatience that a complete reformation has not been accomplished. See E. M. W. Tillyard, *Milton* (New York and London, 1930), p. 137.

1:11-12 CONTROVERSIE OF GREAT IMPORTANCE — The controversy raged in the Anglican Church between the supporters of episcopal church government, which was really Roman Catholic except that the English monarch had become its head, and the supporters of presbyterian church government, which derived from John Calvin. In the *Reason of Church-government* Milton had stated that church government by presbyters was in accord with the doctrine of the Gospel, and was the "only true Church-government" (*Col.* III, 254). In the *Of Prelatical Episcopacy* Milton had attacked the episcopal claims to apostolic precedent and succession. He expected no sound doctrine nor any solution of the problem from the "covetous, and honour-hunting" bishops (*ANIM, Col.* III, 142).

1:13-14 OF WHAT SMALL MOMENT SOEVER I MIGHT BE THOUGHT — Milton is almost proud of his "small repute" (*Apology*, 2:36). Cf. *Apology*, 6:21-26; *Reason of Church-government, Col.* III, 183, "a task too difficult for my yeares"; and *ibid.*, p. 234, "green years." Horace thought that a work of art should be disciplined with many a day and many an erasure, and "refined ten times over" (Horace, *Art of Poetry*, lines 291-94). He and his Renaissance devotees felt that great art was the more probable when the artist had allowed years of experience to temper and mature his judgment. Milton is pleased with the task he has undertaken; he is proud of his abilities and of the accomplishments of his "green yeers."

1:14-16 BOTH THE PLAIN AUTORITY OF SCRIPTURE LEADING, AND ... REASON ... PERSWADING — Because Scripture and reason are against episcopacy Milton is impatient, perhaps bewildered, at men's refusal to see what was to him obvious. In spite of the passage of the Bishops' Exclusion Bill men still supported the bishops, and the King was preparing to oppose Parliament with military force. Milton and the Smectymnuans preferred to "depend upon what is for them the clear and unequivocal authority of scripture" (Arthur Barker, "Milton's Schoolmasters," *MLR*, XXXII (1937), 521), for "one grain of Scripture is of more efficacy & esteeme to faith, then whole volumes of humane testimonies" (Smectymnuus, *Vindication*, p. 114). Milton upheld the authority of the Scriptures in opposition to the "unlearned drudgery" (*RCG, Col.* III, 242) of the prelates who argued from the Fathers and from tradition. He considered the Fathers ignorant (*REF, Col.* III, 34); he detested their "knotty Africanisms... pamper'd metafors... intricat, and involv'd sentences" (*ibid.*). Tradition was to him the "starting hole" (*PRE, Col.* III, 99) of the prelates, "the perpetuall cankerworme to eat out Gods Commandements" (*RCG, Col.* III, 210). Milton's appeal was to be to Scripture (*ibid.*, p. 246), the "onely Book left us of *Divine* authority" (*PRE, Col.* III, 81). Milton's reference to reason is reminiscent of his dictum that "reason is the gift of God" (*ANIM, Col.* III, 126). Such appeals, Barker points out, are rare in the anti-episcopal tracts where Milton's concern is to show rather "the limitations than the prerogatives" of reason (Barker, "Milton's Schoolmasters," p. 522). Robert Lord Brooke in *A Discovrse Opening The Natvre Of That Episcopacie, Which is Exercised In England....* (London, 1641), p. 14, said that "in expounding of Scripture," the "judge" must be "Scripture; but in finding out what is indifferent, *Recto Ratio* right reason, must be the Judge." Although Milton held that the "rule and canon of faith... is Scripture alone" (*Christian Doctrine, Col.* XVI, 267), he did not, in matters of interpretation of the Bible, limit man's reason to matters indifferent, for the believer has "the Spirit for his guide, and the mind of Christ is in him" (*ibid.*, p. 265). Milton used such light as he had (*RCG, Col.* III, 198). For the authority of the Scriptures he had such Bible texts as II Peter 1:21; II Timothy 3:16; Exodus 4:15; Luke 1:70; and I Corinthians 2:7-15. Cf. *Apology*, 31:9-10.

1:16-18 WITH THIS OPINION... COLD NEUTER... LAW OF *SOLON*... STATE— Sir Francis Bacon in *A Wise and Moderate Discourse, Concerning Church-Affaires....* ([London], 1641), pp. 46-47 (Reprinted under the title "An Advertisement, Touching The Controversies, Of The Church, Of England" in *Resuscitatio: Or Bringing [into] Publick Life Severall Pieces, Of*

The Works, Civil, Historical, Philosophical, & Theological, Hitherto Sleeping.... London, 1657, p. 179) wrote: "Neither let them fear *Solons* law which compelled in factions, every particular person to range himselfe on the one side, or the other: nor the fond calumnie of neutrality. But let them know that it was true which was said by a wise man, that neuters in contention were better or worse, then either side."

Solon (*c.* 638-*c.* 558 B.C.) was a celebrated Athenian legislator. In 594 B.C. he was invested with unlimited powers to alleviate the conditions that resulted largely from civil commotion, and instituted a code of laws that embraced both public and private life. Milton approved of Solon's law that, at the first sign of open strife, every citizen should openly choose sides and used it to justify his own boldness in attacking episcopacy. See *The Prose Works of Milton*, ed. by J. A. St. John (London, 1901-04, 5 vols.), III, 95 note.

1:23-24 HONOR A GOOD CAUSE... BY DEFENDING IT — Cf. *Areopagitica, Col.* IV, 311, "I cannot praise a fugitive and cloister'd vertue, unexercis'd & unbreath'd, that never sallies out and sees her adversary"; *Ready and Easy Way, Col.* VI, 111, "I thought best not to suppress what I had written"; Cicero, *De Republica*, Ch. 1, sec. 2, "Nec vero habere virtutem satis est, quasi artem aliquam, nisi utare."

1:28-29 THE CHIEFE AND MOST NOMINATED OPPOSERS — Archbishop James Ussher and Bishop Joseph Hall. See *Second Defence, Col.* VIII, 129, "two bishops of reputation above the rest, who maintained their own cause against certain leading ministers."

2:4-5 INTRAPPING AUTORITY OF GREAT NAMES — See Note 1:28-29, and Masson, *Life*, II, 248 ff.

2:6 GUIFTS OF GODS IMPARTING — Romans 12:6; I Corinthians 12.

2:9-10 WEARISOME LABOURS AND STUDIOUS WATCHINGS — "Wearisome labours" may be a reference to the features of the English educational system which Milton in his student days had found uncongenial. In the *Reason of Church-government* Milton sketched his youthful studies and his aspirations (*Col.* III, 235 ff.). He hoped to do for England "what the greatest and choycest wits of *Athens, Rome,* or Modern *Italy,* and those Hebrews of old did for their country" (*ibid.,* p. 236).

2:15-16 BIG AND BLUNTED FAME OF HIS ELDER ADVERSARY — Joseph Hall had been a defender of the Anglican Church for more than a quarter of a century. The "blunted" may be a reference to his abandonment, as a result of great pressure from Laud, of a conciliatory policy toward the Puritans and his writing of the *Episcopacie By Divine Right* (London, 1640), under Laud's supervision.

2:16 HIS — Both *his*'s refer to "timely spirit."

2:17 SENTENC'T — Judged.

2:19 MY ADVERSARY — Joseph Hall, against whom Milton's *Animadversions* had been written.

2:20 ABROAD — *i.e.,* as a public figure.

2:20-21 OTHER MENS GREAT OPINION OF HIM — Hall was a man much esteemed as a defender of the Anglican Church and as an authority on religion. He had published close to half a hundred separate works, many of them voluminous, before 1640, a score of which had been so popular that two or more editions had been necessitated. See Note 2:15-16.

2:21-22 PROPER LIGHT OF HIS OWNE WORTH — See 21:13-14, "he shall be to me so as I finde him principl'd."

2:22-23 NOW AGAINST THE RANCOR OF AN EVILL TONGUE — Refers to the vicious attacks in the anonymous *Modest Confutation.* Cf. *Ad Patrem, Col.* I, 277, 279, in which Milton defies "merciless Calumny."

2:27 THIS MODEST CONFUTER — The term "Confuter" is used by Milton to designate the author of *A Modest Confutation.*

2:36 SMALL REPUTE — Milton is proud of his youth (cf. 2:12-17; *RCG, Col.* III, 241, "the heat of youth"; *Apology,* 43:12, "The Remonstrant when he was as young as I"; and Note 1:13-14). Milton is probably indulging in meiosis or tapinosis.

2:39 SILENCE AND SUFFERANCE — Aristotle suggested in his *Rhetoric to Alexander* that the employment of self-depreciation was often proper and expedient in gaining a favorable hearing from fellow-citizens. He suggested that the speaker say: "I have risen not owing to confidence in my own ability, but in the belief that the proposal I am about to introduce is advantageous to the community" (Aristotle, *Rhetorica Ad Alexandrum, With An English Translation By H. Rackham,* London, 1937, p. 379). Tacitus said, in alluding to himself, "Let it not be imagined that this is said from motives of vanity" (*Annals,* Bk. xi, ch. 11). Francis Bacon in *A Wise and Moderate Discourse,* p. 46, said: "all Preachers especially such as are of a good temper, and have wisedome, with conscience ought to inculcate and beat upon a place, peace, silence, and sufferance." He urged that "if wee did but know the vertue of silence, and slownesse to speake, commended by Saint *Iames,* our controversies would (of themselves) close up and grow together . . . if we would leave the overweening and turbulent humours of these times, and renue the blessed proceedings of the Apostles and Fathers of the Primitive Church, which was in the like and greater cases, not to enter into assertions and positions, but to deliver counsels and advices, we should need no other remedy at all" (*ibid.,* p. 5). Milton, about to defend his own character, reminds his reader that, were not a blow aimed at truth by the attack on his virtue, he would maintain "silence and sufferance." He points to scriptural authority for "silence and sufferance" in the *Animadversions* (*Col.* III, 105), where he says: *"Wee all know that in private and personall injuries, yea in publique sufferings for the cause of Christ, his rule and example teaches us to be so farre from a readinesse to speak evill, as not to answer the reviler in his language though never so much provok't."* Hall in his *Short Answer* (Sig. [A3] *verso*) expressed much the same attitude that Milton was taking: *"My labour was all for peace,"* but *"I were worse then a worm, if upon this treading upon, I did not turn again; Yet, not so much out of respect to my own poor, and (if need were) despicable reputation, as to the publique cause of God, and his Church, which I saw now ingaged in this unjust brawl."* Cf. 3:20 and 11:26-28.

3:3-4 SLANDEROUS BOLTS, SHOT SO WIDE — The Confuter's charges against Milton were based on inferences that the Confuter had made as a result of reading the *Animadversions*. Cf. 11:3-28.

3:4-6 I HAVE OFT...PERCEAV'D MY FRIENDS CONGRATULATING THEMSELVES IN MY INNOCENCE — Cf. 11:22-24.

3:20 SILENCE, AND SUFFERANCE — See Note 2:39.

3:22-23 THE TRUTH WHICH I HAD WRITTEN — "I could do Religion, and my Country no better service for the time then doing my utmost endeavour to recall the people of God from this vaine forraging after straw" (*PRE, Col.* III, 82). See 11:36-38.

3:26 THAT TRUTH WHEREOF I WAS PERSWADED — Echoes Romans 8:38; 14:5,14.

3:27 OPENLY TO BE A PARTAKER — Milton had confessed presbyterianism "to be the only true Church-government" (*RCG, Col.* III, 254).

3:29-31 NOT TO LEAVE...WIPE IT OFF — See 11:33-34, "[God] now assisting me"; 15:8-9, "garment injur'd and ill bedighted."

3:34 THOSE REVERENT MEN — Milton is referring to Stephen Marshall, Edmund Calamy, Thomas Young, Matthew Newcomen, and William Spurstowe, the five presbyterian ministers who wrote under the pseudonym "Smectymnuus."

3:34-35 WHOSE FRIEND I MAY BE THOUGHT — In 1641 and early 1642 Milton supported the Smectymnuans, partially, no doubt, because of his sympathy with Thomas Young, his former tutor, but more because he held fundamentally the same convictions as the Smectymnuans. Because Milton's ideas in his early pamphlets are essentially those that are found in the writings of the Smectymnuans, it is conjectured that he originally derived them from Thomas Young (Arthur Barker, *Milton and the Puritan Dilemma, 1641-1660*, Toronto, 1942, p. 27. Cf. Barker's unconvincing suggestion in "Milton's Schoolmasters," p. 521 note, that the "freind" to whom *Of Reformation* was addressed was Thomas Young.). Masson (*Life*, II, 244, 359) and W. T. Hale (*Of Reformation Touching Church-Discipline in England by John Milton*, New Haven, 1916, p. liv) held the opinion that Milton was solicited by the Smectymnuans to

enter the controversy. George W. Whiting ("Milton and the 'Postscript'," *MLN*, XXX (1935), 506-08) has shifted the weight of opinion toward Milton's voluntary participation. Frederick Lovett Taft (*Milton and the Smectymnuus Controversy, 1641-42*, Unpublished Ph.D. dissertation in English, Western Reserve University, 1942, pp. 267-72) thinks that the emphasis of *Apology* 3:27-39 shows that Milton's connection was a voluntary one. Milton's own testimony that he wrote the book "to those ends which the best men propose to themselves" together with his further discussion (4:15-5:3) apparently confirms the notion. Milton seems to indicate that one of the chief reasons for entering was that he resented the implication, not infrequently made (Taft, *op. cit.*, pp. 269-72), that bishops only had learning and that those who opposed the bishops were generally ignorant. It seemed an indignity that those men who had answered Hall well from a controversial point of view should be overcome by his facility in writing. Milton, therefore, turned against Hall the levity that Hall had used against the Smectymnuans (5:13); Milton attacked Hall to prove that others besides bishops had learning and to show that that learning which the "Prelats admire and have not, others have and admire not" (5:17-40). Another reason for Milton's entering the controversy was that he was antiprelatical in sympathy. He had already written two antiprelatical pamphlets, the *Of Reformation* and the *Of Prelatical Episcopacy*. It seems probable that Milton was motivated by many considerations to come to the aid of his "respected friends" (4:37) among which may or may not have been a direct appeal. It is certain that the "learning of Usher, and the wit of Hall" must have been keenly felt by the Smectymnuans and Milton (see John Mitford, *The Works of John Milton in Verse and Prose*, London, 1851, 8 vols., I, xlvii). In Milton's opinion Ussher and Hall were superior to the Smectymnuans. Therefore Milton felt constrained to enter the fray (*Second Defence, Col.* VIII, 131).

3:35 *ANIMADVERSIONS* — *Animadversions Upon The Remonstrants Defence, Against Smectymnvvs* (1641).

3:37 COMMON ADVERSARY — Bishop Joseph Hall.

3:39 BABLER — The author of *A Modest Confutation.*

4:1 THERE BE WHO — "there be [those] who."

4:3-6 AS FOR OTHERS ... REASONS OF MY SILENCE — Cf. 19:1-3.

4:8 ANIMADVERSIONS — See Note 3:35.

4:9 THE REMONSTRANT — Bishop Hall's first tract in the controversy was entitled *An Humble Remonstrance To The High Covrt of Parliament, By A dutifull Sonne of the Church.* As a result the author was referred to as the Remonstrant.

4:10 PREFACE — *"The Preface"* to the *Animadversions* (1641), pp. 1-4 (*Col.* III, 105-08).

4:11 NOT THOUGHT APOLOGETICALL ANOUGH — Milton had in *"The Preface"* of the *Animadversions* stated:

I shall adresse my selfe in few words to give notice before hand of something in this booke, which to some men perhaps may seeme offensive, that when I have render'd a lawfull reason of what is done, I may trust to have sav'd the labour of defending or excusing hereafter. (*ANIM* (1641), p. 1; *Col.* III, 105.)

The Confuter answered:

The Preface ... Is apologeticall; and well may it be so. *Satisfaction to tender Consciences,* is that which we look for, and that which you ought to give....

We must suppose you have *undertaken a religious cause.* that is your pretended subject; we shall examine the truth of it by and by; we must now look to your manner of handling it: a suspicious way you think; and so do I. (*Modest Confutation,* p. 1.)

4:13-14 I DO NOT LOOK TO BE ASKT WHEREFORE I WRIT THE BOOK — Milton means to defend the "manner" of writing that he used (4:13); he does not expect to be asked why he wrote the book.

4:17 SPECIUS ANTIQUITY — Milton thought of antiquity as the "cheifest Argument of the Heathen against the Christians" (*REF, Col.* III, 29). In *Of Reformation* Milton challenged those who justify episcopacy on the basis of antiquity and tradition, who trace the ecclesiastical offices back to apostolic times and claim apostolic succession for them (*Col.* III, 14-15). He wrote the *Of Prelatical Episcopacy* to show the folly of the pleas to "that indigested heap, and frie of Authors" (*Col.* III,

82), of "not weighing the Fathers in the ballance of Scripture, but Scripture in the ballance of the Fathers" (*ibid.,* III, 101). He held that all of prelacy's "learned scraping in antiquity ... is but to maintain and set upon our necks a stately and severe dignity, which you call sacred, and is nothing in very deed but a grave and reverent gluttony, a sanctimonious avarice, in comparison of which, all the duties and dearnesses which ye owe to God or to his Church, to law, custome, or nature ye have resolv'd to set at nought" (*RCG, Col.* III, 220-21).

4:19 MILITARY ADVANTAGES — Milton characterizes his method of attack in the *Animadversions* as based upon observing "some kind of military advantages," striking the opponent when he is feeding and watering his horses and when he feels most secure. The *Animadversions* are in dialogue form. Milton quoted sentences or phrases from Hall's *Defence Of The Humble Remonstrance* (1641) which he answered, often resorting to punning, irony, and abuse.

4:20 VEINE — Humor or mood; state of mind or feeling.

4:21 IN DERISION OF — In contempt of.

4:22-23 THE REMEMBRANCE OF THAT WHICH HE HATH LICENC'T HIMSELFE TO UTTER CONTEMPTUOUSLY OF THOSE REVEREND MEN — See Note 4:25-26. In the preface "To the Reader" of the Smectymnuan *A Vindication* (1641) the authors decided to lay before the reader the "bitter invectives, false aspersions, hyperbolicall confidence, selfe contradictions, and such like extravagancies ... rather then to interrupt our following discourse" (Sig. [A4] *recto*). These were the aspersions that Hall had made against the Smectymnuans in *A Defence Of The Humble Remonstrance,* the pamphlet which Milton had had in mind when he had written his *Animadversions.* The Smectymnuans grouped Hall's charges under four categories: (1) Hall has accused them of *"misallegations, misinterpretations, mistranslations, and false quotations"* not only to the ordinary reader but to the King, in such a manner that Hall *"calles God to witnesse ...that hee never saw any Author that would dare to professe Christian sincerity so fowle to overlash"* (Sig. [A4] *recto* and *verso*); (2) Hall has "railed upon, reviled, slighted, and scorned" them (Sig. a *recto*); (3) Hall has attacked them with *"daring protestations,"* "bold *asserrations," "confident slightings,"* and *"scorne-full denyalls"* (Sig. [a] *verso*, a2 *recto*); (4) he has passed over the strongest arguments "either with scorne or silence" (Sig. [a3] *recto*).

4:24-25 OVER AGAINE...FREELY DONE — In the *Animadversions* Milton had considered it nothing *"disagreeing from Christian meeknesse"* to handle one who was a *"notorious enimie to truth and his Countries peace,"* who by a *"voluble and smart fluence of tongue, and in the vaine confidence of that, and out of a more tenacious cling to worldly respects"* justified the *"long usurpation and convicted Pseudepiscopy of Prelates," "in a rougher accent, and to send home his haughtinesse well bespurted with his owne holy-water"* (*Col.* III, 105-06). Although Milton had devoted all of *"The Preface"* of the *Animadversions* to a justification of his manner of writing, yet the Confuter had called for *"Satisfaction to tender Consciences"* (see Note 4:11).

4:25-26 HIS LATEST INSULTING IN HIS SHORT ANSWER — The reference is in particular to "An Answer to *A Calumniatory* Epistle, Directed by way of Preface to the Reader," in Joseph Hall's *A Short Answer To The Tedious Vindication Of Smectymnvvs* (1641). Hall recounts the controversy in brief. He

sent forth a meek and peaceable Remonstrance.... Wherein I could not suppose that any person could finde himself touched, save onely those, who profess friendship to Libells, enmity to the established forms: When all on the sudden, the Smectymnuans, *a strange generation of men, unprovoked, unthought of, cry out of hard measure, and flye in my face, as men wrongfully accused; I know them not, I hurt them not; If their own guilt have galled them, that is no fault of mine.* (Sig. A3 *recto*.)

Hall complains:
Now, inraged with a moderate opposition, they heat their furnace seven times more, and break forth into a not more voluminous, then vehement Invective. I do not see them look fleeringly through their fingers, at their seemingly-unknown, (yet often discovered, and oft vilified) Antagonist; it is all one, so long as he is namelesse; if he be a Consul, they are Senators; Civility is but a Ceremony. (Sig. [A3] *verso*.)

Hall beseeches the Reader to find the "Machiavel" and bring him forth to shame: *"certainly, where the*

falshood lies, there he lurks" (Sig. [A4] *recto*). He charges the Smectymnuans with misapplying his words. *"These men will not see in themselves that true guilt, which they unjustly cry out of, in another"* (Sig. a *recto*). Hall decides that, since they *"offer nothing, but that which hath passed an hundred ventilations,"* he will spend his time to better advantage *"then in drawing this Sawe to and fro, to no purpose."* He challenges them to give a full answer to his treatise *"concerning the Divine Right of Episcopacie"* before they should expect him to trouble himself *"with sweeping away these loose scraps of their exceptions. Till then, let them, if they can, be silent, at least I shall; as one that knows how to give a better account of the remainder of my precious hours"* (Sig. [a4] *verso*).

4:26 THEIR FINALL PATIEUCE — The Smectymnuans had abandoned the controversy. Their *Vindication* of June 1641 was their last contribution thereto.

4:27 AUTHORS OF *SMECTYMNUS* — See Note 3:34.

4:30 PUDDER — To pudder; *i.e.* to dabble, or to meddle.

4:30-31 HE AND HIS — The Remonstrant and his party.

4:31 OUT OF STRATAGEM — The prelates assumed that the Puritans had a deficiency of knowledge in antiquity. The Confuter charged Milton with being "unread in the Counsels" (see 52: 7-8). The antiprelatarians had to prepare themselves to meet the prelates on their own grounds where they commanded respect (see Note 3:34-35). Hall's claims rest on the "scriptural and patristic evidence for episcopacy as the divine discipline" (Arthur Barker, *Milton and the Puritan Dilemma,* p. 22). Hall claimed that the apostles "were through the guidance of Gods Spirit, in the acts of their Function, inerrable. So then, if the foundation [of episcopacy] were laid by Christ, and the wals built up by his Apostles, the Fabrick can be no lesse than divine"; therefore, episcopacy "is not only an holy and lavvful, but a divine Institution; and therefore cannot be abdicated, vvithout a manifest violation of Gods Ordinance" (Hall, *Episcopacie By Divine Right,* pp. 30, 27).

4:33-34 QUIPS AND SNAPPING ADAGIES
— The Smectymnuans were able to rival Hall in
weight of argument and in ponderous citations, but
they could not rival him in eloquence (*Second
Defence*, *Col.* VIII, 131), or in the use of petulant,
peevish, curt maxims and clever, sarcastic turns of
phrase. See 19:20-21; cf. *ANIM, Col.* III, 105
"voluble and smart fluence of tongue."

4:34 TO VAPOUR THEM OUT — To make the
Smectymnuans look ridiculous by destroying the
validity of their arguments; to make them seem a
"baseless fabric." Cf. 7:15-20; 7:24-28.

4:34-35 THEY BENT ONLY UPON THE
BUSINESSE WERE MINDED TO LET
PASSE — The Smectymnuans complained of the
Remonstrant's tactics and admitted the cumber-
someness of their answers. In the *Smectymnuus
Vindication*, p. 31, the *Smectymnuans* said:

We confesse in some passages of that booke [*i.e., An
Answer To ... An Humble Remonstrance*] wee tooke
liberty to use some cheerfull expressions, provoked
thereto by the strange confidence, and little strength of
our Remonstrant, Remembering that of *Tertullian. It
wel agrees with truth to laugh, because it is of a
pleasant disposition, and to sport with her competitors,
because it is secure, and feares not the wals of her
bulwarks.*

4:37 MY RESPECTED FRIENDS — In Mil-
ton's anti-episcopal pamphlets there is little practical
difference between his views and those of the
Smectymnuans. Milton believes that power right-
fully belongs with the laity; he contrasts the primitive and modern bishops (*REF, Col.* III, 16); he
argues for the noble effectiveness of ecclesiastical
censure (*RCG, Col.* III, 257-58). Barker has shown
that Milton is "agreeable to the principals of orthodox English Puritanism," as held by the Smectymnuans (*Milton and the Puritan Dilemma*, p. 31).
Milton and the Smectymnuans insist on one right
discipline prescribed in Scripture, on parity of
ministers, on the importance of the particular congregation, on the desirability of having "unity and
... singleness in doctrine," and on "the layman's
right to a share in the church government" (*ibid.*).
While there is no certainty that Milton collaborated
with the Smectymnuans, his interest in the controversy with Hall and his sympathy with the "respected friends" is beyond doubt.

4:38 UNNECESSARY PATIENCE — The
Smectymnuans had abandoned the controversy, presumably because they were unable to rival Hall in
"sharpe taunts," in "quips and snapping adagies,"
and in "frumps and curtall gibes" (4:32-39). Milton
insists that the "respected friends" had not been
forced, under the duress of the Bishop's arguments,
to abandon it. He feels that they and their cause
have suffered because of their "own unnecessary
patience" with the opponent's "coy flurting stile"
(4:39).

4:39 COY FLURTING STILE — A manner
characterized by disdain and playfulness.

4:39 TO BE GIRDED WITH FRUMPS AND
CURTALL GIBES — To be bound or encircled
with sneers and curt taunts. See *Eikonoklastes, Col.*
V, 212, "Essays & curtal Aphorisms."

4:40-5:1 ONE WHO MAKES SENTENCES
BY THE STATUTE, AS IF ALL ABOVE
THREE INCHES LONG WERE CONFISCAT
— "Bacon used one sort of sentence for his history
and another for his essays... Milton apparently
despised those minor forms for their triviality"
(Elbert N. S. Thompson, "Milton's Prose Style,"
PQ, XIV (1935), 2). Milton is here ridiculing Hall.
Thompson thinks that Milton had Hall's essays and
characters in mind because he refers later to Hall's
"penurious Book of Characters" (11:21). More
than likely, however, Milton was referring to the
"Preface to the Reader" of the *Short Answer*, the
sentences of which have a simplicity which Milton
disparaged. The citations from that preface in Note
4:25-26 indicate the general tone.

5:1 CONFISCAT — Confiscated or forfeited.
Confiscat or *confiscate* was used as a participial
adjective before the verb was introduced (see
OED). Cf. *REF, Col.* III, 57 "... by proscribing,
and confiscating from us all the right we have to
our owne bodies, goods and liberties."

5:1-2 THAT WHOM — "that [the ones] whom."

5:4 THAT BOOKE — The *Animadversions.*

5:5 I MIGHT USE ... THE PATRONAGE —
Milton is entering the prelate's own sanctimonious
realm of antiquity, the "immeasurable, innumerable
... unnecessary, and unmercifull volumes" (*REF,*

Col. III, 34) of the Fathers, in justifying his use of sharp language.

5:6 *GREGORY NYSSEN* — Gregorius Nyssenus, Bishop of Nyssa in Cappadocia (372-395) was probably born A.D. 335 or 336. His older brother was Basil the Great (see Note 5:7 *BASIL.*) The language which Gregory adopted in speaking of Basil was, "as a son to a father" (*A Dictionary of Christian Biography,* ed. by William Smith and Henry Wace, London, 1880-1900, 4 vols., II, 761). Gregory was a noted defender of Trinitarianism against Arianism. His *Against Eunomius* defends the Nicene creed against Arianism and his brother against the charges Eunomius had made.

5:7 *EUNOMIUS* — Eunomius of Cappadocia, Bishop of Cyzicus (360-364), early came under the influence of Aetius whose doctrines he "completed and formulated" with such a preciseness and such "logical consistency" that the Anomean heretics became known by the name Eunomians. His theological convictions were unsullied by the taint of self-interest which characterized many of the extreme or Anomean Arians, especially the Arian court party (see Smith and Wace, *Dictionary of Christian Biography,* II, 286). Eunomius died about 393.

5:7 *BASIL* — (*c.* 330-379), Bishop of Caesarea, called the Great, an older brother of *"Gregory Nyssen."* Basil turned his talents against the Arians, who were numerous in Eastern Europe and Asia Minor and who were favored by the Arian emperor Valens, ruling in Constantinople. Among his works are three books against Eunomius who was the outstanding exponent of Anomian Arianism.

5:8-10 *WAS NOT FOR HIMSELFE ... THEN TO BE COOLER* — "Cum autem plerique aliam fortassis persuasionem habeant, quasi eo simus ingenio, vt eos qui petulanter in nos insurgent, aequo & patiente animo sustinere, & ex disciplina S. Basilii moderationem in moribus, quoad licet, exhibere soleamus; metui ne ex his, quae contra hunc aduersarium scripsimus, lecturibus noui appareremus, tanquam qui ad calumniatorum conuitia facilè inflammemur. An fortè ne tales habeamus, obstabit, quòd non pro nobis, sed pro probrosis in Patrem nostrum dictis irascimur. Nam in huiusmodi rebus maiorem forsitan veniam meretur succensere, quam moderatè agere."

("Sancti Patris nostri Gregorii Episcopi Nysseni Epistola Ad Petrvm Fratrem Svvm, Episcopvm Sebastenvm." One place the work was available to Milton was in *Appendix Ad Sancti Gregorii Episcopi Nysseni Opera Graece et Latina, Non Ita Pridem Evvlgata.* Editore & partim quoque interprete Iacobo Gretsero Societatis Iesu Theologo. Parisiis, 1618, p. 2. (Gregory habitually addressed his brother Basil as father; see Note 5:6.) See Jacques Paul Migne, *Patrologiae Cursus Completus, Graeco-Latina,* Paris, 1857-1903, 161 vols., XLV, 238-39 (Latin).)

5:10-11 THIS CONFUTER ... LEVITY — In the *Modest Confutation,* Sig. A3 *recto,* the Confuter calls the *Animadversions* "*a scurrilous* Mime." On pages 1 and 2 he says:

We must suppose you have *undertaken a religious cause.* That is your pretended subject.... Your defense is, *In such a cause, it is nothing disagreeing from Christian meeknesse, the morall precept of Solomon, the example of Christ.* What? to weary God and man, with lewd profanations, scurrilous jests, slanderous and reproachfull calumnies? What morall precept in *Solomon* countenances such language as this.... Such language you should scarce hear from the mouths of canting beggars, at an heathen altar; much lesse was it looked for in a treatise of controversall Theologie....

5:11-12 I SHALL SHEW YE ... OBJECTED IN PARTICULAR — Milton will defend his method in Section 1 of the *Apology* (20:38-27:2).

5:13 AS LITTLE LIGHTNESSE AS THE REMOUSTRANT HATH GIVEN EXAMPLE — The quotations taken from Hall's *A Defence Of The Humble Remonstrance* which Milton cited in the *Animadversions* and to which he prepared answers therein illustrate the Remonstrant's "lightnesse." Hall's lightness may have been provoked by the Smectymnuan *An Answer To ... An Humble Remonstrance* in which the Smectymnuans "tooke liberty to use some cheerfull expressions" (see Note 4:34-35), and found Hall's retorts so much surpassing theirs that in the *Vindication* they claimed: "But whatever we have done in other places, here (we attest the great Searcher of hearts) it never came into our thoughts to use a light expression" (Smectymnuus, *Vindication,* p. 31).

5:14-16 NOT BEENE SO LIGHT AS THE PALME OF A BISHOP ... BOOK OF ORDINATION — The practicé of simony in the English Church is often referred to by the opponents of prelacy. The *Constitvtions And Canons Ecclesias-*

tical...agreed vpon with the Kings Maiesties Licence in their Synode begun at London Anno Dom. 1603 (London, 1604), Sig. [G3] *verso* ff., stipulated the procedure for ordination, particularly demanding the oath that *"no Symoniacall paiment, contract or promise, directly or indirectly,"* had been made (*ibid.*, Sig. [H4] *verso*-I *recto*). It was frequently charged that much of the evil in the Anglican Church resulted from the evils connected with ordination and preferment. A pamphlet entitled *An Appeale To Every Impartiall, Iudicious, and Godly Reader: Whether The Presbyterie or Prelacie Be the better....* (London, 1641), pp. 4-5, charges that in prelacy the candidate "be made to pay his fees for Ordination, and License; and when hee is to be admitted into his Living, to pay for Institution and Induction, with other gratuities to the Prelates servants, and their gentlemen Apparators; and are forced to sweare Canonicall obedience to their Lordly Authoritie." Ministers are made upon "slight tryall," the ordination consisting of reading questions and answers and of using for prayers "the Letany and some short Collects" (*ibid.*, p. 5). The minister, although ordained, is not allowed to preach without a license. "True Patrons" are often deprived "by cunning shifts of the right of Patronage, to place in whom they please." The chief objective of the prelates is "how to secure themselves in their Lordly standing" (*ibid.*, p. 6). Henry Peacham, in *A Paradox, In The Praise Of A Dunce, To Smectymnuus* (London, 1642), p. 5, says that the tradesman or mechanic may come to preferment as easily as the learned man. Lord Brooke in the *Nature of Episcopacy* (1641), pp. 112-13, gives the opinion of those who oppose episcopacy as follows:

And they conceive 30. or 40. or an 100. Good men of any one or more Congregations, to be as Fit Judges of their parts and abilities every way, as One Lord Bishop and his Ignorant (perhaps Drunken) Chaplaine; who make scruple of admitting any to Orders, but Bowers and Cringers, sincks of Superstition; Yet when they please, they can poze in an Alehouse, and lay hands (well quicknd with angels) on Tapsters, Coblers, Butchers, and many such, that are so farre from the smell of a Colledge, that they never saw an Abcee or Primer to purpose, much lesse a *Ferula* in a Grammer Schoole.

He quotes King James as answering to the question "why hee made so many Bad Bishops" *"That hee was very sorry, but could not helpe it; For, no good*

men would take the Office on them" (*ibid.*, p. 97). See Note 57:4.

5:16-17 FOR THEN CONTRARY TO THAT WHICH IS WONT IN RELEASING OUT OF PRISON, ANY ONE THAT WILL PAY HIS FEES IS LAYD HANDS ON — Note the sarcastic pun — for a fee hands are laid off in releasing out of prison, but, in this case, hands are laid on.

5:18-19 IT WOULD NOT BE AMISSE... REMONSTRANT WERE TOLD — The Remonstrant should know.

5:19 UNUSUALL MANNER BELEAGUER'D — The reference is to the method of attack in the *Animadversions*. See Note 4:19.

5:21-22 ALL WHO ARE NOT PRELATICALL...SHALLOW — Cf. *ANIM* (1641), Sig. [I4] *verso* (*Col.* III, 173), where Milton defends the Smectymnuan's "Postscript" (Smectymnuus, *Answer*, pp. 85 [*i.e.*, 95] -104), which Hall had called a "goodly Pasquin" (Hall, *Defence*, p. 163), by asserting that it "was taken, be it knowne to you, from as authentique authors in this kinde, as any in a Bishops library."

5:22-24 CAN NOTHING...SPEAK GOOD ENGLISH . . . ORDER . . . WORDS JUDICIOUSLY — Cf. 4:31-5:1 and 5:35-40. Milton shows a resentment to the implication that bishops alone have learning. In "An Answer to a *Calumniatory* Epistle," of the *Short Answer* (Sig. a *recto*-[a] *verso*), Hall says: *"Do not think, Readers, that I will be beaten out with words; there is no one line of those passages, which they have recited, that I will not make good against all the clan of* Smectymnuus." He speaks of *"finding nothing in that swollen bulk"* of their *Vindication "but a meer unsound Tympanie...meer verball quarrells, or...disputes of things uncontroverted"* (Sig. a2 *recto*). He disdains them: *"I wis, it is not the force of their argutation, that could move me one foot forward"* (Sig. [a2] *verso*). He states that their charges of levity against him are the result of *"their own mis-understanding"* (Sig. [a2] *verso*) and that their comments *"argue great rashnesse, or much weaknesse of judgement"* (Sig. a3 *recto*). Hall's intimation that the opponents of the bishops were ignorant was a frequently made one (Taft, *Milton and The Smectymnuus Controversy*, pp. 269-72).

5:25 BARBAROUS LATIN — Cf. 20:1; 45:34. Harsh-sounding as compared with classical Latin, particularly that of Cicero.

5:25 TO ILLUMIN A PERIOD — How to shed light upon a complete sentence. The term "period" was usually applied to a sentence consisting of a number of clauses, grammatically connected, and rhetorically constructed (see *OED*). Cf. Aristotle, *Rhetoric* III, ix [1409a].

5:26 WREATH AN ENTHYMEMA — *i.e.*, to strain, to extend unduly a rhetorical argument, that is an argument based on probability rather than on demonstrable facts.

5:27-28 I HAVE HEARD IT OBSERV'D THAT A JESUITS ITALIAN ... IS EVER NAUGHT ... *FLORENTINE* — No exact source has been located. Milton observed that the Jesuits were "the onely corrupters of youth, and good learning" (*REF, Col.* III, 51). He valued Florence above all other Italian cities "for the elegance of its dialect and of its genius" (*Second Defence, Col.* VIII, 123) and spoke of those who regard the "Tuscan tongue" as a "chief delight" (Familiar Letter 8, *Col.* XII, 35), and of the "universally celebrated authors of the Florentine tongue" (*ibid.*, p. 37). Nor was Milton alone in the sentiment. Fynes Moryson, for instance, in *An Itinerary* (London, 1617), p. 155, speaks of learning the "Italian tongue, reputed the most pure in those parts" (*i.e.*, in the "State of *Florence*"). The sense of the observation to which Milton refers seems to be that the Jesuits, who, because their main interest was in scholasticism, spoke and wrote in a Latin of sorts, never became proficient in Italian even when they were born and raised in Florence.

5:29-30 FROM LIKE CAUSES ... STILE OF A PRELAT — The "Prelats," who are "out of the way in philosophy; pestring their heads with the saplesse dotages of old *Paris and Salamanca* ... affecting the comments and postils of Friers and Jesuits" (46:3-6), lack an eloquence because they are far removed from nature (5:30-34). Cf. *ANIM*, (1641), p. 59 (*Col.* III, 167): Learning does not flourish "among your beloved Jesuits, nor their favourers, though you take all the Prelates into the number."

5:30-32 THAT INDEED ACCORDING TO ART ... APPROACHES NEEREST TO NATURE FROM WHENCE IT CAME — See Horace, *Ars Poetica*, lines 1-13; Aristotle, *Physics*, Bk. II, ch. 2 [194a 22], and *Poetics*, Ch. 24 [1460a 18-20]. For a full discussion of "Nature and Art" in the sixteenth century see Marvin T. Herrick, "The Fusion of Horation and Aristotelian Literary Criticism, 1531-1555," *Illinois Studies in Language and Literature*, XXXII, No. 1, pp. 7-27.

5:32-35 THEY EXPRESSE NATURE BEST ... A GOOD MAN — Cf. Note 16:21-23. The notion has its source in Strabo's *Geography*, 1.2.5: Nor can we assume that any excellence of a poet whatever is superior to that which enables him to imitate life through the means of speech. How, then, can a man imitate life if he has no experience of life and is a dolt? Of course we do not speak of the excellence of a poet in the same sense as we speak of that of a carpenter or a blacksmith; for their excellence depends upon no inherent nobility and dignity, whereas the excellence of a poet is inseparably associated with the excellence of the man himself, and it is impossible for one to become a good poet unless he has previously become a good man. (*The Geography of Strabo With An English Translation By Horace Leonard Jones*, London, 1917-32, 8 vols., I, 63. Cf. Aristotle, *Rhetoric*, Bk. I, ch. 1 [1356a], and Bk. II, ch. 1 [1378a]. Aristotle insists that the appearance of virtue in an orator is a powerful factor in persuasion.)

Minturno, *De Poeta* (Venice, 1559), p. 79, says:
Definitur poeta vir bonus dicendi atque imitandi peritus. ... In qua definitione quod principiò ponitur, ipsaque natura potissimum est, ita praecipium mihi videtur, ut non modò qui sit poeta, hunc virum bonum esse oporteat, sed ne futurus quidem sit poeta, nisi vir bonus. (See *ibid.*, pp. 8-9, for the poet's mission.)

Ben Jonson in the "Dedicatory Epistle" to *Volpone* says:
For, if men will impartially, and not à-squint, looke toward the offices, and function of a poet, they will easily conclude to themselues, the impossibility of any mans being the good Poet, without first being a good man. (*The Workes of Beniamin Jonson*, London, 1616, p. 442.)

For comments on the passage see E. H. Visiak, *Milton Agonistes: a Metaphysical Criticism* (London, [1923]), p. 86 note; J. E. Spingarn, *Critical Essays of the Seventeenth Century* (Oxford, 1908-09, 3 vols.), I, 221, 250; J. E. Spingarn, *Literary Criticism in the Renaissance* (New York, 1908), pp. 54-55; Malcolm W. Wallace (ed.), *Milton's*

Prose (London, 1925), p. xxv. Milton's notion is that great writing proceeds from the man, not from greatness of theme nor dexterity in rhetorical manipulation.

5:35-40 NEVER THE LESSE...ADMIRE NOT — A rearrangement of elements in the sentence may clarify: "Never the lesse, as oft as is to be dealt with there be men of those that esteeme Prelaty a figment who pride themselves in their supposed art, to leave thẽ [those others] unexcusable wherin they will not be better'd, who yet can pipe, if they can dance, nor [who] will be unfurnisht to shew that what the Prelats admire and have not, others have and admire not."

5:38 THOSE THAT ESTEEME PRELATY A FIGMENT — *i.e.,* those who claim that the office or superiority of the prelate is a fictitious invention. Cf. "Prelaty or Prelateity" (*RGG, Col.* III, 244).

5:40 WHAT THE PRELATES ADMIRE AND HAVE NOT — *i.e.,* learning and its accompanying attributes.

6:2-3 TO WITHSTAND THE PERVERTERS OF THE GOSPELL — Cf. II John 10; Romans 16:17; Galatians 1:8-9; I Timothy 1:3; Titus 3:10; II Thessalonians 2:15 and 3:6; I Corinthians 16:22.

6:3-4 GAVE THE ANIMADVERSIONS NO LEAVE...VEHEMENCE — Milton claims that the admonitions of the Scripture "to withstand the perverters of the Gospell" left him no choice in his method of attack in his *Animadversions.*

6:5-6 IN TEACHING...SPIRIT OF MEEKNESS...MEEKE ONLY FIT PERSONS TO BE TAUGHT — The notion is Biblical. II Timothy 2:25 cautions to be meek in instructing; Galatians 6:1 exhorts the restoration of a brother overtaken in a fault "in a spirit of meekness." Christ, the great Teacher, was a man of "meekness and gentleness" (II Corinthians 10:1) who blessed the meek (Matthew 5:5; cf. Psalms 37:11). In Isaiah 61:1 the prophet says that the Lord has anointed him "to preach good tidings to the meek." Paul's admonition is to "Mind not high things, but condescend to men of low estate. Be not wise in your own conceits" (Romans 12:16).

6:7-8 THE PROUD...BE TAUGHT THEY WILL NOT — I Corinthians 1:26, "Not many wise men after the flesh, not many mighty, not many noble, *are called.*" See also verse 20: "Where *is* the wise? where *is* the scribe? where *is* the disputer of this world? hath not God made foolish the wisdom of this world?"

6:9-11 HOW CAN THEY ADMIT OF TEACHING...CONDEMNATION OF GOD ...FOR REFUSING DIVINE INSTRUCTION — See Proverbs 1:24-30. Cf. Zechariah 7:11-13; Jeremiah 9:6-7; John 3:18.

6:11 *FILL'D WITH THEIR OWN DEVICES* — Proverbs 1:31.

6:13 *WITH THE FROWARD...FROWARD* — Psalms 18:26, "with the froward thou wilt shew thyself froward"; cf. II Samuel 22:27.

6:14 *THROW SCORNE...SCORNER* — Proverbs 3:34, "Surely he scorneth the scorners"; cf. Proverbs 9:12.

6:14-15 *SCORNE...WILL HEALE* — Scorn, if anything, will heal, for the scorner does not love reproof, nor "will he go unto the wise" (Proverbs 15:12).

6:15-16 *THE RIGHTEOUS...UNGODLY* — Psalms 58:10, "The righteous shall rejoice when he seeth the vengeance." Cf. Job 22:18-19; Psalms 107:42.

6:16 THEY — *i.e.,* the righteous.

6:16 THEIR — *i.e.,* the ungodly, the supporters of prelacy.

6:18-19 PRELATY USURPT — "Prelaty neither hath nor can have foundation in the law, nor yet in the Gospell" (*RCG, Col.* III, 207). In the *Reason of Church-government* Milton had summarized the case against prelacy. He had pointed out that Jerome admitted that "custome only...was the maker of Prelaty" (*ibid.,* p. 208); that it was the "hatefull thirst of Lording in the Church that first bestow'd a being upon Prelaty" (*ibid.,* p. 213); that the "service of Prelaty is perfect slavery, and by consequence perfect falshood" (*ibid.,* p. 272); and that there is not "one good thing in prelaty, either to religion, or civil government, to King or Parlament, to Prince or people, to law, liberty, wealth or learning" (*ibid.,* p. 278).

6:19 THAT JUST GOVERNMENT—*i.e.,* presbyterian, which was older than government by prelates (*RCG, Col.* III, 209). It was established by the apostles who governed the Church by assemblies (*REF, Col.* III, 70) and was still the church government twenty years after St. Paul's death as testified by Clement's Epistle to the Corinthians (*RCG, Col.* III, 211). Milton did not fear that "any crookednes, any wrincle or spot should be found in presbyterial government" (*ibid.,* p. 253). He confessed "it to be the only true Church-government" (*ibid.,* p. 254).

6:20 FETCHES AND PRETENCES — *i.e.,* stratagems and hypocritical pretensions. The prelates' devices, Milton thought, were numerous. They held that "Church discipline ... [was] left to the discretion of men" (*RCG, Col.* III, 184); that episcopacy was patterned upon the Mosaic Law (*ibid.,* p. 195 ff.); that it had its beginning in the priesthood of Aaron (*ibid.,* p. 199 ff.); and that it developed, the bishop being "heav'd above the Presbyter" (*ibid.,* p. 210), to prevent schism. All of these devices were little more than hypocritical pretensions by which the prelates could maintain their position of lordship and wealth. The *Of Prelatical Episcopacy* had as its purpose to prove that episcopacy could not be "deduc't from the *Apostolicall* TIMES" (*PRE, Col.* III, 104), that it had grown up as a result of worldly ambition, and that the "well-tasted Hierarchy" once established was maintained "by what faire pretext soever," for the prelates "had now learnt to defend many other grosse corruptions by as ancient, and suppos'd authentick tradition as Episcopacie" (*ibid.,* p. 84).

6:24 THIS OFFICE GOES NOT BY AGE, OR YOUTH — Cf. Note 2:36.

6:25-26 TO WHOMSOEVER GOD SHALL GIVE ... THE WILL, THE SPIRIT, AND THE UTTERANCE — The Biblical teaching was that spiritual gifts were allotted by God to his followers (I Corinthians 12:1-11; Ephesians 4:11), some to prophesy, some to preach, some to teach, some to heal, some to help (I Corinthians 12:28). Paul's exhortation to the Romans was to use the gifts which God had given (Romans 12:6-8; cf. I Peter 4:10). The utterance of a man who used the gift God gave him was in some instances considered tantamount to God's speaking through him (II Peter 1:21). Many men of Milton's age claimed immediate inspiration from God. Richard Baxter sought "those inward *perceptions* of the verity of the Promises & Rewards of God" which cannot result from "artificial reasonings." Some "are taught of God by the effective sort of Teaching, which reacheth the Heart or *Will,* as well as the Understanding.... And who findeth not need to pray for this effective Teaching of God, when he hath got all Organical Knowledge, and Words and Arguments in themselves most apt, at his fingers ends (as we say?)" (Richard Baxter's *Dying Thoughts Upon Phil. I. xxiii,* London, 1688, pp. 8-9.)

6:26-28 THE REASONS ... CHURCHES WELLFARE — Cf. 43:24-28. Milton, who had been "by the intentions of my parents and friends ... and in mine own resolutions" destined for the Church (*RCG, Col.* III, 242), could not deny to the Church the "meanest under-service, if God by his Secretary conscience injoyn it" (*ibid.*) and felt "the right I have to meddle in these matters" (*ibid.*). Sir Francis Bacon had much the same idea:

It is very true, that these *Ecclesiasticall Matters,* are Things, not properly appertaining, to my *Profession;* which, I was not, so inconsiderate, but to object to my Self: But finding, that it is, many times, seen, that a Man that standeth off, and somewhat removed, from a Plot of Ground, doth better survey it, and discover it, then those which are upon it; I thought it not impossible, but that I, as a Looker on, might cast mine Eyes, upon some Things, which the Actours themselves, (especially, some being *interested,* some *led* and *addicted,* some *declared and engaged,*) did not, or would not see. (Bacon, "Certain Considerations, Touching the Better, Pacification, And Edification, Of The Church Of England," in *Resuscitatio,* p. 234.)

6:27-28 GOOD MEN IN THEIR LABOURS — The Smectymnuans and their *An Answer To ... An Humble Remonstrance* (March 1640/41) and *A Vindication Of The Ansvver To The Hvmble Remonstrance* (June 1641).

6:28-29 TO WHICH IF ANY ONE BROUGHT OPPOSITION, I BROUGHT MY BEST RESISTANCE — Milton answered Hall's *Defence Of The Humble Remonstrance,* which answered the Smectymnuan *Answer,* with his *Animadversions Upon The Remonstrants Defence, Against Smectymnuus,* and Hall's *A Short Answer To The Tedious Vindication Of Smectymnuus,* which answered the Smectymnuan *Vindication,* with some attentions in the *Apology* (*Apology* 4:26; 7:28). Milton was a willing defender of his own and of his friends' ideas, holding himself ready should there be any reply to his *Reason of Church-government* or *Apology* (*Second Defence, Col.* VIII, 131).

6:29-31 IF IN REQUITALL . . . OF MY FRIENDS — "If in requitall of this [resistance] and [if] for that [*i.e.*, because] I have not been negligent toward the reputation of my friends." See Note 6:28-29.

6:31-34 A NAME BESTUCK . . . BEDECKT WITH THE REPROACHES AND REVILES OF THIS MODEST CONFUTER . . . NEITHER STRANGE, NOR UNWELCOME . . . A BETTER TIME — Milton feels that if in the defense of his cause and of his friends he has become the target of the author of the *Modest Confutation* he is not surprised, nor is the attack unwelcome, for "to be generally prais'd is wofull" (11:30-31); furthermore, he has "bin already bitten at" by "this sort of men" (15:3). Because the *Animadversions* has been answered, Milton feels that his writing has been effective (cf. 19:24; 27:3-4); he welcomes the opportunity of defending himself. He feels that the time is propitious for his *Apology*. See 12:8-9.

6:35-36 ANIMADVERSIONS — See Note 3:35.

6:37 CONFUTATIŌ — *A Modest Confutation Of A Slanderous and Scurrilous Libell, Entitvled, Animadversions Vpon The Remonstrants Defense Against Smectymnuus* (1642).

6:37 THĒ — The *Animadversions*.

6:37 CONFUTER — See Note 2:27.

6:37-7:1 WHAT THE . . . FROM HIS OWN TITLE — The opening of this paragraph gives Milton's plan for the *Apology*. He has accounted for the manner in which he wrote the *Animadversions*. He will now consider what the *Modest Confutation* says against the *Animadversions;* but first he will discuss the *Modest Confutation* for the benefit of the Confuter.

6:39-7:1 HE PRETENDS . . . FROM HIS OWN TITLE — The Confuter admitted that he had no knowledge of Milton except what he gleaned from the *Animadversions* (see 11:5-15):

I have no further notice of him, than he hath been pleased, in his immodest and injurious Libell to give of

himself: and therefore, as our industrious Criticks for want of clearer evidence concerning the life and manners of some revived Authours, must fetch his character from some scattered passages in his own writings. (*Modest Confutation,* Sig. A3 *recto.*)

Milton intends to answer in kind by making an inference from the wording of the Confuter's title.

6:39 CONJECTOR — Conjecturer.

7:1 TOLING — Alluring or enticing, intended to lead into a snare.

7:1 SIGNE-POST — Probably a synecdoche, *signe-post* standing for the sign of an inn or shop. Cf. 20:21-23.

7:2 PASSENGERS — Passers-by.

7:4-6 MODEST TITLE SHOULD ONLY INFORME . . . BY READING — See 7:26-28.

7:5 OFFICIOUS — Obtruding information or services not needed.

7:7 FORESTALLING — Stating beforehand.

7:8 SET . . . TO SALE — Placed on exhibition for selling.

7:8 FRONTISPICE — *i.e.*, the title page.

7:12 THE SEQUEL — That which follows the title page; the text of the *Modest Confutation*, particularly the preface "To the Reader."

7:12-13 OMITTED ANY KINDE OF BOLDNESSE IN SLANDERING — See *Apology*, pp. 11-20, Milton's own defense of himself against the Confuter's charges in the preface of the *Modest Confutation* (Sig. A3 *recto*-[A4] *verso*).

7:13-14 FOREHEAD OF HIS TITLE — *i.e.*, the first few words of his title, specifically the words "*A Modest Confutation*" (see 7:2).

7:14-15 THAT HE MIGHT NOT WANT COLOUR TO BE THE MORE IMPUDENT THROUGHOUT HIS WHOLE CONFUTATION — Cf. 20:20-24. "Colour" has a double meaning (cf. 20:22-23 "a certaine red portending signe"). The likening of the title page to a man's face with the first words as the "forehead" which has been rubbed in order to give it color gives the word its meaning in the figure of speech. In the logic of the passage "colour" means a "fair pretence, a pretext, a specious or plausible reason."

7:15-20 NEXT WHAT CAN EQUALLY SAVOUR OF INJUSTICE...NOT STAYING TILL THE READER CAN HEAR HIM PROV'D SO — See Note 7:26-28.

7:17-18 *SLANDEROUS AND SCURRILOUS* — Part of the title of the *Modest Confutation*; see Note 6:37.

7:18 AS THE REMONSTRANTS FASHION IS — Milton sees in the wording of the title a similarity to the methods of Joseph Hall, the Remonstrant. See 7:21-22.

7:18-19 *FRIVOLOUS, TEDIOUS, AND FALSE* — Hall's answer to the Smectymnuan *An Answer To...An Humble Remonstrance* (1641), was *A Defence Of The Humble Remonstrance Against the frivolous and false exceptions of Smectymnvvs* (1641). Hall's answer to the Smectymnuan *A Vindication Of The Ansvver To The Hvmble Remonstrance* (1641) was *A Short Answer To The Tedious Vindication Of Smectymnvvs* (1641).

7:20-22 WHICH IS ONE CAUSE OF A SUSPICION...THE REMONSTRANT WAS NOT UNCONSULTED WITH — Milton sees in the Confuter's use of the word *modest* one of the Remonstrant's techniques to ingratiate himself to the reader. A similar technique is used in his *Defence* and *Short Answer* in the words "frivolous," "tedious," and "false" (see Note 7:18-19) to prejudice his readers against his opponents. These are among his methods of "[vapouring] them out" (*Apology* 4:34). Milton presumes that Bishop Hall aided his son in writing the *Modest Confutation*. See 7:18; 7:31-36; 8:17-18; 10:31-33; 21:2-3; 27:14-15; 34:20; 35:5-6; 36:8.

7:22-23 *AN HUMBLE...CHURCH* — Joseph Hall's *An Humble Remonstrance To The High Covrt Of Parliament, By A dutifull Sonne of the Church* (1640), the first of the pamphlets of the Smectymnuan series (Masson, *Life*, II, 391).

7:24 WHITE-BOY — Favorite or darling boy. The reference is, of course, to Hall's "A dutifull Sonne" (see Note 7:22-23).

7:24-26 HIS NEXT WAS *A DEFENCE...* SITTING — "His next was *a defence* ... [in which the Remonstrant is] sitting," etc.

7:24-26 *A DEFENCE...EXCEPTIONS OF SMECTYMNUS* — See Note 7:18-19.

7:24-25 (A WONDER HOW IT SCAPT SOME PRAISING ADJUNCT) — Milton, with the term "modest" (7:2,14) in mind, suggests that the Bishop lost a good opportunity for self-praise in formulating the title of his *Defence*.

7:26-28 SITTING IN THE CHAIRE OF HIS TITLE PAGE...BEFORE THE JURY OF READERS CAN BE IMPANNELL'D — See 7:3-6; 7:15-20. Milton points out that the wording of the title, "*the frivolous and false exceptions*" (see Note 7:20-22), makes the author, who sits in the place of authority on the title page, both a plaintiff and a judge against his adversary whom he has already condemned, without giving the jury of readers an opportunity of sitting to hear the case.

7:27 CAST — Condemned; defeated in a law suit (*OED*).

7:28-29 *A SHORT ANSWER...VINDICATION* — See Note 7:18-19.

7:29-31 SO LITTLE...PREOCCUPYING DIRECTION — Milton is enjoying the pursuit *ad absurdum*. The Remonstrant does not allow his reader the opportunity to judge for himself whether his *Short Answer* is "short," or whether the Smectymnuan *Vindication* is "tedious" or not (see Note 7:18-19).

7:31-32 FROM HENCE...*LIBELL* — From this source or origin came such a title as the "*modest confutation against a slanderous and scurrilous libell.*"

7:35 CONCEIT — To imagine, to fancy, or to think (*OED*).

7:35-36 I CONCEIT HIM...PASSION SERMON — Milton thinks the author of the *Modest Confutation* closely related to the person who published a "Passion Sermon."

7:36-37 PASSION SERMON...SAVIOUR — The Passion Sermon is a sermon regularly preached on Good Friday. The reference is to Bishop Hall's sermon preached at St. Paul's Cross on Good Friday, April 14, 1609. The formal dedicatory is printed in capital letters:

TO THE ONELY / HONOVR AND GLO- / RIE OF GOD MY DEARE / AND *BLESSED SAVIOVR* / (WHICH HATH DONE AND / SVFFERED ALL THESE / THINGES FOR MY / SOVLE.) / HIS WEAKE AND VN- / *WORTHIE SERVANT HVM-* / BLIE DESIRES TO CONSE- / *CRATE HIM-SELFE AND HIS* / POORE LABOVRS: BE-SEECHING / HIM TO ACCEPT AND BLESSE / THEM TO THE PVBLIKE / GOOD, AND TO THE / PRAISE OF HIS OVVNE / GLORIOVS / NAME. /

(*The Passion Sermon, Preached At Pavles Crosse on Good-Friday. Apr. 14. 1609. By I. H.*, London, 1609, Sig. A3 *recto;* cf. IOS. HALL, *Meditations and Vowes, Divine and Morall; Serving For Direction In Christian and ciuill practice. 3. Centuries*, London, 1614, p. [621]. Available in *"The Works of Joseph Hall, D.D.,* Oxford, 1837-39, 12 vols., V, 21.)

7:38-39 ALL WE DO OUGHT TO BEGIN AND END TO HIS PRAISE AND GLORY — Colossians 3:17; cf. I Corinthians 10:31, Philippians 1:11, Psalms 107:31.

7:39-8:4 TO INSCRIBE HIM ... AN INSULS AND FRIGID AFFECTATION — To inscribe the Saviour on a separate page with flourishes is too much like paying compliment to men from whom favors are desired to be respectful.

7:40 COMPLEMENT — Compliment.

7:40 TO TRICK UP — To dress up, to adorn by using an ingenious expedient or device.

8:1 LORD PARAMOUNT AT COMMON LAW — A person "who exercises supreme power or jurisdiction" (*OED*) in the unwritten law of England; that is, a man of great importance.

8:1-2 BOOK-PATRON — The person who accepted the dedication of a book.

8:2 APPENDANT — "Attached in a subordinate capacity or relationship" (*OED*).

8:2 PRESENTMENT — Presentation.

8:3-4 INSULS ... AFFECTATION — "Insuls," an adjective modifying "affectation," means dull, stupid, absurd.

8:4 AS NO LESSE WAS THAT — No less a stupid and frigid affectation was that dedicatory.

8:4-5 THAT BEFORE HIS BOOK AGAINST THE BROWNISTS — Milton refers to the dedicatory to Joseph Hall's *A Common Apologie of the Church of England, against the Unjust Challenges of the overjust Sect, commonly called Brownists ...* (1610). See Note 8:5-6.

8:5-6 TO WRITE A LETTER ... WHOM HE CALLS MOTHER — The "Letter" prefaced to *A Common Apologie of the Church of England, against ... the ... Brownists* begins:

TO OVR GRATIOVS / AND BLESSED MOTHER, / *THE CHVRCH OF* / ENGLAND / THE MEANEST OF HER CHIL- / DREN DEDICATES THIS HER / *APOLOGY, AND WISHETH* / *All Peace and Happinesse.* (Ios. Hall, *Meditations and Vowes*, 1614, p. [717]; see also *The Works*, 1837-39, X, p. [4].)

8:5 PROSOPOPOEA — A rhetorical figure representing an inanimate or abstract thing as a person, or with the characteristics of a person.

8:6-7 COMPLAINS OF SOME ... TO HER CHARGE — Hall says in the "Letter":

No lesse then a yeare and a halfe is past (Reuerend, Deare, and holy Mother) since I wrote a louing monitory letter to two of thine vnworthy Sons ... one of them hath washt off thy Font-water as vnclean, and hath written desperately both against thee, and his owne fellowes: From the other, I receiued (not two moneths since) a stomackful Pamphlet ... casting vpon thine honourable name blasphemous imputations of Apostasie, Antichristianisme, Whoordome, Rebellion.... (Ios. Hall, *Meditations and Vowes*, 1614, p. [717]; *The Works*, 1837-39, X, [4].)

The two unworthy sons were John Robinson (1576?-1625), pastor of the pilgrim fathers, and John Smith (d.1612), "reputed father of English general baptists." For the epistle, "the louing monitory letter," to Mr. Smith, and Mr. Robinson, "Ring-leaders of the late separation; at Amsterdam," see "Decade iii, Epistle 1, of Ios. Hall, *Meditations and Vowes* (1614), pp. 451-53; also *The Works* (1837-39), VI, 179-81.

8:7-12 HAD HE FOLDED HIS EPISTLE ... MIRACULOUS GREETING.... BRETHREN AND SONS — Had the letter been addressed and delivered to the Church of England by anyone but a clergyman the greeting would have been most extraordinary. The point Milton is making is that no one, other than a clergyman in the English Church would have conceived of addressing the Church as a rhetorized woman. The example of the early teachers of the Church was to address the Churches as "faithfull brethren and sons" (see Colossians 1:2; I Timothy 1:2; II Timothy 1:2).

8:9 POST — Although entries occur in the wardrobe accounts of the Kings of England as early as the thirteenth century to pay royal messengers for the conveyance of letters, the first distinct account of an English postmaster is that of Sir Brian Tuke in 1533.

8:9 UBIQUITARY — Literally, a clergyman having no settled benefice, who takes duty anywhere. To that meaning is added the connotation of one who can be everywhere at once. Hall's see at Exeter, from December 23, 1627, to November 15, 1641, and thereafter at Norwich, did not prevent him from leading a very active public life.

8:10 PRIMITIVE DOCTORS — Teachers of primitive times. The Church as it sprang from Christ and the apostles was the model of the Protestants. Milton turned to the "*Primitive,* and pure times" (*REF, Col.* III, 70) when "Primitive pastors ...labour'd faithfully" (*ibid.,* p. 41), when "many before ever they had receiv'd ordination from the Apostles, had done the Church noble service" (*ANIM, Col.* III, 156). "*Primitive,* and pure times" was for Milton practically limited to the times of the apostles and by the record of the Bible (*PRE, Col.* III, 85-86).

8:12-16 A CLOUDY TRANSMIGRATION OF SEXES ... FOND UTTERANCES BETTER LET ALONE — Milton is referring to Hall's Dedicatory to the Church of England, which Milton has previously termed a "Letter" (8:5), of the *Common Apology against Brownists:*

[cloudy transmigration of sexes] Mine owne wrongs I could haue contemned in silence; but, For Sions sake, I cannot holde my peace: If I remember not thee, O Ierusalem, let my tongue cleaue to the roofe of my mouth. It were a shame, and sin for me, that my zeale should be lesse hote for thine innocency, then theirs to thy false disgrace. [to runne up] How haue I hastened therefore to let the world see thy sincere truth, and their peruerse slanders! [tread the aire in metaphoricall compellations] Vnto thy sacred name then (vvhereto I haue in all piety deuoted my selfe) I humbly present this my speedy and dutifull labour: whereby I hope thy weak Sons may be confirmed, the strong encouraged, the rebellious shamed: And if any shall still obstinately accurse thee, I refer their reuenge vnto thy Glorious Head, who hath espoused thee to himselfe, in truth and righteousnesse: Let him whose thou art, right thee: [fond utterances better let alone] In the meane time, we thy true Sons shall not only defend, but magnify thee: Thou maiest be black, but

thou art comely: the Daughters haue seen thee, and counted thee blessed; euen the Queene, and the Concubines, and they haue praised thee: thou art thy Welbeloueds, and his desire is towards thee. So let it be, and so let thine be towards him for euer; and mine towards you both, who am the least of all thy little ones, IOS. HALL. (Ios. Hall, *Meditations and Vowes,* 1614, p. [717]; *The Works,* 1837-39, X, p. [4].)

Hall's "fond utterances" are based upon the Song of Solomon.

8:16-17 EMBLAZONER OF HIS TITLE PAGE — One who makes his title page illustrious.

8:17-18 (WHETHER IT BE THE SAME MAN OR NO I LEAVE IT IN THE MIDST) — After marshaling all the evidence to prove Hall the author, Milton admits his uncertainty. See Note 7:20-22.

8:18-19 I FINDE HIM PRONOUNCING ... THOSE ANIMADVERSIONS ... *A SLANDEROUS* ... *LIBELL* — See 6:35-37, and 7:17-18.

8:21 WILL ANSWER IN WHAT PLACE OF HIS BOOK — In Section II of the *Modest Confutation,* the Confuter considers libels. Milton answers him in [Section 2] of the *Apology, i.e.,* 27:3-28:15.

8:22 NOT INKE ONLY IN HIS MOUTH — Milton points out that, in the title of the *Modest Confutation,* the author, in using the words "slanderous" and "scurrilous," has, like a cuttlefish, ejected a black, inky liquid in order to help him escape. The figure is apt. The idea is probably borrowed from the Smectymnuan *Vindication,* p. 62: "he [the Remonstrant] deals like the fish *Sepia,* and casteth out a great deal of black inke before the eyes of the Reader, that so hee may escape without observation."

8:22-24 NOR CAN IT ... SLANDERS — "Nor can [the *Animadversions*] be a libell more then [the *Modest Confutation*]." The *Modest Confutation,* which was issued anonymously, stirred Milton's anger with its slanders, which are particularly severe in the preface "To the Reader."

8:24-27 AND IF [it be a libell] IN THIS THAT IT FREELY SPEAKS OF THINGS AMISSE IN RELIGION, BUT ESTABLISHED BY ACT OF STATE ... LIBELLING — Milton asserts the principle that against right and truth there is no law. If his *Animadversions* is a libel because it denounces those things which are amiss in religion, even though they have been established by the government, then all the reformers are guilty of libeling, and all reform is wrong. By implication then, if the prelates denied Milton's logic, they could not justify their own separation from the Roman Catholic Church. A position as part of the Roman Catholic Church the prelates were not willing to admit.

8:25 ESTABLISHT BY ACT OF STATE — The Church of England was, of course, established by law. (See Milton's account of the reformation in England, REF, Col. III, 7 ff.) Milton is, however, certain that there is much amiss (8:24). He is convinced that England has been hindered by episcopacy from obtaining the perfection of reformation, for in the episcopal "Discipline," in its "sencelesse Ceremonies," there is no "Uniforme Consent to the rest of the Churches abroad" (REF, Col. III, 6). Of Reformation has as its objective "to declare those Causes that hinder the forwarding of true Discipline" (ibid., p. 7).

8:25 WICKLEFFE — John Wycliffe (c.1320-1384). To Milton, Wycliffe was highly venerable. He was "that Englishman honor'd of God to be the first preacher of a general reformation to all Europe" (Tetrachordon, Col. IV, 222), who, had he not been suppressed by the "obstinat perversnes of our Prelats," might have made "the glory of reforming all our neighbors...compleatly ours" (Areopagitica, Col. IV, 340). It was at the flame of Wycliffe's preaching that "all the succeding Reformers more effectually lighted their Tapers." And although his "short blaze" was "soone dampt and stifl'd by the Pope, and Prelates," yet he represented to Milton "the Precedencie which GOD gave this Iland, to be the first Restorer of buried Truth" (REF, Col. III, 5). God, having chosen "to purifie and renew his Church," awakened England first "by that glimmering light which Wicklef, and his followers dispers't (ANIM, Col. III, 145). Milton denies "that Bishops were our first Reformers, for Wickliffe was before them, and his egregious labours are not to be neglected" (ibid., pp. 177-78).

8:26 LUTHER — Martin Luther (1483-1546), the great German religious reformer, "whom God made choice of before others to be of highest emi-

nence and power in reforming the Church" (23:31-33), was a great "servant of God" (Tetrachordon, Col. IV, 222). See also Eikonoklastes, Col. V, 63; Means to Remove Hirelings, Col. VI, 75; Second Defence, Col. VIII, 203; Commonplace Book, Col. XVIII, 145, 216; and Apology, 23:31-24:15; 58:37-59:1.

8:27-29 I NEVER THOUGHT THE HUMANE FRAILTY OF ERRING...COUNCELL — Cf. Plato, Apology, 26 (Jowett translation): "If my offence is unintentional, the law has no cognizance of unintentional offences." In setting up the comparison Milton is striking the prelates on the vital spot of tradition. For them as for the Roman Catholics the writings of the Fathers and the decisions of the Church Councils were binding. Milton cannot understand how erring in religion can be a disgrace to a state if it isn't to a Council. The whole reformation was based on a denial of the infallibility of the Councils. Luther refused to deny at the Diet of Worms that the "Councels...haue erred often tymes, and set forthe thinges contrary one to another" and that the Bishop of Rome often erred (Johannes Sleidanus, A Famovse Cronicle of oure time, called Sleidanes Commentaries, concerning the state of Religion and common wealth, during the raigne of the Emperour Charles the fift...Translated...by Ihon Daus, London, 1560, fol. xxx recto). Milton emphasizes that "many opinions in the Fathers...have no ground in Scripture...their own words shall condemn them" (REF, Col. III, 32). Even the Council of Nicea, "the first and famousest of all the rest," must have erred, Milton implies in twitting those who upheld the episcopal church government, when it exhorted the choosing of worthy orthodox bishops by the assent of the people (ibid., p. 17).

8:29-33 IT HAD THEREFORE...FOREFATHERS — It would furthermore be "neither civill, nor Christianly," Milton argues, to dishonor or reproach the State because it erred by establishing false tenets in religion, especially when the Parliament is making great efforts to reform the "defects and oversights of their forefathers." See 38:39-39:12.

8:32-35 DEFECTS AND OVERSIGHTS... MAINTAINING — i.e., the godly and repentant ages of the Jews humbly confessed and bewailed their defects and oversights; the prelates confidently assert and maintain them.

8:33 GODLY... AGES OF THE JEWES —
See the reign of Asa, I Kings 15:8-24 (II Chronicles 14-15); of Hezekiah, II Kings 18-21 (II Chronicles 29-32); of Josiah, II Kings 22-23 (II Chronicles 34-35).

8:35-36 OF THE STATE... HONOURABLE THINGS — Milton claims a deep affection for the State. He speaks very respectfully of the Parliament (see *REF, Col.* III, 57-58, 70; *ANIM, Col.* III, 111-12, 118-19, 137, 159, 170) which would deliver England "from your *Ephesian* beasts, your cruell *Nimrods,* with whom we shall be ever fearelesse to encounter" (*ANIM, Col.* III, 173). He affirms Solomon's dictum that "the throne of a King ... *is establisht in Justice*" (*REF, Col.* III, 49). He speaks of the possibility that "this present King had in all likelyhood never sat on this Throne, and the happy union of this Iland had bin frustrated" (*REF, Col.* III, 68); of the prelates as "the greatest underminers and betrayers of the Monarch" (*RCG, Col.* III, 276). He hopes for the "very jubily, and resurrection of the State" (*ANIM, Col.* III, 112); he expects God to do a "remarkable good to our Church or state" (*ibid.,* p. 144). If the people "cut away ... the noysom, and diseased tumor of Prelacie ... nourishing and cordial restorements to the State will follow" (*REF, Col.* III, 62-63).

8:37 PETITION WITH GOOD MEN THAT PETITION'D — (Cf. *ANIM, Col.* III, 118-19, where Milton mentions the "City Petition.") Milton is no doubt referring to the London Petition against episcopacy presented to the Parliament December 11, 1640. It was signed by 15,000 Londoners, perhaps by Milton, and brought to Westminster by an approving crowd of 1,500 persons. It proposed church reform and the abolition of episcopal government (Gardiner, *History,* IX, 247) that "the government according to God's word may be rightly placed among us" (Masson, *Life,* II, 213).

8:37-38 PRELATS ... THE ONLY SEDUCERS AND MIS-LEADERS OF THE STATE — See *REF, Col.* III, 56. The prelates are "a Tyrannicall crew and Corporation of Impostors, that have blinded and abus'd the World" (*ibid.,* p. 12);

they were the chief hinderers of reform in Elizabeth's days (*ibid.,* p. 14); they have weakened the kingdom by removing such supports of monarchy as "the love of the Subjects, the multitude, and valor of the people, and store of treasure" (*ibid.,* p. 49). They have driven many Englishmen to America and alienated the Protestant Princes abroad (*ibid.,* pp. 50-51); they have sought to "effeminate us all at home" (*ibid.,* p. 52). They "set at nought ... the most sacred, and life blood Lawes, Statutes, and Acts of *Parliament,*" confiscate "from us all the right we have to our owne bodies, goods and liberties," and "affect to be Kings" (*ibid.,* p. 57). They have been "a sad and dolefull succession of illiterate and blind guides," "a wastfull band of robbers," "a continuall *Hydra* of mischiefe, and molestation, the forge of discord and Rebellion" (*ibid.,* p. 67). Their "diabolical Courts" (*ibid.,* p. 75) have added to the tyranny. The monarchy must be saved from the prelates (*ANIM, Col.* III, 115): the "misbestowed wealth" should be taken from them (*ibid.,* p. 143); the dissolving of their order would bring "ease, and happinesse" (*ibid.,* p. 163). Since they fear that their "faire dayes cannot long hold" they possess the King with their "false doctrine," and "ingage his power for them" (*RCG, Col.* III, 202). They are the "greatest underminers and betrayers of the Monarch" (*ibid.,* p. 276). The "worthy Peeres and Commons" know that the prelates are "clippers of regal power and shavers of the Law," and opposers of those "glorious and immortal actions" taken by the Parliament "to repaire the shatter'd and disjoynted frame of the Commonwealth" (*ibid.,* p. 277).

8:40 NOT VEHEMENCE ANOUGH — Milton, who loves *the soules of men,* when he meets with the counterfeiting, dissimulation, and deception of the prelates, becomes *transported with the zeale of truth to a well heated fervencie; especially, seeing they which thus offend against the soules of their brethren, do it with delight to their great gaine, ease, and advancement in this world* (*ANIM, Col.* III, 107). Consequently, he exposes in the *Animadversions* the *"Pseudepiscopy of Prelates"* (*ibid.,* p. 106), points out their "applauding" at the expulsion of Englishmen to New England (*ibid.,* p. 111), accuses them of collusion with the Pope (*ibid.,* p. 116), charges that there is more "savoury knowledge in one Lay-man, then in a dozen of Cathedrall *Prelates*" (*ibid.*, p. 131), labels them the "spirituall adulterers" of the Church of England (*ibid.*, p. 171), and declares that a good prelate is an impossibility (*ibid.*, p. 176). Milton is convinced that, if the prelate is "un-visarded . . . to publick view," prelacy will die (*ibid.*, p. 112) and the "Sacred Monarchy" will be saved "from such friends" (*ibid.*, p. 115), and from their "intolerable yoke" (*ibid.*, p. 145).

9:1-2 TWO OR THREE NOTES . . . TITLE PAGE — See *Apology* 6:40-8:19.

9:2 FIRSTLINGS . . . WHOLE LUMPE — Cf. Romans 11:16.

9:4-5 ALTHOUGH I TELL HIM . . . ME — Milton is in effect challenging the Confuter to follow the argument by suggesting that the Confuter may have the courage to hear the truth. The clauses might be paraphrased: in spite of the fact that I am telling him the bold truth, he may be indulgent toward me.

9:5 CHAFE HIM INTO SOME GOOD KNOWLEDGE — Note the virility as well as the earthiness of the idiom.

9:7-9 AIME . . . STANDER BY — Milton does not forget that as one prepared for the ministry he is essentially a teacher. He insists that the "Churchmans office is only to teach men the Christian Faith" (*REF, Col.* III, 40; cf. *PRE, Col.* III, 86), for the ministry was "set a part to teach and discipline the Church" (*RCG, Col.* III, 197; cf. *Paradise Lost,* XII, 440, 446, and Matthew 28:19). Milton feels he has no choice but to be unpleasant to the Confuter who is at fault in the *Modest Confutation* for "asserting and maintaining" untruths (8:35; cf. 6:1-26). In the process of withstanding the "perverters of the Gospell" (6:2-3) Milton promises "to be usefull in some thing to the stander by" (9:8-9). He may have in mind the Scriptural admonition to "smite a scorner, and the simple will beware" (Proverbs 19:25; cf. Proverbs 21:11 and 22:10), for he had already identified the Confuter with the scorner (*Apology,* 6:14).

9:11 SYCOPHANTING — Calumniating, slandering. Cf. "Sycophants," *ANIM, Col.* III, 113.

9:12 THE WORKE — *i.e.,* Milton's *Animadversions.*

9:12 *MIME* — "A kind of simple farcical drama among the Greeks and Romans characterized by mummery and ludicrous representation of familiar types of character; a dialogue written for recital in a performance of this kind" (*OED*).

9:12-14 *A MIME . . . SMECTYMNUANS* — In the *Modest Confutation,* the Confuter had said in regard to *"the late and hot bickerings between the* Prelates *and* Smectymnuans:*"
To make up [*i.e.,* to close up] *the breaches of whose* [Prelates *and* Smectymnuans] *solemn Scenes, (it were too ominous to say Tragicall) there is thrust forth upon the Stage, as also to take the eare of the lesse intelligent, a scurrilous* Mime, *a personated, and (as himself thinks) a grim, lowring, bitter fool.* ("To the Reader," *Modest Confutation,* Sig. A3 *recto*.)

9:16 HIMSELFE, OR HIS OWN FRIENDS — If the Confuter and the Remonstrant are one and the same person (cf. 7:20-22; 8:17-18), the Confuter has, in his eagerness "to fix a name of ill sound upon another" (9:15), exposed himself; if the two are not one and the same, the Confuter has exposed his friends, particularly the Remonstrant, to ignominy (see 9:16-17).

9:17 THOSE GRAVE CONTROVERSIES — *i.e.,* the pamphlet controversy between the Smectymnuans and the Remonstrant, which the Confuter had called the *"late and hot bickerings"* (*Modest Confutation,* Sig. A3 *recto*).

9:17-18 TO A PIECE OF STAGERY, OR SCENE-WORKE — *"To make up the breaches of whose solemn Scenes, (it were too ominous to say Tragicall) there is thrust forth upon the Stage . . ."* (*Modest Confutation,* Sig. A3 *recto*).

9:18 HIS OWNE REMONSTRANT — *i.e.,* Bishop Hall.

9:19 BUSKIN OR SOCK — Tragedy or comedy.

9:19 [Remonstrant] MUST . . . BE COUNTED THE CHIEFE PLAYER — Milton argues that in degrading the "grave controversies" by likening them to "Stagery, or Scene-worke," the Remonstrant, who had written three pamphlets in the controversy, not counting his part in the *Modest Confutation,* was also degraded. Furthermore in

drawing attention to the trappings of drama, the
Confuter has drawn attention to the Remonstrant
as a chief actor, having written "the idlest and the
paltriest Mime that ever mounted upon banke"
(10:11-12), in a very unpopular aspect of English
life, particularly for a divine, for public sentiment
was growing toward the climax that resulted in the
closing of the theatres in September 1642.

9:20 BOASTING *THRASO* — The braggart
soldier in Terence's *Eunuch*. The Smectymnuans, in
their *Vindication*, Sig. [a3]*recto*, referred to Hall's
"Thrasonicall boasting." Hall, in his *Short Answer*,
Sig. a2 *recto*, defended himself against the alleged
"Thrasonicall boasts."

9:20 *DAVUS THAT TROUBLES ALL
THINGS* — Davus is the stock name in Latin
comedies for the slave or servant who betrays his
master for gain. Milton may have the Davus in
Terence's *Andria* in mind. In "Scholia, quae expli-
cant textum Act: IIII. Scenae. I" of *Andria*, Davus
is described: "Dauus est ommium turbarum & malorum author, aut, perturbat omnia." (Stephanus
Riccius, *In P. Terentii Comoedias Sex Novvis Commentarivs* ... [Leipzig], 1566-82, 2 vols., I, fol.
144 *verso*.)

9:20-21 ONE WHO CAN SHIFT INTO ANY
SHAPE — A general reference to a protean char-
acter. The term was limited neither to the poets nor
to poetry: for example, "But the cardinal [Cajetan]
would hear no Scriptures; he disputed without
Scriptures; he devised glosses and expositions of
his own head; and by distinctions ... , like a very
Proteus, he avoided all things" (*The Acts and
Monuments of John Foxe*, ed. by the Rev. Stephen
Reed Cattley, London, 1837-41, 8 vols., IV, 271).

9:21 EXPLICATE — Explain.

9:22 WHO ... TO A COMEDY — It was the
author of the *Modest Confutation* who had labeled
the argument a comedy as part of his "sycophanting" (9:11). See Note 9:12-14.

9:22 RESEMBL'D — Compared, likened.

9:22-23 FOR *TRAGICALL* ... *WERE TOO
OMINOUS* — See Note 9:12-14. The Confuter had
intimated that the *"late and hot bickerings"* between
the prelates and Smectymnuans were *"solemn
scenes, (it were too ominous to say Tragicall)."* The

"breaches" in those *"solemn scenes,"* the Confuter
had continued, had been closed up by a *"scurrilous
Mime,"* that is, Milton's *Animadversions*. Milton,
however, turns the meaning of the Confuter's
words. Milton says that the Confuter has called the
argument between the prelates and Smectymnuans
"a Comedy, for *Tragicall*, he sayes, *were too ominous.*" Thus Milton evades the charge that his
Animadversions is the Mime, that is, comedy, and
places the Confuter in the position of one who
thinks the church controversy is a comedy.

9:24-26 MIME ... WHEREOF WE HAVE NO
PATTERN ... WISE SENTENCES — Aristotle
said: "There is further an art which imitates by
language alone, without harmony, in prose or in
verse, and if in verse, either in some one or in a
plurality of metres. This form of imitation is to this
day without a name. We have no common name
for a mime of Sophron or Xenarchus and a Socratic
Conversation" (*Poetics*, Ch. 1 [1447a-b], translated
by Ingram Bywater).

9:26 *LAERTIUS* — Diogenes Laertius, generally
believed a native of Laërte, in Cilicia, lived, it is
believed, near the end of the second century A. D.
His work is one of the chief sources of information
for the history of Greek philosophy. In his "Life
of Plato," XIII, Diogenes says: "Plato also appears
to have brought the books of Sophron, the farce-
writer, to Athens, which were previously neglected;
and to have availed himself of them in his Speculations on Morals: and a copy of them was found
under his head" (Diogenes Laërtius, *The Lives and
Opinions of Eminent Philosophers*, translated by
C. D. Yonge, London, 1909, p. 119; see also *"Life of
Plato* according to Diogenes Laertius," 18, in *The
Works of Plato*, Bohn Classical Library, London,
1876-83, 6 vols., VI, 184-85). Olympiodorus, in his
"Life of Plato," after mentioning Plato's delight in
Sophron adds that when Plato "was dead, (copies
of) Aristophanes and Sophron were found on his
couch" (*The Works of Plato*, VI, 235). Athenaeus
in *Deipnosophistae*, xi, 504, speaks of "the writer
... of those *Mimes* which ... were always in the
hands of the wise Plato" (Athenaeus, *The Deipnosophists, With An English Translation By Charles
Burton Gulick*, London, 1927-41, 7 vols., V, 261).
For comments on Milton's use of Diogenes Laertius
see Herbert Agar, *Milton and Plato* (Princeton,

1928), p. 58 note; Irene Samuel, *Plato and Milton* (Ithaca, New York, 1947), pp. 14 note, 15, and 23 note; and Irene Samuel, "Milton's References to Plato and Socrates," *SP*, XLI (1944), 62.

9:26 MIMES OF *SOPHRON* — Sophron flourished about 430 B.C. He wrote in the Doric dialect both serious and humorous prose dialogues containing male and female characters, depicting ordinary scenes from the lives of Sicilian Greeks in popular, colloquial language, full of proverbs. According to Suidas, Plato introduced Sophron's dialogues into Athens and made use of them in his own works. Only fragments of Sophron's dialogues remain. See also Note 9:27-28.

9:27-28 [Mimes] WERE OF SUCH RECKNING...NIGHTLY TO READ ON AND AFTER MAKE THEM HIS PILLOW — "The book of Sophron likewise, the mime-writer, which had been neglected, Plato appears to have brought first to Athens, and to have modelled the manner (of the speakers in his dialogues) after them, which (were said) to have been found under his head" (*"Life of Plato* according to Diogenes Laertius," 18, in *The Works of Plato*, VI, 184-85). Milton has evidently not seen Olympiodorus' account (see Note 9:26 *LAERTIUS*), for Milton does not connect the finding of the book under Plato's head with Plato's death. "Plato's Dialogues," says Irene Samuel, "are like mimes, and Plato enjoyed the humor of mimes" (Samuel, *Plato and Milton*, p. 97).

9:28 *SCALIGER* — Julius Caesar Scaliger (1484-1558), whose own account of his life to 1525 is probably pretty much a tissue of fables, was at his death more highly reputed in scientific and literary endeavor than any other man in Europe. His *Poetics* appeared in 1561.

9:28-29 *SCALIGER* DESCRIBES...LAUGHTER — "Est igitur Mimus, poema quoduis genus actionis imitans ita, vt ridiculum faciat" (*Ivlii Caesaris Scaligeri Viri Clarissimi Poetices libri septem*... Second edition, [Heidelberg], 1581, Part I, ch. x, p. 43).

9:30-31 THIS...MIME — *i.e.*, since the *Animadversions* are neither poem nor ridiculous, having a very serious purpose, it is incorrectly called a mime.

9:31-39 FOR IF EVERY BOOK...THEN A SMILE — Herbert Agar in *Milton and Plato*, p. 62, has pointed out the following passage in the *Deipnosophists* (xi, 112) of Athenaeus:

And in his [Plato's] polity, he banishes Homer from his city, and all poetry of the theatrical kind; and yet he himself wrote dialogues in a theatrical style, — a manner of writing of which he himself was not the inventor; for Alexamenus the Teian had, before him, invented this style of dialogue.... And Aristotle, in his treatise on Poets, writes thus: — "Let us not then call those Mimes, as they are called, of Sophron, which are written in metre, Discourses and Imitations; or those Dialogues of Alexamenus of Teos, which were written before the Socratic Dialogues...." (Athenaeus, *The Deipnosophists*, literally translated by C. D. Yonge, London, 1854, 3 vols., II, 808-09; cf. with Charles Burton Gulick's translation of Athenaeus, *The Deipnosophists* (xi, 505), V, 267.)

9:33 DIALOGUES OF *PLATO* — Irene Samuel has shown that Milton's "own references to Plato up through the publication of the *Apology for Smectymnuus* include specific citations of *Phaedrus*, the *Laws*, the *Sophist*, and *Critias*, with probable allusions to *Protagoras* and the *Symposium*, and general remarks on Plato that suggest a familiarity with all his writings" (Samuel, *Plato and Milton*, p. 17). In *Of Education*, Milton

prescribes the 'moral works of Plato,' perhaps meaning the dialogues which Diogenes Laertius classified as 'ethical': the *Apology, Crito, Phaedo, Phaedrus*, the *Symposium, Menexenus, Clitophon*, the Epistles, *Philebus, Hipparchus*, and the *Rivals*. Perhaps he knew some of these to be spurious. But since he also wished to have the principles of rhetoric 'taught out of the rule of Plato,' he would add at least *Gorgias* to the list. (Samuel, *Plato and Milton*, p. 17.)

In works later than the *Apology* he

specifically mentions the *Symposium, Protagoras, Gorgias*, the *Republic*, and the Eighth *Epistle*.... If we are to include the examples in his *Logic* among his own citations of Plato, other dialogues must be added: *Cratylus* and the *First Alcibiades, Philebus, Crito, Phaedo, Meno*, and the *Statesman*. There are, in addition, numerous places where he cites an opinion of Plato's without naming the dialogue or epistle in which it appears. We have every reason to think him familiar with all the writings commonly ascribed to Plato. (Samuel, *Plato and Milton*, p. 17.)

9:34 DIVINE [Plato] — In Athenaeus' *Deipnosophists*, x, 440b, Plato is called "divine" (see Gulick's translation of Athenaeus' *Deipnosophists*, IV, 495). The works of pseudo-Dionysius the

Areopagite, and of Boëthius, both of whom wrote at the end of the fifth and the beginning of the sixth centuries, as well as references and quotations in the Fathers, determined to a large extent the notion of Platonism generally accepted in the Middle Ages. "These writers bequeathed to the Middle Ages the conception of 'divine Plato,' whose teachings were inspired ... and whose dialogues were full of strange, unfathomable sayings" (Agar, *Milton and Plato,* p. 25). See Note 17:20 DIVINE VOLUMES OF *PLATO.*

9:34-35 THAT DETRACTOR IN *ATHENAEUS* — See *Athenaei Navcratitis, Lvcvlentissimi Elegantissimiqve Scriptoris, Deipnosophistarvm* (Lvgdvni, 1583), p. 376. The "detractor" is probably Pontianus of Nicomedia, one of the conversers in the *Deipnosophists,* who in his detraction (Athenaeus, *Deipnosophists,* xi, 504b-509e; Gulick's translation, V, 261-91) declares that Plato is "unsparing in his accusation" (xi, 506d; Gulick, V, 275), that he says "the most outrageous thing ... without any compelling need" (xi, 505f; Gulick, V, 271), and "that he speaks of the Athenian populace as a hasty and even rash judge" (xi, 506c; Gulick, V, 273). (See Samuel, "Milton's References to Plato and Socrates," p. 62 note, and Samuel, *Plato and Milton,* pp. 15 and note, and 23 note 4.)

9:35 *ATHENAEUS* — A Greek rhetorician and grammarian of Naucratis in Egypt who flourished at the end of the second and the beginning of the third century A.D. His *Deipnosophists* or "Banquet of the Learned" in fifteen books is an account given by the author to his friend Timocrates of a banquet that was held at the home of the scholar and patron of art, Larentius. The discussion, chiefly concerned with matters of the table, digresses to remarks on a great variety of subjects including literary matters. That Milton had read Athenaeus' discussion of Plato is a certainty.

9:35 NO BETTER THEN *MIMES* — Pontianus spoke scornfully of Plato's dialogues stating that Plato was "inimical toward everybody" (Athenaeus, *Deipnosophists,* xi, 506; Gulick's translation, V, 271), that "the day would fail me if I should wish to proceed with all who were abused by the philosopher" (xi, 507; Gulick, V, 277). If, Milton argues, every book that treats a subject sharply is a mime, then Plato's dialogues are, as it has been alleged by

Pontianus in Athenaeus, truly mimes. With that notion Milton is in opposition. See Note 9:31-39.

9:35-36 SCARCE ONE OF THEM — *i.e.,* one of the dialogues of Plato.

9:36-38 ESPECIALLY [those] WHEREIN SOME NOTABLE SOPHISTER ... INEVITABLE, AND MERCILESSE DILEMMA'S OF *SOCRATES* — This passage indicates that Milton has read considerably from the dialogues of Plato and is speaking on the basis of that reading (Samuel, "Milton's References to Plato and Socrates," p. 62, note 4, and Samuel, *Plato and Milton,* p. 23, note 4). The term "Sophister" is scornfully used by Milton. He apparently takes it "from his reading in the dialogues, though the word was common in his time as now." Milton is here associating the "refutation of sophistry with the Socratic method." Milton in his *Author's Defence of Himself* (*Col.* IX, 285) and *The Means to Remove Hirelings* (*Col.* VI, 46) "repeats the argument of Plato that those who deal in truth for hire cannot be true teachers" (Samuel, *Plato and Milton,* p. 14; see Note 57:11-13). In the *Reason of Church-government,* Milton points out that he knows of no sophister who, although he was highly paid, was not refuted by the Socratic school who were not hired (*Col.* III, 202). Sophistry is associated with false learning by Milton. In the Third *Prolusion* Milton identifies scholastic philosophy with the "warty controversies of the sophists" (*Col.* XII, 159) who "please nobody except one who is boorish and quite hairy of chest, and one who, inclined by some secret leanings to controversies and disagreements and moreover to excessive talkativeness, always shudders at and turns from a just and sound wisdom" (*ibid.,* p. 165). Milton's purpose is to avoid the "Lernian swamp of sophisms" (*Prolusion VII, Col.* XII, 277). He says that the "thorny lectures of monkish and miserable sophistry ... [have] stopt and hinderd all true and generous philosophy from entring" (*RCG, Col.* III, 273; see Samuel, *Plato and Milton,* pp. 96, 106).

9:38 *SOCRATES* — Socrates (c. 470-399 B.C.) was a great Athenian philosopher made memorable in the dialogues of Plato and the *Memorabilia* of Xenophon. Socrates in the dialogues often pits his wits against the sophists whom he refutes much to their discomfiture.

9:38 *SATURNE* — In astrology, Saturn, because of its remoteness and slow movement, was supposed the cause of coldness, "sluggishness, and gloominess of temperament in those born under its influence, and in general to have a baleful effect on human affairs" (*OED*). E. H. Visiak thinks that Milton is referring to "the mythical king," Saturn, who after he had introduced civilization and agriculture into Italy, suddenly disappeared, becoming, as some supposed, "a god of the nether world" (E. H. Visiak (ed.) *Milton Complete Poetry & Selected Prose* [London, 1938], p. 846).

9:39 MORE THEN A SMILE — Milton considers Plato masterful in comic invention. In *Tetrachordon, Col.* IV, 76, he refers to "*Plato's* wit."

9:39-40 HE TELLS US THAT *SCURRILOUS MIME . . . FOOLE* — The Confuter had said:

. . . there is thrust forth upon the Stage, as also to take the eare of the lesse intelligent, a scurrilous Mime, *a personated, and (as himself thinks) a grim, lowring, bitter fool.* ("To the Reader," *Modest Confutation,* Sig. A3 *recto.*)

In this loosely constructed sentence the "*scurrilous* Mime," that is the *Animadversions,* and "*a personated, and . . . a grim, lowring, bitter fool,*" presumably Milton, are appositive in their relationships seeming to indicate that the mime and fool are one. Milton interpreted the sentence in that fashion when he transcribed it "that . . . *Mime was a . . . foole.*" The Confuter's statement was a reference in particular to Milton's words:

And although in the serious uncasing of a grand imposture . . . there be mixt here and there such a grim laughter, as may appear at the same time in an austere visage, it cannot be taxt of levity or insolence . . . if it be harmfull to be angry, and withall to cast a lowring smile . . . it will be long enough ere any be able to say why . . . anger and laughter were first seated in the brest of man. (*ANIM* (1641), pp. 3-4; *Col.* III, 107-08.)

9:40 *PERSONATED* — Represented as being of a certain type described. Cf. *ANIM, Col.* III, 165, "the Poet lively personates our Prelates."

10:1-2 HIS OWNE FRIEND . . . THE *REMONSTRANT* — Milton wrenches the words that the Confuter intended against Milton against Bishop Hall. The Confuter's statement is ambiguous (see Note 9:39-40). Milton takes the opportunity to give the Confuter the notoriety of calling Hall a fool, and a mime. See *Apology* 10:32-33.

10:2 THERE — In the *Animadversions.*

10:2-3 THE AUTHOR IS EVER DISTINGUISHT FROM THE PERSON HE INTRODUCES — Milton is asserting the prerogative of the author to introduce any character and to have that character express himself in any way without any reflection whatsoever upon the author himself. The basis of the notion may be in Socrates' notion that a good man cannot imitate evil without suffering loss (see Note 16:21-23). "Milton never lost himself in his characters." By keeping "his intellect in control, he could ward off infection. . . . So fundamental was the platonic notion of *form* that he would have feared impairment if he moved beyond the point where intellect controlled the imitation or where the author excluded himself from his agent's speeches" (Charles W. Jones, "Milton's 'Brief Epic,'" *SP,* XLIV (1947), 219). Milton is emphasizing that the "*Scurrilous Mime,*" that is the *Animadversions,* since it is his own, could not in any way be said to refer to himself as the Confuter had suggested it did when he wrote "*a scurrilous* Mime, *a personated, and . . . a grim, lowring, bitter fool*" (see Note 9:39-40).

10:3 DISTINGUISHT — Individually distinct; separate (*OED*).

10:5-7 THAT HEE MIGHT AT LENGTH CEASE. . . . COULD HE NOT BEWARE — The relationship of the two sentences is clarified if the period after "aide" is replaced by a comma, and the first letter of "Could" made a lower case letter.

10:6-7 HIM WHOM HEE WOULD AIDE — Him, *i.e.,* the Remonstrant; hee, *i.e.,* the Confuter.

10:8 SO UNCIRCUMSPECT, AS NOT TO FORESEE — Cf. 9:16-17.

10:10 WRETCHED PILGRIMAGE OVER *MINSHEWS* DICTIONARY — In both the text and notes of *Mundus Alter et Idem* Hall shows his acquaintance with various languages. Milton twits him with having secured his knowledge from ἩΓΕΜῺΝ ΕἸΣ ΤᾺΣ ΓΛῶΣΣΑΣ, *id est, Ductor in Linguas. . . . The Guide into the tongues. With their agreement and consent one with another, as also their Etymologies, that is the Reasons and Deriua-*

tions of all or the most part of the wordes, in these eleven Languages, viz. English, British or Welsh, Low Dutch, High Dutch, French, Italian, Spanish, Portuguez, Latine, Greeke, Hebrew, &c.... By the Industrie, Study, Labour, and at the charges of Iohn Minsheu Published and Printed (London, 1617). A second edition of Minsheu's work was published in 1625, of which there were two other issues dated 1626 and 1627.

10:11 *MUNDUS ALTER & IDEM* — Joseph Hall's *Mvndvs Alter Et Idem Siue Terra Australis ante hac semper incognita longis itineribus peregrini Academici nuperrime lustrata Auth: Mercurio Britannico* (Frankfort, [1605]). This Latin tract was republished at Hanau in 1607. In 1608 or 1609 an English translation by I. H. (*i.e.,* John Healey) appeared, entitled *The Discovery of A New World or A Description of the South Indies. Hetherto Vnknowne By an English Mercury Imprinted for Ed: Blount. and W. Barrett.* The work is a prose satire upon gluttony, drunkenness, and licentiousness, often scurrilous, that takes bitter thrusts at the Roman Catholic Church. Milton referred to it in the *Animadversions* in answer to the Remonstrant's statement that there were many lands where there had never been bishops as follows:

we can ... tell you where they [the Bishops] have bin ever since *Constantines* time at least, in a place call'd *Mundus alter & idem,* in the spacious, and rich Countries of *Crapulia* [Gutsy-land], *Pamphagonia* [Kingdom of Stomach], *Yvronia* [Dominion of Drink], and in the Dukedome of *Orgilia* [the Choleric], and *Variana* [Fickleness] and their *Metropolis* of *Ucalegonium* [Idleness]. (*Col.* III, 138; cf. Masson, *Life,* II, 259.)

10:11 THE IDLEST AND THE PALTRIEST MIME — Milton considered the *"Mundus alter & idem"* the most worthless and most petty or contemptible representation of life in a ridiculous manner. A number of chapter titles from Healey's translation will indicate the general tone of the satire: "The Discouery of the land of *Tenter-belly* ..."; "The discription of *Carousi-kanikan* the chiefe citty of *Drink-allia,* as also the fashions and conditions of the *Drink-alls*"; "The description of *Shee-lands,* or *Womandecoia* and of the situation thereof"; "Of *Double-sex* Ile, otherwise called Skrat or Hermophrcodite Iland"; "The paradise of *Fooliana* the fatte"; "The conditions of the *Robbers-walders.*" The word "Mime" takes on the force of a

personification in the clause which completes the sentence. See Notes 9:39-40 and 10:31-33.

10:12 BANKE — A bench; a platform or stage from which to speak (*OED*).

10:12-13 LET HIM ASK *THE AUTHOR OF THOSE TOOTHLESSE SATYRS* — Let the Confuter ask *"the Author,"* that is, the Remonstrant, Bishop Joseph Hall. Joseph Hall had first made his reputation as a writer by his verse satires published in 1597 under the title of *Virgidemiarvm, Sixe Bookes. First three bookes of Toothlesse Satyrs* (London by Thomas Creed). In 1598 under the same general title appeared *The three last Bookes. Of byting Satyres* (London by Richard Bradocke for Robert Dexter). New editions of the *Toothlesse Satyrs* appeared in 1598 and 1602; a new edition of *Byting Satyrs* appeared in 1599. On the 1599 edition of the *Byting Satyrs* only was there any indication of authorship; in that edition appeared the words "Corrected and amended with some Additions. by I.H." See *Apology* 32:13-33:32.

10:13-14 WHO WAS THE MAKER ... THE ANTICREATOR OF THAT UNIVERSALL FOOLERY — The "maker ... the anticreator" refer to Hall's authorship of *Mundus Alter et Idem* (*i.e.,* the world different yet the same), which Milton calls that piece of "universall foolery." "Anticreator" shows Milton's real or feigned disdain for Hall as the pretended, spurious, or pseudo-creator of that "universall foolery." Milton is thinking specifically when he speaks of "universall foolery" about the *Mundus Alter et Idem,* which he has already called the "idlest and the paltriest Mime" (10:11). But in a larger sense he is thinking of the *Mundus* as an attempt at writing Utopian literature (see 10:18-26). Hall is, therefore, the "anticreator" of a foolish invention pertaining to the universe. (Cf. "Universal nature" in *Lycidas,* 60.)

10:14 HE — *i.e.,* Hall.

10:14-17 THAT OTHER PRINCIPLE OF THE *MANICHES* THE *ARCH EVILL ONE* ... ALL VERY FOOLISH — The two principles of Manichaeism were light and darkness, both eternal. The two principles were conceived as opposed to each other. The good principle, light, was God; the evil was matter or Hyle, sometimes also called god. The region of each was infinite except on the one side where they met. The encroachment of darkness upon light started the conflict which ultimately resulted in the creation of Jesus by the light, and of man by the darkness. Darkness created man because he could concentrate and maintain in man all the portions of light he had originally stolen. Man is therefore a discordant being, created by darkness, but having within himself the strong spark of light. The ultimate goal of the conflict was to separate darkness from light. Anything that contributed to that end, the ultimate end, was desirable. Mani, a high-born Persian, probably born about 215 A. D., was the formulator of Manichaeism, which he professed was a blending of the teachings of Christ and of old Persian Magism. At the close of the third century A.D. Manichaeism had great strength in Western Europe.

Milton is here collapsing the notions that the Manichaeists held about the arch evil one — *i.e.*, the "god" of darkness, Hyle, who had invaded the region of light, and who had had victories over the emanation of the god of light that had been sent to oppose the invasion — with St. Augustine's refutation of one of the charges of Faustus, the chief proponent of Manichaeism in the time of St. Augustine, against Catholicism. St. Augustine, Bishop of Hippo, in the "Reply to Faustus the Manichaean," Book 22, Section 12, says:

Why should the Manichaeans object to our God seeing His work that it was good, when their god placed a covering before himself when he mingled his own members with the darkness? For instead of seeing his work that it is good, he refuses to look at it because it is evil. (*The Works of Aurelius Augustine, Bishop of Hippo*, translated by the Rev. Marcus Dods, Edinburgh, 1872-76, 15 vols., V, 407.)

Milton might have run across the idea in *Opervm D. Avrelii Avgvstini Hipponensis Episcopi* (Basil, 1596, 10 vols.), VI, 395. (Available in Jacques Paul Migne, *Patrologiae Cursus Completus, Latinae*, Paris, 1844-1900, 221 vols., XLII, 406.) For a recent brief comment on Manichaeism see Martin A. Larson, *The Modernity of Milton* (Chicago, 1927), pp. 38-39.

10:16-17 CONTRARY TO THE DIVINE MOUTH — God, when he created the universe, declared that his work was good (Genesis 1:10, 12, 18, 21, 25).

10:17-28 THAT GRAVE...STEWES — The logic of the sentences becomes lost. "That grave and noble invention...this petty prevaricator...the zanie of *Columbus*... [used, wherefore, it is] no marvell, if he brought us home nothing but...a venereous parjetory for a stewes." Milton laments that a person of "vain thoughts" should use the "grave and noble invention" of "sublimest wits" by which they have taught the "world better and exacter things" than ever before were "known, or us'd," so ineffectively that he contributes only drunken jests and lascivious ornaments for a brothel.

10:18 GRAVE AND NOBLE INVENTION — Milton has in mind those creations of the mind in which one proposes or advocates plans for social improvement.

10:19 *PLATO IN CRITIAS* — Plato's *Critias* begins an exposé of an ideal government on the Island of Atlantis, but the story is broken off shortly after the commencement. Milton recognizes in the *Critias* the pattern for Utopian literature (Samuel, *Plato and Milton,* p. 15). That Milton studied the *Critias* has been demonstrated (Ronald B. Levinson, "Milton and Plato," *MLN,* XLVI (1931), 87). Milton's *Ready and Easy Way to establish a free Commonwealth* (1660) was his contribution to the genre. In it he tried "by sheer power in discourse to lift the Puritan Commonwealth into the classical republic, or rather, into the humanistic Utopia of his own speculation and allegiance" (William Haller, "Review of *The Dignity of Kingship Asserted*, By G. S. Reproduced in facsimile from the edition of 1660, with an Introduction by William R. Parker, New York: Columbia University Press, 1942," *MLN,* LVIII (1943), 402).

10:20 THE ONE IN HIS *VTOPIA*, THE OTHER IN HIS *NEW ATLANTIS* — *i.e.*, Sir Thomas More's *Utopia* (1516) and Sir Francis Bacon's *New Atlantis* (1627).

10:21 CONTINENT — Each of the Utopian experiments took place on a mythical or imaginary continent.

10:22-23 TEACHING THIS OUR WORLD BETTER AND EXACTER THINGS — Milton is convinced that literature on the ideal state is valuable as a teaching agency for the world. See Note 10:19.

10:23-24 THIS PETTY PREVARICATOR OF *AMERICA*, THE ZANIE OF *COLUMBUS*— Milton is referring to Hall's introduction, "The occasion of this trauell," to *The Discovery of A New World* (see Note 10:11 *MUNDUS ALTER & IDEM*) where Hall says:

...and what if I prooue the countrie America *to be* knowne to former ages?... *Now I am fully perswaded that some part of these west* Indies *was that* Ophir, *where* Salamons *and* Hirams *nauy had their gold.* (Sig. [A5] *verso.*)
...I am most firmely perswaded that Senecaes *large continent is yet vndiscouered, and staies to yeeld vs this glorie, if we dare venter on it. For my selfe, I am comming (my world) after so many vowes, and delaies, now I come at last, all fraight with hope and confidence, either to vnmaske thee to* Europe, *or to lay my bones in thee.* (Sig. [A7] *verso.*)
...I hold, that your Drake *and your* Candish *were trauellers, as also* Sebastian Delcano, *the* Portughesse, *because their voyages put girdles about the whole world: Nay I will allow* Chrystopher Colono *that name also, for his discouerie of the West* Indies.... (Sig. A2 *recto and verso.*)

Hall is evading the strict truth in regard to America, and thus makes himself a ludicrous imitator of Columbus.

10:25-26 HUGE TOPOGRAPHY — Hall's work *Mundus Alter et Idem* included several maps on which were delineated the boundaries of the sections of the southern continent of which his book treated.

10:27 TANKARD DROLLERY — Jesting and waggery that accompanies drinking.

10:27-28 A VENEREOUS PARJETORY FOR A STEWES — A licentious ornament in plaster fit for a brothel.

10:28 HE — The author of *Mundus Alter et Idem*, Joseph Hall.

10:29 DEVISE LAWS FOR DRUNKARDS TO CAROUSE BY — Hall, in the *Mundus Alter et Idem*, Bk. I [*i.e.*, Bk. II], ch. 4, presents the laws of "Eatallia and Drinkallia," among which are: *"That hee whome either nature or sicknesse hath made abstinent; bee banished the land"; "That hee that goeth from any publique meeting, without staggering, bee accompted a malefactor in the highest degree"; "That the calling of a Citizen theefe*

or whore-maister, beare no action, that to call him abstayner, shalbe lyable to the lawe"; "That he that sweareth by Bacchus, *and keepeth not his word, bee vtterly disabled from making any will, and bearing any witnesse"* (John Healey's translation, *The Discovery of A New World*, Sig. [F7] *verso* and [F8] *recto*).

10:30 UNLICOUR'D *SILENUS* — Silenus was in Greek mythology the foster father of Bacchus and leader of the Satyrs. He always carried a wine bag with him, and was generally intoxicated. Like the Satyrs he loved sleep, wine, and music. When he was asleep or drunk, he had the power of prophecy. Milton in likening Hall to an "unlicour'd *Silenus*" is calling him a sober drunk-man.

10:31 DRUNK — Drunkenness.

10:31-33 LET HIM...HEARD OF — Milton had conjectured from the title page that Hall had had his hand in phrasing the title (6:40-9:4; see particularly 7:20-22; 7:35-36; 8:17-18; 8:40-9:4). By a careful examination of one of the first statements in the preface "To the Reader" (see Note 9:39-40) Milton has arrived at the conclusion that Hall's hand is there. Milton had turned the statement that that *"Scurrilous Mime was a personated grim lowring foole"* (9:40) against Hall himself (10:1-2). Now he recognizes the original intention of the author of the *Modest Confutation* to brand Milton with the name of "Mime." "Let him [Hall] go now and brand another man [Milton] injuriously...." The word "Mime" is throughout of doubtful signification, as Milton recognized (9:23-24). The mime, usually considered as a kind of drama imitating scenes from life which are generally represented in a ridiculous manner, here becomes the actor or author of such a representation. On the basis of Hall's early satirical works, which Milton has examined, he points out that Hall, who is himself "the loosest and most extravagant *Mime,* that hath been heard of" (10:32-33), has had the effrontery to label Milton with the term. Milton has shifted the emphasis of the argument completely since his declaration that the Confuter's "foolish language unwittingly writes foole upon his owne friend" (10:1). Now it is the Remonstrant who is writing "foole" upon himself.

10:33-35 WHOM NO LESSE... *MIME* IN — Hall's Southern Land occupied all the territory to the south of South America, Africa, and India from which it was separated by a more or less large expanse of water, coming nearest to contiguity with known land at the southern end of South America. Hall's map showed the vast Southern Land as covering almost half the earth, as an expanse of land larger than all the known continents as represented by Hall. The word *"Mime"* has reverted to the meaning "the representation of life in a ridiculous manner."

10:35 ADVISE AGAINE — Reconsider.

10:35-39 AND LET HIM ADVISE... TEACHING IS ADJOYND — Milton challenges Hall to consider again what is wrong with turning the sins of Christendom into a mockery and ripping up vices *"with a laughing countenance,"* particularly if Hall offers no means for reproving nor any better way of teaching. Milton's aim is to improve mankind (9:5-6); Milton has no sympathy for one who offers nothing to better the situation. Hall has become in Milton's mind the author of at least the part of Section I of the *Modest Confutation* from which Milton draws the citation from Sir Francis Bacon which the author of the *Modest Confutation* has used to confute Milton. See Note 10:36-38.

10:36-38 *TURN THE SINNES... LAUGHING COUNTENANCE* — The author of the *Modest Confutation* calls upon Bacon to oppose Milton's claim for laughter as a *"strong and sinewy force in teaching"* (ANIM (1641), p. 3; *Col.* III, 107) by quoting from him:

To leave all reverend compassion towards evils, all religious indignation towards faults, to turn Religion into a Comedy or Satyr, to rip up wounds with a laughing countenance, to intermixe Scripture and scurrility sometimes in one sentence, is a thing far from the devout reverence of a Christian, and scant beseeming the honest regard of a sober man. (Modest Confutation, p. 2.)

The source of the quotation is Bacon's *A Wise and Moderate Discourse, Concerning Church-Affaires* (1641), which was written in 1589 with the title *An Advertisement Touching the Controversies of the Church of England* (see George Whiting, *Milton's Literary Milieu*, Chapel Hill, 1939, pp. 268-69), under which title it still appears in *Resuscitatio* (1657). The piece was not published until 1641.

Bacon said:

But to leave all reverend and religious compassions toward evils, or indignation toward faults, to turne religion into a Comedy or Satyr, to search and rip up wounds with a laughing countenance, to intermix Scripture and Scurrility sometime in one sentence, is a thing farre from the devout reverence of a Christian, and scant beseeming the honest regard of a sober man. ([Sir Francis Bacon], *A Wise and Moderate Discourse,* pp. 7-8; "An Advertisement," in *Resuscitatio,* p. 164.)

See 25:34-37; 27:33-36.

10:39 ADJOYND — Added or appended.

11:1 SHALL — The subject of *shall* is "I" (omitted).

11:1 RESPITED — Delayed or postponed.

11:1-2 TILL I CAN COME TO SOME INSTANCE, WHERETO I MAY GIVE ANSWER — Milton will defend his method later when the opportunity offers (see 22:7-27:2), and asks that the reader withhold judgment.

11:3 HIS FIRST ONSET — The first paragraph of the preface "To the Reader" of *A Modest Confutation*, Sig. A3 *recto*. In the preceding lines of the *Apology* (10:28-39), the Confuter and the Remonstrant have become confused in Milton's mind or stand as one person, the Remonstrant. The "his" here, however, apparently refers to the Confuter (12:29).

11:4 THE BOOK — The *Animadversions* (see 11:7).

11:5 AUTHOR — Of the *Animadversions, i.e.,* Milton.

11:6-7 *HAVING NO CERTAINE NOTICE... AS HE PROFESSES, FURDER THEN... ANIMADVERSIONS* — See Note 6:39-7:1; cf. *Apology,* 11:3-4.

11:7-8 BLUNDERS AT ME... CRIMES AT A VENTURE — Cf. 11:20, "let drive at randome"; 18:24-25, "flyes out beyond all truth & shame"; and see Note 6:39-7:1.

11:9 SERPENT — The word "Serpent" had as a part of its connotation the notion of Devil (see Revelations 12:9; 20:2).

11:9 SUCK — Aristotle notes that the serpent is carnivorous and that it sucks juices from the creatures it captures after it has swallowed them, thereafter ejecting the creature whole (Aristotle, *Historia Animalium*, Bk. VIII, ch. 4 [594a]).

11:10 STUFFT — Cf. *RCG, Col.* III, 241, "men whose learning and belief lies in marginal stuffings"; and *Tenure of Kings and Magistrates, Col.* V, 56, "Thus while they, in a cautious line or two here and there stuft in, are onely verbal against the pulling down or punishing of Tyrants."

11:10 MAGAZIN — Storehouse, repository.

11:11 INVENTIONS — Contrivances or fabrications.

11:12-13 SINGULAR — Particular, special.

11:12-14 SINGULAR . . . SLIGHT SATISFACTION — Cf. 3:4-6, "I have oft with inward contentment perceav'd my friends congratulating themselves in my innocence." Milton has identified himself completely with the cause becoming "a member incorporate into that truth" (3:25-26). He does not want religion to suffer through his "default," nor those "reverent men" to come under reproach because of him (3:32-39). Therefore, he intends not to leave the "least spot" on his garment, nor the least blemish on his name if God gives him the words wherewith to "wipe it off" (3:29-31). He finds now a particular satisfaction in his opponent's admission that all the charges that have been made against him are guesses. It is, furthermore, "no slight satisfaction" "to good men" (11:13) — those "good men" with whom he had associated himself "in their labours toward the Churches wellfare" (6:27-28), the "respected friends" (4:37) for whom he had "gain'd a name bestuck" (6:31), the men who had a "common adversary" (3:37) with him — to be able to count Milton an able assistant to their cause (3:38), and to see how unfounded are the "reproaches and reviles" (6:32) that have been hurled against Milton and the cause. Milton shows a great enthusiasm in identifying himself with the "good men," and in vindicating himself for their sake.

11:14-15 *NO FURDER . . . CONJECTURE* — See Notes 6:39-7:1, and 11:7-8.

11:16 SUCH INFAMOUS WORDS — The author of the *Modest Confutation,* after admitting that he is fetching Milton's character *"from some scattered passages"* in Milton's *Animadversions* (see Notes 6:39-7:1 and 11:7-8), continues:

It seems he hath been initiated in the Arts by Jacke Seaton, *and by Bishop* Downam *confirmed a Logician: and as he sayes his companions did, it is like hee spent his youth, in loytering, bezelling, and harlotting. Thus being grown to an Impostume in the brest of the* Vniversity, *he was at length vomited out thence into a Suburbe sinke about* London; *which, since his comming up, hath groaned under two ills,* Him, *and the* Plague. *Where his morning haunts are I wist not; but he that would finde him after dinner, must search the* Play-Houses, *or the* Bordelli, *for there I have traced him.* . . . ("To the Reader," *Modest Confutation,* Sig. A3 *recto* and *verso.*)

11:17-22 HE DID INQUIRE . . . WOULD FAINE APPLY — The notion that Milton was of such "small repute" (2:36) that inquiry resulted in little tangible evidence is stated by William Haller:

The truth seems to be that Milton was personally little known to the general public, and was not regarded as a person of importance until after he became identified with the revolutionary leaders of 1649.

.   .   .   .   .   .

The ignorance concerning Milton's personal character and affairs, shown during these years by his opponents, is curiously complete. Bishop Hall and his son, who must surely have had means of finding out whatever there was to their purpose to be found out concerning their antagonist in 1642, seem to have relied upon rumor, invention and dubious inferences based upon the raciness of Milton's vocabulary. Except for the replies of the Halls, Milton's antiprelatical tracts went unnoticed in the press. (William Haller, *Tracts on Liberty in the Puritan Revolution, 1638-1647,* New York, 1934, 3 vols., I, 129; see also William Riley Parker, *Milton's Contemporary Reputation,* Columbus, 1940, p. 17.)

Surely the evidence that Milton was little known cannot be proved from this passage, for the emphasis is plainly that the inquiries provided the author or authors of the *Modest Confutation* with little intelligence that was suitable to them for the grounding of the arguments that they had contrived in order to answer in an effective manner the *Animadversions.* Therefore, they chose to pretend ignorance and use their arguments rather than to leave the pamphlet unanswered because Milton's life provided little or no opportunity for an attack that would be convincing.

11:20 LET DRIVE AT RANDOME — See Note 11:7-8.

11:21 PENURIOUS — Barren.

11:21 BOOK OF CHARACTERS — The *character*, dating from Theophrastus (d. 278 B.C.), is a sketch which usually portrays an undesirable social quality, followed by a description of the talk and actions of the man embodying the quality. The language of the street, combined with the "wit," description, and psychological insight, made the genre effective. The Casaubon edition of *Characters* (1592) brought the seventeenth century popularity which in England had as its chief authors Hall, Overbury, and Earle. Elbert N. S. Thompson says: "Joseph Hall's *Characters of Virtues and Vices,* published in 1608, may be called the earliest collection of Theophrastian sketches in English" (Elbert N. S. Thompson, *Literary Bypaths of the Renaissance,* New Haven, 1924, p. 8; cf. Gwendolen Murphy, *A Cabinet of Characters,* London, 1925, "Introduction"; Elbert N. S. Thompson, "The Seventeenth-Century English Essay," *University of Iowa Humanistic Studies,* III, no. 3 (November 1926), ch. VII; and Richard Aldington, *A Book of 'Characters',* London, [1924], "Introduction"). Milton shows his awareness of Hall's *Characters* which he is detracting. The *Characters* were, subsequently, included in Hall's *Works* of which a number of editions and several issues were made prior to 1642.

11:22-26 NOT CARING...PRAISES — Cf. 3: 4-7. The sentence is grammatically connected to the preceding — "he...thought it his likeliest course ...to let drive at randome, lest he should lose his odde ends which...he...would faine apply [, n]ot caring to burden [*i.e.,* that he burdened] me with those vices, whereof, among [those] whom my conversation hath been, I have been ever least suspected; perhaps not without some suttlety [hoping] to cast me into envie [*i.e.,* to make others envious of me, or to make me unpopular], by bringing on me a necessity to enter into mine own praises."

11:23-24 CONVERSATION — Manner of life. Cf. Ephesians 2:3; Hebrews 13:5. See *Apology,* 32:29.

11:26-28 IN WHICH...AVERSE TO HEARE — Cf. 2:38-40.

11:26 ARGUMENT — Subject or theme.

11:28-30 S I N C E I...S L A N D E R O U S TONGUES — Milton is, no doubt, alluding to Matthew 5:11-12. See John 15:20. Cf. Milton's statement here with that in *Ad Patrem,* 101-110 (*Col.* I, 276, 278).

11:30-31 TO BE GENERALLY PRAIS'D IS WOFULL — The reference is to Luke 6:26, "Woe unto you, when all men shall speak well of you!" See also Luke 6:22; Acts 14:22; II Timothy 3:12; I Peter 2:20-21.

11:31-32 PROMISE TO FREE...ASPERSIONS — The idea is a general one for which there is no specific reference. The general notion is present in a number of scriptural passages such as Psalms 52:2-5; Psalms 94; Isaiah 51:7; Deuteronomy 25:1; Job 22:19; Psalms 1:5; 5:12; Matthew 5:10-12.

11:33 HIM — *i.e.,* God.

11:33-34 [God] ASSISTING ME...SELFE — Cf. 3:27-33.

11:34-35 THOSE OTHER MATTERS OF PUBLICK DEBATEMENT — *i.e.,* matters of political and ecclesiastical importance, particularly concerning church government.

11:36-38 HARME THE TRUTH...LYE UNPURG'D — Cf. 3:21-31.

11:38 ESTIMATION — Repute.

11:38 INSOLENT SUSPICIONS — The vicious charges of the Confuter against Milton began with his turning Milton's charge that the students at Cambridge spent their time "loitering, bezzling, and harlotting" (*ANIM* (1641), p. 13; *Col.* III, 119) against Milton himself (see Note 11:16). That charge, though unmentioned in the *Apology,* is one of the most hurtful charges against Milton. Therefore, Milton, in the whole of his digression in defense of himself (14:33-19:3), is concerned with denying the imputations, particularly that of "harlotting," of that charge.

11:39 LARGE — Free, unrestrained.

11:39 UNWONTED — *i.e.,* take extraordinary measures.

12:3 IF IT SO HAPPEN — If the occasion warrants.

12:4-5 (FOR NOW HE SHEWES HIMSELFE TO BE SO) — The rest of Milton's "Preface" (*Apology*, 12:4-20:37) is taken up with aspects of the charges brought by the Confuter, charges which in Milton's opinion make the Confuter a libeler. The Confuter had objected to the *Animadversions* by calling it *"a slanderous and scurrilous libell"* (7:32). Milton had implied that the Confuter libelled (6:35-11:2), but he now makes the charge without reservation.

12:5 INORDINAT AND RIOTOUS — Both adjectives have unusual force because they echo particularly vital and frequently used passages of the Bible. See Colossians 3:5 (cf. Ezekiel 23:11); and Luke 15:13.

12:6-7 *THE VNIVERSITY...VOMITED OUT THENCE* — In the *Modest Confutation*, Sig. [A3] *verso*, the Confuter had said: *"Thus being grown to an Impostume in the brest of the Vniversity, he was at length vomited out thence into a Suburbe sinke about* London." W. R. Parker has opined that by *"vomited out"* the Confuter was thinking of "graduated." To Milton, however, who recalled with bitterness his rustication, the words demanded an answer that should take the stigma out of the charge (W. R. Parker, *Milton's Contemporary Reputation*, pp. 269-70). Milton's rustication from Cambridge, as a result of an altercation with his tutor, William Chappell, in the Lent Term of 1626 seems to have been of small consequence. Milton was allowed to return during the same term under the tutorship of Nathaniel Tovey. Milton's *Elegy* I (*Col.* I, 168-75) gives the most satisfactory commentary on the incident. John Toland in *The Life of John Milton* (1698) said:

It was about this time he wrote from London a Latin Elegy to his intimat Friend Charles Diodati, wherein som Verses reflecting on the University, and preferring the Pleasures of the Town, gave a handle afterwards to certain Persons no less ignorant than malitious to report that either he was expel'd for som Misdemeanor from Cambridg, or left it in discontent that he obtain'd no Preferment: and that at London he spent his time with leud Women, or at Playhouses. (Wm. H. Hulme (ed.), "Two Early Lives of John Milton," *Western Reserve University Bulletin*, XXVII, no. 8 (August 1924), 10.)

John Aubrey, by the interlineation "whip't him" in his "Minutes of the Life of Mr John Milton" (Helen Darbishire, *The Early Lives of Milton*, Lon-

don, 1932, p. 10) gave the occasion for numerous remarks. Dr. Johnson, in *Lives of the English Poets* (ed. George Birkbeck Hill; Oxford, 1905, 3 vols., I, 88), feared "that Milton was one of the last students in either university that suffered the publick indignity of corporal correction." Joseph Wilson in *Memorabilia Cantabrigiae* (London, 1803), p. 203, notes that "John Milton, the greatest Poet of this or any other nation, finished his education in this college; where it is, I fear, too clearly ascertained, that he was the last who underwent the degrading punishment of flagellation." Cf. Masson, *Life*, I, 159-61.

12:7 COMMODIOUS — Convenient, useful.

12:9 APT OCCASION — Milton welcomes every opportunity for self-vindication (see 6:33-34). The charge that he was "vomited out" gives him the opportunity of making known the real story of his college successes.

12:10-11 MORE THAN ORDINARY FAVOUR ...EQUALS — W. R. Parker feels that because Milton was very sensitive to the "opinion that others held of him, we may discount somewhat his references to his unpopularity." He points out that Milton's "certaine nicenesse of nature, an honest haughtinesse, and self-esteem either of what I was, or what I might be" (16:27-29) might contribute to make him self-depreciatory whenever his abilities were not immediately recognized. The rustication that resulted from the quarrel with his tutor William Chappell was not promising. However, when Milton delivered his first *Prolusion* he found those who "wish me well" (*Col.* XII, 121), and if he intentionally was "too biting," (*ibid.*, p. 123) he learned that his remarks were received with applause "beyond my belief" (*Prolusion* VI, *Col.* XII, 207) even by "those who at other times, on account of disagreements over our studies, possessed an absolutely hostile and unfriendly spirit" (*ibid.*). He was "appointed Dictator" (*ibid.*, p. 227) of the banquet at the close of the summer term (1628?), giving the mock oration for the occasion (*ibid.*, pp. 204-47), in which he praised his audience with extravagance (Parker, *Milton's Contemporary Reputation*, pp. 6-7; cf. Phyllis B. Tillyard (trans.), *Milton Private Correspondence and Academic Exercises*, Cambridge, 1932, p. xxx). He "obtained and with applause, the degree of master" (*Second*

Defence, Col. VIII, 121). On the other hand, Milton had little good to say about Cambridge and seems to have made few friendships (Letter 3, To Alexander Gill, Cambridge, July 2, 1628, *Col.* XII, p. 13). Cf. William Haller, *The Rise of Puritanism* (New York, 1938), pp. 297-98.

12:11   EQUALS—Contemporary fellow students.

12:12-14   FELLOWES OF THAT COLLEDGE ...SIGNIFI'D MANY WAYES— Milton said in his *Second Defence, Col.* VIII, 121, "I ... returned home [from Cambridge], leaving behind me among most of the fellows of the college, who had shown me no ordinary attention, even an affectionate regret." Compare Edward Phillips' statement in "The Life of Mr. John Milton" (Darbishire, *Early Lives,* p. 54) that "He was lov'd and admir'd by the whole University" with Milton's statement that he received "the approbation of all good men" at Cambridge (*Second Defence, Col.* VIII, 121). Anthony à Wood says that Milton "performed the collegiate and academical exercise to the admiration of all, and was esteemed to be a vertuous and sober person, yet not to be ignorant of his own parts" (from *Fasti Oxoniensis,* Darbishire, *Early Lives,* p. 36).

12:15   I WOULD STAY — There is no real evidence that Milton was offered a fellowship at Christ's although there may be the implication in the request of the "curteous and learned men" (12:11) that he stay. Haller, in *The Rise of Puritanism,* pp. 293-94, thinks that if Milton "had chosen, he might have been elected a fellow at Christ's." See Francis Peck, *New Memoirs of the Life and Poetical Works of Mr. John Milton* (London, 1740), pp. 34-35; Masson, *Life,* I, 239 and note; and W. R. Parker, *Milton's Contemporary Reputation,* pp. 24-25, 110, who notes that John Eachard as late as 1670 "announced that he was none 'of those occasional Writers, that missing preferment in the University, can presently write you their new ways of Education.'" ([John Eachard], *The Grounds & Occasions of the Contempt of the Clergy and Religion Enquired into. In a Letter written to R. L.,* London, W. Godbid for N. Brooke, 1670, pp. [ii-iii]).

12:15-17   AS BY MANY LETTERS ... TOWARDS ME — The autobiographical note here

given seems to contradict the notion that Milton had made few lasting friendships in college (see Note 12:10-11), particularly with the "Fellows." The letters do not survive. The purpose of the statement may be rhetorical.

12:17   WHICH — *i.e.,* who.

12:18   PROPENSE TO — Biased in favor of, partial to.

12:19-23   I COULD NOT WRONG THEIR JUDGEMENTS ... GOOD PROOFE — Milton feels that he is respected by the "curteous and learned men" because they are sympathetic with the "honest and laudable courses," which Milton has proved he is following, and in which they hope to encourage him. The "honest and laudable courses" probably refer to Milton's virtuous life.

12:23-25   AND TO THOSE INGENUOUS AND FRIENDLY MEN ... COUNTNANCERS OF VERTUOUS AND HOPEFUL WITS — Cf. 12:22. They encouraged Milton to proceed in "honest and laudable courses."

12:25-26   FRIENDS IN ABSENCE ... ANOTHER — See Note 12:12-14.

12:26-30   AS FOR THE COMMON APPROBATION ... RIGHT DISCERNER — "... if he [the Confuter] thinke to obtaine [*i.e.,* win the day] with me, or any right discerner [for the reason] that I should esteeme or disesteeme my selfe or any other the more ... [because of] the common approbation or dislike of that place [*i.e.,* Cambridge], as now it is, [he is] too simple and too credulous."

The Confuter assumed Milton's dislike of the University from the *Animadversions* (see Note 11: 38 INSOLENT SUSPICIONS). He speaks of Milton as "*being grown to an Impostume in the brest of the Vniversity*" (*Modest Confutation,* Sig. [A3] *verso*). The term "*Impostume*" had a very disagreeable connotation denoting "rotting and swellyng." In the medical treatises of the day the postume was thought of as the gathering of "superfluitie of humours in some member," sometimes as a result of an outward cause as a wound, bruise, or burn, "for of all such things, humoures moue ofte and come to the sore place, & putteth and hurleth euery each with other, and wereth hot and rotteth," and sometimes as a result of an inward cause "as of superfluitie of corrupt humors, that oft runneth and commeth togethers to a certaine place" (*Batman vppon Bartholome His Booke De Proprietatibus Rerum*, London, 1582, Bk. VII, ch. 60, "Of a Postume," fol. [110] *verso*. See Note 12:30).

Milton's early protest against the educational system was made in his third Academic Exercise (*Prolusion* III, *Col.* XII, 158-73). In the *Reason of Church-government* he expressed his dissatisfaction with the Universities (*Col.* III, 272-74), with the emphasis on "scragged and thorny lectures of monkish and miserable sophistry," and the lack of emphasis on the "true lore of religion or moral vertue."

Others were disturbed about the Universities. J[ohn] H[all], in *An Humble Motion To The Parliament Of England Concerning The Advancement of Learning* (London, 1649), p. 27, complains that in the English universities there are "hardly Professours for the three principall faculties, and these but lazily read, and carelesly followed." He laments that chemistry, anatomy, "ocular demonstration of herbes," "manuall demonstrations of Mathematicall Theorems or Instruments," history, and languages are still untaught. He says that the English universities "have not yet arrived to the exactnesse of the Jesuits Colledges, and many transmarine Universities" (*ibid.*, p. 28), suggests that "education would thrive the best in any place, that was the least cumbred with unnecessary notions" (*ibid.*, p. 34), and wishes "that there were a place in some University appointed for a collection of all such Papers, Letters, Transcripts, and Relations, which should discover the inner side of Negotiations, and events, and the true face of things, without the adulteration of common policy. And I thought it were profitable rather to take in many needlesse things, then to leave out one needfull, because a judging minde out of many particularities, could draw a better estimate of things, and deduce more certaine, and unquestioned axiomes" (*ibid.*, p. 36).

12:29 THE CONFUTER — Milton is no longer thinking of Bishop Joseph Hall as the author of the *Modest Confutation*.

12:29 OBTAINE — To prevail; to win the victory or gain the day.

12:30 OF SMALL PRACTIZE WERE THAT PHYSITIAN — Kester Svendson points out that Milton mentions the physician with considerable respect (*First Defence, Col.* VII, 67), many times with reference to an ailment (*ANIM, Col.* III, 117; *RCG, Col.* III, 182, 189; *Tetrachordon, Col.* IV, 174; *Brief Notes upon a Late Sermon, Col.* VI, 151-52; *Author's Defence of Himself, Col.* IX, 11), and in this case with reference to the "diagnosis of nausea" (Kester Svendson, "Milton and Medical Lore," *Bulletin of the History of Medicine*, XIII (1943), 160). Robert Burton thought, on the other hand, that the trade of a physician was a "corrupt" one, "no science, art, no profession; the beginning, practice, and progresse of it, all is naught, full of imposture, incertainty, and doth generally more harme then good" (Robert Burton, *The Anatomy Of Melancholy*, Oxford, 1638, Part 2, sec. 4, subsec. I, p. 359). The "encyclopedias of Batman, Bartholomew, and La Primaudaye are extremely useful to the study of Milton's medical lore" (Svendson, *op. cit.*, p. 183. Bartholomew's *De Proprietatibus Rerum* was compiled about 1230, and published in English in 1495 and 1535; Stephen Batman's *Batman vppon Bartholome* was published in London in 1582, and Peter de la Primaudaye's *The French Academie* in London in 1618.). Batman and Primaudaye "depend largely on medieval sources" (Svendson, *op. cit.*, p. 184). See Notes 12:26-30; 12:32-35; 22:38-23:4; 46:31-32.

12:31 SHE OR HER SISTER — *i.e.*, Cambridge and Oxford. Joseph Hall called them the "two best vniuersities of the worlde, both of them my mothers, and one of them my nurse also, and both sisters" ([Joseph Hall], *The Discovery of A New World*, pp. 14-15).

12:32-35 THE WORSER STUFFE... STRONG PHYSICK — In *Tetrachordon* (*Col.* IV, 174), Milton points out that "the physician cures not by the 'middling temper' of nourishing medicine but by the other extreme" (Svendson, "Milton and Medical Lore," p. 180). Batman suggests that giddiness should be treated by letting blood and by using purgatives (*Batman vppon Bartholome*, Bk. 7, ch. 8, fol. [89] *verso*; cf. *Brief Notes upon a late Sermon, Col.* VI, 151-52). He says:

Spuing is good when it commeth of the vertue and

working of kinde, or when it commeth as it shoulde, and when it must bee done by help of medicine... Good spuing cleanseth the stomacke, and helpeth and serueth the vertue of digestion: and dischargeth all kind, and releeueth all the body of man of full many sicknesses and evils. And doth the contrarye if it be not good. (*Batman vppon Bartholome*, Bk. 7, ch. 47, fol. 104 *recto*.)

Milton maintains that the Universities, which have been ill for a long time, have been vomiting out the better, but retaining the worse which is the actual cause of the illness. Since the vomiting as a result of illness comes to naught, a "strong physick" must be given. The analogy is apt. See Notes 12:30 and 46:31-32.

12:33 KECKING AT...QUEASIE — Cf. 12: 32-35 and 19:30.

12:35 *SUBURB SINKE* — The Confuter charged that Milton had been vomited from the University "*into a Suburbe sinke about* London" (*Modest Confutation,* Sig. [A3] *verso*; see Note 12:6-7). Milton was actually living outside the city wall in 1642 in Aldersgate Street. Although some rather reputable people lived in the same neighborhood (see Parker, *Milton's Contemporary Reputation*, p. 270; cf. Merritt Y. Hughes, *John Milton Prose Selections,* New York, 1947, p. 150 note), the Confuter calls it a "*sinke,*" that is, a place in which vice or corruption is rampant. See Masson, *Life,* II, 204-08.

12:36 SCAVINGER — Milton effectively returns blow for blow — the one who knows about the "*sinke*" must be a collector of filth, a dishonorable person. See Masson, *Life,* II, 401.

12:37 *PLAGUE* — See Note 11:16. According to the Confuter the "*Suburbe sinke*" since Milton's coming, "*hath groaned under two ills,* Him *and the* Plague" (*Modest Confutation,* Sig. [A3] *verso*). Milton was probably living in Aldersgate Street by the end of 1640 (Masson, *Life,* II, 204). In the summer of 1641 the plague raged (*ibid.,* p. 272), continuing well into the autumn (*ibid.,* p. 315).

12:37 WORSE PLAGUE ... ENTRAILE — The remark may indicate that Milton had information that the Confuter was not well (see Introduction, p. 3). Masson says that the "middle entraile" is the "heart, or spleen" (Masson, *Life,* II, 401-02).

12:39 HIS UNIVERSITY — Whether Milton is referring to Cambridge or Oxford is not easy to determine unless one is positive who the Confuter is (see Introduction, p. 3). In the paragraph of the *Apology* that begins on page 11, line 3, Milton is again departing more and more from the identification of Bishop Hall with the author of the pamphlet. On page 12, line 29, he takes care to say "Confuter." Milton is usually careful to distinguish between the two. If the Confuter is the youngest of Hall's sons, the University is Oxford. If he is the oldest son, it may be Cambridge or Oxford; if he is Bishop Hall, it may be either, for Hall took degrees at both Universities.

12:39-40 HER BETTER HEALTH — Milton feels that the Universities are becoming progressively more inadequate.

12:40 MINE OWNE YOUNGER JUDGEMENT — See *Prolusion* III, *Col.* XII, 158-73. Anthony à Wood, Milton's unsympathetic biographer, noted that in later years Milton became "a great reproacher of the Universities, scholastical degrees" (Darbishire, *Early Lives,* p. 39). The statement is indeed justified by Milton's attacks on Oxford and Cambridge in the antiprelatical pamphlets. One must, however, be cautious in accepting what Milton says in those pamphlets at face value for Milton had the ecclesiastical-political motive in the foreground. Merritt Y. Hughes says: "How much of a rebel he was against the social and intellectual life of the Cambridge that he knew as an undergraduate, it is hard to tell; but he certainly was not a submissive or uncritical student" (Hughes, *Milton Prose Selections,* p. xix).

12:40-13:1 I NEVER GREATLY ADMIR'D — Milton was a follower of the school of thinking opposed to Scholasticism. Educators like Vives and reformers like Herman Melancthon had advocated the principle of Erasmus that boys should not be forced "to perform dialectical stunts with vague concepts like the Aristotelian principles of form and matter" (Hughes, *Milton Prose Selections,* p. xxi). Peter Ramus' anti-Aristotelianism in France had become very influential in England and was the basis for Milton's *Logic.* In 1585, George Downham, famous for his commentary on Ramist logic, had been made a fellow at Cambridge (see *ANIM*

(1641), p. 10, *Col.* III, 115; *Modest Confutation,*
Sig. A3 *recto*). Bacon in the *Advancement of
Learning* (1605) had shown the way to better edu-
cation.

13:1 CITY — London.

13:2 USURPING — Making assumptions without
evidence.

**13:2-3 BOOK NOTICE, WHICH ONLY HE
AFFIRMES TO HAVE HAD** — See Notes 6:39-
7:1 and 11:7-8.

13:3-4 AND WHERE... HE WISSES NOT —
"Where his morning haunts are I wist not" (*Modest Confutation,* Sig. [A3] *verso*). See Note 11:16
for context.

13:5 UNIVERSITY VOMIT — See Note 12:6-7.

13:6 SUBURB SINKE — See Note 12:35.

13:7 LIMBECK — An alembic, an apparatus used
by alchemists in distilling.

13:7 TO GIVE HIM AND ENVIE — *i.e.,* in
order to give him and the envious. Cf. 11:25.

13:9 CONCOCTING — Digesting (cf. *Of Education, Col.* IV, 289, "concoction"). Hughes, *Milton
Prose Selections,* p. 47 note, points out the relationship of the term "to Aristotle's teaching in his work
On the Parts of Animals that the food in the in-
testine (or its substance) passed to the heart first
in the form of vapor."

13:12 NOT MUCH TARDIER — Cf. *L'Allegro,*
41-44; *Il Penseroso,* 121-30.

13:13 GOOD AUTHORS — See 15:18-18:20;
32:37; 55:24-25; *Il Penseroso,* 85-120.

**13:14-15 THEN WITH USEFULL AND GEN-
EROUS LABOURS** — Milton recommended not
only the alternation of mental and physical activity
but also the value of leisure, "because the spirit of
man cannot demean it selfe lively in this body without some recreating intermission of labour, and
serious things" (*RCG, Col.* III, 239).

13:15-20 PRESERVING... SLAVISH LIFE —
From the evidence of this statement Masson has
inferred that Milton was taking part in military
exercises with the London militia in 1642 (Masson,
Life, II, 481. For Masson's marshaling of evidence

see *ibid.,* pp. 472-88.). Milton in the *Second Defence*
(*Col.* VIII, 9, 11) claimed no part in the "glorious
warfare." Milton felt that leisure time should be
controlled by the magistrates in order that the activities "may inure and harden our bodies by martial
exercises to all warlike skil and performance, and
may civilize, adorn and make discreet our minds by
the learned and affable meeting of frequent Academies... that the call of wisdom and vertu may be
heard every where" (*RCG, Col.* III, 240). Hanford thinks Milton "has been simply taking exercise, his lifelong habit, as a relief from study and
to preserve his health for the kind of service which
he was then rendering and which he was later to
render in his country's cause" (James Holly Hanford, "Milton and the Art of War," *SP,* XVIII
(1921), 244). Compare the emphasis given to exercise in *Of Education, Col.* IV, 287 ff., where,
Hughes, *Milton Prose Selections,* p. 46 note, points
out, "Milton reflects Plato's disapproval of the over-
emphasis on military training in Sparta (*Laws* I,
633, 636), but (as Miss Lockwood pointed out) he
also shared Plato's faith in athletic discipline as a
moral stimulus. (*Laws* VII, 791.)"

13:16 LUMPISH — Sluggish, lethargic.

13:18 FIRME HEARTS IN SOUND BODIES
— A variation of Homer's statement that "a sound
mind in a manly body" is the greatest blessing of
man (*Contest of Hesiod and Homer.* Sec. 320).
Compare "Orandum est ut sit mens sana in corpore
sano" (Juvenal, *Satires* X, line 356).

13:19 PROTESTATION — Rendered *Protes-
tantism* by Masson (*Life,* II, 402) and Joseph Ivimey (*John Milton: His Life and Times, Religious
and Political Opinions,* New York, 1833, p. 47).
Milton is referring to the Protestation of May 3,
1641, in which the members of the House of Commons, after pointing out that attempts were being
made to undermine "the true reformed Protestant
religion," to "subvert the fundamental laws of England and Ireland," to bring the English army into a
misunderstanding of the Parliament in order by its
force "to bring to pass those wicked counsels,"
made the Protestation (see Note 39:40-40:2).

**13:21-22 IN PLAYHOUSES... AND THE
BORDELLOES** — *"... but he that would finde
him after dinner, must search the* Play-Houses, *or*

the Bordelli, *for there I have traced him*; [among old Cloaks, false Beards, Tyres, Cases, Periwigs, Modona Vizzards, night-walking-Cudgellers, and Salt Lotion.] *Many* [times] *of late . . . he is new cloathed in Serge, and confined to a Parlour"* (*Modest Confutation*, Sig. [A3] *verso*). See note 11:16. (The quotation is exact except for "[times]" which is mine.)

13:22 *BORDELLOES* — Houses of prostitution.

13:22 UNFAITHFUL SPIE OF CANAAN — Milton likens the author of the *Modest Confutation* to one of the ten spies "which Moses sent to search the land [Canaan], who returned, and made all the congregation to murmur against him [Moses], by bringing up a slander upon the land" (Numbers 14:36; cf. Numbers 13:25-33).

13:23 *THERE HE HATH TRAC'T ME* — See Note 13:21-22.

13:24 SURETIES — Pledges, guarantees, sureties given as a pledge of fulfilment of an action or undertaking.

13:28 GIN — A device or trap to ensnare game; a cunning stratagem or artifice.

13:28 HAMPER'D — Entangled or caught.

13:28-29 HAMPER'D IN HIS OWNE HEMPE — A variation of an old proverb: "In his own grease I made him fry," Chaucer, *Wife of Bath's Prologue* (*c.*1386), line 487. Cf. John Lydgate, *Temple of Glass* (*c.* 1400), line 14; Thomas Fuller, *Holy and Profane State* (1642), p. 396.

13:29-30 IN THE ANIMADVERSIONS . . . SALT LOTION — See Note 13:21-22. Milton has narrowed the Confuter's gleanings to those which appear in the *Animadversions* (1641), pp. 7-8 (*Col.* III, 112-13). Having cited Bacon's complaint (see Notes 27:3 and 27:28) that the bishops suppressed those pamphlets written against themselves and licensed those against the Puritans (*ANIM* (1641), p. 7; *Col.* III, 111-12), and having pleaded for a free press, Milton points out the advantages of free speech, among which are that Princes and Statesmen will no longer need to disguise themselves and become eavesdroppers in order to learn the truth from the people themselves: "they shall not need heerafter in old Cloaks, and false Beards, to stand to the courtesy of a night-walking

cudgeller for eaves dropping, nor to accept quietly as a perfume, the over-head emptying of some salt lotion" (*ANIM* (1641), pp. 8-9; *Col.* III, 113). Milton chose to recall this particular passage because it gave him a new excuse to pummel Hall again with the *Mundus Alter et Idem* (14:1-9) and because he intended to refer again to the question of free speech and libelling and to use Bacon's statement relative thereto (27:25-28:15).

13:31 ANIMADVERTER — That is, Milton, the author of the *Animadversions*.

13:33-34 A CHILDE . . . EDG'D TOOLES — A common saying:
   Beware how you give any edged tool
   Unto a young child and unto a fool. — William Wager, *Longer Thou Livest* (1568).
   It is not good jesting with edged tools. — Stephen Gosson, *School of Abuse* (1579), 57.
   It is no jesting with edge tools. — *True Tragedy of Richard III* (1594).
   There is no jesting with edge tools.—Beaumont and Fletcher, *The Little French Lawyer* (*c.* 1619), Act II, Sc. iv.
   For secrets are edged tools,
   And must be kept from children and from fools. — Dryden, *Sir Martin Mar-All* (1668), Act II.

13:34 *ANTISTREPHON* — "An argument that is retorted upon an opponent" (*OED*, "Antistrophon").

13:35-36 THE CONFUTER . . . BORDELLOES — Milton charges that since the Confuter recognizes the furniture, that is, the "old Cloaks, false Beards, Tyres, Cases, Periwigs, Modona Vizzards, night-walking-Cudgellers, and Salt Lotion" (see Note 13:21-22), he must himself have some knowledge of them.

13:37-40 WAS IT SUCH A DISSOLUTE SPEECH . . . URINALL? — See Note 13:29-30.

14:1-2 AFORESAID *MIME, MUNDUS ALTER & IDEM* — See Notes 10:11.

14:2 *CEPHALUS* — Cephalus, envied by the gods because of his happiness with his wife, Procris, was carried away by Aurora, goddess of the dawn (Ovid, *Metamorphoses* VII, 700-13).

14:3 *HYLAS* — The story of Hercules' seizure and ravishing of Hylas was a familiar one (Natale Conti, *Natalis Comitis Mythologiae, Sive Explica-*

tionis Fabvlarvm, Libri decem, Frankfort, 1588, p. 704. For other accounts of the Hylas story see Apollonius Rhodius *Argonautica,* I, 1207 *et seq.*; Theocritus *Idyll* XIII; Virgil *Eclogue* VI, lines 43-44).

14:3-4 TROOPE OF CAMPING HUSWIVES IN *VIRAGINIA* ... UXORIOUS VARLET — Hall, having been captured by the inhabitants (Huswives) of Sheelands (Viraginia), just outside their borders in the land of Letcheritania, is held a prisoner because any Letcheritanians whom the Viraginians capture are either hung or given slavish duties in prison. Hall gains his freedom after some time by taking an oath conceding many things to women (*Mundus Alter et Idem,* Bk. II [*i.e.,* Bk. III], ch.2, pp. 92-96; *The Discovery of A New World,* pp. 98-102).

14:5-6 *APHRODISIA* ... SWEET SMELL TO HIS NOSTRILS — In Book II [*i.e.,* Book III], Chapter 5, of the *Mundus,* Hall describes his coming to Aphrodisia, the land of romance, where the air is "as delicately sented, as if all the perfumers in England ... had lately plaied their prizes there for eternal soueraignty" (*Mundus Alter et Idem,* pp. 100-02; *The Discovery of A New World,* pp. 107-10).

14:7 SHAMELESSE COURTEZANS OF *DESVERGONIA* — The "shire towne" of *Aphrodisia* was *Desvergonia.* The houses there were made of glass. The women of the city could be found at home only at dressing time. Otherwise they were at the Playhouse and Tavern where they set their nets for their enemies, the Lecheritanians, some of whom were voluntary servants, and some of whom were attracted by loose allurements and prayers, whereas others were compelled "to serue their wanton desires by force," and kept in custody for that purpose (*Mundus Alter et Idem,* p. 101; *The Discovery of A New World,* pp. 108-09). Milton's treatment of Hall's *Mundus* is, of course, unsympathetic throughout. Cf. *Apology,* 10:10-31 and *ANIM, Col.* III, 138.

14:9 SUCH NECESSITY TO THE HEARSAY — "Necessity" has the meaning in this case of a "constraining or compelling to a definite action." In using the word "hear-say" Milton may be punning, having in mind the greater incongruity that the word "heresy" might contribute to the

already mock-serious cause-effect situation. Milton is stating that the Confuter's contention that, because the Confuter has heard someone speaking of "a Tire, a Periwig, or a Vizard," someone must necessarily have seen plays, is based on evidence that is untrustworthy, and gossipy.

14:10 TIRE — A costume, often a headdress. See Note 13:21-22 for the Confuter's use of the word which the Confuter had gleaned from the *Animadversions* (*Col.* III, 112).

14:10 PERIWIG — Artificial headdress used by actors as part of their make-up. See Note 13:21-22 and *ANIM, Col.* III, 112.

14:10 VIZARD — Mask. See Note 13:21-22 and *ANIM, Col.* III, 112, 152.

14:12 THOSE IN NEXT APTITUDE TO DIVINITY — That is, divinity students. See 14:15-16.

14:13 SO OFT UPON THE STAGE — Dr. Johnson, in commenting on this passage, thought Milton "peevish" for objecting to the acting of plays by academics when he during his exile from college "relates with great luxuriance the compensation which the pleasures of the theatre afford him" (*Lives of the English Poets,* ed. George Birkbeck Hill, I, 90). Milton is, as J. A. St. John pointed out, objecting that the ministers dishonor "their sacred calling by the personation of coarse and indecent characters" (St. John, *Prose Works of Milton,* III, 114-15 note). See 14:26-32.

14:13 UNBONING — Taking the bones out; perhaps, staggering.

14:14 DISHONEST — That is, shameful, indecent, leud.

14:14-15 TRINCULO'S — Drunken jesters. The term probably is a reference not to the drunken sailor in Shakespeare's *Tempest,* III, ii, but to Thomas Tomkys' Trincalo in the play *Albumazor,* which was acted in 1614 at Trinity College, Cambridge. See St. John, *Prose Works of Milton,* III, 114-15 note; Samuel Johnson, "Life of Milton" in *Works of Samuel Johnson* (London, William Pickering, 1825, 11 vols.), VII, 70 note; Alwin Thaler, "The Shakesperian Element in Milton," *PMLA,* XL (1925), 686 note; and Merritt Y. Hughes, *Milton Prose Selections,* p. 153 note.

14:15 BUFFONS—Low jesters; those who practice indecent raillery.

14:15 BAWDS — Procurers or procuresses.

14:15-16 THAT MINISTRY . . . HAVING — Some had already taken orders; the rest were, at least in theory, preparing for priesthood in the Anglican Church (see 14:11-13).

14:17-18 GROOMES AND *MADEMOISELLAES* — *i.e.,* male attendants or servants, and serving-maids, often foreign. See Thomas Keightley, *An Account of the Life, Opinions, and Writings of John Milton* (London, 1855), p. 362 note, who states that Pepys in his *Diary* records that "even *his* wife was accompanied to the theatre by her maid."

14:18 WHILE THEY ACTED, AND OVERACTED — "Milton, while still a Cambridge undergraduate, upheld an exacting standard for actors" (Ida Langdon, *Milton's Theory of Poetry and Fine Art,* New Haven, 1924, p. 84). The custom of performing plays at the Universities as well as at the Inns of Court was a common one, and was still observed so late as 1747 when Christopher Smart's *The Grateful Fair* was performed at Pembroke College, Cambridge.

14:22 *ATTICISME* — The passage beginning "There while they acted, and overacted" (14:18-22) and ending "they were out, and I hist," is the *"atticisme,"* that is, "the peculiar style and idiom of the Greek language as used by the Athenians" (*OED*). Milton is referring to a passage which was his model in Demosthenes' *De Corona* in which Demosthenes speaking to Aeschines bitterly contrasts "their respective fortunes" (Demosthenes, *De Corona,* par. 80. For a translation see *The Crown, The Philippics and ten other Orations of Demosthenes,* translated by C. Rann-Kennedy, Everyman's Library, New York, [1911], p. 48).

14:23 TEXT MEN — Those learned in scriptural texts and apt in quoting them (*OED*).

14:23-24 FALSE BEARDS AND VIZARDS — See Notes 13:29-30 and 14:10 VIZARD.

14:26-32 FOR. . . ACTORS — See Notes 14:13 SO OFT UPON THE STAGE, 14:15-16, and 14:18.

14:27 UNLAWFUL — Contrary to moral standards or spiritual principles. The theatres were not closed until September 1642.

14:33 UPRAIDING — *i.e.,* upbraiding.

14:33 UPRAIDING TO ME THE BORDELLO'S — *i.e.,* reproving me for frequenting the Bordelloes. The apostrophe in "Bordello's" indicates the omission of the *e.*

14:34 OTHER SUSPICIOUS GLANCINGS — The Confuter had charged Milton with riotous living, with making trouble at the University, with causing the *"suburbe sink"* to groan with his activities, with attending the play houses (see *Apology,* pp. 12 ff.), with "blaspheming God and the King," and with drinking and swearing (see Note 18:28-29), and had cited passages from the *Animadversions* to arouse Christians against him (see Note 19:4-5).

14:35-36 ONE WHOSE CUSTOME OF LIFE WERE NOT HONEST, BUT LICENTIOUS — The whole of the preface "To the Reader" of the *Modest Confutation* (Sig. A3 *recto-*[A4] *verso*) as well as the first two paragraphs of Section I (pp. 1-2) are particularly intended to reveal Milton in a very evil light.

14:36 BORN WITH — Indulged, endured.

14:37 IN A WAY NOT OFTEN TROD — Milton is aware that his digressions to justify himself are not the usual procedure, and that few writers attempt to acquaint the reader with the mental and spiritual events in their lives. Though self-praise is "a way not often trod," Milton trod the path frequently, for instance, in the second prologue of the *Reason of Church-government* (*Col.* III, 229-42), in the *First Defence* (*Col.* VII, 2-9), in the *Second Defence* (*Col.* VIII, 117-39), in the *Author's Defence of Himself* (*Col.* IX), and in the prologues to some of the books of *Paradise Lost.* See Note 18:21-22.

14:40 ENVIOUS — Cf. 11:25; 13:7; 15:6; 16:29.

15:1 COMPACT ORDER — *i.e.,* having the parts or numbers so arranged that all lie within a comparatively small compass, without straggling portions or members (*OED*). Merritt Y. Hughes, *Milton Prose Selections,* p. 154 note, explains "to change compact order" as "of soldiers in close order in a square formation when the inner and outer ranks change positions." Note the application of changing outward actions for inward thoughts (15:1-2) and of turning the coat inside out (15:9-10).

15:3 THIS SORT OF MEN — *i.e.*, the envious (14:40).

15:4 FOR — *i.e.*, from.

15:5 Ἀπειροκαλία — False taste, vulgarity; wanting in taste; ignorance in those things that are polite, becoming, and beautiful. I. C. T. Ernesti, in *Lexicon Technologiae Graecorvm Rhetoricae* (Lipsiae, 1795), p. 34, defines the words thus: "affectatum elegantiae et ornatus studium. Dionys. Iud. Demosth. 23. p. 1025."

15:6 ENVIE — See Note 14:40.

15:8-9 OUTWARD GARMENT HATH BIN INJUR'D AND ILL BEDIGHTED — Cf. 3:29-30; 6:32.

15:9 BEDIGHTED — Bedecked, adorned, *i.e.*, badly handled or treated.

15:9 SHIFT — Means available for effecting an end; in this case, garment.

15:9-11 FOR...WHAT HELPE...BETTER — "...for...what helpe [is there] but to turn the inside outwards, especially if the lining be of the same [material as the outside], or...much better."

15:13 DISCOVERY — Revelation.

15:13-14 TWO PURPOSES — To defend himself by the example of his "outward demeanour," and by revealing his "inmost thoughts" (15:11-13).

15:15-18 ALTHOUGH...FAIN — "...although I faile to gaine [the] beliefe [of] others [that I am] such as my perpetuall thoughts shall heere disclose me, I may yet not faile of successe in perswading some, [that they are] such really themselves, [when] they cannot believe me to be more then what I fain."

15:20 THOSE PLACES — The grammar school and the university — in Milton's case, St. Paul's, and Christ College, Cambridge.

15:20-21 WHERE THE OPINION...ATTAIN'D — Cf. 12:26-13:1; 14:11-22; 15:4-5; 37:38-40; 45:32-46:11.

15:22 THOSE AUTHORS...COMMENDED — A notion of what authors Milton considered important from an educational point of view may be gained from the curriculum he outlines in *Of Education* (*Col.* IV, 275 ff.). Although that curriculum may seem overly literary or overly permeated by abstract ethical teachings from the *Dialogues* of Plato or the *Moralia* of Plutarch, it may exemplify the course of reading which Milton himself experienced and which he delineates in his *Apology*, 15:18-18:20 (Hughes, *Milton Prose Selections*, p. xxxi).

15:23 GRAVE ORATORS & HISTORIANS — Milton's reading in the Horton years seems to have been systematically planned and carried out. In the *Apology* (52:9-15), Milton indicates that after having spent "some years...in the stories of those Greek and Roman exploits," reading of "many things both nobly done, [and] worthily spoken," he came "in the method of time to that age wherein the Church had obtain'd a Christian Emperor." Hanford feels that "Milton had...begun with the history of classical antiquity, studying the chief authorities, we may suppose, exhaustively" (James Holly Hanford, "The Chronology of Milton's Private Studies," *PMLA*, XXXVI (1921), 291). The term "grave Orators & Historians" indicates that Milton was thinking of authors whom he considered weighty and authoritative. The Church historians were neither, for they could write, for the most part, only of "ambition, corruption, contention, combustion" (52:11-18). The fact that Milton lists the "grave Orators & Historians" first in the history of his mental growth and states that he, because of his youth, understood them imperfectly (15:23-24) seems further to suggest that he is thinking of the authors of classical antiquity whom he had read early in his educational experience and had since reread (Hanford, "The Chronology of Milton's Private Studies," p. 290). A casual reading in Milton shows that Cicero is one of the "grave Orators & Historians": in the preface to *Samson Agonistes* (*Col.* I, 331), Cicero is bracketed with Plutarch as one of the "philosophers and...gravest writers"; in the *First Defence* (*Col.* VII, 39), he is bracketed with Demosthenes. Cicero was he who "established and determined" the three-fold "function of the speaker" (*Prolusion* III, *Col.* XII, 159). Milton pronounced Quintus Hortensius the "most renowned of all the orators, after Marcus Tullius" (*Prolusion* VI, *Col.* XII, 243; cf. *ibid.*, p. 211); he accorded to Demosthenes and Aeschines the honor of being "the two most distinguished orators" (*ibid.*, p. 211), and to Lucius Crassus that of being "a distinguished orator" (*First Defence, Col.* VII, 183). Among the historians, Milton preferred Sallust "to any other Latin Historian" (*Familiar Letters, Col.* XII, 93, 95) and mentioned him simply as "the Historian" in the *Apology* (25:14; cf. Familiar Letters, *Col.* XII, 101). In the *History of Britain* (*Col.* X, 68), Milton referred to Dion, the "Greek Historian"; in his letter to Henry De Brass, December 16, 1657 (*Col.* XII, 103), he pointed out that "the ancient authors, Polybius, the Halicarnassian, Diodorus, Cicero, Lucian" had "handed down certain stray precepts" concerning the writing of history; and in the *First Defence* (*Col.* VII, 299), he mentioned "Herodotus, Ctesias, Diodorus."

15:25 SMOOTH ELEGIACK POETS — *i.e.*, "The smooth and glowing love poetry of Ovid and his fellows." Milton's "Latin elegies, particularly the First, Fifth, and Seventh, with their strong accent of sensuous feeling and their only partly chastened Ovidian tone," show the influence of the elegiac poets (Hanford, *Handbook*, p. 369).

15:25-26 SCHOOLES ARE NOT SCARCE — *i.e.*, much read in the schools.

15:26 NUMEROUS — Measured, rhythmic, harmonious. Cf. *Paradise Lost,* V, 149-50, "such prompt eloquence/Flow'd from their lips, in Prose or numerous Verse," and *Paradise Regained*, IV, 254-56,

There thou shalt hear and learn the secret power
Of harmony in tones and numbers hit
By voice or hand, and various-measur'd verse.

15:27 IN IMITATION . . . EASIE — See Note 15:25.

15:27-28 MOST AGREEABLE TO NATURES PART IN ME — Milton found that the sensuous love poetry of the elegiac poets struck a vibrant chord in his own life.

15:28 THEIR MATTER — Stories abounding in sensual love and gross enticements told in a highly sensuous manner.

15:29-30 NO RECREATION . . . BETTER WELCOME — Milton's zest for the Ovidian is plainly stated.

15:30-31 THOSE YEARS . . . EXCUS'D — Hanford conjectures that Milton was about nineteen years of age when he became enamoured of the "Elegiack Poets" (Hanford, *Handbook*, p. 369). Milton describes the period of young manhood when emotions are likely to be uncontrollable and passions violent as "those years . . . which are excus'd" (*i.e.*, overlooked or regarded indulgently).

15:31 THOUGH THEY BE LEAST SEVERE — "Severe" has the notion of "difficult," "exacting," "rigorous," "not inclined to indulgence or leniency." The meaning is, therefore, that those years are most inclined toward leniency. Thomas Keightley explains the clause as "most inclined to love, and to light and amorous reading" (Keightley, *Life of Milton*, 364 note).

15:32 REMEMBER — *i.e.*, remind.

15:32 THEM — The elegiac poets.

15:35-36 HIGH PERFECTIONS . . . CELEBRATE — Milton in reading such authors as Ovid, Tibullus, or Propertius has an idealistic reaction wherein he attributes to the authors the desire, which is really his own, to celebrate "high perfections."

15:36-39 I THOUGHT . . . IMBOLDEN ME — Having seen in the elegiac poets the attempt to celebrate "high perfections," Milton feels the challenge.

15:39-16:3 THAT WHAT JUDGEMENT . . . PRAISES — Milton feels that if he exercises greater wisdom and a greater love of virtue in choosing the object of his high praises than the elegiac poets used, his "judgement, wit, or elegance" can surpass theirs, showing itself to best advantage.

16:2 (LET RUDE EARES BE ABSENT) — Merritt Y. Hughes, *Milton Prose Selections*, p. 155 note, finds in these words a "reminiscence of classical warnings," and refers to the seer in Virgil's

Aeneid, VI, 258-59, who exhorts the profane not to approach the hallowed place:

> Procul o, procul este, profani,
> Conclamat vates....

16:5   IDLE — *i.e.,* worthless.

16:6   END IN SERIOUS — Result in matters of serious consequence.

16:12   PROFICIENT — An adept, an expert; one who progresses toward an objective such as virtue.

16:13-16   IF I FOUND ... MEN I DEPLOR'D — Milton reveals that he became an expert at rejecting the "unworthy things" and the "unchaste," deploring the authors of such writing as men, but approving their art. Cf. 17:5-8.

16:17-18   TWO FAMOUS RENOWNERS OF *BEATRICE* AND *LAURA* — Milton refers to Dante (1265-1321) and his idealization of Beatrice in the *Vita Nuova* and in the *Paradiso* of the *Divina Commedia,* and to Petrarch (1304-1374) and his idealization of Laura in his *Canzoniere.*

16:19-20   SUBLIME AND PURE THOUGHTS, WITHOUT TRANSGRESSION — Milton, describing his studies when he was at Cambridge, says that he preferred Dante and Petrarch who never wrote "unworthy things," but displayed "sublime and pure thoughts." Milton was naturally equipped by virtue of his purpose to do all "As ever in my great task Masters eye" (Sonnet VII, *Col.* I, 60), to fathom "the purity and the sublimity of the *Vita Nuova,*" to see that "the blessedness of love lies, not in a reward, but in a homage without thought of self." Dante in his "ecstatic intuition" sees Beatrice in the *Vita Nuova* as "a spiritual power, bringing earthly things into compliance with the divine order of the world" (Charles H. Herford, "Dante and Milton," *Bulletin of John Rylands Library Manchester,* VIII (1924), 193, 196). In the *Paradiso* intellectual illumination and moral purification go hand in hand; and the consummation of Beatrice's work, of the transforming power of that selfless love, is not more to have won for him the vision of God, the crowning experience of the Paradise, than it is to have effected that complete oneness of his will with the Will of the universe, which makes him at length 'concentric with the Love which moves the sun and the other stars.' (*Ibid.,* p. 197.)

16:21-23   HE WHO WOULD NOT BE FRUSTRATE ... A TRUE POEM — Cf. Note 5:32-35. The idea is a favorite one of Renaissance criticism, going back to Strabo, *Geography,* 1.2.5: "it is impossible for one to become a good poet unless he has previously become a good man" (*The Geography of Strabo,* I, 63; cf. Longinus, *On the Sublime,* ed. by Rhys Roberts, Cambridge, 1899, Ch. 9, p. 61). Spingarn says that the notion

is to be found in Ronsard and other French and Italian writers; it is especially noticeable in English literature, and is insisted on by Ben Jonson, Milton.... In this idea Plato's praise of the philosopher, as well as Cicero's and Quintilian's praise of the orator, was by the Renaissance transferred to the poet [see Minturno, *De Poeta,* p. 105]; but the conception itself goes back to ... Strabo." (Spingarn, *Literary Criticism in the Renaissance,* p. 54.)

For further discussions see Samuel Taylor Coleridge, *Table Talk,* August 20, 1833, in *The Complete Works of Samuel Taylor Coleridge,* ed. by W. G. T. Shedd (New York, 1884, 7 vols.), VI, 481; Samuel, *Plato and Milton,* pp. 45-67; and Langdon, *Milton's Theory of Poetry and Fine Art,* pp. 173-75. Charles W. Jones thinks that the "crucial passage" is the statement of Socrates that a poet and "good man ... will adopt a mode of narration such as we have illustrated out of Homer; that is to say, his style will be both imitative and narrative; but there will be very little of the former, and a great deal of the latter" (*The Republic of Plato,* 3.396, Jowett translation), because, according to Socrates, "a good man cannot imitate evil without impairment," (Jones, "Milton's 'Brief Epic,'" p. 219) and "will assume [the likeness of an evil man], if at all, for a moment only when he is performing some good action; at other times he will be ashamed to play a part which he has never practised, nor will he like to fashion and frame himself after the baser models" (*Republic,* 3.396). For Milton, the humanistic doctrine that the poet himself must be a "true poem" already is becoming a self-discipline in the *Sixth Elegy* (*Col.* I, 211, 213) in which Milton states that the epic poet in order to write with "high seriousness must preserve the loftiness of his inspiration and the sacredness of his office by repudiating worldly pleasures for spare living, strict purity, and chastity of life" (Barker, *Milton and the Puritan Dilemma,* p. 8; cf. "How soon hath time," Sonnet VII, *Col.* I, 60). Milton promised "a work ... to be rays'd ... by devout prayer to that eternall Spirit who can enrich with all utterance and knowledge, and sends out his Seraphim with the hallow'd fire of his Altar to touch and purify the lips of whom he pleases" (*RCG, Col.* III, 241).

16:23-24 A COMPOSITION ... THINGS — Plato said two things about poetry: "that poets are the inspired oracles of the gods and that poets ought to be banished from a perfect State" (Samuel, *Plato and Milton*, p. 46). Plato's reason for banishing poetry was because of "its damaging effect on the audience." Plato was stating that "the ultimate function of poetry, as of every activity, must be to make men better" (*ibid.*, p. 47). He questioned "the right of an art to exist in opposition to the end of all other human activity, the happiness that, according to him, is won only through the wisdom synonymous with virtue" (*ibid.*). Milton, by the time he was writing the *Apology*, thought a poem, a "composition, and patterne of the best and honourablest things." In the *Reason of Church-government* (*Col.* III, 181), Milton developed "the argument by which he could assign to poetry the rank of means, not end, and still justify himself as a poet" (Samuel, *Plato and Milton*, p. 50). That argument is "that persuasion is a better instrument than force for the improvement of men" (*ibid.*, p. 51). When "the cause of God and his Church was to be pleaded" Milton did not want to be declared "domb as a beast" (*RCG, Col.* III, 232-33). Milton purposed not to be a writer of "verbal curiosities ... but to be an interpreter & relater of the best and sagest things among mine own Citizens" (*ibid.*, p. 236). The poet, therefore, as a persuader to goodness takes his place with all those who seek to better life. Plato insisted that poetry serve morality, or be banished; Milton accepts for poety the "work to be done in the realms of true doctrine and social good" (Samuel, *Plato and Milton*, p. 59). Milton would provide against the bad in poetry by the "unwritt'n, or at least unconstraining laws of vertuous education" (*Areopagitica, Col.* IV, 318; cf. *Paradise Regained*, IV, 286-92; 318-27), for "doctrine and discipline are one" — the good man leaves his good mark (Samuel, *Plato and Milton*, p. 65). Plato held that honored poets are those "who in themselves are good" (*Laws* 7.829), and Milton held that the poem will be the "composition, and patterne of the best and honourablest things." Cf. 17:5-8.

16:25-26 HE HAVE IN HIMSELFE THE EXPERIENCE ... PRAISE-WORTHY — Cf. *Sixth Elegy* (*Col.* I, 211, 213), and Note 16:21-23.

16:29 ENVIE — *i.e.*, the envious; cf. 13:7; see Note 14:40.

16:29 MODESTY — Reserve arising from knowledge that one in estimating his qualities has not presumed or exaggerated. Hughes, *Milton Prose Selections*, p. 127 note, suggests Milton may have in mind the modesty attributed by Plato to the white horse (*Phaedrus*, 253), that symbol of the "soul's best aspirations," or Seneca's suggestion at the ending of Epistle XI, "On Shame," that serious men might well follow the advice of Epicurus "to choose some revered person and live constantly as if they were in his presence." Milton says in the *Reason of Church-government*:

It was thought of old in Philosophy, that shame or to call it better, the reverence of our elders, our brethren, and friends was the greatest incitement to vertuous deeds and the greatest dissuasion from unworthy attempts that might be. (*Col.* III, 259.)

16:30 NOT IN THE TITLE PAGE — The word "modesty" reminds Milton of the *Modest Confutation*. Milton had severely criticized the use of the word *modest* in a title (7:2-15) because its use prejudices the reader before he has considered the piece itself.

16:31 TO MAKE SOME BESEEMING PROFESSION — Cf. 14:37.

16:31-32 ALL THESE ... AIDE TOGETHER — Milton is summarizing the account of his moral development. His reasonings have made him aware that he can excel as a poet if he chooses wisely, and with a love of virtue, his object of celebration (16: 1-3). He determines that when the good and the fair meet in one person (16:9), that person can write sublime and pure thoughts. Milton has made a determined effort to "have in himselfe the experience and the practice of all that which is praiseworthy" (16:25-26). These reasonings have been supported by Milton's own personality, by his ambition, and by his modesty (16:27-29). The united force of these tendencies has always kept Milton above the "low [descent] of minde" which is the point of departure for those who force themselves into "salable and unlawfull prostitutions" (16:32-34). Milton is emphasizing that he did not at any time approach that mental state which would permit him to fall into sin. He has in mind the Confuter's charge of "harlotting" (*Modest Confutation*, Sig. A3 *recto*; see Note 11:16), and of frequenting the "Bordelloes" (*Modest Confutation*, Sig. [A3] *verso*; see Note 13:21-22). See Note 17:13-17.

16:35-36 WHETHER MY YOUNGER FEET WANDER'D — See Note 16:31-32.

16:36-37 LOFTY FABLES AND ROMANCES — Milton is thinking of the literature of chivalry. The Breton cycle has diverted and charmed him.

16:37-39 DEEDS OF KNIGHTHOOD... CHRISTENDOME — Milton is not now interested chiefly in diversion but in the moral problems and the moral values which were recounted and made famous throughout Christendom. He occupied himself seriously in the best Renaissance manner with the interpretation and moralization of these stories. Foremost in his mind are "the 'solemn cantos' of the 'sage and serious' Spenser" (Hanford, *Handbook*, p. 370; cf. M. M. Ross, *Milton's Royalism*, Ithaca, New York, 1943, pp. 48-49), who became a dominant influence which is witnessed not only in the allegory of *Comus,* but also in Milton's aspirations to write an Arthurian epic. In *Paradise Lost* (IX, 27-38) there is a reflection of Milton's early interest in the Arthurian legend which he considered at one time a fit subject for his "British" epic (*Mansus, Col.* I, 293).

16:38 KNIGHTHOOD... VICTORIOUS KINGS — Although Milton's chief interest is probably the legendary order of knighthood instituted by King Arthur, namely, the Knights of the Round Table, he seems also to be thinking of the Order of Garter, founded by King Edward III in 1334, and the Order of Bath, the foundation of which is generally attributed to Henry IV in 1399.

17:3 NOBLE VERTUE CHASTITY SURE MUST BE — The reading of the romances and fables confirmed Milton's judgments that the way of chastity that he followed was a noble one.

17:5-8 AND IF I FOUND... UNDECENT THINGS OF THE GODS — Again Milton becomes a law unto himself. Instead of becoming disillusioned and skeptical when an oath is broken, Milton blames the author for his failure to maintain

the moral standard. The moral law remains valid. Cf. 16:13-16; 17:13-17. Milton is referring to Plato's *Republic,* 2.377 ff., in which Plato accuses Homer of misrepresenting the gods when he recounts their quarrels and jealousies and attributes to them the evil in the world. Plato would not permit the Homeric tales in his State even though they were supposed by many to have an allegorical value. The passage is a detraction on poets who praise virtue but represent it as difficult and unpleasant, who portray the advantages of injustice over justice, who despise the poor who are admittedly superior in virtue, who show that the gods often direct misfortune against the virtuous while they favor the wicked. Plato could not permit poets in his *Republic* because they were a demoralizing factor; Milton held that lapses from morality in the work of poets is the fault of the poet, not of the virtue. Had Plato had all Miltons in his *Republic* he need not have worried about the evil effects of the inspiration of the poet. See Note 16:23-24.

17:9-13 EVERY... SPIRIT... OUGHT TO BE BORNE A KNIGHT... CHASTITY — Milton asserts that true virtue exists in the heart apart from all external ceremonies. The truly virtuous person will as a result of the inward urge "secure and protect the weaknesse of any attempted chastity."

17:10 GUILT — *i.e.,* gilt.

17:11 COUNSELL — *i.e.,* deliberate purpose; intent.

17:12 SECURE — *i.e.,* guard; make safe.

17:12-13 ANY ATTEMPTED CHASTITY — *i.e.,* anyone who attempted to live in a chaste manner.

17:13-17 EVEN THOSE BOOKS... BORDELLO'S — Milton's experience is one of constant growth toward the virtuous life as a result of a certain nicety of judgment that was able to discern and unify those things of eternal significance. Milton suggests that through God's particular favor he is destined to "the love and stedfast observation of that vertue." Milton's position has much in common with the Calvinistic doctrine of "irresistible grace": God, having elected and foreordained and predestined that certain individuals, irrespective of

their own merits, would be saved, infilled them with an irresistible grace which dominated their lives and made impossible the loss of their salvation. The great problem for the devotee was to ascertain that he was one of the elect. Any evidence that God was working through him was encouraging. Milton seems to feel that he has in some manner or another been the object of divine favor, that he has been directed by "divine indulgence" so that "those books which to many others have bin fuell of wantonnesse and loose living" become to him incitements toward virtue. Cf. 16:13-16; 17:5-8. The whole process of his mental and spiritual development has led away from the possibility of his indulging "the society of Bordello's." Cf. 16:31-33; 16:36-37; 17:39-18:2; 18:20. See Note 13:21-22 for the Bordello charge.

17:14 FUELL OF WANTONNESSE AND LOOSE LIVING — Keightley suggests that Milton was thinking in particular of the works of Ariosto (Keightley, *Life of Milton*, p. 365 note).

17:15 INDULGENCE — *i.e.*, favor.

17:18 LAUREAT — "Distinguished for excellence as a poet, worthy of the Muses' crown" (*OED*). Cf. *Lycidas*, 151, "To strew the Laureat Herse where *Lycid* lies." Milton is thinking chiefly of Dante, Petrarch (16:17-18), and Spenser. The title *poet laureate* was generally given to eminent poets. Petrarch was crowned poet laureate of Rome, April 8, 1341.

17:19 CEASELESSE ROUND OF STUDY AND READING — Cf. 13:11-14 and the "industrious and select reading" of *Reason of Church-government* (*Col.* III, 241). Milton's "ceaselesse round of . . . reading," particularly in Spenser, who had assimilated and embodied the Platonic concepts, led Milton chiefly to the "abstracted sublimities" (17:28) of Plato and Xenophon.

17:19-20 SHADY SPACES OF PHILOSOPHY — Ronald B. Levinson points out that this phrase seems

to bespeak [Milton's] acquaintance with Thomaso Aldobrandini's Latin version of Diogenes Laertius, Rome, 1594, where, in the life of Plato (Lib. III, p. 71 of the Stephanus-Casaubon edition, London, 1664), occurs the phrase "umbrosis spaciis Ecademi Dei," translating εὐσκίοις δρόμοισιν, a line from a play of Eupolis. In the Loeb Library version of Diogenes Laertius (I, 283), εὐσκίοις δρόμοισιν is given its literal

meaning, "shady walks." (Levinson, "Milton and Plato," p. 89.)

Keightley has suggested for spaces "*Spatia*, courses or rounds of the circus" (Keightley, *Life of Milton*, p. 365 note). "Spatium" also had the notion of the "bigness of anything" (Adam Littleton, *A Latine Dictionary*, London, 1678, 2 vols.) and may have the notion of "reaches."

17:20 PHILOSOPHY — Milton's interest in romantic poetry with its emphasis on the knight and on the oath to defend the "honour and chastity" of the lady leads by a sort of inevitable progression to the "high doctrine of love and virtue" found in the philosophy of Plato (see Hanford, *Handbook*, p. 370).

17:20 DIVINE VOLUMES OF *PLATO* — Milton seems to have studied Plato directly without recourse to the Platonism of the Alexandrians and their disciples in the Renaissance, and, consequently, to have seen Plato with "unprejudiced eyes" (Agar, *Milton and Plato*, pp. 31-32). He probably went to the Greek text, in which he discovered for himself what Plato had said. In *Comus* Milton had used what he had learned about chastity and love from Plato. Irene Samuel feels that the force of Milton's epithet "divine" shows that Milton's use of Plato is no longer that of conventionality, but that of an enthusiastic initiate into the "abstracted sublimities" (17:28): "For this is the language of an initiate, of one for whom the heart of an ethical doctrine has come alive," of a philosophical convert (Samuel, "Milton's Reference to Plato and Socrates," p. 56; cf. Samuel, *Plato and Milton*, p. 11). The "divine volumes" confirm the truth that had been growing in Milton that moral truth is unalterable. The notion, rather vague in Milton's earlier works, grows more distinct. In *Paradise Lost* "the eternal decrees of Justice . . . illustrate the absolute validity of *principles* as opposed to the fluctuations of occurrence, and so, too, in *Paradise Regained* the triumph of Good through Truth, Wisdom, and Justice" (Samuel, *Plato and Milton*, p. 145). Milton's emphasis on Plato in the *Apology* (9:27-39; 10:19) shows his debt to Plato. To no other writing except the Bible does he pay the high compliment of being divine. Furthermore, he places the writings of Plato in a position only less important than the

Bible (18:2-3), which is last in his account as "perfection is last" (17:35-36).

17:20-21 *PLATO . . . XENOPHON* — From Plato's works, especially *Phaedrus*, 246-56, and *The Symposium*, 202-12, and from Xenophon, Milton learned the doctrine of true love. Xenophon is secondary to Plato and is used for the purpose of emphasis. Irene Samuel (*Plato and Milton*, p. 22, note 29) has pointed out that only for the single passage in *Animadversions* beginning "so *Xenophon* writes of *Socrates*," (*Col.* III, 161), did Milton rely solely upon Xenophon as the authority (Xenophon, *Apology*, 26; *Memorabilia* I.2.1-8; I.6.11-13). However, he no doubt valued highly Xenophon's *Memorabilia*, a collection of the teachings wherewith Socrates had defended himself against the charge of corrupting the youth of Athens.

17:21 *EQUALL* — *i.e.*, contemporary; cf. 12:11 "equals."

17:21-27 *WHERE IF . . . THE SOULE* — The nature of this reference makes fairly certain that Milton has the tale of love of Diotima in mind as recounted in *The Symposium*, 202-12. Milton follows Plato in linking the "high mystery" of true love and the doctrine of chastity (see *Symposium*, 206-10a; cf. *Comus*, 784-88). In *Paradise Lost*, VIII, 588-94, Milton applies Plato's theory of love (cf. with eulogy to wedded love, *Paradise Lost*, IV, 750-70). Plato described love generally "as the love of the everlasting possession of the good" (*Symposium*, 206, Jowett translation), as the interpreter between the gods and men: "through [love] all the intercourse and speech of God with man . . . is carried on" (*ibid.*, 203). But Plato envisioned the progress from the appreciation of "fair forms to fair practices, and from fair practices to fair notions, until from fair notions [one] arrives at the notion of absolute beauty" (*ibid.*, 211). Once the person has the ability of "beholding beauty with the eye of the mind, he will be enabled to bring forth, not images of beauty, but realities (for he has hold not of an image but of a reality), and bringing forth and nourishing true virtue to become the friend of God and be immortal, if mortal man may" (*ibid.*, 212).

17:22 *THAT WHICH IS TRULY SO* — Milton is distinguishing between love and lust. Love "re-fines/The thoughts . . . hath his seat/In reason . . . is the scale/By which to heav'nly Love thou maist ascend" (*Paradise Lost*, VIII, 589-92); lust is the surrender of reason and will to the appetite. In the *Comus* Milton represents a rather negative doctrine of chastity. Milton promises, however, the "abstracted sublimities" (17:28). In his outlines for a tragedy on the subject of *Paradise Lost* he included in three drafts a figure "Heavenly Love" which may have been the intended representation of "love that is truly so" (see *Col.* XVIII, 228-29). That tragedy remained unwritten. However, in the epic *Paradise Lost*, " 'Heavenly Love,' the doctrine of the 'divine volumes' of Plato, is a major theme in the explanation Milton gives of the loss of happiness" (Samuel, *Plato and Milton*, pp. 161-62, is the basis for this discussion).

17:22-23 *WHOSE CHARMING CUP . . . VERTUE* — Levinson says that the passage describing "Love whose charming cup is only virtue," which he calls "Milton's miniature myth," reflects a "peculiarly Platonic style of allegory" (Levinson, "Milton and Plato," p. 89). Plato said that "all desire of good and happiness is only the great and subtle power of love" (*Symposium*, 205); and that "creative souls . . . conceive that which is proper for the soul to conceive or retain," that is "wisdom and virtue" (*ibid.*, 209). The lesser mysteries of love, Plato thought, could be enjoyed by the undisciplined soul. The "higher mysteries" could be gained by undergoing careful disciplining and by proving oneself worthy. There is the possibility that Milton's emphasis upon virtue may have a source in Seneca's *Of a Happy Life* (see 26:7) wherein Seneca shows that "*human happiness* is founded upon *wisdom* and *virtue*," and that there can be no happiness without virtue.

Virtue is that perfect good, which is the compliment of a *happy life*; the only immortal thing that belongs to mortality: it is the knowledge both of others and itself; it is an invincible greatness of mind, not to be elevated or dejected with good or ill fortune. It is sociable and gentle, free, steady, and fearless; content within itself; full of inexhaustible delights; and it is valued for itself. (*Seneca's Morals*, ed. by Sir Roger L'Estrange, Philadelphia, 1834, pp. 80 ff.)

17:23-24 *TO THOSE WHO ARE WORTHY* — Plato distinguishes between those whose bodies only are creative and those whose souls are creative.

The former strive for immortality by procreation; the latter strive to conceive wisdom and virtue. The offspring of the latter are the fairer and the more immortal. "These are the lesser mysteries of love" (*Symposium*, 209-10). He that is worthy (Diotima was not certain that Socrates could attain) can gain the greater and more hidden mysteries of love which crown the lesser, progressing from love of one beautiful form to the recognition of beauty in general, subsequently, to the love of all beautiful forms. Love of beautiful forms leads to the love of beauty of the mind, and that in turn to the beauty of the concept. Thereafter "he arrives at the notion of absolute beauty and at last knows what the essence of beauty is" (*ibid.*, 210-12; see Note 17:21-27). In the *Phaedrus*, Plato says: "Now he who has not been lately initiated or who has become corrupted, is not easily carried out of this world to the sight of absolute beauty in the other" (*Phaedrus*, 250, Jowett translation).

17:24-26 THE REST...CARRIES ABOUT — Having mentioned the charming cup of Platonic love, Milton turns to the "baneful cup" (*Comus*, 524) of Ovidian love. Having already distinguished the love "which is truly so," Milton turns to lust (see Note 17:22). In *Comus* Milton had dealt similarly with "saintly Chastity" and "lust" (*Comus*, 452-68). Comus was "Of Bacchus, and of Circe born" from whom he inherited the "witcheries" and the "baneful cup,/...whose pleasing poison/ The visage quite transforms of him that drinks" (*ibid.*, 521-26).

Although the Circe episode has its foundations in Book X of Homer's *Odyssey*, Milton was following Ovid, *Metamorphoses*, Book XIV, lines 1-69. The allegorizing of Circe's herd into men subdued by sensuality, probably beginning in Greek times, became "a commonplace of the Christian classicizers," and "a medieval possession through Boethius" (E. M. W. Tillyard, "The Action of *Comus*," *Essays and Studies by Members of the English Association,* XXVII (1942), Oxford, 1943, p. 28). Hanford says that the allegorizing of the Circe myth "had a precedent in the Platonizing mythographer, Heraclitus Ponticus, of whose *Allegoriae* [Milton] is known to have owned a copy" (Hanford, *Handbook*, p. 161). But Spenser's Bower of Bliss (*Faerie Queene*, Book II, Canto xii) is a "more immediate suggestion," for, as Hanford points out,

Acracia, "a Circe-like figure, the symbol of intemperance," is surrounded by those "who have been transformed to beasts" (Hanford, *Handbook*, p. 161). Milton's sorceress is

>   ...Circe
> The daughter of the Sun? Whose charmed Cup
> Whoever tasted, lost his upright shape,
> And downward fell into a groveling Swine.
>   (*Comus*, 50-53.)

According to the Ovidian account, the love of the sea-god Glaucus for Scylla having been spurned by her, he turns to the goddess Circe who, he knows, can with her "wonder-working Herbs" stir an "equal Flame" in Scylla. The story continues:

But Circe, (who of all her Sex had a Temper the most susceptible of this Passion, whether the Cause springs from herself, or that Venus, offended at the Discovery made by her Father, inflicted this Punishment in Revenge) thus replies: Pursue rather a willing Maid, whose Wishes correspond with your own, and who is smitten with a like Passion. You was worthy of a better Fate, and might justly claim to have been first sued to by her; nay, give but Hopes of your Compliance, and you shall be sued to in your Turn; doubt not of Success, but boldly confide in your Beauty. Lo! I a Goddess, the Daughter of the bright Sun, powerful by magic Charms, powerful by the Juice of Herbs, covet to be yours. Despise one that slights you, make a due Return to the Passion of one that loves you, and by this Act avenge us both.

Glaucus' reply to her soliciting is: "Sooner shall verdant Leaves grow on the Surface of the Deep, and Sea-Weed repair to the Tops of the Mountains, than any Passion for Scylla change." Circe thereupon compounds a charm from herbs to "wreak her Vengeance on her happier Rival." But after the revenge, Glaucus "shuns the Embraces of Circe, who had thus cruelly exerted the Power of Herbs against her Rival." (See *A New Translation of Ovid's Metamorphoses into English Prose*, London, 1748, pp. 482-85.)

The account presents two types of love: that love of Glaucus for Scylla which is proved to be a pure love, and that love of Circe for Glaucus which is proved to be passion. The same opposition of love and passion is pictured by Plato in *Phaedrus* in the two natures of the horses in the famous charioteer passage. Cf. *Paradise Lost*, V, 468-87; XII, 82-101.

17:26-27 THE FIRST AND CHIEFEST OFFICE OF LOVE, BEGINS AND ENDS IN THE SOULE — Plato ranks the creative soul above the creative body. The soul which is implanted with temperance and justice seeks the beautiful. When he is touched by the beautiful or comes into the presence of it "he brings forth the beautiful which he conceived long before, and the beautiful is ever present with him" (*Symposium,* 209). The "first and chiefest office of love" is to perceive the nature of beauty in its fullness. When love has led to ideal beauty, when the individual can behold beauty with the eye of the mind, he can bring into being not merely "images of beauty, but realities," and "bringing forth and educating true virtue to become the friend of God" (*ibid.,* 210-12). The soul, therefore, implanted with love, has a sense of imperfection until it attains to a measure of beauty. In its longing for perfection, it needs "for its satisfaction not so much outward acts as inward assurance" (Samuel, *Plato and Milton,* p. 154; see Milton's Letter to Diodati, dated September 23, 1637, in Phyllis B. Tillyard (trans.), *Milton Private Correspondence and Academic Exercises,* p. 13; cf. *Col.* XII, 25). Although physical beauty has a part in the progression toward ideal beauty, it is the "inward beauty of the noble soul which, Plato had taught, more truly reflects the perfect Idea of Beauty" (Samuel, *Plato and Milton,* p. 156) that attracted Milton (see Phyllis B. Tillyard (trans.), *Milton Private Correspondence and Academic Exercises,* p. 14; and *Col.* XII, 27). In *The Doctrine and Discipline of Divorce* Milton applies the notion that the "first and chiefest office of love, begins and ends in the soule," for true marriage can only exist where "the fit union of their souls be such as may incorporate them to love and amity; but that can never be where no correspondence is of the minde" (*Col.* III, 477-78), for from the mind "must flow the acts of peace and love" (*ibid.,* p. 393). Marriage is, therefore, a union of souls (see *Tetrachordon, Col.* IV, 90), and approximates the love which Christ has for his Church (*ibid.,* p. 192). Any other union is lustful. (For a full discussion see Irene Samuel, "The Doctrine of Love" in *Plato and Milton,* pp. 149-71.)

17:27-28 THOSE HAPPY TWINS . . . KNOWLEDGE AND VERTUE — Milton is probably referring to Diotima's statement that creative souls conceive wisdom and virtue (*Symposium,* 209). In *Meno, Protagorus,* and *Republic,* 10.618-19, Plato distinguishes between the "moral law of the community" and the "moral law of the uni-

verse." A knowledge of the latter constituted for Plato *virtue,* and was alone true knowledge, for "the moral law of the universe" alone was immutable and perfect. Any man who observed it secured happiness and was virtuous irrespective of the opinion of society. Any man who sinned against it, did so, Plato argued, because he was ignorant of it. Milton referred to the notion that "no *man is wicked willingly*" in *The Doctrine and Discipline of Divorce* (*Col.* III, 464).

17:28 SUEH — Printer's error for "such."

17:28 ABSTRACTED SUBLIMITIES — Reflects Diotima's words as she turns from earthly to heavenly love:

These are the lesser mysteries of love, into which even you, Socrates, may enter; to the greater and more hidden ones which are the crown of these, and to which, if you pursue them in a right spirit, they will lead, I know not whether you will be able to attain. (*Symposium,* 210; see also "perfect mysteries" of *Phaedrus,* 249.)

17:29-30 AS I MAY . . . STILL TIME — Milton is hinting that he shall celebrate the "abstracted sublimities," the "perfect mysteries," the "greater and more hidden" mysteries of love when he is not disturbed by the political and religious events and by personal defenses. Milton's early plans for a tragedy show "Heavenly Love" as one of the characters (see Note 17:22). *Paradise Lost,* in a sense, celebrates the "abstracted sublimities" (see *Paradise Lost,* IV, 750-57; VIII, 415-19; 449-51; 472-77; 551-53; 561-66; 586-94; 604-06; 610-13; 620-21). For Milton's ambitions in poetry see *Of Reformation, Col.* III, 78; *Reason of Church-government, Col.* III, 237 ff., and Note 37:12-13.

17:31 THE ADVERSARY — *i.e.,* the author of the *Modest Confutation.*

17:32 BURDELLO'S — See Notes 13:21-22 and 13:22.

17:33-35 LOST HIMSELFE . . . INQUIRE FOR SUCH A ONE — Milton insinuates that the Confuter has in his naive inquiry concerning Milton (cf. 11:15-16) at the "Bordelloes" become lost, and has forced the "prioress," who although rheumatic is wise in such matters, as well as her profligate laymen, to arise in order to answer his questions. The "*Prelatesse*" is a figure for the prelates; the

"Corinthian Laity," for those who support prelacy. In representing the bawd as a *"Prelatesse"* and the strumpets as a *"Corinthian Laity,"* Milton is bitterly satirizing the English Church. The name Corinthian, meaning prostitutes, relates to the licentious manners of Corinth.

17:35-36 LAST OF ALL ... AS PERFECTION IS LAST — Milton is giving the highest importance in the account of his moral development to the "precepts of Christian Religion." Cf. Note 17:20 DIVINE VOLUMES OF *PLATO.*

17:37-38 NOT TO BE NEGLIGENTLY TRAIN'D IN THE PRECEPTS OF CHRISTIAN RELIGION — Haller has attempted to re-create in a measure the religious life of the Miltons. The Bread Street house was in the parish of All-hallows and the church was a short distance away. The preacher must have played an important part in the Milton household. Richard Stock, who had received his M.A. at Cambridge about 1594, preached in the vicinity for more than thirty years. He died soon after Milton departed for Cambridge. He was depicted as a "perfect exemplar in pulpit and parish of all the familiar Puritan ministerial virtues," gaining the "highest praise that could come to the preacher, namely, that he was not only a winner of souls but a winner of such as proved winners of others." No doubt his teaching had an effective influence on Milton. Furthermore, there were other noted preachers within easy reach whom the Miltons went to hear (cf. 45:1-5). Godly living was the daily routine in the home. Thomas Young, a godly divine, became Milton's tutor. In his seventeenth year the young Milton left for Cambridge to enter the ministry (Haller, *Rise of Puritanism,* pp. 290-93). Milton stated that "by the intentions of my parents and friends I was destin'd of a child" to the service of the Church (*RCG, Col.* III, 242). Symmons "confidently [conjectures]" that Milton in the early period of his life "imbibed that spirit of devotion which actuated his bosom to his latest moment upon earth: and we need not extend our search beyond the limits of his own house for the fountain from which the living influence was derived" (Charles Symmons, *The Life of John Milton,* London, 1810, p. 53).

17:39 THOUGH — Even if.

17:39-18:2 THOUGH ... BURDELLO — Milton again affirms the power of a "reserv'dnesse of naturall disposition, and morall discipline learnt out of the noblest Philosophy," apart from religious training, to keep him from incontinence (cf. 16:31-33; 16:35-36; 17:13-17).

18:1 NOBLEST PHILOSOPHY — Cf. *Comus,* 475, "How charming is Divine Philosophy"; Seneca, *Of a Happy Life,* Chapter IV, that philosophy is the guide of life; and *Apology,* 17:21-24.

18:3-4 THE DOCTRINE OF HOLY SCRIPTURE UNFOLDING THOSE CHASTE AND HIGH MYSTERIES — Diotima turned from the "lesser mysteries ... to the greater and more hidden" (see Note 17:28 ABSTRACTED SUBLIMITIES), often called the "higher mysteries" of love. But to Milton the "chaste and high mysteries" are scriptural, for the Scriptures are "last" as "perfection is last" (17:35-36). Peter de la Primaudaye spoke of a similar distinction: He saw

two sorts of goods, the one which is the last end, the other is the meanes to attaine thereunto. The first is the souereigne, supreme, most perfect, and eternall good, which we expect and hope for in the immortalitie of the second life.... That which we call the meanes whereby we come to the first is vertue onely ... which is the proper effect of our regeneration by the spirit of God dwelling in vs.... Vertue ... is a disposition and power of the reasonable part of the soule, which bringeth into order and decencie the vnresonable part. ... Vertue is a proportion and vprightnes of life in all points agreeable to reason. The diuision thereof is altogither like to that of philosophie. For they are so linked togither, that it is all one to be vertuous, and to be a philosopher, the one thing being the matter and substance of the other. Vertue therefore is diuided into *Contemplatiue* and into *Morall.* The eternall Wisedome by the operation of his spirit, guideth and lifteth vp the contemplatiue vertue to hir proper end, which is that happie and immutable knowledge, that concerneth the maiestie of God.... [Socrates] could [not] finde amongst the race of men any greater vertue than religion and pietie towards God, whose honor is the foundation of euerie good worke.... Yea religion is not onely the head of iustice and vertue, but also is as it were the soule to giue vigor and strength vnto it." (Peter de la Primavdaye, *The French Academie,* London, 1586, pp. 52-53.)

It is important to realize that chastity meant in Milton's day monogamy as well as virginity. E. M. W. Tillyard, in "The Action of *Comus,*" has pointed out that Milton made changes in the *Comus* to accommodate his changing ideas. In the first version *Comus,* after praising the Lady's beauty, suggests, in order to turn her into a wanton, that her beauty was not given her so that she should become, as by intent she meant to become, a model of chastity. Later Milton saw that both the Lady's and Comus' ambitions were wrong, that the real meaning of her gifts was marriage. In the revision, therefore, "Comus advocates incontinence ... the Lady advocates abstinence. The Attendant Spirit gives the solution, advocating the Aristotelian middle course, which for the Lady is the right one; and it is marriage" (E. M. W. Tillyard, "The Action of *Comus,*" p. 35).

In the *Apology,* Milton with Plato's aid, passes from the natural level to the regions where the natural meets the religious; then with the help of the Scriptures he gains the fullness of the religious level. As he goes from level to level the doctrine of continence changes to the doctrine of chastity and then to the doctrine of virginity. Continence, taught by good poets, can be achieved on the basis of natural ethics. "Chastity, even in its 'abstracted sublimities,' may be learned from the wise and virtuous pagan philosophers ... who move likewise on the natural level but strain upwards to the very verge of the religious.... But above the natural level is the religious and there Christian doctrine is the only guide" (A. S. P. Woodhouse, "The Argument of Milton's *Comus,*" *University of Toronto Quarterly,* XI (1941), p. 51). Milton has described how he progressed upward as a result of his readings, arriving finally at the "high mysteries" of Christianity which confirmed those things he had learned on the natural level and which transcended them. His "reserv'dnesse of naturall disposition, and morall discipline" (17:40) was enough to cause him to disdain incontinence and love chastity. On the religious level he found the doctrine of virginity: considering the "high rewards of ever accompanying the Lambe" not granted to those who were "defil'd with women, which doubtlesse meanes fornication: For mariage must not be call'd a defilement" (18:13-17). Thus the broad scheme, continence, chastity, virginity (including marriage) which was basic in the revised *Comus* is basic also in the *Apology* (Woodhouse, *op. cit.,* p. 51. For the development of the implied doctrine of virginity in *Comus,* see also *ibid.,* pp. 60-61.). The "abstracted sublimies" (17:28) and

"those chaste and high mysteries" (18:3-4) are paralleled in *Comus* by "The sublime notion, and high mystery" (*Comus,* 784). Milton repudiated wisdom on the natural level when he turned to the religious level; he repudiated even the wisdom of ancient Greece and its philosophers. In *Paradise Regained,* IV, 288-92, he said:

> ... he who receives
> Light from above, from the fountain of light,
> No other doctrine needs, though granted true;
> But these are false, or little else but dreams,
> Conjectures, fancies, built on nothing firm.

18:4-5 *THE BODY ... THE BODY* — I Corinthians 6:13. Denis Saurat has seen in Milton's use of the Apostle Paul's words the first germs of the doctrine that "the body is not only *from,* but *of* the Lord: the body is a part of God, matter is a part of the Divinity." Milton, by virtue of his "pride and chastity," came to consider his body holy, as a part of the "substance of God" (Denis Saurat, *Milton, Man and Thinker,* New York, 1925, p. 46).

18:6-7 UNCHASTITY IN A WOMAN ... BE SUCH A SCANDALL AND DISHONOR — Milton is considering unchastity chiefly from the Biblical point of view in this instance. Unchastity in a woman was declared in the Hebrew Law to be punishable by death (Leviticus 20:10; 21:9). The scandal and dishonor of unchastity is reflected in such passages as Deuteronomy 22:13-27; Ezekiel 16:35-41; Leviticus 18:20; Job 31:9-10; and Proverbs 6:29.

18:6-7 GLORY OF MAN — I Corinthians 11:7.

18:8 BOTH THE IMAGE AND GLORY OF GOD — I Corinthians 11:7; cf. *Apology,* 18:12.

18:8-9 THOUGH COMMONLY NOT SO THOUGHT — Milton is witnessing to the tendency to look more leniently upon unchastity in men than in women.

18:9-10 DISHONOURABLE. IN — Modern usage demands that the clause, "In that he sins...." be connected to the preceding sentence of which it is syntactically a part.

18:10 SINS BOTH AGAINST HIS OWNE BODY — I Corinthians 6:18, "he that committeth fornication sinneth against his own body."

18:11 PERFETER SEX — Refers to I Corinthians 11:7-10 where Paul declares that man is "the image and glory of God: but the woman is the glory of the man. For the man is not of the woman; but the woman of the man. Neither was the man created for the woman; but the woman for the man." In Castiglione's *Book of the Courtier,* the most influential of all courtesy books, the assumption is made that "women are unperfect creatures, and consequently of lesse worthinesse than men" (Baldassare Castiglione, *The Book of the Courtier,* translated by Sir Thomas Hoby, Everyman's Library, London, 1928, p. 196). Milton accepted the view, but he was also aware of I Corinthians 7:11-12 which asserts the oneness and equality of man and woman in the Lord, Milton urged that the law should give "liberty and . . . human dignity" taking into account not only "mans right above the woman," but also "womans just appeal against wrong, and servitude" (*Tetrachordon, Col.* IV, 121), for the wife is not a servant (*ibid.,* p. 76).

18:11 HIS OWN GLORY WHICH IS IN THE WOMAN — I Corinthians 11:7, "but the woman is the glory of the man."

18:12-13 IMAGE AND GLORY OF GOD WHICH IS IN HIMSELFE — See Note 18:8.

18:13-16 THAT PLACE . . . WOMEN — Milton is referring to Revelation 14:3-4. Milton has turned from Platonic love to Christian chastity, finding special significance in the song which "no man could learn" except those "not defil'd with women" who have followed the Lamb of God. The "celestiall songs" which are sung to the Lamb of God celebrate the marriage of the Lamb with those who, because they have through their redemption become worthy of Him, are to become his bride (see Revelation 19:1-8). Hanford has judged that the *Comus* (1634) is the outcome of Milton's "elevated yet fervid imaginings" for there one can trace "the correlative influences of Spenserian, Platonic, and Apocalyptic allegory" (Hanford, *Handbook,* p. 371. See Note 18:3-4 for other comments on the relationship between *Comus* and this passage.). The theme of the Attendant Spirit's Epilogue (*Comus,* 975-1022) is the "mystic marriage of the pure soul with God" (Hanford, *Handbook,* p. 371), portrayed in Spenserian and Platonic imagery. To the "unex-

pressive nuptial Song" Milton refers in *Lycidas* (1637), 176, and in *Damon's Epitaph* (1640), 215-19 (*Col.* I, 316-17).

18:16 WHICH DOUBTLESSE MEANES FORNICATION — Cf. I Corinthians 6:18; 7:2. Fornication is sin against one's own body as distinguished from other sins that are "without the body"; therefore, Paul suggests, *"to avoid* fornication let every man have his own wife, and let every woman have her own husband."

18:17 MARIAGE MUST NOT BE CALL'D A DEFILEMENT — Saurat calls this statement the "corrective to *Comus,* to the hymn to total chastity" (Saurat, *Milton, Man and Thinker,* p. 46), and Tillyard more cautiously says that this statement shows that Milton "no longer considers marriage a defilement (as in some sort he appears to have considered it in *Comus)"* (E. M. W. Tillyard, *Milton,* p. 139. For comments that show the harmony of ideas in *Comus* and the *Apology* see Note 18:3-4.). Milton's defense of marriage, based scripturally on Hebrews 13:4, emphasizes the distinction, much discussed by the Elizabethans, between "love commanded and love forbidden, love and lust" (Saurat, *Milton, Man and Thinker,* p. 46). Lust is here considered the "lowest degradation of men" (*ibid.;* see Notes 18:16, 17:22, and 17:24-26). Milton had the full support of Calvin in the stand he took on marriage, for Calvin declared: "the Apostle doth without exception boldly pronounce, that marriage is honorable among all men, but that for whoremongers, and adulterers abideth the iudgement of God" (*The Institution of Christian Religion, written in Latine by M. John Caluine, and translated into English . . . by Thomas Norton,* London, 1587, IV, xii, 25).

18:17 LARGE — *i.e.,* lengthy, copious.

18:19-20 TENNE-FOLD SHAME — Milton is calling down upon himself a curse if what he said is not truth. He accepts the full responsibility in thus accounting for his life, even as those who accused Jesus before Pilate, who declared, "His blood *be* on us, and on our children" (Matthew 27:25).

18:20 OPPROBRIOUS WORD — The word which has been anathema to Milton, and which he has spent his pages (15:18-19:3) refuting because

it negates the idealism upon which he has founded
his life, is "Bordello" (17:17, 18:2, 18:36-38; see
also Note 17:13-17).

18:21-22 I MAY . . . I HAVE PROFEST — Milton feels that if he has proved by his revelation of
the development of his inward thoughts, and he is
confidently certain he has, that no "opprobrious
word, or suspicion" can be attached to himself, he is
free to proceed openly in practicing those things he
has professed. Cf. 3:27-31.

18:24-25 BEYOND ALL TRUTH & SHAME —
Cf. 11:5-15; 11:20.

18:25-26 FROM THE SINGLE NOTICE . . .
CLOATHS I WEARE — The Confuter, having
said: "*I have no further notice of him, than he hath
been pleased, in his immodest and injurious Libell*
[*i.e., the *Animadversions*] *to give of himself*"
(*Modest Confutation*, Sig. A3 recto), departs from
the policy of fetching Milton's "*character from some
scattered passages in his own writings*" (*ibid.*) to
make an application to Milton of Stilpo's remark to
Crates: "'ὦ κράτης, εἶπε, δοκεῖς μοι χρείαν ἔχειν ἱματίου
καινοῦ.' ὅπερ ἦν νοῦ καὶ ἱματίου." (Diogenes Laertius,
"Stilpo," 6, translated by C. D. Yonge, " 'Crates,
you seem to me to want a new dress,' meaning, both
a new mind and a new garment," in Diogenes
Laërtius, *The Lives and Opinions of Eminent Philosophers*, p. 102), which the Confuter copies on
the margin (*Modest Confutation*, Sig. [A3] verso)
thus: "ὦ κράτης, δοκεῖς μοι χρείαν ἔχειν ἱματίου καινοῦ,
ὅπερ ἦν νοῦ καὶ ἱματίου Lae't. lib. 2. in vita Stilpon."
The Confuter's implication is that Milton, who has
lately needed "a new mind and a new garment," has
now assumed a role of importance and a new re-
spectability. Therefore the Confuter says of Milton:
"*Many* [times] *of late, since he was out of Wit
and Cloaths, as Stilpo merrily jeered the poore
Starveling* Crates, *he is new cloathed in Serge, and
confined to a Parlour*; *where he blasphemes God
and the King, as ordinarily as erewhile he drank
Sack or swore*" (*ibid.*). The application emphasized
the previously made Bordello charge, which became
the reason not only for the autobiographical passage
(see Note 18:20) but for much of the *Apology*.

18:27 HE BE MUCH MISTAKEN IN MY
WARDROBE — Milton emphasizes again how far
afield the Confuter has been in connecting him in

any way with the "Bordellos" (see Notes 17:13-17,
18:20, and 18:25-26). The Confuter had inferred
that Milton was a churchman, a "small Clerk," from
Milton's references to the "great Clarks" (*ANIM,
Col*. III, 118) and from his prayer (*ibid.*, pp. 146-
48). That matter Milton considers in Section ten
(*Apology*, 42:1-46:29). For the moment he reminds the Confuter that the Confuter has completely mistaken Milton's wardrobe.

18:27-28 SON OF BELIAL WITHOUT THE
HIRE OF *IESABEL* — See I Kings 21:9-10,
"And she [Jezebel] . . . set two men, sons of Belial,
before him, to bear witness against him, saying,
Thou didst blaspheme God and the King."

18:28-29 *OF BLASPHEMING . . . AND
SWEARE* — "*. . . he is new cloathed in Serge, and
confined to a Parlour; where he blasphemes God and
the King, as ordinarily as erewhile he drank Sack
or swore*" (*Modest Confutation*, Sig. [A3] verso).
The Confuter may have been thinking of Falstaff
when he mentioned drinking and swearing.

18:30 COMMON PLACE-BOOK — Frequently
written "commonplace-book." A blank book often
used for the collection of interesting or valuable
literary extracts. Cf. Note 36:32.

18:31 EMPIRICK — A member of the sect
among ancient physicians called Empirici, who,
unlike the Dogmatici and Methodici, drew their
rules of practice entirely from experience, to the
exclusion of philosophical theory.

18:33 WHOM WHAT — "Whom" stands for
"him"; "what" seems to stand for the Latin "quid"
meaning "why" (Thompson, "Milton's Prose Style,"
p. 3).

18:34 THAT BOOK — *i.e.*, the *Animadversions*.

18:34 HIS ONLY TESTIMONY — Cf. 11:5-15
and 18:25-26.

18:34-36 RETURNES THE LYE . . .
SWEARER, OR A SACK DRINKER — A sec-
ond time Milton protests (see 18:25-26) that nothing in the *Animadversions,* from which the Confuter
claims to draw his information (18:25), gives the
least hint that its author is a "swearer, or a Sack
drinker." Milton is cautious in choosing not to deny
the charge of blaspheming "*God and the King*" (18:

28), for the evidence that the Confuter presents (see Note 19:4-5) *might* be construed if closely inspected to be blasphemy. Milton prefers to draw attention where he is perfectly safe, throwing discredit upon the Confuter there and allowing the effects of the discrediting to negate those statements which cannot be closely scrutinized.

18:36-38 AND FOR THE READERS ... NOR UNCHASTE — Cf. Notes 17:13-17, 18:20, and 18:21-22. Again Milton pleads that the reader believe him honest and chaste on the basis of his revelation of himself (15:18-18:36). He is approaching the end of his defense of himself from the dreadful charge of frequenting the "Bordelloes." He has, as it were, opened his inward thoughts to the reader. He has discredited the Confuter. He can ill afford to let the reader forget the contumely with which the Confuter has attacked him; on the other hand, he can ill afford to allow the reader's sympathy to wane. See also 32:30-33.

18:39-40 SOBER ... OF WINE, AND OF WORD — Note that "sober" carries the connotations "habitually temperate" and "serious," respectively, as applied to its phrasal modifiers.

19:1-3 BETTER THRIFT ... NEEDLESSE HEARING — Cf. 4:3-6.

19:4 GING — Company, pack — the simple sense of the word has been transferred boldly to the analogical use.

19:4-5 GING OF WORDS AND PHRASES NOT MINE, FOR HE HATH MAIM'D THEM — Milton is complaining that he has been misrepresented. The Confuter's words are paralleled with Milton's to show that the complaint is partially justified:

"Our Liturgie runnes up and down like an English galloping Nun, *Pag.* 16." — *Modest Confutation,* Sig. [A3] *verso.*

"And indeed our *Liturgie* hath run up and downe the world like an English galloping Nun, proffering her selfe, but wee heare of none yet that bids money for her." — *ANIM* (1641), p. 16 (*Col.* III, 122).

"While shee prankes her selfe in the weeds of Popish Masse, she provokes the jelousie of God, no otherwise than a Wife affecting Whorish attire, *Pag.* 22." — *Modest Confutation,* Sig. [A3] *verso.*

"... so long as she symbolizes in forme, and pranks her selfe in the weeds of *Popish* Masse, it

may be justly fear'd shee provokes the jealousie of God, no otherwise then a wife affecting whorish attire kindles a disturbance in the eye of her discerning husband." — *ANIM* (1641), p. 22 (*Col.* III, 129).

"Liturgie a bait for them (*Papists* to bite at, *Pag.* 23." — *Modest Confutation,* Sig. [A3] *verso.*

"... you should have given so much honour then to the word preach't, as to have left it to Gods working without the interloping of a Liturgy baited for them to bite at." — *ANIM* (1641), p. 23 (*Col.* III, 130).

"A Pharisaicall and vain-glorious project, *Ibid.*" — *Modest Confutation,* Sig. [A3] *verso.*

"It was Pharisaicall, and vain-glorious, a greedy desire to win Proselites...." — *ANIM* (1641), p. 23 (*Col.* III, 130).

"God hath taught them (*the People*) to detest your Liturgie and Prelacy, *Pag.* 24." — *Modest Confutation,* Sig. [A3] *verso.*

"... God hath now taught them [the Christian multitude] to detest your *Liturgie* and *Prelacie:*" — *ANIM* (1641), p. 24 (*Col.* III, 131. Words within brackets are mine.).

"Is Liturgie good or evill? Evill? *Pag.* 26." — *Modest Confutation,* Sig. [A3] *verso.*

"It is evill:" — *ANIM* (1641), p. 26 (*Col.* III, 133).

"A Meditation of yours observed at Lambeth from the Archiepiscopall Kittens, *Pag.* 29." — *Modest Confutation,* Sig. [A3] *verso.*

"A Meditation of yours doubtlesse observ'd at *Lambeth* from one of the *Archiepiscopall Kittens.*" — *ANIM* (1641), p. 29 (*Col.* III, 137).

"The Prelates would have Saint *Pauls* words ramp one over another, *Pag.* 40." — *Modest Confutation,* Sig. [A3] *verso.*

"... But surely the *Prelates* would have Saint *Pauls* words rampe one over another, as they use to clime into their Livings and *Bishopricks.*" — *ANIM* (1641), p. 40 (*Col.* III, 150).

"Let not those wretched Fathers think they shall impoverish the Church of willing and able supply, though they keep back their sordid sperm, begotten in the lustinesse of their avarice, *Pag.* 57." — *Modest Confutation,* Sig. [A3] *verso.*

[Essentially as quoted] — *ANIM* (1641), p. 57 (*Col.* III, 165).

"Lest thinking to offer them as a Present to God, they dish them out for the Divell, *Pag.* 58." — *Modest Confutation,* Sig. [A3] *verso* and [A4] *recto.*

"... lest, thinking to offer him as a present to God, they dish him out for the Devill." — *ANIM* (1641), p. 58 (*Col.* III, 165).

"Your Confutation hath atchieved nothing against it, (*The Reply by* SMECTYMNUUS) left nothing upon it, but a foule taste of your Skillet foot; and a more perfect and distinguishable odour of your Socks than of your Night-cap, *Pag. 67*" — *Modest Confutation*, Sig. [A4] *recto*.

> [Practically verbatim] — *ANIM* (1641), p. 67 (*Col.* III, 176) ; see Note 19:18-19.

19:6 LIMBO — The abode of the just who died before Christ's coming and of unbaptized infants in a region on the border of Hell. The meaning here is of an unfavorable place, a place of oblivion for the absurd, useless, or outworn. Cf. *Paradise Lost,* III, 440-98; see Note 49:21.

19:6-7 W O R S E . . . *D E I P H O B U S . . . AENEAS* — See Virgil's *Aeneid,* Book VI, 494-547. The ghost of Deiphobus appears to Aeneas, its features so marred and lacerated that Aeneas scarcely recognizes him. The ghost, to Aeneas' queries, relates how he was betrayed and killed on the night Troy fell.

19:8 REPAIRE — Go; resort.

19:9 THAT BOOKE — The *Animadversions.*

19:9-10 TORMENTER OF SEMICOLONS — The meaning of the word "semicolon" may be illustrated by the following quotations:

"At a comma, stop a little . . . At a semi-colon, somewhat more." — Hodges *English Primrose* N3 (1644) (see *OED*, "Semicolon").

"A Semicolon is a distinction of an imperfect Sentence, wherein with somewhat a longer Breath, the Sentence following is included." — B. Jonson's "English Grammar," in *The Works* . . . London, 1692, p. 690.

The Confuter in the preface "To the Reader" of the *Modest Confutation*, Sig. A3 *recto*-[A4] *verso*, uses the semicolon (1) to separate a subordinate clause having parenthetical elements from its dependent clause, (2) to separate coordinate clauses, (3) to separate a preposition having a series of objects from the rest of the sentence, (4) to separate the latter of two phrasal objects of a preposition from the former, (5) to separate an adjective subordinate clause from the element it modifies, (6) and to separate the latter verb of a compound predicate from the former.

19:10 DISMEMBRING AND SLITTING SENTENCES — See 19:4-5. Note the paralleling with "stigmatizing & slitting noses" (19:11-12).

19:11-12 PRELATES . . . NOSES — The allusion is to the cruel persecutions of the Puritans with a special reference to the case of Alexander Leighton which was long remembered by Laud's enemies. Alexander Leighton had in 1628 put forth the pamphlet *An Appeal To the Parliament: Or Sions Plea against the Prelacie,* proposing the immediate abolition of prelacy root and branch. Upon the order of Star Chamber he was fined, imprisoned, and scourged; his ears were cropped, his nose was slit, and his forehead was branded.

19:12 THIS — *i.e.,* "dismembering and slitting sentences" (19:10).

19:12 TRADUCE — Deduce; bring forth.

19:13-14 ONLY . . . SMELLING — A variation of the proverb commonly phrased "The fox smells his own stink first" (see William George Smith, *The Oxford Dictionary of English Proverbs,* Oxford, 1935, p. 438, who cites no earlier instance than that in Swift's *Polite Conversations*). In John Bridges' *A Defence Of The Government Established In The Chvrch Of England For Ecclesiasticall Matters* (London, 1587), p. 7, is an allusion to the proverb: " . . . as the old saying accordeth, the Foxe the first fynder." Joseph Hall in his *Defence Of The Humble Remonstrance* (1641), p. 36, said: "Wanton wits must have leave to play with their owne sterne." That statement Milton repeated and answered in the *Animadversions* (1641), p. 29 (*Col.* III, 137). In *Colasterion* (*Col.* IV, 257) Milton said: "it offends him that rankest should signify ought, but his own smell."

19:14 BESTOW HIS FOOT AMONG US — Hall, in "To the Postscript" of *A Defence Of The Humble Remonstrance,* p. 167, applies the proverb concerning the bishop's foot (see Note 19:18-19) by saying: "*The Bishops foot hath been in your Book,* for I am sure it is quite spoiled by this just confutation." Hall is calling his own *Defence* the bishop's foot, which he has placed in "*your Book,*" that is, the Smectymnuan *Answer To . . . An Humble Remonstrance,* and "*spoiled*" it. Robert Lord Brooke mentions the proverb (*Nature of Episcopacy,* p. 47): "What Our Bishops did in Queene Maries dayes (Bloody Times!) we all know; sure it was an unhappy Proverb that was then learnt, *The Bishops foote hath trodden here.*"

19:15 NOT ALLOW US TO THINK HE WEARES A SOCK — *i.e.,* not allow us to think that he hides anything. The sock hides the actual condition of the bishop's foot (see 19:25-30), and is metonymical for the surplice even as the foot stands for the bishop himself. Although the sock hides the foul conditions it covers, it takes to itself the odor thereof, which, though only a token of what is concealed, is offensive to the bishop himself, to others, and to heaven.

19:15-16 ENDEAVOUR IT MAY BE — Try to make it.

19:17 GRAVE AND REVEREND MEN HIS ADVERSARIES — *i.e.,* the Smectymnuans. See Note 3:34.

19:18-19 THE BISHOPS FOOT...CONFUTED IT — The Smectymnuans in *An Answer To...An Humble Remonstrance,* pp. 103-04, started the business of the bishop's foot. They claimed that the prelates designed

to hinder all further reformation; to bring in doctrines of Popery, Arminianisme, and Libertinisme, to maintaine, propagate and much encrease the burden of humane ceremonies: to keepe out, and beate downe the Preaching of the Word, to silence the faithfull Preachers of it, to oppose and persecute the most zealous professours, and to turne all Religion into a pompous out-side. And to tread downe the power of godlinesse. Insomuch as it is come to an ordinary Proverb, that when any thing is spoyled wee use to say, *The Bishops foot hath beene in it.* And in all this (and much more which might be said) fulfilling Bishop *Bonners* Prophesie, who when hee saw that in King *Edwards* reformation, there was a reservation of ceremonies and Hierarchy, is credibly reported to have used these words; *Since they have begun to tast of our Broath, it will not be long ere they will eat of our Beefe.*

Hall answered in *A Defence Of The Humble Remonstrance,* p. 167:

if whatsoever is spoiled, they say, *The Bishops foot hath been in it*; I doubt not but they will say, *The Bishops foot hath been in your Book,* for I am sure it is quite spoiled by this just confutation. After your own pottage (for your Proverb; *sapit ollam*) you tell us of *Boner's broath*; I should have too much wondred at this conclusion, but that I hear it is the fashion in some Countries, to send in their Keal in the last service; and this, it seems, is the manner amongst our *Smectymnuans.*

Hall's words were quoted in part by Milton in the *Animadversions* (1641), pp. 66-67 (*Col.* III, 176),

who, after having turned Hall's words to make a favorable comparison between bishops and "a *Scurra* in *Trivio,* or som Ribald upon an Ale-bench" (see Note 19:21-23), answered:

Spoyld quoth ye? indeed it is so spoyld, as a good song is spoyld by a lewd singer, or as the saying is, God sends meat, but the Cooks worke their wills; in that sense we grant your Bishops foot may have spoyld it, and made it *Sapere ollam* [to savor of the pot], if not *Sapere aulam* [to savor of princely power, or dignity], which is the same in old Latin, and perhaps in plaine English. For certaine your confutation hath atchiev'd nothing against it, and left nothing upon it, but a foule taste of your skillet soot, and a more perfect and distinguishable odour of your socks, then of your night-cap. And how the Bishop should confute a book with his foot, unless his braines were dropt into his great toe, I cannot meet with any man that can resolve me, onely they tell me that certainly such a confutation must needs be goutie. So much for the Bishops foot. (*ANIM* (1641), pp. 66-67; *Col.* III, 176-77. The term "skillet soot" was transcribed "Skillet foot" by the Confuter (see the Confuter's quotation which concludes this note), and has been likewise transcribed in the Columbia edition of Milton. In the *OED,* under the word "skillet," it has been correctly transcribed. When the term is considered in its context and in its background, there is no compelling reason to assume that the word "foot" was intended. The term "skillet soot" does not have the doubtful signification or unintelligibility that the term "skillet foot" presents. Milton makes no reference to the "skillet foot" when he questions "what odor a Sock would have in such a painfull businesse," and concludes that he quite innocently touched the Remonstrant "more nearly then I was aware" (19:16-24). The truth of the matter seems to be that Hall's quotation concerning "pottage...*sapit ollam*...*Boner's broath*" reminded Milton that the Latin word *olla* meaning "pot" had an old form *aula* which was identical with the word *aula* meaning "princely power, dignity." It further reminded him of the saying "God sends meat, but the Cooks worke their wills." Milton's retort to the "you tell us of *Boner's broath*...*Smectymnuans*" develops the cook and kitchen theme (*ANIM* (1641), p. 67; *Col.* III, 177). Therefore, the term "skillet soot" seems to be logical and necessary.)

The Confuter in the *Modest Confutation* (Sig. [A4] recto) selected a part of the passage from the *Animadversions* to include in his quotations to prove that Milton "*blasphemes God and the King, as ordinarily as erewhile he drank Sack or swore*" (see Note 18:28-29):

Your Confutation hath atchieved nothing against it, (*The Reply by* SMECTYMNUUS) left nothing upon it, but a foule taste of your Skillet foot; and a more perfect and distinguishable odour of your Socks than of your Night-cap, *Pag.* 67.

19:19 ARROGATE — Claim an advantage without just reason.

19:19-21 TO HAVE DONE...OF HIS HEAD — Cf. 4:31-34.

19:20 HEELES — Metonymical for foot.

19:21 TO SPURN A CONFUTATION — "Spurn", that is, to treat contemptuously, is an apt word in the context for in its literal meaning there is the idea of "kick" (cf. Note 19:38). The confutation in this case is the Smectymnuan *An Answer*.

19:21 RESPECTED MEN — See Notes 3:34 and 19:17.

19:21-23 I QUESTION'D...BUSINESSE — *i.e.*, I did not think it unlawful to disturb his jollity by calling to his attention what an "odor a Sock would have in such a painfull businesse." The jollity Milton has in mind is Hall's attempt to discountenance the proverb *"The Bishops foot hath beene in it"* (see Note 19:18-19) by saying:

As for that base and scurrilous Proverb, to which you say it is now comme (whereas the World knows it is elder then your Grandsires, and was taken up, in the popish times) it were more fit for a *Scurra in trivio* [buffoon on the street corner], or some rivald [ribald] upon an Ale-bench, then for grave Divines. (Hall, *Defence,* p. 166.)

Milton had quoted from the passage,

As for that proverb, the Bishops foot hath been in it, it were more fit for a *Scurra* in *Trivio*, or som Ribald upon an Ale-bench (*ANIM* (1641), p. 66; *Col.* III, 176),

and had answered: "The fitter for them then of whom it was meant" (*ibid.*). Milton had then proceeded to quote Hall's statement that *"The Bishops foot hath been in your Book,"* and had answered that the bishop's foot had "atchiev'd nothing," but had left the "foule taste of your skillet soot, and a more perfect and distinguishable odour of your socks" (see Note 19:18-19).

19:22 TO BETHINK HIM — An obsolete reflexive meaning "to remind himself"; cf. *Eikonoklastes, Col.* V, 309, "To bethink themselves, and recover."

19:24 THIS...AWARE — "This" refers to the previous line: "What [an] odor a Sock [surplice] would have in such a painfull businesse [contro-

versy]." Bishop Hall had turned the proverb, *"The Bishops foot hath beene in it,"* spoken of anything that was spoiled, against the Smectymnuans by saying of their *Answer, "The Bishops foot hath been in your Book,* for I am sure it is quite spoiled by this just confutation." Milton had picked up the statement in the *Animadversions* and, elaborating upon the figure of speech, had said in effect that Hall's confutation had not spoiled the Smectymnuan *Answer,* but had left the taste of his soot and the disagreeable odor of his socks rather than the fresh odor of his nightcap. Milton now conjectures that the author of the *Defence* feels that he has been recognized as a bishop and that the figure of speech is too applicable to the position of the bishop for comfort (19:25-30), wherefore he has in the *Modest Confutation* repeated the apt figure of speech to prove that Milton *"blasphemes God and the King"* (see Note 19:18-19).

19:24 NEERLY — *i.e.*, closely.

19:25 MAUGRE — Notwithstanding, from French *malgre.*

19:27 PLURALIST — A clergyman who holds two or more benefices or offices at one time. Hall, on December 23, 1627, had been consecrated to the see of Exeter, and allowed because of "the small revenue of the see, to hold the living of St. Breoc *in commendam"* (*DNB*, VIII, 961). In fact, as early as 1616 he had become a pluralist, holding the Deanery of Worcester and the living at Waltham (George Lewis, *A Life of Joseph Hall,* London, 1886, pp. 173-74). Only a few months prior to Milton's writing of the *Apology,* on November 15, 1641, Hall had been translated to the see of Norwich.

19:28-29 FOURE BENEFICES BESIDES THE METROPOLITAN TOE — The large toe Milton likens to the position as head of an ecclesiastical province which in England is approximately coextensive with the domain of the Archbishop, and the small toes to lesser preferments held at the same time.

19:29 FOULER STENCH — The practice of holding more than one living had long been under attack. See 57:33-58:15.

19:29-30 FOULER STENCH...THEN THAT ...RECHES AT — Milton is saying that the "pluralist...sends a fouler stench to heaven, then that [stench, *i.e.*, the collection of quotations that the Confuter has selected from the *Animadversions* (see Note 19:4-5) to prove that Milton *'blasphemes God and the King'* (see Note 18:28-29)] which this young queasinesse [*i.e.*, the Confuter, who has pretended nausea at Milton's stench] reches at." The "reches at" refers to the Confuter's statement, after he had listed the quotations from the *Animadversions* to which he objected most violently:

Christian, doest thou like these passages? or doth thy heart rise against such unseemly beastlinesse? (*Modest Confutation*, Sig. [A4] *recto*.)

19:30 QUEASINESSE RECHES AT — Cf. 12:33, "kecking at, and is queasie." *Batman vppon Bartholome*, Bk. VII, ch. 47, fol. 104 *recto* and *verso,* gives a description "Of Spuing" as

...mooving and quaking of lippes, and forcing and anguishe of the spirituall members, wambling and abhomination, opening of the mouth, stretching of the tongue, stretching of veines, of pipes, and of sinewes, teares in the eyen, running out of sweate, chaunging of the throate, and bitternesse and infection of the tongue, of the palat, and of the mouth.

19:31-32 AS PERFET AN HYPOCRITE AS *CAIAPHAS,* ERE HE [the Confuter] BE A HIGH PRIEST — See Matthew 26:57-66. Milton likens the Confuter, not yet a high priest, yet charging blasphemy (*Apology*, 18:28-29), to the hypocritical Caiaphas, the high priest, who charged Jesus with blasphemy.

19:32-33 *HORRID BLASPHEMY!* — Blasphemy, the speaking of God or sacred things in a profane manner, was to be punished with death according to the Hebrew Law (see Leviticus 24:16; I Kings 21:10; Matthew 26:65-66). Milton is referring to the Confuter's climactic words in the preface:

[This is nothing disagreeing from Christian meeknesse, *Pag.* 2. Not unauthorised from the Morall precept of *Solomon,* — Nor from the example of Christ, and all his Followers, in all ages, *Ibid.*] *Horrid blasphemy! You that love Christ, and know this miscreant wretch, stone him to death, lest your selves smart for his impunity.* (*Modest Confutation,* Sig. [A4] *recto.* The brackets in the quotation are the Confuter's, the citations in the bracketed portion were taken by the Confuter from *Animadversions* (1641), p. 2 (*Col.* III, 106).)

19:33 LIKE A RECREANT JEW CALLS FOR *STONES* — See previous Note. Observe Milton's

matching of "recreant Jew" with the Confuter's "miscreant wretch."

19:33 RECREANT — Apostate, unfaithful to one's duty, false; cf. "Turn'd recreant to God, ingrate and false" (*Paradise Regained*, III, 138).

19:34 RESOLVE — *i.e.,* assure or convince one on some point.

19:35 CHRISTIAN MEEKNESSE — See Galatians 5:22-23; 6:1; Ephesians 4:2; Colossians 3:12; I Timothy 6:11; II Timothy 2:25; Titus 3:2; Matthew 5:5.

19:36 WHEN AS...TRADITIONS — Matthew 23:1-33; Mark 7:5-13; Luke 11:37-54. See *Apology,* 23:24-26.

19:37 DUNGHILL — Luke 14:35 (cf. Luke 13:8).

19:37 JAKES — *i.e.,* a privy, used synonymously with "Dunghill."

19:38 WINCER — *i.e.,* a kicker; cf. Note 19:21 TO SPURN A CONFUTATION.

19:40 MUSK, NOR BENJAMIN — "Musk" is the odoriferous substance, secreted in the gland or sac by the male musk-deer, that is used as the basis of many perfumes. "Benjamin," a corruption of "benjoin," is a dry, brittle, resinous substance, having a fragrant odor (*OED*).

19:40-20:2 THUS DID THAT FOOLISH MONK...WINES — When Petrarch learned that Nicole Oresme had been sent by Charles V of France to Pope Urban V to attempt to influence the Pope not to return the residence of the Pontificate to Rome, Petrarch wrote the Pope a letter in order to establish the relative merits of the two rival countries, France and Italy ("Epistolarum de rebus senilibus," Liber IX, Epistola 1), much to the discredit of France. Petrarch's letter was answered anonymously by a Frenchman. A. Mézières (*Petrarque,* Paris, 1895, p. 314-15) says of the Frenchman and Petrarch:

Notre défenseur, dont le talent n'égale pas la bonne volonté, s'indigne surtout qu'on se permette de traiter les Français de barbares. Qu'est-ce que la barbarie, sinon l'ignorance, la rudesse, la grossièreté? Rien de plus poli, au contraire, de plus aimable et de plus civilisé que les Français. C'est leur adversaire qui parle en barbare. Ne montre-t-il pas sa barbarie en disant du mal du vin de Beaune, "le plus doux, le plus salutaire, les plus agréable des vins?"

The Frenchman was probably Jean de Hesdin, *Magister* at the University of Paris, and attached to the home of Cardinal Gui de Boulougne, one of Petrarch's friends of the days before Petrarch advocated the return of the Papacy to Rome (Pierre de Nolhac, *Pétrarque et L'Humanisme*, Paris, 1907, 2 vols., II, 303-12, "Le 'Gallus Calumniator'"). Hesdin had in mind the letters in which Petrarch encouraged the return of the papacy to Italy, particularly the letter to Clement VI, published among the familiar letters, Book V, Epistle 19, and two to Urban V, published among the "Epistolarum de rebus senilibus," Book VII, Epistle 1, and Book IX, Epistle 1 (Nolhac, *op. cit.*, p. 306). It was the last of the three, written toward the end of 1367, that the Frenchman attacked in particular. Petrarch's answer, published in 1371, intimated that the anonymous Frenchman had spent four years compiling his pamphlet against Petrarch.

The two letters to Urban V, the Frenchman's pamphlet under the title *Galli cvivsdam anonymi in Franciscvm Petrarcham invectiva,* and Petrarch's answer, the *Contra cvivsdam anonymi Galli calvmnias . . . Apologia,* were available to Milton in *Francisci Petrarchae Florentini . . . Opera quae extant omnia,* Basil, [1581].

20:3 BEDLAM STUFFE . . . *DEMONIACK LEGION* — Hall in *A Defence,* p. 1, refers to the plural authorship of the Smectymnuan *An Answer* by citing from the Bible account of the demon-possessed man in the land of the Gadarenes: *"My name is Legion, for we are many"* (see Mark 5:9; cf. Luke 8:30). Milton had in the *Animadversions* (1641), p. 5 (*Col.* III, 109), turned Hall's statement to show that the Legion was esteemed by Hall as brethren.

20:3-5 THIS IS . . . FOR HIM — The reference is to the Confuter's call to those *"that love Christ"* to stone Milton to death (see Note 19:32-33). The group which is to do the stoning, the true *"Demoniack Legion,"* says Milton, shifting the term from the Smectymnuans (see Note 20:3), who were against Hall, is on Hall's side.

20:5-6 *YOU THAT LOVE CHRIST . . . IMPUNITY* — See Note 19:32-33.

20:8 OUT OF HIS SHOP, OUT OF HIS TROJAN HORSE — "Shop" and "Trojan horse" are figurative terms for prelacy or episcopacy. Milton is implying that as Troy was overcome by permitting the Trojan horse within the city, so religion is being betrayed by the prelates. For the Trojan horse story see Virgil's *Aeneid,* II, 1-56.

20:9 LIKE *A GUISIAN OF PARIS* . . . MASSACRE — *"A Guisian of Paris"* was a follower of the duc de Guise in the Massacre of St. Bartholomew. The immediate cause for the Massacre of St. Bartholomew, which began August 24, 1572 at Paris, was the result of Catherine dé Medici's attempt to maintain control of France through her son Charles IX. The House of Guise in the persons of the Duke of Guise and the Cardinal of Lorraine had dominated her first son, Francis II, who had married Mary Stuart, daughter of Marie of Guise. Catherine determined to protect the Huguenots in order to maintain them as a counterpoise against the Guises. Hoping to marry the Duke of Anjou to Queen Elizabeth of England, and her daughter Margaret to Henry of Navarre, she permitted the Huguenot Admiral Coligny to re-enter the council, only to find that the attachment which grew up between Charles IX and Admiral Coligny threatened her control over Charles. When her attempt to have Coligny assassinated failed, she turned to the Catholic leaders, and frightened Charles into authorizing the massacre of all Huguenot leaders. In England, the massacre was seen from another point of view. The long struggle of Mary Stuart to get the English throne, the conspiracies of the Roman Catholics against Queen Elizabeth, and the activity of the Cardinal of Lorraine were particularly onerous. The fear of France under the wily hands of the Duke of Guise was great.

20:10 *CRUSADA* — Milton has likened the Confuter's *"stone him to death, lest you smart for his impunity"* (20:6) to the watchword for a religious crusade against the antiprelatical party.

20:11-12 IF HE DO [like such words] . . . JESUIT — "Do" is the regular subjunctive form. The Jesuits were very much hated, particularly in England, because they were the active agent of the counter reformation, often effecting their ends through political meddling. They fanned the flames of political hatred against the Huguenots; they plotted against England in the reign of Elizabeth, and helped bring disaster to the Stuarts. Their activities in relation to the religious struggle in Bohemia, their share in the Thirty-Years' War, their instrumentality in the revocation of the Edict of Nantes and the resulting expulsion of the Huguenots, and their radical antimonarchical doctrine made them the focal point of the opposition as viewed by the English churchmen, politicians, and middle class.

20:13-14 REBELS HAVE DONE IN *IRELAND* TO THE PROTESTANTS — The Irish insurrection and massacre of Protestants began in October 1641 (see Masson, *Life,* II, 308-14). The wildest stories reached England early in November. The lowest estimates of contemporary writers places the number of English and Scotch Protestant victims at 30,000. Gardiner calculates, however, that perhaps four or five thousand were slain in cold blood, and about twice that number died from ill-treatment (Gardiner, *History,* X, 68-69). Milton states that the number massacred in Ulster was 154,000 (*Eikonoklastes, Col.* V, 188). See Note 40:39-40.

20:16 CELL OF *LOYOLA* — Cf. *REF, Col.* III, 47, "Jesuites Cell." The "cell" was a small room in a monastery or nunnery which served as the dwelling of a single person. Sometimes the word "cell" referred to the monastery or nunnery itself. St. Ignatius of Loyola (1491-1556) was the founder of the Society of Jesus.

20:17 ONE...SPAKE NOT — Milton alleges that, in contrast with the Confuter who like a Jesuit suggests stoning, he has never suggested that anyone be put to torture.

20:17-18 SKIN SHOULD BE RAIS'D — R. Fletcher amended "rais'd" to read "grazed" (Robert Fletcher (ed.), *Milton. I Prose Works. II Poetical Works.* "The Prose Works of John Milton; with an Introductory Review," London, 1844, p. xviii). The stretching or raising of the skin was an oft used means of torture. Cf. *REF, Col.* III, 72, "not the least skin rais'd." See also, *ANIM, Col.* III, 121, "A little pulley would have stretch'd your ... frame it may be three inches further."

20:18-19 CURSING *SHIMEI*...RAYLER — II Samuel 16:5-8. Milton may also have remem-

bered that Hall in the sixteenth book of his *Contemplations* had a meditation named "Shimei *cursing*" (*Contemplations, The Sixth Volume, By I. H. D.D.,* in *The Works Of Joseph Hall,* London, 1625, pp. 1231-33). Cf. 19:30-33.

20:20 *DESPAIR'D OF VICTORY UNLESSE A MODEST DEFENCE WOULD GET IT HIM* — *Modest Confutation* [A4] *recto,* "I ... must despaire of victory, unlesse it may be gotten by the strength of a good cause, and a modest defense of it."

20:21-23 WHEN FIRST...SIGNE — See 6:40-7:15. "Red portending signe"; *i.e.,* violent, warning sign.

20:24-27 *HE DARES NOT SAY ...I HAVE* — *Modest Confutation* [A4] *recto,* "I dare not say but there may be hid in my nature, as much venemons Atheisme and profanation as hath broken out at his lips; (Every one that is infected with the Sicknesse, hath not the Sores running upon him:)"

20:28-29 PLUMING AND FOOTING... STROKES — Milton turns to the phraseology of falconry. The hawk [*i.e.,* Milton] is weary of plucking the feathers from the seagull [*i.e.,* the Confuter], and of seizing it with his talons because its lack of opposition offers little incentive to the attack. See *OED,* "plume" and "foot"; cf. Visiak, *Milton,* p. 347, who thinks that "pluming and footing" means "plucking, and taking away the claws."

20:30 DORRE — Ridicule (*OED*).

20:30-37 FOR IF THE SORE...VENOME — Bartholomew (*De Proprietatibvs Rervm,* London, 1535, fol. [cviii] *verso*) sheds light on Milton's metaphor: "And than Triacle shall be layed to fresshe often tymes, tylle the postume break: And whan it is broke, it is no drede of peryll." Cf. "For a fester hathe a depe wounde within, and a streyghte and a narowe withoute" (*ibid.* fol. cviii *recto*). Cf. *Samson Agonistes,* 617-28, on sores; and see Svendson, "Milton and Medical Lore," pp. 176-77, to which this note is indebted.

20:33 HE — *i.e.,* the Confuter.

SECTION 1

20:38-39 A KIND OF JUSTICE...EVILL — Ronald B. Levinson ("Milton and Plato," pp. 87-

88) has traced the idea to Plato's *Republic*, 352c: "there must evidently have been some remnant of justice in them [gangs of evil-doers], or they would have injured one another as well as their victims" (Jowett translation). Cicero (*De Officiis*, Bk. ii, ch. 11, sec. 40) said: "Quin etiam leges latronum esse dicuntur, quibus pareant, quas observent." Cf. Luke 16:1-8.

20:39 THIS MAN — The Confuter.

20:40 ALL THIS WHILE — The whole preface "To the Reader" (which Milton has discussed, 9:10-20:37) of the *Modest Confutation* was spent abusing Milton.

21:1 ADVERSARY — *i.e.,* Milton.

21:1-2 IN REVENGE OF — *i.e.,* to avenge.

21:2 REMONSTRANT — Bishop Joseph Hall.

21:2-3 IF THEY BE NOT ... SON — Cf. 8:17-18; 27:14-20; 36:8. The problem of authorship is discussed in the Introduction, p. 3.

21:3 THIS — See Note 20:40.

21:3-4 CALLS FOR SATISFACTION ... FARDING — The Confuter, who has already abused Milton considerably (see Note 20:40), now says (*Modest Confutation*, p. 1):

Satisfaction to tender Consciences, is that which we look for, and that which you ought to give; as having done violence through all your book to the person of an holy and religious Prelate, the eares of all good Christians within our Church, the established Laws of the Kingdom, the pretious and dear name of our common Master and Saviour Christ Jesus.

The Confuter, in calling for *"Satisfaction to tender Consciences,"* no doubt took the suggestion from Milton's *Animadversions* (1641), p. 1 (Col. III, 105):

ALTHOUGH it be a certaine truth that they who undertake a Religious Cause need not care to be Men-pleasers; yet because the satisfaction of tender and mild consciences is far different from that which is call'd Men-pleasing, to satisfie such, I shall adresse my selfe in few words to give notice before hand of something in this booke, which to some men perhaps may seeme offensive, that when I have render'd a lawfull reason of what is done, I may trust to have sav'd the labour of defending or excusing hereafter.

21:4 FARDING — *i.e.,* farthing.

21:4-6 VIOLENCE ... PRELAT — See Note 21:3-4.

21:6-8 S. *PAUL* ... WOULD BE PRELATS — In Acts 23:5, Paul said: "I wist not, brethren, that he was the high priest: for it is written, Thou shalt not speak evil of the ruler of thy people." Milton's paraphrase of the latter part of the Biblical verse is interesting in showing his facility in turning phrases to a wholly new emphasis without losing any of the spirit and without losing many of the words of the original passage. The bitter insinuation of the modified quotation of the first part of the scriptural passage is that Milton knew that the Confuter was a prelate, but he did not know that the prelate was *"holy and religious."* Among the evil things written of prelates is that by Robert Lord Brooke in the *Nature of Episcopacy*, p. 97:

While I heare the sad groanes, and see the bleeding wounds of Three Kingdomes at once, by their [the prelates'] Schismes; I have almost forgotten the parting sighs, and farewell teares of ten thousand poore Christians, by Their Tyranny forc'd to abandon their native Country, and dearest acquaintance; while others were here violently detained in Fetters, some smoothered in Dungeons, some Dismembred, some driven out of house and Living, and forced to beg: All which yet would have bin born patiently, had not only all Good men, but Goodnes it self, Learning, Religion, Piety, All that speaks any worth, been altogether, not only discountenanced, but suppressed, smoothered, and by most exquisite Tortures almost forced to breath its last.

21:7 *ANANIAS* — Acts 23:2-5. Visiak is in error in saying that Ananias is "a slip for Caiaphas" (Visiak, *Milton*, p. 847).

21:9-10 IN DISGUISE ... *HOLY* OR *PRELAT* — Hall's pamphlets, *An Humble Remonstrance, A Defence,* and *A Short Answer,* were issued anonymously. "Superscription" is used figuratively by Milton. A "superscription" is a piece of writing or an inscription upon or above something (see Matthew 22:20, Luke 20:24; Mark 15:26, Luke 23:38). The "Phylactery" was a square leathern box worn by Jews, one on the head and one on the left arm during prayer. Milton may have had the term in mind as a result of his previous reference to Christ's "speaking of unsavory traditions" (see Note 19:36), for the term appears (Matthew 23:5) in the denunciation of the scribes and Pharisees.

21:10-11 IT WERE NO SINNE ... *DOVER* — According to Holinshed, Longchamp, Bishop of

Elie, was given the Lord Chancellorship of England when Richard the First went to the Holy Land. The Bishop, attended by a thousand horsemen, traveled from place to place, demanding lodging, and oppressing the people so much that a civil war ensued. The Bishop took refuge from his enemies in the Tower, from which, after a long siege, he escaped, hastening to Canterbury

where he promised to receiue the crosse of a pilgrime to go into the holie land, and to render vp the crosse of his legatship, which he had vsurped a yeare and a halfe after the death of pope Clement, to the preiudice of the church of Rome, and to the detriment and great hinderance of the English church. For there was not any church within the realme, which had not béene put to fine and ransome by that crosse, nor any ecclesiasticall person went frée, but the print of the crosse appeared in him and his purse.

From Canterbury he went to Dover, hoping to escape to France. Fearing lest he be discovered, he disguised himself as a woman. He

got a web of cloth on his arme, as though he had beene some housewifelie woman of the countrie: but by the vntowardlie folding and vnconning handling of his cloth (or rather by a lewd fisherman that tooke him for an harlot) he was suspected and searched so narrowlie, that by his priuie members he was prooued to be a man, and at length knowne, attached, and committed to prison, after he had beene reprochfullie handled by them that found him, and by the wiues of the towne, in such vnséemlie apparell. (*Holinshed's Chronicles of England, Scotland, and Ireland,* London, 1807-08, 6 vols., II, 228; see also St. John, *Prose Works of Milton*, III, 126 note.)

In Smectymnuus, *An Answer*, p. 88, a reference was made to the Bishop of Elie:

Next the pride of *W. Longchamp*, Bishop of Elie was notorious, who would ride with a thousand horse, and of a Governour in the Kings absence, became a Tyrant; for which flying in Womans apparell he was taken. [Margin] *Richard I. Pag.* 129. 130. 132.

21:12 HE HATH...NAMELESSE — Bishop Hall began the controversy with the anonymous *An Humble Remonstrance To The High Covrt Of Parliament, By A dutifull Sonne of the Church.*

21:12-13 WHEN HE PLEASES...AS WE ARE — Milton challenges the Remonstrant and Confuter to declare their authorship whereupon he will make himself known. Milton's phraseology has the familiar echo of Scripture (cf. II Corinthians 5:10; I Corinthians 13:12; I John 3:2).

21:13-14 AND LET HIM...PRINCIPL'D — When the true authorship is revealed Milton will not be cowed by the importance or rank of the man, for Milton will consider him according as he finds him established in principles.

21:14-17 FOR NEITHER MUST PRELATS ...EXEMPTS — Milton maintains that the station of man does not raise him above the bases upon which common or ordinary people are judged. That man alone can hope for exemption from judgment on such a basis who has "true wisdome and the contempt of vulgar opinions." Milton's hierarchy is one based on wisdom. Cf. *RCG, Col.* III, 229, on the lower and higher wisdom; *REF, Col.* III, 29, "wisdome the gift of God"; *REF, Col.* III, 37, training in true wisdom grows toward *"godlines"; Doctrine and Discipline of Divorce, Col.* III, 378, the "high gift of wisdom"; and *Tetrachordon, Col.* IV, 85, "wisdom is as a high tower of pleasure." See also *Comus,* 374; *Paradise Lost,* III, 706; IV, 491; VII, 9, 83, 130; VIII, 194; XI, 636.

21:18-19 PSALMES...PERISH — See Psalms 49:12.

21:19-20 *THE MANNER...SUSPICIOUS — Modest Confutation*, p. 1, "We must suppose you have *undertaken a religious cause.* that is your pretended subject; we shall examine the truth of it by and by; we must now look to your manner of handling it: a suspicious way you think; and so do I. Here we agree." (See Note 21:3-4 for the statement in the *Animadversions* to which the Confuter is referring.)

21:22-23 WHERE IS THE OFFENCE... FOLLY? — Milton had said in the *Animadversions* (1641), pp. 1-2 (Col. III, 105-06):

Yet in the detecting, and convincing of any notorious enimie to truth and his Countries peace ... it will be nothing disagreeing from Christian meeknesse to handle such a one in a rougher accent, and to send home his haughtinesse well bespurted with his owne holy-water. Nor to do thus are we unautoritied either from the morall precept of SALOMON to answer him thereafter that prides him in his folly; nor from the example of Christ, and all his followers in all Ages....

The Confuter had answered thereto (*Modest Confutation,* p. 1):

Your defense is, *In such a cause, it is nothing disagreeing from Christian meeknesse, the morall precept of* Solomon, *the example of Christ.*

21:24 REMONSTRANT . . . *SCUM* — Milton defends himself against the Confuter's charge that no "morall precept" gives Milton the liberty of using such words as "froth" and "scum" (see previous Note). The Remonstrant, Bishop Hall, started the discussion of "froth" and "scum" by saying of "some verball exceptions" in the Smectymnuan *An Answer*:

Those other verball exceptions are but light froth, and will sink alone; that scum may be worth taking off, which followes.... (Hall, *Defence*, p. 4.)

To the "froth" part of Hall's sentence, Milton said (*ANIM*, (1641) p. 9; *Col.* III, 114):

O rare suttlety . . . when I beseech you, will light things sink? when will froth sink alone.

To the "scum" part, Milton said (*ibid.*):

Spare your Ladle Sir, it will be as bad as the Bishops foot in the broth [see Note 19:18-19]; the scum will be found upon your own *Remonstrance*.

Of Milton's comments in the *Animadversions,* the Confuter questioned:

What morall precept in *Solomon* countenances such language as this [*Scum, Ladles.....*] (*Modest Confutation*, pp. 1-2. The brackets are the Confuter's.)

21:25 *SPARE HIS LADLE* — See Note 21:24.

21:25-26 MESSE WITH *KEALE, BEEF,* AND *BREWESSE* — "Keale," *i.e.,* kale; "Brewesse," *i.e.,* broth. The Smectymnuans in *An Answer,* p. 104, having indicated the origin of the proverb *"The Bishops foot hath beene in it"* (see Note 19:18-19) had continued:

And in all this (and much more which might be said) fulfilling Bishop *Bonners* Prophesie, who when hee saw that in King *Edwards* reformation, there was a reservation of ceremonies and Hierarchy, is credibly reported to have used these words; *Since they have begun to tast of our Broath, it will not be long ere they will eat of our Beefe.*

Hall retorted (*Defence*, p. 167),

After your own pottage (for your Proverb; *sapit ollam*) you tell us of *Boner's Broth*; I should have too much wondred at this conclusion, but that I hear it is the fashion in some Countries, to send in their Keal in the last service; and this, it seems, is the manner among our *Smectymnuans.*

Well; to shut up all, let them of their own *Boners beef and broath,* make what Brewesse they please for their credulous guests....

Milton in *Animadversions* (1641), p. 67 (*Col.* III, 177), pounced upon the phrase "last service" to say: Your latter service at the high Altar you mean; but

soft Sir, the feast was but begun, the broth was your owne, you have been inviting the Land to it this fourescore yeares, and so long we have been your slaves to serve it up for you, much against our wils, we know you have the Beefe to it, ready in your Kitchins... this broth was but your first service: Alas Sir, why doe you delude your guests? Why doe not those goodly Flanks and Briskets march up in your stately chargers? doubtlesse... the Pope that owes you for mollifying the matter so well with him, and making him a true Church, will furnish you with all the fat Oxen of *Italy.*

The Confuter (*Modest Confutation*, pp. 1-2) lists among those words to which he objects on moral grounds, "Beef," "Flanks," and "Briskets."

21:27 FLANKS AND BRISKETS — See Note 21:25-26.

21:27-31 CAPON AND WHITEBROTH... BUT INTERRUPT? — *Modest Confutation*, pp. 1-2, "What morall precept in *Solomon* countenances such language as this [... *Christ and his Apostles, Capon and white-broath in the same leaf* ....]" The Confuter is objecting to Milton's usage of the term, "Capon, and whitebroth" on the same page as "*Christ,* and his *Apostles,*" that is, on page 33 of the *Animadversions* (*Col.* III, 141-42).

21:30 CONTINU'D — *i.e.,* continuous.

21:33 SUPERFLUITIES — Superabundance.

21:38-39 *OF OLD BOTTLES ... CLOATHS* — Matthew 9:16-17; Mark 2:21-22; Luke 5:36-39.

21:40 *COMMING ... NIGHT* — Matthew 24:42-44; Luke 12:37-40; cf. I Thessalonians 5:2; Revelation 16:15.

21:40-22:1 RIGHTEOUS MANS *WISDOME ... STEWARD* — Luke 16:8.

22:2-3 *HIS CANTING BEGGARS ... ALTAR* — *Modest Confutation*, p. 2:

Such language you should scarce hear from the mouths of canting beggars, at an heathen altar; much lesse was looked for in a treatise of controversall Theologie, as yours might have been thought, had you not thus prevented it.

22:3 CRITICISME OF *BOMOLOCHUS* — Milton refers to the marginal note in the *Modest Confutation*, p. 2, in which the Confuter points out that the "canting beggars, at an heathen altar" (cf. Note 22:2-3) is an "allusion to the primary signification of βωμολόχοι (buffoons)" (Visiak, *Milton*, p. 847). The marginal reference is as follows:

οἱ μὲν οὖν τῷ γελοίῳ ὑπερβάλλοντες βωμολόχος [βωμολό-χοι] δοκοῦσιν ἔιναι [εἶναι]. Arist. Eth. *l.4.c.8*. βωμολόχος Latinis *Scurra* dicitur, sumtâ metaphora à mendicantibus, qui ad aras & templa Deum sedebant & jacebant, & à sacrificantibus stipem mendicabant. Interea autem seipsos multis jocis & scommatis vexabant, & interdum praetereuntes convitiis prosequebantur. à βωμὸς ara, & λέχομαι jaceo seu accubo. *Vid. Mag. Com. in Eth, Arist.* [Those men who hurl jests at them seem to be (or are called) Bomolochoi. Aristotle, *Nicomachean Ethics*, *Bk.* IV, *ch.* 8 (1128a 3-5) in Latin *Scurra*, which is used metaphorically of beggars, who were in the habit of sitting and lying at the altars and temples of the gods and begging alms of those who made sacrifice. Meanwhile they railed upon each other with many jokes and jeers, and sometimes they hurled jibes at passers-by; from *Bomos*, altar, and *lechomi*, I lie or I recline. See Magirus, *Commentary on Nicomachean Ethics of Aristotle* (see Joannis Magiri, *Aristotelis Ethica Nicomachea Commentationes*, edited by Ricardus Walker, Oxonii, 1842, p. 204).]

E. H. Visiak thinks the "canting" refers to the beggars' solicitations of "alms from those who sacrificed." He opines that "λέχομαι is a spurious form, and the source is probably λοχάω [lurk]" (Visiak, *Milton*, p. 847).

22:4 IMPORTUNITY — From Latin *importunitas* meaning "unsuitableness."

22:5 GREEK DERIVATION — Refers to the last part of the marginal note transcribed in Note 22:3, *i.e.*, "à βωμὸς ara, & λέχομαι jaceo seu accubo."

22:5 TILL...FRESH MEN — Seems to indicate that Milton considers the Confuter a man who teaches freshmen (see Introduction, p. 3).

22:8-10 NOTWITHSTANDING . . . DEFENDED — In "The Preface" to the *Animadversions* Milton defended his manner of writing (see Note 21:3-4):

And although in the serious uncasing of a grand imposture ... there be mixt here and there such a grim laughter, as may appear at the same time in an austere visage, it cannot be taxt of levity or insolence: for even this veine of laughing (as I could produce out of grave Authors) hath oft-times a strong and sinewy force in teaching and confuting; nor can there be a more proper object of indignation and scorne together then a false Prophet taken in the greatest dearest and most dangerous cheat, the cheat of soules: in the disclosing whereof if it be harmful to be angry, and withall to cast a lowring smile, when the properest object

calls for both, it will be long enough ere any be able to say why those two most rationall faculties of humane intellect anger and laughter were first seated in the brest of man. (*ANIM*, (1641), pp. 3-4; and *Col.* III, 107-08.)

22:11 CONFUTER ... DISAPPROVES — Milton had declared in the *Animadversions* (1641), p. 3 (*Col.* III, 107), that his writings were "*without all private and personall spleene.*" The Confuter answered (*Modest Confutation*, pp. 5-6):
Nor would I have done you the injury to have called it so [libels], were it not too too manifest. For that which even you professedly disavow (private and personall spleen, p. 3. lin. 18) is the greatest matter in your book; the other businesse being handled but by the by, or not at all: and where it is, in such a wretched, loathsome manner, as once I did almost doubt me, whether or no you did not jeer at both sides, at Religion, and God, and all.

22:15 *IDEAS* — Forms. For Milton's theory of Ideas see Irene Samuel, *Plato and Milton*, pp. 131-42.

22:22-23 THE BAPTIST...LIFE — Matthew 3:4; Mark 1:6.

22:23-24 OUR SAVIOUR ... HIM — Cf. Matthew 28:18; Ephesians 1:22; I Timothy 6:17.

22:25-26 MILDE . . . CONVERSE — See Matthew 13.

22:26-28 SOMETIMES . . . RESPECT — See Matthew 15:1-14, especially verse 12.

22:26-27 HOME-SPEAKING — *i.e.*, talk on domestic or everyday matters in a humble manner.

22:28-30 WITH BITTER...IMPUGNERS — See Matthew 23:13-33.

22:30-31 DIVIDED...CHURCH — See I Corinthians 12; Mark 6:7-13; Luke 9:1-6; 24:49; Acts 1:8.

22:32 SUCH — *i.e.*, the austere and grave.

22:34 AND STILL...LARGE — "and[,] still as it were[,] at large [*i.e.*, unrestrained]."

22:35 UNTRESPASSING HONESTY — "Untrespassing" has the notion of "unoffending."

22:36 MAY HAVE BY WHOM — "May have [those] by whom."

22:38-23:4 NO MAN...VERTUES — Milton argues against attempting to alter completely the conjunction of the humors in the body. He doubts that "any man can with the safety of his life... alter his natural temperament, and disposition of minde" (*Colasterion, Col.* IV, 250; cf. *REF, Col.* III, 63, "nor are the elements or humors in Mans Body exactly *homogeneall*"; *RCG, Col.* III, 260, "this pious and just honouring of our selves... may be thought as the radical moisture"; see also *Paradise Lost,* II, 274-77, where Milton suggests that alteration of humors is possible. For a discussion of Milton's use of the concept of the humors as well as of the medical lore background in Bartholomew *De Proprietatibus Rerum,* and *Batman vppon Bartholome,* see Kester Svendson, "Milton and Medical Lore," pp. 165-66). Peter de la Primavdaye, in *The Second Part Of The French Academie* (London, 1594), p. 384, said of the "radical humor":

... there is in a liuing body a certaine humiditie that holdeth of the nature of the aire, which moisture is very good, and is dispersed throughout the whole body, hauing his propagation of the seede, and ioyning together all the parts of the body.

Primavdaye warned that

wee must labour to correct, and bridle [our vices], and to quench such inclinations, as much as wee can, through sobrietie, vigilancie, and continuall practise to the contrary: least wee nourish and encrease them, when as wee ought to diminish and wholy to abolish them. (*Ibid.,* p. 382.)

See Preface to and lines 600-01 of *Samson Agonistes* for the homeopathic theory of tragedy and humors, as well as Ingram Bywater, "Milton and the Aristotelian Definition of Tragedy," *Journal of Philology,* XXVII (1900), no. 54, pp. 267-75.

23:7 YET NOT THEREFORE — *i.e.,* yet that was not therefore.

23:11 PROUD RESISTANCE...DOCTORS — Cf. *Tetrachordon, Col.* IV, 150, "carnall Doctors"; and *Areopagitica, Col.* IV, 313, "Priests and Doctors." Hall cited in his *Humble Remonstrance* (pp. 32 ff.) the praise of the flourishing estate of the English Church, given by the Geneva Professors. The Smectymnuans maintained, on the other hand (*Answer,* pp. 63 ff.), that ecclesiastical history had proved that riches usually resulted in the clergy's neglect of the ministry, and "ushered in... stately and pompous attendance." Hall answered thereto (*Defence,* p. 127) that "some such ill use hath beene made, by some, of their abundance: but surely... the fault is rare, and hardly instanceable." Milton maintained:

If in lesse noble and almost mechanik arts... he is not esteem'd to deserve the name of a compleat Architect ... that beares not a generous mind above the peasantly regard of wages, and hire; much more must we thinke him a most imperfect, and incompleate Divine... [whose] whole divinity is moulded and bred up in the beggarly, and brutish hopes of a fat Prebendary, Deanery, or Bishoprick. (*ANIM* (1641), p. 65; *Col.* III, 162.)

Milton asked: Can a man who is the "Herald of heavenly truth... find himselfe discontented, or dishonour'd for want of admittance to have a pragmaticall voyce at Sessions, and Jayle deliveries? ... would he tugge for a Barony to sit and vote in Parliament"? (*ANIM* (1641), p. 57; *Col.* III, 164.) Thereto the Confuter answered (*Modest Confutation,* p. 40): "That man that was and could have still been content without those honours, will be very loath now to let them go."

23:12 (THAT I...POETS USE) — Cf. 42:37-38.

23:13 ZEALE — Cf. *ANIM, Col.* III, 107, "*zeale of truth*"; *RCG, Col.* III, 225, "Watchfulnesse and Zeale"; *Apology,* 1:21-22, "zeale... disparag'd"; 51:26, "those who in zeale."

23:13-14 ARMING... DIAMOND — Arming itself completely in a substance of extreme hardness.

23:14 FIERY CHARIOT — Milton may have been influenced by the Helios myth, as well as by the fiery chariots of the Bible (Isaiah 66:15; II Kings 2:11, 6:17).

23:15 ZODIACK — The belt of the celestial sphere is divided into twelve parts in which the twelve signs of the zodiac are represented by twelve figures some of which are beasts.

23:15-23 BEASTS... RESEMBLING... WHEELS — Ezekiel 1:10; and Saint John in The Revelation 4:7. The phrase "Brusing their stiffe necks" seems to echo Proverbs 29:1.

23:23-24 THUS...THE FALSE — Milton probably has in mind the account of Elijah's challenging the prophets of Baal: "And call ye on the name of your gods, and I will call on the name of the

Lord: and the God that answereth by fire, let him be God" (I Kings 18:24). When the efforts of the followers of Baal proved futile, Elijah "cast derision and scorne upon perverse and fraudulent seducers" (*Apology*, 23:18-19). "Elijah mocked them, and said, Cry aloud: for he *is* a god; either he is talking, or he is pursuing, or he is in a journey, *or* peradventure he sleepeth, and must be awaked" (I Kings 18:27).

23:24 CHRIST...MEEKNESSE — See Matthew 11:29; 21:5 (Zechariah 9:9); II Corinthians 10:1; Philippians 2:7-8.

23:25-26 ACRIMONY ANOUGH...PRELATICALL PHARISEES — See Matthew 15:12; 23: 1-35; Luke 11:37-44; 16:15; Matthew 5:20. The "Prelaticall Pharisees" are well described in Matthew 23:4-7; Luke 11:43. Luther, when attempting to stimulate reform within the Church, started to purge his order, that is the Augustinian, as early as 1515 of Pharisaism (Preserved Smith, *The Age of the Reformation*, New York, 1920, pp. 65-66). Joseph Hall published a pamphlet on the subject *Pharisaisme And Christianitie: Compared and set forth in a Sermon at Pauls Crosse, May 1, 1608. ...Vpon Matth. 5.20* in 1608. See Note 44:29.

23:28-29 SANCTIFI'D...TRUTH — See Matthew 11:20-24; 21:12-13; 23:13-33; Mark 11:15-17; Luke 10:13-15. See Note 22:8-10.

23:29 INSPIRATION — *i.e.*, a supernatural influence that communicates divine truth.

23:31 THE EXAMPLE OF *LUTHER* — See 8:26. The example of Luther in using unrestrained language is not paralleled or approached by any other popular religious writer. In licentiousness of language he stands quite apart (see Hartmann Grisar, *Luther*, trans. E. M. Lamond, St. Louis, 1914-17, 6 vols., III, 228-41).

23:33-37 WHO NOT OF REVELATION... SPIRIT — One ready source for Milton's defence of Luther was Sleidan's *Commentariorum de Statu Religionis et Republicae, Carolo Quinto Caesare*; cf. Milton's *Commonplace Book*, fol. 76 (*Col. XVIII*, 145): "Nec acerbitate, nec scommatis abstinuit Lutherus interdum etiam parùm verecundis Sleidan. 1.16. p. 261" (Hanford, "The Chronology of Milton's Private Studies," p. 271, note 65, has

pointed out that Milton's page references do not agree with those of the Latin editions he has examined, nor with those of the English translation of 1560). The *de Statu Religionis* (Argentorati [Strasbourg]: Theodosius Rihelius, [1559?], Bk. III, pp. 55-62) covers in general what Milton has to say about Luther (see also Ihon Daus' translation of Sleidan's *de Statu Religionis* under the title *A Famovse Cronicle of oure time*, fol. xxviii *recto*-[xxxi] *verso*). Another most common source for information about Luther was John Foxe's *Acts and Monuments,* printed in Latin in 1559 and in English in 1563. By 1632, seven English editions had appeared.

The cited passage, however, is probably taken from, or the result of the dissemination of knowledge from, an edition of Luther's *Works*, either in Latin or German, a number of which were available in the second half of the sixteenth century, for Milton appears to have in mind Luther's letter to "an unnamed correspondent," Wittenberg, August 28, 1522 (available, for instance, in...*aller Bücher und Schrifften des thewren seligen Mans Doct: Mart: Lutheri*, Jhena, 1555-64, 8 vols. and index, II, fol. 149), in which Luther said:

You ask why I have answered the King of England so sharply, so that you can reply to my opponents. I would have you know that I did it purposely, and will henceforth show no more gentleness to blasphemers and liars.... You know that Christ and Peter and Paul were not always gentle....I have made the most humble overtures, and run after those men and appeared before them at great difficulty and expense, and have borne their measureless lies and slanders. But the more I have humbled myself the more they rave and slander me and my doctrine.... If anyone is so minded that he disregards and despises my long patience and my many offers, why should I care if he takes offence at my rebukes?... Therefore...do not be surprised that many take offence at what I write. So it should and so it must be....it will clear in due time why I have been so harsh.... My work is not that of one who can take a middle course, and yield this or give up that, as I have done hitherto, fool that I was. (From Preserved Smith, *Luther's Correspondence and Contemporary Letters,* Philadelphia, 1913-18, 2 vols., II, 133-34.)

23:37-24:1 YET HE BEING CITED... THEREIN — *Ioannis Sleidani Commentariorvm de Statv Religionis & Reipublicae, Carolo Quinto Caesare, Libri XXVI* (Argentorati, [1559?]), pp. 57-58; see also Ihon Daus' translation, *A Famovse Cronicle of oure time,* fol. xxix. Milton is, as he tells us, drawing his material concerning Luther's plea before the Emperor directly from Sleidan (24:1).

24:1 *SLEIDEN* — Johannes Philippson, Sleidanus (1506-1556), born at Schleiden from which he took his name, was appointed by Philip of Hesse, at the suggestion of Martin Bucer, historian of the Reformation and given access to the necessary documents. He finished his *Commentariorum de Statu Religionis* in 1554, and had it printed in 1555. The book was a source "not only for Milton's knowledge of German history, but also for his citations from the writings of Luther" (William Talbot Allison, (ed.), *The Tenure of Kings and Magistrates By John Milton*, New York, 1911, pp. xlii-xliii). Sleidan was considered an authority in Milton's day as evidenced by Milton's references to him (*Judgment of Martin Bucer, Col.* IV, 6; *Tenure of Kings and Magistrates, Col.* V, 27, 46; *Means to Remove Hirelings, Col.* VI, 82, and the numerous references in the *Commonplace Book* which Hanford, "The Chronology of Milton's Private Studies," pp. 268, 271, has noted). An indication of the importance of Sleidan is shown by the fact that John Foxe in his *Acts and Monuments*, the Latin edition of which was completed in 1559 and the English edition in 1563, used Sleidan as a source. See Note 23:33-37.

24:2 *OF AN ARDENT SPIRIT...A DULL STILE* — See Luther's letter to Spalatin, Wittenburg (between February 15 and 18), 1520, "calidus sum et stylum habeo non penitus obtusem" (*D. Martin Luthers Werke...Briefwecksel*, Letter no. 255, Weimar, 1930-38, 8 vols., II, 44; see also Preserved Smith, *Luther's Correspondence*, I, 288, "I am naturally warm, and have a pen which is not at all blunt.").

24:3-5. *HEE THOUGHT IT ... FORGOT* — Luther to Wenzelaus Link in Nürnberg [Wittenberg], August 19, 1520, "Omnes ferme in me damnant mordacitatem, sed mihi idem sensus ist, qui tibi, scilicet Deum forte hoc modo revelare hominum figmenta. Video enim ea, quae nostro saeculo quiete tractantur, mox cadere in oblivionem, nemine ea curante" (Luther, *Briefwecksel*, Letter no. 328, II, 168).

24:5-8 HOW USEFULL ... CONTEMPT — See Note 23:33-37.

24:9 *CAJETAN ... ECCHIUS* — Cajetan (1468-1534) was born in Gaeta in the Kingdom of Naples. His proper name was Tommaso de Vio, but he adopted that of Gaetanus (*i.e.,* Cajetan) from his birthplace. He was made a cardinal and archbishop of Palermo in 1517 by Pope Leo X. In 1518 he was sent to Germany as legate in order to quiet the turmoils that Luther was causing. It was to Cajetan that Luther appeared at the Diet of Augsburg (October 1518); and it was Cajetan who helped draw up the bull excommunicating Luther.

Johann Dobneck, Cochlaeus (1479-1552), who became dean of Liebfrauenkirche at Frankfurt in 1520, became a controversialist against Luther's party. He developed a bitter hatred for the Reformation, attributing the movement to mean motives. Luther refused to discuss the issues with him publicly in 1521. Cochlaeus was present at the Diet of Worms. He was particularly active in the meetings in John Eck's room, subsequent to Luther's appearance before the Emperor, in attempting to convince Luther to recant.

Johann Maier Eck, Bishop of Triers (1486-1543), was an important and indefatigable defender of the Roman Church. In July 1520 he became papal nuncio. Because the bull *Exsurge Domine,* directed against Luther's writings was ineffectual, Eck appealed to the Emperor to use force, particularly in his *Epistola ad Carolum V* (February 18, 1521). The result was the Edict of Worms against Luther. Eck acted as prosecuter for the Emperor and the Pope at the Diet of Worms (1521).

Erasmus (1466?-1536), though not in attendance at either the Diet of Augsburg or the Diet of Worms, is included by Milton in the group who poured contempt on Luther. Erasmus recognized much good in Luther's work. His early position toward Luther was favorable except as it seemed to Erasmus the cause of learning was being adversely affected (see Preserved Smith, *Luther's Correspondence*, I, Letters 141, 142, 149, 155, 156). However, he did not desire to be connected with Luther or the movement; he pleaded, when he was accused of belonging to Luther's camp, that he did not know Luther, and that he had not read his works (*ibid.*, Letters 155, 156, 187, 192, 212). By 1520

Erasmus felt that Luther's lack of civility and moderateness were detrimental to the cause of peace and learning (*ibid., Letters* 258, 273, 281). When the opposition to Luther mounted, Erasmus feared the worst for Luther, but refused to take sides actively (*ibid., Letters* 294, 297, 298, 311, 312, 313, 314).

Erasmus preferred to be a spectator rather than an actor in the tragedy that he felt was inevitable (*ibid., Letters,* 33, 333), yet he hoped that Luther would not be crushed by mere vociferations and conspiracies (*ibid., Letters* 345, 346) and that odium would not come on learning (*ibid., Letter* 356). Erasmus was, therefore, careful not to stand opposed to Luther (*ibid., Letter* 385) or reform (*ibid., Letter* 399). He thought that the peace of Christendom could be attained if the Emperor imposed silence on both the Catholic and Lutheran parties (*ibid., Letter* 422). He felt that moderation might have done more than anything else (*ibid., Letters* 429, 477: Vol. II, Letter 581), for "Luther cannot perish without a great part of evangelical purity perishing with him" (*ibid.,* II, Letter 581). Yet the sympathy of Erasmus for the reformers waned (*ibid.,* II, Letters 597, 620, 624), and, with his book *On the Free Will* (1524), active opposition was begun.

According to Sleidan, Erasmus wrote to Luther expressing his pleasure in Luther's writings and trusting "that they shall profit many ... but of one thing he would admonishe him, that a man shall more preuaile with a certeine ciuile modestie, then if he be to vehement: And that he muste rather thunder against them which abuse the bishop of Romes authoritie, then against the Bishoppes themselues" (Sleidan, *A Famovse Cronicle of oure time,* fol. xvi *verso*).

24:10-11 INSOMUCH . . . ERROR — See Note 23:33-37.

24:11-14 IF AT OTHER TIMES...FERVENT MINDE — Sleidan (*A Famovse Cronicle of oure time,* fol. xxix *verso*) records that Luther confessed "to haue bene more vehement then became me" (see also *Aller Bücher und Schrifften des thewren seligen Mans Doct: Mart: Lutheri,* I, fol. 490 *recto*). Luther himself made excuses for his vehemence upon several occasions, though he usually tried to justify his harshness (see Luther to Spalatin, Wit-

tenberg (between February 12 and 18), 1520, discussed in Note 23:33-37; Luther to Elector Frederic of Saxony at Worms, Wittenberg, March 3, 1521, Preserved Smith, *Luther's Correspondence,* I, 478-81; Luther to Hans von der Planitz, Wittenberg, February 4, 1523, *ibid.,* II, 167-68; and Luther to the Elector Frederick of Saxony, Wittenberg, May 29, 1523, *ibid.,* II, 183-85).

24:19 WORDS NOT CIVILL . . . SPOK'N — Cf. 25:10-13. See Note 23:31. Milton is justifying in his own mind, on the basis of Luther who "did not refrain from bitter remarks or from jests that were at times somewhat lacking in good taste" (*Commonplace Book,* fol. 76; *Col.* XVIII, 145), "the deliberate adoption of the worst controversial habits of the times, and doing so, moreover, before he had himself written anything to incur severe reprobation on this ground" (Hanford, "The Chronology of Milton's Private Studies," p. 307).

24:20-22 NUMBERS ... *ZIMRI AND COSBI . . . PHINEAS . . . WORD* — Numbers 25:7-8. Harris F. Fletcher has used this passage to prove that Milton was able to read the rabbinical commentaries on the Scripture (see Harris F. Fletcher, *Milton's Rabbinical Readings,* Urbana, 1930, pp. 20 ff., and Harris F. Fletcher, *Milton's Semitic Studies,* Chicago, 1926, pp. 78-79). Milton is saying that the rabbis explain the passage in Numbers 25:7-8 by using "a more obscene word than the text itself contains" (Harris F. Fletcher, *Milton's Rabbinical Readings,* p. 22). Milton was reading Buxtorf's Rabbinical Bible wherein Rashi's comment which names the actual parts of the body is much more obscene than the text itself (*ibid.,* pp. 25-26).

24:22-25 DEUTERONOMY . . . OPENLY — Deuteronomy 28:30; Isaiah 13:16; Zechariah 14:2; Jeremiah 3:2.

24:24 IMMODEST — *i.e.,* "too indecent" (H. F. Fletcher, *Milton's Rabbinical Readings,* p. 27).

24:24 COOLE — *i.e.,* cold.

24:25-27 BUT THESE ... CAN PROVE — The objectors will say that the words that seem obscene now were "honest" ones "when they were spok'n." But even the Rabbis who point out that the marginal reading or "*Keri*" (see Note 25:5-6) lessened "the vigor of the original expression in an attempt to refine the text" (H. F. Fletcher, *Milton's Rabbinical Readings,* p. 29) cannot prove that. To the "rabbinical softenings of the original . . . Milton objected . . . on the grounds that the text is sacred and can say what it pleases" (*ibid.,* p. 30).

24:29-32 *DAVID . . . WALL* — I Samuel 25:22, 34.

24:33-34. AGGRAVATE HIS INFIRMITY — *i.e.,* increase the gravity of David's weakness of character.

24:34-36 FIRST OF KINGS . . . *WALL* — I Kings 14:10.

24:36-39 WHICH HAD IT BEENE . . . THE TONGUE — *i.e.,* if that speech, made "in the heat of an earnest expression," is indecent, then Jonathan and Onkelos "were of cleaner language" than God who made the language. Milton is arguing that the use of strong language is completely justified when there is a *"proper object of indignation and scorne"* (*ANIM, Col.* III, 107; see 25:1-3; 25:10-13).

24:36 UNSEEMELY — Indecent.

24:37-38 *IONATHAN . . . THE TARGUMISTS* — Jonathan Ben Uzziel, said to have been Hillel's most prominent pupil, seems to have been the author of a Targum, that is a translation or paraphrase of a portion of the Old Testament into the Aramaic language, which became the foundation of the present Targum to the Prophets, and which, although Palestinian in origin, gained general recognition in Babylonia in the third century A.D. From the Babylonian academies it was spread throughout the Diaspora. After the fourteenth century, the authorship of the Palestinian Targum to the Pentateuch was also attributed to Jonathan Ben Uzziel.

24:38 *ONKELOS THE TARGUMISTS* — The title "Targum Onkelos" is derived from the well-known passage in the Babylonian Talmud which attributed the Targum to the proselyte Onkelos who lived in the first century A.D. The Targum is the Aramaic translation of the Bible which forms a part of Jewish traditional literature and which because it gained general acceptance in Babylonian schools was called the Babylonian Targum. Because hardly anything was known about the proselyte Aquila, who actually composed the Targum, and because Onke-

los was known through tannaitic tradition, legends that were really connected with the former were attributed to the latter.

24:39-40 *I WILL CUT OFF . . . DISCRETION* — Harris F. Fletcher (*Milton's Rabbinical Readings,* pp. 32-33) points out that Jonathan and Onkelos the Targumists actually changed the text to read as Milton indicates. Fletcher proceeds to prove that Milton was using Buxtorf's *Biblia Hebraica,* which included an enormous amount of rabbinical material including the Targums Jonathan, Onkelos, and Uziell.

25:1-3 WHEREAS GOD . . . HE SPAKE — See Note 24:36-39.

25:3 PLAINE WORD — See 24:35.

25:4 FORBORNE — *i.e.,* avoided.

25:4-6 WHICH THE *MASORETHS* . . . ATTENDING . . . MARGENT — *i.e.,* since "the *Masoreths* and Rabbinical *Scholiasts*" have given little heed to all this, they have often been accustomed to blur the margin.

25:4-5 *MASORETHS* AND RABBINICALL *SCHOLIASTS* — The Masoreths were the Jewish scholars who contributed to the Masora, that body of traditional information pertinent to the text of the Hebrew Bible, which was compiled prior to the eleventh century. The Scholiast was a writer of *scholia,* that is, commentaries.

25:5-6 BLURRE THE MARGENT WITH *KERI,* INSTEAD OF *KETIV* — In the Hebrew text of the Old Testament the *Keri* (to be read) is the word, given in the margin, to be substituted in reading for the *Ketiv* (what is written), the traditional wording in the text. Cf. *Areopagitica, Col.* IV, 312, "what ails the modesty of his marginall Keri"; *Author's Defence of Himself, Col.* IX, 111, "Not the writings of Solomon the elegant, nor even of the prophets could escape your proscription of every petty indelicacy, indeed sometimes even of broad obscenity, whenever the Masorets and Rabins think proper to write their marginal *Keri,* to note the eloquent plainness of the text."

25:6 INSULS — *i.e.,* absurd. Cf. *PRE, Col.* III, 89, "insulse, and ill-layd comparison"; *Apology,* 8:3-4, "an insuls and frigid affection."

25:6-8 INSULS RULE...*CIVILL WORDS*— Harris F. Fletcher (*Milton's Rabbinical Readings*, p. 33) has pointed out that Milton probably took the "insuls rule" not directly from the Talmud itself but from the Introduction to Buxtorf's *Rabbinical Bible* in which the "principle of softening the vigor of the text by substituting in the margin words which are less offensive" was stated twice.

25:8-10 FOOLS...WRITE— "Fools," together with its adjective clause, is in apposition with "*Masoreths* and Rabbinicall *Scholiasts*" (25:4-5).

25:10-13 AND THUS...USE— Cf. 24:36-37. Milton feels he has proved that there may be "a sanctifi'd bitternesse against the enemies of truth" (23:28-29).

25:13 THAT YE MAY KNOW— These words are part of the oft-repeated passage of Scripture, "These things have I written unto you...that ye may know" (I John 5:13). No doubt the great familiarity with the passage made the omission of the first clause (which is the main clause of the sentence) unimportant to Milton or his reader who would automatically supply them.

25:14 THE HISTORIAN SPEAKS— *i.e.*, Gaius Sallustius Crispus (86-34 B.C.), commonly known as Sallust. At the age of 36, having already been in succession the quaestor and tribune, he was expelled from the Roman Senate. Three years later he regained his seat by being elected to the praetorship. Through Caesar's influence he became governor of Numidia, where by oppressive and extortionate measures he gained for himself great wealth. After returning to Rome he retired from public life and devoted himself to literary pursuits.

25:14-15 *THAT ALL THOSE THINGS ... OBEY VERTUE*— "Quae homines arant, navigant, aedificant, virtuti omnia parent."—Sallust, *The War with Cataline*, II, 7.

25:16 UNWONTED— *i.e.*, unusual.

25:18-19 NOW THAT THE CONFUTANT... LAUGHTER— Milton, who spoke of "*anger and laughter*" as the "*two most rationall faculties*" of the human mind (see Note 22:8-10), begins the justification of his use of satire (cf. 27:38-39). The Confuter had quoted Milton's words: "*even this veine of laughing (as I could produce out of grave*

Authors) hath oft-times a strong and sinewy force in teaching" (*ANIM* (1641), p. 3; *Col.* III, 107) and had retorted that doubtless Milton meant "*in teaching*...Atheism. For what else it can teach I am as far to seek, as you are of those grave Authors that defend it" (*Modest Confutation*, p. 2; see Note 25:20). He had then quoted Sir Francis Bacon to prove that the intermixing of "*Scripture and scurrility...is a thing far from the devout reverence of a Christian, and scant beseeming the honest regard of a sober man*" (*Modest Confutation*, p. 2). Thereafter he had taunted Milton:

Is this your *noble jealousie*, your *dear love* to the *souls* of weak Christians! this your *well-heated fervency*! for shame render not that holy fire of zeal, which burned as bright in our fore-fathers breasts, as it lyes dead in ours, any further suspected to the world; lest anon, men think it nothing but a name, and *ignis fatuus*, or the lying and false bragge of some vainglorious fools. (*Ibid.*)

The Confuter is referring to the *Animadversions* (1641), p. 3; *Col.* III, 107):

And therefore they that love the soules of men, which is the dearest love, and stirs up the noblest jealousie; when they meet with such collusion, cannot be blam'd though they bee transported with the zeale of truth to a well heated fervencie; especially, seeing they which thus offend against the soules of their brethren, do it with delight to their great gaine, ease, and advancement in this world....

25:20 LAUGHTER...ANSWERING— Since the Confuter has gone to Bacon as an authority, Milton is interested in proving Bacon's point indefensible, particularly the notion that laughter was a force in teaching atheism (see Note 25:18-19). Bacon had said:

The majestie of religion, and the contempt and deformity of things ridiculous, are things as distant as things may be. Two principall causes have I ever knowne of Atheisme, curious controversies and prophane scoffing. Now that these two are joyned in one, no doubt that Sect will make no small progression. And here I do much esteem the wisedome and religion of that Bishop, which replied to the first pamphlet of this kinde, who remembred that a foole was to be answered, but not by becomming like unto him, and considered the matter hee handled, and not the person with whom he dealt. (Bacon, *A Wise and Moderate Discourse*, p. 8; "An Advertisement" in *Resuscitatio*, p. 165; see Note 27:25-27.)

Bacon's reference to "that Bishop, which replied to the first pamphlet of this kinde," is to Thomas Cooper, Bishop of Winchester, who wrote *An Ad-*

monition to the People of England (1589) in answer to the Epistle of Martin Marprelate (1588). Bacon, in alluding to the "foole," was thinking of Proverbs 26:4; Milton turns to Proverbs 26:5 to refute him (see Notes 25:20-22 and 25:34-37).

25:20-22 *A FOOLE ... CONCEIT* — Proverbs 26:5, "Answer a fool according to his folly, lest he be wise in his own conceit." Milton is by implication calling the Confuter the fool (see 26:8-11).

25:23 DOCUMENT — *i.e.*, precept.

25:24 IT TEACHES THE HEARERS — Proverbs 19:25; 21:11.

25:25 PUNISHMENTS ... WISE — *i.e.*, punishments which are the lot of the carnally wise.

25:26 OFT IN SCRIPTURE DECLAR'D — See Proverbs 3:34; 9:12; 19:29; 22:10; Isaiah 29:20; Psalms 1:1; Luke 16:14-15.

25:26-27 *THE SIMPLE* ... TRUE — Proverbs 21:11.

25:28 *ELIAH* MOCKT THE FALSE PROPHETS? — I Kings 18:27.

25:30-31 HE THERE DID — Milton's reference is to Elijah and the gathering of the four hundred fifty prophets of Baal at Mount Carmel to prove whether the god of Baal or Jehovah was the true God (I Kings 18:17-40).

25:34-37 CONFUTANT ... *COUNTENANCE* — See Note 10:36-38. Milton began the paragraph in order to prove that Bacon's statement, aptly used by the Confuter, that the pouring of contempt upon religious matters led to atheism, based upon Proverbs 26:4, "Answer not a fool according to his folly, lest thou also be like unto him," was untrue. Milton turned for his retort to Proverbs 26:5, "Answer a fool according to his folly, lest he be wise in his own conceit." Then he instanced Elijah and the Martyrs to support himself and returned to another statement from Bacon, which he had already discountenanced (10:36-38), to ask the Confuter, in effect, whether he still maintained, with Bacon, that there was no justification for the type of writing Milton had defended in the "Preface" to the *Animadversions*.

25:38 HIS AUTHOR HERE — Sir Francis Bacon.

26:1-4—*LAUGHING* ... FIRST SATIR — From Quintus Horatius Flaccus' (Horace, 65-8 B.C.) *Satires*, Bk. I, Satire I, lines 24-26:
— quamquam ridentem dicere verum
Quid vetat? ut pueris olim dant crustula blandi
Doctores, elementa velint ut discere prima; —

26:4-6 AND IN HIS TENTH ... *EARNEST CAN* — From Horace's *Satires*, Bk. I, Satire X, lines 14-15:   Ridiculum acri
Fortius et melius magnas plerumque secat res.

26:7 I COULD URGE ... *CICERO* — Milton may be thinking of Cicero's *De Oratore*, II, 54: "Suavis autem est, et vehementer saepe utilis jocus et facetiae.... Verumtamen, ut dicis, Antoni, multum in causis persaepe lepore et facetiis profici vidi." See also *De Oratore*, II, 56.

26:7 AND *SENECA* — Milton may be thinking of the single satire of L. Annaeus Seneca (*c.* 4 B.C.- 65 A.D.) entitled the *Apocolocyntosis,* which is his "Pumpkinification" of the Emperor Claudius. The conduct of the Emperor was disturbing to the staid philosopher. Consequently, Seneca made the postmortem attack in which Claudius is "ejected from heaven and sent back by way of earth to Hades" (J. Wight Duff, *Roman Satire*, Berkeley, 1936, p. 91). The account of Claudius' rejection in heaven when he made his application "to be enrolled as a god" is clever and amusing. Although the *Apocolocyntosis* scornfully ridicules Claudius in particular, it satirizes the whole idea of deification. The *Apocolocyntosis* did not appear in print until 1513, but it gained currency by virtue of three editions edited by Erasmus appearing from Basle in 1515, 1529, and 1537. Another important editor of the work was Justus Lipsius whose first edition from Antwerp was issued in 1605. (See *Seneca Apokolokyntosis,* Testo e versione de Augusto Rostagni, Torino, 1944, and *Selected Essays of Seneca and the Satire on the Deification of Claudius,* ed. by Allan P. Ball, New York, 1916.)

26:8-11 AND HENCE FORWARD ... THEM BOTH — Milton rests his case by asserting that he has indicated "the bounds, and objects of laughter and vehement reproofe" though he doubts the ability of the Confuter to understand them even though he has known how to deserve them. Milton has explained the "force of teaching there is sometimes in laughter" (25:19) to the "Foole" (25:20-22), who Milton intimates is still the fool, for Milton doubts that the Confuter "can learn" (26:8).

26:8-9 MAY KNOW — The unexpressed subject is "he."

26:11-14 BUT LEST...BOUNTY FOR? — Milton anticipates the question: "Why are you so concerned that you have appointed yourself to teach by means of 'laughter and reprehension'?" See 26:30-35.

26:16-18 HEATHEN PHILOSOPHERS . . . BEFORE HIM — Socrates spoke of the oracle or sign that came to him forbidding him to do certain things but never commanding anything (Plato, *Apology*, 31; Xenophon, *Apology*, 3-9). Socrates thought of the sign as the genius of the individual, to whom the individual actually belonged during life, and who, after the individual's death led him to the place where the dead were gathered for judgment (Plato, *Phaedo*, 107-8, 113). It was this genius who had made Socrates the gadfly of the state, given by God to stir the state into life (Plato, *Apology*, 31), and it was this spiritual agency or demigod to which he bore witness when Miletus charged him of atheism (Plato, *Apology*, 27). It was for the directing voice of this genius that Socrates listened until he learned what he ought to do and what he ought not (Plato, *Symposium*, 175, 220; Xenophon, *Memorabilia*, 1.4.15-16; 4.3.12; 4.8.1.). (See also "Discourses of Epictetus," Bk. III, ch. 22, in Whitney J. Oates (ed.), *The Stoic and Epicurean Philosophers*, New York, 1940, p. 382, "destroy the Messenger and Spy and Herald of the gods that is in him.")

26:19-20 STOICKS, TO ACCOUNT REASON ...HEGEMONICON — The word "Hegemonicon" is the Greek τὸ ἡγεμονικὸν which means the "guiding faculty." Justus Lipsius, quoting from Nemesius "De Anima" gives a notion of what Milton means: *"Zeno Stoicus, inquit, octonarum partium Animam esse censet, partiens eam in Principem facultatē (τὸ ἡγεμονικὸν) in quinque Sensus, & Vocis mittendae, Procreandią; vim.* [Zeno, he says, considers the mind to be made up of eight parts, dividing it into the principal faculty — the Hegemonicon — the five senses, the power of speak-

ing, and of procreating.]" See Ivsti Lipsi, *Physiologiae Stoicorum Libri Tres*: . . . Antverpiae, 1604, Book III, Dissertation XVII, p. 182, in Justus Lipsius, [*Opera historica, politica, philosophica et epistolica*] (Antwerp, 1596-1625, 8 vols.), Vol. VI. Lipsius quotes furthermore from Stobaeus, providing a Latin rendering:

τὸ ἡγεμονικὸν αρχοντος χώραν ἔχειν, τὰ δὲ ἄλλα μέρη ἐν ὑπηρέτου τάξει ἀπεδ ίδοσαν: *Principale imperantis vice fungi, reliquas partes in ministri loco quamque ducebant* [They (the Stoics) allowed reason to hold the place of leadership; the other parts (faculties) they put in the rank of helpers] (*ibid.*, 183).

26:21 *MERCURY* — The guide or conductor who shows the way. Mercury, the Latin god of commerce, whose cult was derived from that of Hermes, took over, consequently, many of the characteristics of Hermes including those of conducting departed souls, and of being the messenger of the gods. It is interesting to note that Joseph Hall in the anonymous *Mundus Alter et Idem* indicated the book as written by Mercurio Britannico [an English Messenger], thus originating the name used by several English news sheets of the middle of the seventeenth century (see Note 10:11 *MUNDUS ALTER & IDEM*).

26:23-25 I COULD NOT ESTEEME... WARRANT — See Romans 2:15; 8:16; 9:1; II Corinthians 1:22; 5:5; Hebrews 10:14-15; I John 5:10. The Scripture teaches that God in addition to providing the conscience as a guide left his Spirit to be a witness.

26:28 TO MAKE US THE MOST AT A STAND — To place us in a state of arrested progress.

26:30 THE QUESTION ERE WHILE MOV'D — See 26:11-14.

26:34 JERK—"A lash of sarcasm; a cutting gibe" (*OED*).

26:35-37 NEITHER CAN RELIGION . . . AMITY — Cf. 42:7-11; 43:39-44:32; 45:26-46:7; 57:21-58:15; and Note 21:6-8.

26:38 THEIR STRIPES MUST HEALE HER — Echoes Isaiah 53:5, "and with his stripes we are healed"; cf. I Peter 2:24.

26:38-27:2 *ELECTRA . . . WORDS* — A quite
literal translation of Electra's sophism in Sophocles,
Electra, lines 624-25:

οὔ τοι λέγεις νιν, οὐκ ἐγώ. σὺ γὰρ ποιεῖς
τοὔργον· τὰ δ᾽ ἔργα τοὺς λόγους εὑρίσκεται.

[SECTION 2]

27:3-4 IF THEREFORE . . . RIGHT AIM'D —
The second section of the *Apology,* which Milton
did not formally caption "*Sect. 2,*" begins with this
sentence. The section is an answer to Section II of
the *Modest Confutation.*

27:3 REMONSTRANT COMPLAINE OF LI-
BELS — Section II of the *Modest Confutation* begins by charging that Milton's intent in the *Animadversions* was "to maintain and defend libelling."

The Smectymnuans in *An Answer To . . . An
Humble Remonstrance,* p. 1, criticized the "Preface" of *An Humble Remonstrance* as undertaking
to support "two things, which seeme . . . to bee
threatened with danger of a present precipice, *the
Liturgy, and the Hierarchie.*" Hall in *A Defence*
(p. 3) said in answer that their "censure [was]
palpably mistaken";

for that which you mis-call the *Preface,* is one of the
maine pieces of the substance of that intended Discourse, which was a too just complaint of the shamefull number of Libels, lately dropped from our lawlesse
Presses. . . .

Hall's reference to the "shamefull number of Libels"
became Milton's cue to show that the libeling was
done by the bishops and under the control of the
bishops. In doing so Milton turned to Bacon's,
A Wise and Moderate Discourse (1641), pp. 10-11,
"Neverthelesse, I note, there is not an indifferent
hand carried toward these pamphlets as they deserve. For the one sort flieth in darknesse, and the
other is uttered openly," in order to lend weight to
his own argument. Milton said (*ANIM,* (1641),
p. 7; *Col.* III, 111-12):

How long is it that you, and the Prelaticall troop
have bin in such distast with Libells? aske your *Lysimachus Nicanor* what defaming invectives have lately
flown abroad against the Subjects of *Scotland,* and our
poore expulsed Brethren of *New-England,* the Prelates
rather applauding, then shewing any dislike: and this
hath bin ever so, in so much, that Sir *Francis Bacon* in
one of his discourses complaines of the Bishops uneven
hand over these Pamflets, confining those against Bishops to darkness, but Licencing those against Puritans

to be utter'd openly, though with the greater mischeife
of leading into contempt the exercise of Religion in the
persons of sundry Preachers, and disgracing the higher
matter in the meaner person.

The Confuter was thinking of Milton's strictures
when he wrote:

Not to tarry longer in your Preface [*i.e.,* the "Preface"
of the *Animadversions*]; the intent of it was, as of
other passages in your book, rather to maintain and
defend libelling, than to give any pretended satisfaction [see Note 21:3-4]: yet at the same time you condemn it too: condemn it on the Bishops side, defend it
on your own. (*Modest Confutation,* p. 3.)

Milton's opinion is that the Remonstrant's complaint
against libels was made with great insistence because
the Remonstrant was being hit in a vital spot. Cf.
19:24.

27:4-5 AS BEFORE IN THE ANIMADVER-
SIONS, HOW LONG . . . DIS-RELISHT LI-
BELS? — See the passage from the *Animadver-
sions* in Note 27:3.

27:8 HE — Milton is identifying the Confuter
with the Remonstrant. The Remonstrant it was who
was answered in the *Animadversions,* but it was the
Confuter who "*mislikt and censur'd*" (27:9). In
the next sentence the Remonstrant is specifically indicated again as the Confuter (cf. 8:17-18).

27:8-9 *LYSIMACHUS NICANOR*—"Lysimachus Nicanor" was the pen-name of John Corbet
(1603-1641), the well-known, contemporary antipresbyterian writer, as well as the catch title of a
tract he published (see Note 27:3). The author of
the *Modest Confutation,* p. 3, had copied in the
margin Milton's "*Ask your Lysi*-machus Nicanor
what defaming invectives &c. p. 7," in connection
with which he said:

If any of their [the bishops'] party . . . do chance to
write, then their writings are *defaming Invectives*; if
any of yours, then it is *liberty of speaking, permission
of free-writing: nothing more injurious, nothing more
pinching, than the restraint of them to freeborn spirits,*
p. 8. (The Confuter took the italicized words from
the *Animadversions* (1641), pp. 7-8; *Col.* III, 111-13.)

The references to *Lysimachus Nicanor* are to *The
Epistle Congratulatorie Of Lysimachus Nicanor Of
the Societie of Jesu, To The Covenanters In Scotland. Wherein is paralleled our sweet Harmony and
correspondency in divers materiall points of Doctrine and Practice* (1640), written anonymously by

the antipresbyterian author, John Corbet, who had been expelled from the presbyterian ministry. As the title indicates Corbet paralleled the Scottish Covenanters with the Jesuits. Of Corbet, Robert Baillie said, in *Ladensivm ΑΥΤΟΚΑΤΆΚΡΙΣΙS, The Canterbvrians Self-Conviction . . . With a postscript for the Personat Jesuite Lysimachus Nicanor, a prime Canterburian,* of which there were two editions in 1640:

Yee are the first of the *Canterburians* I know, who for the hatred of their party was content avowedly to enter the Iesuits Order, and put on their habit, that from under the maske of their broad Hat, might be spued out on the face of the Covenanters, such a torrent of pestiferous venome, as none would suspect could flow from any other fountaine, then the heart of a very Iesuit. . . . In this your Pamphlet yee vent so much impudency, so many lies and slanders, so much spight and cruelty, and disdainfull pride, so salt and bitter scoffings, mockings, railings, and which is worst of all, so prophane and blasphemous abuse of holy Scripture, for yee make it alway the channell wherethrough your wicked humours must run, for the overwhelming of your enemies. . . . (Quoted from 3rd edition, "Printed for NATHANIEL BVTTER, 1641," "Postscript," pp. 2-3.)

27:9 THAT HE MISLIKT AND CENSUR'D — The Confuter, having claimed that Milton calls anything written by the bishops' party *"defaming Invectives,"* and anything written by his own party *"liberty of speaking,"* etc. (see the quotation from the *Modest Confutation* in Note 27:8-9), continues:

For my own part, I dislike them [libels] equally in both [parties], unless in you somewhat worse, than in all that in this kinde have wrote before, because you stand up to justifie it. That *Lysimachus Nicanor,* which you instance in, (is but one, and truly to my remembrance I have seen no more; one of theirs to an hundred of yours is oddes:) I misliked and censured as much as any that I have read. (*Modest Confutation,* p. 3.)

The Confuter has placed Milton in the same group with Nicanor against whom Milton has railed as typical of the "Prelaticall troop" (see Note 27:3). The Confuter has "misliked and censured" Nicanor; but he thinks Milton's libels "somewhat worse, than in all that in this kinde have wrote before."

27:9-10 NO MORE BUT OF ONE ... REMEMBER — See Note 27:9.

27:11-12 WHEREOF THE REMONSTRANT ...AUTHOR — Milton, whom the Confuter grouped with Nicanor (Note 27:9), proceeds to

show that the Remonstrant, who at present is identified with the Confuter (Note 27:8), belongs in the same category with Nicanor because he is the author of a pamphlet, which he has chosen to forget, which compares favorably with that of Nicanor in its defamation of the antiprelatical party (27:12-20). The Remonstrant — a writer of calumnies himself — has had the boldness to say that there was only one instance when the prelates were guilty of writing *"defaming Invectives."*

27:13-14 A SURVEY ... PROTESTED? — [Joseph Hall], *A Survay Of That Foolish, Seditious, Scandalous, Prophane Libell, The Protestation Protested* (London, 1641), was the anonymous answer to Henry Burton's anonymous *The Protestation Protested: Or, A Short Remonstrance, shewing what is principally required of all those that have or doe take the last Parliamentary Protestation* (1641), which proposed a plan for the coexistence of a national church and of voluntary independent congregations apart from the national church, allowing "a due respect ... to those *Coneregations* and Churches, which desire an exemption and liberty of enjoying Christs *ordinances* in such a purity, as a *Nationall* Church is not possibly capable of" (*Protestation Protested,* Sig. [C3] *verso*). Burton stated that the

particular church, or *Congregation* rightly collected and constituted, consists of none, but such as are visible living Members of Christ the head, and visible Saints under him, the one and only King of Saints: but so it is not with a Nationall Church: all Members thereof are not visible Saints, or visible living *Members,* wherein the greatest part of a Nation commonly is found to consist of persons either ignorant or *profane.* (*Ibid.,* Sig. B3 *recto.*)

The Confuter alleged that "the designe of your dear friend, the Authour of *The Protestation protested,* and some since him, is, to have the Church at length sifted and winnowed, and the grain laid apart by it self, that is your faction" (*Modest Confutation,* p. 29).

27:14-17 THE CHILD ... DELIGHT — "The child [son of Bishop Hall] doth not more expresly refigure the visage of his Father [Bishop Hall], then that book [*A Survay of ... The Protestation Protested*] resembles the stile of the Remonstrant [Bishop Hall], in those idioms of speech, wherein he [Hall] seemes most to delight" (cf. Note 7:20-

22). (Note that the title with its *"Foolish, Seditious, Scandalous, Prophane Libell"* is typical of Hall's titles; cf. 7:15-32. Such words as *"mother the Church"* (Joseph Hall, *A Survay*, Sig. A2 *recto*), *"cursed Shimei"* (*ibid.*, p. 7), *"most glorious Church in the world"* (*ibid.*), and *"boutefeux"* (*ibid.*, p. 13) are idioms in which Hall "delights"; see Note 27:21-23.)

27:18-20 SEVENTEENTH PAGE...FROM HIMSELFE — In *A Survay Of ... The Protestation Protested* (p. 17) occur three lines:

Meane time what a death it is to thinke of the sport and advantage our watchfull enemies will be sure to make of our self-confession ...?

which Milton notes are borrowed from Hall's *An Humble Remonstrance* (pp. 37-38) "word for word":

What a death it is, to think of the sport, and advantage these watchfull enemies will be sure to make of our sins, and shame?

27:20-21 WHO EVER IT BE...WRITES — "Who ever it [*i.e.*, the author of *A Survay Of ... The Protestation Protested*] be, he [the same author] may as justly be said to have libell'd, as he [*i.e.*, Henry Burton, the anonymous author of the *Protestation Protested*] against whom he writes...."
The author of *A Survay Of ... The Protestation Protested* (Sig. A2 *recto*) had considered *The Protestation Protested* a libel:

It is true their scale [position as bishops, etc.] *may expect a more proportioned adversarie, but they, do not mean time consider that Libels the more vulgar, because fitted to that capacity, be the more dangerous; silence appears guilty or timorous to this talkative age. ... This Comet points also at the State, for the loose rain'd popularity the Libeller aims at, is no lesse dangerous to the liberty of the Subject, then a too high tun'd prerogative.*

27:21-23 THERE...WHINES — "There," *i.e.*, in *A Survay Of ... The Protestation Protested*; "here," *i.e.*, in *A Modest Confutation*. Milton, having discovered similarities between the two books (27:14-20), now intimates that there are differences: the author of the *Survay* "bites"; the author of the *Confutation* "whines." Milton insinuates that Bishop Hall wrote the former, the Bishop's son, the latter. A few excerpts from the former will indicate that its tone has much in common with Hall's:

[The Parliament] will in due time provide against these monstrously absurd Libells, that heap of non-

sense, from the which such a vapor of stupiditie and ignorance is exhaled; that who are strangers to our better times, if they behold this Iland thorow the same, shall verily thinke it under universall Lunacie. (Joseph Hall, *A Survay*, pp. 3-4.)

... you idolize onely the calves of your owne making, that is, of your crazed imagination. (*Ibid.*, p. 9.)

... the roaring and out-cries of such braying schismatikes as your selfe.... (*Ibid.*, p. 12.)

But the honourable House of Commons ... will provide for that fire, that gangrene of yours, which hath already inflamed the bed-straw.... (*Ibid.*, p. 15.)

... it will be three ages yet ere you attaine to so much judgement as to understand [the discourses of Mason, Hooker, etc.].... (*Ibid.*, p. 17.)

... fall you once upon the businesse of reformation, you rave perfectly, like these Lunaticks who will perhaps speak sense, doe they encounter with the purpose that first chased them out of their witts, then streight they run out. (*Ibid.*, p. 32.)

... all are *Dogges* and *Swine* to you that will not be of your kennell, nor wallow in your Puddle.... (*Ibid.*, p. 34.)

27:23-24 *VINEGAR ... VIPERS* — Joseph Hall, *A Survay* (p. 3):
If the Reader complaine of Vinegar in the Inke, let him remember that the bite of the Viper (and such they are that rend the bowels of their mother the Church) is best helped by the antidote of Vipers: a phrensie is hardly cured but by the lance, the scourge, the whipping-post....

27:24-25 *LAUGHING ... MELANCHOLY* — Joseph Hall, *A Survay* (p. 32):
Sir, by laughing at you, you have spared me the cost of Physick for expelling malancholy.

27:25-27 IN THE MEANE TIME...UTTER'D OPENLY — Milton is referring to his use of Sir Francis Bacon's testimony in the *Animadversions* (1641), p. 7; *Col.* III, 111-12 (see Note 27:3). Thereto the Confuter answered:

... you have wronged the noble ingenuity and fair memory of that wonder of our age, Sir *Francis Bacon*, whom you here bring in as a witnesse against the Bishops: He complains (you say) *of the Bishops uneven hand over these kind of pamphlets.* You say so: Hear him.

The Confuter then proceeded to quote from Bacon (*A Wise and Moderate Discourse*, p. 8):

[And here I do much esteem the wisedome and religion of that Bishop, which replyed to the first Pamphlet in this kinde; who remembred that a fool was to be answered, but not by becomming like unto him; and considered the matter he handled, and not the person with

whom he dealt.] (Quoted from the *Modest Confutation*, pp. 3-4; the brackets are the Confuter's. See Note 25:20 for the direct quotation from Bacon.)

The Confuter continued, "You will say perhaps, this was but one Bishop: Hear him again in the name of them all," and turned again to Bacon (*A Wise and Moderate Discourse*, p. 10):

[*I hope assuredly that my Lords of the Clergie have no intelligence with these other Libellours, but do altogether disallow, that their dealing should be thus defended: For though I observe in him many glozes, whereby the man would insinuate himself into their favour, yet I find too ordinary, that many pressing and fawning persons do misconjecture of men in authority; and many times Veneri immolant suem, they seek to gratifie them with that they most dislike.*] — [*For I have great reason to satisfie my self touching the judgment of my Lords the Bishops in this matter, by that which was written by one of them, whom I mentioned before with honour.*] (Quoted from *Modest Confutation*, p. 4; the brackets are the Confuter's. See Note 27:28 for the direct quotation from Bacon.)

Then the Confuter concluded: "Whom have you wronged most now? your Authour, your Reader, or the Bishops? Beleeve me, who ever you are, such collusion as this is unchristian" (*Modest Confutation*, p. 4).

Bacon had continued in the passage that the Confuter was quoting by pointing out that "there is not an indifferent hand carried toward these pamphlets as they deserve. For the one sort flieth in darknesse, and the other is uttered openly" (see Note 27:28). That was the sentence that Milton had used as the basis for his charge of the "Bishops uneven hand over ... Pamflets" in the *Animadversions* (see Note 27:3), having in mind the plea for freedom of the press that he was about to make (*ANIM* (1641), pp. 7-9; *Col*. III, 112-13. Notice that Milton connected "Sr Fran. Bacon in a discours of church affairs" with "prohibition of books not the wisest cours" in his *Commonplace Book*, fol. 184 (*Col*. XVIII, 180), and that in this *Apology*, 28-1-7, the mentioning of the "Bishops uneven hand" is followed by a summary of Milton's ideas on "free permission of writing."). It is obvious that Milton had turned Bacon's sentence to his own purposes for Bacon did not favor free discussion (see Whiting, *Milton's Literary Milieu*, p. 269). It is obvious also that Milton quoted only so much from Bacon as would support his party. The author of the *Modest Confutation* noted and exposed Milton's method

stating that "such collusion as this is unchristian" (*Modest Confutation*, p. 4). Milton attempted, somewhat ineffectually, to turn aside the charge by directing attention to Bacon's contradiction of himself and his "aspersiou upon *Iob*" (27:27-31). (See Barker, *Milton and the Puritan Dilemma*, p. 343.)

27:28 *HAD NO INTELLIGENCE WITH THE LIBELLOURS* — Milton is taking his quotation from the *Modest Confutation*, p. 4 (see Note 27: 25-27), the author of which was citing from Bacon, *A Wise and Moderate Discourse* (1641), pp. 10-11 (see also "An Advertisement" in *Resuscitatio*, pp. 165-66). Bacon said:

...I hope assuredly, that my Lords of the Cleargy have no intelligence with these other libellers; but do altogether disallow that their dealing should be thus defended: For though I observe in him many glozes, whereby the man would insinuate himselfe into their favour; yet I finde too ordinary, that many pressing & fawning persons, do misconjecture of the humours of men in authority, and many times *venerie immolant suem,* they seeke to gratifie them with that they most dislike. For I have great reason to satisfie my selfe touching the judgement of my Lords and Bishops in this matter, by that which was written by one of them, whom I mentioned before with honor. Neverthelesse, I note, there is not an indifferent hand carried toward these pamphlets as they deserve. For the one sort flieth in darknesse, and the other is uttered openly. (Cf. Notes 25:20 and 27:25-27.)

27:28-29 *HE DELIVERS ... OPINION* — See Note 27:28, particularly the "I hope assuredly" and "For I have great reason to satisfie my selfe."

27:29 *HAD HE CONTRADICTED HIMSELFE* — Milton points out a seeming contradiction in Bacon in that Bacon admitted that the censorship maintained by the two archbishops and the Bishop of London was partial and yet hoped that the prelates "*had no intelligence with the libellours*" (27:28). The contradiction is averted because the latter idea is only an opinion.

27:30 *ASSOIL* — *i.e.*, refute.

27:30-31 *MORE THEN A LITTLE BEFORE ... IOB* — Cf. Notes 10:36-38; 25:34-37; 27:33-36; 27:37-38.

27:33-36 *THERE ... UPON HIM* — Bacon in *A Wise and Moderate Discourse*, p. 8, had said: "*Non est major confusio quam serii & joci*: there is no greater confusion then the confounding of jest and earnest." That statement he had followed with his discussion on the distance between the majesty of religion and the "contempt and deformity of things ridiculous" and his comment concerning that Bishop who "considered the matter hee handled, and not the person with whom he dealt" (see Note 25:20). Immediately following that he had written:

Iob speaking of the majesty and gravity of a Iudge in himselfe, saith: *If I did smile, they believed me not*; as if he should have said: If I diverted or glanced unto conceit of mirth, yet mens mindes were so possessed with a reverence of the action in hand, as they could not receive it. (See also "An Advertisement" in *Resuscitatio*, p. 165.)

If Bacon has narrowly avoided contradicting himself in regard to the bishops and libels (see Note 27:29), he has, Milton says, in these two statements succeeded in "entangling himselfe" (27:31). The Biblical reference is to Job 29:24. Cf. Note 10: 36-38.

27:37-38 *IOB ... HIM NOT* — Job 29:24, "If I laughed on them, they believed *it* not."

27:38-39 TO DEFEND LIBELS ... ACCUS'D — See Note 27:3.

28:1-4 THE SUMME ... AS NOW THEY HAVE—It was Hall's statement that his "Preface" (see Note 27:3) in the *Humble Remonstrance* had been concerned with the "shamefull number of Libels, lately dropped from our lawlesse Presses; A point no lesse considerable, nor lesse essentiall to that proposed *Remonstrance*" (Hall, *Defence*, p. 3) that gave Milton the opportunity to express himself on freedom of the press. In the *Animadversions* (1641) p. 8, *Col.* III, 113, Milton maintained:

whereas now this permission of free writing, were there no good else in it, yet at some times thus licenc't, is such an unripping, such an Anatomie of the shiest, and tenderest particular truths, as makes not only the whole Nation in many points the wiser, but also presents, and carries home to Princes, and men most remote from vulgar concourse, such a full insight of every lurking evil, or restrained good among the Commons....

The Confuter answered in a long tirade (*Modest Confutation*, pp. 4-5):

This permission of free-writing (so you are pleased to stile the most bitter and Atheisticall libels) *were there no good else in it, yet at some time thus licenced, is such an unripping, &c.*

Let the good be what it will, I am sure it is the most unworthy way of procuring it that may be.... [*These

courses* (saith Master *Sandys*) *are base and beggarly, even when singlenesse of mind and truth do concurre with them....*] ... both which are wanting here in your cause.... (The brackets are the Confuter's.)

. . . . . .

The good that arises of these libels ... is, to incite the people to fury and tumult, to breed hatred, sidings, factions, ruine.

28:5-7 NOT AS WHEN THE PRELATS ... PEN OR PAPER — The use of pen and paper was not generally denied those in custody. However, the occasions upon which it was denied were used to the best advantage by the opponents of prelacy. Thomas May in *The History Of The Parliament Of England: Which began November the third, M.DC.XL.* (London, 1647), Bk. I, pp. 79-80, records that Prynne, Burton, and Bastwicke "were afterward banished to remote places of the Kingdom, and there kept in close and solitary confinement, not allowed pen and paper" (cf. *Calendar of State Papers, Domestic, 1637*, p. 343). William Prynne, in "The Epistle Dedicatoire" of *The Antipathie Of The English Lordly Prelacie, Both To Regall Monarchy, And Civill Unity* (London, 1641), Sig. [¶4] *recto* & *verso*, related:

But the *Arch Prelate of Canterbury* not long after, presenting me afresh in the *Starchamber* without any just occasion, procured me there, not onely to bee most inhumanely censured, but likewise to be sent thence close prisoner, first to *Carnarvan*, then to *Mount-Orguile* Castle in Isle of *Jersie*, and there cloystered up so narrowly that I could neither have the use of pen, inke, paper, writings nor Bookes to benefit my selfe or others....

28:8 *DIVINE ... EPISCOPACY ... ASSERTED* — The claim of superiority for bishops by divine right was first made by Richard Bancroft in 1589. Milton probably has in mind Hall's *"expostulation"* of the doctrine in *An Humble Remonstrance* (1641), pp. 25 ff., and particularly Hall's book entitled *Episcopacie By Divine Right* (1640), which, written at the recommendation of Laud and revised twice under his direction, was considered a statement of the Church's position. Hall states, in "The Epistle Dedicatorie" to the *Episcopacie By Divine Right*, Sig. a *recto*, that his *"zeale was the more stirred"* by learning

that one M. G. Grahame *Bishop of* Orkney *had openly, before the whole body of the Assembly, renounced his Episcopall Function, and craved pardon for having accepted it, as if thereby he had committed some hainous offence; this uncouth act of his was more than enough

*to inflame any dutifull son of the Church, and to oc-
casion this my ensuing (most just) expostulation.* (For
references to Bishop George Grahame see John Rushworth, *Historical Collections. The Second Part*, London, 1680, p. 957; William Laud, *The Works of the
Most Reverend Father in God, William Laud, D. D.* in
"Library of Anglo-Catholic Theology," vols. 56-64, Oxford, 1847-60, 7 vols., III, 178; and Hew Scott, *Fasti
Ecclesiae Scoticanae*, Edinburgh, 1915-28, 7 vols., VII,
353.)

28:8-9 HE WHO WOULD HAVE BEEN RE-
SPONDENT — The "he who would have [de-
fended the thesis]" means, in the general sense,
anyone who would have attempted to write in opposition to the prelates or to the divine right of
prelacy; it may mean, in the particular sense, "M. G.
Grahame, *Bishop of* Orkney" (see Note 28:8).

28:10 REFUTE — *i.e.,* avoid.

28:10 *CLINK,* OR THE *GATE-HOUSE* — The
Clink was a noted prison in Clink Street, South-
wark; the Gate-house was the apartment over the
gate of the palace of Westminster which was used
as a prison. The author of the Marprelate Tracts
wrote: "you ... cry out, 'Down with that side that
favoureth the Gospel so! Fetch them up with pur-
suivants; to the Gatehouse, to the Fleet, to the
Marshalsea, to the Clink, to Newgate, to the
Counter, with them!'" (William Pierce (ed.), *The
Marprelate Tracts 1588, 1589*, London, 1911, p.
151.)

28:10-14 IF NOW THEREFORE ... ACTION
— Milton in defense of freedom of writing points
out satirically that if they who persecuted others
with bad deeds receive in return bad words, or
libels, tumult has been decreased by the anger's
spending itself and failing to result in action.

28:14 THOUGH *MACHIAVELL* ... CITES —
The Confuter made the general statement (*Modest
Confutation*, p. 5): "The good that arises of these
libels, (as the Florentine informs me) is, to incite
the people to fury and tumult, to breed hatred,
sidings, factions, ruine. [Margin] *Mach. discourses
upon Livio, lib.*I.c.8" (*Machiavels discovrses upon
the first Decade of T. Livius translated out of the
Italian ... By E. D.,* London, 1636, is a possible
source). Hall, in *A Short Answer To The Tedious
Vindication* (Sig. [A4] recto), after citing the "mis-
inferences" that the Smectymnuans had made in

their *Vindication*, suggested that there was a
"*Machiavel somewhere*" who should "*be brought
forth to shame.*" Niccolò Machiavelli (1469-1527)
became famous for his *Principe*, which is an analysis of the methods that might be used to gain
sovereign power. It seems to derive from his *Dis-
corsi sopra la prima deca di Tito Livio,* which was
begun earlier than the *Principe,* but was completed
after, and which contained his speculations and
observations on the nature of principalities and on
the qualities of the ruler. That Milton himself was
particularly interested in Machiavelli's *Discourses* is
evident from his many references to it in his *Commonplace Book* (*Col.* XVIII, 160, 183, 197, 199,
200, 210, 211, 212, 215, 217). Machiavelli himself
embodied the spirit of the Renaissance: he was the
impartial searcher for truth, he welcomed the heri-
tage of the ancients, he sought to preserve the state,
whatever its form, and outlined the policies which
would accomplish that end.

SECTION 3

28:18 CHAPLAINE AT HAND — The chap-
lain at hand conducted religious services in the private chapel of a sovereign, lord, or high official.
Milton maintained that the

... Chaplain is a thing so diminutive, and inconsider-
able, that how he should come heer among matters of
so great concernment ... is to be smil'd at. ... The
Scripture ownes no such order. ... In State perhaps
they may be listed among the upper Servingmen of
som great household, and be admitted to som such
place, as may stile them the Sewers, or the Yeomen-
Ushers of Devotion, where the Maister is too restie,
or too rich to say his own prayers, or to bless his own
Table. (*Eikonoklastes, Col.* V, 259.)

28:18-19 SQUIRE ... PRELAT — The squire of
the body was an officer whose duty was personal
attendance upon a sovereign, a nobleman, or other
high dignitary. Milton is derogatory in pointing out
that the prelate's "Squire of the body" is not only
an assistant in the church services, but particularly
officiates at the "Court cup board." Milton is, of
course, opposed to the lordly position and life of the
prelates. Cf. 57:30-58:15.

28:20 HE WILL BESTOW ... HIMSELF —
The Confuter described himself as follows (*Modest
Confutation*, p. 6):
Only first let me satisfie you concerning my engage-
ments and dependencie, which perhaps you may pos-

sibly think might have wrought me to this vindication. I am free, as you, or any true subiect may or need be: I have a fortune therefore good, because I am content with it: and therefore content with it, because it neither goes before, nor comes behind my merit. God hath given me a soul, eager in the search of truth; and affections so equally tempered, that they neither too hastily adhere to the truth, before it be fully examined, nor too lazily afterward. Such excesse fills the world with furious, hot-braind Hereticks, Schismaticks, &c. the defect, with cold speculative Atheists. I have always resolved that neither person nor cause shall improper me, further than they are good; and so far it is my duty to give evidence.

28:21-22 SOBS ME OUT . . . CONVULSION FITS — See the "hopping short" mottoes in the Confuter's "modell of himselfe," Note 28:20.

28:21 TIZICALL — *i.e.*, phthisical, consumptive.

28:21-22 WHERE EVER . . . THEM — *i.e.*, no matter where he got them.

28:24 PERIODS — Well-proportioned, harmonious sentences, containing several clauses.

28:24-25 THUM-RING POSIES — Short mottoes or sentences (originally a line or verse of poetry), often in patterned language, that might be engraved on a thumb ring (*OED*).

28:25 *HE HAS A FORTUNE . . . WITH IT* — See Note 28:20.

28:26 BRAIN OF A FRUIT-TRENCHER — *i.e.*, the brain of one who carries a fruit-trencher, a wooden tray, formerly used as a dessert-plate (*OED*); therefore, the brain of a menial servant.

28:28-31 FOR BY THIS RULE . . . AND THE LIKE — Aristotle (*Nicomachean Ethics*, Bk. IV, ch. 3 [1123b-1124b]) observed that the good man only deserves honor. People who have gifts of fortune, without virtue, can neither be worthy of great things, nor be highminded, for greatness and highmindedness are impossible without complete virtue.

28:31-32 *AND THEREFORE . . . MERIT* — See Note 28:20.

28:36-38 IF A WISE MANS . . . WORLD? — Milton implies that few wise men have a fortune commensurate with their merits (see Note 57:18-19; and Plato, *Laws*, 5.743).

28:39 BOARD — Assail, accost.

28:39-40 *THE SEVEN . . . GREECE* — The story of the wise men of Greece, met with in Plato's *Protagoras*, 343a, is unhistorical. No seven wise men were acknowledged by their contemporaries as the wisest. The names of the seven wise men are variously given including at least twenty-two belonging to widely separated periods. Four men, Thales, Bias, Pittacus, and Solon, are included in all the enumerations. Others frequently mentioned are Cleobulus, Myson, Chilon, Periander, and Anacharsis. The story was referred to and elaborated upon by Plato in *Theaetetus* and Pseudo-Plato in *Hippias major*, by Aristotle, Herodotus, Plutarch, Cicero, Strabo, Diodorus, Diogenes Laertius, and Stobaeus. The sayings of the Seven Sages were taught as a regular part of the sixteenth century grammar school curriculum (see T. W. Baldwin, *William Shakspere's Small Latine & Lesse Greeke*, Urbana, 1944, 2 vols., I, 214) and were common knowledge through such books as Elio Antonio de Lebrija's, *Sapientvm Dicta Vafre Et Acvtissime Cvm Glosemate Aelij Antonij Nebrissensis* (Antiqvariae, 1577). (A good modern study of the subject is Bruno Snell, *Leben and Meinungen der Sieben Weisen*, München, 1938.)

28:40-29:3 ATTRIBUTING . . . *LAZILY AFTERWARD* — See Note 28:20. For the reference to Solomon see I Kings 11:1-8; cf. Nehemiah 13:26.

29:4 CORRUPT . . . *ADAM* — Echoes the comparison made by Paul between Adam and Christ; see I Corinthians 15:22, 47, 48, 50, 53.

29:4-5 BORNE . . . ACTUALL — Among the scriptural passages which deny the possibility of being "borne without sinne originall, and living without actually" are: Job 15:14; 25:4-6; Psalms 51:5; John 3:6; Romans 3:9; 5:12; Galatians 3:22; I John 3:8.

29:6 INSTANCE IN THE WISEST — Solomon was commonly considered the wisest man that ever lived. See I Kings 3:12-13; 4:30-31.

29:6-7 TRANSCENDENT SAGE — *i.e.*, preeminent wise man because of his boast that his *"equally temper'd"* *"affections"* led him inerrantly to the truth (29:1-3).

29:8 *NOT ADHERING . . . TRUTH* — See Note 28:20.

29:8-9 GOD WARN'D ... HALTING IN IDOL-ATRY — I Kings 6:12; 9:6-7; 11:11.

29:10 AFFECTIONS ... TRUTH — I Kings 11: 2; Nehemiah 13:26.

29:12 *STOICK APATHY* — "According to the Stoics, *apathy* meant the extinction of the passions by the ascendancy of reason" (William Fleming, *The Vocabulary of Philosophy,* Philadelphia, 1860, p. 34). One of the opposites to patience is "a stoical apathy; for sensibility to pain, and even lamentations, are not inconsistent with true patience" (*Christian Doctrine, Col.* XVII, 253; cf. *Paradise Lost,* II, 564). The Stoics maintained that things external to the mind were of no consequence to the good man, that is to the man who had subdued all his passions to the power of his reason; they held that all happiness consisted in virtue, in well-doing.

29:13 DIM GLASSE OF HIS AFFECTIONS — The word "affections" frequently has in the Bible a derogatory connotation. See Romans 1:26, 31; Galatians 5:24; Colossians 3:5; II Timothy 3:3.

29:13-14 FRAIL MANSION OF FLESH — The notion that the flesh is weak is based on Scripture. See Romans 7:18, 25; 8:3; II Corinthians 10:2; Galatians 5:17; Ephesians 2:3.

29:16-17 H O W F A R R E ... *P R E F A C E* SPEAKE — Milton refers to the preface "To the Reader" of *A Modest Confutation.* In that preface the Confuter, this man who boasts of "affections so equally tempered that they neither too hastily adhere to the truth, before it be fully examined, nor too lazily afterward" (see Note 28:20), fetched Milton's *"character from some scattered passages"* (*Modest Confutation,* Sig. A3 *recto*) in Milton's *Animadversions.* Since the "fetchings" were completely wrong, the boast is disproved — the boaster does not know his own inaptitudes.

29:18 SUCH STRANGE ... ANIMADVER-SIONS — See Note 11:16.

29:19 WHEREOF ... FROM THENCE — Milton's sarcasm grows. This man, whose eagerness in the search of truth and whose equable temper have been proclaimed (see Note 28:20), has from the *Animadversions* gathered strange facts, none of which are true.

29:20-21 OF *SUBURB SINKS ... AND SWEARING* — See Notes 11:16; 13:21-22; 18:25-26; 18:28-29.

29:23 FENELL RUB'D SERPENT — Herbal lore attributed to the fennel, a perennial herb, many virtues. The notion that the serpent, the eyes of which had been rubbed with fennel, could see very well found its aptest expression and derived its authority from Pliny, *Natural History,* Bk. 20, ch. XXIII.

As for Fenell, the Serpents haue woon it much credit, and brought it into name, in this regard, That by tasting thereof ... they cast their old skin, and by the juice that it yeeldeth do cleare their eies: whereby we also are come to know, that this herbe hath a singular property to mundifie our sight, and take away the filme or web that ouercasteth and dimmeth our eyes. (*The Historie Of The World: Commonly called, The Natvral Historie of C. Plinivs Secvndvs Translated into English by Philemon Holland,* London, 1634, 2 vols., II, 77; see also Edvvard Topsell, *The History Of Serpents,* London, 1608, p. 17, "As concerning their eyesight, they [serpents] naturally doe take the iuyce of Fennel, which they eate, and by that recouer their seeing againe: and if it happen that they cannot finde sufficient, they rubbe their dimme eyes there-vpon"; cf. Visiak, *Milton,* p. 847.)

29:23-24 *THAT NEITHER PERSON ... IMPROPER HIM* — See Note 28:20.

29:25 *IMPROPER* — Perhaps a pun. The verb has the notion of assigning as a private possession. The Confuter has said that only if a person or cause is good will he take it as his own (see Note 28:20). Milton thinks the Confuter's sentence may have a deeper meaning than the Confuter would willingly admit.

29:26 PERSONAGE, OR IMPROPRIATION — Both terms indicate ecclesiastical property that has been converted to private use and profit. "Personage" is an obsolete form of "Parsonage." An "Impropriation" is the possession of a benefice or of the revenues thereof.

29:26-27 BOUGHT OUT ... *IMPROPER* HIM — Milton questions whether a parsonage or benefice secured for the Confuter would not *improper* him, in the true sense of the word.

29:28 CANONIST — *i.e.,* one skilled in the ecclesiastical law laid down by papal decrees and by statutes formulated in Church councils.

SECTION 4

29:30-32 SHORT . . . ATTAINTED — Milton maintains that the one occasion when praise of self need not be short "in breath, and extent" is when "a good name hath bin wrongfully attainted." See 3:27-31; and Notes 14:37; 18:21-22. The Confuter's "dissection of himselfe" (see Note 28:20) was hardly more than fourteen lines long.

29:33 *THAT TEMPER . . . AFFECTIONS* — See 28:30-29:17 and notes thereon.

29:36 NEXT REMOVALL — *i.e.,* Section IV of the *Modest Confutation.*

29:37 THIS DESCRIPTION OF HIMSELFE — See Note 28:20.

29:38-39 STAND . . . MARGENT [margin] — Section III has no marginal notations.

29:39 SLUCE — The sluice is a structure that impounds water and regulates its flow.

30:1 *ARME FULL OF WEEDS* — Milton refers to the *Modest Confutation,* p. 6:

He that shall weed a field of corn, bind the weeds up in sheaves, and present them at once to the eye of a stranger, that is ignorant how much good wheat the field bears, beside those weeds, may very well be deceived in censuring that field; especially if he which presents them hath put into the heap such weeds as came from elsewhere Thus it fares with men, when the evill actions of the best are picked and culled out from their virtues, and all presented in grosse together to the eye or ear of him who is otherwise ignorant of the persons whose vices or faults they are; what monsters do they seem! This and more have you done to our Prelate: This, in pinning upon his sleeve the faults of others: More, in that those which you pretend faults are indeed virtues.

30:2 DOUGH KNEADED — Probably has the notion of impressionable, amorphous, spineless.

30:3 *SYNTAXIS* — Milton's own definition is the "right-joyning of words" (*Accidence Commenc't Grammar,* Col. VI, 287).

30:4-5 *THE STRANGER . . . THE FIELD* — See Note 30:1.

30:6 HIP-SHOT — *i.e.,* clumsy.

30:7-8 *REDDITION* — The clause containing the application of a comparison (*OED*).

30:8-10 *THE FAULTS . . . FAULTS OF OTHERS* — See Note 30:1.

30:14 CONVEIANCE — Conveyance; *i.e.,* manner of expression.

30:14 HIS [nonsense] — The Confuter's. The Confuter and the Remonstrant may be one and the same person in this passage.

30:15 LOOSING — *i.e.,* losing.

30:16-17 WHAT OF OTHER MENS FAULTS . . . LET HIM SHEW — See Note 30:1. The Confuter supposes that Milton by his question in the *Animadversions* (see Note 30:18) "Are not these [martyrs] they which one of your Bishops in print scornfully termes the *Foxian* Confessors?" is pinning upon his, the Remonstrant's, sleeve the faults of others (see Note 30:1). Milton asks the Confuter to produce the evidence.

30:16 HIS [sleeve] — The Remonstrant's.

30:17 HIM [shew] — The Confuter.

30:17 HE [were] — The Remonstrant.

30:18 *FOXIAN* CONFESSORS — The *"Foxian"* refers, of course, to John Foxe and his *Acts and Monuments.* The English bishop who termed the martyrs "Foxian confessors" and who pointed out the similarities between the Roman Catholic Mass and the English liturgy is almost certainly Bishop Richard Montagu, who defended the Anglican Church from both the Puritans and the papists by showing "that the Anglican position was derived from 'ancient founts'" (*DNB,* XIII, 713) and by maintaining that the Anglican Church was a true and sound Church of Christ whereas the "Church of *Rome* is a *true,* though not a *sound* Church of CHRIST" (Richard Mountagu, *Appello Caesarem. A Ivst Appeale From Two Vniust Informers,* London, 1625, p. 113). The Puritans charged him with Arminianism and popery. The reading of Robert Baillie's *A Parallel Or Briefe Comparison Of The Liturgie With The Masse-Book, The Breviarie, the Ceremoniall, and other Romish Rituals* (London, 1641), pp. 1-3, suggests that one or both of the citations — one by the Smectymnuans, one by Milton — attributed to the English bishop (see below) may appear in Montagu's *Antidiatribae ad priorem partem diatribae J. Caesaris Bulengeri* (Cambridge,

1625), which I have not seen. The background of the term "*Foxian* confessors" as used in the *Apology* begins in Hall's *Humble Remonstrance* (pp. 9-10) with Hall's statement:

The Liturgie of the Church of *England* hath been hitherto esteemed sacred, reverently used by holy Martyrs, daily frequented by devout Protestants, as that, which more then once hath been allowed and confirmed by the Edicts of religious Princes, and by your own Parliamentary Acts. . . .

The Smectymnuans in their *Answer* (pp. 5-6) replied:

. . . if these holy Martyrs that once so reverently used the Liturgy should revive and looke for their Letany stampt by Authority of Parliament, they would be amased, and wondering say; *England* had forgotten her selfe and brought forth, &c. Martyrs? what doe we speake of Martyrs when we know Sir, that one of your owne Bishops said it in the hearing of many not so long since, but you may well remember it. *That the service of the Church of England was now so drest, that if the Pope should come and see it, he would claime it as his owne, but that it is in English.*

Hall retorted in his *Defence* (pp. 9-10):

And why should not I speake of Martyrs, as the authors, and users of this holy Liturgy? why should not we glory in their name and authority? sleight you them as you please, we blesse God for such Patrons of our good cause? what a poore return is this? Whiles I tell you what our holy Martyrs did, You tell me what one of our Bishops said; As if we were bound to make good every word that falls from the mouth of every Bishop . . . If a Bishop have said, that our Liturgy hath beene so wisely and charitably framed, as that the Devotion of it yeeldeth no cause of offence to a very Popes eare, as onely ayming at an uncontroversory Piety, I see not what hainous fault can herein be imputed to the speech, or the author. . . .

Milton quoted from Hall's *Defence* and answered (*ANIM* (1641), p. 14; *Col.* III, 120):

Remonst. Slight you them as you please, we blesse God for such Patrons of our good cause.
Answ. O Benedicte! Qui color ater erat, nunc est contrarius atro. Are not these they which one of your Bishops in print scornfully termes the *Foxian* Confessors? Are not these they whose Acts and Monuments are not onely so contemptible, but so hatefull to the *Prelates,* that their Story was almost come to be a prohibited *book,* which for these two or three Editions hath crept into the world by stealth, and at times of advantage, not without the open regret and vexation of the Bishops. . . . (For Archbishop Laud's refusal to license John Foxe's *Acts and Monuments,* see Rushworth, *Historical Collections,* II, 450; *The Works of Laud,* IV, 265-66, 405; Leslie M. Oliver, "The Seventh Edition of John Foxe's *Acts and Monuments,*" *The*

Papers of the Bibliographical Society of America, XXXVII (1943), 243-60; and *DNB,* VII, 588.)

The Confuter defended the Remonstrant from Milton's attack (*Modest Confutation,* p. 6-7):

What hath the Remonstrant to answer for the [Marginal notation: "*Foxian confess. p.* 14"] scorn that is by some thrown upon our Martyrs; while it is known to all, that will not be ignorant, that he doth both honour their memories, and tread in their steps; and that he doth not, as they did, in an holy zeal sacrifice his blood to his God, is not that he is backward to it, but that it is not yet required at his hands.

Cf. Note 51:39.

30:18-19 HE THAT SHALL . . . DEFEND A CHURCH-GOVERNMENT — Bishop Hall, by virtue of his *Episcopacie By Divine Right* and his *An Humble Remonstrance To The High Court Of Parliament,* had become a chief defender of episcopacy. In his *Survay Of . . . The Protestation Protested* he emphasized that bishops were of divine institution. He showed "the Divine institution of *Episcopacy* [to be] from *Christ* himselfe, not from the precept and practices of the Apostles." He held that the "apostolicall office it self, in its proper & *reciprocal* acts, was nothing els but the *Episcopall* . . . as it is now a dayes exercised in the church of England" (Hall, *A Survay,* p. 25), and that the Church of England maintained "a visible succession in the ministery from the very Apostles times." Since the English Church derived directly from the Roman Catholic, it was necessary to declare, as Hall did, that "the Church of Rome though in her old age more faulty" was also a true Church (*ibid.,* p. 29).

30:19-20 WANTS . . . ONLY A NAME — Milton charges that the Church of England is Roman Catholic in all but name (for Milton's notions concerning the English liturgy, see 49:8-50:7). The charge was the more pertinent because Laud had reaffirmed some of the practices that were associated with the Roman Catholic Church. The church government of the Church of England was like that of the Roman Catholic from which it derived except that it was headed by the King of England rather than by the Pope. The author of the Marprelate Tracts in "The Epistle" (1588) stated the case thus:

Martin . . . reasoneth thus. Those that are petty popes and petty antichrists ought not be maintained in any Christian commonwealth. But . . . all the Bishops in England, Wales and Ireland, are petty popes and petty antichrists. . . . [for they] usurp authority of pastors over them who, by the ordinance of God, are to be under no pastors. For none but antichristian popes and popelings ever claimed this authority unto themselves; especially when it was gainsaid, and accounted antichristian, generally, by the most churches in the world. . . . [Yet the prelates] claim pastoral authority over other ministers and pastors, who by the ordinance of God are appointed to be pastors and shepherds to feed others; and not sheep, or such as are to have shepherds, by whom they are to be fed and overseen; which authority the Bishops claim unto themselves. For they say that they are pastors of all the pastors within their diocese. (Pierce (ed.), *The Marprelate Tracts*, pp. 23-26.)

30:21-22 FATHERLY . . . CHRIST — Milton thought the "government of the Gospell . . . economicall and paternall" (*RCG, Col.* III, 267); he thought Church discipline "beyond the faculty of man to frame," being "the worke of God as father, and of Christ as Husband of the Church" (*ibid.,* p. 189). He conceived of the ministry as "set a part to teach and discipline the Church" (*ibid.,* p. 197). He felt that prelacy had "[smothered and extinguished] the spirituall force . . . in the discipline of [the] Church with the boistrous and carnall tyranny of an undue, unlawfull and ungospellike jurisdiction" (*ibid.,* p. 268), for God "has left unto the church no arms but patience and innocence, prayer and the teaching of the gospel" (*First Defence, Col.* VII, 211). He instanced that Christ himself was "called 'the Shepherd,' by reason of his protecting and teaching the church" (*Christian Doctrine, Col.* XVI, 65). Cf. 44:23-29 and 56:3-6.

30:23 POPE ANTICHRIST — The Puritans' ideas concerning the Pope were antithetical to those of the bishops' party. The latter regarded the Roman Church as a true church which had no doubt fallen into great errors, but errors that were not insurmountable. The Puritans believed the Pope to be anathema and Anti-Christ. Robert Lord Brooke (*Nature of Episcopacy,* p. 61) boldly affirmed that . . . He (who ever he be) that Commands the least title of Doctrine or discipline . . . without Licence or Warrant from Scripture, or Right Reason, (where the Scripture hath beene silent) though the Thing he so commands should happen to be good in it selfe: Yet He in his so Commanding, is not onely *Tyrannicall,* but *Antichristian,* properly *Antichristian*; Encroaching on the Royall Office of Christ, which is truly High Treason against God. . . . I care not whether we call

him a *Pope, Papist, Romanist,* or any other name; I call him *Antichrist.* . . .

30:24 THOSE — The prelatical group.

30:25 THAT UNDUE GOVERNMENT — *i.e.,* episcopal church government.

30:25-27 WHICH THEY . . . DESTROY — Milton sees within episcopacy the seeds of its own dissolution.

30:27-28 HE BY PLAUSIBLE WORDS AND TRADITIONS AGAINST THE SCRIPTURE — Hall, in common with the episcopal party, depended upon what Milton called "uncertaine, or unsound antiquity" and the "broken reed of *tradition*" — "needlesse tractats stuff't with specious names of *Ignatius,* and *Polycarpus,* with fragments of old *Martyrologies,* and *legends,* to distract, and stagger the multitude of credulous readers, & mislead them from their strong guards, and places of safety under the tuition of holy writ" (*PRE, Col.* III, 81-82). Milton agreed perfectly with William Fulke, who, in the anonymous *A Briefe and plaine declaration, concerning the desires of all those faithfull Ministers, that haue and do seeke for the Discipline and reformation of the Church of Englande* (London, 1584), p. 80, stated: "wee search the Scripture, the onelye rule whereby the Church of God oughte to be gouerned" (see Note 31:9-10).

30:38-39 HE THAT . . . SCATTERS — Milton is quoting Luke 11:23 (cf. Matthew 12:30). He is depending, as he usually does for his Biblical citations in English, on the King James version. For a study of Milton's quotations from the Bible, see Harris F. Fletcher, "The Use of the Bible in Milton's Prose," *University of Illinois Studies in Language and Literature,* XIV (1929), no. 3. For Fletcher's listing on this particular quotation, see page 96.

30:40 THAT MAN — Milton is thinking in generalities, but the specific application is to Bishop Hall.

30:40-31:2 WHO SO IS WITH HIM . . . SCATTERS MORE FROM HIM? — *i.e.,* who is so diligent for Christ, that he hinders Christ's cause, and gathers so diligently for him, that he "scatters more from him."

31:3-4 THE PHARISEES...HOLY PROPH-
ETS — Milton is referring to Matthew 23:29-31; cf.
Luke 11:47-48.

31:7-8 *GENERATION OF VIPERS...
WRATH TO COME* — Luke 3:7.

31:9-10 PURITY OF SCRIPTURE...ONLY
RULE OF REFORMATION — The Reformation
thinkers and the Puritans were not interested in
creating new precepts in religion; they were interested in removing the abuses which had grown up
within the Church. Both Luther and Calvin were
eager to restore Christianity to the purity that was
supposed to have existed in the third and fourth
centuries. Almost everything that was condemned
by the reformers had come into existence after the
fifth century. St. Augustine (354-430 A.D.) was
the authority to whom they returned, for in his
writings he systematized and summarized the patristic thought of three centuries. What Augustine considered orthodox, the reformers accepted. And
Augustine's measuring stick was the Scriptures. The
reformers, having denied validity to antiquity and
to the acts of the councils, turned to the Scriptures
as the only source of truth. Wycliffe maintained
"that the simple and plain truth doth appear and
consist in the Scriptures, whereunto all human traditions, whatsoever they be, must be referred"
(Foxe, *Acts and Monuments,* II, 800). Luther
affirmed and reaffirmed his inability to submit to
"anything contrary to the gospel of God" (Preserved Smith, *Luther's Correspondence,* "Luther to
the Emperor Charles V at Worms, Friedberg, April
28, 1521," I, 548; see also "Luther to Count Albert
of Mansfeld, Eisenach, May 3, 1521," I, 555).
Luther, upon one occasion, after citing "the place
in Gal.ii, that if an angel from heaven do bring any
other gospel than that we received, he ought to be
accursed," further

alleged the place of Austin unto Jerome, where the
said Austin saith, That he was wont to give this honour
only to the books of canonical Scripture, that whoso-
ever were the writers thereof, he believeth them verily
not to have erred. But as touching all other men's
writings, were they ever so holy men, or learned, he
doth not believe them therefore, because they so say;
but in that respect as they do agree with the canonical
Scripture, which cannot err. (Foxe, *Acts and Monuments,* IV, 269.)

Thomas Cartwright complained that *"The heauenly*

*doctrine of our Sauiour Christ was so buried in the
darkenesse of schoole-learning,* that no man tasted
the sweetnes of it," that

Reason is highlie sett vp against holie scripture, and
reading against preaching, the church of Rome favour-
ablie admitted to bee of the house of God. Calvin with
the reformed churches full of faults: & most of all
they which indeuoured to be most remoued from con-
formitie with the church of Rome: Almost all the
principall pointes of our English creede, greatlie
shaken and contradicted. (Thomas Cartwright, *A
Christian Letter of certaine English Protestants...
vnto that Reverend and learned man, Mr. R. Hoo*[ker],
1599, p. 42-43.)

Joseph Hall pictured the Church of England as the
object of attack by the papists on the one hand for
refusing to maintain Roman Catholic orders, and
by the antiprelatists on the other for "want of purity, because we doe not renounce all continuation
and orders of the Chu[r]ch" (Joseph Hall, *A Survay,* p. 29). Milton stands "on that side where [he
sees] ...the plain autority of Scripture leading" (1:
14-15), for "Scripture...is...the onely Book left
us of *Divine* authority" (*PRE, Col.* III, 81). Milton
proposes "to hold to the Scriptures against all
antiquity" (*ibid.,* p. 101), to let others "chaunt
while they will of prerogatives, we shall tell them of
Scripture" (*RCG, Col.* III, 246), the perfect "rule,
and instrument of necessary knowledge" (*ANIM,
Col.* III, 139). See Notes 31:15-16 and 31:30-32.

31:10 OLD VOMIT — Echoes Proverbs 26:11;
II Peter 2:22.

31:11-12 EITHER TROUBL'D ... GOSPELL
— Cf. I Corinthians 5:6; Matthew 13:33; 16:6,
11-12; Mark 8:15; Luke 13:21. See *Apology,* 51:
36-39.

31:13 MASSE-BORROW'D LITURGIES — Cf.
49:8-13, 30-35. The charge that the English liturgy
was little more than a translation of the Romish
Latin liturgy was a common one. To one such
charge Bishop Hall answered (*A Survay,* p. 16):

Doe you thinke we may not use what is in the Masse
booke consonant to Scripture, and purest antiquity? to
say otherwise, were to deny the Lords prayer and the
Decalogue, because they are there: Indeed I thinke you
intend no lesse then a perfect reformation from *Rome,*
that is, a flat denyall of all that ever *Rome* maintained...God grant you doe not deny Christ to be
the Sonne of God, because the Devills confessed him
to be so.

31:15-16 RELYE ONLY...SCRIPTURES —
See Note 31:9-10. The reliance upon the Scripture
was stated with great insistence by the antiprelatical
party. The validity of the teachings of the Scripture,
however, depended upon the individual interpretation of key passages. Laud admitted that the
"*Ancient Fathers* relied upon the Scriptures," which
had not failed them. He himself "set the *Mysteries
of Faith* above Reason, which is their proper place;
yet I would have no man thinke They contradict
Reason, or the *Principles thereof*" (William
[Laud], *A Relation Of The Conference between
William Lawd...And Mr. Fisher the Jesuite*,
London, 1639, p. 76; cf. *Apology*, 1:13-16). Hall
twitted the author of the *Protestation Protested* by
asking: "are not you and your Bible the onely Judge
of Controversies? can any one finde out the true
meaning of Scripture, except your selfe, who hath
monopolized ... the Spirit of truth? To say otherwise, were to preferre *Rome* to *Amsterdam*"
(Joseph Hall, *A Survay*, p. 3). To many, whatever was not expressly "commanded in scripture"
was considered "*contramandat*" (*ibid.*, p. 25).

31:19-23 *FIRST ... UNTRULY* — In the *Modest Confutation*, p. 7, the Confuter said:

I know what it is that hath rendred many Martyrs and
their stories so suspected as they are, to wary and
uncredulous men: Sometimes a wrong cause; when
Traytours shall engage God in a conspiracy, and then
being detected and brought to execution, dye for it no
lesse undauntedly than if it were for the dearest truth;
unhappily priding themselves in that, for which they
ought rather to have repented.... Sometimes the seeking their own deaths in a good cause, out of ambition
of obtaining that honour, which those first times of
the Church had set upon Martyrdome.... Otherwhiles
the ignorant or malitious unfaithfulnesse of the Mar-
tyrologers, in transmitting to us those Church-stories,
big-swoln with untrue Legends, as so many invincible
arguments of the truth of that cause, which those
Martyrs sealed with their blood.

31:25 *PATRONS...CAUSE* — Milton is refer-
ring to Hall's *A Defence*, p. 9; see Note 30:18. Cf.
"Neither doth the Author [John Foxe] of our
Church History [*Acts and Monuments*] spare to
record sadly the fall...and infirmities of these
Martyrs, though we would deify them" (*REF, Col.
III*, 68).

31:30-32 THE TESTIMONY...WORD OF
GOD — This sentence is a concise, comprehensive

statement of Milton's belief concerning the Bible.
See Note 31:9-10.

SECTION 5

31:33-36 AGRIEV'D...*HE KNOWES* — Hall
in *A Defence*, p. 7, started the discussion:

It is a foule sclander to charge the name of Episcopacie with a faction.... Fie, brethren, are ye Presbyters of the Church of England, and dare challenge
Episcopacie of faction? Had you spoken but such a
word in the time of holy *Cyprian* ... what had become
of you?

To the latter question Milton answered (*ANIM*
(1641), p. 12; *Col.* III, 117):

They had neither bin hal'd into your Gehenna at *Lambeth*, nor strappado'd with an Oath *Ex Officio* by your
bow men of the Arches....

Thereto the Confuter retorted (*Modest Confutation*, p. 8):

After you have born the people in hand, that our Remonstrant hath defamed the old ones [martyrs; see
Note 30:18], it is an easie thing to perswade them
that he hath made new. So you do; [*haled* some *into
the Gehenna at Lambeth, strappado'd* others *with an
oath ex officio* —] If that Court [of High Commission]
hath been illegall, either in the constitution of it, or in
its proceedings, it is more than I know: but if so, the
Remonstrant is as guiltlesse of such illegalities, as I am
ignorant: And a fault committed there can no more
prejudice *Him*, than the Divine right of Episcopacy.
Though your *Bow-men* here were quick in the delivery
of their arrows, yet they were wide of the mark. (First
and last bracketed passages are mine.)

31:35 OATH *EX OFFICIO* — By means of the
ex officio oath the extraordinary courts compelled
victims to bear witness against themselves.

31:37 THAT TYRANNY — *i.e.*, the Court of
High Commission. The Court of High Commission,
as well as the Star Chamber, was abolished July 5,
1641. With that abolition the extraordinary courts
upon which the Tudor monarchy had depended
were no more. Thereafter the King had to exercise
his prerogatives "in accordance with the decisions
of the common law judges" (Gardiner, *History*, IX,
404-05). It was the Court of High Commission
which had been an active agent against the opponents of the Church of England, which had enforced
the desires of the King in matters ecclesiastical, and
which had forced many to flee to Holland and
America. On its bench many a bishop, including
Joseph Hall, had sat to protect the King's preroga-

tive and to perpetuate episcopal authority. The effectiveness of the Court really came to an end with the attack of the London mob on October 20, 1640, which "tore down the benches, seized upon the books, and threw the furniture out of the window" (*ibid.* IX, 215), but it remained a very real threat until its abolition.

32:1-2 THORN-EATER — Devourer of thorns. The inference is that the Confuter is demented. The notion of the "thorn-eater" probably derives at least in part from the Old Testament account of Nebuchadnezzar's being driven from men and eating grass as the oxen (Daniel 4:1-33).

32:2 *QUODLIBETS* — Scholastic exercises in argument or disputation.

32:2-3 *SOPHISMS* — A sophism is a "specious but fallacious argument, either used deliberately in order to deceive or mislead, or employed as a means of displaying ingenuity in reasoning" (*OED*).

32:4-5 THIS SOPHISTER — *i.e.*, a specious reasoner; evidently the Confuter.

32:6-7 WASH HIS HANDS OF — Originally an allusion to Pilate's washing his hands of the blood of Jesus (Matthew 27:24).

32:8-9 THEY SCOURG'D . . . SCOURGERS GARMENTS — Echoes Acts 22:20; cf. Acts 7:58; 8:1. The prelates, acting as members of the extraordinary courts, scourged those who were antiprelatical. The outstanding cases of such scourging were those of Leighton, Prynne, Burton, and Bastwick.

32:9-10 HE . . . WITH THE OATH — *i.e.*, the *ex officio* oath; see Notes 31:35; 31:37; 32:30.

32:11 DID IT — *i.e.*, made possible the scourging.

32:11 CEREMONIES . . . CAUSE OF IT — The antiprelatical party objected violently to the ceremonies that smacked of Rome, which were an integral part of the Church of England as it had been established under the influence of the ritual-loving Queen Elizabeth. The objection to the ceremonies had become more pronounced as Laud, whose idea was to make the English Church as similar to the Roman Catholic in organization as possible, made innovations which seemed to indicate a return to Rome. Although Hall did not

belong to the High Church party, his writings upheld episcopacy in general (see Note 28:8).

SECTION 6

32:14 BATING OF A *SATIR* — Milton is playing upon the confusion between the words "satyr" and "satire" that resulted from the common notion that there was a connection between "satire" and the chorus of satyrs which gave its name to "satyric" drama. It was supposed that the satyrs of the satyric drama gave, of necessity, satiric speeches. Because *i* and *y* were used as interchangeable symbols in the sixteenth and seventeenth centuries, the play on words was facilitated. The "bating of a *Satir*" is the "harrassing" or "worrying" of the Satyr, a woodland god or demon, partly human and partly bestial, and frequently the companion of Bacchus. Milton had in his *Animadversions* (1641), p. 9 (*Col.* III, 113-14), referred to the three books of *Toothlesse Satyrs*, first published by Joseph Hall in 1597 under the general title *Virgidemiarvm* (see Note 10:12-13), by saying: "You love toothlesse Satyrs; let me informe you, a toothlesse Satyr is as improper as a toothed sleekstone, and as bullish [nonsensical]." The Confuter objected to Milton's bringing to light of the Remonstrant's early works, which were not representative of the Remonstrant's maturity, by saying: "If you missed before [in libeling him], now you will be sure to hit him." Thereupon the Confuter quoted Milton's: *"You love toothlesse Satyrs; Let me inform you, a toothlesse Satyre is as improper as a toothed sleek-stone, and as Bullish,"* and commented:

I wonder you go no lower; perhaps his cradle might have yeelded you some worthy observation: It was reckoned amongst Saint *Augustines* faults, that in his infancy he did *morosiùs flere*. Such a note had not been amisse here: but *vixit* is enough for that; an happy time, that you cannot invent a slander to fixe upon. You begin therefore with his youth; the sport and leisure of his youth, even that must be raked up out of the dust, and cited to witnesse against him, as it were to disparage the holinesse of his Age and Calling. (*Modest Confutation*, p. 8.)

32:16-18 FOLLY OF THIS CONFUTER . . . BLAZE OF IT — Milton alleges that he intended the remark concerning "toothlesse Satyrs" only for the Remonstrant, but, because the Confuter devoted all of Section VI of the *Modest Confutation* to prove that a "toothlesse Satyr" is not improper, nor bullish, Milton will elaborate on the subject that must be distasteful to the Remonstrant (see Notes 32:14 and 32:22).

32:17 PRIVATE—*i.e.*, "Intended only for . . . the person . . . directly concerned" (*OED*).

32:18-21 I HAD SAID . . . SLEEKSTONE — Hall in *A Defence* (p. 3) had stated that his so-called preface to *An Humble Remonstrance* was a "too just complaint of the shamefull number of Libels," a point of considerable importance to the Remonstrant (for background see Note 27:3). Milton pointed out in the *Animadversions* (1641) pp. 7-9 (*Col.* III, 112-14) that the reason the Remonstrant objected vehemently to the alleged libels was that he felt they were right aimed:

Wee know where the shoo wrings you, you fret, and are gall'd at the quick, and O what a death it is to the Prelates to be thus un-visarded, thus uncas'd, to have the Periwigs pluk't off that cover your baldnesse, your inside nakednesse thrown open to publick view.

He then pleaded for "permission of free writing" as a means of making the nation "in many points the wiser" and of giving the rulers an insight into the conditions in the land. He added:

Who could be angry therefore but those that are guilty, with these free-spoken, and plaine harted men that are the eyes of their Country, and the prospective glasses of their Prince?

These are the very writers, Milton pointed out, who irritate the prelates, although their books do not reveal half the doings of the prelatical group. Milton therefore charged that the Remonstrant loves "toothlesse Satyrs," that is, harmless satires. But in Milton's opinion "a toothlesse Satyr is as improper as a toothed sleekstone, and as bullish." For the comment on "toothlesse Satirs" see Notes 10:12-13 and 32:14.

32:20-21 TOOTHED SLEEKSTONE — The sleekstone was a "smooth stone used for smoothing and polishing" (*OED*; see Note 32:25-26); "toothed Sleekstone" is, therefore, a contradictory term.

32:21 CHAMPION . . . ARRAS — The allusion is to *Hamlet,* Act III, Scene iv, in which Polonius hides behind the arras in order to overhear the conversation between Hamlet and his mother so that he can determine Hamlet's mental condition. Alwin

Thaler, "The Shakesperian Element in Milton," p. 645, has noted that "it is characteristic of the working of Milton's creative imagination that he fused — or transfused, into something new and strange — the rich and varied stories of his memory." Milton's "Champion" does not cry out "O, I am slain," as Polonius did, but rants about "toothlesse Satyrs." The "Champion" is the Confuter, hidden by the arras of his anonymity, crying out in defense of the Remonstrant.

32:22 THOSE TOOTHLESSE SATYRS . . . MAKING — Since the *Toothlesse Satyrs* had been published anonymously (see Note 10:12-13), few people knew that Bishop Hall was the author. The Confuter revealed to the public by his discussion of the satires that the Remonstrant had written them. Milton insinuates that he, Milton, would have preferred not to show or remind the world that the Bishop of Norwich had written works such as these satires in his youth, that he preferred to twit Hall privately (see Note 32:16-18). But the Confuter with naïveté and indiscreetness had admitted Hall's connection (see Note 32:14) and had elaborated thereupon:

[*When my early sinnes are done away as a morning cloud, they shall never obscure or darken my setting Sun: God will never impute them to me, man may*] hath been the comfort of many a dying Saint, in the day of evill, when the iniquity of their heeles have encompassed them; many, whose first years have been as famous for debauchednesse, as their latter for devotion: whiles this *Remonstrant* no sooner came to be capable of the more violent impressions of sin, but his nature and it fell foul; and because he had overcome vices in himself, he took liberty to whip them in others. Which timely zeal, as it did not mis-become his youth, so can it not disparage his Prelacy; no, not as Poesie, not as Satyr. (*Modest Confutation*, p. 8. The brackets are the Confuter's.)

32:23-24 ARMES HIMSELFE . . . SATIRS — The Confuter devotes a number of pages (*Modest Confutation*, pp. 9 ff.) to the defense of the term "toothlesse Satyrs" citing that *Satyra* designated "anciently any kind of miscellaneous writing," that, since "*dens* or *dentatus*" cannot be considered in their "primitive or proper signification" when placed in connection with "Satyre," "we must seek then some other sense for it; where I finde teeth and horns to signifie strength, used to defense or injury. Nothing is more familiar in Scripture, than *horn* for *strength* . . . *He hath raised up an horn of salva-*

tion; a strong salvation." After calling upon Martial, Horace, and others to support his thesis, he adds: "...it is no *Bull* to say a toothlesse Satyr, *i.e.*, an harmlesse Poem, that doth...spare the person, but strike the vice." (Note Milton's use of the idiom "tooth and naile" in connection with the verb "armes." The "naile" has no significance other than as part of the idiom; the "tooth" and *"horne"* have, as has already been pointed out, other significance.)

32:25-26 *SHEWES*...*LAUNDRESSE* — In the *Modest Confutation*, p. 9, the Confuter said:

To let passe therefore your simile of the *sleek-stone* (which shews that you can be as bold with a Prelate [*i.e.*, the Remonstrant], as familiar with your Laundresse,) why, in the name of Philology, is a toothlesse Satyr improper? why Bullish?

Since the sleekstone was commonly used for ironing clothing, Milton's reference to sleekstone in the *Animadversions* (see Note 32:18-21) brought to the Confuter's mind the *"Laundresse,"* and offered the Confuter another opportunity to attack Milton's virtue. Milton answers that the Confuter's simile merely shows the "lascivious promptnesse" of the Confuter's fancy (32:26-27).

32:28-30 NEIGH OUT... *VIRAGINIAN* TROLLOPS? — Cf. Note 14:3-4. The Confuter's folly (32:16) has made public Hall's early verse satires. It does more. It calls attention also to his prose satire. Milton charges that the "lascivious promptnesse" of the Confuter's fancy has somehow, at the mention of the word "sleekstone," caused the Confuter to think Milton *"familiar with a Laundresse"* (see Note 32:25-26), prompted no doubt by his remembrance of conversations with the slatterns in Viraginia (Shee-lands), where Hall had once been prisoner of the viragoes, and had subjected himself to their manner of life.

32:29 CONVERSATION — *i.e.*, manner of living; behavior; conduct. Cf. 11:23-24.

32:30 HIS OWNE OATH — Milton maintains that Hall has "defended the government with the oath" (see Note 32:9-10) that made possible the "cruelties exercis'd by the Prelats" (32:7), the oath *ex officio*, which is therefore Hall's own oath (32:6-12).

32:31-33 OATH *EX OFFICIO*...THEM ALL — Milton declares that he is innocent of such in-

sinuations as the Confuter has made against his character (32:25-26). Furthermore, if the Confuter give him reason, Milton will, by the use of the *ex officio* oath, force "any Priest or Prelat" to show by revealing his own life that Milton's virtue is unassailable as is that of the "best and chastest" of the priests and prelates. Cf. 18:36-38.

32:33 EXCEPTION — *i.e.*, objection.

32:33 WHICH I MADE... SATIRS — See 32: 18-21 and Notes 32:14; 32:18-21.

32:34 [That exception...] THE CONFUTER HOPES I HAD FROM THE *SATIRIST* — See *Modest Confutation*, p. 9:

Euge novam Satyram, Satyrum sine cornibus euge!
Monstra, novi monstri, haec; & Satyri & Satyrae!

The Authour himself furnished you with the exception: and had you had but so much life or quicknesse in your pallade, as to have tasted an Epigram, you might have understood he speaks there in the person of such carping Poetasters as you, and your now-despised Tribe, are....

32:34 THE *SATIRIST* — Joseph Hall in the "Prologue" of Book I of the anonymous [*Virgidemiarvm, Sixe Bookes. First three bookes of Toothlesse Satyrs*, London, R. Bradocke for R. Dexter, 1598], Sig. B *recto*, declared:

I First aduenture, with fool-hardy might,
To tread the steps of perilous despight:
I first aduenture: follow me who list,
And be the second English Satyrist.

32:35 HOBBLING *DISTICK* — The Confuter copied with minor changes one of three epigrams from the *Virgidemiarvm* (see Notes 32:34). Hall's distich from the "De suis Satyres" read:

Ecce nouam Satyram: Satyrū sine Cornibus! Euge Monstra noui monstri haec, & Satyri & Satyrae. [Behold the new satire, a satyr with horns! Hail these monsters of a new monster, both of satyr and of satire.] ([*Virgidemiarvm, Toothlesse Satyrs,* 1598], Sig. [A8] *recto*.)

Milton used either the 1597 or 1598 editions of *Virgidemiarvm, Sixe Bookes. First three bookes of Toothlesse Satyrs,* because the poems "His Defiance to Enuy" and the "De suis Satyris" which are prefaced to the 1597 and 1598 editions of *Toothlesse Satyrs* were omitted from the 1602 edition. They appeared, however, prefixed to the three books of *Byting Satyres,* 1599 edition of *Virgidemiarvm*:

The three last Bookes. Of Byting Satyres. See Notes 33:5-6; 33:11; and 43:16-19.

32:39-40 RATHER NICE...THEN PATIENT — *i.e.,* "[being] rather nice [fastidious] and humorous [influenced by humour or mood, perhaps, humoring] ... [than] patient."

33:1 *TOOTHLESSE SATIRS* — See Note 10: 12-13.

33:3 SUCKING SATIR — Note the confusion between the words *satire* and *satyr* (see Note 32: 14). Milton is using the word "Satir" to designate one of the woodland gods or demons.

33:4 CORALL — "A toy made of polished coral, given to infants to assist them in cutting their teeth" (*OED*).

33:4 AN END OF BREEDING — *i.e.,* completed his education. Cf. *Means to Remove Hirelings, Col.* VI, 91-92, "boyes ... had the most of their breeding both at schoole and universitie by schollarships."

33:5 WEILD A SATIRS WHIP — Because of the confusion of the words *satiric* and *satyric,* the sixteenth and seventeenth centuries frequently attributed censoriousness to the satyr (see Note 32: 14). The "Satirs whip" is *satire.*

33:5-6 *SCOURING THE RUSTED SWORDS OF ELVISH KNIGHTS* — From Hall's poem "His Defiance to Enuy," prefaced to [*Virgidemiarvm, Toothlesse Satyrs,* 1598], Sig. [A5] *recto:*
> *Or scoure the rusted swords of Eluish knights*
> *Bathed in Pagan blood....*

"referring to Spenser." See Spingarn, *Critical Essays,* I, 250.

33:8-9 *SCORNEFULL MUSE ... FOR TO HIDE* — From Book I, Satire I, of [*Virgidemiarvm, Toothlesse Satyrs,* 1598], p. 1.
> Nor euer could my scornfull Muse abide
> VVith Tragick shooes her ankles for to hide.

33:8 *TRAGICK SHOOS* — *i.e.,* buskin; the high thick-soled boot worn by the actors in ancient Athenian tragedy.

33:8-9 *ANKLES FOR TO HIDE* — Hall is saying that his muse which is scornful (satiric) in nature could not wear "tragick shoos" (the lofty style of tragedy) for any length of time in order to

hide her ankles. The alternative is to wear the sock, the light, low shoes worn by comic actors on the ancient Greek and Roman stage.

33:9 PACE OF THE VERSE — Milton may have in mind Book I, Satire VI, of *Toothlesse Satyrs* in which Hall satirizes the pace of English verse:
> The nimble *Dactils* striuing to out-go
> The drawling *Spondees* pacing it below.
> The lingring *Spondees,* labouring to delay,
> The breath-lesse *Dactils* with a sudden stay.
>
> .   .   .   .   .   .
>
> If *Ioue* speak English in a thundring cloud,
> *Thwick thwack,* and *rif raf,* rores he out aloud.
> Fie on the forged mint that did create
> New coyne of words neuer articulate.
> ([*Virgidemiarvm, Toothlesse Satyrs,* 1598], pp. 13-14.)

33:9-10 MAUKIN KNUCKLES — Unshapely, slatternly ankles. E. H. Visiak equates the word "maukin" with "morkin (diseased, scabrous)" (Visiak, *Milton,* p. 848).

33:10 ROYALL BUSKIN — Tragic vein.

33:11 SIXTH SATYR...SECOND BOOK — Milton's reference (33:12) is actually in Book II, Satire VII, which represents "the signs of the Zodiac as twelve inns in the high-street of heaven: the names of the taverns and of the thoroughfare (Bridge Street) are derived from those in Cambridge; and the astrologers, who are in attendance, are hostlers, tapsters, and chamberlains" (Spingarn, *Critical Essays,* I, 250). Milton's error in the number of the Satire furnishes further proof (see Notes 32:35 and 33:12-14) that he used the 1597 or 1598 *Virgidemiarvm* in which Satire VII of Book II was erroneously numbered Satire VI. Milton, probably glancing hastily through the volume, evidently did not check the correctness of the Satire number (see [*Virgidemiarvm, Toothlesse Satyrs,* 1598], pp. 43-46). In the 1602 edition the correction had been made.

33:12-14 *IN HEAVENS ... OSTLER OF HEAV'N* — In Book II, Satire VII, of [*Virgidemiarvm, Toothlesse Satyrs,* 1598], pp. 43-45, Hall says:
> In th'heauens vniuersall Alphabet,
> All earthly things so surely are foreset

That who can read those figures, may foreshow
What euer thing shall afterwards ensue.

. . . .

In th'heauens *High-streete* are but a dozen roomes,
In which dwels all the world, past and to come:
Twelue goodly *Innes* they are, with twelue fayre
   signes,
Euer wel tended by our *Star-diuines*.
Euery mans head Innes at the horned *Ramme*,
The whiles the necke the *Black-buls* guest became:
Th'arms by good hap, meet at the wrastling twins,
Th'heart in the way at the *Blew-lion* innes.
The legs their lodging in *Aquarius* got,
That is the *Bridge-streete* of the heauen, I wot.
The feete tooke vp the *Fish* with teeth of gold:
But who with *Scorpio* lodg'd, may not be told.
What office then doth the *Star-gazer* beare?
Or let him be the heauens *Ostelere*:
Or *Tapsters* some or some be *Chamberlaines*.

In the 1602 edition *Bridge-street* has become *Bride-street*, which it remains in *The Complete Poems Of Joseph Hall, D. D.*, volume VIII of "Occasional Issues of Unique or Very Rare Books," edited by the Rev. Alexander B. Grosart, Printed For The Subscribers, 1879, p. 57, further indicating that Milton used the 1597 or 1598 edition (see Notes 32:35; 33:11; 43:16-19).

33:15 CATCH HIM A HEAT — Give him intensity or great warmth of feeling.

33:15-16 IN THE FROZEN *ZONE* MISERABLY BENUMM'D — *i.e.*, miserably uninspired. Cf. "frigidity" (33:13).

33:16-19 WITH THOUGHTS ... PITTIFULL — *i.e.*, the author of *Virgidemiarvm*, "with thoughts lower then any Beadle[,] betakes him" "in a straine as pittifull [*i.e.*, miserably insignificant]" "to whip the signe posts of *Cambridge* Alehouses, [which are] the ordinary subject of freshmens tales." The twelve signs of the Zodiac are, in Book II, Satire VII, the signs or sign posts for twelve inns. The taverns, the *Ramme*, the *Black-buls*, the *Blew-lion*, etc., on Bridge-street, Cambridge, which are patronized by the students studying for the priesthood, that is, "Euer wel tended by our *Star-diuines*," are "whipped," that is, afflicted or tormented, by being forced into the scheme of the "twelue goodly *Innes*" in "heauens *High-streete*" (see Note 33:12-14).

33:19-20 *THE FIRST ENGLISH SATYR* — See Note 32:34 THE *SATIRIST*.

33:20 ABASE — *i.e.*, debase.

33:22 *VISION . . . PLOWMAN* — William Langland (*c*.1332-*c*.1400) is the supposed author of *The Vision of Piers Plowman*. The author of *The Creed of Piers Plowman*, which appeared with the *Vision* in the 1561 edition, imprinted at London by Owen Rogers, is unknown.

33:24-26 FOR A SATYR ... PERSONS — Aristotle spoke in the *Poetics*, Ch. 4 [1449a], of the development of old tragedy through the satyric stage to a position of magnitude and dignity. Ancient grammarians early derived the Latin word *Satira* from the Greek σατυρος (satyr) which had given Greek satyric drama its name. Horace, following the current derivation of *tragoedia*, that is, *goat song*, connected satyric drama closely with tragedy, insisting that it maintain a certain dignity and reserve in view of its high origin (Horace, *The Art of Poetry*, 220 *et seq.*). See St. John, *Prose Works of Milton*, III, 141 note.

33:27 EVERY BLINDE TAPHOUSE — *i.e.*, obscure alehouse. Milton is referring to the Cambridge taverns which Hall mentioned in Book II, Satire VII, of *Virgidemiarvm* (see Note 33:16-19).

33:29 A BULL — A self-contradictory proposition; a blunder. The Confuter in referring to the "Epigrams" (see Note 32:35) to the *Virgidemiarvm* said: "They say, they are Monsters; you, that they are Bulls: you mean, I suppose, Chymaera's; absurd and ridiculous compositions of words, inconsistible with sense" (*Modest Confutation*, p. 9). Cf. Note 35:14-15.

33:30-31 FOR IF IT BITE ... IF IT BITE EITHER — The Confuter had defined the "toothlesse Satyr" as "an harmlesse Poem, that doth ... spare the person but strike the vice" (*Modest Confutation*, p. 10; see Note 32:23-24).

33:33-34 LEARNED COMMENT ... *HORNS* — See Note 32:23-24.

33:34-35 *PEDANTICK* KINGDOME OF *CORNUCOPIA* — In defending the term "toothlesse Satyrs" the Confuter digresses to show that, if the obvious sense of the words does not apply, "we must seek then some other sense" (*Modest Confutation*, p. 9). Using *"horn"* as an example of a word used in various senses, he cites authorities in both text and margin using *"cornu"* several times as well as "Keren," "κέρας," and "cornupetis." The term *"Cornucopia"* has the flavor, in this instance, of a pun meaning "an abundance of *'cornu's.'* "

33:35-36   GLOSSING...*HEBREW ROOT* — In the margin of the *Modest Confutation*, p. 10, the Confuter noted: "Luk.I.69. Hebraeis familiare est (*Karen*) id est cornu, pro vi & robore usurpare, sumpta metaphora ab animalibus cornupetis. *Beza ad loc.*" A part of Beza's comment on Luke 1:69 was: "Est enim Hebraeis familiare קרן (*keren*) id est cornu, pro vi & robore vsurpare, translatione sumpta ab animalibus cornupetis" (Theodori Bezae, *Annotationes Maiores*, [Geneva], 1594, Part I, p. 248).

33:37-38   LECTURER ... DETFORD — Milton proposes that the Confuter's ability in "glossing upon *hornes*" be rewarded by allowing him to lecture upon them on "S. *Lukes* day." Because the representations of St. Luke in sculpture and painting usually portrayed him in the act of writing, with an ox or cow by his side, the horns of which were very conspicuous, horns or the horned ox came to be thought of as the symbol of St. Luke. On St. Luke's Day, October 18, in the village of Charlton, about eight miles from London, and very near Deptford, an annual fair was held. King John originated the fair by a grant to the inhabitants of Charlton. The fair was primarily intended for the sale of goods made of *horn*. The original significance of the horns was lost as the years passed, whereupon the horns became associated with horns on the head and cuckolds. Thus the fair became an occasion for "unusual licence." Men, dressed in women's clothing, amused themselves, particularly while making their way across Blackheath, by "lashing the women with furze, it being proverbial that 'all was fair at Horn Fair'" (R. Chambers, *The Book of Days*, London & Edinburgh, 1914, 2 vols., I, 645; cf. T. F. Thiselton Dyer, *British Popular Customs Present and Past*, London, 1911, pp. 386-87; John Brand, *Observations on the Popular Antiquities of Great Britain*, arranged, revised, and enlarged by Sir Henry Ellis, London, 1888-95, 3 vols., II, 194; and W. Carew Hazlitt, *Faiths and Folklore*, London, 1905, 2 vols., I, 326). One procession of holiday-makers started at Cuckold's Point and marched through Deptford to Charlton. Other processions, beginning at the inns of Bishopsgate-

street and other places passed through Eastcheap before crossing London Bridge, gathering merrymakers as it went. The riotous paraders, wearing horns of various kinds on their heads, proceeded through Deptford and Greenwich to Charlton where they marched around the church three times and proceeded to the green opposite the church. Horns were everywhere in evidence: the vendors' booths were decorated with horns, the gingerbread figures had horns. It appears that the stained-glass windows of the church featured St. Luke and horns. (See William Hone, *The Every-day Book*, London, 1826-27, 2 vols., I, 1386-89; Fred Emil Ekfelt, "The Graphic Diction of Milton's English Prose," *PQ*, XXV (1946), 55.) The "tribute" which Milton mentions probably refers to the "horns" which people of Eastcheap wore in tribute to St. Luke, although Visiak thinks it refers to "the toll paid to the King on the sale of goods in the Fair" (Visiak, *Milton*, p. 848). Milton is perhaps suggesting that the Confuter might use his absurdly learned comments on "horns" in Eastcheap on St. Luke's Day when there would be few to listen to him. Visiak suggests that in the

Middle Ages on feast days displays of learning were common in the pulpits of Festival churches: hence the reference to "lecturer". If the lecturing in this case took place in a church, that church was almost certainly St. Clement's in Clement's Lane; but, more probably, it took place in the open air. (*Ibid.*)

33:39   SCAPE — *i.e.*, escape.

33:39-34:1   WORME OF *CRITICISME...OF INK* — Milton's reference is to the Confuter's words (*Modest Confutation*, p. 12):

And *Suetonius*...tells us how the Romans used the old Germane word (*Rutters*) which they still use to signifie horsemen in war. And so perhaps our English word (Meat) is but *Mattya* fashioned to our dialect .... So the Italian Inciostro from the Latine word *Encaustum*, as likewise our English word (Inke.)

In addition to these statements, together with supporting evidence from Martial, the Confuter adds Latin marginal notes of some length for each of the words "*Rutters*," "*Mattya*," and "*Encaustum*" (*ibid.*).

34:1-2   *RUTTERS*...HEALE — Milton is thinking of the strange concoctions used as curative agents. He suggests rutters, meat, and ink mixed with gall. See Note 33:39-34:1.

34:2 TETTER — A general term for pustular skin diseases. Cf. *REF, Col.* III, 21, "What a universal tetter of impurity hath invenom'd every part, order, and degree of the Church."

34:3 *TENASMUS* — Thomas Cooper in *Thesaurus Linguae Romanae & Britannicae* (London, 1565), defines the word as a "vayne desire to goe oftē to the stoole, and yet can doo nothyng."

34:4 ARMINIAN — A follower of the doctrine of Jacobus Arminius (1560-1609), the Dutch theologian. Arminius was the formulator of the modified reformed theology which held that because Christ died for all men, any man could be saved; nevertheless, any man could resist salvation, and any man possessing salvation could fall from divine grace; therefore, eternal life was predestined to those who were faithful. Arminius proposed freedom of the will for man as opposed to Calvinistic predeterminism. The Arminians had become hated by the Calvinistic Protestants, particularly because Andrewes, Laud, and others, in their desire to establish the hierarchy of the Church of England and the English liturgy on a firm basis, insisted on the adoption of Arminian principles in place of Calvinistic (Masson, *Life,* I, 518). The Arminian Anglicans were, of course, "passionately devoted to the royal prerogative and the defence of the Divine right of Kings" (A. H. Drysdale, *History of the Presbyterians in England,* London, 1889, p. 243), which resulted in much opposition (Masson, *Life,* I, 216). The Confuter noted: "If some Bishops be Arminians, and some Scholars at either University, that infection came from beyond sea, though not in the same ship with your Presbytery" (*Modest Confutation,* p. 35).

34:4 DENY ORIGINALL SINNE — Whereas Luther and Calvin believed that God accounted man guilty because of the indwelling sin inherited from Adam, the Arminians rejected the idea of the imputation of Adam's sin to his descendants.

34:5-6 *ETYMOLOGIES* ... TAINTED WITH THAT INFECTION — Note the pun on *original sin.* Milton is saying that all the Confuter's etymologies indicate that his brain is tainted considerably with the sin of originating.

SECTION 7

34:7 CAVILL OUT — Do away with.

34:9-10 *CIVILL POLITY ... ARBITRARY* — Bishop Hall in *An Humble Remonstrance,* p. 8, made the statement that

if you finde it passe for one of the maine accusations against some great persons ... that they endeavoured to alter the forme of the established government of the Common-wealth; how can these Pamphleteers seem worthy of but an easie censure, which combine their counsels and practises, for the changing of the setled form of the government of the Church? Since, if Antiquity may be the rule, the civill Politie hath sometimes varied, the sacred, never. ...

The Smectymnuans noted in their *Answer,* p. 4:

the comparison ... between the two Governments, the Civill which with us *is Monarchie:* and the sacred which with *him is Episcopacy.* Of the first he saith, *if Antiquity may be the Rule;* (as he pleades it for Episcopacy) or if Scripture (as he interprets Scripture) it is VARIABLE, and ARBITRARY: but the other DIVINE and VNALTERABLE, so that had men petitioned for the altering of *Monarchicall* Government, they had (in his Iudgement) beene lesse culpable, hoth by Scripture, and Antiquity, then in petitioning the alteration of *Hierarchicall:* Had he found but any such passage in any of his *Lewd Libellers* ... certainly ... *the whole Christian world, and no small part beyond it,* had rung with the lowd cryes of no lesse then *Treason, Treason.*

The Remonstrant defended himself (*Defence,* pp. 4-5):

In comparing of Governments of Churches and States, I had said, that if Antiquity may be the rule, the Civill Politie (as in generall notion) hath sometimes varied, (as that of the State of Rome had done to seven severall formes) the Sacred, never; The Civill came from arbitrary imposers, the Sacred from men inspired: these gracious Interpreters would needs draw my words to the present, and particular Government of our owne Monarchie, as if I implyed that to be variable and arbitrary; and are not ashamed to mention that deadly name of *Treason.* ...

Milton added to the Remonstrant's woes (*ANIM* (1641), p. 10; *Col.* III, 115):

Bishop *Downam* in his *Dialecticks* will tell you it is a generall axiome, though the universal particle be not expres't and you your selfe in your defence so explaine in these words as in general notion. Hence is justly inferr'd he that saies civil polity is arbitrary, saies that the civil polity of *England* is Arbitrary. The inference is undeniable, *a thesi ad hypothesin,* or from the general to the particular, an evincing argument in Logick.

The Confuter came to the defense of the Remonstrant, resolving the points into a "Darii" syllogism (*Modest Confutation*, p. 14):

NExt you impugne his Logick: The Remonstrant had said,

> Da- *Civill Polity in generall notion is variable and arbirtary*; you subsume, *But*
> ri- *The Polity of our Kingdome is Civill Polity*: Ergo,
> i. *The Polity of our Kingdome is variable*, &c.

And thereupon you cry, *Treason*! and want of *Logick*! In the first you are uncharitable; in the last, irrationall, only guilty of that failing which you impute to the Remonstrant. For look you upon your syllogism; there is in the major proposition *fallacia ad plures interrogationes*: For either we ask, what is possible only; or what is possible and lawfull. The Remonstrant answers; It is possible Civill Polity may vary; or, It is in the generall notion left of God to a various administration; subject to divers forms, Monarchy, Aristocracy, Democracy. You answer; It may be lawfully done at any time, or by any what ever undertakers: For so much is inferred in your conclusion.

> *Civill Polity is at any time, or by any undertakers variable and subject to a lawfull alteration*:
> *But the Polity of England, &c* Ergo,
> *It is at any time, by any undertakers, &c.*

This makes the Treason, this you must and do inferre, or else you charge him with Treason unjustly. In this sense, *as lawfull,* and, *at any time,* and, *by any undertakers,* the Remonstrant denyes the particular to be inferred upon his generall. But in his own he grants it, *viz.* That it is *possible,* subject to a condition of variation, though it be Treason against the highest Majesty of heaven, whose substitute the King is, in him or them who do attempt a change.

34:16-17 DOUBLE DEALING PROPOSITIONS TO THE PARLAMENT — The *An Humble Remonstrance* was addressed to "The High Covrt Of Parliament."

34:20 HE OR HIS SUBSTITUTE — The Remonstrant or his substitute, the Confuter. See Note 7:20-22.

34:20-22 LAY THE INTEGRITY ... UPHOLD THE INFERENCE — The syllogism as posed has the inevitable answer that English civil polity is both variable and arbitrary. The Smectymnuans and Milton pointed out the inference, which the Remonstrant denied. Milton feels that the Remonstrant or his substitute, seeing the outcome of the Remonstrant's statement, has pointed to a fallacy in the major premise, where, Milton claims, there is none,

rather than be forced to uphold the completely logical conclusion.

34:22 *MAJOR* — Major premise.

34:23 *OF POSSIBLE AND LAWFULL* — "For either we ask, what is possible only; or what is possible and lawfull" (see Note 34:9-10). The Confuter is maintaining that it is possible to vary the civil polity, but not lawful. He points out that the Remonstrant grants that "it is *possible,* subject to a condition of variation, though it be Treason against the highest Majesty of heaven, whose substitute the King is, in him or them who do attempt a change" (see Note 34:9-10).

34:26 *ARBITRARY* — "*Civill Polity in generall notion is variable and arbitrary*" (see Note 34:9-10).

34:27 *AT ANY TIME ... UNDERTAKERS* — "In this sense, *as lawfull,* and, *at any time,* and, *by any undertakers,* the Remonstrant denyes the particular to be inferred upon his generall" (see Note 34:9-10).

34:28 TWO LIMITATIONS ... SINCE — The Confuter's first distinction had been that it is possible that civil polity be varied but it is not lawful (see Note 34:23). He now adds two additional limitations, namely: it cannot be varied "*at any time or by any undertakers.*"

34:29-30 SECOND EDITION *CIVILL ... UNDERTAKERS* — The major premise of the Confuter's second syllogism of the position of Smectymnuus and Milton is that "*Civill Polity is at any time, or by any undertakers variable and subject to a lawfull alteration.*" Since the Confuter denies the "*at any time,*" the "*lawfull,*" and the "*by any undertakers*" (Note 34:27), Milton formulates the major premise that the Confuter proposed, namely: "*civill polity is variable but not at any time or by any undertakers.*"

34:31 THEN AT SOME TIME ... MAY — Milton has pursued the Confuter's logic until he has turned it against the Confuter. By using the Confuter's negative in the Confuter's syllogism, as reconstructed by Milton, Milton gains the answer he wants.

34:32-33 MEETS ... *BACON* — From Sir Francis Bacon's "Certain Considerations, Touching the

Better, Pacification, and Edification, of the Church of England" (in *Resuscitatio*, p. 237) the Confuter quotes:

All civill governments are restrained from God unto the generall grounds of justice and manners, but the Policies and forms of them are left free; (*Modest Confutation*, p. 15.)

34:33-34 HIS *MAJOR* AT LARGE — With the help given by Bacon, the Confuter displays publicly his major premise that civil polity in general is variable:

[*All civill governments... are left free*;] free, and to the arbitrement of a people, met together and consenting by the secret impression and instinct of God... to take what form of government they please: which being setled according to the generall rules of justice, and particular rules of the best advancement of publike good, is so immediately ratified by God, by his infusion of soveraignty into him or them, who by the joint consent of all is advanced to the helm.... (*Modest Confutation*, p. 15. The brackets are the Confuter's.)

34:34 AT LARGE — *i.e.*, publicly.

34:36-37 CONTRADICT HIMSELFE... *ONCE SETTL'D* — The Confuter, after explaining that the people are free to set up the type of government that they desire, points out that God not only ratifies that government by giving sovereignty, but also by "laying so many injunctions upon the people, to obey and honour all those in authority, not for wrath, but for conscience sake; that it is a sinne of the highest degree, onely but in thought to meditate an alteration" (*Modest Confutation*, p. 15). The phraseology *"either variable or arbitrary, being once settl'd"* is Milton's statement of the Confuter's position.

34:36 IN DIAMETER — In direct opposition. Cf. *Doctrine and Discipline of Divorce, Col.* III, 500, "To hinder...those deep and serious regresses of nature...is in diameter against both nature and institution."

34:37-38 THIRD SHIFT — For first shift see Note 34:23; for second shift, Note 34:28.

35:1 *AFTER SETLING* — See Note 34:36-37.

35:1-2 HIS FORMER ASSERTION — *"Civill Polity in generall notion is variable and arbitrary"* (see Note 34:9-10).

SECTION 8

35:4-7 THIS CONFUTATION WAS NOT MADE...BELIEVE — See Notes 7:20-22 and 34:20.

35:8-9 *NOT HAVING... PARLAMENT* — Section VIII of the *Modest Confutation* (p. 15) begins: "ENvie is a make-bate, always doing ill offices: if it cannot compasse its own ends one way, it will another. You, not having any thing to accuse the Remonstrant to the King, do it to the Parliament."

35:9-10 KING OUT OF THE PARLAMENT ...ONE — The idea of a single "body-politic" in which the interests of all classes of society were represented had grown up in the Tudor period. The King was the head of the state. His vast and undefined powers could be used only for the common good, not for the advancement of the Crown itself. Though the King was the most important individual in the state, he was less important than the sum total of his people. In the Parliament, the King as head and the Lords and Commons were joined to secure the best interests of the state. The King was as necessary a part of the Parliament as the House of Lords or the House of Commons, and no one of the three parts could act without the others. Since every Englishman was intended to be present in Parliament either in person or by representation, from the King down to the lowest person in England, the consent of Parliament was, therefore, every man's consent. (Frederick C. Dietz, *A Political and Social History of England*, New York, 1935, p. 236.)

James I, by claiming that the King controlled the state, that he was bound by the law only as he chose to be, started the breakdown of the "body-politic" idea. Yet in the mundane business of government he did little to change practices. In critical cases, however, he asserted and insisted upon his absolute power. His successors by their insistence upon ruling without Parliament brought to the fore men like Sir Edward Coke and the Supremacy of the Law idea. Cf. John A. R. Marriott, *The Crisis of English Liberty* (Oxford, 1930), Ch. II, "Crown and Parliament"; and David Ogg, *England in the Reign of Charles II* (Oxford, 1934), Ch. XIII, "The Crown in Parliament."

35:11-13 EPISTLE... *CONCERNMENTS* — Joseph Hall in "An Answer to *A Calumniatory*

Epistle, Directed by way of Preface to the Reader" of *A Short Answer to the Tedious Vindication of Smectymnuus*, published anonymously, said:

It is ... an unreasonably envious suggestion of theirs [the Smectymnuans] *that in dedicating my Book* [*A Defence*] *to His Sacred Majestie, I did, ever the more, flye from the judgement of Parliament; when in that very Epistle, I made confident mention of my secure reliance upon the noble justice of their Iudicature; Besides, that it is not too wise, nor too loyall an intimation of these men, which would imply such a distance betwixt Soveraign, and Parliamentary interest: For me, I would ever suppose such an entire union betwixt them, as the head and the body; that they neither should nor can be severed in the rights of their severall concernments.* (*Short Answer*, Sig. [a] *verso*.)

Hall's *Short Answer* was by his own statement his last contribution to the controversy on episcopacy, hence Milton's "his last *short answer*" (*ibid.*, Sig. [A4] *verso* and pp. 102-03).

35:13-16 IF . . . CONCERNMENTS — Milton has again wrenched the Remonstrant's statement. By "severall concernments," the Remonstrant meant "common concernments." Milton by clever phrasing emphasizes the aspect of "severall" and then shows the ridiculousness of the Confuter's argument.

35:14-15 BULS EYE . . . SATYRS — By "Buls eye" Milton may mean a small but important piece of nonsense to be joined with the "toothlesse Satyrs," which Milton had already called a "bull," that is, a blunder (Note 33:29).

35:16 DUE — *i.e.*, dutiful.

35:16-18 SUCH AS ARE THE COMMON GRIEVANCES . . . TO BE ONE — Milton is turning to the common practice of "namecalling."

35:19-20 INTO THE DISH OF I KNOW NOT WHOM — Milton rejects for himself and the Smectymnuans the implication made by the Confuter (see 35:20-22).

35:20-22 THEY FLATTER . . . PROCEEDINGS — The Confuter charged in the *Modest Confutation*, p. 16:

Doubtlesse the Remonstrant, and those which you esteem his faction, are as glad of, and wish as well to this Honourable Assembly, as you and yours do. It is not the Parliament they make head against, but you [Milton] and your furious complices [the Smectymnuans, in particular] who between soft flattery towards some of that House, and rough violence to others (wit-

nesse your Libels against so many of them, as their consciences made Vote contrary to some proceedings) are like to over-turn all.

35:22-23 THOSE SOME PROCEEDINGS . . . DEPUTIES EXECUTION — *i.e.*, the proceedings which led to the execution of the Earl of Strafford, May 12, 1641.

35:26 THAT PUBLICK TRIUMPH — The proceedings against Strafford were based upon the accusation that he had endeavored to subvert the fundamental laws of the land. The Commons were convinced that Strafford's death was essential to the liberties of the kingdom. Strafford, however, might have been saved but for the King's ill-advised conduct and the revelation of the Army Plot on May 5 which caused the Lords to pass the Bill of Attainder against Strafford. The King's consent was given May 10. The execution attracted a multitude of 200,000 people, perhaps the largest group of people that had ever assembled in England, for in the common mind Strafford was the symbol of the tyranny that they had endured.

35:28-29 SOME PROCEEDINGS — See Note 35:22-23.

35:29-30 HEE FALLS TO GLOZING . . . TIMES — See 35:33-35.

35:31 THEM — *i.e.*, the Parliament.

35:32 FOPPERY — Absurdity.

35:32-33 DISCOVERS — Discloses.

35:33-35 THAT THE SUN . . . COMMONS — Milton is referring to the Confuter's praise of the Parliament which inspired (37:7-9) his own eulogy (36:40-41:28). The Confuter in his encomium said: They [the Remonstrant and his faction] know, and so do I, That the Sunne looks not upon a braver, nobler Convocation, than is that of King, Peeres, and Commons; whose equall Justice, and wise moderation, shall eternally triumph, in that they have hitherto deferred to do, what the sowre exorbitancies on one hand, and eager solicitations on the other, not permitting them to consult with reason, would have prompted them to: who know how to ponder wise and grave sentences, not from the number, but the worth of them that propound them. (*Modest Confutation*, p. 16.)

He spoke of the members of the Parliament as the "pattern and example to future times" because they were not swayed by the "prejudice of this present," because they, in spite of the people's praise, granted the people their desires on the basis of the justice of the cause, rather than on the basis of the vehemence of the requests. He thought that discreet action of the Parliament conspired

unanimously, so to advance the pure Religion of our dearest Saviour, that it be not dispirited on one hand by gaudy ceremonious Formalists; nor lost on the other amids a Crowd of sullen and ignorant Sectaries: and after that ... the divine soveraignty and royall Immunities of our most Gratious Master [the King]. (*Modest Confutation*, pp. 16-17.)

35:36-37 *DECORUM* — That which is proper and befitting.

35:39 LUBBER — A drudge; a scullion.

35:40 LOZEL — Good-for-nothing.

35:40 BACHELOUR OF ART — Cf. 46:14; see Introduction, p. 3.

36:1-2 TO TERME ... CONVOCATION? — See Note 35:33-35.

36:2 CONVOCATION — In England the Convocation was, in the ecclesiastical government, the counterpart of the Parliament in the civil government. The Convocation, made up of the spirituality or clergy of the kingdom, was summoned to deliberate on ecclesiastical matters by the Archbishops of Canterbury and York within their respective provinces, pursuant to the King's writ, whenever the Parliament was summoned, was continued when and if the Parliament was prorogued, and discharged when the Parliament was dissolved. The Convocation was considered a necessary though independent part of "Parliament considered in its totality." Since no Parliaments were summoned from 1628/9 until 1640, no Convocations assembled, giving Laud a freer hand than he might have had if he had been subject to the criticism and actions of such assemblies (Masson, *Life*, I, 391 note). The divine who wrote the anonymous *An Appeale to Every Impartial, Iudicious, and Godly Reader* (pp. 10-11) gives a contemporary description of a Convocation which is representative of the tone of the antiprelatical party. He says that Convocation meets in two Provinces; one at *Yorke*, in which the Arch-Bishop of *Yorke* is President; and the other at *London*, where the Archbishop of *Canterbury* is President; ruling and commanding, or cunningly contriving to bring about what ever pleaseth him. Here meet all the Prel-

ates, all the great Deanes and Archdeacons, and the rest of the Prelaticall body; and to these come two Ministers called Clerks out of every Diocesse, to represent all the rest of the Ministers: chosen these should be freely by the rest of their brethren; but are appointed by the Lording Prelates, such as they best like of. The Nobles and Gentry have nothing to doe here; the Prelates have ever had the Laitie ... in contempt, scorning they should meddle in causes Ecclesiasticall, though never so learned and wise. ...

36:3 *SYNONYMA'S* — Thomas Cooper in *Thesaurus Linguae* (1565) defines "Synonyma" as "woordes of one signification." Milton's plural form is analogical.

36:3 VOLUMINOUS *PAPERS* ... *FOLIOS* — Although Milton is persuaded that Hall had little to do with Section VIII (35:4-7), he here identifies the Confuter with Hall, whose works are voluminous, many in folio editions. Cf. Hall, *Virgidemiarvm, Toothlesse Satyrs*, Bk. II, Satire I, line 29, "With *Folio-volumes*, two to an Oxe hide."

36:4-5 WINDING SHEETES ... PILCHERS — *i.e.*, wrapping paper for pilchers, a small sea fish, closely related to the herring, caught in large numbers on the coasts of Devon and Cornwall. Cf. "On Salmasius," in *Second Defence, Col.* VIII, 57. See Ekfelt, "The Graphic Diction of Milton's English Prose," p. 55.

36:6 CLAP — The equivalent of *put* or *place* with the implication that the action is energetically and easily performed.

36:6 HATCHES — *i.e.*, subjection, humiliation, degradation.

36:6-7 THE KING ... MONKISH HOODS? — Milton charges that, in using the word *Convocation* for the Parliament, the Confuter has subjected or humiliated the King, peers, and gentry, by making them churchmen.

36:8 CHIP OF THE OLD BLOCK — Milton feels that he has discovered another similarity between the author of the *Modest Confutation* and the author of the *Virgidemiarum*. The Confuter tries to humiliate the Parliament by making of it a "Convocation"; Hall placed *"Bridge street and Alehouses in heav'n."* If the author of the *Modest Confutation* is Hall's son, he is a "Chip of the old block" (cf. Note 7:20-22). A variation of the

"Chip of the old block" is: "Am not I a child of the same Adam, a vessel of the same clay, a chip of the same block, with him?" (Robert Sanderson, *Sermons*, I, 283, 1627; see W. G. Smith, *Oxford Dictionary of English Proverbs*, p. 4, and *OED*.)

36:9 *BRIDGE STREET ... HEAV'N* — See Note 33:12-14.

36:9-11 WHY DIDST THOU NOT ... DOCTORS — Milton pursues the theme of the Confuter's degradation of the King and Parliament, shifting the notion of Convocation to that type held in the university. As the type of Convocation under consideration becomes less important, the degradation of the Parliament grows, and the satire becomes the more effective.

36:12-13 THAT INVIOLABLE RESIDENCE OF JUSTICE AND LIBERTY — Parliament in its inclusive sense.

36:13-17 ODIOUS NAME ... THROUGHOUT THE LAND — It was the Convocation that assembled with the convening of the Short Parliament (April 13, 1640) that gained particular odium, for it did not come to an end with the Parliament (May 5, 1640), as was the custom, but continued to hold sessions until May 29, during which time it voted a "benevolence" of £20,000 annually to the King for a period of six years, and revised the Canons of the Church, finally authenticating a body of seventeen new canons, one of which (Canon VI) required that all clergymen, schoolmasters, divinity graduates, and "all that are licensed to practice physic, all register actuaries and proctors" (William H. Hutton, *The English Church From the Accession of Charles I. to the Death of Anne*, London, 1903, p. 82), take an oath, to be known as the Etcetera Oath, before November 2, 1640, approving the doctrine and discipline of the established Church "as containing all things necessary to salvation," and swearing that they would never consent to the altering of "the government of this Church by Archbishops, Bishops, Deans, and Archdeacons, &c." (For an account of the Convocation see Thomas Fuller, *The Church-History Of Britain; From the Birth of Jesus Christ, Untill the Year M.DC.XLVIII*, London, 1656, Bk. XI, pp. 168-71; see also Masson, *Life*, II, 131-32.) The intent of the oath was to prevent innovations. So great and im-

mediate was the opposition that Charles proclaimed that the oath "should be forborne" until the next Convocation (Hutton, *op. cit.*, p. 84). The implication of the continuance of the Convocation was that "the Church had a kind of separate, superior legislative life" (Taft, *Milton and the Smectymnuus Controversy*, p. 157). The new canons were offensive to the Puritans, and to many ordinary Protestants. The required obeisance upon entering the church, the railing around the communion table, the kneeling at the reception of the sacraments, all were objectionable. The first Canon defended the Divine Right of the King, stipulating that "for subjects to bear arms against their king, offensive or defensive, upon any pretense whatsoever, is at least to resist the powers which are ordained of God; and ... they shall receive to themselves damnation" (see Gardiner, *History*, IX, 142-47).

The Long Parliament was determined to pass a condemnation upon the Convocation, but other issues intervened. On December 15 and 16, 1640, resolutions were considered against the Canons of 1640 in particular, and against the power of the clergy to act in Convocation without the "common consent of Parliament" (John Rushworth, *Historical Collections. The Third Part*, London, 1692, p. 1365; cf. *Commons' Journal*, II, 51-52, and *Lords' Journal*, IV, 273). In April 1641 a bill was introduced in Commons to punish the members of the Convocation. On the fourth of August the formal impeachment of thirteen bishops for their cooperation with Laud in the Convocation was sent to the Lords (Masson, *Life*, II, 269-70).

The feeling against the Convocation was not a thing of the moment. The author of *A Briefe and plaine declaration* (1584), p. 134, complained that the general Convocations were "stuffed full of Popish and prophane Chauncelloures, and other Lawyers, which beeing meere laye men, and vnlearned in Diuinitie, by their owne Lawe, ought to be no members of the Synode: And yet these will beare the greatest sway in all thinges." William Prynne, in 1628, complained that the Convocation failed to avenge the Church "of those treacherous, corrupt and *Cozening watchmen, who haue smitten her to the heart*, and almost betrayed her to her Roman enemies" (William Prynne, *A Briefe Svrvay And Censvre Of Mr Cozens His Couzening*

Deuotions, London, 1628, "The Epistle," Sig. [¶¶] *verso*).

Milton mentions the "bad and slippery men" that "are wont to be in our Convocations" (*PRE, Col.* III, 83), and insinuates that the Convocation of 1640 would not have declared the Pope Antichrist (*ANIM, Col.* III, 116).

36:19 THIS PARLAMENT — The Parliament commonly known as the Long Parliament, which convened November 3, 1640.

36:21-22 NOT FOR ANY THING DOING... TO DO — See the Confuter's statement in Note 35:33-35.

36:22-23 FOR DEFERRING... *COMPRIESTS* — Milton refers to the attempts made by the Parliament to punish the Convocation of 1640 (see Note 36:13-17).

36:22 LEUD — *i.e.,* lewd, meaning lawless or unprincipled. The continued sitting of the Convocation of 1640 after the dissolution of the Parliament was considered a lawless act.

36:23 *COMPRIESTS* — Fellow priests.

36:23 NOT THAT THEY HAVE DEFERR'D ALL — The Confuter's hope that the "equall Justice, and wise moderation" of the Parliament "shall eternally triumph, in that they have hitherto deferred to do, what the sowre exorbitancies on one hand, and eager solicitations on the other, not permitting them to consult with reason, would have prompted them to" (see Notes 35:33-35; 36:13-17) seems to indicate, as Masson has suggested, that the "Bishops' Ejection Bill had not yet been passed by the Peers and the King" (Masson, *Life,* II, 398) at the time the *Modest Confutation* was written. The twelve Bishops, including Hall, had, however, already been impeached on December 30, 1641. Since the Peers passed the Ejection Bill on February 5, 1641/2, and since the King gave his assent on February 12, Milton, at the time of composing the *Apology,* could say that the Parliament had not "deferr'd all."

36:24 HE HOPES... BEHIND — Milton thinks that the Confuter hopes the Parliament will forgive those things that remain. Milton himself was disappointed with the action that had been taken (see

39:7-8). The Ejection Bill deprived the bishops of their seats in the House of Lords, but it left the whole episcopal hierarchy. The Root and Branch Bills had had as their objective the elimination of that hierarchy. Milton was a Root and Branch man.

36:24-25 REST OF HIS ORATORY THAT FOLLOWES — See Note 35:33-35 for the summary of the Confuter's "oratory."

36:25 STALL EPISTLE — An "open letter" or pamphlet sold at a bookstall.

36:26-27 NON SENSE... DOUBLET — The Confuter credited the members of Parliament with the ability to consider

grave sentences, not from the number, but the worth of them that propound them. Among whom, even the youngest and unskilfullest may stand a pattern and example to future times, teaching State-Novices, rather to inform their judgments to the good of the next Assembly, than to use them to the prejudice of this present. The gravest and most experienced, to be what they are thought, and to deserve all that praise, with which the people load them. So to satisfie their desires as they are just, not as they are vehement: considering that the multitude crave only out of the sense of evils; of which so long they will have a sense, as they are willing to obey. (*Modest Confutation,* p. 16.)

Much of the above citation deserves Milton's disparagement: "stall epistle non sense, that if he who made can understand it ... he may deserve ... a cast Doublet" (cf. 36:36-38).

36:27 CAST DOUBLET — *i.e.,* a castoff Doublet. The "doublet" was a close-fitting body-garment. The "cast Doublet" may be anticipatory of the following sentence in which Milton maintains that the Confuter relies upon the "odde remnants," that is, cast-off garments of another.

36:28 LOOKE — Expect.

36:30-31 DECLARES IT BY ALPHABET — The four marginal notes for the passage (quoted in Note 36:26-27) are comparatively full and are related to the "odde remnants" in the text by the letters a, b, c, d. See Note 36:33-36.

36:31-32 REFERRES US... IN HIS TOPICKS — Milton declares that the Confuter hides his "barren stupidity" by citing learned quotations in the margin in order to support the trivialities of the text.

36:32 TOPICKS — *i.e.,* commonplace-book. Cf. Note 18:30.

36:32-33 NOR YET CONTENT . . . TEXT — On page 16 of the *Modest Confutation* the marginal notes beginning about the middle of the page are indented into the normal space for the text almost an inch to make the "large docks." The last two lines of the notes continue the full line length of the page to make the "creek."

36:33-36 TO UNLADE . . . THEM DO — Having likened the physical arrangement of the marginal notes to docks and creeks, Milton continues the figure with the ship-unloading at the dock. The cargo of the "foolish frigate" is the "unseasonable antorities," Pliny, Seneca, and Filesac — the last, one of the faculty of the Sorbonne in Paris who died in 1636. Milton charges that the citations are not in praise of the Parliament, but are instructions to the Parliament telling "what [the Confuter] would have them do." The citations follow:

a Numerantur sententiae, non ponderantur: nihil est tam inaequale, quàm aequalitas ipsa: nam cum sit impar prudentia, par omnium jus est. *Plin. l.*3 [2]. *epist.* 12. ["Votes go by number, not weight: nothing is more unequal than that equality which prevails in them; for though every member has the same right of suffrage, every member has not the same strength of judgement to direct it" (*Pliny Letters, With An English Translation by William Melmoth*, London, 1915, 2 vols., I,137)]. (See Bacon's reference to the quotation, Note 52:36-39.)

b Rudes nos & imperitos reducta libertas deprehendit, cujus dulcedine accensi, cogimur quaedam facere antequam nosse. *Idem. l.*8.ep.14. ["Liberty at her return found us ignorant and inexperienced; and kindled by her charms, we are sometimes impelled to action, ere we know how to act" (Melmoth translation of *Pliny Letters,* II, 127)].

c Senatus, humano generi reverendus, Orbis terrae consilium, Asylum mundi, Fidum & altum reipublicae pectus. *Vide Filesacum l.*3. *select.* [orum] T.*t. Senectus Ven. Sen.* §.4,5,&c. [The Senate, respectful of the human kind, council of the terrestrial globe, asylum of the world, faithful and old heart of the republic.]

d Non considerandum est quid vir optimus in praesent â velit, sed quid semper sit probaturus. *Plin.lib.* I.*ep.*7. Sunt quae non dare, sed negare, beneficium est. Poscit aeger frigidam, iratus ferrum, &c. exorari in pernitiem regantium, saeva est bonita. *Sen. de Benef* [iciis, II, xiv]. [What the best man desires at present is not so much to be considered as what that man will always approve (Pliny). There

are those things which it is a benefit not to give, but to deny. The sick one requests coolness; the angry man, the sword, etc. It is a savage kind of benevolence to be persuaded to grant things that are harmful to men, even though men beg for those things (Seneca).]

36:36-38. WHAT ELSE . . . PIECE UP — See Note 36:26-27. Milton may be referring to the phrase beginning "considering that the multitude."

36:40 ALTHOUGH IT BE A DIGRESSION FROM THE ENSUING MATTER — Milton quoted part of the *"Encomium"* of the Confuter to Parliament (see Note 35:33-35). He now introduces his own encomium, comparing the repulse given by Parliament to the prelates (39:7) with the exploits of liberators "of highest fame in Poems and *Panegyrics* of old" (39:10-11). He lauds the calling "out of darknesse and bonds, the elect Martyrs and witnesses of their Redeemer" (39:18-20) and the "repulse of an unholy *hierarchy*" resulting in the replenishing of the country with "saving knowledge" (39:28-31). See 37:7-9.

37:2-3 HARSH DISCORD . . . SMOOTHER STRING — Ida Langdon (*Milton's Theory of Poetry and Fine Art,* p. 48) has cited the terms "harsh discord" and "smoother string" as musical metaphors.

37:4 FIT — *i.e.,* strain of music.

37:4 LEST — A variant spelling of *least.*

37:5-6 GRATITUDE . . . COUNTRY — Milton thoroughly approved of the Long Parliament membership and the legislative efforts that they were making.

37:7-9 I SHALL BE SO TROUBLESOME . . . IN THEIR PRAISE — See 35:35-37.

37:12-13 YET IF HEREAFTER . . . GREAT MERITS — E. M. W. Tillyard notes that the epic which Milton was considering when he wrote the "panegyric on the ruling majority in the Long Parliament" (E. M. W. Tillyard, *Milton,* p. 118) was "still to be patriotic and contemporary . . . he hopes he may some day commemorate their deeds more worthily" (E. M. W. Tillyard, *The Miltonic Setting,* p. 198; cf. E. M. W. Tillyard, "Milton and the English Epic Tradition," p. 230). See also 17:29-31 for another reference to Milton's poetic intentions.

37:15 WEIGHTS — A variant spelling of *waits* (*OED*).

37:15-18 NOBLE DEEDS, THE UNFINISH-ING WHEREOF ... AGES — The Long Parliament had by April of 1642 already accomplished a considerable revolution. Those men who were the symbols of tyranny were gone: Strafford had been beheaded; Laud was languishing in prison. The Court of High Commission and the Star Chamber had been abolished. The Parliament had secured itself from dissolution; it had provided against attempts by the King to rule without Parliament by the Bill for Triennial Parliaments. The King's monopolies had been swept away and the rights of the Parliament to control the levying of subsidies, customs, and imposts had been re-established. The bishops had been excluded from the House of Lords. The King had fled Westminster. The two Houses of Parliament had concurred in declaring certain acts of both Houses the law of the land without the King's signature.

37:25 TIMES ... DESPERAT — The times of real desperation coincide pretty well with the years of Laud's paramount influence in the government of England, that is, from 1632 to 1640 (Masson, *Life,* I, 385 ff.), designated by Masson as "The Reign of Thorough" (*ibid.*, pp. 664-732).

37:26-27 THE MOST OF THEM ... ANCESTRY — The composition of the two Houses of Parliament is discussed by Masson in his *Life of Milton,* II, 150-73.

37:28-30 A GREAT ADVANTAGE ... VERTUE ONE WAY ... A HINDRANCE ANOTHER WAY — Aristotle maintained that nature gives the capacity for receiving virtues, and that the capacity for moral virtue is perfected by habit (Aristotle, *Nicomachean Ethics,* Bk. II, ch. 1 [1103a]. In one way those of "well reputed ancestry" have not only the greater capacity, but the greater opportunity for the perfecting of the capacity. Aristotle further held that intellectual virtue is both originated and fostered chiefly by teaching (*ibid.*). The "nice and tender education" with its attendant "welth, ease, and flattery" is not, therefore, an effective agent for the development of intellectual virtue.

Aristotle reasoned that the effect of good birth on a character was to make the one who had it the more ambitious. He noted that the well-born man often looks down upon those who are as good as his ancestors were. He felt that being well-born, that is, coming from fine stock, was to be distinguished from nobility, that is, being true to the family nature — a quality rarely found in the well-born, who are usually inferior creatures. Upon occasion, where the stock is good, sons will emulate or surpass the virtues of their fathers, but decadence soon sets in (Aristotle, *Rhetoric,* Bk. II, ch. 15 [1390b]).

37:35-36 INBRED GOODNESSE . . . NO MEANE PURPOSES — Milton is reflecting Calvinistic doctrine. Certain people, elect before the foundation of the world, were predestined to do certain things and fortified with God's "irresistible grace" to carry them out. Cf. *Paradise Lost,* III, 183-202.

37:38-38:8 THOSE PLACES ... ANY THING GOOD — Cf. 12:26-13:1; 14:11-32; 15:20-21; 53:21-26. See also *ANIM, Col.* III, 119, "unprofitable questions, and barbarous sophistry."

38:5-6 AS *DAVID* ... TEACHERS — I Samuel 18:30. Cf. Robert Lord Brooke, *The Nature of Episcopacy,* p. 47, "That Admirable young Prince [Edward VI], was even in his Infancie, with King *David,* wiser then his Teachers; and could weepe, though not yeeld to Their perswasions."

38:12 BAITS OF PREFERMENT — Cf. *REF, Col.* III, 75; *ANIM, Col.* III, 161, 165; *RCG, Col.* III, 274; *Eikonoklastes, Col.* V, 183, 303; *History of Britain, Col.* X, 135. See Notes 53:34-36 and 54:29.

38:18-20 (SOME ALSO . . . COUNTREY) — Milton may be thinking of William Strode, Denzil Holles, Eliot, Selden, Benjamin Valentine, William Coriton and others, who, in consequence of their part in the famous closing scene of the Parliament of 1628/9, in which the Speaker, Finch, was forced to remain in his chair in spite of the King's order for adjournment until the Three Resolutions, one against innovations in religion, and two in connection with tonnage and poundage, had been imprisoned (Gardiner, *History,* VII, 67-76). Of the group, a number including Holles and Selden were members of the Long Parliament. Another member was John Hampden, who in 1627 had suffered the disgrace of imprisonment for refusing to contribute to a forced loan.

38:25 THIS — *i.e.*, service in the Parliament. See 38:28-31.

38:34 GLOBE — "Complete or perfect body" (*OED*). Cf. *On The Morning of Christ's Nativity*, 110, "A Globe of circular light"; *Paradise Lost*, II, 512, "Globe of fierie Seraphim"; *ibid.*, III, 418, "firm opacous Globe"; *RCG, Col.* III, 260, "glob it self upward."

38:36 THEIR ENEMIES . . . SUTTLE — The King and his party, including particularly Laud and Strafford.

38:37 HER — *i.e.*, tyranny.

38:37 BLOCK. WITH — In modern usage the phrasal modifier beginning "With" would probably be separated from the preceding element by a comma.

38:37-38 WITH ONE STROKE WINNING — The one stroke, perhaps the "two-handed engine" of *Lycidas*, 130, seems to refer to the passing of the two Bills for the abolition of the Courts of Star Chamber and High Commission to which the King gave his assent July 5, 1641. Since the other extraordinary courts such as the Council of the North and the Council of Wales had already been voted down, the extraordinary courts which were the support of the monarchy were gone. Milton speaks of the "illegall proceedings of the high Commission, and oath *Ex officio*" as "that tyranny which the Parlament in compassion of the Church and Commonwealth hath dissolv'd" (31:34-40). He accuses Hall of being a party to the scourging of the "confessors of the Gospell," if in no other way, by defending the "government with the oath" that made the scourging possible (32:6-12). Milton can think of no worse tool to use in his own defense against his contemners than the "oath *Ex officio*" (32:30-33). He resented violently, with many Englishmen, being "hal'd into your [the prelates'] Gehenna," and being "strappado'd with an Oath *Ex Officio*" (*ANIM, Col.* III, 117). The oath *ex officio* was the chief tool of the Star Chamber and the Court of High Commission, upon which rested the King's power of binding the people by proclamation, the

strong symbol of the King's arbitrary power. With the passing of the extraordinary courts the "lost liberties and Charters" (38:38) were restored. For instance, the established system of controlling the press died with the abolition of these courts. The constitutional limitations which the Great Charter and the Petition of Rights, the latter of which Charles himself had approved in June 1628, imposed, had been flaunted by the King from 1628 to 1640 during which time no Parliament had met, and during which time the extraordinary courts were the King's mainstay.

38:40 SECOND LIFE OF TYRANNY — Whereas the first life of tyranny (see Note 38:37-38) lay in the suppression of civil rights, the second life lay in the imposition of the Arminian creed and the innovations in discipline that seemed to point toward a return to the Roman Catholic Church. Laud's insistence upon uniformity of ceremony in the churches, the persecutions of those who objected to the forcing of conscience, the popularity of Roman Catholicism at the Court, and the intrigues of Charles' Catholic Queen seemed to indicate that the King only awaited an opportune time to return England to Rome. The agent that made possible the King's tyranny was the "ambiguous monster," (39:1) the extra-ordinary courts. The Court of Star Chamber originally concerned itself with civil matters; the Court of High Commission with ecclesiastical affairs. In the years of Laud's ascendancy the jurisdictions had become confused, the Star Chamber taking over many of the matters originally within the jurisdiction of the Court of High Commission. As a result of the decisions of these courts many fled to Holland and America. Leighton, Lilburne, Prynne, Bastwick, and Burton suffered degradation and imprisonment at their hands. Open opposition to episcopacy was suppressed.

39:5 HER BESTIALL HORNES — Milton's reference to "bestiall hornes" may be to one of a number of things: Milton may be likening the prelates to Moses in his character as lawgiver and leader, to whom horns were attributed (Exodus 34:29-30 Douay); since "horn" was a name often given to part or the whole of headdresses, Milton may be using "hornes" to refer to the mitre; or Milton may have in mind Revelation 13 in which two beasts are mentioned, one with seven heads and ten horns (papacy), the other with two horns (prelacy), the latter of which had the power of the former, and forced all to worship the former.

39:6 UNBEND — Relax the severity of.

39:6-7 WHICH REPULSE ONLY . . . PRELATS — Milton is referring to the Bishops' Exclusion Bill which became law February 14, 1641/2.

39:7-8 (THAT WE MAY . . . REMOVALL WOULD BE) — Milton belonged to the group who advocated the complete abolition of episcopacy in the several Root and Branch Bills which had failed to receive approval in the House of Lords. Milton's program is delineated in the closing pages of the *Apology* (57:27-59:10). See Note 36:24.

39:8-9 PRODUCEMENT . . . CHURCH — When Milton had written the *Animadversions,* at least three-quarters of a year before this passage was written, he had been elated with the religious progress that the measures passed by the Long Parliament had brought. He had said:

God hath reform'd his Church after many hundred yeers of *Popish* corruption; in this Age hee hath freed us from the intolerable yoke of *Prelats,* and *Papall* Discipline; in this age he hath renewed our *Protestation* against all those yet remaining dregs of superstition: Let us all goe every true protested *Brittaine* . . . and render thanks to God. (*ANIM, Col.* III, 144-45.)

The effects and consequences of the passage of the Exclusion Bill on February 14, 1641/2, were spiritually great. The great religious reform seemed to be finally under way. The bishops, who were felt to be the hinderers to the passage of desirable legislation, could no longer obstruct. Furthermore, the King professed to welcome reform. A new hope surged through the populace, and a new zeal pervaded the antiprelatical group. The relative freedom that had existed since the imprisonment of Laud in December 1640 had been followed by the discarding of objectionable aspects of discipline and creed. The Exclusion Bill seemed to offer assurance that the good work which had begun would not end abortively. See Note 39:29.

39:10 THEM — *i.e.,* the "effects and consequences in the Church" (39:9).

39:11 IT — The comparison.

39:12 ARGUMENT — Proof or evidence.

39:12-13 THOSE ANCIENT WORTHIES . . . TYRANTS — For a lengthy discussion of ancient writers and tyrannicide see William T. Allison (ed.), *The Tenure of Kings and Magistrates by John Milton,* "Appendix," pp. 156-72.

39:15-16 DOCTRINE OF TYRANNY . . . PERSUASION — Laud's policy of securing uniformity by making metropolitan visitations resulted in the closest supervision that the clergy and people had ever experienced. Laud as the head of the Church was quickly aware of irregularities and took action without delay. His thoroughness was accomplished by close attention to every aspect of the ecclesiastical hierarchy including the relatively insignificant details. He instituted ceremonial innovations such as the moving of the communion tables to the east chancel of the church where it was to be railed in, in order to secure it against profanation. The innovations were deemed significant by his opponents because they were in the Roman Catholic direction. Those who refused to comply with Laud's innovations were imprisoned and excommunicated. Although Laud had his way, a fixed belief grew that, under the cloak of providing decency, Laud was bringing the Church back to Rome. The bringing of the foreign churches under the control of the Church of England, the appointing of a commission to control all religious activities in the English colonies, the excommunication, mutilation, and imprisonment of objectors, the insistence on the adoption of a new prayer book in Scotland — all contributed to make Laud the more despised and the consciences of the people not in the least assuaged. Hundreds of the clergy unwillingly administered the Communion at the rails. Dissatisfaction was suppressed but not overcome. The sullen ill-feeling of the gentry and middle class grew. In 1639 Laud admitted that he was unable to keep down the Separatists and Anabaptists in his own diocese. On May 11, 1640, Laud should have been made aware of the intense feeling against him, for he was forced to flee from Lambeth to Whitehall by the "rascal routers" who rioted outside his palace.

39:18-20 OPENING THE PRISONS AND DUNGEONS . . . REDEEMER — Within ten days after the convening of the Long Parliament on November 3, 1640, Strafford was in custody. Before any other business was transacted, orders were issued for the liberation of Prynne, Bastwick, Burton, Leighton, and Lilburne, in order to give them the opportunity to bring their complaints before the Commons.

39:21-22 FREEDOME ... GOSPELL — Echoes John 8:32,36; Galatians 4:31; 5:1; Romans 8:2.

39:24 UPON OUR NECKS — *i.e.*, as a yoke. T. Holt White in *A Review of Johnson's Criticism on the Style of Milton's English Prose* ([London], 1818), p. 12 note, relates the phrase to Cicero's "Itaque *posiustis in cervicibus nostris* sempiternum dominum, quem dies et noctes timeremus," in *De Natura Deorum*, I, 54. Cf. Acts 15:10, and Note 50:30-33.

39:24-26 BY THE STRANGE ... INDIFFERENCE — Many of the practices in the English Church which differed from those in the continental churches were defended on the basis of being "things indifferent," that is, non-essential to the ultimate goals of religion, but useful or expedient in reference to other values. The Canons of 1640 explained that although the position of the communion-table was "in its own nature indifferent," all churches "should conform ... to the example of the cathedral or mother churches" (Gardiner, *History*, IX, 143). Joseph Hall affirmed that the episcopal calling was justifiable and holy, that every Church capable of the form "may, and ought to affect it," but he held that those churches abroad which did not have the same organization lost "nothing of the true essence of a Church, though they misse something of [the] glory and perfection" (Hall, *Humble Remonstrance*, p. 31). In Section 14 of his *Defence*, Hall clarified the position: "the Divine or Apostolical right, which wee hold, goes not so high, as if there were an expresse command, that, upon an absolute necessity there must be either Episcopacy, or no Church; but so far only, that it both may, and ought to be" (Hall, *Defence*, p. 132). Many of the innovations demanded by Laud were defended on the basis of securing uniformity and decency, being in themselves "things indifferent." Milton felt it a great shame that some continued to trouble "Gods Church with things by themselves confest to be indifferent, since true charity is af-

flicted, and burns at the offence of every little one" (*ANIM, Col.* III, 131). He said:

what numbers of faithful, and freeborn Englishmen, and good Christians have bin constrain'd to forsake their dearest home, their friends, and kindred, whom nothing but the wide Ocean, and the savage deserts of *America* could hide and shelter from the fury of the Bishops. O Sir, if we could but see the shape of our deare Mother *England* ... how would she appeare ... but in a mourning weed, with ashes upon her head, and teares abundantly flowing from her eyes, to behold so many of her children expos'd at once, and thrust from things of dearest necessity, because their conscience could not assent to things which the Bishops thought *indifferent*. What more binding then Conscience? what more free then *indifferency*? cruel then must that *indifferency* needs be, that shall violate the strict necessity of Conscience, merciles, and inhumane that free choyse, and liberty that shall break asunder the bonds of Religion. (*REF, Col.* III, 49-50; cf. Notes 46:32; 49:10-11.)

39:25 NEEDLESSE — T. Holt White, in *A Review of Johnson's Criticism on the Style of Milton's English Prose* (1818), p. 13 note, questions whether "needlesse" is not "an errour of the Press for 'heedless'." The sense of the sentence is apparently clear, however, as it stands.

39:25 JOLLY — *i.e.*, overweeningly self-confident (*OED*).

39:27-28 PRESERVING . . . FAMINE OF CORNE — One of Solon's enactments to relieve the conditions in Athens in 594 B.C. was to supply corn at reduced rates and to make frequent public donations and distributions from the public granaries. Gaius Gracchus, who became tribune in Rome in 132 B.C., by the *lex frumentaria* gave to those who had the Roman franchise the right to purchase monthly from the public stores at a little more than half price.

39:28 ONLY — *i.e.*, one.

39:28 ONLY REPULSE OF AN UNHOLY HIERARCHY — See Note 39:6-7.

39:29 ALMOST IN A MOMENT REPLENISHT — The people of London expressed the general feeling of many an Englishman when in November 1641 they petitioned the House of Commons "that the bishops, who were the main obstacles to the passage of good laws in the Upper House, might be deprived of their votes" (Gardiner,

History, X, 71). And on January 25, 1641/2, Pym lashed the Peers by reiterating time and again that their policy was "Obstruction." On February 4, the Women's Petition charged that there was great danger as "long as Popish Lords and superstitious Bishops are suffered to have their voice in the House of Peers" (Masson, *Life*, II, 348). The next day the Lords passed the Bishops' Exclusion Bill. The popular rejoicing was great, for after more than a year the first measure of church reform had passed the two Houses. The King not only assented to the Bill on February 14, but by a gracious message to the two Houses he indicated his willingness to "gratify their desires for religious reformation in every way" (*ibid.*, p. 353). He said he would enforce the laws against the Roman Catholics, and that he would leave to the Parliament the revision of the government and liturgy of the Church. The Parliament was duly thankful. New hopes stirred the nation. See Note 39:8-9.

39:31   TWO ARMIES — The Second Bishops' War was a complete fiasco for the King. The skirmish on August 28, 1640, resulted in panic. The Scotch held the field. The King resolved to leave Northumberland and Durham to the Scots who took possession. The English Parliament was summoned. At Ripon, thirteen preliminary articles were agreed upon by the English and Scotch negotiators, one of which provided that the Scotch army would remain on English soil, at a cost of £850 a day to the English, until a treaty was concluded. In the meantime, the English army was maintained in Yorkshire, for it "could hardly, for shame's sake, be disbanded while an army nominally of invaders was on the English soil" (Masson, *Life*, II, 190). It was not until August 1641 with the formal signing of the treaty with Scotland that the two armies were disbanded.

39:32   THE ONE IN REVERENCE — *i.e.*, the Scottish army.

39:33   DISLODG'D — Withdrew; cf. *Paradise Lost*, V, 668-69.

39:33-35   THE OTHER . . . HOME — The English army, assembled by Charles in preparation for the Second Bishops' War, was first made up almost exclusively of raw recruits. The laborers and small handicraftsmen resented having to leave their homes. There was no enthusiasm. The officers, many of them Roman Catholics and many of them fresh from the Court, were not respected. The men were indifferent to a Scottish invasion which would probably not disturb their homes. Furthermore, since the payment of the soldiers was erratic, many doubted that there was any intention to remunerate them for their service. In London and the counties nearby, resistance to the troop levy was universal. Desertions were so numerous that only half the numbers raised appeared for duty. Many who came were ill-clothed, but their needs could not be supplied. In the eastern counties unruly soldiers invaded churches and pulled down communion rails.

At the last minute, on August 19, the Northern and Midland trained bands were called out. Those who held knight's service under the King were summoned. Strafford was placed in command. When the King joined the army some of the grievances were laid aside. The Yorkshire gentlemen offered for two weeks' pay to follow the King anywhere within the county. The motley, undisciplined, ill-affected army met the Scotch on August 28, 1640.

It was components of the same army that were maintained at Yorkshire until August 1641. There is little doubt that Charles was sending money to York in April 1641 to conciliate the troops. He seems to have believed that he could expect "the help of the Northern army in the event of a breach with Parliament." The King's talk of going in person to take command of the army fostered the belief "that he intended first to attack the Scots, and then to turn his arms against those who resisted his authority in England." Other plans included one for a violent dissolution of Parliament with the help of the Northern army, which was to advance on London, and the Irish army, which the King had repeatedly refused to disband (Gardiner, *History*, IX, 342-43). In early May when the Parliament began to become aware of the pretended gathering of soldiers in London for the Portuguese service, of Capt. Billingsley's attempt to take possession of the Tower, that ancient fortification of London where Strafford was imprisoned and munitions were stored, and of Suckling's levies of armed men, a letter was sent to the Northern army promising the arrears in salary in a short time. On May 5, 1641, Pym revealed the design, known as the Army Plot, the aim of which was "not only to disaffect the army, but to bring it up to overawe the Parliament" (*ibid.*, p. 357; Masson, *Life*, II, 183).

39:38   SINGLE — Honest, sincere; free from duplicity or deceit.

39:39-40   OVERAWE . . . HIR'D AGAINST THEM — See Note 39:33-35.

39:40-40:2   SOLEMNE PROTESTATION . . . SERVICE — With the first rumors of the Army Plot, Pym had suggested that a manifesto be drawn up to show that the Parliament was united. The Lords, shocked as a result of investigations of their own, were ready to align themselves with the Commons. On May 3, 1641, the signing of the Protestation began. It was signed by the Protestant Lords and by the Commons and was circulated in London. The text of the Protestation was as follows:

I, *A.B.* do, in the Presence of Almighty God, promise, vow, and protest, to maintain and defend, as far as lawfully I may, with my Life, Power, and Estate, the true Reformed Protestant Religion, expressed in the Doctrine of the Church of *England,* against all Popery and Popish Innovations, within this realm, contrary to the same Doctrine, and according to the Duty of my Allegiance, His Majesty's Royal Person, Honour, and Estate, as also the Power and Privileges of Parliaments, the lawful Rights and Liberties of the Subjects, and every Person that maketh this Protestation, in whatsoever he shall do in the lawful Pursuance of the same; and to my Power, and as far as lawfully I may, I will oppose, and by all good Ways and Means endeavour to bring to condign Punishment, all such as shall, either by Force, Practice, Counsels, Plots, Conspiracies, or otherwise, do any Thing to the contrary of any Thing in this present Protestation contained; and further, that I shall, in all just and honourable Ways, endeavour to preserve the Union and Peace betwixt the Three Kingdoms of *England, Scotland,* and *Ireland*; and, neither for Hope, Fear, nor other Respect, shall relinquish this Promise, Vow, and Protestation. (*Lords' Journal,* IV, 234; Gardiner, *History,* IX, 354; and Samuel R. Gardiner, *The Constitutional Documents of the Puritan Revolution, 1625-1660,* Oxford, 1906, pp. 155-56.)

40:3-4   PREVENTED THE DISSOLUTION . . . UNTIMELY BREAKING UP — Milton refers to the Bill securing the Parliament against dissolution by the King, to which Charles assented May 10, 1641. Among the "designes" of the moment were the Attainder Bill against Strafford, church reform, civil reform, and the Scottish treaty.

40:5-6   TREASONOUS PLOTS . . . INVASION — Rumors on May 4 and 5, 1641, were rife. One rumor was that preparations were completed to supply the Northern army with ammunition. There was talk of the movement of French troops on the French coast, evidently as a result of Charles' wife's negotiations with her brother, the King of France. Charles himself talked of joining the army in the North. News of the Queen's intended flight to Portsmouth was not taken lightly, for it was likely her intention to summon French aid.

40:8   OWNE SAFETIES — The purpose of the Army Plot seems to have been to force the Parliament into subjection, perhaps in the midst of a clash of arms to dissolve it, so that the King could rule again without hindrance.

40:11   DAILY PETITIONS — According to D'Ewes the number of petitions presented to Parliament from November 3, 1640, to June 15, 1641, numbered nine hundred (see William H. Shaw, *A History of the English Church during the Civil Wars and under the Commonwealth 1640-1660,* London, 1900, 2 vols., I, 13-14).

40:13-14   ALL GENTLE AFFABILITY AND CURTEOUS ACCEPTANCE — An instance of the "affability" may be cited from Pym's answer in behalf of the House of Commons to the Petition from Gentlewomen (see Note 40:18-19):

Good Women; Your Petition, with the Reasons, hath been read in the house, and is thankfully accepted of, and is come in a seasonable time. You shall, God willing, receive from us all the satisfaction which we can possibly give to your just and lawful desires. We intreat you, therefore, to repair to your houses, and turn your Petition, which you have delivered here, into prayers at home for us; for we have been, are, and shall be, to our utmost power, ready to relieve you, your husbands, and children; and to perform the trust committed unto us, towards God, our king and country, as becometh faithful Christians and loyal subjects. (*The Parliamentary History of England, from the earliest period to the year 1803,* London, 1807-1820, 36 vols., II, 1076.)

40:18   MEANEST ARTIZANS AND LABOURERS — Among the petitions against bishops in January and early February 1641/2 were one by the Prentices and Sailors of London and one by the Street Porters. Such petitions, which later became subjects for jests among the Royalists, indicate the "meanness" of many of the petitioners (Masson, *Life*, II, 349).

40:18-19 WOMEN — Milton is referring to "The Humble Petition of the Gentlewomen, Tradesmen's Wives, and many other of the Female Sex, all Inhabitants of the City of London, and the Suburbs thereof, With the lowest submission shewing, for Redress of Grievances," presented to the House of Commons, February 4, 1641/2, in which these women stated the "great danger and fear" that they felt as long as

Popish Lords, and superstitious Bishops are suffered to have their voice in the house of peers; that accursed and abominable Idol of the mass suffered in the kingdom; and that arch-enemy of our prosperity and reformation, (abp. Laud) lieth in the Tower, yet not receiving his deserved punishment.

Having recounted the insolencies accorded their sex in the Irish Rebellion (see Note 40:39-40), they alleged their fears that

unless the blood-thirsty faction of the Papists and Prelates be hindered in their designs, ourselves in England, as well as they in Ireland shall be exposed to that misery which is more intolerable than that which is already past; as, namely, to the rage, not of men alone, but of devils incarnate, as we may so say, besides the thraldom of our souls and consciences concerning God, which, of all things, are most dear unto us. (*Parliamentary History of England*, II, 1072-76; Masson, *Life*, II, 348-49.)

40:23 DISTASTED — Disapproved.

40:32-33 STILL REFERRING...TO HIM — The Parliament, lest people place too much confidence in their bequests to it, exhorted the people to direct their prayers to Christ. See Note 40:13-14.

40:33 TO HIM...ALL — Milton alludes to Christ's promise to give to those who believe the things that they desire. See Mark 11:24; John 14:13; 15:7; 16:24; Jude 24.

40:34 THE MONTHLY RETURN OF PUBLICK FASTS AND SUPPLICATIONS — On January 3, 1641/2, a warrant for the preparation of a proclamation was given to the Attorney-General

commanding a fast to be kept throughout all England, London and Westminster only excepted, where it has already been observed, on the 20th of January, and after that a general fast to be held throughout this whole kingdom on the last Wednesday of February, and every month on the same day during the troubles

in Ireland. (*Calendar of State Papers, Domestic, 1641-1643*, p. 235.)

40:36 BY MANIFEST . . . TESTIMONIES — Echoes scriptural passages like "Through mighty signs and wonders" (Romans 15:19; cf. Acts 2:22; 5:12; II Corinthians 12:12; Hebrews 2:4).

40:37 MEDIATORS . . . COV'NANT — Cf. Hebrews 8:6; 9:15; 12:24.

40:37-38 THIS . . . OFFERS . . . TO RENEW — Milton felt that the ceremonies and liturgy of the Anglican Church, the reliance upon tradition, were reminiscent of the covenant between God and Adam, which rested on the basis of obedience to God's laws, moral and ceremonial. The new covenant, instituted by Christ (Luke 22:20; I Corinthians 11:25), supplanted the old covenant, offering redemption through faith without recourse to the fulfillment of rigid disciplines and the carrying out of elaborate ceremonies. Milton said that the papists by the "snare and pitfall of imitating the ceremonial law, fel into that irrecoverable superstition, as must needs make void the cov'nant of salvation to them that persist in this blindnesse" (*RCG, Col.* III, 199). Milton pointed out that the Saviour detested the customs held by the ritualists

though never so seeming harmlesse, and [charged] them severely that they had transgrest the Commandments of God by their traditions and worshipt him in vain. How much more then must these, and much grosser ceremonies now in force delude the end of Christs comming in the flesh against the flesh, and stifle the sincerity of our new cov'nant which hath bound us to forsake all carnall pride and wisdom especially in matters of religion. (*Ibid.*, p. 248.)

He held that prelacy was "sayling in opposition to the main end and power of the Gospel," for it did not join

in that misterious work of Christ, by lowliness to confound height, by simplicity of doctrin the wisdom of the world, but contrariwise hath made it self high in the world and the flesh to vanquish things by the world accounted low, and made it self wise in tradition and fleshly ceremony to confound the purity of doctrin which is the wisdom of God. (*Ibid.*)

40:38-39 WICKED MEN . . . HURT — Milton is probably thinking of such occasions as the "supposed Popish Plot." The horrors of the Irish Rebellion revived the belief in a plot to murder all the Protestants in the three Kingdoms. On November 15, 1641, Pym informed the Commons that two priests had been taken. The Lords learned from a Thomas Beale that he "had overheard some persons talking of their intention to murder no less than 108 members of the two Houses, and of a general rising to take place on the 18th" (Gardiner, *History*, X, 72-73; see *Lords' Journal*, IV, 439).

40:39-40 REBELLION RAGES ... PROVINCE — The Irish Rebellion began in Ulster on October 23, 1641. The news reached London on November 1. The accounts of the atrocities were horrible. The English army in Ireland amounted to about 3,000 men scattered in small detachments. Dublin was saved, but all Ulster was overrun. The Parliament immediately on November 1 voted that £50,000 should be borrowed to suppress the rebels, and that 8,000 men should be raised. But the question was, "Who should control the army?" In the King's hands it would become a danger to Parliament. On November 11 the news from Ireland indicated that savagery was increasing. The multitude had taken over the English homesteads, leaving the possessors to shift for themselves. English officials and clergy had become the special victims of the wild brutality. Estimates of the number of English murdered ranged from 40,000 to 200,000. Parliament voted on the 11th to send 10,000 foot and 2,000 horse from England and requested the Scots to furnish 10,000 men. On December 8, letters were read in the Commons indicating that the rebellion was gaining ground in the South of Ireland. On December 27 it seemed evident that the Catholic Lords of the Pale were joining forces with the rebels. Before the end of December the first 1,500 men arrived in Ireland under the command of Sir Simon Harcourt, and, in February 1641/2, 400 horse under Sir Richard Grenville and 1,500 men under George Monk were added to the English forces in Ireland.

40:40 MIRACULOUS AND LOSSELESSE VICTORIES — The fighting in Ireland was anything but noble. The rebels were driven back by the English troops; the inhabitants were cut down or hanged without mercy. The Irish, who were badly armed or not at all, were no match for the English soldiers. The formidable numbers of Irish, however, made the struggle appear endless. Every Irishman knew that his religion and land were at stake, and that no mercy could be expected. The "losselesse

victories" began in February. On March 19, 1641/2, the English Parliament enacted sweeping confiscations in Ireland which were approved by the King.

41:2-3 SLACKNESSE OF OUR NEEDFULL AIDS — Milton is restive because the amount of aid sent to Ireland seems to him inadequate.

41:4-5 GOD VOUTSAFES ... GRACIOUS WILL — Cf. Romans 6:13; I Corinthians 3:9; II Corinthians 6:1. See *Apology* 41:12-13.

41:5-6 SUCH ACCEPTATION ... HIM — Milton is thinking of scriptural passages that indicate God's pleasure with the prayers of some. See, for instance, I Kings 9:3; II Chronicles 7:12; Proverbs 15:8; Isaiah 58:9; Acts 10:4.

41:12-13 INFERIOR OFFICERS ... FROM GOD — See 41:4-5.

[SECTION 9]

41:34-35 OFFENDING THE EARE ... HARMONY — Cf. 37:2-3. The passage gives hints of Milton's intimacy with music. Cf. *ANIM, Col.* III, 133, "As for the words ... variety (as both Musick and Rhethorick teacheth us) erects and rouses an Auditory, like the maisterfull running over many Cords and divisions; whereas if men should ever bee thumming the drone of one plaine Song, it would bee a dull Opiat to the most wakefull attention."

41:36-37 MOURNFULL ELEGY — The Confuter, in *A Modest Confutation*, p. 17, selected from the *Animadversions* (1641) a number of the statements that Milton had made about the Remonstrant, citing the page number from which he took the statement, preparatory to making a defense. He said:

We ... if we *will*, may beleeve the Remonstrant to be [*a notorious enemy to truth*, pag.2. *a false Prophet*, pag.3. *a belly-god, proud and covetous*, pag.5 *squeezed to a wretched, cold, and hollow-hearted confession of some Prelaticall ryots*, pag.15. *whose understanding nothing will cure but Kitchin-physick*, pag.17. *a Laodicean*, pag.24. *a dissembling Joab*,pag.28 *a dawber with untempered morter*,pag,62.] (The brackets are the Confuter's. For the citations from the *Animadversions* in the Columbia edition, see *Col.* III, 105, 107, 109, 121, 123, 132, 136, and 170 respectively.)

The defense which followed began as a "mournfull elegy":

Good God! thou that hast promised to direct the steps

of the humble, and to be with those that are of a meek heart, instruct me how to chuse some path to walk in towards my Eternity; for this my soul hates! Let me for ever be shut out of that heaven, that is the reward of such black calumny, such malitious and divellish slanders! And, O you my dear brethren, who are disaffected towards the Prelate, look upon and give evidence to the man! How is he an enemy to the truth, unlesse the Gospel of Christ be a lye! How is he a false Prophet, unlesse your selves who professe the same faith be impostors? View well that heap of age and reverence, and say whether that clear and healthfull constitution, those fresh cheeks and quick eyes, that round tongue, agile hand, nimble invention, stay'd delivery, quiet calm and happy bosome, be the effects of threescore yeers surfeits and gluttony. (*Modest Confutation*, p. 17.)

41:37 PASSIONAT SOLILOQUIES — See the first line of the "mournfull elegy" quotation, Note 41:36-37. Compare the following passages:

Worthy you of your chains and fagots, O ye Martyrs, that commended this government unto us; perish and rot the memories of those famous Assemblies, that confirmed it, and bound us to the maintenance of superstition and Antichristianisme! And now that I finde them so ungratefull to the dead, it lessens my wonder, though not their impiety, that they are so to the living. Away with those cheap as numerous leaves, that image forth to us his ravished and devout thoughts; away with the clear and bright mirrour of a dispassioned soul, a rectified understanding, a liberall and Christian charity; with that sweet and heavenly eloquence that prepares a way for the Spirit of God. (*Modest Confutation*, pp. 19-20.)

Froward spite, that makes us therefore hate, because we cannot love enough; therefore revile, because we cannot sufficiently praise. (*Ibid.*, p. 21.)

41:37-38 TWO WHOLE PAGES OF INTER-GATORIES — Much of the Confuter's defense of the Remonstrant on pages 18 and 19 of the *Modest Confutation* is in the form of questions such as:

Must he be therefore luke warm, because his zeal burns not as hot as hell? must his conscience be therefore cauterized and seared, because he brands not every Christian out of the Church of England with the marks of reprobation? writes not the dreadfull doom of God in the forehead of all Popishly given, in France, Spain, Italy, Germany? (*Modest Confutation*, p. 18.)

41:39-40 HIS FRESH CHEEKS ... INVENTION — See Note 41:36-37.

[SECTION 10]

42:1 ERECT FIGURES — In Section X of the *Modest Confutation* the author sets out to delineate

Milton's character from inferences taken from the *Animadversions*. See Note 42:2.

42:2 I AM NO BISHOP ... TO IT — The Confuter's statement was:

Forsooth you would give the world to know these two things: First, that you are no Bishop: Secondly, that you can pray *ex tempore*. Surely a man of strong parts, and a mortified ambition! It was thought of old, that the Philosophers did therefore contemn and speak ill of riches and pleasures and high places, because they were never born to them; as the Fox cursed the Grapes that were out of his reach. But we will not think so uncharitably of you; A rich Widow, or a Lecture, or both, contents you. (*Modest Confutation*, p. 22.)

42:5 HIS IDOL A BISHOPRICK — Milton assumes from certain things he reads in the *Modest Confutation* and perhaps knows as a matter of common knowledge or as a result of investigation that the Confuter's "Idol" is a "Bishoprick." The Confuter speaks with some authority for the "*great Clerks*" when he denies (*Modest Confutation*, p. 22) Milton's statement that the "great Clarks" think that those men who have a trade cannot "attaine to some good measure of knowledge" (*ANIM* (1641) p. 13; *Col.* III, 118). Furthermore, he defends the liturgy, the prelates, the Universities, the granting of bishopricks and deaneries to young scholars, the seeking of preferment, and the political activities of the bishops (*Modest Confutation*, pp. 24-40). He says that he is "one of those young Scholars," presumably, who has petitioned for a bishoprick or deanery (*ibid.*, p. 36; see Introduction, p. 3).

42:12 FAMILIAR — Masson thinks the "familiar" is "Hall's informant respecting Milton" (Masson, *Life*, II, 408). It may as well be the Confuter's familiar spirit, for Milton has already spoken of the Confuter as a "wizzard" who "[tells] fortunes" (42:1-3) and is about to mention "his art of divining" (42:14).

42:12 BELIKE — *i.e.*, probably.

42:12-13 A RICH WIDOW ... CONTENT ME — See Notes 42:2 and 55:5.

42:14 MORE IGNORANT ... ANY GIPSY — Gypsies were and have been noted for their pretences to fortune-telling, particularly to the art of palmistry, which they probably derived from their Indian home. They first appeared in England about the beginning of the sixteenth century. In the seventeenth century proponents of systems of palmistry were appealing to Scripture for support, especially to Exodus 13:16, Job 37:7, and Proverbs 3:16.

42:17 NOT BIN UNEXPENSIVE IN LEARNING, AND VOYAGING ABOUT — Milton's education began early. According to his own statement he was destined by his father "from a child for the pursuits of polite learning" for which he showed such "instinctive ardour" that his father provided "in addition to the ordinary instructions of grammar school, masters to give me daily lessons at home" (*Second Defence, Col.* VIII, 119, 121). The anonymous biographer of Milton records that the young Milton "had his institution to learning both under public and private Masters" (Darbishire, *Early Lives,* p. 18). The only private tutor about whom anything is known is Thomas Young. Some time before 1620 Milton entered St. Paul's School. On February 12, 1624/5 (Masson, *Life,* I, 111-12), Milton was admitted to Christ College, Cambridge, at which he took the B.A. degree on March 26, 1629, and the M.A. on July 3, 1632. Thereafter he spent six years at his father's home in Horton (*Second Defence, Col.* VIII, 121), where by virtue of very diligent study he became a very learned man. In 1638 Milton set out on a Grand Tour to complete his education. The itinerary was to include France and Italy, Greece and Sicily. He was accompanied by a male companion. How long he intended to travel is unknown. He did not visit Greece or Sicily because he was "restrained by the melancholy tidings from England of the civil war" (*ibid.,* p. 125). He returned to England, having spent about fifteen months on the trip.

The cost of an education such as that which the elder Milton provided for his son was very considerable. Until the end of the Italian trip the young Milton was financially dependent upon his father. He could boast that he was "ever bred . . . up in plenty" (42:16).

42:22 *RICH HOPES* — The Confuter had charged that Milton's prayer in the *Animadversions* (1641), pp. 37-39 (*Col.* III, 146-48; cf. Masson, *Life,* II, 267-68 and Notes 42:30-31; 42:33-34) was intended to gain "A rich Widow, or a Lecture, or both" (see Note 42:2). He continued:

To the first you make way, by a long, tedious, theatricall, big-mouthed, astounding Prayer, put up in the name of the three Kingdomes; not so much either to please God, or benefit the weal-publike by it, as to intimate your owne good abilities to her that is your *rich hopes.* (*Modest Confutation,* p. 22.)

42:24 WIDE ALL THE HOUSES OF HEAV'N — In astrology the heaven is divided into twelve "mundane houses" by great circles through the north and south points of the horizon. These "houses" are used by astrologers to note the positions of heavenly bodies, and to cast horoscopes and nativities. Each "mundane house" has a heavenly body as its lord. *Batman vppon Bartholome,* Bk. VIII, ch. 9, fol. 124 *recto* and *verso,* says:

Zodiacus is a circle that passeth aslont, & is departed euen in twelue partes, the which twelue partes Philosophers call signes. And these signes shewe to vs in what parte of heauen the Sunne and the Planettes are in. . . . And these signes bee called houses: for they bee the home and dwelling places of Planettes.

42:26 *RICH HOPES* — See Note 42:22.

42:27-28 A VIRGIN . . . HONESTLY BRED — Masson thinks that Milton is posting "a marriage-advertisement" (Masson, *Life,* II, 408). Milton had celebrated the "sublime notion," the "high mystery," the "serious doctrine of Virginity" (*Comus,* 784-86). He felt the high significance of Scripture language which pictured Christ, the bridegroom, expecting the Church "to be presented before him a pure unspotted virgin," for which reason it was most unfit that a virgin "be left to an uncertaine and arbitrary education" (*RCG, Col.* III, 188). From Plato and Xenophon he learned of "chastity and love, I meane that which is truly so" (17:20-22). From St. Paul he had learned the "chaste and high mysteries," that "unchastity in a woman" was a "scandall and dishonour" (18:3-7). The defense of his own virtue, which the *Apology* in a large measure is (18:37-40), led him to look upon the ideal side of marriage, to prefer "a virgin of mean fortunes honestly bred" to the *"rich Widow."*

42:29 *CHALDEAN* — The Chaldeans were reputed for their skill in occult learning, astrology, divination. Hence the term Chaldean came to mean a seer, astrologer, soothsayer.

42:30-31 A PRAYER . . . IN THE ANIMADVERSIONS — Milton in his prayer (*ANIM* (1641), pp. 37-39; *Col.* III, 146-48) said:

O if we freeze at noone after their earely thaw, let

us feare lest the Sunne for ever hide himselfe, and turne his orient steps from our ingratefull Horizon justly condemn'd to be eternally benighted. Which dreadfull judgement O thou the ever-begotten light, and perfect Image of the Father, intercede may never come upon us, as we trust thou hast; for thou hast open'd our difficult and sad times, and given us an unexpected breathing after our long oppressions; thou hast done justice upon those that tyranniz'd over us, while some men waver'd, and admir'd a vaine shadow of wisedome in a tongue nothing slow to utter guile, though thou hast taught us to admire onely that which is good, and to count that onely praise-worthy which is grounded upon thy divine Precepts. (*Ibid.*, (1641), p. 37; *Col.* III, 146.)

It concluded:

Come forth out of thy Royall Chambers, O Prince of all the Kings of the earth, put on the visible roabes of thy imperiall Majesty, take up that unlimited Scepter which thy Almighty Father hath bequeath'd thee; for now the voice of thy Bride calls thee, and all creatures sigh to bee renew'd. (*Ibid.*, (1641), p. 39; *Col.* III, 148.)

The Confuter described the prayer as "long, tedious, theatricall, big-mouthed, astounding" (see Note 42:22). In explaining the disadvantages of *"ex tempore"* prayers, the Confuter said:

Though the language be not in it self unknown, yet the harshnesse of it in some, the length and tediousnesse of stile in others, the affected heighth of forced Allegories and Tropes, not to say the nonsense and ridiculously absurd variations of many pretenders to the faculty, renders it altogether as unintelligible, as it were Latine or Greek. If I were to make good this assertion by a particular instance, I would go no farther than your prayer you have given us, *pag* 36, 37, 38. which infinite of honest and simple Christians would no more know how to understand, than they would doe a Scene out of *Iohnsons Cataline.* (*Modest Confutation*, p. 27.)

42:32 SERVICE BOOK — *i.e.*, the *Book of Common Prayer.*

42:33 *IT WAS THEATRICALL* — See Note 42:22.

42:33-34 MOST OF SCRIPTURE LANGUAGE — Reminiscent of many books of the Bible — the books of history, Job, the Psalms, the prophets, the Gospels, the Pauline epistles, the Revelation — in verbal echoes, as well as in detail and imagery, is a passage such as the following:

Who is there that cannot trace thee now in thy beamy walke through the midst of thy Sanctuary, amidst those golden *candlesticks*, which have long suffer'd a

dimnesse amongst us through the violence of those that had seiz'd them, and were more taken with the mention of their gold then of their starry light; teaching the doctrine of Balaam to cast a stumbling-block before thy servants, commanding them to eat things sacrifiz'd to Idols, and forcing them to fornication. Come therefore O thou that hast the seven starres in thy right hand, appoint thy chosen *Preists* according to their Orders, and courses of old, to minister before thee, and duely to dresse and powre out the consecrated oyle into thy holy and ever-burning lamps; thou hast sent out the spirit of prayer upon thy servants over all the Land to this effect, and stirr'd up their vowes as the sound of many waters about thy Throne. (*ANIM* (1641), pp. 37-38; *Col.* III, 147.)

42:34 *RUBRICK* TO BE SUNG — Directions for being sung. In the liturgical books, the directions for the conduct of the service were frequently written or printed in red.

42:34 COAPE — A vestment resembling a long cloak worn by ecclesiastics in procession, at vespers, and on other occasions.

42:35 HIGH ALTAR — *i.e.*, the chief altar in a cathedral or church.

42:35 *IT WAS BIG-MOUTH'D* — See Note 42:22.

42:36 VOICE OF THREE KINGDOMES — With the coming to the English throne of James VI of Scotland as James I of England, terms such as "all three kingdoms," and "all three realms" came into popular usage. Francis Bacon wrote *A Briefe Discourse, Of the Happy Union, of the Kingdomes, of England, and Scotland,"* (1603) and *Certain Articles, or, Considerations, Touching the Union of the Kingdomes, of England, and Scotland* (1603), wherein he helped popularize the term the "three Kingdomes" (see *Resuscitatio*, pp. 197-220). Milton in the *Animadversions* (*Col.* III, 145) says: "Let us all goe every true protested *Brittaine* throughout the 3. *Kingdoms,* and render thanks to God." The Confuter charges that Milton's prayer is "put up in the name of the three Kingdomes" (see Note 42:22).

42:37-38. A HYMNE IN PROSE ... HUMANE AUTHORS — Milton claims that his "prayer" in the *Animadversions* (see Note 42:30-31) was actually a "hymne in prose." The language is largely inspired by the Old Testament. Visiak says that it is the language of the Bible which has undergone "a marvellous mental change; it is still the voice of Milton...but it is his voice, as it were, attuned to the rhythmical strains of a magnific organ, themselves a transmutation of his own individual quality" (E. H. Visiak, "Milton's Prose," *Nineteenth Century*, CXXIII (1938), 505-06). In the "hymne" Milton forecasts that

When thou hast settl'd peace in the Church, and righteous judgement in the Kingdome, then shall all thy Saints address their voyces of joy, and triumph to thee.... And he that now for haste snatches up a plain ungarnish't present as a thanke-offering to thee... may then perhaps take up a Harp, and sing thee an elaborate Song to Generations. (*ANIM* (1641), p. 38; *Col.* III, 148.)

In the *Reason of Church-Government*, Milton promises to "celebrate in glorious and lofty Hymns the throne and equipage of Gods Almightinesse" (*RCG, Col.* III, 238. For Milton's epic plans as evidenced in the *Apology*, see 17:29-31 and 37:12-13). When Milton speaks of the "hymne in prose" as frequent in the Prophets he may be thinking of such passages as Isaiah 40 and Ezekiel 34. Of the "humane authors," Plato is outstanding.

42:38 HUMANE — *i.e.*, human as opposed to divinely inspired by God to utter His Word. The spelling "humane" remained until the beginning of the eighteenth century, when "human," of which isolated examples occur in the seventeenth century, was substituted, leaving to "humane" a distinct pronunciation and a specialized meaning.

42:39-40 *IT WAS ... PRAYER* — See Note 42:22.

43:4-7 *IT WAS MADE ... YOUR MARO-NILLA* — The Confuter had charged that Milton had appealed to the rich widow by means of the "prayer" (see Note 44:22),

not so much either to please God, or benefit the weal-publike by it, as to intimate your owne good abilities to her that is your *rich hopes.*

> *Petit Gemellus nuptias Maronilla,*
> *Et cupit, & instat, &* Precatur.
> (*Modest Confutation*, p. 22.)

The lines on Maronilla are from Martial's *Epigrams*, Book I, Epigram X. Milton would have recognized them and realized their significance:

> Petit Gemellus nuptias Maronillae,
> Et cupit, & instat, & precatur, & donat.

Adeóne pulchra est? immo foedius nil est.
Quid ergo in illa petitur & placet? tussit.
> (Taken from M. Val. Martialis *Epigrammation Libri*...London, 1615, p. 16, Bk. I, Epigram XI.)

Walter C. A. Ker's translation is as follows: "Gemellus seeks wedlock with Maronilla: he desires it, he urges her, he implores her, and sends her gifts. Is she so beautiful? Nay, no creature is more disgusting. What then is the bait and charm in her? Her cough." (*Martial Epigrams With An English Translation by Walter C. A. Ker*, London, 1925, 2 vols., I, 37, Bk. I, Epigram X.)

43:8 TO KEEPE HIS TONGUE FROM FOLLY — Cf. Proverbs 26:4.

43:9 MISERABLE ... *MARONILLA* — The Confuter's insinuation by referring to Martial's epigram is that Milton's "prayer" is aimed to gain a rich widow who is afflicted with consumption (see Note 43:4-7), that he has "urged and implored" her by means of that "prayer."

43:9-12 COURTER ... OF SUCH A HAP-LESSE INVENTION ... ORISONS — Milton thinks it were miserable if he had to resort to such an unfortunate device as a prayer, as if no way were left him to express himself except by becoming a candidate for the ministry who prays in a sing-song manner. The Confuter had charged him with wishing to become a lecturer (see Notes 42:22 and 43:25-26).

43:13-14 *TEACH EACH ... CHANGELESSE WORD* — Joseph Hall in "His Defiance to Enuy" prefixed to [*Virgidemiarvm, Toothlesse Satyrs*, 1598], Sig. [A6] *recto*, wrote:

VVould we but breath within a wax-bound quill,
Pans seuenfold Pipe, some plaintiue Pastorall:
To teach each hollow groue, and shrubby hill,
Ech murmuring brooke, each solitary vale
To sound our loue, and to our song accord,
VVearying Eccho with one changelesse word.

43:16-19 *TEACH EACH.... MY LOVES* — Hall, in "His Defiance to Enuy" ([*Virgidemiarvm, Toothlesse Satyrs*, 1598], Sig. [A7] *recto*), wrote:

VVhether so me list my louely thought to sing,
Come daunce ye nimble Dryads by my side:
Ye gentle wood-Nymphs come: & with you bring
The willing Faunes that mought your musick guide.
Come Nimphs & Faunes, that haunt those shady groues,
vvhiles I report my fortunes or my loues.

The *"teach each"* is repeated from the previous citation from Hall (see Note 43:13-14). The fact that Milton indicated that this citation and the preceding one (43:13-14) were taken from the *Toothlesse Satyrs* points to Milton's use of the 1597 or 1598 edition of *Virgidemiarum . . . Toothlesse Satyrs* (see Notes 32:35 and 33:11).

43:21 MORRICE OR AT MAY POLE — The "morris" was a grotesque dance performed by persons dressed in fantastic costumes. The "May pole" was a high pole, painted gaily with spiral stripes and decked with flowers, placed in an open space for May-day merry-makers to dance around.

43:23 MY LITURGY — *i.e.,* in general, the rites which Milton approved for public worship; in particular, Milton's "prayer" (see Note 42:30-31).

43:23-24 LADIES PSALTER — *i.e.,* our Lady's Psalter. John Foxe said that the author of our Lady's Psalter, Bonaventure, a bishop and cardinal, canonized in 1482, in order to prove himself

a devout servant to his Lady [the Virgin Mary], hath taken every psalm of David's Psalter (which he peculiarly made and referred to Almighty God), and hath in divers of the said psalms and verses put out the name of the Lord, and hath placed in the name of our Lady. This being done through the whole psalms and every one of them, it is now called our Lady's Psalter, used to be sung and said in the praise and service of our Lady.

Foxe then cites passages from the Psalter including: "In thee, O Lady, do I put my trust"; "To thee, O Lady, do I lift up my soul"; "They that put their trust in thee, O mother of God, shall not be afraid." (Foxe, *Acts and Monuments,* VII, 131-36.)

Milton is playing upon words, making "Ladies" refer both to the Maronilla and to the Virgin Mary. He says that the Confuter attributes such impoverishment of speech to Milton that Milton must turn his own liturgy into the blasphemous praise of his Lady even as the author of the Lady's Psalter had done, and his own prayer to the unworthy objective of winning a rich widow.

43:24 GRADUAT — The term may be used in the sense of being a proficient. In this case, Milton would be using the term sarcastically to ridicule the Confuter's advanced position as "figure-caster" (43:21).

43:25-26 FARRE DISTANT . . . LAICK — The Confuter has imagined Milton to be a lesser "Clerk" on the basis of Milton's statement that the "great Clarks" think men who have a trade cannot "attaine to some good measure of knowledge, and to a reason of their actions" (*ANIM* (1641), p. 13; *Col.* III, 118-19). He charges Milton with attempting to gain a lectureship "by flattery and rayling." Addressing Milton he says:

Truly, small Clerk, you know but little of those mens [great Clerk's] mindes: I will insure you they do not think so. But why should you plead this? Methinks it were much better for you, and more conducible to your ends if it were so: For could they not attain to a reason of their actions, there were great hopes they would choose you to be their Minister. But I know not how unluckily you have spoyled your own market; if that be true which you elsewhere affirm of them [*That they are competent Judges of a Ministers abilities, as it will not be denyed that he may be the competent Judge of a neat picture or elegant Poem, that cannot limne the like,*] unlesse in your simile you recover your selfe and abuse them. (*Modest Confutation,* pp. 22-23. The italicized passage is taken from *Animadversions* (1641), p. 50; *Col.* III, 157, and is bracketed by the Confuter.)

Milton retorts that he is as far from a lecturer as the most humble layman. See Note 53:34-36.

43:27-28 YET I SHALL NOT DECLINE . . . NEXT MOV'D — Although Milton has no intention of becoming a churchman, he feels qualified to give his opinion. He had been trained for the ministry and "Church-outed by the Prelats"; therefore, he felt that he had "the right . . . to meddle in these matters" (*RCG, Col.* III, 242; see 3:27-31).

43:28-29 *WHETHER THE PEOPLE . . . MINISTERS ABILITY* — Milton said in the *Animadversions* (1641), p. 50 (*Col.* III, 157):

For many may be able to judge who is fit to be made a minister, that would not be found fit to be made Ministers themselves, as it will not be deny'd that he may be the competent Judge of a neat picture, or elegant poem, that cannot limne the like.

Part of Milton's statement was used by the Confuter to point out how Milton argued to his own detriment (see Note 43:25-26). Milton's statement in both the *Animadversions* and the *Apology* indicates the good opinion Milton had of the lower classes. Milton was in agreement with those mentioned by Robert Lord Brooke who "conceive 30. or 40. or an 100. Good men of any one or more Congregations, to be as Fit Judges of their [the ministers'] parts and abilities every way, as One Lord Bishop and his Ignorant (perhaps Drunken) Chaplaine" (Brooke, *Nature of Episcopacy*, pp. 112-13). Milton's good opinion was not destined to survive.

43:30-31 GOD HATH PROMIS'D...KNOWL-EDGE — Among the scriptural passages that promise God's outpouring of knowledge and wisdom are: Acts 2:17-18; James 1:5; Luke 21:15; I John 2:27; Romans 15:14; I Corinthians 1:5; 12:8; Ephesians 1:17; Colossians 1:9.

43:32-34 HOW SHOULD THE PEOPLE EX-AMINE...BID THEM DO? — See I Thessalonians 5:21; I John 4:1; II John 8-12; I Timothy 6:3-6; II Corinthians 13:5; John 7:17; I Corinthians 11:28; Galatians 1:6-9; I Peter 3:15.

43:34-35 *DISCERNE AND BEWARE...TRY EVERY SPIRIT* — Milton seems primarily to have I John 4:1 in mind: "Beloved, believe not every spirit, but try the spirits whether they are of God: because many false prophets are gone out into the world." Cf. Matthew 7:15; 24:4-5, 11, 24; I Corinthians 12:10.

43:37-39 *WERE CALL'D IN CHRIST...IN THE MYSTERY OF GOD* — Milton seems to be referring to Colossians 1:28, "[Christ] Whom we preach, warning every man, and teaching every man in all wisdom; that we may present every man perfect in Christ Jesus," and to Colossians 2:2-3, "That their hearts might be comforted, being knit together in love, and unto all riches of the full assurance of understanding, to the acknowledgment of the mystery of God, and of the Father, and of Christ; In whom are hid all the treasures of wisdom and knowledge." Cf. Colossians 1:9 and I Corinthians 1:2-5.

43:39-44:2 BUT THE NON-RESIDENT AND PLURALITY-GAPING PRELATS [,] THE GULPHS AND WHIRLE POOLS OF BENE-FICES, BUT THE DRY PITS OF ALL SOUND DOCTRINE...ARE — Francis Bacon took much the same stand as Milton. He said:

FOR *Non-Residence*, except it be, in Case of necessary Absence, it seemeth, an *Abuse*, drawn out of *Covetousnesse*, and *Sloth*: For that Men should *Live* of the *Flock*, that they do not *Feed*; Or of the *Altar*, at which they do not *Serve*; Is a Thing, that can hardly receive,

just *Defence*. And to the Exercise, the *Office*, of a *Pastour*, in Matter of the *Word*, and *Doctrine*, by Deputies; Is a Thing not warranted.... (Bacon, "Certain Considerations, Touching the Better, Pacification, And Edification, Of The Church Of England," in *Resuscitatio*, p. 250).

44:1-2 PREACH WHAT THEY LIST — The censure was of old standing. Martin Marprelate complained that the Archbishop of Canterbury, in licensing a catechism by a Mr. Davison blotted out the word "preached" in the place of the book where "the means of salvation was attributed to the Word preached...so ascribing the way to work men's salvation to the Word read. Thus they do to suppress the truth and to keep men in ignorance" (Pierce (ed.), *The Marprelate Tracts*, p. 73). John Bridges, in *A Defence Of The Government Established In The Chvrch Of Englande* (1587), p. 12, deplored that the abundance of spiritual food given by God in his Holy Word was not delivered to the people. Milton said that

while Protestants, to avoid the due labor of understanding thir own religion are content to lodge it in the breast or rather in the books of a clergie man, and to take it thence by scraps and mammocks as he dispences it in his sundays dole, they will be alwaies learning and never knowing, alwaies infants, alwaies either his vassals, as lay-papists are to their priests, or at odds with him, as reformed principles give them som light.... (*Means to Remove Hirelings, Col.* VI, 99-100.)

44:4 *THE VERY BEASTS...CALLS THEM* — The Confuter said, "Who but you, against the command of God himself, dare bring not the Congregation onely, but the very beasts of the people, within the borders of the Mount?" (*Modest Confutation*, p. 23) in referring to Milton's statement that "many may be able to judge who is fit to be made a minister, that would not be found fit to be made Ministers themselves" (see Note 43:28-29). The Confuter is thinking of Exodus 19:12-13. He has changed the emphasis on the word "beasts." God's caution was that any beast or man that touched the border of the mount should not live. Milton notes the Confuter's use of the phrase the "beasts of the people" to mean the most despicable of the people, and capitalizes upon it.

44:9-11 BOTH BY SUPPRESSING...ENG-LISH BIBLE — Because the opponents of prelacy considered preaching the "only ordinary means" to salvation (cf. Pierce (ed.), *The Marprelate Tracts,* p. 65), they had long been eager that preaching have a free course and deplored the "silencing of so many learned and worthy preachers" (*ibid.,* p. 64). William Fulke in *A Briefe and plaine declaration* (1584), p. 66, had urged that, since the right use of public prayer could not be known until the people were taught the Word of God, public preaching should be established, and public prayers would necessarily follow. He suggested that all unlearned pastors be removed from their charges: "O Lorde how miserable is the state of many flockes in this lande, who either seldome or neuer heare the worde of God truely preached, and therefore know not how to beleeue that they might be saued" (*ibid.,* pp. 36-37). He objected that the pastor's office should be thought to consist in reading a number of Psalms and following the appointed forms of prayer "which a Childe of ten yeares olde maye doe" (*ibid.,* p. 40). The author of *An Appeale To Every Impartiall, Iudicious, and Godly Reader* (1641), p. 11, complained of the suppression of preaching "as it of late hath beene." Pyrnne charged that

some of our unpreaching, domineering secular Prelates ... not onely give over preaching themselues, as no part of their function; and suppresse most weekday Lectures in divers Countries; but have likewise lately shut up the mouthes of sundry of our most godly, powerfull, painefull Preachers (who have woon more soules to God in a yeare, than all the Lord Bishops in *England* or the world have done in divers ages) *out of meere malice to Religion, and the peoples salvation;* contrary to the very Lawes of God and the Realme; strictly prohibit-bited, under paine of suspention, in sundry Diocesse, all afternoone Sermons on :he Lords own Day; that so the prophane vulgar might haue more time to *dance, play, revell, drinke, and prophane Gods Sabbatbs,* even in these dayes of plague and pestilence, *to draw downe more plagues & judgements on us....* ([William Prynne], *Newes from Ipswich,* 1636, Sig. [***] verso.)

He stated that some of the lordly prelates "did not so much as preach one Sermon in sundry yeares ... yea, most of them have by themselves and their instruments *written* and *preached* against *frequent preaching;* suppressed all week-day Lectures, and Sermons, on Lordsday afternoones throughout their Diocesses" (William Prynne, *The Antipathie Of The English Lordly Prelacie,* Sig. ¶¶¶*recto*). Robert Lord Brooke in 1641 wrote:

... through the whole Kingdome, Preaching, Praying, Expounding, and the like exercises, both in publick and private, are severely suppressed, and in many places altogether forbidden (except such and such, more pernicious than profitable;) and all This by the Fathers of our Church, the Lords our Bishops. (Brooke, *Nature of Episcopacy,* p. 95.)

The licensing authority of the two Archbishops and the Bishop of London had since the days of Elizabeth protected the Church of England by suppressing antiprelatical literature. By the Canons of 1640, Canon IV, it was decreed that "no Stationer, Printer, or Importer of [Socinian] Books, or any other person whatsoever, shall print, buy, sell or disperse any book [broaching] or maintaining of the said abominable Doctrine or Positions." Canon V decreed and ordained that the clause concerning "Books of Socinianism, shall also extend to the Makers, Importers, Printers and Publishers, or Dispersers of any Book, Writing, or scandalous Pamphlet devised against the Discipline and Government of the Church of *England,* and unto the maintainers and Abettors of any Opinion or Doctrine against the same" (*A Collection Of Articles, Injunctions, Canons, Orders, Ordinances,* London, 1675, pp. 355-59). Under such a restriction the attempts by the antiprelatical party to defend their position by appealing to the Bible were suppressed. The result was a flood of unlicensed pamphlets.

44:12-15 *ISAIAH ... FROM HIS QUARTER* — Milton's quotation of Isaiah 56:10-11 illustrates how he often fitted Bible passages "into the context of his writings ... in such a way that they became parts of his own sentences" (H. F. Fletcher, "The Use of the Bible in Milton's Prose," p. 38). The author of *A Briefe and plaine declaration,* p. 44, complained in a vein similar to Milton's:

We ... allow such for Pastours of mens soules, whom no carefull owner of Cattell, woulde make ouerseer of his sheepes bodyes. Which thing almightye God hath always detested, and ... sayeth by the Prophet Esaye, complayning of the vnlearned Pastours of Israell, which was the onelye cause of their affliction and miseries. *Their watchmen are all blinde, they haue no knowledge, they cannot barke, they lye and sleepe and delight in sleeping, and these greedie dogges can neuer haue ynough, and these sheepheardes cannot vnderstande, for they all looke to their owne way, euery one for his aduauntage and for his owne purpose.*

44:16 SINCERE MILKE — See I Peter 2:2, "sincere milk of the word."

44:18-19 WASTE PLACES...*SHADOW OF DEATH* — Milton's source is Matthew 4:15-16, which he has condensed.

44:20 LIGHT—Cf. *ANIM, Col.* III, 153, "light of his truth"; *RCG, Col.* III, 226, "if the sacred Bible may be our light"; *Doctrine and Discipline of Divorce, Col.* III, 434, "certain and true light for men to walk in"; *Paradise Regained*, IV, 288-90,

> he who receives
> Light from above, from the fountain of light,
> No other doctrine needs....

See I John 1:7.

44:20-23 BEASTS TO MAKE THEM MEN... *IUDAIZING* BEASTS — Cf. *ANIM, Col.* III, 173, "our just Parliament will deliver us from your *Ephesian* beasts" (I Corinthians 15:32). Milton charges that the prelates by their "sorcerous doctrine of formalities" (*Apology*, 44:21) transform rational followers of Christ into irrational conformers to the doctrines and observances of the Jews, into "beasts that perish" (21:19). In the *History of Britain, Col.* X, 134-35, Milton cites Gildas to describe the clergy:

... Pastors in Name, but indeed Wolves; intent upon all occasions, not to feed the Flock, but to pamper and well line themselves... teaching the people, not by sound Doctrin, but by evil Example... seeking after preferments and degrees in the Church more then after Heav'n.... they have thir niceties and trivial points to keep in aw the superstitious multitude; but in true saving knowledge leave them still as gross and stupid as themselves; bunglers at the Scripture, nay forbidding and silencing them that know; but in worldly matters, practis'd and cunning Shifters; in that only art and symony, great Clercs and Maisters, bearing thir heads high, but thir thoughts abject and low.... gluttonous, incontinent, and daily Drunkards. And what shouldst thou expect from these, poor Laity... these beasts, all belly?... Leave them... as bids our Saviour, lest ye fall both blind-fold into the same perdition.

44:23-25 HAD THEY BUT TAUGHT... DISPENSATION OF THE WORD — Cf. Matthew 28:19; Luke 4:18-19; 9:2; 10:1; 24:47; II Timothy 4:2.

44:23 SUFFER'D IT TO BE TAUGHT — After Laud had become Archbishop of Canterbury, August 6, 1633, one of his first objectives was to bring the ordination of puritan chaplains and lecturers to a halt.

44:26-27 DISCERN'D... FALSE — See Galatians 1:7-9; II John 8-10; Matthew 15:9; 24:11, 24; II Peter 2:1; Mark 13:22; Luke 20:47; John 10:5.

44:28 THEY WHO HAVE PUT OUT THE PEOPLES EYES — Cf. Matthew 15:3, 9, 14; 23:13.

44:28-29 REPROACH THEM... BLINDNESSE — The Confuter used a similar figure of speech in accusing the presbyterians of blindness: "Blind men! that will not see our own good; that shut our eyes, and then complain that we want the Sunne!" (*Modest Confutation*, p. 20.) Milton could not stand by and see the prelate train "*on the easie Christian insensibly within the close ambushment of worst errors,*" and leave him "*under the sevenfold possession of a desperate stupidity*" (*ANIM, Col.* III, 106-07).

44:29 PHARISEES THEIR TRUE FATHERS — Christ described the Pharisees thus: "Ye are they which justify yourselves before men; but God knoweth your hearts" (Luke 16:15). Upon another occasion Christ declared: "Ye are of *your* father the devil, and the lusts of your father ye will do" (John 8:44). See Note 23:25-26.

44:30-31 WHO COULD NOT INDURE... CHRISTS DOCTRINE — See Matthew 4:16; 15:10; Luke 19:37-39; John 9:22, 28-34; 12:42; 19:38.

44:31-32 THEY JUDG'D FARRE BETTER... RABBIES — See Matthew 16:16; 27:54; John 4: 29, 42; 6:14, 69; 11:27; 12:42; Acts 4:1-4.

44:32-33 *YET THIS PEOPLE... IS ACCURST* — John 7:49.

44:33-34 AUTHORITY OF *PLINY* — The Confuter brought Pliny to prove Milton wrong in saying that the people were "*competent judges of a ministers ability*" (see Note 43:28-29). He quoted from Pliny (*Modest Confutation*, p. 23):

Ut de pictore, fictore, sculptore, nisi artifex judicare, ita nisi sapiens non potest perspicere sapientem, Plin. lib 1, epist. 10 ["... as none but those who are skilled in Painting, Statuary, or the plastic art, can form a right judgement of any master in those arts; so a man must himself have made three advances in philosophy, before he is capable of forming a just notion of a philosopher" (Melmoth's translation of *Pliny Letters*, I, 35)].

Pliny's full name was Gaius Plinius Caecilius Secundus (61 or 62 - *c*. 113 A.D.). He was educated in rhetoric under Quintilian.

44:35   FOR AS NONE CAN JUDGE OF A PAINTER — Milton accepts Pliny's authority (44:33-35) and shows the Confuter that Pliny's statement upholds Milton's original contention concerning the competence of the people to judge (44:35-45:15).

44:36   *PRACTICK* — *i.e.*, practise.

45:1   MEANEST — Undistinguished in position (*OED*). Milton has said that Englishmen bear "a naturall disposition of much reverence and awe towards the Deity," that if they "get the benefit once of a wise and well rectifi'd nurture . . . the English people . . . may deserve to be accounted a right pious, right honest, and right hardy nation" (*RCG, Col.* III, 224-25). Milton is upholding the notion insisted upon by Henry Burton in the *Protestation Protested* (see Note 27:13-14) that average people have the ability to set up a congregation, to select their minister, and to worship in their own way. Hall, however, denounced the voice of the "mutinous rabble" (see Note 45:17-18) as the "hummings of a factious congregation" (*A Survay*, p. 26). He asked whether Burton would allow "the meanest chimney-sweeper amongst you his calling to preach, to expound scripture, to give the Sacraments" (*ibid.*, p. 30). Milton proclaims that the "meanest Christians" have the capacity to elect their ministers, and that the "plaine artizan" is a "competent discerner" (45:13-15; cf. Wolfe, *Milton in the Puritan Revolution*, New York, 1941, pp. 54, 249).

45:6-7   TO READE . . . BOOKS — Of the many references that might be cited, the following will suffice: II Chronicles 34:30; Nehemiah 8:8; Matthew 12:3; 19:4; 21:16; 22:31; Mark 12:10, 26; Acts 13:27; 15:21; Colossians 4:16; I Thessalonians 5:27.

45:9   BY THE LIFE HE LEADS — See James 2:14-26; Matthew 7:16, 20; John 15:16; Colossians 1:10.

45:11   WHEN HE WHO JUDGES . . . HIMSELFE — See I Corinthians 2:15; Galatians 6:1; Colossians 1:9-10.

45:13   PLAINE ARTIZAN — See Note 45:1. Preserved Smith, in *The Age of the Reformation*, p. 90, has indicated that about the time of the beginning of the Reformation in Germany, or slightly before, the peasant who had been mocked and insulted began to be courted and flattered. In the pamphlet literature he became an ideal figure, the "plain, honest, God-fearing man." "Carlstadt and other learned men proclaimed that the peasant knew better the Word of God and the way of salvation than did the learned."

45:15   COMPETENT DISCERNER — See Note 45:1.

45:16   *METAPHYSICALL* FUME — A vapor made up of overly-subtle, overly-abstract ideas.

45:17-18   *THE MUTINOUS RABBLE . . . VNIVERSITY* — The Confuter had said:

Go you then to your mutinous rabble, and if you can appease their furies, enthrone their sage wisedomes upon some stall or bench, and cite before them the Clerks of either University: those competent Judges, I guesse, will do like themselves, reject one as unsufficient . . . onely for that he hath too little haire on his upper lip, or too much upon his fore-head; because he useth not to wear wrought night-caps, or mastick patches. In the mean while another . . . shall be thought fitter to cleave blocks than divide a Text, because he hath a sowre or crabbed countenance; because either his learning is too much, or that little he hath lodges, as their Prentices do, in an ugly Garret: Whiles a third shall be deeply suspected of Arminianism, because he hath a squint-eye, or is of the Arch-bishops Colledge. (*Modest Confutation*, p. 24.)

45:19   I DOUBT ME — I am afraid.

45:23   TO SEND THE SIMPLEST OF THEIR SONNES — Since the first son in the English families inherited the estates, the other sons had to seek their fortunes in other fashions. The Petition of the University of Oxford, May 12, 1641, deplored among other things the attacks on the Cathedral Establishments which were "a motive and encouragement" to divinity students, and a method of rewarding scholars, as well as "many younger brothers of good parentage who devote themselves to the ministry of the Gospel" (Masson, *Life*, II, 228). Haller conjectures that Milton as a boy may very well have heard Richard Stock, who preached in the Bread Street neighborhood for near three decades, "urge parents to dedicate their most gifted children, not those good for nothing else, to the ministry" (Haller, *Rise of Puritanism*, p. 292).

45:25-26 TWO CORPORATIONS — Oxford and Cambridge.

45:28-29 FOR ANY CUSTOME — For want of business patronage.

45:33 *IDEA'S* — See Note 22:15.

45:34-35 *SOLECISMS* — "The use of incorrect or ungrammatical speech or diction" (*OED*).

45:37 GAY RANKNESSE OF *APULEIUS*, *ARNOBIUS* — Lucius Apuleius, born about A.D. 125, is the only example extant in Latin literature of the accomplished sophist. The *Metamorphoses* or *Golden Ass* are marked by fancy and feeling, by affectation and tawdry ornamentation, and by a mixture or sequence of dignity, ludicrousness, sensuousness, and horribleness. Apuleius' Latin is African in tone. Obsolete words are a marked characteristic of it.

Arnobius, the elder, was a Christian writer who seems to have flourished in the late third and early fourth centuries A.D. He taught rhetoric at Sicca Venerea in proconsular Africa during the reign of Diocletian. His apology for Christianity, *Adversus Gentes,* is an answer to those who claimed that the misfortunes of the age could be attributed to Christianity and to the impiety of Christians. Part of his work is devoted to a detraction of the legends concerning the Greek and Roman gods. Milton includes him among the "ancient fathers of the church, Clemens Alexandrinus ... Lactantius, Eusebius" who uncovered and "cast derision upon the obscene mysteries of the old religion!" (*Author's Defence of Himself, Col.* IX, 111). In *Of Reformation,* Milton shows his dislike for the "knotty Africanisms, the pamper'd metafors; the intricat, and involv'd sentences ... the fantastick, and declamatory flashes; the crosse-jingling periods which cannot but disturb, and come thwart a setl'd devotion worse then the din of bells, and rattles" (*Col.* III, 34; see Kathleen Ellen Hartwell, *Lactantius and Milton,* Cambridge, Mass., 1929, pp. 39-40).

45:37 FUSTIANIST — One who writes in a ridiculously lofty, bombastic, pompous manner.

45:38 *LATINISMS* OF *CICERO* — The writers and stylists of the Renaissance considered the works of Marcus Tullius Cicero (106-43 B.C.) the supreme example of pure Latinity, and attempted to recapture its excellences by imitating its style and vocabulary.

45:40 *ATTICK* MAISTERS OF MORALL WISDOME AND ELOQUENCE — Milton frequently mentions or alludes to the "*Attick* maisters." In a letter to Leonard Philaras of Athens, June 1652, he confessed "that whatever literary advance I have made I owe chiefly to steady intimacy with [the] writings" of the "many men of supreme eloquence ... produced by that city" (*Col.* XII, 57). He praises the "eloquent writers" who glorified the "small deeds" of Athens (*RCG. Col.* III, 237), the "Orator renound In *Athens* or free *Rome,* where Eloquence Flourished" (*Paradise Lost,* IX, 670-72), and the writers of "*Attic* Tragedies of stateliest and most regal argument" (*Of Education, Col.* IV, 285; see also *Paradise Regained,* IV, 261-63). Among the "maisters" are Socrates, "pronounced by the oracle the wisest of mankind" (*Author's Defence of Himself, Col.* IX, 53; cf. *Second Defence, Col.* VIII, 193, "wisest Athenian"), "*Plato,* and his equall *Xenophon*" (17:20-21; cf. *Of Education, Col.* IV, 284, "the moral works of *Plato, Xenophon*"), Aristotle, one of "the best interpreters of nature and morality" (*Tenure of Kings and Magistrates, Col.* V, 12), Themistocles (*Doctrine and Discipline of Divorce, Col.* III, 464), and "the two most distinguished orators, Demosthenes and Aeschines" (*Prolusion* VI, *Col.* XII, 211; cf. *Author's Defence of Himself, Col.* IX, 147, "most renowned of the Athenians for eloquence"). In more general references, Milton praises the "sage and severe Judges of *Athens*" (*ANIM, Col.* III, 110), the "greatest and choycest wits of *Athens*" (*RCG, Col.* III, 236), the "*Athens* where Books and Wits were ever busier then in any other part of *Greece*" (*Areopagitica, Col.* IV, 299), and Greece itself where "flourished ... many worthies distinguished for their wisdom" (*First Defence, Col.* VII, 313).

46:2 THEIR LIPS ... UNCIRCUMCIS'D — *i.e.,* the clerks are totally unfamiliar; their lips are not spiritually purified.

46:4 *PARIS AND SALAMANCA* — Centers of the scholasticism for which Milton had little sympathy. See 37:37-38:1.

46:5 AFFECTING — Showing a fondness for.

46:6 POSTILS — Marginal notes or comments, especially upon scriptural texts.

46:9 EITHER OF THEIR GREAT CHURCHES — The great church of Oxford University was and still is St. Mary's Church (see Charles E. Mallet, *A History of the University of Oxford,* New York, 1924, 2 vols., I, 140, and John Pointer, *Oxoniensis Academia: or, the Antiquities and Curiosities of the University of Oxford,* London, 1749, pp. 173-75; see also Sir T. G. Jackson, *The Church of St. Mary the Virgin Oxford,* Oxford, 1897). The church which at Cambridge "has always been the scene of the great religious ceremonials observed by the Academical Body" is "Great St. Mary's," the history of which goes back to 1478 (J. J. Smith, *The Cambridge Portfolio,* London, 1840, pp. 447-56).

46:12 QUEASIE — See 12:33.

46:14 *MATRICULATED CONFUTANT* — The phrase seems to indicate that Milton thought the Confuter enrolled at a university. The Confuter has spoken in behalf of the clerks of the Universities (see Notes 43:25-26; 45:17-18) and will defend the Universities (see Note 53:21-22).

46:20 *LATINIZING* BARBARIAN — One who uses an impure type of Latin. Some of the dictionaries of the time included a "Dictionarium Latino-barbarium" (see Littleton, *A Latine Dictionary* (1678); cf. 45:36-38).

46:20 GOOSERY — *i.e.,* silliness.

46:21 SERMON-ACTOR — *i.e.,* the insincere priest, who acts the part of the sermonizer but has no message to give.

46:21-22 *STARRES ... OF EITHER HORI-ZON* — The Confuter, after he had poked fun at the "mutinous rabble," whom Milton had claimed competent to judge ministers, pointed out the ridiculousness of bringing before them the "Clerks of either University" (see Note 45:17-18). Then he continued by calling the University clerks "lights" and "stars," and the "competent Judges" the "Areopagi":
Briefly all those glorious lights, and bright stars of

eminence and lustre in either Horizon, shall be no better esteemed of, than *Tyro* in *Gellius* observes the *Hyades* were, which by his Clownish Ancestors were taken for so many sucking-pigs.... But I leave these grave Censors, these *Areopagi,* if you will, to their own discretion; lest while I am busied in observing of theirs, I forfeit mine. (*Modest Confutation,* p. 24.)

46:22-23 *OF EITHER HORIZON ... HEMI-SPHERE* — The Confuter in mentioning the "lights" and "stars" "in either Horizon" was referring to the clerks of either University. The application of the name "star" to clergymen, especially to bishops, was based on an interpretation of Revelation 2:1 (see "The *Originall* of Bishops and *Metro-politans,* set down By Iames *Arch-Bishop* of Armagh" in *Certain Briefe Treatises,* Oxford, 1641, p. 55). Milton pretends to miss the point, taking "Horizon" to mean "the celestial hemisphere within the horizon of any place" (*OED*). See Note 46:25-26.

46:24 RATIONALL HORIZON — "A great circle of the celestial sphere, the plane of which passes through the centre of the earth and is parallel to that of the sensible horizon of a given place" (*OED*). See Note 46:24-25.

46:24-25 SENSIBLE HORIZONS — "The boundary-line of that part of the earth's surface visible from a given point of view; the line at which the earth and sky appear to meet" (*OED*).

46:25-26 YOUR ALLUSION ... YOUR STARRES — Milton concludes against the Confuter that his allusion to "horizons" is as erroneous as his appellation "stars" is for clerks.

46:26 BUT THAT YOU DID WELL — The sentence construction is complete without the word "that."

46:29 SINKING ... SOCKET — The words present an interesting condensation of two figures: "sinking in the western sky" and "wasted to snuff in their socket."

46:29 SNUFFE — "That part of a wick ... which is partly consumed in the course of burning to give light ..." (*OED*).

46:29 SOCKET — That "part of a candlestick in which the candle is placed" (*OED*).

SECTION 11

**46:31-32 PHLEGMATICK SLOTH . . .
HEAVIE PULSE** — Cf. Note 12:30. The "phlegmatick sloth" and "heavie pulse" that Milton attributes to his opponent refers to "phlegm" and
"melancholy" in their medical connotations. Milton
prefers in *Colasterion* not to "spend words with this
fleamy clodd of an *Antagonist*" (*Col.* IV, 254).
Kester Svendson ("Milton and Medical Lore," p.
165) traces the references to Bartholomew's *De
Proprietatibus Rerum.* "Bartholomew's treatment of
the humour phlegm reveals what was in Milton's
mind:"

For a very flewmatyke man is of bodye vnlusty, heuy,
and slowe, dulle of witte, and of thought foryeteful,
nesshe of fleshe and quauy, of colour whyte in the
face, ferfull of hert, full of spyttynge, sneuelyd and
rookinge, ful of slouth and slepinge, and of lytell
appetyte, and of lytel thyrst but if the fleme be salte.
(Bertholomeus, *De Proprietatibus Rerum* (1535), Bk.
IV, ch. IX, fol. [xxx] *verso*; *Batman vppon Bartholome,* fol. 32 *recto.*)

46:32 *EXPEDIENCE OF SET FORMES* — In
Section XI of the *Modest Confutation,* the Confuter
turns to the consideration of liturgy. He begins by
quoting from St. Paul (I Corinthians 6:12), "All
things are lawfull, but all things are not expedient,"
and then says:

A thing in its own nature indifferent, and so lawfull,
doth sometimes . . . become inexpedient, and so unlawfull. . . . For that set forms of Prayer are in themselves
at least indifferent, the precept and practice of Christ
confirms, and no man in his right wits ever denyed.
. . . The question is therefore of the expediency, not of
the lawfulnesse of such prayers. . . . (*Modest Confutation,* pp. 24-25.)

**47:1-2 *GOD IN HIS PROVIDENCE . . . PAS-
TORS*** — The Confuter in considering the *"conveniencies and inconveniencies"* of the set form of
prayer instanced that God's "own proceedings in the
government of his Church" seem to indicate the
"conveniencies" of the set form, for

it hath pleased his divine wisdom so to order the
matter, that (since all men are not alike capable of
knowledge, nor have the same abilities,) his providence
should as it were conform it self to this unequall condition of men: whence it is, he hath made choice of
some to teach others, and pray for others; chose some
to be Apostles, some Ministers, Pastors, Teachers;
whereas had he not had respect to this, and purposed
to go along with this weaknesse of mans nature, he
could as well have infused abilities (I mean super-

naturall) into the brest and brain of the most ignorant
despicable member of the Church, sufficient without
other teachings or helps, to have raised him to converse with God here, and possesse God hereafter, as
ever he did into the ablest of the Apostles. (*Modest
Confutation,* p. 25.)

**47:2-6 WHENCE I GATHER . . . MENS AP-
POINTED WORDS** — Milton, by carefully choosing from the Confuter's words a thought, and by
isolating it from its context, is able to show that the
Confuter, whose "bounty still is to his adversary,"
(46:39-40) contradicts himself (see Note 47:1-2
for the Confuter's actual statement). The syntax of
the cited passage becomes clear if it is read as
follows:

Whence I gather, that however [*i.e.,* whatever] the
faculty of others may be, yet [it is certain] that they
whom God hath set apart . . . are by him endu'd with
an ability of prayer . . . because their office is to pray
for others [, a]nd not to be the lip-working deacons. . . .

**47:11-12 IF PRAYER BE THE GUIFT OF
THE SPIRIT** — See Romans 8:26-27; I Corinthians 14:14-15; Ephesians 6:18. Prayer is not listed
among the gifts of the spirit in I Corinthians 12
to which the Confuter (see Note 47:1-2) was referring. Note Milton's "if."

47:22 LOITERING BOOKS — Books which
cause one to dawdle. Cf. *Areopagitica, Col.* IV, 335,
"interlinearies, breviaries, *synopses,* and other
loitering gear."

**47:27 *THE PRESERVING OF ORDER,
UNITY, AND PIETY*** — The Confuter said that
liturgy is

Most expedient to attain the end such worship drives
at; Order, Unity, Piety, and the best advancement of
Gods glory: Whereas an unbounded liberty in ex-
temporall and fanaticall Prayers, brings forth the quite
contrary; disorder [,] dis-union of affections between
man and man, impiety, atheism, and anarchy. (*Modest
Confutation,* pp. 28-29.)

**47:29-31 OBEDIENCE . . . CHRISTIAN CAN
OBSERVE** — Cf. Acts 5:29 and 4:19.

**47:31-32 IF THE SPIRIT OF GOD MANI-
FEST THE GUIFT OF PRAYER** — See Note
47:11-12.

47:39 COMMUNION OF SAINTS — Cf.
Christian Doctrine, Col. XVI, 59, "From this our
fellowship with Christ arises the mutual fellowship

of the members of Christ's body among themselves, called in the Apostles' Creed THE COMMUNION OF SAINTS." Milton follows the statement by quoting Romans 12:4-5; I Corinthians 12:12-13; and I Corinthians 12:27.

47:40-48:1 FOR WHAT OTHER . . . DOES NOT RATHER DISLIKE IT? — The implication that some other reformed Church does hold communion with the English by using the English liturgy, which it does not like, is not intended. Milton simply asks, "[What] other reformed Church holds communion with us by our liturgy [? What other reformed Church] does not rather dislike it?"

48:2-3 PERPETUALL CAUSE OF DISUNION — Milton's contention that the English liturgy was the old Mass translated into English (*ANIM, Col.* III, 119-20) was far from unique. Elements in the Church of England who wished the Reformation in England to approximate that which had been effected on the continent were not satisfied with the half-way measures of Henry VIII and Edward VI. From the dislike of vestments, which resulted in the vestment controversy of 1558-1560, it was only a step to the dislike of the service book. Many considered that all set forms of prayer were unlawful because they fell under the suspicion of popery. Therefore, the revision of the prayer book, upon Elizabeth's accession, gave little satisfaction. Elizabeth's Act of Uniformity, which became effective June 24, 1559, only minimized the open opposition. The "Cathedral mode of worship," the singing of prayers, and the antiphonal chanting of psalms, were still disallowed by the purifiers, who bided their time. (See Daniel Neal, *The History of the Puritans, or Protestant Nonconformists,* New York, 1843-44, 2 vols., I, 107.)

48:5-6 AS THE DAILY POWRING . . . NATURALL HEAT — The exact origin of the statement has not been found. Milton is, of course, alluding to medical lore. If the body is artificially warmed by the continued "powring in of hot waters," it loses its ability to maintain its "naturall heat." "For life is preserued in the body by heate, which is the chiefe instrument thereof: so that as soone as heat is gone, it becommeth starke dead" (La Primaudaye, *The Second Part Of The French Academie,* p. 110; for other references to "naturall

heat" and its relationship to moisture, as well as for reference to the agreement between the "temperature of the body, and the affections of the soule" see *ibid.,* pp. 230-31, 336, 384-85).

48:9 LOOSE — *i.e.,* lose.

48:10 LEGS — *i.e.,* supports. Cf. "Not a leg to stand on."

48:12 ENGLISH LITURGY — Cf. Notes 31:13; 49:9-10; 49:30.

48:16 *RESPONSORIES* — The responsories were those portions of the divine service, often prescribed in liturgy, in which the people or choir sung or said a response to the words of the clergyman. As early as June 27, 1554, the English exiles at Frankfort on the Main had "concluded, by universal consent of all present, not to answer aloud after the minister, nor to use the litany and surplice" (Neal, *History of the Puritans,* I, 66). Cf. *Eikonoklastes, Col.* V, 262, "Which if I should repeat again, would turn my answers into *Responsories,* and begett another Liturgie, having too much of one already."

48:21 PROPERTY — *i.e.,* propriety; appropriateness.

48:22-23 TWO PERSONS AND TWO BODIES — That is, the priest by turns represents the body and the body represents the priest, making a real priest and a representative one, a real body and a representative one.

48:25 THE *LITANY* — Milton is thinking of *The Litany and Suffrages* appointed for use in the *Book of Common Prayer,* consisting of invocations and supplications with alternate responses.

48:27 I KNOW NOT WHAT TO NAME IT — Milton does not want to repeat the word *"Litany,"* and, because he disapproves of the Litany, he is at a loss for a word.

48:33 WARRANTED PRAYER — In this instance, a prayer based on Biblical sanction. Milton is citing that there is no instance of nor any authority for the alternation of invocation or supplication with the response in the Bible.

48:34 JIG — Milton is probably thinking of the alternating dialogues of the jig drolls.

48:36-37 *PATHETICALL* — earnest; passionate. Cf. "the pathetical words of a Psalme can be no certaine decision to a poynt" (*Tenure, Col.* V, 13).

48:40 SOAR UPON THE WINGS OF ZEALE — Cf. 23:13, "Zeale whose substance is ethereal"; *ANIM, Col.* III, 107, *"zeale of truth"; RCG, Col.* III, 225, "Watchfulnesse and Zeale"; 51:26, "those who in zeale."

49:1-2 WOMANS CHURCHING — Milton refers to "The Thanksgiving of Women after Child-Birth; commonly called, The Churching of Women" in the *Book of Common Prayer.*

49:2-3 DELIVERY FROM SUNBURNING AND MOONBLASTING — Milton charges the liturgy with "errors, *tautologies,* impertinences," citing as an example from the "Churching of Women" the passage, repeated by the priest, from Psalm 121: "So that the sonne shall not burne the by daye, neither the moon by night" (Quotation taken from William Benham (ed.), *The Prayer Book of Queen Elizabeth 1559,* Edinburgh, 1911, p. 140). "In 1661 the Psalms cxvi. and cxxvii. were substituted for Psalm cxxi." (Leighton Pullan, *The History of the Book of Common Prayer,* London, 1914, p. 247; cf. W. K. Lowther Clarke (ed.), *Liturgy and Worship,* London, 1932, p. 426.) The rite is based upon the example of the Virgin Mary as recorded in Luke 2:22-24 and upon Leviticus 12. Of the rite the author of *A Briefe and plaine declaration* (1584), p. 74, said:

And as for Churching of Women, because it sauoureth of the Iewish purification, and of Popish institution, it ought altogether to bee omitted, for it breedeth and nourisheth many superstitious opinions in the simple peoples hearts: as, that the woman which hath born a child, is vncleane or vnholy: whereas the Apostle pronounceth, that Godlye women are sanctified and saued by bearing of children.

49:9-10 THIS OUR LITURGY WHERE ... WE LEFT IT — Robert Baillie produced a pamphlet on the liturgy the title of which is revealing: *A Parallel Or Briefe Comparison Of The LITVRGIE With The Masse-Book, The Breviarie, the Ceremoniall, and other Romish Ritualls. Wherein is clearly and shortly demonstrated, not onely that the LITVRGIE is taken for the most part word for word out of these Antichristian Writts; but also that not one of the most abominable passages of the*

Masse can in reason be refused by any who cordially imbrace the Liturgie as now it stands, and is commented by the Prime of our Clergie (London, 1641). In the pamphlet he endeavored to show

not so much that the Liturgie is in the Masse, whereof none doe doubt, as that the Masse is in the Liturgie: that the matter and the forme, that the substance and the accidents of the Masse are here; that of the integrall parts those which are incomparably the worst, doe actually and expresly appeare in our Service; that all the portions of the Masse better and worse are in our Booke, if not expresly (as very may be) yet virtually such a seed of them being sowne that for their bud, blossome, and fruit, they needed no more but a command from a Bishops mouth to the Printer, upon a privie Warrant from Court, purchased by false information.... (Ibid. Sig. [a] *verso-[a2] recto.)*

Milton's emphasis is that the English liturgy was found in the Roman Catholic Church service in England at the time of Henry VIII's break with Rome. From the Roman service the English reformers took it, adapted and translated it, and left it as the major component of the Church of England service. See Note 49:23-26.

49:10-11 STILL SERVING ... ANTICHRISTIAN TEMPLE — Cf. Note 5:14-16. Robert Lord Brooke said:

That which they [the prelates] have most sounded in the Peoples Eares, is the Church, the Church, the Temple of the Lord, the Temple of the Lord.... But now their Vizard beginnes to fall off; and Men beginne to see the true power of the True Church; and the Tyranny of that Antichristian Mock-Church; which under the Maske of *Indifference,* hath brought in most abominable Superstitions, and most intolerable slavery on the Persons, Liberties, Bodies, and *Soules of Men.* For they have pressed Consciences, even unto Gasping: yea, and would not be satisfied, though they daily heard the sighes and groanes of those bleeding hearts, which themselves had stabd with the poysoned sword of *Church-Indifference.* (Brooke, *Nature of Episcopacy,* Sig. [k] *verso-k2 recto.)*

49:10 WERE — Printer's error for "where."

49:15-18 WHEREAS OTHER CORRUPT LITURGIES ... *BASIL* — The Roman Rite which was the Rite of the Roman Catholic Church was in the popular mind traced back to St. Peter. Although the Greek Liturgy of St. Peter which seems to have been used by the first Christians at Rome, who were a Greek-speaking community, is the Roman Canon of the Mass in an Eastern liturgical framework and may be represented by the so-called liturgy attributed to St. Clement I, the Latin liturgy does not derive therefrom but seems to be a survival of an intermediate form. Milton maintained that it "had no being that wee can know of, but from the corruptest times" (*ANIM, Col.* III, 129).

St. James, the brother (cousin) of Jesus, is said to have originated the liturgy from which the Syrian or Antiochene family of liturgies, that is, the liturgies originally used in the Patriarchate of Antioch, derived. St. Mark, according to the tradition of the Church of Egypt, was the first Bishop of Alexandria, and formulated the parent liturgy of the Patriarchate of Alexandria. According to the tradition of the Church of Constantinople, the oldest of its two liturgies is ascribed to St. Basil the Great. St. John Chrysostum modified the Rite of Basil. He left his reformed liturgy and the unreformed of Basil as the two liturgies of Constantinople, the former used more generally, the latter specified for certain occasions. The Chrysostum liturgy gained general acceptance in the orthodox world as Constantinople gained prestige in the eastern world.

49:18-20 OURS HATH BIN NEVER ... LEAST OFFENSIVE — The Anglican Church, in maintaining its continuity with the Apostolic Church, went to considerable trouble to prove the antiquity of its discipline and its liturgy. The Prayer Book was, in fact, an abbreviated and condensed form of the four chief Roman Catholic service books: the Missal, Breviary, Manual, and Pontifical. The Arminians, who were more ready to admit that the Roman Church was the true Church fallen into error than those who were Calvinistic in creed, might trace their liturgy boldly to Roman Catholic origins. Such boldness, however, resulted in great denunciations by the Puritans, and by the anti-Arminian element in the Church of England. The latter sought to stress the purer times of the Church, particularly the times before the Bishop of Rome had become ascendant, to support the Establishment. The Puritans were interested chiefly in following the prescriptions contained in the Bible, particularly in the New Testament. Hall, in defending the liturgy of the Church of England, said:

Surely, our blessed Saviour, and his gracious Forerunner ... plainly taught ... a direct forme of prayer; and such, as that part of the frame prescribed by our Saviour, was composed of the formes of devotion then formerly usuall; And Gods people ever since *Moses* his daies, constantly practised it; and put it over unto the times of the Gospel; under which, whiles it is said that *Peter* and *Iohn* went up to the Temple at the ninth houre of prayer, we know the prayer wherewith they joyned was not of an extemporary, and sudden conception, but of a regular prescription; the formes whereof are yet extant, and ready to be produced.... (Hall, *Humble Remonstrance,* pp. 10-11.)

He pleaded that the English liturgy was "selected, out of ancient models, (not Romane, but Christian) and contrived by the holy Martyrs, and Confessors of the blessed Reformation of Religion" (*ibid.,* p. 13). In the *Defence Of The Humble Remonstrance,* pp. 8-32, Hall went to considerable trouble to trace the liturgy, citing the forms extant "under the names of St. *Iames* ... of *Basil,* and *Chrysostome,* though they have some intersertions which are plainly spurious, yet the substance of them cannot be taxed for other then holy, and ancient" (Hall, *Defence,* p. 19), as well as the customs at several churches and the actions of the Councils.

Milton may be thinking of Hall's position that the English liturgy, selected out of ancient models, not "Romane, but Christian," "had no relation either to the place, or religion of Rome, but onely to the Christian and holy matter of those godly prayers" (*ibid.,* pp. 20-21; for the antiprelatical point of view, the Smectymnuan *An Answer To ... An Humble Remonstrance,* pp. 5-14, is an obvious source).

49:20-21 TWO CREEDS — The Nicene Creed, based upon an ancient eastern baptismal confession, was formulated as a defense against Arianism at the first ecumenical synod of Nicaea in 325 A.D. The Apostles' Creed, attributed to the apostles themselves and probably expressive of apostolic teaching, seems to be the amplification of a statement used at baptismal services in apostolic times. It is quoted by Tertullian about 200 A.D. in an early form. The present form dates from the seventh century. The Nicene and Apostles' Creeds found general acceptation by the reformed religious leaders. Milton spoke of the Apostles' Creed as "the most ancient and universally received compendium of belief in the possession of the Church" (*Christian Doctrine, Col.* XIV, 357).

49:21 TE DEUM ... LIMBUS PATRUM —The "Te Deum laudamus" of the Roman Catholic liturgy was in translation made a Morning Prayer in the *Book of Common Prayer*. The word "smach" probably shows a printer's error for "smack." The *"Limbus Patrum"* is a temporary place or state of happiness, apart and distinct from purgatory, where the just who had attained perfect holiness prior to the coming of Christ had to remain awaiting the resurrection of Christ. See Notes 19:6 and 49:22-23.

49:22-23 *OPEN'D THE KINGDOME OF HEAVEN...DEATH* — Milton is referring to the statement in the "Te Deum laudamus": "When thou hadst overcome the sharpness of death; thou didst open the Kingdom of Heaven to all believers." Milton's view is that Christ opened the kingdom of heaven *before* he overcame death. In the *Christian Doctrine,* Milton says that Christ's "kingdom of grace, indeed, which is also called 'the kingdom of heaven,' began with his first advent, when its beginning was proclaimed by John the Baptist, as appears from testimony of Scripture" (*Col.* XVI, 359). Therefore, the "Te Deum" reminds Milton of the temporary state or place of happiness in which the just must wait until Christ has fulfilled his mission on earth and defeated death by his resurrection.

49:23-26 SO THAT HAVING RECEAV'D IT ...ILL TO BE TRUSTED — Milton reiterates many times that the English liturgy is "an extract of the Masse book translated" (*RCG, Col.* III, 216). He cites King Edward VI's confession that it was "no other then the old Mass-Book don into English" (*Eikonoklastes, Col.* V, 220). He maintains that, since the English "order of the Service, and the use thereof in the English Tongue is no other then the old Service was, and the same words in English which were in Latine" (*ANIM, Col.* III, 119-20), it might be rejected. He is confident that it "had no being that wee can know of, but from the corruptest times" (*ibid.,* p. 129), and that the "essence of it, [is] fantastick, and superstitious, the end sinister, and the imposition violent" (*ibid.,* p. 130). His stand is that no true Christian can "find a reason why Liturgie should be at all admitted, a prescription not impos'd or practis'd by those first Founders of the Church, who alone had that authority" (*Eikonoklastes, Col.* V, 221). See 49:30 and 55:36-38.

49:24 OUGHT — *i.e.,* nought.

49:26-27 IF GOD LOATHE . . . IDOLATERS PRAYER — Cf. Ephesians 5:5; I Corinthians 6:9; Proverbs 21:27; 28:9; Psalms 66:18; Amos 5:21-22. The reformers did not doubt that the Roman Catholic service was idolatrous. The Hebrew law was specific in forbidding the making and worshipping of idols (see Leviticus 19:4; 26:1). The statuary of the Roman Catholic Church and the ceremonies in which the statuary played an important part became anathema. The charge of idolatry, however, rested upon an inclusive basis. On April 4, 1550, John Knox in his "Vindication" gave his reasons for affirming the Mass to be idolatry. He maintained that "All wirschipping, honoring, or service inventit by the braine of man in the religioun of God, without his own express commandment, is Idolatrie: The Masse is inventit be the braine of man, without any commandement of God: Thairfoir it is Idolatrie" (*The Works of John Knox,* ed. by David Laing, Edinburgh, 1846-64, 6 vols., III, 34).

49:27 MUCH MORE . . . FANGLE—*i.e.,* "much more [doth he loathe] the conceited fangle."

49:27 FANGLE — Fantastic contrivance (*OED*).

49:28-30 A COMMUNITY . . . *CHURCH TRULY ONE* — The Confuter questioned:
What order can ever be expected? what uniformity looked for? what consent and harmony betwixt Church and Church, when every one shall differ in that which should make them truly one? a Communion of Saints, even their community of Prayers? How, while some are starved, shall others be pampered? and then what likenesse? Tell me not, that they that will shall use the Churches set forms; for either they will be wholly neglected . . . discountenanced . . . by publike authority, & depraved, condemned, damned, by private persons; or else, whiles both are in use, it will nourish a continuall enmity betwixt the users of each. It is a requisite in the Church of Christ, that the particular Congregations which are the members of that mysticall body, be of one heart and one minde, especially in their Prayers to, and Praises of God.... (*Modest Confutation,* p. 29.)

49:30 LITURGY FARRE MORE LIKE TO THE MASSE-BOOK — Milton calls the English liturgy "the motley incoherence of a patch'd Missall" (*ANIM, Col.* III, 132). See Note 49:23-26.

49:32 *ROMISH* — Roman Catholic.

49:36 GOD IN HIS JEALOUSIE — Cf. Exodus 20:5; 34:14; Deuteronomy 4:24; 5:9; 6:15; Joshua 24:19; Nahum 1:2.

49:37-38 WHO DETESTED . . . OFFER'D TO IDOLS — Upon a number of occasions God indicated his detestation of gold: Deuteronomy 7:25 and Joshua 7:15, 21-26. At other times He commanded the destruction of the spoil: Deuteronomy 13:16-18; Joshua 6:17-21; I Samuel 15:1-23. Among the admonitions concerning the eating of things offered to idols are those in the following passages: Acts 15:20, 29; I Corinthians 8:9-10; 10: 18-20, 28; Revelation 2:14, 20.

50:5 IDOLATROUS MOTHER — The Roman Catholic Church. See Note 49:26-27.

50:6-7 TRUE CHURCH — Milton thought of the true Church as composed of invisible and visible aspects. The invisible or mystical Church consisted in the believer's "UNION and FELLOWSHIP with the Father through Christ the Son," and his "glorification after the image of Christ" (*Christian Doctrine, Col.* XVI, 57). The result of such "UNION and FELLOWSHIP" consisted "in a participation, through the Spirit, of the various gifts and merits of Christ," and in a "mutual fellowship of the members of Christ's body among themselves, called in the Apostles' Creed THE COMMUNION OF SAINTS" (*ibid.*, p. 59). The fellowship of the members of the invisible or mystical Church was also mystical, being composed of "individuals of widely separated countries, and of all ages from the foundation of the world" (*ibid.*, p. 63). The visible Church, the tokens of which were "pure doctrine; the proper external worship of God; genuine evangelical love, so far as it can be distinguished from fictitious by mere human perception; and a right administration of the seals of the covenant" (*ibid.*, p. 221), Milton conceived as being the "ASSEMBLY OF THOSE WHO ARE CALLED" (*ibid.*, p. 219). The visible Church, in its universal aspect, included all believers "IN EVERY PART OF THE WORLD . . . WHO OPENLY WORSHIP GOD THE FATHER THROUGH CHRIST IN ANY PLACE WHATEVER, EITHER INDIVIDU-ALLY, OR IN CONJUNCTION WITH OTHERS" (*ibid.*, p. 233). It was upon the visible

Church, the government of which Milton in 1641 and 1642 was certain was prescribed in Scripture (*RCG, Col.* III, 189-95) to be presbyterial in form (*ibid.*, p. 253), that Milton relied to "new mould a better and more pious Liturgy then this which was conceav'd and infanted by an idolatrous Mother" (50:3-5).

50:8 MOTHER OF ENGLAND — A common appellation used by the prelates for the Church of England. Cf. Note 8:5-6.

50:8 CHRIST HATH TAUGHT HER TO PRAY — See Matthew 6:9 and Luke 11:2.

50:9-10 TEACHING OF ANTICHRIST — See Notes 30:23; 49:9-10; 49:23-26.

50:10-11 STIPEND OF ROME — There was much fear that Laud and the Arminian prelates were awaiting an opportune moment to make the Church of England again subservient to Rome. Robert Lord Brooke (*Nature of Episcopacy*, p. 99) preferred to

hazzard the comming in of [Anabaptisme, Brownisme, Separatisme, etc.], than still to suffer our soules and bodies, to be groun'd to powder by these Tyrannicall, Antichristian Prelates, that under pretence of keeping out *Separatisme*, introduce downe-right *Popery*, and a sinck of almost all Errors and Heresies.

50:13-15 *ABRAHAM* DISDAIN'D . . . WICKED KING — Milton has in mind Genesis 14:21-23.

50:18-19 SPIRIT . . . UNCERTAINE WIND — Cf. Ephesians 4:14 "carried about with every wind of doctrine." See Acts 2:2-4.

50:19-20 GUIFTS PROMIS'D . . . ELECT — See I Corinthians 12.

50:21 ACCEPTABLE . . . AND ABOUND — The phraseology is reminiscent of many scriptural passages, but it is not directly drawn from any of them. See Philippians 4:18. The phrase "acceptable unto God," or its equivalent, occurs in Romans 12:1-2; Ephesians 5:10; I Timothy 2:3; 5:4; I Peter 2:5, 20. Milton's use of the word "abound" recalls passages such as Philippians 4:12, 17; I Thessalonians 3:12; 4:1; II Thessalonians 1:3; II Peter 1:8.

50:30 FOOLISH *GALATIANS* — Milton is referring to Galatians 3:1.

50:30-33 FOR THAT WHICH THE APOSTLES TAUGHT . . . THE REDEEMED OF CHRIST — The Apostles Peter and Paul, having returned to a Council at Jerusalem, were confronted by the Pharisees who insisted that converted Gentiles conform to the Mosaic law of circumcision (Acts 15). Peter answered the Pharisees: "Now therefore why tempt ye God, to put a yoke upon the neck of the disciples, which neither our fathers nor we were able to bear?" (Acts 15:10). After Paul and Barnabas had likewise testified concerning the gift of salvation to the Gentiles, James, one of the "pillars" of the Church at Jerusalem and cousin of Jesus declared that, since the Gentiles were not under the law, circumcision could not be demanded "For it seemed good to the Holy Ghost, and to us, to lay upon you no greater burden than these necessary things" (Acts 15:28; cf. Ephesians 2:15, and Colossians 2:14, 20). See Note 39:24.

50:35-38 THE VERY ACT OF PRAYER . . . DECENCY THAT CAN BE IMAGIN'D — Ida Langdon (*Milton's Theory of Poetry and Fine Art*, p. 9) comments that "Milton's disdain of churchly ritual is nothing else than his disdain of all deception, and in particular his scorn of that violation of the law of form called hypocrisy." Cf. *REF, Col.* III, 12, "what doe wee suffer mis-shapen and enormous *Prelatisme*"; and *PRE, Col.* III, 91,

we doe injuriously in thinking to tast better the pure Evangelick Manna by seasoning our mouths with the tainted scraps, and fragments of an unknown table; and searching among the verminous, and polluted rags dropt overworn from the toyling shoulders of Time, with these deformedly to quilt, and interlace the intire, the spotlesse, and undecaying robe of Truth.

50:36-37 FREE AND UNIMPOS'D EXPRESSIONS . . . UNBIDDEN COME — Milton may be thinking of such scriptural verses as John 4:23-24; Romans 8:26; and I Corinthians 1:5. Cf. II Corinthians 8:7; Ephesians 6:19; Colossians 4:3.

50:38-39 WHICH TO DRESSE UP . . . DISCLAM'D BY THE GOSPELL — The Hebrew law provided definite and specific detail for the carrying on of the worship service. The tabernacle, the ark of the covenant, the altar, and the curtains were made in accordance with God's prescription. The garments that the priests wore had to meet the specified requirements. The sacrifices and ceremonies were carried on as demanded by the law (see Exodus 25-40; Leviticus 1-18). There was no place for "devis'd" ostentation or splendor. The failure of a person to follow the prescription in the minutest detail resulted in his being "cut off from his people" (see, for instance, Exodus 30:33, 38; Leviticus 17:4, 9-10, 14). The Gospel, that is, the New Testament, renounces the ritualism and legalism of the law emphasizing that "Christ *is* the end of the law" (Romans 10:4), that "true worshippers shall worship the Father in spirit and in truth" (John 4:23), and that salvation is "by the foolishness of preaching" (I Corinthians 1:21).

50:39 BRAVERY — *i.e.,* ostentation, splendor (*OED*).

50:39 ABOLISHT — *i.e.,* suppressed.

50:39-40 ADDES NOTHING. . . . AND HATH EVER — Modern usage would not permit that the parallel predicates be separated by a period.

51:3-6 JEWES FIGUR'D UNDER . . . DESIRABLE TO THE EYE? — Milton is alluding to Ezekiel 23.

51:7-8 *TO MAKE* . . . S. *PAULS* WORDS ARE? — Quoted directly from Galatians 6:12.

51:11 THEY — Probably used as an indefinite pronoun meaning "they who are left."

51:12 PARTING FROM ROME? — *i.e.,* breaking away from the Roman Church.

51:14-15 THESE LETTERS . . . ORNAMENTS — The Anglican Church continued to use the discipline and ceremony of the Roman Catholic Church in a modified form.

51:25-27 WE CRY OUT *SACRILEDGE AND MISDEVOTION* . . . UNCLEANE WALLOWINGS — The Smectymnuans called attention in *An Answer*, p. 6, to Calvin's opinion that there were "sundry *Tolerabiles Ineptiae*" in the English liturgy. The Remonstrant answered that those of the prelatical party

honor the name of that noble instrument of God's glory in his Church [*i.e.,* the liturgy], yet withall, we feare not to say, without any disparagement to his [Calvin's] worth, that our Liturgie both in the frame, and survay of it, passed the judgement of no lesse reverend heads then his owne." (Hall, *Defence*, p. 11.)

Milton replied in the *Animadversions* (1641), p. 16 (*Col.* III, 122), that the English liturgy "brib'd their judgement with worldly ingagements and so past it." To Milton's statement the Confuter countered:

O the inconsideratenesse of eager and headlong ambition! that men, who but now were, some returned from banishment, others drawn out of prison, should in an instant be so turned about, that they would forfeit their Religion, their Wisedomes, their Credits, yea their Souls, in obtruding upon a Church superstitious and damnable Rules for Devotion; and all this to get a narrow incompetent Bishoprick. If they had minded preferment, why looked they not abroad, where sacriledge and misdevotion had not so streightned their walkes, nor demolished their goodly prospects, nor washed out their gilded titles? they could not have been worse there, if they were superstitious at home. (*Modest Confutation*, pp. 31-32.)

Cf. *REF, Col.* III, 70, "Wee count it Sacrilege to take from the rich *Prelates* their Lands, and revenu's which is Sacrilege in them to keep . . . !" See 57:25-26.

51:26-27 DENS AND CAGES . . . UNCLEANE WALLOWINGS — The ideas and phraseology are suggestive of scriptural passages such as II Peter 2:22; Jeremiah 48:26; Matthew 21:13; Mark 9:20; Revelation 18:2.

51:27-28 ARK OF OUR COV'NANT — The ark of the covenant was an oblong chest, covered with gold, which supported the mercy seat and the two cherubim of gold (Exodus 25). In the chest Moses placed the two stone tablets upon which were the ten commandments. The ark of the covenant was kept in the most sacred place in the sanctuary, for through it God communed with the children of Israel. Milton is lamenting that the English permit a popish liturgy to be the instrument through which they commune with God.

51:30-31 PRAYER . . . TO THE PARLAMENT — Milton is thinking of the many petitions to Parliament (see Notes 8:37 and 40:11), particularly those sent by the episcopal party in defense of the Establishment. Joseph Hall's *An Humble Remonstrance To The High Court Of Parliament* had

been one such "prayer" by a defender of "praying by rote."

51:32 PRAYERS OF OTHER MEN — *i.e.*, the prayers formulated in the *Book of Common Prayer*.

51:33 OUR CREED — The Apostles' Creed.

51:34 CREED HAD BIN OF THE APOSTLES — See Note 49:20-21. The Apostles' Creed was anciently ascribed to the twelve apostles, each of whom supposedly contributed one of the twelve tenets into which it was divided. Milton, although he considered it "the most ancient and universally received compendium of belief in the possession of the Church" (*Christian Doctrine, Col.* XIV, 357), felt that no "modern church" nor magistrate was "entitled to impose on believers a creed nowhere found in Scripture, or which is merely inferred from thence by human reasons carrying with them no certain conviction" (*ibid.*, XVI, 281). Consequently, he asserts that if the Apostles' Creed is Rome's, "let her take it. We can want no Creed, so long as we want not the Scriptures" (51:35-36).

51:38-39 LEVEN TO . . . SOURE OUR WHOLE LUMPE — See I Corinthians 5:6; Galatians 5:9; Matthew 13:33; Luke 13:21.

51:39 *THEY WERE MARTYRS* — Cf. Note 30:18. Upon one occasion Hall boasted "that the restauration of the *English* Church, and eversion of Popery next under God, and our Kings is chiefly to be ascribed, and owed to the learning and industry of our *Bishops*; some whereof being crowned with *Martyrdome*, subscribed the *Gospell* with their *blood*" (Hall, *Defence*, pp. 167-68). Milton retorted:

You boast much of Martyrs to uphold your Episcopacy, but if you would call to minde that *Eusebius* in his 5.1. recites from *Apolinarius* of *Hierapolis*, you should then heare it esteem'd no other then an old hereticall argument, to prove a position true, because some that held it were martyrs: this was that which gave boldnesse to the *Marcionists,* and *Cataphryges* to avouch their impious heresies for pious doctrine, because they could reckon many Martyrs of their sect, and when they were confuted in other points, this was ever their last and stoutest plea. (*ANIM* (1641), p. 68; *Col.* III, 178.)

Hall in *A Survay*, pp. 7-8, instanced that "*Cranmer, Ridley, Latimer,* and numbers more of religious and learned martyrs, [sealed] their departure from the

Church of *Rome* by their dearest blood." He continued, speaking to the author of the *Protestation Protested* (see Note 27:13-14):

must your sacrilegious hands throw their sacred dust in the ayre, by perswading us, that they dyed popish, not as members only, but (in some kind) authors of that Church, that publique service wee now enjoy? (Hall, *A Survay*, p. 8.)

In *An Humble Remonstrance,* p. 17, Hall said:

And if our holy Martyrs heretofore went to heaven with a Litany in their mouth; Let not an ill advised new-fanglenesse be suffered to put scorn upon that, wherein they thought themselves happy.

Cf. *REF, Col.* III, 9, "These men were *Martyrs.*"

51:40   BOOK OF GODS PROVIDENCE — The Bible. Milton conceived the providence of God to extend "to all things, and that certain immutable laws have been enacted, by which every part of the creation is administered" (*Christian Doctrine, Col.* XV, 91).

51:40-52:2   IF HE READ THERE . . . UPON THIS CHURCH, AND ON THEMSELVES — Cf. Isaiah 59:1-4, 9-15; Numbers 32:13; Genesis 13:10-13; 19:24-25; Judges 13-16; I Samuel 15; I Kings 11:1, 9, 14, 31, 41; Nehemiah 13:26; II Kings 17:1-23; II Chronicles 28:2-5; II Kings 21:1-18.

52:1   THEIR — The reference is to "those who in reforming" (51:36-37).

52:3   AT THE LAST DAY — See the following scriptural verses for the phrase: John 6:39-40, 44, 54; 11:24; 12:48.

SECTION 12

52:7-8   UNREAD IN THE COUNSELS — Bishop Hall commented in *A Defence,* p. 16:

The words of the Councel are full and affirmative . . . that the prayers or orisons which are allowed in the Synod, &c. shall be used or celebrated by all men . . . and that no other shall be used in the Church. . . . Lest perhaps something may be composed . . . through ignorance, or want of care, contrary to the faith.

Milton replied:

Set the grave councels up upou their shelvs again, and string them hard, lest their various, and jangling opinions put their leavs into a flutter. I shall not intend this hot season to bid you the base through the wide, and dusty champaine of the Councels, but shall take councel of that which counsel'd them, reason. . . . (*ANIM* (1641), p. 19; *Col.* III, 126.)

The Confuter exulted:

I Was glad at my heart when I heard you cry out [*set the grave Councels upon their shelves, string them hard*] for from such your slighting of them, I conjectured your ignorance in that kind of learning to be, though not so ingenuously confessed, yet altogether as much and great as mine. (*Modest Confutation,* p. 34. The brackets are the Confuter's.)

52:10   THOSE GREEK AND ROMAN EXPLOITS — Milton may be referring to Homer's *Iliad* and *Odyssey* and to Virgil's *Aeneid*. He may be thinking of the Greek and Roman historians. See Note 15:23.

52:11   ADD — Printer's error for "and."

52:13   CHRISTIAN EMPEROR — *i.e.,* Constantine the Great in the first quarter of the fourth century A.D.

52:17   EXCEPTING IN SOME VERY FEW — Milton's comments on the "prime fathers *Austin, Jerom*" (*Tetrachordon, Col.* IV, 195) are consistently sympathetic (cf. *RCG, Col.* III, 208, "*Jerome* the learned'st of the Fathers"). On Clement of Alexandria (*RCG, Col.* III, 211) and Ignatius (*REF, Col.* III, 30), they are often respectful.

52:19   HISTORIAN *SOCRATES* — Socrates Scholasticus, born in Constantinople about 380 A.D., wrote a continuation of the history of the Church begun by Eusebius. Socrates' *Ecclesiastical History* covers the years 306-439 A.D.

52:20-22   *HE WAS FAINE TO INTERMIXE . . . COUNTERPLOTTINGS OF THE BISHOPS* — In "The Proëme" to Book 5 of *The Ecclesiasticall Historie of Socrates Scholasticvs, Comprised in Seven Books . . . Written in the Greeke tongue aboue a thousand yeares agoe, and translated by M.* [eredith] *H.* [anmer] (London, 1607), the following statement appears:

Before we enter into the discourse of our fift booke of ecclesiastical history, we desire the reader to be admonished not to blame vs, for that our special drift being to deliuer to posterity in writing the ecclesiasticall affaires, we haue also (as farre forth as we could learne) mingled therewithall battels and bloody warres, at seuerall times waged in sundry parts of the world. For this haue we done for divers causes. First that things done in wars might come to knowledge of posteritie: secondly lest the Reader by continuall consideration of the Bishops affaires, and their practices euery where one against another, should be overcome with tediousness: but chiefly that it may appear how when the common weale hath bene tossed and turmoiled with troublesome dissention and discord, the Church of God likewise . . . hath bene altogether out of quiet. (*The Avncient Ecclesiasticall Histories Of The First Six Hvndred Yeares After Christ, written in the Greeke tongue by three learned Historiographers, Eusebius, Socrates, and Euagrius. . . . All which Authors are faithfully translated out of the Greeke tongue by Meredith Hanmer,* London, 1607, p. 339.)

52:25 THERE — In Socrates Scholasticus' *Ecclesiastical History.*

52:33 S. *MARTIN* — St. Martin was Bishop of Tours in the latter part of the fourth century. For information concerning his life Sulpicius Severus' *Historia Sacra* is practically the only authority. St. Martin was born in 316 or 317 and died within the years 397-401. He was noted for his plea before the Emperor Maximus in behalf of the followers of Priscillian, whose system of doctrines was Gnostic and Manichaean in character, not because he favored their belief, but because he felt they were being unjustly treated. When he learned, however, that a raid on the Priscillians was contemplated he withdrew his plea lest he be charged a sympathizer with the heresy. His action brought the lives of innocent men and his own religion into danger. An angel appeared to him confirming his action, but he felt that his "power of working miracles and of relieving the oppressed was diminished. . . . In order to escape such risks in the future, he never, for the remaining sixteen years of his life, attended any synod or gathering of bishops." (Smith & Wace, *Dictionary of Christian Biography,* III, 842-43.)

52:33-35 LAST SIXTEENE YEARES . . . ANY COUNCELL OF THE BISHOPS — Sulpicius Severus said of St. Martin:

Sedecim postea vixit annos: nullam synodum adiit, ab omnibus episcoporum conventibus se removit. (Sulpicius Severus, *Dialogus* III, Cap. xiii, in Migne, *Patrologiae Cursus Completus* (Latinae), XX, 219.)

Compare *Of Reformation, Col.* III, 26:

And in the end of his [Sulpicius'] History thus he concludes, all things went to wrack by the *faction, wilfulnesse,* and *avarice* of the *Bishops,* and by this means *Gods people,* & every *good man* was had in scorn and derision: which S. *Martin* found truly to be said by his friend *Sulpitius;* for being held in admiration of all men, he had onely the *Bishops* his enemies, found God lesse favorable to him after he was *Bishop*

then before, & for his last 16. yeares would come at no *Bishops* meeting.

(See W. T. Hale (ed.), *Of Reformation Touching Church-Discipline In England by John Milton,* p. 125, note 26.29. Milton may have used the Elzevir edition of Sulpicius Severus, Leyden, 1635: see James Holly Hanford, "The Chronology of Milton's Private Studies," p. 263 note; Jacques-Charles Brunet, *Manuel Du Librairie,* Paris, 1860-80, 6 vols. and 2 supplements, V, 322; and Jean George Théodore Graesse, *Trésor de Livres Rares et Precieux,* Paris, 1859-1900, 7 vols. and supplement, VI, 376.)

52:35 *GREGORY NAZIANZEN* — Saint Gregory of Nazianzus (*c.* 329-*c.* 389 A.D.) was bishop of Sasima and of Constantinople. He was a friend of Basil the Great. Because he was a born orator and a master of theological language, he was one of the great defenders of Trinitarianism at a time when Arianism was in ascendancy in Byzantium.

52:36 *PROCOPIUS* — Procopius was a friend of Gregory Nazianzen and the recipient of a number of epistles from him. He was perhaps the son-in-law of the emperor Valens.

52:36-39 *THAT OF ANY COUNCELL . . . NO TONGUE IS ABLE TO EXPRESSE* — In Gregory of Nazianzen's *Epistola* CXXX, Novus Ordo, to Procopius, he said:

Ego, si vera scribere oportet, hoc animo sum, ut omnem episcoporum conventum fugiam, quoniam nullius concilii finem laetum et faustum vidi, nec quod depulsionem malorum potius, quam accessionem et incrementum habuerit. Semper enim sunt contentiones, et dominandi cupiditates (ac ne me, quaeso, gravem et molestum existimes, haec scribentem), nec ullis quidem verbis explicari queunt; citiusque aliquis improbitatis arguetur, dum aliis se judicem praebet, quam illorum improbitatem comprimat. (Migne, *Patrologiae Cursus Completus* (Graeco-Latina), XXXVII, 225-26.)

Cf. Bacon, *A Wise and Moderate Discourse,* p. 18, [*i.e.,* 26]:

It is hard in all causes, especially in matters of religion, when voyces shall be numbred and not weighed. [See Note 36:33-36.] *Equidem* (saith a wise Father) *ut verè quod res est scribam, prorsus decrevi fugere omnem conventum Episcoporū: nullius enim consilii bonum exitum unquā vidi: consilia enim non minuunt mala, sed augent potius.* To say the truth, I am utterly determined never to come to any Councell of Bishops: for I never yet saw good end of any Councell: for Councels abate not ill things, but rather increase them.

... (See also "An Advertisement," in *Resuscitatio,* pp. 171-72.)

52:39-40 I HAVE NOT... READ MORE OF THE COUNCELS SAVE HERE AND THERE — In quoting from the patristic sources Milton was playing the bishops' game, and although he did not "complain ... of any insufficiency to the matter in hand" (*RCG, Col.* III, 234), he did make clear that his reading in the "Councels" was sporadic. Perhaps because he recognized that some of his opponents, particularly Ussher and Hall, exceeded him in the field of patristic learning, he preferred, for the most part, to substitute for patristic citations an emotional, common sense appeal. Milton felt the futility of wasting

pretious howrs in the endles conferring of Councels and Conclaves that demolish one another, although I know many of those that pretend to be great Rabbies in these studies have scarce saluted them from the strings, and the titlepage, or to give 'em more, have bin but the Ferrets and Moushunts of an Index.... (*REF, Col.* III, 34-35.)

53:4-7 DEFENCE OF *MURAENA* ... EXPERT COUNCELIST — Cicero, in *Oratio Pro L. Murena,* Chapter XIII, paragraph 28, in order to humble Sulpitius, who esteemed highly his knowledge of civil law, says:

Itaque si mihi homini vehementer occupato stomachum moveritis, triduo me jurisconsultum esse profitebor.

(See Hanford, "The Chronology of Milton's Private Studies," p. 301; Saurat, *Milton Man and Thinker,* p. 266; St. John, *Prose Works of Milton,* III, 163 note; Charles E. Vaughan (ed.), *Areopagitica and Other Prose Works of John Milton,* Everyman's Library, London, [1927], p. 156 note.)

53:10 MARGENT — See 25:6; 29:39; 36:32.

53:10 DO — *i.e.,* if ye do.

53:10-11 WINNOW THEIR CHAFFE FROM THEIR WHEAT — Cf. Bacon, *A Wise and Moderate Discourse,* p. 1, "by contrary blastes of doctrine, doth sift and winow mens faith"; *Modest Confutation,* p. 29, "the designe of ... the Authour of *The Protestation protested,* and some since him, is, to have the Church at length sifted and winnowed, and the grain laid apart by it self, that is your faction; and for the chaffe, all else, let them do or be what they will, it matters not"; *REF, Col.* III, 1,

"that Doctrine of the *Gospel,* planted by teachers Divinely inspir'd, and by them winnow'd, and sifted, from the chaffe of overdated Ceremonies." See Matthew 3:12 and Luke 3:17.

53:12-14 WHEREFORE I SHOULD BLAME ... AS FAULTY — The author of the *Modest Confutation,* p. 35, said:

[I] confess with you, that there is nothing more intolerable, more justly abominable in the eys of God and man, than a lewd, vicious, or lying Prophet; that there is nor higher nor lower among them, nor Priest nor Prelate, but some of them hath been and is so: What, shall we therfore have no more Ministers? Is it the office, or the man, that bears this cursed fruit? you say the office. I ask of Prelacy only: why is it then that the inferiour Clergy is most faulty?

53:17 GOVERNMENT — *i.e.,* discipline.

54:18 *NONCONFORMISTS* — The nonconformist early in the seventeenth century was one who refused to conform to the discipline and practice of the Church of England, although he accepted the doctrine thereof (*OED*). To Milton the term seems to have been synonymous with Puritan. He speaks of "those faithful witnesses commonly call'd Puritans, and Nonconformists" (*Tenure, Col.* V, 30; cf. *ibid.,* pp. 45-46, "branded with the name of Puritans and Nonconformists"). Robert Lord Brooke said that the three main divisions of the Church of England were "The *Conformists,* the *Non-Conformists,* and the *Separatists.*" "The *Conformist,*" Brooke said,

hath the *Orthodox* Divine, contending with the *Arminian, Socinian, Pelagian, Anabaptist,* and divers others; who yet All stile themselves Sonnes of the Church of England. The *Non-conformist* is uncertaine what he scrupleth; for some can dispence with one of the three Grand Nocent-innocent Ceremonies; some with another; some with neither. The *Separatist* is subdivided too (as they say) into *Seperatist* and *Semi-seperatist.* (Brooke, *Nature of Episcopacy,* p. 90.)

53:20-21 THEY ARE IN THE TRUTH... ERROR — Cf. Matthew 7:16, 20; John 15:2-6; II Corinthians 11:15; James 2:17, 20, 26.

53:21-22 *WHAT THE CORRUPTIONS ... PRELATS* — Milton in the *Animadversions* (1641), p. 53 (*Col.* III, 160), after commenting on the "lazinesse" of the Priests, "their Tavern-hunting, their neglect of all sound literature, and their liking of doltish and monasticall Schoolemen," said:

What should I tell you how the Universities, that men looke should be fountaines of learning and knowledge, have been poyson'd and choak'd under your governance?

The Confuter copied the quotation and continued:

Fair and pure may those living streams ever flow, both *Isis* and *Chame*! but who, I wis, hath troubled them? yea, who goes about to dry them up? if either they fail, or be pudled, you can not blame Episcopacy for either. If some Bishops be Arminians, and some Scholars at either University, that infection came from beyond sea, though not in the same ship with your Presbytery. Was *Arminius* a Bishop? surely no more than Mr *Calvin*: Why then should that be objected to them or the cause? Or pray tell me, do you think if you have pulled down Episcopacy that those opinions will dye? (*Modest Confutation,* p. 35.)

53:23-24 THE REMONSTRANT HAVING SPOK'N ... REMOVALL OF PRELATS — The Smectymnuans in *An Answer,* p. 64, in decrying the wealth and power of the Church commented that when the churches "*had woodden Chalices,* they had *golden Priests*; but when their *Chalices were golden, their Priests were wooden.*" Hall answered:

But, Brethren, take no care for this danger [of having wooden Priests, and golden Chalices]; Our last age hath begun to take sufficient order for the redresse of this evill: and if in time you shall see wooden Chalices, and wooden Priests, thank your selves. (Hall, *Defence,* pp. 126-27.)

Milton took up the topic, saying:

It had beene happy for this land, if your priests had beene but onely wooden, all *England* knowes they have been to this Iland not wood, but wormewood, that have infected the third part of our waters, like that Apostate starre in the Revelation; that many soules have di'd of their bitternesse; and if you meane by wooden, illiterate, or contemptible, there was no want of that sort among you, and their number increasing daily, as their lazinesse, their Tavern-hunting, their neglect of all sound literature, and their liking of doltish and monasticall Schoolemen daily increase. (*ANIM* (1641), p. 53; *Col.* III, 159-60.)

53:24-26 I SHEW'D HIM ... UNDER THEIR GOVERNMENT—Milton, in the *Animadversions,* had pointed out that the Universities had "been poyson'd and choak'd under [the] governance" of the prelates, that there could not be anywhere found, even "in the Church of *Rome* it selfe a baser brood of flattering and time-serving priests." And as for the

young schollers that petition for Bishopricks and Deaneries to incourage them in their studies, and that

many Gentlemen else will not put their sons to learning, away with such young mercenary stripplings and their Simoniacall fathers, God has no neede of such, they have no part or lot in his Vineyard, they may as well sue for Nunneries, that they may have some convenient stowage for their wither'd daughters, because they cannot give them portions answerable to the pride and vanity they have bred them in; this is the root of all our mischiefe, that which they alleage for the incouragement of their studies, should be cut away forthwith as the very bait of pride and ambition, the very garbage that drawes together all the fowles of prey and ravin in the land to come, and gorge upon the Church; how can it be but ever unhappy to the Church of *England,* while shee shall thinke to intice men to the pure service of God by the same meanes that were us'd to tempt our Saviour to the service of the devill, by laying before him honour and preferment. Fit professors indeed are they like to be, to teach others that godlinesse with content is great gaine, whenas their godlinesse of teaching had not been but for worldly gaine. The heathen Philosophers thought that vertue was for its owne sake inestimable, and the greatest gaine of a teacher to make a soule vertuous.... Was morall vertue so lovely, and so alluring, and heathen men so enamour'd of her, as to teach and study her with greatest neglect and contempt of worldly profit and advancement; and is Christian piety so homely and so unpleasant, and Christian men so cloy'd with her, as that none will study and teach her, but for lucre and preferment! O stale-growne piety! O Gospell rated as cheap as thy Master. (*ANIM* (1641), pp. 53-54; *Col.* III, 160-61.)

To the possible objection that "piety may thrive," but learning decay unless "wealth," "honour," "dainty fare," and "lofty houses" be the prize, Milton replied:

Certainly never any cleare spirit nurst up from brighter influences with a soule inlarg'd to the dimensions of spacious art and high knowledge ever enter'd there but with scorn, & thought it ever foule disdain to make pelf or ambition the reward of his studies, it being the greatest honor, the greatest fruit and proficiency of learned studies to despise these things. (*Ibid.,* pp. 54-55; *Col.* III, 161-62.)

Those who study merely for money "can have neither true wisdom nor grace." That divine is "most imperfect, and incompleate ... who is so farre from being a contemner of filthy lucre." Those who mix their "poore and low pitch't desires" for a "fat Prebendary, Deanery, or Bishoprick," "with those other heavenly intentions that draw a man to this study," will "bring forth a baseborn issue of Divinity like that of those imperfect, and putrid creatures that receive a crawling life from two most unlike procreants the Sun, and mudde" (*ibid.,* p. 55; *Col.* III, 162).

The "learned foole," or the "learned Hypocrite," arises from such an educational system. The first spends his time in "empty speculations" or sows "the World with nice, and idle questions"; the other uses his "sophisticated arts" and bends his studies "to make his insatiate avarice, & ambition seem pious, and orthodoxall by painting his lewd and deceitfull principles with a smooth, and glossy varnish in a doctrinall way to bring about his wickedest purposes" (*ibid.,* pp. 55-56; *Col.* III, 162-63). Milton points out that nowhere in the Christian world does learning flourish more than in Geneva, and where the "Churches of *Belgia* and *Helvetia*" uphold true ideals (*ibid.,* p. 59; *Col.* III, 167). He says that "all noble sciences attending upon the traine of Christian doctrine" can be made to flourish, that "able professors of every Art" can be paid "ample stipends . . . honestly provided," and that measures can be taken to insure that "hearers may benefit," all "without the Prelates" (*ibid.,* p. 59; *Col.* III, 167; cf. Bishop Hall's opinion, *Humble Remonstrance,* p. 38, that "no one Clergy in the whole Christian world, yeelds so many eminent Scholars, learned Preachers, grave, holy, and accomplished Divines, as this Church of *England* doth at this day.").

53:27-28 HE SEEKS TO JUSTIFIE . . . UPHELD SOVERANTY — To Milton's allegation that there could not be found "among all the reformed Churches, nay, in the Church of *Rome* it selfe a baser brood of flattering and time-serving priests" (*ANIM* (1641), p. 53; *Col.* III, 160), the Confuter retorted:

What is that which you call flattery? standing up by the King. Is it not their duty? and yours too, were ye not so great Patrons of popularity? If the Kings Soveraignty be inviolable, may it not lawfully be published? may not a Minister dare preach it? yea, and if your Parlour Oratours have defamed, may not the Pulpit vindicate? There is difference, I hope, between a Libell clapt upon Whitehallgates, and a Panygirick at *Pauls*: In my opinion those flatterers shall do very ill to be silent, till either their Prince be lesse vertuous, or you lesse malitious. (*Modest Confutation,* p. 36.)

53:28 THEY — *i.e.,* the clergy; cf. "their" (53: 30) and "they" (53:32).

53:28-34 ALL CHRISTIAN SOVERANTY . . . TYRANNIZ'D PEOPLE — The theory of the

mixed state was mainly the development of the Greek historian Polybius, who brought "into conjunction the three ideas of divided power, balance, and permanence in government." Polybius saw in Sparta and Rome the sharing of monarchial, aristocratic, and democratic elements in such a manner that "the degenerative tendency which led every pure form of government to destruction had little room to operate, and in which, therefore, permanence and stability were attained" (Zera S. Fink, "The Theory of the Mixed State and the Development of Milton's Political Thoughts," *PMLA,* LVII (1942), 705-06; cf. Zera S. Fink, "Venice and English Political Thought in the Seventeenth Century," *MP,* XXXVIII (1940), 168; Zera S. Fink, *Classical Republicans,* Evanston, 1945, pp. 95-99, and E. M. Clark (ed.), *The Ready and Easy Way to Establish a Free Commonwealth by John Milton,* New Haven, 1915, pp. lviii-lix). Milton accepted the theory (*REF, Col.* III, 63). He judged that no "Civill *Goverment*" was "more divinely and harmoniously tun'd, more equally ballanc'd" than the "Common-wealth of *England*: where under a free, and untutor'd *Monarch,* the noblest, worthiest, and most prudent men, with full approbation, and suffrage of the People have in their power the supreame, and finall determination of highest Affaires (*ibid.*; cf. *Ready and Easy Way, Col.* VI, 118 ff.). The clergy, Milton indicated, were "commonly the corrupters of kingly authority turning it to tyrannie by thire wicked flatteries even in the pulpit" (*Commonplace Book, Col.* XVIII, 175), therefore destructive to the state. The clergy sought the "dissolution of law" and the "erecting of an arbitrary sway" (53:30-32), thus undermining the liberty of the people. At the same time the clergy tended toward the "destruction of Monarchy" (*REF, Col.* III, 41). Episcopacy was, therefore, the wen, the tumor (*ibid.,* pp. 47-49) in the state which aggrandized the civil power with the purpose of ultimately taking over that power (*ibid.,* pp. 41-47). Milton was not a little concerned when he noticed in "most men" a "carelessenes of knowing what they, and others ought to do" (*Apology,* 1:3-4; cf. Fink, "The Theory of the Mixed State," p. 730), for episcopacy was "incompatible with, and ultimately destructive of, such a mixed government as Milton conceived England to have" (Fink, "The Theory of the Mixed State," p. 714; cf. Fink, *Classical Republicans*, p. 98).

Milton considered that "all Christian soverainty is by law" (53:28-29). The Church was in no way to usurp the jurisdiction of the magistrate (*ibid.*, pp. 65). It should not "invade worldly possession, which is the rightfull lot and portion, even of the wickedest men, as frankly bestow'd upon them by the al-dispensing bounty, as *rain* and *Sunshine.*" It was "not to bereave or destroy the body, it seekes to save the Soule by humbling the body, not by Imprisonment, or pecuniary mulct, much less by stripes or bonds, or disinheritance" (*REF, Col.* III, 71-72). Both the "Liberty of the subject, and the supremacie of the King" (*ibid.*, p. 56) were dependent upon the law. The prelates were, however, attempting to exalt the King by the "dissolution of law" and by demanding an "arbitrary sway according to privat will" which would sooner or later be their will. To Milton the end was tyranny and a "tyranniz'd people" (53:30-34). The united tyranny of King and bishop was unendurable. Furthermore, it was ruinous to the Church, for

when the Church without temporal support is able to doe her great works upon the unforc't obedience of men, it argues a divinity about her. But when she thinks to credit and better her spirituall efficacy, and to win her self respect and dread by strutting in the fals visard of worldly autority, tis evident that God is not there.... (*RCG, Col.* III, 251-52.)

Milton said in his *Observations upon the Articles of Peace, Col.* VI, 250, that

the Church began then most apparently to degenerate, and goe to ruine, when shee borrow'd of the Civill power more then fair encouragement and protection; more then which Christ himself and his Apostles never requir'd.

53:33-34 KNOWN DEFINITION OF A TYRANT — Cf. *Second Defence, Col.* VIII, 27, 29:

But if every good man is a king, as a certain sect of the ancients magnificently philosophized [Plato, *Republic*, 5.473], it follows, by parity of reason, that every bad man, according to his proportion, is a tyrant: and that he may not be puffed up with this name let it be observed, that a tyrant, so far from being anything great, is the meanest of earthly things; that as far as he surpasses all in the elevation of his rank, so far is he the vilest of all, and the most a slave. For others are the willing slaves, only of their own vices; he is obliged to be the slave, even against his will, not of his own vices only, but of the most importunate profligacies of his ministers and satellites; he is obliged

to yield the subordinate branches of his tyranny to the most worthless of his creatures. Tyrants, therefore, are the most abject of slaves; they are slaves even to their own slaves.

53:34 A LITTLE BENEATH — A little further down on the same page, that is, page 36 of the *Modest Confutation*.

53:34-36 DENIES THAT GREAT RICHES... PRIDE & AMBITION — Cf. Note 38:12. The Confuter quoted Milton's denunciation of the practice of giving young scholars "Bishopricks and Deaneries," and his plea that those "[encouragements] *should be cut away forthwith, as the very bait of pride and ambition, the very garbage that draws together all the fowls of prey*" (see Note 53:24-26). He answered, taking the occasion to ridicule Milton as the supposedly "small Clerk" (see Note 43:25-26), and as the seeker of a rich widow (42:12-13):

It is one of those young Scholars that asks your Eldership, whether there were not birds and beasts of prey, that did devour the flock, before ere the Church were so much beholding to the bounty of Princes and Nobles as now she is? Whether the Devill can allure never a Cobler from his *awl* and *last* under a fat Prebendary? Whether a Widows house [may be an allusion to Milton's supposed ambition to get a rich widow] be not as tempting as a Bishops Palace? or there be not of those degenerate sort of men [*i.e.*, Milton], who will desire the Priesthood for a morsell of bread? If so, how are we, or shall we be then more safe than now? Poor soul! how envie and anger befools thee! Bethink your self better; are not Parsonages, Vicarages, and Lectures prey too? and do we not see halt and dumb too often possesse the former, and crazed men the latter? away with them then by any means. No, but away with those fowls and beasts rather, and then that prey will be meat for honest and able Preachers.... But in good earnest Sir, for Bishopricks and Denaries, they are in too wise a Dispencers hands to be given to Vultures; had it been otherwise, perhaps yours and your fellows mouths ere this had been stopt. (*Modest Confutation*, pp. 36-37.)

53:36-37 REPUTED DIVINE AUTORITY — Possibly Pope Melchiades, immediate predecessor of Pope Sylvester I (see Note 54:4-25). A spurious letter purports that Melchiades affirms that Constantine decreed the building of churches, including the one at Rome, and bestowed great wealth, resulting in corruption in the Church (see Migne, *Patrologie Cursus Completus* (Latinae), VIII, 566-68).

53:37 *CONSTANTINE*—Constantine, the Great (288?-377). According to Eusebius's *Life of Constantine,* Constantine boldly attacked Rome in 312 after having seen the Vision of the Flaming Cross with the legend "By this conquer," and defeated his opponent, Maxentius. The experience led to his conversion to Christianity. In 313 toleration for Christianity throughout the Empire was secured by the edict of Milan. In 325 Constantine ruled as sole emperor in East and West, and in 326 he chose to make his seat of empire at Byzantium. In 330 Constantinople was dedicated to the Blessed Virgin, and Christianity became the official religion of the empire. Milton charged Constantine with neglect for not having curbed the "Pride, Avarice, and Luxury" of the clergy who took advantage of their position in the state religion (*REF, Col.* III, 23), and of the "stately Palaces, rich furniture, delicious fare, and *Princely* attendance" that came with Constantine's wealth (*ibid.,* p. 25). Constantine's doings "marr'd all in the Church" (*ibid.,* p. 26). For the prelates, however, Constantine was a man of great importance (*ibid.,* pp. 21-23). When

the *Prelates* cry out Let the Church be reform'd according to *Constantine,* it should sound to a judicious eare no otherwise, then if they should say Make us rich, make us lofty, make us lawlesse, for if any under him were not so, thanks to those ancient remains of integrity, which were not yet quite worne out, and not to his Government. (*Ibid.,* p. 28.)

53:37-38 HIS LOVE TO ANTIQUITY — For examples of the Confuter's "love to antiquity" see Notes 22:3; 33:35-36; 33:39-34:1; 36:33-36.

53:39 *GOWER* — John Gower (d. 1408), author of the *Confessio Amantis* (1390).

54:2 A VOICE FROM HEAV'N — See 54:17. Cf. Matthew 3:17; Mark 1:11; Luke 3:22; John 12:28. See also Matthew 17:5; Mark 9:7; Luke 9:35.

54:4-25 THIS CONSTANTINE . . . NONE OTHER SKILL — The passage is taken from the tale of Constantine and Sylvester, which is based on the legend of the Donation of Constantine. The tale comprises the final story of Book II of *Confessio Amantis,* the passage, lines 3475-96 of Book II. (See G. C. Macaulay, *The Complete Works of John Gower,* Oxford, 1899-1902, 4 vols., II, 223-24.) One or more of three editions of Gower's *Confessio Amantis* may have been available to Milton.

The passage may have been taken from *tHis Book is intituled confessio amantis* . . . compyled, by Johan Gower [Colophon: Emprynted at Westmestre by me Willyam Caxton and fynyssht the ii day of Septembre the fyrst yere of the regne of Kyng Richard the thyrd/the yere of our lord, a thousand,/CCCC/lxxxxiij/ (*i.e.,* 1483)], fol. 51 *recto*; from *Jo. Gower de confessione Amantis,* Imprinted at London in Flete-strete by Thomas Berthelette Printer to the kingis grace, AN. M.D.XXXII., fol. [46] *verso* and 47 *recto*; or from *Jo. Gower de confessione Amantis.* Imprinted at London in Flete-strete by Thomas Berthelette the. XII. daye of Marche. AN. M.D.LIIII., fol. [46] *verso* and 47 *recto.* Milton probably used the 1532 or 1554 edition, for the folio references to Gower in the *Commonplace Book* (*Col.* XVIII, 211) fit either of those editions.

54:4 HEAL — Salvation.

54:9 YAFE — Gave.

54:15 CRONICK — *i.e.,* chronicle.

54:16 YEFT — Gift.

54:19 SHAD — Shed.

54:23 SOOTH — *i.e.,* truth.

54:26-27 BEASTS OF PREY . . . ON THE CHURCH — See Note 53:34-36.

54:27 WHAT THOUGH? — *i.e.,* what of it?

54:27 VULTURS — See Note 53:34-36 for the Confuter's use of "Vultures"; cf. 55:15.

54:29 FOR LUCRE . . . CREEPE INTO THE CHURCH — Cf. *REF, Col.* III, 56; *ANIM, Col.* III, 162, 170; *RCG, Col.* III, 274; *Means to Remove Hirelings, Col.* VI, 67. See Note 38:12.

54:31 THE GOLDEN MEAN — Horace *Odes,* Bk. II, Ode X, line 5.

54:31-32 FOR SO, GOOD PASTORS WILL BE CONTENT — Milton felt that the good minister often has reason to wish away much of the "prosperity of this life . . . as a diet puffing up the soul with a slimy fleshinesse, and weakning her principall organick parts" (*RCG, Col.* III, 264). The maintenance of ministers under the gospel was, he argued, left to "charity and Christian freedom" in church (*Means to Remove Hirelings, Col.* VI, 50-51), for Christ "ordained no certain maintenance for his apostles or ministers" (*ibid.*, p. 62). The example of Christ and Paul was evidence that it is well, in order that no burden be laid on the church, for the minister to have a trade (*ibid.*, pp. 80-81). Recompense made to ministers should be distributed "according to thir several labors" out of the church treasury (*ibid.*, pp. 73-74). He showed that it is the duty of "richer congregations, where most commonly they abound with teachers, to send som of thir number to the villages round" (*ibid.*, p. 77). He argued that the "necessary Consequence" of "Liberty of Conscience" was "the removal of a forc'd Maintenance from Ministers" (*Letter to a Friend, Col.* VI, 104-05). Admitting that "a certain recompense is both reasonable in itself, and sanctioned by the law of God and the declarations of Christ and his apostle" (*Christian Doctrine, Col.* XVI, 293), he insisted that ministers rely not on the "edicts of civil power" but on the "spontaneous good-will and liberality of the church in requital of their voluntary service" (*ibid.*, p. 297; cf. *Proposalls, Col.* XVIII, 6). Ministers who have any thought of "*Gods glory* and the advancement of Christian Faith" will, Milton asserted, be satisfied with a "moderate maintenance" (*REF, Col.* III, 55). See 57:11-19; 58:15-21.

54:32 BE CONTENT — Cf. Philippians 4:11; I Timothy 6:8; Hebrews 13:5; Luke 3:14.

54:32 HAVING NEED OF NO MORE — Cf. Philippians 4:19; Acts 4:35.

54:32-33 KNOWING WITHALL... CHRIST AND HIS APOSTLES — Christ himself was a carpenter (Mark 6:3); Paul was a tent-maker (Acts 18:3). Christ not only taught that the servant of God should not worry about material things (Matthew 6:19, 25; 8:20; 19:21), but that riches were a hindrance to entering the Kingdom of Heaven (Matthew 19:24; Luke 6:24; 12:16-21; 16:19-23). He sent out his followers telling them to "eat such things as are set before you," and to lodge with those who offer lodging (Luke 10:1-11; cf. Luke 9:1-6 and Matthew 10:5-14). In the early Church a system of sharing was devised which extended to the needy at home and abroad (Acts 4: 34-35; 11:29; 24:17; Romans 15:26; II Corinthians 8:1-4; Galatians 2:10; James 1:27; I John 3:17). Paul outlined a system for making contributions

for the saints (I Corinthians 16:1-2; II Corinthians 9:7-12). Paul thought it no shame to "hunger, and thirst, and [be] naked, and [be] buffeted" for Christ (I Corinthians 4:9-13); his admonition was not to trust in "uncertain riches" (I Timothy 6:17; Philippians 4:6; cf. I Peter 5:7). Cf. *Apology,* 55: 39-56:2.

55:5 A WIDOWS HOUSE... PALACE — See Note 53:34-36. Cf. Matthew 23:14; Mark 12:40; Luke 20:47; II Timothy 3:6; Titus 1:11. In the Hebrew law provisions were made for the alleviating of the difficult life of the widow (Deuteronomy 24:19-22; 26:12; 16:11). The provision that the "widow's raiment" should not be taken in pledge (Deuteronomy 24:17), together with the reference to the evil of taking "the widow's ox for a pledge" (Job 24:3), established certain rights for the widow. In the New Testament there are references concerning the care of widows (see Acts 6:1). Christ charged that the Pharisees robbed the most needy and defenseless of the last remaining necessities of life under the pretence of religion (Matthew 23: 14). The Confuter's mentioning of widows' houses was probably intended to have a sting, for the Confuter presumed Milton to be looking for a rich widow (*Apology,* 42:12-13), but Milton preferred to ignore the innuendo.

55:7 OCCASION TAKEN OF EVILL — *i.e.,* occasion for evil.

55:12-13 YEA BUT... DISPENSERS HAND — See Note 53:34-36.

55:15 VULTURES — See Note 54:27 VULTURS.

55:16-22 BUT THIS WHICH COMES NEXT IN VIEW... BETTER CLOTH'D — To Milton's comments in the *Animadversions* that the "heathen Philosophers thought that vertue was for its owne sake inestimable," but that "Christian piety" seemed to have become "so homely and so unpleasant... that none will study and teach her, but for lucre and preferment" (*ANIM* (1641), p. 54; *Col.* III, 161; see Note 53:24-26 for the full quotation), the Confuter answered:

Now I see you know somewhat: and were I not assured that other passions distracted you, I could easily be enclined to think that this volley of expressions proceeded from a love of *goodnesse*: indeed so much the more easily inclined, by how much I would fain have it so. For were there no guile in them, as I do continually nourish such thoughts, so would I never desire to have them better cloathed: if at any time a floud of eloquence becomes us, it is when we expresse such a love, or such an indignation! But it is one thing that you say, and another thing that you prove: the means is often times rested and taken up in stead of the end; therefore the means is not the means; or therefore the means cannot be looked at as the means: illogical and absurd! (*Modest Confutation*, p. 37.)

55:23 BEST RHETORICIANS — Among the more important rhetoricians Milton mentions are Aristotle (*Art of Logic, Col.* XI, 465; *Familiar Letters, Col.* XII, 101), Cicero (*Tetrachordon, Col.* IV, 75; *Art of Logic, Col.* XI, 113, 167, 239), Hermogenes (*Of Education, Col.* IV, 286), Quintilian (*Art of Logic, Col.* XI, 113, 129, 205, 209, 213, 223), Ramus (*Art of Logic, Col.* XI, 117, 127, 131, 147, 215, 217). Other men identified as rhetoricians by Milton are Demetrius (*Doctrine and Discipline of Divorce, Col.* III, 491), Callicles (*ibid.*, p. 500), and Eumenius (*History of Britain, Col.* X, 90). No attempt has been made to make the references inclusive.

55:24-25 PRIME AUTHORS OF ELOQUENCE — Cf. *First Defence, Col.* VII, 39, Cicero and Demosthenes; *Prolusion* VI, *Col.* XII, 211, Demosthenes and Aeschines; *Author's Defence of Himself, Col.* IX, 175, Cicero; *Prolusion* VI, *Col.* XII, 243, Q. Hortensius; *First Defence, Col.* VII, 183, Lucius Crassus.

55:25-32 TRUE ELOQUENCE . . . THEIR OWN PLACES — Milton favored a prose that was "sober, plain, and unaffected," after the manner of the Scriptures (*REF, Col.* III, 34). He disliked a "coy flurting stile" that "girded with frumps and curtall gibes" (4:39), but he was not opposed to the use of *"grim laughter,"* which *"hath oft-times a strong and sinewy force"* (*ANIM, Col.* III, 107). He was not, in general, impressed by a "paroxysm of citations" (*REF, Col.* III, 33; *Apology*, 36:27-36). He felt that *"there is no doubt but that, wholsom* matter, and good desires rightly conceav'd in the heart, wholesom words will follow of themselves" (*Eikonoklastes, Col.* V, 220-21), and that a copiousness of words often signified an emptiness of matter (*First Defence, Col.* VII, 3). Fred Emil Ekfelt points out that Milton disclaims "the neces-

sity for art in true eloquence." True eloquence is the natural outpouring of the mind which possesses "the serious and hearty love of truth," and which has the desire to "infuse the knowledge" of "good things" "into others" (Ekfelt, "The Graphic Diction of Milton's English Prose," p. 46; *Apology*, 55: 26-29).

55:33-34 CHRIST REFUS'D . . . DEVILS HAND — In answering Milton's allegation that "none will study and teach [Christian piety], but for lucre and preferment" (see Note 55:16-22), the Confuter said:

But that offends you, that our Church should use the same means to entice men to the pure service of God, that were used to tempt our Saviour to the service of the Devill. Those means were neither in themselves, nor as enticements, any way dangerous; but so far as they were tendered by him, from whom it was a sin to receive them; to him, who could make no use of them; for such an end, as it had been a sin to accept them. Otherwise how could God entice the children of Israel with the promise of Canaan; or *Solomon*, with riches and honours and all kind of abundance? But these *desires mixe.* As subordinate they may: The holy Ghost witnesseth of *Moses*, that he had an eye to the reward; I ask whether in that *Moses* sinned. . . . (*Modest Confutation*, pp. 37 and 39 [*i.e.*, 38].)

Both the Confuter and Milton refer to the account of the temptation of Christ in the wilderness by Satan, particularly to that temptation in which Satan offered Christ the kingdoms of the world together with the glory of them (Matthew 4:8-9; Luke 4:5-7).

55:34-35 *AS THEY WERE TENDER'D . . . RECEAVE THEM* — See Note 55:33-34; Luke 4:6; and Matthew 4:9.

55:36-38 WHY IS IT NOT THEREFORE . . . FOR THE GIVER? — See Notes 49:9-10; 49: 23-26; 49:30.

55:38 *BUT HE COULD MAKE NO USE OF SUCH A HIGH ESTATE* — See Note 55:33-34.

55:39 THE SERVANT — *i.e.*, the priest or minister.

56:1-2 THAT HEE MIGHT TEACH HIS MINISTERS TO FOLLOW HIS STEPS — Cf. Note 54:32-33.

56:2-3 *THEY WERE OFFER'D . . . END* — See Note 55:33-34; Luke 4:7; and Matthew 4:9.

56:3-6 PRELATS; WHO AFTER THEIR PREFERMENT ... AND PURSES — Cf. 5:14-16; 30:21-22; 56:34; 57:1-3. The author of *An Appeale To Every Impartiall, Iudicious, and Godly Reader* (1641), p. 6, said that the prelates

seek out and search for the fattest Parsonages to feed themselves, and to fit their carnall mindes, carefully preferring their Sonnes, their Chaplaines, their Friends, Kinsmen, and Favorites; endeavouring sometime to deprive true Patrons by cunning shifts of the right of Patronage, to place in whom they please; respecting mens persons, and not the spirituall good of the people.

He complained that they "study carnally to their utmost power, that they may hold up their owne greatnesse, and not nourish people in goodnesse: they strive not against sinne, but rather how to secure themselves in their Lordly standing." Henry Peacham in *A Paradox*, p. 1, said:

had I bin *Dunce* [*i.e.*, a prelate], without question, I had long ere this, perhaps bin double or treble benefic'd, bin a lasie Prebend, or Deane of some Cathedrall my selfe, or kept a fellowship with a good Living to boote in some Colledge or other, as long as I had lived.

Robert Lord Brooke (*Nature of Episcopacy*, p. 98) opined that the "mad outrage" of the bishops

in all the three Kingdomes, of late, hath so incensed the Common People, that in all mens eyes they are become most vile: and while all men reflect on their constant trade of mischeivous practices, the wisest begin to conclude, The very Calling hurt the Men, as much as These disgrace the Calling. (Cf. *REF, Col.* III, 11-12.)

56:4-5 TEACHING LABOUR OF THE WORD — Cf. I Timothy 5:17; I Thessalonians 1:3; Hebrews 6:10; II Timothy 4:2; Matthew 28:19; Acts 5:42; I Corinthians 4:17; Colossians 1:28.

56:6-7 *GOD ENTIC'T ... CANAAN*—See Note 55:33-34; Genesis 17:8; Exodus 6:4.

56:8 JEWES BROUGHT [slavish mindes] OUT OF EGYPT — See Exodus 14:11; 15:24; 16:2; 17:2-3; 32:1; 33:4; Numbers 13:28-33.

56:10-13 SAINT *PAUL* ... CHILDISH ENTICEMENTS — "But before faith came, we were kept under the law, shut up unto the faith which should afterwards be revealed. Wherefore the law was our schoolmaster *to bring us* unto Christ, that we might be justified by faith. But after that faith is come, we are no longer under a schoolmaster" (Galatians 3:23-25).

56:13 THE GOSPELL IS OUR MANHOOD — See Galatians 4:1-9.

56:15 SO BASELY TO PLEAD FOR EARTHLY REWARDS — Milton calls the Confuter's plea (see Note 55:33-34) for earthly rewards base.

56:15-16 *BUT GOD ... SALOMON WITH THESE MEANS* — See Note 55:33-34. The account of Solomon's acquisition of wisdom, riches, and honor, found in I Kings 3:5-15, is recorded as a dream. The Confuter considers the dream the enticement: "how could God entice ... *Solomon*, with riches and honours and all kind of abundance" (*Modest Confutation*, p. 39 [*i.e.*, 38]).

56:16 THE WISEST MAN *SALOMON* — See I Kings 10:24.

56:17-18 *SALOMON* ASKT AN UNDERSTANDING HEART — I Kings 3:9.

56:19-21 [Salomon askt] NO RICHES ... WITHOUT ASKING — I Kings 3:10-14.

56:23 HEE — The Confuter.

56:24 *MOSES HAD AN EYE TO THE REWARD* — See Note 55:33-34. The Confuter, in the margin opposite his quotation "The holy Ghost witnesseth of *Moses*, that he had an eye to the reward," cites "*Heb.* 11.29" in error for Hebrews 11:26. (*Modest Confutation*, p. 39 [*i.e.*, 38].)

56:25 LOOKST WITH *BALAAMS* EYES — Numbers 22:22-31. Balaam, who has stirred God's anger by disobedience, cannot understand why the ass which he is riding refuses to advance until his eyes are opened and he sees the angel of the Lord in the way. Cf. *ANIM, Col.* III, 137, "*Balaams* disease, a pearle in your eye."

56:25 TO WHAT REWARD — Cf. 56:29-30 "incorruptible reward."

56:26 FAITH OF *MOSES* — Milton is thinking of Hebrews 11, the "faith" chapter, particularly verses 23-28.

56:26-27 FORSAKEN ALL THE GREATNESSE OF *EGYPT* — See Hebrews 11:26; Exodus 11:3.

56:27-28 CHOSE A TROUBLESOME JOURNEY ... WILDERNESSE — Hebrews 11:24-29; Exodus 7:7; 12:31-19:25; 24:1-18; 31:1-36:7; Numbers 9:1-28:23; 31:1-Deuteronomy 3:29; Deuteronomy 34:1-12.

56:28-29 AND YET ARRIV'D NOT AT HIS JOURNIES END — Moses was not permitted to enter the Promised Land because he had sinned, but he was allowed to view it from Mount Nebo (Deuteronomy 32:51-52; 34:4).

56:29-31 INCORRUPTIBLE REWARD, PROMIS'D TO *ABRAHAM* AND HIS SEED IN THE *MESSIAH* — See Genesis 12:3; 18:18; 22:18; 26:4; 28:14; Acts 3:25; Galatians 3:8. Through the seed of Abraham came the Messiah who brought eternal life, the "incorruptible reward" (I Corinthians 9:25), the "promise" of Hebrews 11, the heavenly country (Hebrews 11:16), the "city which hath foundations, whose builder and maker *is* God" (Hebrews 11:10).

56:31 A HEAV'NLY REWARD — See Note 56:29-31.

56:32-33 TO SUCH A REWARD ... RESPECT — See Hebrews 11:26, "...he had respect unto ... the reward."

56:34 SUCH REWARDS ... HAPPY — See Note 56:3-6.

56:35 *IACOB* A PRINCE BORNE — See Genesis 25:23; 27:29.

56:35-37 VOW'D ... *THE LORD SHOULD BE HIS GOD* — Genesis 28:20-21.

56:37-38 PRELATS OF MEANE BIRTH — *i.e.*, average birth. Neither Laud nor Hall were of high birth. Laud was the son of a master-tailor of Reading; Hall's father was an officer under the President of the North. It was a custom of Laud's enemies to remind him of the meanness of his birth. Milton called the prelates "a numerous faction of indigent persons, crept for the most part out of extream want and bad nature" (*Means to Remove Hirelings*, Col. VI, 99). Cf. Note 45:23.

56:38-39 MAKING SHEW AS IF THEY WERE CALL'D — Cf. Exodus 28:1; Numbers 16:1-44; I Timothy 2:7; Hebrews 3:1; 5:1, 4; 8:3. See Note 57:12-13.

57:1-3 HARD SERVICE ... PRINCES — See Notes 56:3-6 and 57:21-23.

57:4 *SIMON MAGUS,* FOR HE PROFFER'D A REWARD — The Biblical account of Simon Magus is found in Acts 8:9-24. Eusebius in his *Ecclesiastical History,* Book II, Chapters xii-xv, discussed him. (Five editions of Meredith Hanmer's translation of *The Avncient Ecclesiastical Histories,* in which Eusebius' *Ecclesiastical History* was available, appeared between 1576 and 1637; see Note 52:20-22.) Because Simon Magus offered Peter a sum of money for the power of conferring the Holy Spirit through the laying on of hands, the term "simony" became applied to the buying or selling of church offices (see *RCG, Col.* III, 263, "proud simoniacall Courts"; *ANIM, Col.* III, 160, "Simoniacall fathers"; *The ready and easy way,* Second edition, London, 1660, p. 12, "follow *Iscariot or Simon* the magician.").

Milton taunted the prelates by saying: "If we [the antiprelates] fishing with *Simon* the Apostle can catch nothing; see what you [the prelates] can catch with *Simon Magus*; for all his hooks, & fishing implements he bequeath'd among you" (*ANIM, Col.* III, 151).

In the *Constitvtions And Canons Ecclesiasticall* (1604), Section XL, *"An oath against Symonie at institution into Benefices"* was provided "To auoid the detestable sinne of Symonie, because buying & selling of Spiritual and Ecclesiasticall Functions, Offices, Promotions, Dignities and Liuings is execrable before God." The oath "to be taken by euery one whom it concerneth in his owne person" was:

I N.N. do sweare, That I haue made no Symoniacall paiment, contract or promise, directly or indirectly, by my selfe or by any other to my knowledge, or with my consent, to any person or persons whatsoever, for or concerning the procuring and obtaining of this Ecclesiasticall Dignitie, Place, Preferment, Office or Liuing ... nor will at any time hereafter performe or satisfie any such kind of payment, contract or promise made by any other without my knowledge or consent, So helpe mee God through Jesus Christ.

See Note 5:14-16.

57:5-6 MEANLY — *i.e.*, in a moderate or average capacity.

57:6 HE — The Confuter.

57:6 *MEMBERS OF CHRIST* — Cf. Romans 12:4-5; I Corinthians 6:15; 12:27; Ephesians 5:30.

57:6-7 *ARE NOT THE CLERGY ... THRIVE ALIKE?* — Milton, after proposing the dissolution of episcopacy, said that

a true Pastor of Christs sending hath this especiall mark, that for greatest labours, and greatest merits in the Church, he requires either nothing, if he could so subsist, or a very common and reasonable supply of humane necessaries: Wee cannot therefore doe better then to leave this care of ours to God, he can easily send labourers into his Harvest, that shall not cry, Give, give, but be contented with a moderate and be-seeming allowance; nor will hee suffer true learning to be wanting, where true grace, and our obedience to him abounds.... He can stirre up rich Fathers to bestow exquisite education upon their Children, and so dedi-cate them to the service of the Gospell; he can make the sons of Nobles his Ministers, and Princes to be his Nazarites.... (*ANIM* (1641), p. 56; *Col.* III, 163-64.)

The Confuter exclaimed:

No man doubts of what God can do.... He can rain Manna into our mouths, as well as dew upon the earth. ... no doubt he could have immediately from himself supplyed the necessities of his Ministers; is it not as well that he doth it by others? doth he not make a virtue out of what we have, in their hands through which it passeth? is it not liberality, is it not muni-ficence in them that give it? why should we envie good men their piety? or are these virtues out of date, were they only ceremoniall? hath God impropriated all the riches of the earth for the use of Lay men only? are not Glergy-men members of the body of Christ, why should not each member thrive alike? if these must be poor and naked, so let the rest be.... (*Modest Con-futation*, pp. 39, 38 [*i.e.*, 38-39].)

57:7 CARNALL TEXTMAN — *i.e.*, one who in-terprets the Biblical text in such a manner as to justify temporal or worldly values.

57:8-9 AS IF WORLDLY THRIVING ... IN CHRIST — Christ taught that those who are "per-secuted for righteousness' sake" are blessed (Mat-thew 5:10-12). Paul was of the opinion that "all that will live godly in Christ Jesus shall suffer per-secution" (II Timothy 3:12). Cf. Acts 5:41; Romans 5:3; 8:17-18; II Corinthians 1:7; 12:10; Philippians 1:29; 3:8-10; Colossians 1:24; Hebrews 10:33-34; I Peter 4:13; Revelation 1:9.

57:9-11 A PROVIDENCE ... TO THE CHRIS-TIAN — Cf. Deuteronomy 23:6; Job 12:6; Psalms 73:3, 12; Jeremiah 5:26-28; 12:1; Matthew 5:45.

57:11-13 THEREFORE MUST THE MINIS-TERS OF CHRIST ... SPIRITUALL, NOT SECULAR — Milton agrees with Plato that it is impossible for one who deals in truth for money to be a true teacher. In Plato's dialogue *Protagoras,* two of the sophists, Hippias and Protagoras, who are paid for teaching virtue, are "refuted with out hire" by Socrates (*RCG, Col.* III, 202; cf. *Apology,* 9:35-39). Two things that in Milton's opinion worked "much mischief to the church of God, and the advancement of truth" were "force on the one side restraining, and hire on the other side corrupt-ing the teachers thereof" (*Means to Remove Hire-lings, Col.* VI, 46). In the teachings of those who pass from flock to flock in consideration of "far higher emoluments," who abandon the Church be-cause of the advantage to themselves, Milton has no confidence (*Author's Defence of Himself, Col.* IX, 285). Milton was one of those who objected when they saw

many *Civill Lawyers* take Livings, and have the Cure of Soules: Yea, and all their Lord Bishops have Two Callings, Two severall (opposite) Studies; and yet for all Those Two, They can spend as much, or more time at Cards and Dice (or worse) than at either of their Callings. (Brooke, *Nature of Episcopacy*, p. 113.)

Milton noted from "*Chrysostome,* that when Minis-ters came to have Lands, Houses, Farmes, Coaches, Horses, and the like Lumber, then Religion brought forth riches in the Church, and the Daughter de-vour'd the Mother" (*Eikonoklastes, Col.* V, 233). He pointed out that the Church which Constantine vastly enriched, "began to fall in love with offices, absolute rule, and secular power, and then the Christian religion went to wrack" (*First Defence, Col.* VII, 257). Luxury, sloth, heresies, and vices followed.

Pastors and Bishops, and sometimes those Fathers whom we admire, each a leader of his flock — those very men ... would fight for a bishopric as if for a tyrant's throne; priests and laymen promiscuous would clash swords now throughout the city, now in the very church at the very altar, and keep up their carnage sometimes with great slaughter on both sides. (*Ibid.,* p. 259.)

Milton felt that the good of the Church was served by removing the "baits of preferment" (38: 12). Christ's instructions to those He sent forth to teach indicated that, although "the labourer is worthy of his hire," the minister was to accept such things as were willingly given, and to make no other provision for his security (see Luke 10:1-12; Mat-thew 10:7-15; Luke 9:1-5). Paul witnessed that he "was chargeable to no man," that "in all *things* [he]

... kept [himself] from being burdensome" (II Corinthians 11:9). Milton developed his notions concerning the maintenance of the clergy in *Considerations Touching The likeliest means to remove Hirelings out of the Church* (1659), *Col.* VI, 43-100). See Note 57:18-19.

57:12-13 CALLING IS SPIRITUALL — Cf. I Corinthians 1:26, Ephesians 1:18; 4:1; Philippians 3:14; II Thessalonians 1:11; II Timothy 1:9; Hebrews 3:1; I Peter 2:9. See Note 56:38-39.

57:13-18 SPECIALL WARFARE ... SUBDUE MIGHTY ONES — See Matthew 10:16-42; 16:24-26; Cf. Matthew 11:25; 13:11; Mark 4:11; I Corinthians 1:19, 27.

57:18-19 A MIDDLE ESTATE IS MOST PROPER TO THE OFFICE OF TEACHING — Irene Samuel says in connection with this passage:

Milton demands of the clergy what Plato demanded of his philosopher-kings: both groups, dedicated to a life of service, are to be free from worldly concerns, not by embracing the life of poverty, but by being maintained in a 'middle estate,' untroubled by need, and unimpeded by wealth. (Samuel, *Plato and Milton,* p. 81; see Plato, *Republic,* 5.473.)

Plato held that a man cannot be "very rich and very good at the same time." "He who spends on noble objects, and acquires wealth by just means only can hardly be remarkable for riches, any more than he can be very poor" (Plato, *Laws,* 5.743).

The care of riches should have the last place in our thoughts. For there are in all three things about which every man has an interest; and the interest about money, when rightly regarded, is the third and lowest of them: midway comes the interest of the body; and, first of all, that of the soul. (*Ibid.*)

Plato said further:

May I never pray the gods to find the hidden treasure, which a man has laid up for himself and his family, he not being one of my ancestors, nor lift, if I should find, such a treasure. And may I never have any dealings with the diviners ... who in any way or manner counsel me to take up the deposit intrusted to the earth, for I should not gain so much in the increase of my possessions, if I take up the prize, as I should grow in justice and virtue of soul, if I abstain; and this will be a better possession to me than the other; for the possession of justice in the soul is preferable to the possession of wealth. (Plato, *Laws,* 11.913.)

Milton is certain that until the

Simonious decimating clergie; who shame not ... in a point of covetousnes and unjust claim to other mens

goods; a contention foul and odious in any man, but most of all in ministers of the gospel, in whom contention, though for thir own right, scarce is allowable.... be remov'd and religion set free from the monopolie of hirelings. I dare affirme, that no modell whatsoever of a commonwealth will prove succesful or undisturbed. (*Means to Remove Hirelings, Col.* VI, 45.)

Plato was sure that not "until ... philosophers are kings, or the kings and princes of this world have the spirit and power of philosophy, and political greatness and wisdom meet in one ... will this our State have a possibility of life and behold the light of day" (Plato, *Republic,* 5.473; cf. *Second Defence, Col.* VIII, 27, and Note 53:33-34), for "the insatiable desire of wealth, and the neglect of all other things for the sake of money getting" is ruinous (Plato, *Republic,* 8.562). Milton "echoes the conviction of Plato that from wealth flows ill, not good, that the just man, group, or nation will not be concerned with acquiring riches" (Samuel, *Plato and Milton,* p. 82), for "wealth and plenty in a land where Justice raignes not, is no argument of a flourishing State, but of a neerness rather to ruin or commotion" (*Eikonoklastes, Col.* V, 154). See Note 57:11-13.

57:20 HIGHER DIGNITY ... BLINDES THE TEACHER — See Note 57:18-19.

57:21-23 *THE PRELATS ... PARLAMENT* — Milton maintained that no employment was "more honourable, more worthy to take up a great spirit, more requiring a generous and free nurture, then to be the messenger, and Herald of heavenly truth from God to man" (*ANIM* (1641), p. 56; *Col.* III, 164). He questioned whether a man who had raised the hearts of listeners "out of darksome barrennesse" to "a delicious, and fragrant Spring of saving knowledge, and good workes" could "find himselfe discontented, or dishonour'd for want of admittance to have a pragmaticall voyce at Sessions, and Jayle deliveries ... or be discourag'd though men call him not Lord ... would he tugge for a Barony to sit and vote in Parliament ... ?" (*Ibid.,* p. 57; *Col.* III, 164.) The Confuter answered:

Yes, marry, what else? That man that was and could have still been content without those honours, will be very loath now to let them go; yet not so much that he loves the honours or means that accompany them, as that he would not have his countrey made guilty of so shamefull a depriving him of them. Why should sacriledge and injustice triumph over Gods cause, whiles he hath tongue or pen to defend it? (*Modest Confutation*, p. 40.)

57:23 *GODS CAUSE* — See Note 57:21-23.

57:24-26 *NOT THAT THEY LOVE THE HONOURS . . . SACRILEGE AND INJUSTICE* — See Note 57:21-23. Martin Marprelate argued that "it is utterly unlawful for a minister to be a 'Lord'; that is for any 'Lord Bishop' to be in the ministry" by referring to Luke 22:25-26, Geneva version: "The kings of the Gentiles reign over them [apostles or ministers], and they that bear rule over them are called gracious lords; but you shall not be so" (Pierce (ed.), *The Marprelate Tracts*, p. 89).

57:28 SACRILEGE — The Confuter considers the depriving of a prelate or of the prelates of the right "to have a pragmaticall voyce at Sessions, and Jayle deliveries," to be judges in ecclesiastical courts, to be called Lord, to seek for preferment, and to sit in Parliament (*ANIM* (1641), 57; *Col. III*, 164), to be sacrilege (*Modest Confutation*, p. 40; cf. 58:11-15 and Note 57:21-23).

57:30 [sacrilege] THE PRELATS ARE GUILTY OF — Laud was, for instance, a member of the Privy Council and one of the Commissioners of the Treasury. He served on the Committee on Foreign Affairs, and on the Commission of the Admiralty. He sat in the Court of High Commission, and in the Star Chamber. Juxon, Bishop of London, was in 1836 made Lord High Treasurer. (See W. T. Hale (ed.), *Of Reformation Touching Church-Discipline in England by John Milton*, pp. 97-98.)

57:31 DISCHARGE OF ONE SINGLE DUTY — The bishops claimed their superiority to lie in the power of ordination which they received by apostolic succession (*REF, Col. III*, 6; Hall, *Defence*, pp. 123-24). The right of ordination inevitably gave the right of jurisdiction. Milton did not think that ordination should "be a cause of setting up a superiour degree in the Church" (*RCG, Col. III*, 200); in fact, he considered the keeping up of "a superiour degree" on such pretenses "a meere folly" (*ANIM, Col. III*, 155), for he considered "the winning of soules" the duty of every minister, "an ability above that which is requir'd in ordination" (*ibid.*, p. 157; see also *ibid.*, p. 156 and *RCG, Col. III*, 201).

57:33-34 WHO POSSESSE HUGE BENEFICES — Godfrey Davies says, speaking of the Church of Ireland: "Simony and pluralism were the order of the day. A certain bishop was reported to have held twenty-three benefices, but the curates in charge to have received only a few pounds a year" (Godfrey Davies, *The Early Stuarts 1603-1660*, Oxford, 1937, p. 110). Cf. *Apology*, 19:28-29.

57:36-37 MANY PLURALITIES UNDER A NON-RESIDENT — Cf. 19:27-30. On February 25, 1640/1 a bill was introduced into the Commons "concerning pluralities" to regulate pluralities and "its necessary attendant non-residence," but after many interruptions in its legislative history it was finally rejected by the King almost two years later (Shaw, *History of the English Church*, I, 110-12). Attempts to eliminate pluralities could not be opposed on idealistic grounds (see Note 43:39-44:2), but they were opposed on the grounds that the small value of many ecclesiastical livings made pluralities and non-residence necessary. Furthermore, it was argued, "neither the cathedrals nor professors in the universities, could subsist without them" (Neal, *History of the Puritans*, I, 173-74). Bacon held that pluralities "were, in no sort, tollerable" if the "*Number, of Able Ministers . . . and the Valew of Benefices* were sufficient."

But we must take heed, we desire not Contraries. . . . And to desire, that *Pluralities*, be, forthwith, taken away, is to desire Things contrary; Considering, *De Facto*, there are not, *Sufficient Preachers*, for every *Parish*: Whereto adde likewise, that there is not, *Sufficient Living*, and *Maintenance*, in many *Parishes*, to maintain a *Preacher*; And it maketh, the *Impossibility*, yet much the greater. (Bacon, "Certain Considerations, Touching the Better, Pacification, And Edification, Of The Church Of England," in *Resuscitatio*, p. 251.)

See *RCG, Col. III*, 274; *Tenure of Kings and Magistrates, Col. V*, 6, 58-59; *Eikonoklastes, Col. V*, 205.

57:37 SLUBBRING — Hasty or careless.

58:4-11 THEY WHO CHASE AWAY . . . CHURCH — The Smectymnuans maintained that the design of the prelates was

to hinder all further reformation; to bring in doctrines of Popery, Arminianisme, and Libertinisme, to maintaine, propagate and much encrease the burden of humane ceremonies: to keepe out, and beate downe the Preaching of the Word, to silence the faithfull Preachers of it, to oppose and persecute the most zealous professours, and to turne all Religion into a pompous out-side. And to tread downe the power of godlinesse. (Smectymnuus, *Answer,* pp. 103-04.)

58:12 SINNE OF SACRILEGE — See Note 57:28.

58:14-15 REMOV'D . . . PRELATY AND SAC-RILEGE — Milton favors the total abolition of episcopacy. He is a Root and Branch man. See Notes 39:7-8, and 39:8-9.

58:15-16 A TRUE DEFENDER OF THE FAITH — Milton is making a play on the King's title. The title *"Fidei Defensor"* was conferred by Pope Leo X upon Henry VIII in 1521 for his tract, *Assertions of the Seven Sacraments,* against Luther. The title was later withdrawn by the Pope. The English Parliament conferred the title upon Henry in 1544. Since that year it has been used by English sovereigns.

Milton was not the first who made an appeal to the King as Defender of the Faith. William Prynne, for instance, said:

O our most pious King *Charles,* as thou hast in two severall *Declarations,* protested . . . *That thou wilt never give way to the licensing or authorising of any thing whereby* ANY INNOVATION IN THE LEAST DEGREE *may creepe into our Church; nor never connive at* ANY BACKSLIDING TO POPERY; *and that is my hearts desire to bee found worthy of that title which thou esteemest the most glorious in all thy Crowne, Defender of the faith*; so now behold these desperate innovations, purgations, and Romish practises, of thy Prelates, in open affront of these thy *Declarations*; & now or never shew thy selfe . . . a Prince more worthy of this glorious *Title,* than any of thy royall progenitors, by rooting all Popery, superstition, idolatry, errors, innovations, out of this Church and Kingdome, by restoring the Preaching, the Preachers of Gods Word, and purity of his worship, and *taking vecgeance on* these perfidious Prelates, who have . . . oppressed and grieved thy faithfull Subjects, dishonoured thy God, betrayed thy religion, increased the plague among thy people, & . . . robbed thee both of thy Gods and peoples loves, & pulled thy Crowne off thy Royall head, to set it on their owne trayterous ambitious pates, by exercising all ecclesiasticall power, yea Papal jurisdiction over thy subjects in their own names, and rights alone: and by trampling all thy lawes and Subjects liberties like Cob-webs, thy Subjects like Dogs and dirt, under their tyrannicall Papall feete. (Prynne, *Newes from Ipswich,* Sig. [*₊*3] *verso*-[*₊*4] *recto.*)

Many of Milton's ideas in his concluding statement against the prelates (57:30-58:24) seem to reflect in

a fashion hardly accidental the ideas presented by Prynne.

No doubt Milton's reference to the King as the Defender of the Faith was occasioned by the fact that the author of *A Modest Confutation,* p. 40, had defended the prelates in their "[tugging] for a Barony," and demanding their vote in Parliament (*ANIM, Col.* III, 164), by concluding:

Me thinks if all other arguments failed, it were sufficient proof of the goodnesse of it, that it hath him to be its Defender that is *Defender of the Faith*: A Prince, who if for nothing else, will therefore keep the *munificence* of his Predecessors inviolate, that he may teach succeeding ages a *reverence* to his *Own.* . . .

58:15-23 AND HEREIN WILL THE KING . . . OPPUGNERS OF THE FAITH — The syntax of the sentences seems to be least violently served by making the "scandall of Ceremonies," and the "usurpation of Prelats" parallel with "distributing": "And herein will the King be a true defender of the Faith . . . by distributing in due proportion the maintenance of the Church . . . [by] the scandall of Ceremonies thrown out . . . . [a]nd [by] the usurpation of Prelats laid levell. . . ."

58:27-28 PRIDE AND COVETOUSNESSE . . . FALSE PROPHETS WHICST ARE TO COME — Cf. II Peter 2:1-3, 18; Romans 16:17-18; Titus 1:10-11.

58:28 WHICST — Printer's error for "which," perhaps as a result of foul case.

58:29-30 AS GREAT SEDUCERS, AS ANY OF THE LATTER TIMES — See II Timothy 3:13.

58:30-31 JUDGEMENT DAY — Cf. Matthew 10:15; 11:22, 24; 12:36; Romans 14:10; II Corinthians 5:10; Hebrews 9:27; II Peter 2:9; 3:7; I John 4:17; Jude 6.

58:31 ARCH DECEAVERS — Milton may be thinking of scriptural passages such as II John 7; I John 2:22; 4:1-3; Revelation 13.

58:31 SPIGHT — Variant spelling of "spite."

58:37-38 THAT COURSE WHICH *ERASMUS* . . . POPE AND MONKS — Elector Frederick "the Wise," who was Luther's defender, in November 1520, shortly after the crowning of Charles V Emperor, sought Erasmus' opinion concerning

Luther. As a consequence an interview was arranged. To the Duke's question whether in Erasmus' judgment Luther "had erred in his published opinions," Erasmus answered evasively with a clever epigram: "Lutherus peccavit in duobus; nempe, quod tetigit coronam pontificis, et ventres monachorum." (See John J. Mangan, *Life, Character, and Influence of Desiderius Erasmus of Rotterdam,* New York, 1927, 2 vols., II, 158 ff.; Philippo Melancthone, *Chronicon Carionis,* Geneva, 1625, Bk. V, p. 937; "Colloquia oder Tischreden," in *Dr. Martin Luthers Sammtliche Schriften,* St. Louis, 1881-1910, 23 vols., XXII, Selection 123, "Churfürst Friedrichs Rede von Erasmo," p. 1081; *D. Martin Luthers Werke . . . Tischreden,* Weimar, 1912-21, 6 vols., I, no. 131; IV, no. 4899; Karl Eduard Förstemann, *D. Martin Luther's Tischreden oder Colloquia,* Leipzig, 1844-46, 3 vols., III, sec. 37, no. 123, p. 417; John Jortin, *The Life of Erasmus,* London, 1808, 3 vols., I, 226 and note; Preserved Smith, *Erasmus,* New York and London, 1923, p. 235 and note; and Preserved Smith, *Luther's Correspondence,* I, 564-67, Letter of Erasmus to Justus Jonas, Louvain, May 10, 1521.)

59:1 MITERS — The miter is a liturgical head-dress forming part of the insignia of a bishop and used as the symbol of the episcopal office (*OED*).

59:1 BELLIES — Philippians 3:18-19; Romans 16:18; cf. *REF, Col.* III, 14, "why the *Prelats* labour'd it should be . . . thought" that putting down bishops would infringe on the Queen's prerogative "ask their Bellies"; *ANIM, Col.* III, 109, "shew us any one point of your *Remonstrance* that do's not more concern superiority, pride, ease and the belly, then the truth and glory of God"; and *Lycidas,* 114-15, "for their bellies sake,/Creep . . . into the fold."

59:2 *TURBANT* — Variant spelling of "turban."

59:3 *HELMET OF SALVATION* — See Ephesians 6:17; Isaiah 59:17; cf. I Thessalonians 5:8.

59:4 METTLE AND HORN-WORK — *i.e.,* metal-work and horn-work.

59:5-6 CERTAINE KINDE . . . VOICE IN THEIR BELLIES — Milton is thinking of ventriloquists. The art of ventriloquism has a great antiquity. Traces of it have been found in Egyptian and Hebrew archaeology. Eurykles of Athens was one of the celebrated Greek ventriloquists who were called *Engastrimanteis,* that is, belly-prophets. The term *ventriloquism* itself derives from the Latin *venter,* belly, and *loqui,* to speak. Reginald Scot in his *Discovery of Witchcraft,* 1584, traced the art of ventriloquism as far back as the early Hebrews:

[The Hebrew] word *Ob,* is translated *Pytho,* or *Pythonicus spiritus*: Deut. 18, Isay. 19. 1 Sam. 28. 2 Reg. [Kings] 23. &c. sometime, though unproperly, *Magus,* as 2 Sam. 33. But *Ob* signifieth most properly a bottle and is used in this place, because the *Pythonists* spake hollow; as in the bottome of their bellies, whereby they are aptly in Latin called *Ventriloqui. . . .* (Reginald Scot, *Scot's Discovery of VVitchcraft . . . all written and published in Anno 1584. by Reginald Scot, Esquire,* 1651, Bk. 7, ch. I, p. 94.)

The voice in the belly was associated with demon possession. Among the cases cited by Reginald Scot is one of a young girl possessed of Satan. Several ministers gathered to exorcise the spirit which possessed her. After making "praiers unto God," they "commanded Satan in the name of the eternall God, and of his son Jesus Christ, to speak with such a voice as they might understand, and to declare from whence he came." Those who were present witnessed that "Satans voice did differ much from the maids voice" (*ibid.,* pp. 94 and 99 [*i.e.,* 96]). Milton, by the reference to those who "have their voice in their bellies" associates the prelates with those who are demon possessed.

59:7-8 BEING WELL DRAIN'D . . . DUMBE — Milton is confident that when the clergy came to be "fed at the publick cost" they became idle, and "that idlenes with fulnes of bread begat pride and perpetual contention with thir feeders the despis'd laitie." Milton thinks it will never be otherwise while they are thus upheld undepending on the church . . . and are by the magistrate publickly maintaind a numerous faction of indigent persons, crept for the most part out of extream want and bad nurture, claiming by divine right and freehold the tenth of our estates, to monopolize the ministry as their peculiar, which is free and open to all able Christians, elected by any church. (*Means to Remove Hirelings, Col.* VI, 98-99.)

59:8-9 *DIVINE RIGHT OF EPISCOPACY* — Cf. Note 28:8.

Conversion Chart

Bibliography

BOOKS OF THE SEVENTEENTH CENTURY AND EARLIER

Short-title catalogue numbers when available have been provided. The abbreviation "STC" refers to *A Short-Title Catalogue Of Books Printed In England, Scotland, & Ireland, And Of English Books Printed Abroad 1475-1640*, compiled by A. W. Pollard & G. R. Redgrave, *et al.* (London: Printed by The Bibliographical Society for Bernard Quaritch LTD, 1926); the abbreviation "Wing" refers to *Short-Title Catalogue Of Books Printed In England, Scotland, Ireland, Wales, And British America And Of English Books Printed In Other Countries 1641-1700*, compiled by Donald Wing (New York: Printed for The Index Society by Columbia University Press, 1945——), two of the three volumes of which have been completed.

Wing C-5607   ALMONI. A Compendious Discourse, PROVING EPISCOPACY TO BE OF APOSTOLICALL, AND CONSEQVENTLY OF DIVINE INSTITUTION. . . . By Peloni Almoni, Cosmopolites. *LONDON*, Printed by *E. G.* for *Richard Whitaker* at the Kings Armes in *Pauls* Church-yard, 1641.

STC70   THE ANSWERS OF Some BRETHREN of the Ministerie to the REPLIES of the Ministers and Professours of Divinitie in ABERDENE, CONCERNING THE LATE COVENANT. ALSO, DUPLIES OF The Ministers and Professors of ABERDENE, to the second ANSWERS of some reverend BRETHREN, CONCERNING THE LATE COVENANT. Printed by *R. Y.* His Majesties Printer for Scotland. *Anno Dom.* 1638.

Wing A-3512   AN ANTI-REMONSTRANCE, TO THE LATE HVMBLE REMONSTRANCE TO THE HIGH COVRT OF PARLIAMENT. The second Edition, enlarged. *Printed Anno* 1641.

Wing A-3548   AN APOLOGY FOR THE *English Presbyterians*, WITH A DEFENCE OF THE Heads of Agreement Assented to by the *United Ministers* in the Year 91. *London*, Printed, and are to be Sold by the Bookselle[rs] of *London* and Westminster, 1699.

Wing D-2098   AN APPEALE TO Every Impartiall, Iudicious, and Godly *READER*: WHETHER THE Presbyterie or Prelacie Be the better Church-Government, according to the Word of God; being duely compared the one with the other. *By a judicious and learned Divine. LONDON*, Printed for *Francis Coules*, and *Henry Twyford*, Anno Dom. 1641. [By Calybute Downing.]

Wing A-4078   ASTON, SIR THOMAS. A Remonstrance, AGAINST PRESBITERY. . . . By Sir THOMAS ASTON, Baronet. . . . Printed for *Iohn Aston.* 1641.

———   ATHENAEUS. ATHENAEI NAVCRATITIS, LVCVLENTISSIMI ELEGANTISSIMIQVE SCRIPTORIS, DEIPNOSOPHISTARVM libri quindecim, variis omnium ferme rerum narrationibus iucundissimi, lectúque dignissimi, quanta maxima fieri potui cura, diligentia, fide in Latinum sermonem versi à IACOBO DALECHAMPIO CADOMENSI. . . . LVGDVNI, APUD ANTONIVM DE HARSY, M. D. LXXXIII. [Lyons.]

———   AUGUSTINE, AURELIUS. OPERVM D. AVRELII AVGVSTINI HIPPONENSIS EPISCOPI, Continens ΤΆ ΠΟΛΕΜΙΚΆ, hoc est, Decertationes aduersus Haereses, praecipuè Iudaeorum, Manichaeorum, Priscillianistarum, Origenistarum, Arrianorum, & Iouiniani, nunc multis in locis summo studio emendatus. *Basileae, Ex Officina Frobeniana, Anno Salutis humanae,* M.D.LXIX. [Ten volumes.]

STC10574   THE AVNCIENT ECCLESIASTICAL HISTORIES OF THE FIRST SIX HVNDRED YEARES AFTER CHRIST, written in the Greeke tongue by three learned Historiographers, Eusebius, Socrates, and Euagrius. . . . translated by MEREDITH HANMER. . . . The third Edition. . . . *LONDON*, Printed by RICHARD FIELD, dwelling in the Blackfriers, 1607.

Wing B-319   BACON, SIR FRANCIS. RESUSCITATIO: Or Bringing [into] PUBLICK LIFE SEVERALL PIECES, OF THE WORKS, *Civil, Historical, Philosophical, & Theological,* HITHERTO SLEEPING Of the Right Honourable *FRANCIS BACON*, Baron of *Verulam*, Viscount Saint *Alban*. . . . By WILLIAM RAW-

LEY. . . . *LONDON*, Printed by *Sarah Griffin*, for *William Lee*, and are to
be sold at his Shop in *Fleetstreet*, at the sign of the Turks-head, neer the Mitre
Tavern, 1657.

Wing B-343   [BACON, SIR FRANCIS]. A Wise and Moderate Discourse, Concerning *Church-Affaires*. As it was written, long since, by the famous Authour of those Considerations, which seem to have some reference to this, *Now published for the common good*. Imprinted in the yeere 1641.

Wing B-461   [BAILLIE, ROBERT]. LADENSIVM AYTOKATÁKPIΣIS, THE CANTERBVRIANS SELF-CONVICTION: OR, An evident demonstration of the avowed *Arminianisme, Poperie, and tyrannie of that faction, by their owne confessions* . . . Printed for NATHANIEL BVTTER, 1641. [3rd edition.]

Wing B-465   BAILLIE, ROBERT. A PARALLEL *OR BRIEFE* COMPARISON OF THE *LJTURGJE* WITH THE *MASSE*-BOOK, The Breviarie, the Ceremoniall, and other Romish Ritualls. VVherein is clearly and shortly demonstrated, not onely that the LITURGIE is taken for the most part word by word out of these Antichristian Writts; but also that not one of the most abominable passages of the *Masse can in reason be refused by any who cordially imbrace the* Liturgie *as now it stands, and is commented by the Prime of our Clergie*. . . . By R. B. K. *LONDON*, Printed by *Thomas Paine*, and are to be sold at the Castle in *Cornehill*. 1641.

STC1593   [BANCROFT, RICHARD]. DAVNGEROVS POSITIONS AND PROCEE-dings, published and practised within this Iland *of Brytaine, vnder pretence of Reformation, and for the Presbiteriall Discipline*. LONDON, Imprinted by Iohn Wolfe. 1593.

STC1536   BARTHOLOMEUS. Bartholomeus de proprietatibus rerum. [Translated by J. Trevisa.] [Westminster, W. de Worde, 1495.]

STC1537   BARTHOLOMEUS. ANNO. M. D. XXXV BERTHOLOMEVS DE PROPRIETATIBVS RERVM. LONDINI IN AEDIBVS THOMAE BERTHELETI REGII IMPRESSORIS. . . .

STC1538   BATMAN, STEPHEN. BATMAN vppon Bartholome, His Booke *De Proprietatibus Rerum*, Newly corrected, enlarged and amended . . . 1582. LONDON Imprinted by Thomas East, dwel=ling by Paules wharfe.

Wing B-1257   BAXTER, RICHARD. *RICHARD BAXTER's* DYING THOUGHTS, UPON PHIL. I. xxiii. Written for his own Use in the latter Times of his Corporal Pains and Weakness. The Second Edition. *LONDON*, Printed by *H. Clark*, for *Benjamin Cox*, at the *Prince's-Arms* in *Ludgate-street*, 1688.

Wing B-1370   BAXTER, RICHARD. Reliquiae Baxterianae: OR, MR. RICHARD BAXTER's NARRATIVE OF The most Memorable Passages Of His Life and Times. Faithfully Publish'd from his own Original Manuscript, By MATTHEW SYLVESTER. *LONDON*: Printed for *T. Parkhurst*, *J. Robinson*, *J. Lawrence*, and *J. Dunton*. M DC XC VI.

————   BEZA, THEODORE. THEODORI BEZAE ANNOTATIONES MAIORES In Nouum Dn. Nostri Iesu Christi TESTAMENTVM. *In duas distinctae partes, quarum prior explicationem in quatour Euangelistas & Acta Apostolorum: Posterior verò in Epistolas & Apocalypsin continet*. . . . Anno M D XCIIII. [Geneva.]

STC16309?   THE Booke of *Common Prayer, and* administration of the Sacraments, and
(IU copy   other Rites and Ceremonies in the Church of England. Imprinted at London
is octavo)   by Christopher Barker, Printer to the Queenes Maiestie. [1583.]

STC3734   BRIDGES, JOHN. A DEFENCE OF THE GOVERNMENT ESTABLISHED IN THE CHVRCH OF ENGLANDE FOR ECCLESIASTICALL MATTERS. . . . *AT LONDON*, Printed by *Iohn VVindet*, for *Thomas Chard*. 1587.

Wing B-4911   BROOKE, ROBERT LORD. A DISCOVRSE OPENING THE NATVRE OF THAT EPISCOPACIE, WHICH IS EXERCISED IN ENGLAND. . . . LONDON, Printed by *R. C.* for *Samuel Cartwright* . . . , 1641.

Wing B-6171A   [BURTON, HENRY]. THE PROTESTATION PROTESTED; OR, A short Remonstrance, shewing what is principally required of all those that have or

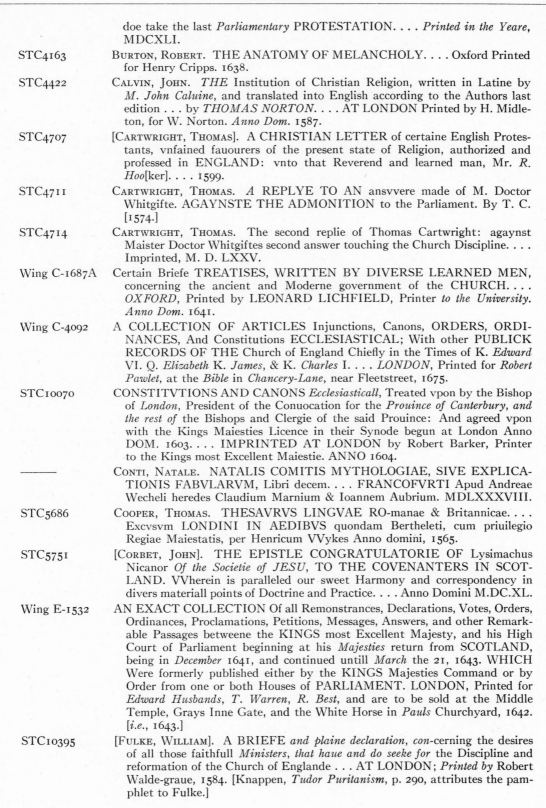

doe take the last *Parliamentary* PROTESTATION. . . . *Printed in the Yeare*, MDCXLI.

STC4163   BURTON, ROBERT. THE ANATOMY OF MELANCHOLY. . . . Oxford Printed for Henry Cripps. 1638.

STC4422   CALVIN, JOHN. *THE* Institution of Christian Religion, written in Latine by *M. John Caluine*, and translated into English according to the Authors last edition . . . by *THOMAS NORTON*. . . . AT LONDON Printed by H. Midleton, for W. Norton. *Anno Dom.* 1587.

STC4707   [CARTWRIGHT, THOMAS]. A CHRISTIAN LETTER of certaine English Protestants, vnfained fauourers of the present state of Religion, authorized and professed in ENGLAND: vnto that Reverend and learned man, Mr. *R. Hoo*[ker]. . . . 1599.

STC4711   CARTWRIGHT, THOMAS. *A* REPLYE TO AN ansvvere made of M. Doctor Whitgifte. AGAYNSTE THE ADMONITION to the Parliament. By T. C. [1574.]

STC4714   CARTWRIGHT, THOMAS. The second replie of Thomas Cartwright: agaynst Maister Doctor Whitgiftes second answer touching the Church Discipline. . . . Imprinted, M. D. LXXV.

Wing C-1687A   Certain Briefe TREATISES, WRITTEN BY DIVERSE LEARNED MEN, concerning the ancient and Moderne government of the CHURCH. . . . *OXFORD*, Printed by LEONARD LICHFIELD, Printer *to the University*. *Anno Dom.* 1641.

Wing C-4092   A COLLECTION OF ARTICLES Injunctions, Canons, ORDERS, ORDINANCES, And Constitutions ECCLESIASTICAL; With other PUBLICK RECORDS OF THE Church of England Chiefly in the Times of K. *Edward* VI. Q. *Elizabeth* K. *James*, & K. *Charles* I. . . . *LONDON*, Printed for *Robert Pawlet*, at the *Bible* in *Chancery-Lane*, near Fleetstreet, 1675.

STC10070   CONSTITVTIONS AND CANONS *Ecclesiasticall*, Treated vpon by the Bishop of *London*, President of the Conuocation for the *Prouince of Canterbury, and the rest of* the Bishops and Clergie of the said Prouince: And agreed vpon with the Kings Maiesties Licence in their Synode begun at London Anno DOM. 1603. . . . IMPRINTED AT LONDON by Robert Barker, Printer to the Kings most Excellent Maiestie. ANNO 1604.

———   CONTI, NATALE. NATALIS COMITIS MYTHOLOGIAE, SIVE EXPLICATIONIS FABVLARVM, Libri decem. . . . FRANCOFVRTI Apud Andreae Wecheli heredes Claudium Marnium & Ioannem Aubrium. MDLXXXVIII.

STC5686   COOPER, THOMAS. THESAVRVS LINGVAE RO-manae & Britannicae. . . . Excvsvm LONDINI IN AEDIBVS quondam Bertheleti, cum priuilegio Regiae Maiestatis, per Henricum VVykes Anno domini, 1565.

STC5751   [CORBET, JOHN]. THE EPISTLE CONGRATULATORIE OF Lysimachus Nicanor *Of the Societie of JESU*, TO THE COVENANTERS IN SCOTLAND. VVherein is paralleled our sweet Harmony and correspondency in divers materiall points of Doctrine and Practice. . . . Anno Domini M.DC.XL.

Wing E-1532   AN EXACT COLLECTION Of all Remonstrances, Declarations, Votes, Orders, Ordinances, Proclamations, Petitions, Messages, Answers, and other Remarkable Passages betweene the KINGS most Excellent Majesty, and his High Court of Parliament beginning at his *Majesties* return from SCOTLAND, being in *December* 1641, and continued untill *March* the 21, 1643. WHICH Were formerly published either by the KINGS Majesties Command or by Order from one or both Houses of PARLIAMENT. LONDON, Printed for *Edward Husbands*, *T. Warren*, *R. Best*, and are to be sold at the Middle Temple, Grays Inne Gate, and the White Horse in *Pauls* Churchyard, 1642. [*i.e.*, 1643.]

STC10395   [FULKE, WILLIAM]. A BRIEFE *and plaine declaration*, con-cerning the desires of all those faithfull *Ministers, that haue and do seeke for* the Discipline and reformation of the Church of Englande . . . AT LONDON; *Printed by* Robert Walde-graue, 1584. [Knappen, *Tudor Puritanism*, p. 290, attributes the pamphlet to Fulke.]

Wing F-2417   FULLER, THOMAS. THE CHURCH-HISTORY OF BRITAIN; From the Birth of JESUS CHRIST, Untill the YEAR M.DC.XLVIII. ENDEAVOURED By *THOMAS FULLER. LONDON*, Printed for IOHN WILLIAMS at the signe of the Crown in St. *Paul's* Church-yard, Anno 1656.

Wing F-2440   FULLER, THOMAS. THE HISTORY OF THE WORTHIES OF ENGLAND. Endeavoured by Thomas Fuller, D. D. LONDON, Printed by *J. G. W. L.* and *W. G.* MDCLXII.

STC12143   GOWER, JOHN. Jo. Gower de confessione Amantis. Imprinted at London in Flete-strete by Thomas Berthelette Printer to the kingis grace, AN. M.D.XXXII.

STC12144   GOWER, JOHN. Jo. Gower de confessione Amantis, Imprinted at London in Flete-strete by Thomas Berthelette the. XII. daie of Marche. AN. M.D.LIIII.

STC12142   GOWER, JOHN. tHis Book is intituled confessio amantis . . . compyled, by Johan Gower [Colophon: Emprynted at Westmestre by me Willyam Caxton and fynyesht the ii day of Septembre the fyrst yere of the regne of Kyng Richard the thyrd the yere of our Lord, a thousand,/CCCC/lxxxxiij/ (*i.e.*, 1483)].

————   GREGORY OF NYSSA, SAINT. APPENDIX AD SANCTI GREGORII EPISCOPI NYSSENI OPERA GRAECE ET LATINE, NON ITA PRIDEM EVVLGATA. Editore & partim quoque interprete IACOBO GRETSERO Societatis IESV Theologo. PARISIIS, Apud MICHAILEM SONNIVM, via Iacobaea, Sub Scuto Basiliensi. M D C XVIII.

Wing H-350   HALL, JOHN. An Humble Motion To The PARLIAMENT OF ENGLAND Concerning The ADVANCEMENT of *Learning*: And *Reformation of the* Universities. By J. H. *LONDON*, Printed for *John Walker*, at the Starre in *Popes-Head-Alley*. MDCIL.

Wing H-378   [HALL, JOSEPH]. A DEFENCE OF THE Humble Remonstrance, Against the frivolous and false exceptions of SMECTYMNVVS. *WHEREIN* The right of *Leiturgie* and *Episcopacie* is clearly vindicated from the vaine cavils, and challenges of the ANSWERERS. By the Author of the said *Humble Remonstrance. Seconded (in way of appendance) with the judgement of the famous Divine of the Palatinate, D. ABRAHAMVS SCVLTETVS*, Late Professor of DIVINITIE in the UNIVERSITIE of HEIDELBERG: Concerning the Divine Right of EPISCOPACIE, and the No-right of LAY-ELDERSHIP. *Faithfully Translated out of his Latine.* LONDON, Printed for NATHANIEL BUTTER in *Pauls* Church-yard at the pyde-Bull neare *St. Austins gate.* 1641.

STC12686   [HALL, JOSEPH]. *THE DISCOVERY of A NEW WORLD or A Description of the South Indies. Hetherto Vnknowne By an English Mercury. Imprinted for Ed: Blount and W. Barrett.* [1609.]

STC12661   HALL, JOSEPH. EPISCOPACIE BY Divine Right. ASSERTED, *BY* JOS. HALL, B. of *Exon. LONDON*, Printed by *R. B.* for *Nathanael Butter*, at the Pide-Bull by *S. Augustine's* Gate. 1640.

STC12675   [HALL, JOSEPH]. AN HUMBLE REMONSTRANCE TO THE HIGH COVRT OF PARLIAMENT, BY A dutifull Sonne of the *Church. LONDON*, Printed by *M. F.* for *Nathaniel Butter* in *Pauls* Church-yard at the pyde-Bull neare *St. Austins gate.* 1640.

STC[12682a]   HALL, JOSEPH. MEDITATIONS AND VOWES, *DIVINE* and *MORALL*; SERVING FOR DIRECTION IN Christian and ciuill practice. 3. *Centuries.* By IOS. HALL. AT LONDON Printed by *Humphrey Lownes*, for *Arthur Iohnson, Samuell Macham*, and *Lawrence Lisle*. 1614.

Wing H-393   [HALL, JOSEPH (?)]. A MODEST CONFUTATION OF A Slanderous and Scurrilous LIBELL, *ENTITVLED*, ANIMADVERSIONS VPON THE REMONSTRANTS *DEFENSE* AGAINST SMECTYMNUUS. Printed in the yeer M.DC.XLII.

STC12685   [HALL, JOSEPH]. MVNDUS ALTER ET IDEM *Siue* Terra Australis ante *hac semper incognita longis itineribus peregrini Academici nuperrime lustrata Auth:* Mercurio Britannico. FRANCOFVRTI APUD *haeredes de Rinialme* [1605.]

STC12694a   HALL, JOSEPH. THE PASSION SERMON, PREACHED AT PAVLES CROSSE on Good-Friday. *Apr.* 14. 1609. By *I. H.* LONDON Printed by *W. S.* for *Samuell Macham*, and are to be sold at his Shop in Pauls Church-Yard at the Signe of the Bull-head. ANNO. 1609.

STC12701   HALL, JOSEPH. PHARISAISME AND CHRISTIANITIE: Compared and set forth *in a Sermon at Pauls* Crosse, May 1, 1608, By *I. H.* Vpon MATTH. 5.20. . . . LONDON, Printed by *H. L.* for *Samuel Macham.* . . . ANNO 1609 [3rd edition.]

Wing H-417   [HALL, JOSEPH]. A SHORT ANSWER TO THE Tedious Vindication OF SMECTYMNVVS. BY The *AVTHOR* of the *Humble Remonstrance. LONDON*, Printed for NATHANIEL BUTTER in *Pauls* Church-yard at the pyde-Bull neare *St. Austins gate.* 1641.

Wing H-418   [HALL, JOSEPH]. A SURVAY OF THAT Foolish, Seditious, Scandalous, Prophane LIBELL, THE PROTESTATION PROTESTED. . . . LONDON, Printed in the Yeare, 1641.

STC12717   [HALL, JOSEPH]. [Virgidemiarvm, Sixe Bookes. First three bookes of Toothlesse Satyrs. London: R. Bradock for R. Dexter, 1598.]

STC12635b   HALL, JOSEPH. THE WORKS OF *JOSEPH HALL* . . . LONDON, Printed for *Nath. Butter*, dwelling neere Saint *Austins* Gate. 1625.

Wing H-1681A HEYLYN, PETER. *AERIUS REDIVIVUS*: OR, THE HISTORY OF THE Presbyterians. CONTAINING The Beginnings, Progress and Successes of that active Sect. Their Oppositions to Monarchical and Episcopal Government. Their Innovations in the Church: and, Their Imbroylments of the Kingdoms and Estates of Christendom in the pursuit of their Designes. *From the Year* 1536, *to the Year* 1647 By Peter Heylyn D. D. . . . *OXFORD*: Printed for *John Crosley*, and are to be sold in *London* by *Thomas Basset*, at the Signe of the *George* neer *Cliffords*-Inne in Fleetstreet. MDCLXX.

Wing H-1700 HEYLYN, PETER. *CYPRIANUS ANGLICUS*: OR, THE HISTORY OF THE Life and Death, OF The most Reverend and Renowned PRELATE WILLIAM By Divine Providence, Lord Archbishop of *Canterbury*, Primate of all ENGLAND, and Metropolitan. . . . By *P. Heylyn.* . . . *LONDON*, Printed by *J. M.* for *A. Seile.* . . . M DC LXXI.

STC14751   JONSON, BENJAMIN. THE WORKES OF Beniamin Jonson. . . . LONDON, *Printed by William Stanby*, An° D. 1616.

Wing J-1216 *Jus Divinum Ministerii Evangelici.* OR THE DIVINE RIGHT OF THE Gospel-Ministry. . . . *LONDON*, Printed for *G. Latham, J. Rothwell, S. Gellibrand, T. Underhill*, and *J. Cranford*, 1654.

Wing J-1218 *Jus Divinum Regiminis Ecclesiastici*: OR, THE DIVINE RIGHT OF Church-Government, Asserted and evidenced by the holy SCRIPTURES. . . . By sundry Ministers of CHRIST within the City of LONDON. . . . *London*, Printed by *J. Y.* for *Joseph Hunscot* and *George Calvert.* . . . 1647.

STC15233   LA PRIMAUDAYE, PETER DE. THE FRENCH ACADEMIE, wherin is discoursed the institution of maners, and whatso-*euer els concerneth the good and hap*-pie life of all estates and callings, by *preceptes of doctrine, and exam*-ples of the liues of ancient *Sages and famous* men: *By* PETER de la PRIMAVDAYE Esquire. . . . Imprinted at London, By Edmund Bollifant for G. *Bishop and Ralph* Newbery. 1586.

STC15238   LA PRIMAUDAYE, PETER DE. THE SECOND PART OF THE FRENCH ACADEMIE. Wherein, as it were by a naturall historie of the bodie and soule of man, the creation, *matter, composition, forme, nature, profite and vse of all* the partes of the frame of man are handled, with *the naturall causes of all affections, vertues and vices*, and chiefly the nature, powers, workes and immortalitie of the Soule. By PETER DE LA PRIMAVDAYE Esquier. . . . And translated out of the second Edition, which was reuiewed and augmented by the Author. AT LONDON Printed by G.B. R.N. R.B. *1594.*

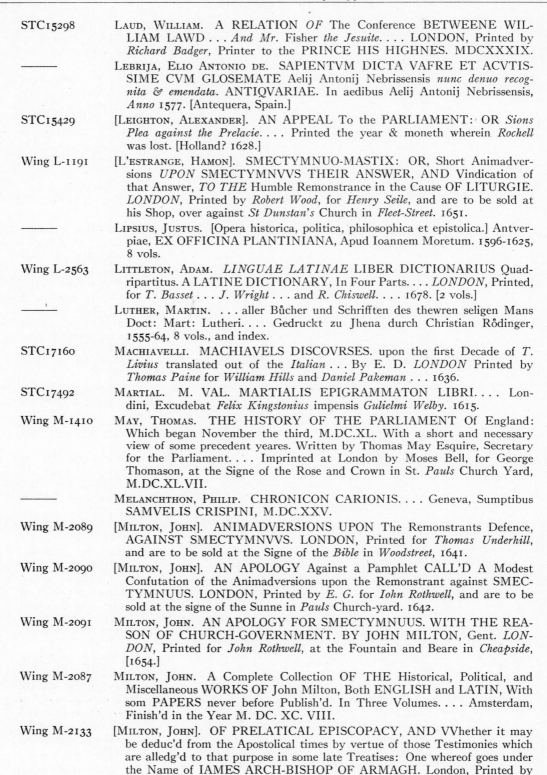

STC15298   LAUD, WILLIAM. A RELATION *OF* The Conference BETWEENE WIL-
            LIAM LAWD . . . *And Mr.* Fisher *the Jesuite.* . . . LONDON, Printed by
            Richard Badger, Printer to the PRINCE HIS HIGHNES. MDCXXXIX.

———   LEBRIJA, ELIO ANTONIO DE. SAPIENTVM DICTA VAFRE ET ACVTIS-
            SIME CVM GLOSEMATE Aelij Antonij Nebrissensis *nunc denuo recog-
            nita & emendata.* ANTIQVARIAE. In aedibus Aelij Antonij Nebrissensis,
            Anno 1577. [Antequera, Spain.]

STC15429   [LEIGHTON, ALEXANDER]. AN APPEAL To the PARLIAMENT: OR *Sions
            Plea against the Prelacie.* . . . Printed the year & moneth wherein *Rochell*
            was lost. [Holland? 1628.]

Wing L-1191 [L'ESTRANGE, HAMON]. SMECTYMNUO-MASTIX: OR, Short Animadver-
            sions *UPON* SMECTYMNVVS THEIR ANSWER, AND Vindication of
            that Answer, *TO THE* Humble Remonstrance in the Cause OF LITURGIE.
            LONDON, Printed by *Robert Wood*, for *Henry Seile*, and are to be sold at
            his Shop, over against *St Dunstan's* Church in *Fleet-Street.* 1651.

———   LIPSIUS, JUSTUS. [Opera historica, politica, philosophica et epistolica.] Antver-
            piae, EX OFFICINA PLANTINIANA, Apud Ioannem Moretum. 1596-1625,
            8 vols.

Wing L-2563 LITTLETON, ADAM. *LINGUAE LATINAE* LIBER DICTIONARIUS Quad-
            ripartitus. A LATINE DICTIONARY, In Four Parts. . . . *LONDON*, Printed,
            for *T. Basset . . . J. Wright . . .* and *R. Chiswell.* . . . 1678. [2 vols.]

———   LUTHER, MARTIN. . . . aller Bůcher und Schrifften des thewren seligen Mans
            Doct: Mart: Lutheri. . . . Gedruckt zu Jhena durch Christian Rōdinger,
            1555-64, 8 vols., and index.

STC17160   MACHIAVELLI. MACHIAVELS DISCOVRSES. upon the first Decade of *T.
            Livius* translated out of the *Italian* . . . By E. D. *LONDON* Printed by
            Thomas Paine for *William Hills* and *Daniel Pakeman* . . . 1636.

STC17492   MARTIAL. M. VAL. MARTIALIS EPIGRAMMATON LIBRI. . . . Lon-
            dini, Excudebat *Felix Kingstonius* impensis *Gulielmi Welby.* 1615.

Wing M-1410 MAY, THOMAS. THE HISTORY OF THE PARLIAMENT Of England:
            Which began November the third, M.DC.XL. With a short and necessary
            view of some precedent yeares. Written by Thomas May Esquire, Secretary
            for the Parliament. . . . Imprinted at London by Moses Bell, for George
            Thomason, at the Signe of the Rose and Crown in St. *Pauls* Church Yard,
            M.DC.XL.VII.

———   MELANCHTHON, PHILIP. CHRONICON CARIONIS. . . . Geneva, Sumptibus
            SAMVELIS CRISPINI, M.DC.XXV.

Wing M-2089 [MILTON, JOHN]. ANIMADVERSIONS UPON The Remonstrants Defence,
            AGAINST SMECTYMNVVS. LONDON, Printed for *Thomas Underhill*,
            and are to be sold at the Signe of the *Bible* in *Woodstreet*, 1641.

Wing M-2090 [MILTON, JOHN]. AN APOLOGY Against a Pamphlet CALL'D A Modest
            Confutation of the Animadversions upon the Remonstrant against SMEC-
            TYMNUUS. LONDON, Printed by *E. G.* for *Iohn Rothwell*, and are to be
            sold at the signe of the Sunne in *Pauls* Church-yard. 1642.

Wing M-2091 MILTON, JOHN. AN APOLOGY FOR SMECTYMNUUS. WITH THE REA-
            SON OF CHURCH-GOVERNMENT. BY JOHN MILTON, Gent. *LON-
            DON*, Printed for *John Rothwell*, at the Fountain and Beare in *Cheapside*,
            [1654.]

Wing M-2087 MILTON, JOHN. A Complete Collection OF THE Historical, Political, and
            Miscellaneous WORKS OF John Milton, Both ENGLISH and LATIN, With
            som PAPERS never before Publish'd. In Three Volumes. . . . Amsterdam,
            Finish'd in the Year M. DC. XC. VIII.

Wing M-2133 [MILTON, JOHN]. OF PRELATICAL EPISCOPACY, AND VVhether it may
            be deduc'd from the Apostolical times by vertue of those Testimonies which
            are alledg'd to that purpose in some late Treatises: One whereof goes under
            the Name of IAMES ARCH-BISHOP OF ARMAGH. London, Printed by

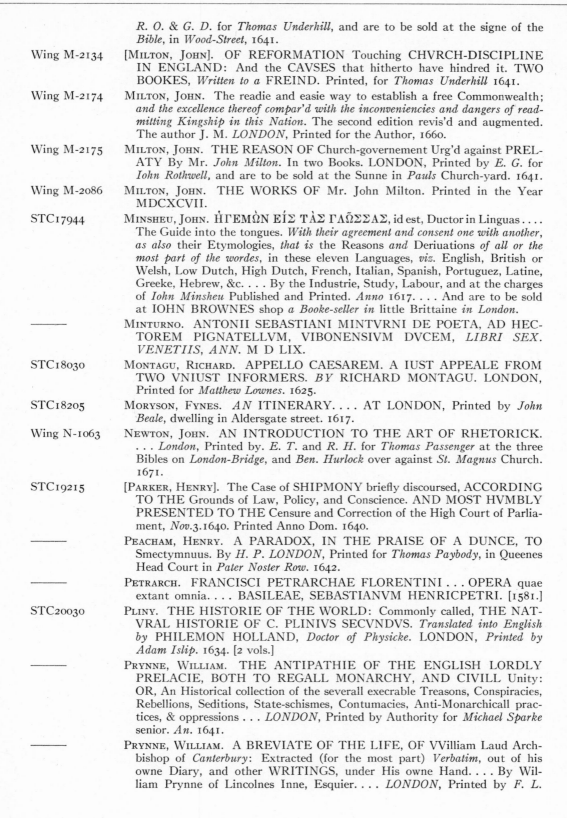

R. O. & G. D. for *Thomas Underhill*, and are to be sold at the signe of the *Bible*, in *Wood-Street*, 1641.

Wing M-2134   [MILTON, JOHN]. OF REFORMATION Touching CHVRCH-DISCIPLINE IN ENGLAND: And the CAVSES that hitherto have hindred it. TWO BOOKES, *Written to a* FREIND. Printed, for *Thomas Underhill* 1641.

Wing M-2174   MILTON, JOHN. The readie and easie way to establish a free Commonwealth; *and the excellence thereof compar'd with the inconveniencies and dangers of readmitting Kingship in this Nation.* The second edition revis'd and augmented. The author J. M. *LONDON*, Printed for the Author, 1660.

Wing M-2175   MILTON, JOHN. THE REASON OF Church-governement Urg'd against PRELATY By Mr. *John Milton.* In two Books. LONDON, Printed by *E. G.* for *Iohn Rothwell,* and are to be sold at the Sunne in *Pauls* Church-yard. 1641.

Wing M-2086   MILTON, JOHN. THE WORKS OF Mr. John Milton. Printed in the Year MDCXCVII.

STC17944   MINSHEU, JOHN. ἩΓΕΜῺΝ ΕΊΣ ΤᾺΣ ΓΛῶΣΣΑΣ, id est, Ductor in Linguas.... The Guide into the tongues. *With their agreement and consent one with another, as also* their Etymologies, *that is* the Reasons *and* Deriuations *of all or the most part of the wordes*, in these eleven Languages, *viz.* English, British or Welsh, Low Dutch, High Dutch, French, Italian, Spanish, Portuguez, Latine, Greeke, Hebrew, &c. . . . By the Industrie, Study, Labour, and at the charges of *Iohn Minsheu* Published and Printed. *Anno* 1617. . . . And are to be sold at IOHN BROWNES shop *a Booke-seller in* little Brittaine *in London.*

———   MINTURNO. ANTONII SEBASTIANI MINTVRNI DE POETA, AD HECTOREM PIGNATELLVM, VIBONENSIVM DVCEM, *LIBRI SEX. VENETIIS, ANN.* M D LIX.

STC18030   MONTAGU, RICHARD. APPELLO CAESAREM. A IUST APPEALE FROM TWO VNIUST INFORMERS. *BY* RICHARD MONTAGU. LONDON, Printed for *Matthew Lownes.* 1625.

STC18205   MORYSON, FYNES. *AN* ITINERARY. . . . AT LONDON, Printed by *John Beale,* dwelling in Aldersgate street. 1617.

Wing N-1063   NEWTON, JOHN. AN INTRODUCTION TO THE ART OF RHETORICK. . . . *London,* Printed by. *E. T.* and *R. H.* for *Thomas Passenger* at the three Bibles on *London-Bridge,* and *Ben. Hurlock* over against *St. Magnus* Church. 1671.

STC19215   [PARKER, HENRY]. The Case of SHIPMONY briefly discoursed, ACCORDING TO THE Grounds of Law, Policy, and Conscience. AND MOST HVMBLY PRESENTED TO THE Censure and Correction of the High Court of Parliament, *Nov.*3.1640. Printed Anno Dom. 1640.

———   PEACHAM, HENRY. A PARADOX, IN THE PRAISE OF A DUNCE, TO Smectymnuus. By *H. P. LONDON,* Printed for *Thomas Paybody,* in Queenes Head Court in *Pater Noster Row.* 1642.

———   PETRARCH. FRANCISCI PETRARCHAE FLORENTINI . . . OPERA quae extant omnia. . . . BASILEAE, SEBASTIANVM HENRICPETRI. [1581.]

STC20030   PLINY. THE HISTORIE OF THE WORLD: Commonly called, THE NATVRAL HISTORIE OF C. PLINIVS SECVNDVS. *Translated into English by* PHILEMON HOLLAND, *Doctor of Physicke.* LONDON, *Printed by Adam Islip.* 1634. [2 vols.]

———   PRYNNE, WILLIAM. THE ANTIPATHIE OF THE ENGLISH LORDLY PRELACIE, BOTH TO REGALL MONARCHY, AND CIVILL Unity: OR, An Historical collection of the severall execrable Treasons, Conspiracies, Rebellions, Seditions, State-schismes, Contumacies, Anti-Monarchicall practices, & oppressions . . . *LONDON,* Printed by Authority for *Michael Sparke* senior. *An.* 1641.

———   PRYNNE, WILLIAM. A BREVIATE OF THE LIFE, OF VVilliam Laud Archbishop of *Canterbury*: Extracted (for the most part) *Verbatim,* out of his owne Diary, and other WRITINGS, under His owne Hand. . . . By William Prynne of Lincolnes Inne, Esquier. . . . *LONDON,* Printed by *F. L.*

for *Michaell Sparke* Senior, and are to bee sold at the Blew-Bible in *Green-Arbour*. 1644.

STC20454   [PRYNNE, WILLIAM]. A Breviate of the Prelates intolerable usurpations, both upon the Kings Prerogative Royall, and the Subjects Liberties. . . . Published by W. HUNTLEY, Esquier. Edition 3. much enlarged. In the Yeare 1637.

STC20455   PRYNNE, WILLIAM. A BRIEFE SVRVAY AND CENSVRE OF Mr COZENS His Couzening *Deuotions*. . . . Printed at *London*. 1628.

STC20469   [PRYNNE, WILLIAM]. *Newes from* Ipswich. Discovering certaine late detestable practises of some domineering Lordly Prelates, to undermine the established doctrine and discipline of our Church, extirpate all Orthodox sincere Preachers and preaching of Gods Word, usher in Popery, Superstition and Idolatry. . . . Printed at Ipswich, An. 1636.

————   [PRYNNE, WILLIAM]. ROMES MASTER-PEECE. *OR*, The Grand Conspiracy of the Pope and his Iesuited Instruments, to extirpate the Protestant Religion. . . . Printed at London for *Michael Sparke, Senior*. 1643.

————   PRYNNE, WILLIAM. THE SOVERAIGNE POWER OF *PARLIAMENTS* and *KINGDOMES*. . . . Printed at *London* for *Michael Sparke* Senior. 1643.

————   THE REASONS Presented by the Dissenting Brethren *AGAINST CERTAIN* PROPOSITIONS CONCERNING Presbyteriall GOVERNMENT. And the PROOFS of them Voted by the *Assembly of Divines*, sitting by authority of PARLIAMENT, at *Westminster*. Together with the ANSWER of the *Assembly of Divines* to those REASONS of Dissent. *LONDON*, Printed by *T. R.* and *E. M.* for *Humphrey Harward*. . . . 1648.

————   RICCIUS, STEPHANUS. *IN P. TERENTII COMOEDIAS SEX* NOVVIS COMMENTARIVS, Ex publicis praele-CTIONIBVS DOCTISSIMORVM VIRORVM, QVI OLIM IN CELEBERRIMA Academia VVitebergensi floruerunt, In vsum scholasticae Iuuentutis magno studio & labore collectus. Et nunc primum aeditus A M. STEPHANO RICCIO. TOMVS PRIMVS Continet argumenta, Grammaticas annotationes, & scholia textus in Andriam & Eunuchum. Cum Gratiat Priuilegio Illustriss. Electoris Saxoniae ad Decennium. M.D.LXVI. [Leipzig, 2 vols., Vol. II dated 1582.]

————   RUSHWORTH, JOHN. Historical Collections. The Second Part, Containing the PRINCIPLE MATTERS Which happened from the Dissolution of the PARLIAMENT, On the 10*th of March*, 4. *Car.* I 1628/9. Until the Summoning of another *Parliament*, which met at *Westminster*, *April* 13. 1640. With an Account of the Proceedings of *That* PARLIAMENT; and the Transactions and Affairs from That Time, until the meeting of another *PARLIAMENT*, *November* the 3*d* following. With some Remarkable Passages therein during the first Six Months. . . . *LONDON*, Printed by *J. D.* for *John Wright* at the Crown on *Ludgate-Hill*, and *Richard Chiswell* at the Rose and Crown in St. *Paul's* Church-yard, 1680.

————   RUSHWORTH, JOHN. Historical Collections. The Third Part; in Two Volumes. Containing the PRINCIPLE MATTERS Which happened from the MEETING of the PARLIAMENT, *November* the 3d. 1640. To the End of the YEAR 1644. . . . *LONDON*: Printed for *Richard Chiswell* and *Thomas Cockerill*, at the Rose and Crown in St. *Paul*'s Church-yard, and at the Three Legs over-against the *Stocks-Market*. M DC XC II.

————   SALTMARSH, JOHN. GROANES FOR LIBERTY. *PRESENTED* From the Presbyterian (formerly Non-conforming) Brethren, reputed the ablest and most learned among them, in some Treatises called Smectymnuus, to the high and Honorable Court of Parliament in the yeare 1641, by reason of the Prelates Tyranny. Now awakened and presented to themselves in the behalf of their now Non-conforming Brethren. WITH A BEAM of LIGHT, discovering a way to peace. ALSO *SOME QUAERES*. . . . By IOHN SALTMARSH. . . . London, Printed for *Giles Calvert*, at the black spread-Eagle at the West end of *Pauls*. 1646.

——— SCALIGER. IVLII CAESARIS SCALIGERI VIRI CLARISSIMI Poetices libri septem . . . Editio Secvnda, Apud Petrum Santandreanum, 1581. [Heidelberg.]

——— SCOT, REGINALD. SCOT'S Discovery of VVitchcraft . . . all written and published in *Anno* 1584. by *Reginald Scot*, Esquire. *Printed by R. C. and are to be sold by* Giles Calvert, *dwelling at the Black Spread-Eagle at the West-end of* Pauls, 1651.

——— SLEIDAN, JOHN. IOANNIS SLEIDANI COMMENTARIORVM DE STATV RELIGIO-nis & Reipublicae, Carolo Quinto Caesare, Libri XXVI, ARGENTORATI Excudebat Theodosius Rihelius. [Strasbourg, 1559?]

STC19848 SLEIDAN, JOHN. A Famovse Cronicle of oure time, called Sleidanes Commentaries, concerning *the state of Religion and common wealth, during the raigne of the Emperour Charles the fift.* . . . *Translated out of Latin into Englishe, by Ihon Daus.* . . . [Colophon: Imprinted at London by Ihon Daye for Abraham Ueale, and Nicholas England. 1560.]

Wing M-748A SMECTYMNUUS. AN ANSWER TO A BOOK ENTITVLED, AN HUMBLE REMONSTRANCE. *In which*, The Originall of LITURGY [and] EPISCOPACY is discussed. . . . Written by SMECTYMNVVS. Printed in the yeare 1641.

Wing M-748 SMECTYMNUUS. AN ANSWER TO A BOOKE ENTITVLED, AN HVMBLE REMONSTRANCE. *In which*, The Originall of LITURGY [and] EPISCOPACY is discussed. . . . Written by SMECTYMNVVS. *LONDON*, Printed for *I. Rothwell*, and are to be sold by *T. N.* at the Bible in Popes-Head-Alley. 1641.

Wing M-784 SMECTYMNUUS. SMECTYMNUUS REDIVIVUS. BEING An Answer to a Book, entituled, AN HUMBLE REMONSTRANCE. In which, The Originall of LITURGY [and] EPISCOPACY is discussed. . . . LONDON, Printed by *T. C.* for *John Rothwell*, at the Fountaine and Beare in *Goldsmiths-row* in *Cheapside*. 1654.

Wing M-785 SMECTYMNUUS. Smectymnuus Redivivus. Being an Answer to a Book, entituled *AN HUMBLE* REMONSTRANCE. *In which*, The Original of LITURGY [and] EPISCOPACY is discussed. . . . *Composed by five Learned and Orthodox Divines.* LONDON, Printed for *John Rothwell*, at the *Fountain* in *Goldsmiths-Row* in *Cheapside*. And now republished, 1660.

Wing M-786 SMECTYMNUUS. Smectymnuus REDIVIVUS. Being an Answer to a Book, entituled *AN HUMBLE* REMONSTRANCE. *In which The Original of* LITURGY [and] EPISCOPACY is discussed. . . . *Composed by five Learned and Orthodox Divines.* . . . LONDON, Printed for *John Rothwell*, at the *Fountain* in *Goldsmiths Row* in *Cheapside*, [space] 1660.

Wing M-798A SMECTYMNUUS. A VINDICATION OF THE ANSVVER TO THE HVMBLE REMONSTRANCE, FROM THE VNIVST IMPVTATIONS OF FRIVOLOVSNESSE AND FALSEHOOD: *Wherein* The cause of *Liturgy* and *Episcopacy* is further debated, BY THE SAME *SMECTYMNVVS.* Printed in the yeare 1641.

Wing M-798 SMECTYMNUUS. A VINDICATION OF THE ANSWER TO THE HUMBLE REMONSTRANCE FROM THE UNJUST IMPUTATION OF FRIVOLOUSNESSE AND FALSHOOD. *Wherein*, The cause of LITURGY and EPISCOPACY is further debated. By the same SMECTYMNUUS. *LONDON*, Printed for *John Rothwell* at the Fountaine and Beare in *Cheapside*. [1654?]

STC22867 SMITH, THOMAS. THE COMMONWEALTH OF *ENGLAND.* . . . LONDON, Printed by *R. Young* for *J. Smethwicke*, and are to be sold at his shop in *S. Dunstans Church-yard*. 1640.

STC23345 STOW, JOHN. THE SURVEY OF LONDON: Contayning The Originall, Increase, Moderne Estate, and Government of that City, Methodically set downe. . . . Begunne first by the paines and industry of IOHN STOVV, in the yeere 1598. . . . LONDON, Printed by ELIZABETH PVRSLOVV, and are to be sold by NICHOLAS BOVRNE, at his Shop at the South Entrance of the ROYALL EXCHANGE. 1633.

STC24124   TOPSELL, EDWARD. THE HISTORY OF SERPENTS. . . . LONDON, *Printed
               by William Jaggard*, 1608.

————   USSHER, JAMES. THE IUDGEMENT OF Doctor RAINOLDES touching
               the Originall of EPISCOPACY. More largely confirmed out of *Antiquity* By
               IAMES Archbishop of *ARMAGH. LONDON*, Printed by *G. M.* for THOMAS
               DOVVNES, and are to be sold by *William Lee* at the Turkes head in *Fleet-
               street*. 1641.

STC25801   WILSON, THOMAS. The Arte of *Rhetorique*, for the use of all soche as are studious
               of Eloquence, set forth in Englishe, by THOMAS Wilson. 1553. And now
               newlie sette foorthe againe, with a Prologue to the Reader. Anno Dñi. 1562.
               Imprinted at London, by Ihon Kingston.

STC26115   [YOUNG, THOMAS]. DIES DOMINICA, *SIVE* Succincta narratio ex S. Scrip-
               turarum, & venerandae antiquitatis Patrum testimoniis concinnata. . . .
               ANNO 1639.

————   [YOUNG, THOMAS]. THE Lords-Day. OR, A SUCCINCT NARRATION
               Compiled Out of the Testimonies of H. SCRIPTURE, and the Reverend
               FATHERS. . . . *London*, Printed by *E Leach*, and are to be sold by *Nevil
               Symmons*, at the Princes Arms in St. *Pauls Church-yard*. 1672.

LATER BOOKS

AGAR, HERBERT. *Milton and Plato*. Princeton: Princeton University Press, 1928

AIRY, OSMOND, and C. A. BRIGGS. "Presbyterianism" [England], *The Encyclopedia Britannica*,
    9th edition. New York: The Henry G. Allen Company, 1890, 24 vols. and index, vol. XIX.

ALDINGTON, RICHARD. *A Book of 'Characters'*. London: George Routledge & Sons Ltd, [1924].

ARISTOTLE. *Rhetorica Ad Alexandrum, With An English Translation By H. Rackham*. "The Loeb
    Classical Library"; London: William Heinemann Ltd, 1937.

ATHENAEUS. *The Deipnosophists*. Literally translated by C. D. Yonge. "Bohn Classical Library";
    London: Henry G. Bohn, 1854, 3 vols.

ATHENAEUS. *The Deipnosophists, With An English Translation By Charles Burton Gulick*. "The
    Loeb Classical Library"; London: William Heinemann Ltd, 1927-41, 7 vols.

AUGUSTINE, AURELIUS. *The Works of Aurelius Augustine, Bishop of Hippo*. Translated by the
    Rev. Marcus Dods. Edinburgh: T & T Clark, 1872-76, 15 vols.

BAILLIE, ROBERT. *The Letters and Journals of Robert Baillie, A. M. Principle of the University
    of Glasgow M.DC.XXXVII.-M.DC.LXII.* Edited by David Laing. Edinburgh: The Ban-
    natyne Club, 1841-42, 3 vols.

BALDWIN, THOMAS WHITFIELD. *William Shakspere's Small Latine & Lesse Greeke*. Urbana:
    University of Illinois Press, 1944, 2 vols.

BARKER, ARTHUR. *Milton and the Puritan Dilemma*, 1641-1660. Toronto: The University of
    Toronto Press, 1942.

BELLOC, HILLAIRE. *Milton*. Philadelphia: J. B. Lippincott Company, 1935.

BENHAM, WILLIAM (ed.). *The Prayer-Book of Queen Elizabeth 1559*. Edinburgh: John Grant, 1911.

BLUNT, JOHN HENRY. *The Reformation of the Church of England*. London: Longmans, Green,
    and Co., 1896-97, 2 vols.

BOSWELL, JAMES. *Boswell's Life of Johnson*. Edited by George Birkbeck Hill; revised by L. F.
    Powell. Oxford: Clarendon Press, 1934, 6 vols., vols. 1-4 published.

BRAND, JOHN. *Observations on the Popular Antiquities of Great Britain*. Arranged, revised, and
    enlarged by Sir Henry Ellis. London: George Bell and Sons, 1888-95, 3 vols.

BROOKE, STOPFORD A. *Milton*. London: Macmillan and Co., 1916.

BRUNET, JACQUES-CHARLES. *Manuel Du Librairie*. Paris: Librairie de Firmin Didot Frères,
    Fils et Cie, 1860-80, 6 vols. and 2 supplements.

BURKE, SIR BERNARD. *The Book of Orders of Knighthood*. London: Hurst and Blackett, 1858.

BURNET, JOHN. *Early Greek Philosophy*. London and Edinburgh: David and Charles Black, 1892.

BURRAGE, CHAMPLIN. *The Early English Dissenters in the Light of Recent Research (1550-1641)*.
    Cambridge: University Press, 1912, 2 vols.

CARPENTER, WILLIAM. *The Life and Times of John Milton*. London: Wakelin, 1836.

CARTER, EDMUND. *The History of the University of Cambridge From its Original To the Year 1753*. London, Printed for the Author, 1753.

CASTIGLIONE, BALDASARE. *The Book of the Courtier*. Translated by Sir Thomas Hoby "Everyman's Library"; London: J. M. Dent & Sons Ltd, 1928.

Catalogue of the McAlpin Collection of British History and Theology. Compiled and edited by Charles Ripley Gillett. New York: Published by the Union Theology Seminary, 1927-30, 5 vols.

Catalogve of Original and Early Editions of some of the Poetical and Prose Works of English Writers from Wither to Prior. New York: Grolier Club, 1905, 3 vols.

Catalogue of the Pamphlets, Books, Newspapers, and Manuscripts relating to the civil war, the Commonwealth, and Restoration, collected by George Thomason, 1640-1661. London: Printed by order of the Trustees, 1908, 2 vols.

CAWLEY, R. R. *Milton's Literary Craftsmanship*. Princeton: Princeton University Press, 1941.

CHAMBERS, ROBERT. *The Book of Days*. London and Edinburgh: W. & R. Chambers, Ltd, 1914, 2 vols.

[CHANNING, WILLIAM ELLERY]. *Remarks on the Character and Writings of John Milton; occasioned by the Publication of His Lately Discovered 'Treatise on Christian Doctrine,' From the Christian Examiner, Vol. III, No. 1*. Boston: Isaac R. Butts and Co., 1826.

CHAUVET, PAUL. *La Religion de Milton*. Paris: H. Didier, 1909.

CHURCHILL, W. A. *Watermarks in Paper in Holland, England, France, etc., in the XVII and XVIII Centuries and their interconnection*. Amsterdam: Menno Hertzberger & Co., 1935.

CLARENDON, EDWARD [HYDE] Earl of. *The History of The Rebellion and Civil Wars in England*. Oxford: University Press, 1839.

CLARK, DONALD LEMEN. *John Milton at St. Paul's School, A Study of Ancient Rhetoric in English Renaissance Education*. New York: Columbia University Press, 1948.

COFFIN, ROBERT P. TRISTRAM. *Laud*. New York: Brentano's, 1930.

COLERIDGE, SAMUEL TAYLOR. *The Complete Works of Samuel Taylor Coleridge*. Edited by William Greenough Thayer Shedd. New York: Harper and Brothers, 1884, 7 vols.

CORSON, HIRAM. *An Introduction to the Prose and Poetical Works of John Milton*. New York: The Macmillan Company, 1899.

DALE, R. W. *History of English Congregationalism*. New York: A. C. Armstrong and Son; London: Hodder and Stoughton, 1907.

DARBISHIRE, HELEN (ed.). *The Early Lives of Milton*. London: Constable & Co. Ltd, 1932.

DAVIES, GODFREY. *The Early Stuarts 1603-1660*. Oxford: Clarendon Press, 1937.

DEMOSTHENES. *The Crown, The Philippics and ten other Orations of Demosthenes*. Translated by C. Rann-Kennedy. "Everyman's Library"; London: J. M. Dent & Sons Ltd, [1911].

D'EWES, SIR SYMONDS. *The Autobiography and Correspondence of Sir Simonds D'Ewes*. Edited by James Orchard Halliwell. London: Richard Bentley, 1845, 2 vols.

———. *College Life in the Time of James the First, as illustrated by an Unpublished Diary*. London: John W. Parker & Son, 1851.

———. *The Journal of Sir Simonds D'Ewes from the beginning of the Long Parliament to the opening of the trial of the Earl of Strafford*. Edited by Wallace Notestein. New Haven: Yale University Press, 1923.

———. *The Journal of Sir Simonds D'Ewes From the First Recess of the Long Parliament to the Withdrawal of King Charles from London*. Edited by Willson Havelock Coates. New Haven: Yale University Press, 1942.

DEXTER, HENRY MARTYN. *The Congregationalism of the Last Three Hundred Years, As Seen in its Literature*. New York: Harper & Brothers, 1880.

The Dictionary of National Biography. Edited by Sir Leslie Stephen and Sir Sidney Lee. Oxford: University Press, 1937-38 reprint, 25 vols. and index.

DIEKHOFF, JOHN S. *Milton on Himself. Milton's Utterances upon himself and his works*. New York: Oxford University Press, 1939.

DIETZ, FREDERICK C. *A Political and Social History of England*. New York: The Macmillan Company, 1935.

DIOGENES LAËRTIUS. *The Lives and Opinions of Eminent Philosophers*. Translated by C. D. Yonge. "Bohn Classical Library"; London: George Bell and Sons, 1909.

DODD, HUGH TOOTEL. *Dodd's Church History of England From the Commencement of the Sixteenth Century to the Revolution in 1688*. With notes, additions, and a continuation by the Rev. M. A. Tierney. London: Charles Dolman, 1839-43, 5 vols.

DOWDEN, EDWARD. *Puritan and Anglican: Studies in Literature*. London: Kegan Paul, Trench, Trübner & Co., Ltd, 1901.

DRYSDALE, A. H. *History of the Presbyterians in England*. London: Publication Committee of the Presbyterian Church of England, 1889.

DUFF, J. WIGHT. *Roman Satire*. Berkeley: University of California Press, 1936.

DUNNING, WILLIAM ARCHIBALD. *A History of Political Theories from Luther to Montesquieu*. New York: The Macmillan Company, 1916.

DYER, T. F. THISELTON. *British Popular Customs Present and Past*. London: G. Bell and Sons, Limited, 1911.

EDMONDS, CYRUS R. *John Milton: A Biography Especially Designed to Exhibit the Ecclesiastical Principles of that Illustrious Man*. London: Albert Cockshaw, 1851.

ERNESTI, IO. CHRIST. THEOPH. *Lexicon Technologiae Graecorvm Rhetorica*. Lipsiae: Caspari Fritsch, 1795.

FINK, ZERA S. *Classical Republicans*. Evanston: Northwestern University, 1945.

FLEMING, WILLIAM. *The Vocabulary of Philosophy, Mental, Moral, and Metaphysical*. Philadelphia: Smith, English & Co., 1860.

FLETCHER, HARRIS FRANCIS. *Milton's Rabbinical Readings*. Urbana: University of Illinois Press, 1930.

——. *Milton's Semitic Studies*. Chicago: University of Chicago Press, 1926.

FLETCHER, JOSEPH. *The History of the Revival and Progress of Independency in England, since the Period of the Reformation*. London: John Snow, 1847-49, 4 vols.

FÖRSTEMANN, KARL EDUARD. *D. Martin Luther's Tischreden oder Colloquia*. Leipzig: E. Schimmel, 1844-46.

FOSTER, JOSEPH. *Alumni Oxonienses: The Members of the University of Oxford, 1500-1714*. Oxford: James Parker & Co., 1891, 4 vols.

FOXE, JOHN. *The Acts and Monuments of John Foxe, with a Preliminary Dissertation by the Rev. George Townsend*. Edited by the Rev. Stephen Reed Cattley. London: R. B. Seeley and W. Burnside, 1837-41, 8 vols

FRY, ALFRED A. *A Lecture on the Writings, Prose and Poetic and the Character, Public and Personal of John Milton*. London: Henry Hooper, 1838.

FULLER, THOMAS. *The History of the University of Cambridge from the Conquest to the year 1634*. Edited by the Rev. Marmaduke Prickett and Thomas Wright. Cambridge: University Press, 1840.

GARDINER, SAMUEL RAWSON. *The Constitutional Documents of the Puritan Revolution, 1625-1660*. Oxford: Clarendon Press, 1906.

——. *History of England From the Accession of James I. To The Outbreak of the Civil War 1603-1642*. London: Longmans, Green, and Co., 1894-1900, 10 vols.

GARNETT, RICHARD. *Life of John Milton*. London: Walter Scott, 1890.

GARRETT, CHRISTINA H. *The Marian Exiles 1553-1559: A Study of the Origins of Elizabethan Puritanism*. Cambridge: University Press, 1938.

GEFFROY, AUGUSTE. *Étude sur les pamphlets politiques et religieux de Milton*. Paris, 1848.

GILBERT, ALLAN H. *Literary Criticism, Plato to Dryden*. New York: American Book Company, 1940.

GOWER, JOHN. *The Complete Works of John Gower*. Edited by G. C. Macaulay. Oxford: Clarendon Press, 1899-1902, 4 vols.

GRAESSE, JEAN GEORGE THÉODORE. *Trésor de Livres Rares et Precieux*. Paris: H. Welter, éditeur, 1859-1900, 7 vols. and supplement.

GRIERSON, SIR HERBERT J. C. *Milton and Wordsworth*. New York: The Macmillan Company, 1937.

GRISAR, HARTMAN. *Luther*. Translated by E. M. Lamond; edited by Luigi Cappadelta. St. Louis: B. Herder, 1914-17, 6 vols.

GUERLE, EDMOND DE. *Milton: sa vie et ses oeuvres*. Paris, 1868.

HALL, EDWIN. *The Puritans and Their Principles*. New York: Baker and Scribner, 1846.

HALL, JOSEPH. *The Complete Poems of Joseph Hall, D. D.* "Occasional Issues of Unique or Very Rare Books," edited by the Rev. Alexander B. Grosart, vol. VIII; Printed For The Subscribers, 1879.

———. *The Works of Joseph Hall, D. D.* Oxford: D. A. Talboys, 1837-39, 12 vols.

HALLAM, HENRY. *The Constitutional History of England From the Accession of Henry VII. To The Death Of George II.* New York: W. J. Widdleton, 1865, 3 vols.

HALLER, WILLIAM. *The Rise of Puritanism Or, The way to the New Jerusalem as set forth in pulpit and press from Thomas Cartwright to John Lilburne and John Milton, 1570-1643.* New York: Morningside Heights, Columbia University Press, 1934.

———. *Tracts On Liberty in the Puritan Revolution, 1638-1647.* Edited, with a commentary, by William Haller. New York: Columbia University Press, 1934.

HANFORD, JAMES HOLLY. *A Milton Handbook*. 4th edition. New York: F. S. Crofts & Co., 1946.

———. "The Youth of Milton," in *Studies in Shakespeare, Milton and Donne by Members of the English Department of the University of Michigan.* New York: The Macmillan Company, 1925, pp. 87-163.

HARDELAND, GERTRUD. *Miltons Anschauungen von Staat, Kirche, und Toleranz.* Halle (Saale): Niemeyer, 1934.

HARTWELL, KATHLEEN E. *Milton and Lactantius*. Cambridge, Mass : Harvard University Press, 1929.

HAYLEY, WILLIAM. *The Life of Milton*. London: T. Cadell, Jr. and W. Davies, 1796.

HAZLITT, W. CAREW. *Faiths and Folklore*. London: Reeves and Turner, 1905, 2 vols.

HILL, CHRISTOPHER. *The English Revolution, 1640.* London: Lawrence & Wishart Ltd, 1940.

Holinshed's Chronicles of England, Scotland, and Ireland. London: Printed for J. Johnson, etc., 1807-08, 6 vols.

HONE, WILLIAM. *The Every-Day Book; or, Everlasting Calendar of Popular Amusements.* London: Published for William Hone, 1826-27, 2 vols.

HOOD, EDWIN PAXTON. *John Milton: The Patriot and Poet.* London: Partridge & Oakey, 1852.

HUME, DAVID. *The History of England from The Invasion of Julius Caesar To The Abdication of James The Second, 1688.* Boston: Crosby, Nichols, Lee and Company, 1861, 6 vols.

HUTTON, WILLIAM HOLDEN. *The English Church From the Accession of Charles I. To the Death of Anne. (1625-1714).* London: Macmillan and Co., 1903.

IVIMEY, JOSEPH. *John Milton: His Life and Times, Religious and Political Opinions.* New York: D. Appleton & Co., 1833.

JACKSON, SIR T. G. *The Church of St. Mary the Virgin Oxford.* Oxford: Clarendon Press, 1897.

JOHNSON, JOHN. *Typographia Or The Printer's Instructor.* London: Longman, Hurst, Rees, Orme, Brown & Green, [1824].

JOHNSON, SAMUEL. *Lives of the English Poets*. Edited by George Birkbeck Hill. Oxford: Clarendon Press, 1905, 3 vols.

———. *Works of Samuel Johnson.* London: William Pickering, 1825, 11 vols.

JONES, I. DEANE. *The English Revolution, An Introduction to English History, 1603-1714.* London: William Heinemann, Ltd, 1931.

JORTIN, JOHN. *The Life of Erasmus.* London: Printed by Richard Taylor and Co., 1808, 3 vols.

KEIGHTLEY, THOMAS. *An Account of the Life, Opinions, and Writings of John Milton.* London: Chapman and Hall, 1855.

KELLETT, E. E. *Suggestions. Literary Essays.* Cambridge: University Press, 1923.

KNAPPEN, M. M. *Tudor Puritanism*. Chicago: University of Chicago Press, 1939.

KNIGHT, G. WILSON. *The Burning Oracle*. London: Oxford University Press, 1939.

———. *Chariot of Wrath: The Message of John Milton to Democracy at War.* London: Faber and Faber, 1942.

KNOX, JOHN. *The Works of John Knox.* Edited by David Laing. Edinburgh: The Bannatyne Club, 1846-64, 6 vols.

[LAING, DAVID]. *Biographical Notices Of Thomas Young, S.T.D. Vicar of Stowmarket, Suffolk. By The Editor Of Principal Baillie's "Letters And Journals."* Edinburgh, 1870.

LANGDON, IDA. *Milton's Theory of Poetry and Fine Art.* New Haven: Yale University Press, 1924.

LARSON, MARTIN A. *The Modernity of Milton: A Theological and Philosophical Interpretation.* Chicago: The University of Chicago Press, 1927.

LAUD, WILLIAM. *The Works of the Most Reverend Father in God, William Laud, D. D.* "Library of Anglo-Catholic Theology," vols. 56-64; Oxford: John Henry Parker, 1847-60, 7 vols.

LAWRENCE-ARCHER, J. H. *The Orders of Chivalry.* London: W. H. Allen and Co., 1887.

LEWIS, C. S. *A Preface to Paradise Lost.* London: Oxford University Press, 1942.

LEWIS, GEORGE. *A Life of Joseph Hall, D. D., Bishop of Exeter and Norwich.* London: Hodder and Stoughton, 1886.

LILJEGREN, S. B. *Studies in Milton.* Lund: C. W. D. Glurup, 1918.

LONGINUS, CASSIUS. *Longinus On the Sublime: the Greek text edited after the Paris manuscript with introduction, translation, facsimiles and appendices, by W. Rhys Roberts.* Cambridge: University Press, 1899.

LOOTEN, CHANOINE. *John Milton. Quelques aspects de son genie.* Lille: Desclée De Brouwer, 1938.

LOWTHER CLARKE, W. K. (ed.). *Liturgy and Worship.* London: Society for promoting Christian Knowledge, 1932.

LUTHER, MARTIN. "Colloquia oder Tischreden," in vols. 22-23 of *Dr. Martin Luthers Sammtliche Schriften.* Herausgegeben von Dr. Joh. Georg Walch. St. Louis: Concordia Publishing House, 1881-1910, 23 vols.

———. *D. Martin Luthers Werke . . . Briefwechsel.* Weimar: Hermann Böhlaus Nachfolger, 1930-38, 8 vols.

———. *D. Martin Luthers Werke . . . Tischreden.* Weimar: Hermann Böhlaus Nachfolger, 1912-21, 6 vols.

LYON, T. *The Theory of Religious Liberty in England 1603-39.* Cambridge: University Press, 1937.

MACAULAY, ROSE. *Milton.* New York and London: Harper & Brothers, 1935.

MAGIRI, JOANNIS. *Aristotelis Ethica Nicomachea Commentationes.* Edited by Ricardus Walker. Oxonii: J. Vincent, 1842.

MALLETT, CHARLES E. *A History of the University of Oxford.* New York: Longmans, Green and Co., 1924, 2 vols.

MANGAN, JOHN JOSEPH. *Life, Character, and Influence of Desiderius Erasmus of Rotterdam.* New York: The Macmillan Company, 1927.

MARRIOTT, JOHN A. R. *The Crisis of English Liberty: A History of the Stuart Monarchy and the Puritan Revolution.* Oxford: Clarendon Press, 1930.

MARSDEN, J. B. *The History of The Early Puritans: From the Reformation To the Opening of the Civil War in 1642.* London: Hamilton, Adams & Co. 1850.

MARTIAL. *Martial Epigrams, With An English Translation By Walter C. A. Ker.* "The Loeb Classical Library"; London: William Heinemann Ltd, 1925, 2 vols.

MARTYN, W. CARLOS. *Life and Times of John Milton.* New York: American Tract Society, 1866.

MASSON, DAVID. *The Life of John Milton: narrated in connexion with the political, ecclesiastical, and literary History of his time.* London and New York: Macmillan and Co., 1859-96, 6 vols. and index. Vol. I revised 1881.

MASTERMANN, J. H. B. *The Age of Milton.* London: George Bell and Sons, 1906.

McCOLLEY, GRANT. *Paradise Lost, An Account of its Growth and Major Origins.* Chicago: Packard and Company, 1940.

McDILL, JOSEPH MOODY. *Milton and the Pattern of Calvinism.* Ph.D. dissertation in English, Vanderbilt University, 1938. Nashville, Tennessee, 1942.

McKERROW, RONALD B. *An Introduction to Bibliography.* Oxford: Clarendon Press, 1927.

———. *Printers' & Publishers' Devices in England & Scotland, 1485-1640.* London: Printed for the Bibliographical Society at the Chiswick Press, 1913.

MÉZIÈRES, A. *Pétrarque*. Paris: Librairie Hachette et Cie, 1895.

MIGNE, JACQUES PAUL. *Patrologiae Cursus Completus, Graeco-Latina*. Paris, 1857-1903, 161 vols.

———. *Patrologiae Cursus Completus, Latinae*. Paris, 1844-1900, 221 vols.

MILTON, JOHN. *An Annotated Edition of John Milton's "The Reason of Church-Government,"* by Ralph Abbott Haug. Unpublished Ph.D. dissertation in English, Ohio State University, 1944.

———. *Areopagitica and Other Prose Works of John Milton*. Edited by Charles Edwyn Vaughan. "Everyman's Library": London: J. M. Dent & Sons Limited, [1927].

———. *A Common-Place Book of John Milton . . With an Introduction* by A. J. Horwood. Chiswick Press: Charles Whittingham, 1876.

———. *The Complete Poetical Works of John Milton*. Edited by Harris Francis Fletcher. "The New Cambridge Edition"; Boston, etc.: Houghton Mifflin Company, 1941.

———. *Facsimile of the Manuscript of Milton's Minor Poems. Preserved in the Library of Trinity College Cambridge*. Edited and Transcribed by William Aldis Wright. Cambridge: University Press, 1899.

———. *John Milton, Prose Selections*. Edited by Merritt Y. Hughes. New York: The Odyssey Press, 1947.

———. *John Milton's Complete Poetical Works Reproduced in Photographic Facsimile: A Critical Text Edition* Compiled and Edited by Harris Francis Fletcher. Urbana: The University of Illinois Press, 1943-48, 4 vols.

———. *Milton. I Prose Works. II Poetical Works*. Edited by Robert Fletcher. London: Henry G. Bohn, 1844.

———. *The Milton Anthology Selected from the Prose Writings*. Prefaced by F. Hurd. New York: Henry Holt and Company, 1876.

———. *Milton Complete Poetry & Selected Prose . . . With a Foreword by Sir Arnold Wilson*. Edited by E. H. Visiak. [London:] The Nonesuch Press, [1938].

———. *Milton on Education. The Tractate "Of Education" with Supplementary Extracts from Other Writings of Milton*. Edited by Oliver Morley Ainsworth. "Cornell Studies in English"; New Haven: Yale University Press, 1928.

———. *Milton Private Correspondence and Academic Exercises*. Translated from the Latin by Phyllis B. Tillyard With an Introduction & Commentary by E. M. W. Tillyard. Cambridge: University Press, 1932.

———. *Milton's Prose*. Selected and edited by Malcolm W. Wallace. London, etc.: Humphrey Milford, Oxford University Press, 1925.

———. *Of Education, Areopagitica, The Commonwealth, By John Milton With Early Biographies of Milton*. Edited by Laura E. Lockwood. Boston, etc.: Houghton Mifflin Company, 1911.

———. *Of Reformation Touching Church-Discipline in England by John Milton*. Edited by Will Taliaferro Hale. New Haven: Yale University Press, 1916.

———. *Prose of Milton*. Selected and edited by Richard Garnett. London: Walter Scott Ltd, 1894.

———. *The Prose Works of John Milton*. Edited by J. A. St. John. "Bohn Edition"; London: George Bell and Sons, 1901-04, 5 vols.

———. *The Ready and Easy Way to Establish a Free Commonwealth by John Milton*. Edited by Evert Mordecai Clark. New Haven: Yale University Press, 1915.

———. *Selected Prose Writings of John Milton*. Edited by Ernest Myers. London: Kegan Paul, Trench & Co., 1884.

———. *Selections from the Prose Works of John Milton with Critical Remarks and Elucidations*. Edited by the Rev. James J. G. Graham. London: Hurst and Blockett, 1870.

———. *The Tenure of Kings and Magistrates by John Milton*. Edited by William Talbot Allison. New York: Henry Holt and Company, 1911.

———. *A Treatise On Christian Doctrine, Compiled From The Holy Scriptures Alone; By John Milton*. Translated by Charles R. Sumner. Cambridge: University Press, 1825.

———. *The Works of John Milton* (Frank Allen Patterson, General Editor). New York: Columbia University Press, 1931-38, 18 vols.

————. *The Works of John Milton in Verse and Prose Printed from the Original Editions with a Life of the Author* by the Rev. John Mitford. London: William Pickering, 1851, 8 vols.

————. *John Milton, A Sketch of Milton and His Prose Works, in the Form of a Lecture.* London: W. J. Johnson, 1866.

MORAND, PAUL PHELPS. *De Comus à Satan: L'oeuvre poétique de John Milton expliquée par sa vie.* Paris: [Imprimerie Ch.-A. Bedu], 1939.

————. *The Effects of his Political Life upon John Milton.* Paris: [H. Didier], 1939.

MOXON, JOSEPH. *Mechanick Exercises, London, 1683.* New York: Typothetae, 1896, 2 vols.

MOZLEY, J. F. *John Foxe and His Book.* London: Society for Promoting Christian Knowledge, 1940.

MULLINGER, JAMES BASS. *The University of Cambridge.* Cambridge: University Press, 1873-1911, 3 vols.

MURPHY, GWENDOLEN. *A Cabinet of Characters.* London: Humphrey Milford, 1925.

MURRAY, JAMES A. H. *A New English Dictionary On Historical Principles Founded Mainly On The Materials Collected By The Philological Society.* Edited by James A. H. Murray, Henry Bradley, William A. Craigie, C. T. Onions. Oxford: Clarendon Press, 1888-1933.

————. *The Oxford English Dictionary: being a corrected re-issue . . . of A New English Dictionary on Historical Principles. . . . edited by James A. H. Murray, Henry Bradley, W. A. Craigie, C. T. Onions.* Oxford: Clarendon Press, 1933.

MUTSCHMANN, HEINRICH. *Der Andere Milton.* Bonn und Leipzig: Kurt Schroeder, 1920.

————. *Milton's Eyesight and the Chronology of his Works.* Tartu (Dorpat), 1924.

————. *Milton's Projected Epic on the Rise and Future Greatness of the Brittanic Nation together with a Reprint of the Anonymous Pamphlet "Great Britain's Ruin Plotted by Seven Sorts of Men," 1641.* Tartu: J. G. Krüger, Ltd, 1936.

————. *The Secret of John Milton.* Dorpat (Tartu), 1925.

————. *Studies Concerning the Origin of "Paradise Lost."* Dorpat, 1924.

NEAL, DANIEL. *The History of the Puritans, Or Protestant Nonconformists; From The Reformation in 1517, to the Revolution in 1688.* Revised by John O. Choules. New York: Harper & Brothers, 1843-44, 2 vols.

NOLHAC, PIERRE DE. *Pétrarque et L'Humanisme.* Paris: Librairie Honoré Champion, Éditeur, 1907, 2 vols.

OATES, WHITNEY J. (ed.). *The Stoic and Epicurean Philosophers.* New York: Random House, 1940.

OGG, DAVID. *England in the Reign of Charles II.* Oxford: Clarendon Press, 1934.

OVID. *A New Translation of Ovid's Metamorphoses into English Prose.* London: Printed for Joseph Davidson, 1748.

PAGE, WILLIAM (ed.). *The Victoria History of London.* London: Constable and Company Limited, 1909.

PARKER, WILLIAM RILEY. *Milton's Contemporary Reputation: An Essay together with A Tentative List of Printed Allusions to Milton, 1641-1674, and facsimile reproductions of five contemporary pamphlets written in answer to Milton.* Columbus: The Ohio State University Press, 1940.

The Parliamentary History of England, from the earliest period to the year 1803. London: Printed by T. C. Hansard . . . For Longman, Hurst, Rees, Orme, & Brown; etc., 1807-20, 36 vols.

PATTERSON, FRANK ALLEN, and FRENCH ROWE FOGLE. *An Index To The Columbia Edition of the Works of John Milton.* New York: Columbia University Press, 1940, 2 vols.

PATTISON, MARK. *Milton.* "English Men of Letters"; New York: Harper & Brothers, 1880.

PECK, FRANCIS. *New Memoirs of the Life and Poetical Works of Mr. John Milton.* London, 1740.

PETRARCH. *Francisci Petrarcae Epistolae De Rebus Familiaribus Et Variae.* Edited by Iosephi Fracassetti. Florence, 1859-63, 3 vols.

————. *Lettere Di Francesco Petrarca Delle cose Familiari.* Edited by Giuseppe Fracassetti. Firenze, 1863-67, 5 vols.

————. *Lettere Senili Di Francesco Petrarca.* Edited by Giuseppe Fracassetti. Firenze, 1869-70, 2 vols.

PIERCE, WILLIAM (ed.). *The Marprelate Tracts 1588, 1589.* London: James Clarke & Co., 1911.

PLATO. *The Dialogues of Plato.* Translated into English with Analysis and Introductions by B. Jowett. Oxford: Clarendon Press, 1875, 5 vols.

———. *The Republic of Plato.* Translated by B. Jowett. Oxford: Clarendon Press, 1888.

———. *The Works of Plato. A New and Literal Version, Chiefly from the text of Stallbaum, translated by Henry Cary, Henry Davis, and George Burges.* "Bohn Classical Library"; London: George Bell & Sons, 1876-83, 6 vols.

PLINY. *The Letters of Pliny the Younger.* Edited by John Earl of Orrery. London: Printed by J. Bettenham for P. Vaillant, 1751, 2 vols.

———. *Pliny Letters, With An English Translation by William Melmoth, revised by W. M. L. Hutchinson.* "The Loeb Classical Library"; London: William Heinemann, 1915, 2 vols.

PLOMER, HENRY R. *A Dictionary of the Booksellers and Printers Who were at Work in England, Scotland and Ireland From 1641 to 1667.* London: Printed for the Bibliographical Society, 1907.

———. *English Printers' Ornaments.* London: Grafton & Co., 1924.

———. *A Short History of English Printing, 1476-1898.* London: Kegan Paul, Trench, Trübner, 1900.

POINTER, JOHN. *Oxoniensis Academia: or, the Antiquities and Curiosities of the University of Oxford.* London: Printed for S. Birt, 1749.

PRITCHARD, JOHN PAUL. *The Influence of the Fathers Upon Milton with Especial Reference to Augustine.* Abstract of Ph.D. dissertation in English, Cornell University, [1925?].

PULLAN, LEIGHTON. *The History of the Book of Common Prayer.* London: Longmans, Green, and Co., 1914.

RALEIGH, SIR WALTER. *Milton.* London: Edward Arnold, 1900.

RAYMOND, DORA NEILL. *Oliver's Secretary: John Milton in an Era of Revolt.* New York: Minton, Balch & Company, 1932.

REESE, M. M. *The Tudors and Stuarts.* London: Edward Arnold & Co., 1940.

RICHARDSON, CAROLINE FRANCES. *English Preachers and Preaching 1640-1670.* London: Society for Promoting Christian Knowledge, 1928.

ROGERS, EDWARD. *Some Accounts of the Life and Opinions of a Fifth-Monarchy-Man. Chiefly extracted from the writings of John Rogers, preacher.* London: Longmans, Green, Reader and Dyer, 1867.

ROSEDALE, H. G. "Milton: His Religion and Polemics, Ecclesiastical as well as Political," *Milton Memorial Lectures, 1908. Read before the Royal Society of Literature.* Edited, With an Introduction by Percy W. Ames. London: Henry Frowde, Oxford University Press, 1909, pp. 109-90.

ROSS, M. M. *Milton's Royalism.* Ithaca, New York: Cornell University Press, 1943.

SAMPSON, ALDEN. *Studies in Milton and an Essay on Poetry.* New York: Moffat, Yard & Co., 1913.

SAMUEL, IRENE. *Plato and Milton.* Ithaca, New York: Cornell University Press, 1947.

SAURAT, DENIS. *Milton, Man and Thinker.* New York: The Dial Press, 1925.

SCOTT, HEW. *Fasti Ecclesiae Scoticanae: The Succession of Ministers in the Church of Scotland From the Reformation.* Edinburgh: Oliver and Boyd, 1915-28, 7 vols.

SENECA. *Apokolokyntosis.* Testo e versione di Augusto Rostagni. Torino, 1944.

———. *Selected Essays of Seneca and the Satire on the Deification of Claudius.* Edited by Allan P. Ball. New York: The Macmillan Company, 1916.

———. *Seneca's Morals. By Way of Abstract. To which is added, A Discourse, under the Title of An Afterthought.* By Sir Robert L'Estrange. Philadelphia: Grigg & Elliot, 1834.

SENIOR, H. L. *John Milton, the Supreme Englishman.* London: W. H. Allen, 1944.

SHAW, WILLIAM A. *A History of the English Church during the Civil Wars and under the Commonwealth 1640-1660.* London: Longmans, Green, and Co., 1900, 2 vols.

SHAW, WILLIAM A. (ed.). *Minutes of the Manchester Presbyterian Classis, Part I.* "Remains Historical and Literary connected with the Palatine counties of Lancaster and Chester," vol. 20, new series; Manchester: Printed for the Chetham Society, 1890.

SMITH, JOHN JAMES. *The Cambridge Portfolio.* London: John W. Parker, 1840.

SMITH, LOGAN PEARSALL. *Milton and His Modern Critics.* Oxford: University Press, 1940.

SMITH, PRESERVED. *The Age of the Reformation.* New York: Henry Holt and Company, 1920.

―――. *Erasmus.* New York & London: Harper & Brothers, 1923.

―――. *Luther's Correspondence and other Contemporary Letters.* Philadelphia: The Lutheran Publication Society, 1913-18, 2 vols.

SMITH, WILLIAM, and HENRY WACE. *A Dictionary of Christian Biography.* London: John Murray, 1880-1900, 4 vols. (Vol. 1 — 1900).

SMITH, WILLIAM GEORGE. *The Oxford Dictionary of English Proverbs.* Oxford: Clarendon Press, 1935.

SNELL, BRUNO. *Leben und Meinungen der Sieben Weisen.* München: Ernst Heimeran, 1938.

SPINGARN, J. E. *Critical Essays of the Seventeenth Century.* Oxford: Clarendon Press, 1908-09, 3 vols.

―――. *Literary Criticism in the Renaissance.* 2nd edition. New York: The Columbia University Press, 1908.

STEARNS, RAYMOND PHINEAS. *Congregationalism in the Dutch Netherlands: The Rise and Fall of The English Congregational Classis, 1621-1635.* Chicago: The American Society of Church History, 1940.

STERN, ALFRED. *Milton und Seine Zeit.* Leipzig: Duncker & Humblot, 1877-79, 2 vols.

STEVENS, DAVID HARRISON. *Reference Guide to Milton.* Chicago: University of Chicago Press, 1930.

STOUGHTON, JOHN. *History of Religion in England from the Opening of the Long Parliament to 1850.* London: Hodder and Stoughton, 1901, 6 vols.

STRABO. *The Geography of Strabo, With An English Translation By Horace Leonard Jones.* "The Loeb Classical Library"; London: William Heinemann, Ltd, 1917-32, 8 vols.

STRONG, AUGUSTUS HOPKINS. *The Great Poets and Their Theology.* Philadelphia, etc.: The Griffith & Rowland Press, 1897.

SYMMONS, CHARLES. *The Life of John Milton.* 2nd edition. London: T. Bensley, 1810.

TACITUS. *The Works of Cornelius Tacitus With An Essay On His Life And Genius, Notes, Supplements, &c. By Arthur Murphy.* New York: Robert Carter & Brothers, 1849.

TAFT, FREDERICK LOVETT. *Milton and the Smectymnuus Controversy, 1641-42.* Unpublished Ph.D. dissertation in English, Western Reserve University, 1942.

TANNER, J. R. *English Constitutional Conflicts of the Seventeenth Century, 1603-1689.* Cambridge: University Press, 1928

TARRANT, W. G. *Milton and Religious Freedom.* London: P. Green, 1908.

THOMPSON, ELBERT N. S. *Essays on Milton.* New Haven: Yale University Press; London: Humphrey Milford, Oxford University Press, 1914.

―――. *John Milton: Topical Bibliography.* New Haven: Yale University Press, 1916.

―――. *Literary Bypaths of the Renaissance.* New Haven: Yale University Press, 1924.

TILLYARD, E. M. W. "The Action of Comus," *Essays and Studies by Members of the English Association,* XXVIII (1942), 22-37. Oxford: Clarendon Press, 1943.

―――. *Milton.* New York: The Dial Press: London: Chatto and Windus, 1930.

―――. "Milton and the English Epic Tradition," *Seventeenth Century Studies Presented to Sir Herbert Grierson.* Oxford: Clarendon Press, 1938, pp. 211-34.

―――. *The Miltonic Setting.* Cambridge: University Press, 1938.

TIXERONT, J. *A Handbook of Patrology.* Translated by S. A. Raemers. St. Louis: B. Herder Book Co., 1939.

TODD, REV. H. J. *Some Account of the Life and Writings of John Milton.* London: C. and J. Rivington, 1826.

A Transcript of the Registers of the Company of Stationers of London; 1554-1640 A. D. Edited by Edward Arber London: Privately Printed, 1875-77; Birmingham, 1894, 5 vols.

A Transcript of the Registers of the Worshipful Company of Stationers; From 1640-1708 A. D. London: Privately Printed, 1913-14, 3 vols.

TREVELYAN, GEORGE MACAULAY. *England Under the Stuarts.* London: Methuen & Co., 1926.

USHER, ROLAND G. *The Presbyterian Movement in the Reign of Queen Elizabeth as illustrated by the Minute Book of the Dedham Classis 1582-1589.* London: Offices of the Royal Historical Society, 1905.

VENN, JOHN and J. A. *Alumni Cantabrigienses. Part I, from earliest times to 1751.* Cambridge: University Press, 1922-27, 4 vols.

VISIAK, E. H. *Milton Agonistes: a Metaphysical Criticism.* London: A. M. Philpot, Ltd, [1923].

VODOZ, JULES. *An Essay on the Prose of John Milton.* Winterthur: G. Binkert, 1895.

VOGT, KARL F. *Milton als Publizist.* Würzburg: Buchdruckerei R. Mayr, 1933

WHITE, T. HOLT. *A Review of Johnson's Criticism on the Style of Milton's English Prose.* [London]: R. Hunter, 1818.

WHITING, GEORGE WESLEY. *Milton's Literary Milieu.* Chapel Hill: University of North Carolina Press, 1939.

WILLIAMSON, GEORGE C. *Milton.* London: George Bell & Sons, 1905.

WILLIS, WILLIAM. *John Milton: Political Thinker & Statesman.* London: W. H. Bartlett & Co., 1909.

WILSON, JOSEPH. *Memorabilia Cantabrigiae.* London: Edward Harding, 1803.

WOLFE, DON M. *Milton in the Puritan Revolution.* New York, etc.: Thomas Nelson and Sons, 1941.

WOOD, ANTHONY À. *Athenae Oxonienses. An exact History of all the writers and Bishops who have had their education in the University of Oxford.* Edited by Philip Bliss. London: F. C. and J. Rivington, etc., 1813-20, 4 vols.

WYLD, HENRY CECIL. *History of Modern Colloquial English.* New York: E. P. Dutton and Company, 1920.

ZELLER, EDWARD. *Outlines of the History of Greek Philosophy.* Translated by Sarah Frances Alleyne and Evelyn Abbott. New York: Henry Holt and Company, 1890.

PERIODICALS

ALLEN, DON CAMERON. "Some Contemporary Accounts of Renaissance Printing Methods," *The Library*, Fourth Series, XVII (1937), 167-71.

["Atticism"], *The Portfolio*, Fifth Series, II (1816), 420-21.

BALDWIN, EDWARD CHAUNCEY. "The Authorized Version's Influence Upon Milton's Diction," *Modern Language Notes*, XXXVI (1921), 376-77.

———. "An Instance of Milton's Debt to the Greek Philosophers," *Classical Weekly*, XI (1918), 121-25.

———. "Milton and Ezekiel," *Modern Language Notes*, XXXIII (1918), 211-15.

———. "Milton and the Psalms," *Modern Philology*, XVII (1919), 97-103.

BARKER, ARTHUR. "Milton's Schoolmasters," *Modern Language Review*, XXXII (1937), 517-36.

BAXTER, WYNNE E. "Milton's *Paradise Lost*," *The Bibliographer* (New York), II (1903), 73-91.

———. "Report on a Paper entitled 'Early Editions of Milton'," *Transactions of the Bibliographical Society* (London), VI (1903), Part 2, 152-55.

BENN, ALFRED W. "Milton's Ethics," *The International Journal of Ethics*, XXI (1911), 422-47.

BOND, WILLIAM H. "Imposition by Half-sheets," *The Library*, Fourth Series, XXII (1942), 163-67.

BOWERS, FREDSON T. "Notes on Running-Titles as Bibliographical Evidence," *The Library*, Fourth Series, XIX (1939), 315-38.

BRUNNER, HILDEGARD. "Miltons Persönliche und Ideelle Welt in Ihrer Beziehung zum Aristokratismus," *Bonner Studien zur Englischen Philologie*, XIX (1933), 1-50.

BYWATER, INGRAM. "Milton and the Aristotelian Definition of Tragedy," *Journal of Philology*, XXVII (1900), no. 54, 267-75.

CAMERON, KENNETH W. "Milton's Library," *Times Literary Supplement*, October 24, 1936, p. 868.

CARLSON, LELAND H. "A History of the Presbyterian Party from Pride's Purge to the Dissolution of the Long Parliament," *Church History*, XI (1942), 83-122.

"Character of Chaplains," *Monthly Magazine*, XLIV (1817), 526.

CLARK, DONALD LEMEN. "Milton's Schoolmasters: Alexander Gill and his Son Alexander," *Huntington Library Quarterly*, IX (1946), 121-47.

CLYDE, WILLIAM M. "Parliament and the Press, 1643-7," *The Library*, Fourth Series, XIII (1933), 399-424, and XIV (1934), 39-58.

CONACHER, W. M. "The Puritanism of Milton," *Queen's Quarterly*, XXXII (1924), 69-80.

COOK, ALBERT S. "Milton's View of the Apocalypse as a Tragedy," *Herrig's Archiv*, CXXIX (1912), 74-80.

DARBISHIRE, HELEN. "The Columbia Edition of Milton," *Review of English Studies*, IX (1933), 61-62.

————. "Pen-and-ink Corrections in Books of the Seventeenth Century," *Review of English Studies*, VII (1931), 72-73.

————. "The Printing of the First Edition of *Paradise Lost*," *Review of English Studies*, XVII (1941), 415-27.

DAVIES, GODFREY. "Arminian versus Puritan in England, *ca.* 1620-1640," *The Huntington Library Bulletin*, no. 5 (April, 1934), 157-79.

DIEKHOFF, JOHN S. "Critical Activity of the Poetic Mind: John Milton," *Publications of the Modern Language Association*, LV (1940), 748-72.

————. "The Function of the Prologues in *Paradise Lost*," *Publications of the Modern Language Association*, LVII (1942), 697-704.

DOBRÉE, BONAMY. "Milton and Dryden: A Comparison and Contrast in Poetic Ideas and Poetic Method," *English Literary History*, III (1936), 83-100.

DONALDSON, GORDON. "The Relations between the English and Scottish presbyterian movements to 1604," Summary of London University Thesis, *Bulletin of the Institute of Historical Research*, XVII (1939-40), 39-41.

DOWDEN, EDWARD. "The Idealism of Milton," *Contemporary Review*, XIX (1872), 198-209.

EKFELT, FRED EMIL. "The Graphic Diction of Milton's English Prose," *Philological Quarterly*, XXV (1946), 46-69.

FINK, ZERA S. "The Theory of the Mixed State and the Development of Milton's Political Thoughts," *Publications of the Modern Language Association*, LVII (1942), 705-36.

————. "Venice and English Political Thought in the Seventeenth Century," *Modern Philology*, XXXVIII (1940), 155-72.

FIRTH, SIR CHARLES. "Milton as An Historian," *Proceedings of the British Academy*, III (1907-08), 227-57.

FLETCHER, HARRIS FRANCIS. "Contributions to A Milton Bibliography 1800-1930," *University of Illinois Studies in Language and Literature*, XVI (1931), no. 1.

————. "The First Edition of Milton's *History of Britain*," *Journal of English and Germanic Philology*, XXXV (1936), 405-14.

————. "Milton and Thomas Young," *Times Literary Supplement*, January 21, 1926, p. 44.

————. "Milton's Use of Biblical Quotations," *Journal of English and Germanic Philology*, XXVI (1927), 145-65.

————. "Review of *Miltons Anschauungen von Staat, Kirche, Toleranz*. By Gertrud Hardeland. *Studien zur Englischen Philologie* LXXXI, Halle (Saale): Niemeyer, 1934," *Journal of English and Germanic Philology*, XXXIV (1934), 120-21.

————. "Review of *The Works of John Milton*. F. A. Patterson, General Editor. New York: Columbia University Press, 1930—. [19?] volumes. Volumes III, IV, V, VI, X," *Journal of English and Germanic Philology*, XXXIII (1934), 300-05.

————. "The Use of the Bible in Milton's Prose," *University of Illinois Studies in Language and Literature*, XIV (1929), no. 3.

FRENCH, J. MILTON. "Milton as a Historian," *Publications of the Modern Language Association*, L (1935), 469-79.

————. "Milton as a Satirist," *Publications of the Modern Language Association*, LI (1936), 414-29.

————. "Milton, Needham, and 'Mercurius Politicus'," *Studies in Philology*, XXXIII (1936), 236-52.

————. "Some Notes on Milton," *Notes and Queries*, CLXXXVIII (1945), 52-55.

GILBERT, ALLAN H. "The Cambridge Manuscript and Milton's Plans for an Epic," *Studies in Philology*, XVI (1919), 172-76.

————. "Milton on the Position of Woman," *Modern Language Review*, XV (1920), 7-27, 240-64.

————. "Milton Quotes from Petrarch?" *Modern Language Notes*, LX (1945), 496.

————. "Some Critical Opinions on Milton," *Studies in Philology*, XXXIII (1936), 523-33.

GILMAN, WILBUR ELWYN. "Milton's Rhetoric: Studies in His Defense of Liberty," *University of Missouri Studies*, XIV (1939), no. 3.

"The Golden Age of English Prose (A Review of Dowden, *Puritan and Anglican* and Sir Henry Craik, *English Prose Selections*)," *Quarterly Review*, CXCVI (1902), 97-99.

GRIERSON, SIR HERBERT J. C. "Milton and Liberty," *Modern Language Review*, XXXIX (1944), 97-107.

———. "Milton and Thomas Young," *Times Literary Supplement*, February 11, 1926, p. 99.

HALLER, WILLIAM. "Before *Areopagitica*," *Publications of the Modern Language Association*, XLII (1927), 875-900.

———. "Review of *The Dignity of Kingship Asserted*, By G. D. Reproduced in facsimile from the edition of 1660, with an Introduction by William R. Parker, New York: Columbia University Press, 1942," *Modern Language Notes*, LVIII (1943), 401-02.

HANFORD, JAMES HOLLY. "The Chronology of Milton's Private Studies," *Publications of the Modern Language Association*, XXXVI (1921), 251-314.

———. "Milton and the Art of War," *Studies in Philology*, XVIII (1921), 232-66.

———. "Milton in Current Criticism," *English Journal*, College Edition, XXVIII (1939), 342-48.

HARDER, J. H. "Milton, Puritan or Calvinist?" *Neophilologus*, IX, no. 3 (April, 1924), 199-203.

HAUG, RALPH A. "Milton and Archbishop Ussher," *Notes and Queries*, CLXXXV (1943), 66-67.

———. "Milton and Bishop Williams," *Notes and Queries*, CLXXXIV (1943), 193.

———. "Milton and Sir John Harington," *Modern Language Quarterly*, IV (1943), 291-92.

HEAWOOD, EDWARD. "Papers Used in England after 1600," *The Library*, Fourth Series, XI (1931), 263-99, 466-98.

HERFORD, CHARLES H. "Dante and Milton," *Bulletin of John Rylands Library Manchester*, VIII (1924), 191-235.

HERRICK, MARVIN T. "The Fusion of Horatian and Aristotelian Literary Criticism, 1531-1555," *University of Illinois Studies in Language and Literature*, XXXII (1946), no. 1.

HINMAN, CHARLTON. "Principles Governing the Use of Variant Spellings as Evidence of Alternate Setting by Two Compositors," *The Library*, Fourth Series, XXI (1941), 78-94

HOWARD, LEON. " 'The Invention' of Milton's 'Great Argument': A Study of the Logic of 'God's Ways to Men'," *Huntington Library Quarterly*, IX (1946), 149-73.

HUGHES, MERRITT Y. "Milton as Revolutionary," *English Literary History*, X (1943), 87-116.

HULME, WILLIAM H. (ed.). "Two Early Lives of John Milton," *Western Reserve University Bulletin*, XXVII (1924), no. 8.

HUNTER, WILLIAM B., JR. "Milton's Materialistic Life Principle," *Journal of English and Germanic Philology*, XLV (1946), 68-76.

JONES, CHARLES W. "Milton's 'Brief Epic,'" *Studies in Philology*, XLIV (1947), 209-27.

JONES, IDA B. "Popular Medical Knowledge in Fourteenth Century English Literature," *Bulletin of the Institute of the History of Medicine*, V (1937), 405-51, 538-88.

LARSON, MARTIN A. "Milton and Puritanism — Clarified," *Philological Quarterly*, IX (1930), 308-11.

———. "Milton's Essential Relationship to Puritanism and Stoicism," *Philological Quarterly*, VI (1927), 201-20.

LAWSON, EVANGELINE. "Milton's Theology," *Open Court*, XLII (1928), 407-13.

LEVINSON, RONALD B. "Milton and Plato," *Modern Language Notes*, XLVI (1931), 85-91.

LOOTEN, CHANOINE. "Les Débuts de Milton pamphlétaire," *Études Anglaises*, I (1937), 297-313.

———. "Milton et l'idée du poète," *Revue Anglo-Américaine*, IX (1931), 1-15.

———. "Milton et la musique," *Revue Anglo-Américaine*, VIII (1931), 393-408.

LUMIANSKY, R. M. "Milton's English Again," *Modern Language Notes*, LV (1941), 591-94.

MABBOTT, T. O. "Milton and Archbishop Ussher," *Notes and Queries*, CLXXXV (1943), 293-94.

MACK, JESSE F. "The Evolution of Milton's Political Thinking," *Sewanee Review*, XXX (1922), 193-205.

McKERROW, R. B. "Edward Allde as a Typical Trade Printer," *The Library*, Fourth Series, X (1929), 121-62.

"Milton's English Prose Works," *North American Review*, XXV (1827), 73-89.

NEWMANN, JOSHUA H. "Milton's Prose Vocabulary," *Publications of the Modern Language Association*, LX (1945), 102-20.

OLIVER, LESLIE M. "The Seventh Edition of John Foxe's *Acts and Monuments*," *The Papers of the Bibliographical Society of America*, XXXVII (1943), 243-60.

PARKER, WILLIAM RILEY. "A Cancel in an Early Milton Tract," *The Library*, Fourth Series, XV (1934), 243-46.

———. "Contributions toward a Milton Bibliography," *The Library*, Fourth Series, XVI (1936), 425-38.

———. "Milton and Thomas Young, 1620-1638," *Modern Language Notes*, LIII (1938), 399-407.

———. "Milton, Rothwell, and Simmons," *The Library*, Fourth Series, XVIII (1937), 89-103.

———. "On Milton's Early Literary Program," *Modern Philology*, XXXIII (1935), 49-53.

PERSHING, JAMES HAMMOND. "The Different States of the First Edition of *Paradise Lost*," *The Library*, Fourth Series, XXII (1941), 34-66.

———. "Storage of Printed Sheets in the Seventeenth Century," *The Library*, Fourth Series, XVII (1937), 468-71

PETAGORSKY, DAVID. "Milton as a Social Philosopher," *The New Republic*, CIV (1941), 606.

PETTIGREW, RICHARD C. "Lowell's Criticism of Milton " *American Literature*, III (1932), 457-64.

PLOMER, H. R. "A Printer's Bill in the Seventeenth Century," *The Library*, Fourth Series, VII (1906), 32-45.

POLLARD, GRAHAM. "Notes on the Size of the Sheet," *The Library*, Fourth Series, XXII (1942), 105-37.

PRITCHARD, JOHN PAUL. "The Fathers of the Church in the Works of John Milton," *The Classical Journal*, XXXIII (1937), 79-87.

RAND, E. K. "Milton in Rustication," *Studies in Philology*, XIX (1922), 109-35.

SAMUEL, IRENE. "Milton's References to Plato and Socrates," *Studies in Philology*, XLI (1944), 50-63.

SILLMAN, DONALD G. "Milton as Proof Reader," *Modern Language Notes*, LIV (1939), 353-54.

SILVETTE, HERBERT. "Medicine in Utopia," *Bulletin of the History of Medicine*, VII (1939), 1013-36.

STARNES, D. T. and E. W. TALBERT. "John Milton and Renaissance Dictionaries," *University of Texas Studies in English*, 1943, pp. 50-65.

SVENDSEN, KESTER. "Milton and the Encyclopedias of Science," *Studies in Philology*, XXXIX (1942), 303-27.

———. "Milton and *Malleus Maleficarum*," *Modern Language Notes*, LX (1945), 118-19.

———. "Milton and Medical Lore," *Bulletin of the History of Medicine*, XIII (1943), 158-84.

TAYLOR, GEORGE COFFIN. "Milton's English," *Notes and Queries*, CLXXVIII (1940), 56-57.

THALER, ALWIN. "The Shakesperian Element in Milton," *Publications of the Modern Language Association*, XL (1925), 645-91.

THOMPSON, ELBERT N. S. "Milton's Prose Style," *Philological Quarterly*, XIV (1935), 1-15.

———. "The Seventeenth-Century English Essay," *University of Iowa Humanistic Studies*, III (1926), no. 3.

TILLYARD, E. M. W. "Review of *Milton and Wordsworth, Poets and Prophets*, by Sir Herbert J. C. Grierson," *Modern Language Notes*, LIII (1938), 381-83.

VISIAK, E. H. "Milton and Archbishop Ussher," *Notes and Queries*, CLXXXV (1943), 146.

———. "Milton's Prose (as represented in the 'Compendious' *Milton*)," *Nineteenth Century*, CXXIII (1938), 499-508.

WHITING, GEORGE W. "Milton and the 'Postscript'," *Modern Language Review*, XXX (1935), 506-08.

———. "Milton and Lord Brooke on the Church," *Modern Language Notes*, LI (1936), 161-66.

———. "Milton's Prelatical Pamphlets," *Times Literary Supplement*, September 5, 1935, p. 552.

———. "The Politics of Milton's Apostate Angels," *Notes and Queries*, CLXIII (1932), 384-86.

————. "A Pseudonymous Reply to Milton's *Of Prelatical Episcopacy*," *Publications of the Modern Language Association*, LI (1936), 430-35.

————. "The Satire in *Eikonoklastes*," *Notes and Queries*, CLXX (1936), 435-38.

WILLIAMS, CHARLES. "The New Milton," *London Mercury*, XXXVI (1937), 255-61.

WOLFE, DON M. "Milton and Hobbes: A Contrast in Social Temper," *Studies in Philology*, XLI (1944), 410-26.

————. "Milton Lilburne, and the People, ' *Modern Philology*, XXXI (1934), 253-72.

————. "Milton's Conception of the Ruler," *Studies in Philology*, XXXIII (1936), 253-72.

WOODHOUSE, A. S. F. "The Argument of Milton's *Comus*," *University of Toronto Quarterly*, XI (1941), 46-71.

————. "Milton and His Age," *University of Toronto Quarterly*, IV (1935), 130-39.

————. "Milton, Puritanism, and Liberty, ' *University of Toronto Quarterly*, IV (1935), 483-513.

WRIGHT, B. A. "The Alleged Falsehoods in Milton's Account of his Continental Tour," *Modern Language Review*, XXVIII (1933), 308-14.

————. "Milton's First Marriage," *Modern Language Review*, XXVI (1931), 383-400; XXVII (1932), 6-23.

WRIGHT, NATHALIA. "Milton's Use of Latin Formularies," *Studies in Philology*, XL (1943), 390-98.

CHIEF EDITIONS AND ISSUES OF THE *APOLOGY*

An Apology Against a Pamphlet Call'd A Modest Confutation of the Animadversions upon the Remonstrant against Smectymnuus. London, Printed by *E. G.* for *Iohn Rothwell*, and are to be sold at the signe of the Sunne in *Pauls* Church-yard. 1642.

An Apology For Smectymnuus. With The Reason Of Church-Government. By John Milton, Gent. London, Printed for *John Rothwell*, at the Fountain and Beare in *Cheapside*, [1654].

The Works of Mr. John Milton. Printed in the Year MDCXCVII., pp. 325-61.

A Complete Collection Of The Historical, Political, and Miscellaneous Works Of John Milton, Both English and Latin. With som Papers never before Publish'd. Amsterdam, Finish'd in the Year M. DC. XC. VIII., 3 vols., I, 169-200.

A Complete Collection Of The Historical, Political, and Miscellaneous Works Of John Milton: Correctly printed from the Original Editions. With An Historical and Critical Account Of The Life and Writings of the Author; Containing several Original Papers of His, Never before Published. London: Printed for A. Millar, 1738, 2 vols., I, 103-34.

The Works of John Milton, Historical, Political, and Miscellaneous. London: Printed for A. Millar, 1753, 2 vols., I, 109-41.

The Prose Works of John Milton, With A Life of the Author, Interspersed With Translations And Critical Remarks, By Charles Symmons. London: Printed by T. Bensley, 1806, 7 vols., I, 207-72.

The Prose Works Of John Milton; Containing His Principal Pieces, With New Translations And An Introduction. By George Burnett. London: Printed for John Miller, 1809, 2 vols., I, 96-126.

A Selection From the English Prose Works of John Milton. Boston: Bowles and Dearborn, 1826, 2 vols., I, 217-96.

The Prose Works of John Milton; with an Introductory Review by R. Fletcher. London: [Westley & Davis], 1833, pp. 75-97.

Extracts from the Prose Works of John Milton, Containing The Whole of His Writings on the Church Question. Edinburgh: William Tait, 1836, pp. 188-247.

Milton. I, Prose Works. II, Poetical Works. Paris: A. and W. Galignani, [*ca.* 1836], pp. 75-97.

The Prose Works of John Milton With a Biographical Introduction. By Rufus Wilmot Griswold. Philadelphia: Hooker, 1845, 2 vols., I, 121-58.

The Prose Works of John Milton . . . With A Preface, Preliminary Remarks, and Notes, By J. A. St. John. London: Henry G. Bohn, 1848-53, 5 vols., III, 93-168.

The Works of John Milton in Verse and Prose Printed from the Original Editions with a Life of the Author by The Rev. John Mitford. London: William Pickering, 1851, 8 vols., III, 250-326.

John Milton's Politische Hauptschriften, Uebersetzt und mit Anmerkungen versehen von Dr. Wilhelm Bernhardi. Leipzig: Erich Koschny (L. Heimann's Verlag), 1874-79, 3 vols., III, 67-125.

The Student's Milton. Edited by Frank Allen Patterson. New York: Printed for F. S. Crofts & Co., 1930, pp. 540-73.

Milton Complete Poetry & Selected Prose . . . With a Foreword by Sir Arnold Wilson. Edited by E. H. Visiak. [London]: The Nonesuch Press, [1938], pp. 567-628.

The Works of John Milton (Frank Allen Patterson, General Editor), New York: Columbia University Press, 1931-38, 18 vols., III, 280-366.

Complete Poetry and Selected Prose of John Milton. "The Modern Library"; New York: Random House, 1948 pp. 547-614.

Index